Pension Planning

Pension Planning

Pensions, Profit-Sharing, and Other Deferred Compensation Plans

Everett T. Allen, Jr., L.L.B.
Retired Vice President and Principal
Towers Perrin

Joseph J. Melone, Ph.D., CLU, ChFC, CPCU
President and Chief Operating Officer
The Equitable

Jerry S. Rosenbloom, Ph.D., CLU, CPCU
Frederick H. Ecker Professor and Chair, Department of Insurance and Risk Management
Wharton School, University of Pennsylvania
and Academic Director, Certified Employee Benefit Specialist Program

Jack L. VanDerhei, Ph.D., CEBS
Associate Professor and Joseph E. Boettner Senior Research Fellow in Risk Management and Insurance
Temple University

Seventh Edition

IRWIN

Homewood, Illinois 60430

© RICHARD D. IRWIN, INC., 1966, 1972, 1976, 1981, 1984, 1988, and 1992

Senior sponsoring editor: Michael W. Junior
Project editor: Jess Ann Ramirez
Production manager: Ann Cassady
Designer: Larry J. Cope
Printer: R. R. Donnelley & Sons Company

Library of Congress Cataloging-in-Publication Data

Pension planning / Everett T. Allen, Jr. ... [et al.].—7th ed.
    p.   cm.
  Rev. ed. of: Pension planning / Everett T. Allen, Jr. 6th ed. 1988.
  Includes index.
  ISBN 0-256-08296-0
  1. Old age pensions—United States. 2. Pension trusts—United States. I. Allen, Everett T. II. Allen, Everett T. Pension planning.
HD7105.35.U6A44 1992
658.3'253—dc20   91-44319

Printed in the United States of America

1 2 3 4 5 6 7 8 9 0 DOC 9 8 7 6 5 4 3 2

Preface

The seventh edition of this book has been completely restructured in response to the dynamic developments in the pension field. Instead of developing the basic concepts of retirement plans from the standpoint of defined benefit plans, we have chosen to introduce the reader to the elements of plan design considerations through the defined contribution paradigm before adding the additional complexities inherent in the defined benefit approach.

Another major change in this edition is the expansion of the coverage of the tax law qualification requirements for retirement plans into two chapters. As regulatory clarification of concepts introduced by the Tax Reform Act of 1986 continues to take shape, the need for precise explanation and illustrative examples resulted in this amplification. The reader should be aware that there are many rules, regulations, and interpretations of the recent legislation still to come that could affect some of the material in this text.

We want to express our appreciation once again to the many individuals who assisted us in prior editions of the text. Many of their contributions have survived in this seventh edition. We are also very much indebted to the individuals in the insurance, financial, and consulting professions who have reviewed portions of this text and made many valuable suggestions, and to the many teachers and students who over the years have given us extremely constructive comments and have enabled us to improve the readability and quality of the text. Special thanks are also due representatives of The American College, the College for Financial Planning, the International

Foundation of Employee Benefit Plans, the Society of Actuaries, and the Life Office Management Association for their comments and review over the years. We are particularly grateful to Professor Sandra L' H. Phillips, Academic Associate, Academic Programs, College for Financial Planning for her detailed analysis of the previous edition of this book.

A special debt of gratitude is owed to Robert J. Myers, one of the world's leading authorities on Social Security for writing the chapter on Social Security and Medicare. We also wish to acknowledge specifically the contribution of George W. Cowles, Senior Vice President, Bankers Trust Company, for reviewing the chapter on Trust Fund Plans. Specific thanks are also due to Frederick R. Karp and Cornelius T. Moylan, both Assistant Vice Presidents of Insurance Products and Services at The Equitable, for their review of the chapters on Special Insurance and Annuity Products and Section 403(b) Plans and to Dennis F. Mahoney, Manager of Benefits, University of Pennsylvania, for his review of the chapter on Section 403(b) Plans. We also would like to express our appreciation for the comments provided by four individuals from TIAA-CREF: Michael Fegan, Vice President; Elihu H. Joyner, Jr., Vice President-Marketing Department; Francis P. King, Senior Research Officer; and Bernard Slack, Assistant Advisory Officer. Several individuals currently or formerly affiliated with the Employee Benefit Research Institute provided much appreciated input over the last four years, particularly Dallas Salisbury, Nora Super Jones, Laura Bos, Joseph Piacentini, Emily Andrews, Jennifer Davis, Stephanie Poe, Bonnie Newton, and Christine Dolan.

Finally, the authors greatly appreciate the cooperation of Towers Perrin in providing material from their forthcoming title concerning Section 401(k) plans.

Everett T. Allen, Jr.
Joseph J. Melone
Jerry S. Rosenbloom
Jack L. VanDerhei

Contents

PART ONE

Environmental Influences on Private Pension Plans

Private pension plans are designed and maintained in a highly complex tax, legal and financial environment. To understand the full implications of this environment, it is helpful to have a general understanding of the history of these plans and the overall objectives they serve.

Chapter 1 documents the growth of private plans, the reasons for this growth and the rationale for their existence. It also includes a brief review of the major legislation that has been enacted with respect to these plans in recent years.

Social Security is a major source of retirement benefits -- not only in the form of income, but in the form of health care coverages. Because of the importance of their benefit to retirees and the role it plays in meeting income-replacement objectives, it is described in detail in Chapter 2. Knowledge of the nature and level of Social Security benefits is essential for a complete understanding of the way in which private pension plans are designed.

It is essential that a private pension plan be designed to support the employer's overall objectives. Employer objectives, in turn, are influenced by the environment in which the employer exists as well as the employer's overall attitude and philosophy with respect to a number of key issues. These environmental factors and employer attitudes, along with specific employer objectives, are covered in Chapter 3.

Chapter 4, the final chapter in this part, deals with a basic issue that has been or is being considered by most employers -- the question of whether to use a defined benefit and/or defined contribution approach to providing pension benefits.

1. Development of Private Pension Plans

Individuals generally seek means to enhance their economic security. One cause of economic insecurity is the probable reduction of an individual's earning power at an advanced age. In this country, this risk is met through one or more of the following means: personal savings (including individual insurance and annuities), employer-sponsored pensions, and social insurance programs. When these three elements are combined, they produce a multifaceted approach to economic security sometimes referred to as the "tripod of economic security," the "three-legged stool of economic security," or the "pillars of economic security." The dramatic growth of private plans since the 1940s has focused considerable interest on this form of income maintenance.[1]

1.1. GROWTH OF PRIVATE PLANS

The beginnings of industrial pension plans in the United States date back to the establishment of the American Express Company plan in 1875.[2] The second formal plan was established in 1880 by the Baltimore and Ohio

---

[1]*Private plans*, as used in this text, refers to plans established by private agencies, including commercial, industrial, labor, and service organizations, and nonprofit religious, educational, and charitable institutions. Social security is covered in Chapter 2.

[2]Murray Webb Latimer, *Industrial Pension Systems* (New York: Industrial Relations Counselors, Inc., 1932), p.21.

Railroad Company. During the next half century, approximately 400 plans were established. These early pension plans were generally found in the railroad, banking, and public utility fields. The development of pensions in manufacturing companies was somewhat slower, largely because most manufacturing companies were still relatively young and therefore not confronted with the superannuation problems of the railroads and public utilities.

Insurance companies entered the pension business with the issuance of the first group annuity contract by the Metropolitan Life Insurance Company in 1921.[3] The second contract was issued by the Metropolitan in 1924 to an employer who already had a retirement plan on a "pay-as-you-go" basis.[4] In 1924, The Equitable Life Assurance Society of the United States announced its intention of offering a group pension service, thus becoming the second company to enter the field.[5]

Although the beginnings of private pensions date back to the 1800s, the significant growth in these programs has come since the 1940s. In 1988, nearly 60 million nonagricultural wage and salary workers worked for an employer that sponsored a pension or retirement plan; one-half of these workers were currently entitled to receive a benefit upon retirement.[6] At the end of 1989, the financial assets of private pension funds exceeded $1.7 trillion and were growing by more than 12 percent per year.[7]

1.2.   ECONOMIC PROBLEMS OF OLD AGE

Longevity is a source of economic insecurity in that individuals may outlive their financial capacities to maintain themselves and their dependents. The extent to which an aged person will have the financial capacity to meet self-maintenance costs and those of dependents relies upon the standard of living desired during retirement years, employment opportunities, and other resources (e.g., personal savings, social insurance and inherited assets) available to meet this contingency.

---

[3]Kenneth Black, Jr., *Group Annuities* (Philadelphia: University of Pennsylvania Press, 1955), p. 9.
[4]Ibid., p.11.
[5]Black, *Group Annuities*, p.11.
[6]Joseph S. Piacentini and Timothy J. Cerino, *EBRI Databook on Employee Benefits* (Washington, DC: Employee Benefit Research Institute, 1990), p. 40.
[7]Employee Benefit Research Institute, *EBRI Quarterly Pension Investment Report* (Washington, DC: Employee Benefit Research Institute, April 1991), p. 42.

1.2.1. Standard of Living after Retirement

The assumption usually is made that the financial needs of an individual decrease after retirement. To some extent, this assumption is valid. The retired individual may have no dependent children, and a home and its furnishings generally have been acquired by retirement age. However, the actual aggregate reduction in the financial needs of a person upon retirement has probably been overstated. Personal expectations and preferences discourage any drastic change in one's standard of living upon retirement, and an increasing tendency exists for retired persons to remain fairly active, particularly in terms of civic, social, travel, and other recreational activities. Furthermore, urbanization, geographic mobility, demographics and changing culture minimize the prospect of retired parents moving in with their children.

Another major factor preventing a decrease in the financial needs of retirees is the likely cost of long term care. It is estimated that one out of every 4 persons over age 65 will someday enter a nursing home and nearly every family will have some direct experience with this financial planning problem.[8] Although the federal government briefly experimented with the possibility of assuming a greater portion of this burden through the Medicare Catastrophic Coverage Act of 1988, the manner in which this additional coverage was financed proved to be politically unpalatable and was repealed the following year. Even if retirees are fortunate enough to have comprehensive health insurance coverage continued by their employers after retirement, recent changes in the accounting standards applied to these plans are likely to cause modifications in either the type of coverage, cost-sharing or financing of this benefit.

The authors are not suggesting that retired workers require income benefits equal to their earnings levels immediately preceding retirement, nor even the level of preretirement take-home pay. Presumably, at least at the higher income levels, these individuals were allocating a portion of their take-home pay to individual savings. However, it is suggested that the reduction in standard of living after retirement is not very great; and, more importantly, the trend in social thinking seems to be in the direction of not expecting retired workers to have to take much of a reduction in standard of living after retirement. The effect of inflation also has militated against a lower standard of living. Therefore, it is questionable whether one should assume any significant decrease in basic financial needs upon retirement, at least for individuals in the low- and middle-income categories.

---

[8] James Edmunds Wilson, "Health Care for the Elderly," *Business & Economic Review* 36, no. 2 (January-March 1990), pp. 42-3.

1.2.2.   Employment Opportunities

The proportion of persons 65 and over with some income from active employment is currently about 10 percent, and this percentage has been declining in recent years.[9] Obviously, many reasons account for the withdrawal of the aged from the labor force. A large number of older workers voluntarily retire. If workers have the necessary financial resources, they may wish to withdraw from active employment and live out their remaining years at a more leisurely pace. Others find it necessary for reasons of health to withdraw from the labor force at an advanced age. The aging process takes its toll, and many individuals are physically unable to operate at the level of efficiency attainable at the younger ages. Disabilities at the older ages tend to be more frequent and of longer duration.

Voluntary retirement and the physical inability to continue employment are undoubtedly important reasons for the decrease in the percentage of older persons participating in the labor force. However, these are probably not the most important factors affecting employment opportunities for the aged. The effects of industrialization and the development of the federal Old-Age, Survivors, Disability, and Health Insurance (OASDHI) program, private pensions, and other employee benefit programs probably have had a more significant impact on this problem.

The rapid pace and dynamic evolution of industrial employment operate to the disadvantage of older persons. Automation and the mass-production assembly lines put a premium on physical dexterity and mental alertness. Employers generally are of the opinion, justifiable or not, that the younger workers are better suited to the demands of industrial employment. In an agricultural economy the able-bodied older person could continue to work, at least on a part-time basis.

The OASDHI program and private pension plans, although created to alleviate the financial risk associated with excessive longevity, have actually aggravated the problem. These programs have tended to institutionalize age 65 as the normal retirement age, although the 1986 amendments to the Age Discrimination in Employment Act (ADEA) banned mandatory retirement (at any age) for most employees. The 1983 amendments to The Social Security Act will gradually raise the normal retirement age for social security benefits to age 67 by the year 2027.[10] Also, some employers may hesitate to hire older workers on the assumption that these employees

---

[9]The corresponding figure was 25 percent as recently as 1978. Susan Grad, *Income of the Population 55 or Older, 1986,* U.S. Department of Health and Human Services, Social Security Administration, pub. no. 13-11871, (Washington, DC: U.S. Government Printing Office, 1988).

[10]The retirement benefits provided under The Social Security Act are discussed in detail in Chapter 2.

would increase pension and other employee benefit plan costs. It is difficult to generalize as to the impact of the older worker on employee benefit plan costs. Nevertheless, it must be recognized that an employer's attitude toward the hiring of older workers may be influenced by the assumption, justified or not, that employee benefit costs will be adversely affected.

Self-employed members of the labor force have greater control as to the timing of their retirement from active employment. For example, physicians and lawyers frequently continue in practice, at least on a part-time basis, until advanced ages. Owners of businesses also continue to be active in the firm until relatively old ages. The fact remains, however, that employment opportunities for the majority of older workers have become more limited. It is quite likely that this will be a temporary phenomenon for many employees given the expected impact of changing demographics and the potential shortage of certain segments of the work force as early as the year 2000.

1.2.3.   Individual Savings of the Aged

If employment opportunities for the aged are decreasing and financial needs are still substantial at advanced ages, the need for savings becomes quite apparent. However, studies indicate that a substantial proportion of the homes owned by the aged are clear of any mortgage. Home ownership reduces the income needs of the aged insofar as normal maintenance costs and taxes are less than the amount of rent required for comparable housing accommodations. It has been estimated that the maintenance costs for an unencumbered home are about one third to forty percent less than the costs of renting comparable facilities. Furthermore, there is the possibility that the home can be used in part as an income-producing asset or that a home equity loan can be used to provide additional cash.

There is growing interest in the concept of a so-called reverse annuity. Under this approach, the homeowner receives a lifetime monthly income in exchange for the title to the home at the homeowner's death. The amount of the monthly annuity payment depends on the equity in the home and the life expectancy of the homeowner.

Jacobs and Weissert analyzed the potential for using home equity to finance long-term care. Their results strongly suggest that a significant number of elderly Americans could use their homes' equity to meet their health care expenses. They also conclude that those in the highest risk group and those with the lowest incomes, who are often the same individuals, also can be significantly helped by the use of reverse annuity mortgages.[11]

Pricing this type of financial instrument has proven to be extremely difficult and a major obstacle to its widespread use. Another problem faced by private institutions is the possibility that the outstanding balance on the mortgage will eventually exceed the value of the property.

As a result of the Housing and Community Development Act of 1987 the federal government began an experimental program in which the Department of Housing and Urban Development (HUD) will insure a maximum of 2,500 reverse mortgages. However, the complexity of the HUD program, the inherent risks, and the small profit potential have reduced the number of original lenders. [12]

Personal savings rates have been running at historically low levels in recent years. The distribution of savings by savings media has changed considerably over the years. The change that is most pertinent to this discussion is the relative increase in private pension reserves in relation to purely individual forms of saving. Annual employer contributions to private pension funds now amount to about $50 billion, and the net contributions to pension funds have averaged over 35 percent of personal savings in recent years.[13] The tremendous increases in disposable income over the last quarter century, therefore, have not resulted in any increase in the proportion of personal savings. There have been many forces at work that have restricted the growth of savings. Advertising, installment credit, and the media of mass communications encourage individuals to set their sights on a constantly increasing standard of living. This competition from consumption goods for current income dollars results in a lower priority being placed on the need for accumulating savings for old age. Also, the high levels of federal income tax rates reduce an income earner's capacity to save. In recent decades, inflation has been an additional deterrent to increased levels of saving. Inflation is a particularly serious threat to the adequacy of savings programs of persons who already are retired. For employed persons, increases in the cost of living may be offset, in part or in whole, by increases in current earnings; however, inflation protection is

---

[11]Bruce Jacobs and William Weissert, "Using Home Equity to Finance Long-Term Care," *Journal of Health Politics, Policy & Law* 12, no. 1 (Spring 1987), pp. 77-95. However, a more recent study analyzes the potential of reverse annuity mortgages to increase the current income of the elderly and concludes that most low-income elderly also have little housing equity. See, Steven F Venti, and David A Wise, "Aging and the Income Value of Housing Wealth," *Journal of Public Economics* 44, no. 3 (April 1991), pp. 371-397.

[12]Robert J Pratte, "A Mortgage for the 21st Century," *Mortgage Banking* 50, no. 8 (May 1990), pp. 45-52.

[13]Jack L. VanDerhei, "What Do We Get from Today's Programs? Savings and Capital Formation, " paper prepared for Employee Benefit Research Institute policy forum, "The Retirement Policy Challenge," May 4, 1989.

likely to be less comprehensive for most aged persons.[14] Therefore, the aged are faced with the alternatives of accepting a lower standard of living or more rapidly liquidating their accumulated savings.

The proportion of individual (as opposed to group) savings, then, is decreasing at a time when the pattern of living of the aged is becoming increasingly more costly. Under such circumstances, the tremendous importance of pension programs in meeting the economic risk of old age is obvious.

1.2.4. Increasing Longevity

Still another dimension to the overall economic problem of old age is the number of aged in the population. The fact that life expectancy has been increasing is well recognized. However, that this increase in longevity is a recent and quite dramatic development often is not appreciated. Since 1900 the life expectancy at birth has increased from 47 years to approximately 74.3 years. The rates of mortality at the earlier ages are now so low that further improvements in mortality at these ages would have little impact on further extensions of the average length of life. If additional improvements in longevity are to be realized, reductions in mortality at the older ages are required. This impediment to further extensions in life expectancy may be overcome if medical advances result from the current concentration of research in the areas of the chronic and degenerative diseases.

One effect of the improvements in longevity in the 20th century has been an absolute and relative increase in the population of persons age 65 and over. In 1900, there were approximately 3 million persons age 65 and over, whereas there were about 25 million such persons in 1980. The proportion of the U.S. population age 65 and over currently is about 11.5 percent, whereas the proportion of the population in these age brackets in 1900 was about 4 percent.

Another important dimension in the analysis of the changing demography of the elderly -- those age 65 and over -- is their age distribution. A generation ago, 68 percent of the elderly were 65 to 74 years old, 27 percent were 75 to 84, and only 5 percent were 85 or older. However, today's elderly population reflects a shift toward the upper end of the age scale: approximately 10 percent are over 85, nearly a third are 75 to 84, and less than 60 percent are 65 to 74.[15]

---

[14]Chapter 2 describes the inflation protection inherent in social security payments and Chapter 14 analyzes the techniques used by many private plan sponsors to provide partial ad hoc relief.

[15]Peter K. Francese, "Demographic Trends Reshaping Retirement Security," in *Search for a National Retirement Income Policy*, ed. Jack L. VanDerhei (Homewood, Ill.: Richard D. Irwin, 1987).

The problem of old-age economic security, therefore, is of concern to an increasing number and percentage of the U.S. population.

1.3.   REASONS FOR GROWTH OF PRIVATE PENSIONS

From the above discussion it can be seen that the problem of economic security for the aged is a serious and increasingly important one. However, the mere existence of the problem does not explain the phenomenal growth of private pensions. In other words, given the existence of the old-age economic problem, why did employers and employees choose to meet the need, at least in part, through the vehicle of private pension programs? In a broad sense, the major reason is the fact that private pensions offer substantial advantages to both employers and employees. Without this foundation of mutual benefit, the private pension movement could not have achieved the prolonged and substantial growth it has enjoyed. In addition, for several decades, government officials recognized the social desirability of pension programs and acted to encourage the growth of these plans through favorable treatment under the tax system and by other means. Recently, however, it appears that this attitude has changed and many commentators have speculated that the resulting tax law modifications may curb the growth of these arrangements.

The specific factors generally considered as having influenced the growth of private pensions are discussed below. It must be recognized that the reasons giving rise to the establishment of one plan might be quite different from those in the case of another plan.

1.3.1.   Increased Productivity

A systematic method of meeting the problem of superannuated employees can be easily justified on sound management grounds. Practically every employee eventually reaches a point where, because of advanced age, he or she is a liability rather than an asset to the employer. That is, at some advanced age, an employee's contribution to the productivity of the firm is less than the compensation he or she is receiving.

The employer has several courses of action when an employee reaches this point. One, the employee can be terminated without any further compensation or any retirement benefits as soon as the value of the employee's services is less than the salary being paid. For obvious reasons, this course of action is seldom followed by employers. Two, the employer can retain the superannuated employee in the employee's current position and at current level of compensation. The difference between the employee's productivity and salary is absorbed by the employer as a cost of doing business. This alternative is also undesirable. Such an approach would undoubtedly prove to be the most costly method of meeting the problem of superannuated employees. Furthermore, the longer range indirect costs that would be incurred from the resultant inefficiencies and poor employee morale among the younger workers would be significant. Three, the employer could retain the superannuated worker, but transfer the employee to a less demanding job at the same or a reduced level of compensation. In the former case, the direct costs would be similar to alternative two, but the indirect costs would be reduced in that a younger and more capable person would now be staffing the more demanding position.   If the employee's salary is reduced, the direct costs of superannuation also would be reduced.

Most employers who do not have a pension plan generally handle the problem of the older worker in the latter manner. The effectiveness of this approach to the problem has certain important limitations. First, a firm usually has only a limited number of positions to which aged workers can be transferred. For a large or even medium-sized firm, only a fraction of the superannuated employees can be efficiently employed. With automation and the increasingly higher levels of skill required in most jobs, the limitations of this solution are apparent. Furthermore, the superannuated employee is generally still overpaid in the less demanding jobs since, for practical purposes, reductions comparable to the decrease in employee productivity are seldom made. Lastly, this approach does not solve the problem of superannuation; it merely defers it, since a point will be reached where the employee's productivity is considerably below even a minimum level of wage.

The fourth alternative available to the employer in meeting the problem of superannuation is to establish a formal pension plan. A pension plan permits employers to provide superannuated employees with an acceptable alternative to continued employment in a humanitarian and nondiscriminatory manner, and the inefficiencies associated with retaining employees beyond their productive years are reduced. Furthermore, the sense of security derived from the knowledge that provision is made, at least in part, for their retirement income needs should increase the morale and productivity of employees. Also, systematic retirement of older workers will keep the channels of promotion open, thereby offering opportunity and incentive to the young, ambitious employees -- particularly those aspiring to executive positions. Therefore, a pension plan should permit an employer to attract and keep a better caliber of employee.

The problem of superannuation, then, exists in all business firms. Any solution, except the unlikely alternative of arbitrary termination of older workers without any retirement benefit, results in some cost, direct or indirect, to the employer. Unfortunately, some employers assume that the pension plan solution is the only approach that carries a price tag. The hidden costs of the other alternatives must be recognized. The decision, therefore, is which solution is best suited to the needs and financial position of the employer. For a large number of employers, the formal pension plan approach has proved to be the superior solution.

1.3.2.   Tax Considerations

The bulk of the growth in private pension plans has occurred since 1940. One reason for the growth of these plans during the World War II and Korean War periods was that normal and excess profits tax rates imposed on corporations during these years were extremely high. Since the employer's contributions to a qualified pension plan are deductible (within limits) for federal income tax purposes, a portion of the plan's liabilities could be funded with very little effective cost to the firm. Furthermore, the investment income earned on pension trust assets is exempt from federal income taxation until distributed.[16]

The tax advantages of qualified pension plans are attractive from the standpoint of employees covered under the plan; for example, the employer's contributions to a pension fund do not constitute taxable income to the employee in the year in which contributions are made. The pension benefits derived from employer contributions are taxed when distributed to the employee. In addition, under limited circumstances, distributions from a pension plan may be taxed on a favorable basis.

Therefore, qualified pension plans offer significant tax advantages to participants generally, and, prior to 1988, employees in high income tax brackets received greater advantages.[17] Since the high-salaried senior officers of corporations often make the decision regarding the establishment and design of employee benefit plans, their role as participants under the plan may have influenced their decisions on these matters. However, in the case of large corporations, cost and other considerations minimized or eliminated the personal tax situations of key employees as factors influencing the establishment or design of a pension plan. In the case of a small, closely held corporation, on the other hand, one can readily see how the tax implications for stockholder-employees might have been a decisive factor in the establishment and design of a pension plan. Lastly, tax

---

[16]For a complete discussion of the tax aspects of qualified pension plans, see Chapter 23.

[17]As recently as 1986, the federal income tax law had 14 progressive tax brackets and a maximum rate of 50 percent. The Tax Reform Act of 1986 reduced the number of tax brackets to two (15 percent and 28 percent), effective in 1988. The maximum tax bracket has since been increased to 31 percent.

considerations are certainly one reason, although not the most important, why some labor leaders negotiate for establishment and liberalization of employee benefit programs in lieu of further wage increases.

Although it is too early to know the full implications of the Tax Reform Act of 1986, benefits available to highly compensated employees will be substantially restricted, perhaps to the point where alternative forms of compensation (such as cash or nonqualified retirement arrangements) will be more desirable. Management of smaller organizations might be tempted to terminate existing plans and use the money to compensate executives in some other way.

1.3.3. Wage Stabilization

The second wartime development that helped to stimulate the growth of pensions was the creation of a wage stabilization program as part of a general price control scheme. Employers, in competing for labor, could not offer the inducement of higher wages. Under these conditions, union leaders found it difficult to prove to their membership the merits of unionism.

Therefore, the War Labor Board attempted to relieve the pressure on management and labor for higher wage rates by permitting the establishment of fringe benefit programs, including pensions. This policy further stimulated the growth of pension plans during the period.

1.3.4. Union Demands

Labor leaders have had mixed emotions over the years regarding the desirability of employer-financed pension plans. In the 1920s, labor generally did not favor such plans for its membership. It held the view that pensions represented an additional form of employer paternalism and were instituted to encourage loyalty to the firm. Labor leaders felt that the need would be best met through the establishment of a government-sponsored universal social security system; in the absence of that solution, unions should establish their own pension plans for their members. The former objective was achieved with the passage of The Social Security Act of 1935. By the 1930s, several unions had established their own plans. However, many of these plans were financed inadequately, a condition that became quite apparent during the depression years. Recognition of the financial burden of a pension program and enactment of wage controls led some labor leaders, in the early 1940s, to favor establishment of employer-supported pension plans.

From 1945 to 1949, the rate of growth of new plans fell off markedly. During this postwar period, employee interest centered upon cash wage increases in an attempt to recover the lost ground suffered during the period of wage stabilization. In the latter part of the 1940s, union leaders once again began expressing an interest in the negotiation of pension programs. The renewal of interest in pensions probably came about because of two factors. First, there was increasing antagonism on the part of the public toward what were viewed by many persons as excessive union demands for cash wage increases. The negotiation of fringe benefits was one way of possibly reducing pressures from this quarter. Second, some union leaders argued that social security benefits were inadequate, and a supplement in the form of private pension benefits was considered to be necessary. Also, certain labor officials believed the negotiation of employer-supported pensions would weaken the resistance of the latter toward liberalizations of social security benefit levels. Thus, pension demands became a central issue in the labor negotiations in the coal, automobile, and steel industries in the late 40s. Although unions had negotiated pension benefits prior to this period, it was not until the late 40s that a major segment of labor made a concerted effort to bargain for private pensions.

Labor's drive for pension benefits was facilitated by a National Labor Relations Board ruling in 1948 that employers had a legal obligation to bargain over the terms of pension plans. Until that time, there was some question whether employee benefit programs fell within the traditional subject areas for collective bargaining; that is, wages, hours, and other conditions of employment. The issue was resolved when the National Labor Relations Board held that pension benefits constitute wages and the provisions of these plans affect conditions of employment.[18] Upon appeal, the court upheld the NLRB decision, although it questioned the assumption that such benefits are wages.[19] The result of these decisions was that an employer cannot install, terminate, or alter the terms of a pension plan covering organized workers without the approval of the authorized bargaining agent for those employees. Furthermore, management has this obligation regardless of whether the plan is contributory or noncontributory, voluntary or compulsory, and regardless of whether the plan was established before or after the certification of the bargaining unit.

Labor was quick to respond to these decisions, and the 1950s were marked by union demands for the establishment of new pension plans, liberalization of existing plans, and the supplanting of employer-sponsored programs with negotiated plans. Undoubtedly, labor's interest in private

---

[18]*Inland Steel Company v. United Steelworkers of America*, 77 NLRB 4 (1948).
[19]*Inland Steel Company v. National Labor Relations Board*, 170 F.(2d) 247, 251 (1949).

pensions has been an important factor in the tremendous growth in plans since 1949.

1.3.5. Business Necessity

Employers hire employees in a free, competitive labor market. Therefore, as the number of plans increases, employees come to expect a pension benefit as part of the employment relationship. Employers who do not have such a plan are at a competitive disadvantage in attracting and holding personnel. Therefore, some employers feel they must install a plan even if they are not convinced that the advantages generally associated with a pension plan outweigh the cost of the benefit. Admittedly, this is a negative reason for instituting a plan. In other words, these employers feel that little evidence exists that pension plans truly result in improved morale and efficiency among their work force; but they feel that there would clearly be an adverse employee reaction if they did not offer a pension. Also, in contrast to situations where a plan is established in response to labor demands, an employer may offer a pension plan as part of an employee relations objective aimed at keeping a union out of the firm.

1.3.6. Reward for Service

There is a tendency to argue that employers never provide any increase in employee benefits unless they can expect an economic return in some form. Although this philosophy may generally prevail in a capitalistic system, the fact remains that many employers have established plans out of a sincere desire to reward employees who have served the firm well over a long period of service. Also, some employers may feel a moral responsibility to make some provision for the economic welfare of retired employees.

1.3.7. Efficiency of Approach

Part of the growth of private pensions must be attributed to the belief that a formal group savings approach has certain inherent advantages. The advantages are not such that they eliminate the need for individual savings; but the merits of private pensions as a supplement to social security benefits and individual savings programs are indeed significant. First, the economic risk of old age derives from the fact that a point is reached when an employee is unable or unwilling to continue in active employment. A formal plan as an integral part of compensation arrangements and employment relationships, therefore, is quite logical. There is no additional wage cost to the employer to the extent that pension benefits are provided in lieu of other forms of compensation. If pension benefits are provided in addition to prevailing wage rates, the employer's extra wage costs resulting from the pension plan may be able to be passed on to the consuming public in the form of higher prices.

It has been argued that from a broad social point of view, the private pension system is the lowest cost method of providing economic security for the aged. In addition to the administrative efficiency of group saving arrangements, it is argued that the small increase in consumer prices that might be required to provide pension benefits is a relatively painless method of meeting the risk. In other words, the burden of retirement security is spread over a large number of people and over a long period of time. Still another aspect to the argument is the assumption that private pensions increase consumption levels among the aged, which in turn helps to maintain a high level of economic activity.

Lastly, private pensions constitute a form of forced savings. This advantage is extremely important in view of the apparent desire of many people to maintain a relatively high standard of living during their active employment years. Thus, it may be argued that it is economically more efficient if at least part of the risk is met through a forced saving private pension scheme.

1.3.8.   Sales Efforts of Funding Agencies

For all the previously mentioned reasons, there has been a considerable demand over the years for private pensions. However, in many instances, the advantages of these programs had to be called to the attention of specific employers. This function of creating effective demand for the pension product has been aggressively performed by those parties interested in providing services in this area. Insurance companies, through agents, brokers, and salaried representatives, were undoubtedly instrumental in the growth of pensions, particularly in the decades of the 20s and 30s. The trust departments of banks also are equipped to handle pension funds, and many corporate trustees and asset managers have been actively soliciting pension business, particularly since the early 1950s.

1.4.   RATIONALE OF PRIVATE PENSIONS

The growth of private pensions is attributable, as seen above, to a variety of reasons. It is difficult to determine the extent to which each factor contributed. Indeed, it seems reasonable to conclude that the dominant reasons leading to the establishment of specific plans vary depending on the circumstances surrounding each case. In other words, productivity considerations were dominant forces leading to the creation of some plans, while labor pressures, tax considerations, or other factors encouraged establishment of still other plans. With such variety of motivation, it is difficult to characterize private pensions in terms of a single philosophy or rationale. Nevertheless, attempts have been made over the years to explain private pensions in terms of an underlying concept or philosophy.[20]

Early industrial pension plans were viewed as gratuities or rewards to employees for long and loyal service to the employer. Closely related to this view is the concept that private pensions constitute a systematic and socially desirable method of releasing employees who are no longer productive members of the employer's labor force. Regardless of the view taken, it is clear that these early plans were largely discretionary, and management made it quite evident that employees had no contractual rights to benefits under the plans. Continuation of the pension plan was dependent upon competitive conditions and management policy. Furthermore, management reserved the right to terminate benefit payments to pensioners for misconduct on the part of the beneficiary or for any other reasons justifying such action in the opinion of the employer.

Thus, the growth of early pensions might be best categorized by a single concept: business expediency. Business expediency, by the very nature of the concept, implies that the establishment of a plan is a management prerogative and that the primary motivation for the creation of such plans was the economic benefit, direct or indirect, that accrued to the employer. But as the economy became more and more industrialized and pension plans became more prevalent, there was increasing interest in the view that employers had a moral obligation to provide for the economic security of retired workers. This point of view was expressed as early as 1912 by Lee Welling Squier, as follows: "From the standpoint of the whole system of social economy, no employer has a right to engage men in any occupation that exhausts the individual's industrial life in 10, 20, or 40 years; and then leave the remnant floating on society at large as a derelict at sea."[21]

This rationale of private pensions has come to be known as the human depreciation concept. It was the point of view taken by the United Mine Workers of America in their 1946 drive to establish a welfare fund:

---

[20]For an excellent discussion of pension philosophies, see Jonas E. Mittelman, "The Vesting of Private Pensions" (Ph.D. dissertation, University of Pennsylvania, 1959), Chapter 2.

[21]Lee Welling Squier, *Old Age Dependency in the United States* (New York: Macmillan, 1912), p.272.

The United Mine Workers of America has assumed the position over the years that the cost of caring for the human equity in the coal industry is inherently as valid as the cost of the replacement of mining machinery, or the cost of paying taxes, or the cost of paying interest indebtedness, or any other factor incident to the production of a ton of coal for consumers' bins. . . . [The agreement establishing the Welfare Fund] recognized in principle the fact that the industry owed an obligation to those employees, and the coal miners could no longer be used up, crippled beyond repair, and turned out to live or die subject to the charity of the community or the minimum contributions of the state.[22]

This analogy between human labor and industrial machines also was made in the report of the president's fact-finding board in the 1949 steelworkers' labor dispute in support of its conclusion that management had a responsibility to provide for the security of its workers: "We think that all industry, in the absence of adequate Government programs, owes an obligation to workers to provide for maintenance of the human body in the form of medical and similar benefits and full depreciation in the form of old-age retirement -- in the same way as it does now for plant and machinery."[23] The report continues as follows: "What does that mean in terms of steelworkers? It should mean the use of earnings to insure against the full depreciation of the human body -- say at age 65 -- in the form of a pension or retirement allowance."[24]

The validity of the human depreciation concept of private pensions has been challenged by many pension experts.[25] The process of aging is physiological and is not attributable to the employment relationship. Admittedly, the hazards of certain occupations undoubtedly shorten the life span of the employees involved. In those instances, the employer can logically be held responsible only for the increase in the rate of aging due to the hazards of the occupation. More importantly, the analogy between humans and machines is inherently unsound. A machine is an asset owned by the employer, and depreciation is merely an accounting technique for allocating the costs of equipment to various accounting periods. Employees, on the other hand, are free agents and sell their services to

---

[22]United Mine Workers of America Welfare and Retirement Fund, *Pensions for Coal Miners* (Washington, D.C., n.d.), p. 4.

[23]Steel Industry Board, *Report to the President of the United States on the Labor Dispute in the Basic Steel Industry* (Washington, D.C.: U.S. Government Printing Office, September 10, 1949), p.55.

[24]Ibid., p.65.

[25]For example, see Dan M. McGill and Donald S. Grubbs, Jr., *Fundamentals of Private Pensions*, 6th ed. (Homewood, Ill.: Richard D. Irwin, 1989), pp. 18-19. See also Charles L. Dearing, *Industrial Pensions* (Washington, D.C.: Brookings Institution, 1954), pp. 62-63 and 241-43; and Mittelman, "Vesting of Private Pensions," pp. 28-34.

employers for a specified wage rate. An employee, unlike a machine, is free to move from one employer to another. The differences between humans and machines are so great that one must question the value of the analogy as a basis for a rationale of private pensions. As Dearing notes: "Any economic or moral responsibility that is imposed on the employer for the welfare of workers after termination of the labor contract should be grounded on firmer reasoning than is supplied by the machine-worker analogy."[26]

In recent years, a view of private pensions that has achieved broader acceptance is the deferred wage concept. This concept views a pension benefit as part of a wage package that is composed of cash wages and other employee fringe benefits. The deferred wage concept has particular appeal with reference to negotiated pension plans. The assumption is made that labor and management negotiators think in terms of total labor costs. Therefore, if labor negotiates a pension benefit, the funds available for increases in cash wages are reduced accordingly. This theory of private pensions was expressed as early as 1913:

> In order to get a full understanding of old-age and service pensions, they should be considered as a part of the real wages of a workman. There is a tendency to speak of these pensions as being paid by the company, or, in cases where the employee contributes a portion, as being paid partly by the employer and partly by the employee. In a certain sense, of course, this may be correct, but it leads to confusion. A pension system considered as part of the real wages of an employee is really paid by the employee, not perhaps in money, but in the forgoing of an increase in wages which he might obtain except for the establishment of a pension system.[27]

The deferred wage concept also has been challenged on several grounds. First, it is noted that some employers who pay the prevailing cash wage rate for the particular industry also provide a pension benefit. Thus, it can be argued that in these cases the pension benefit is offered in addition to, rather than in lieu of, a cash wage increase. Second, the deferred wage concept ignores the possible argument that the employer is willing to accept a lower profit margin to provide a pension plan for employees. Third, it is sometimes argued that if pension benefits are a form of wage, then terminated employees should be entitled to the part of the retirement benefit that has been earned to the date of termination. In practice, one finds that only a small proportion of the plans provides for the full and immediate vesting of all benefits. However, it can be argued that the

---

[26]Dearing, *Industrial Pensions*, p.243.
[27]Albert de Roode, "Pensions as Wages," *American Economic Review* III, no. 2 (June 1913), p. 287.

deferred wage concept does not necessarily require the full and immediate vesting of benefits. Proponents of this concept view pension benefits as a wage the receipt of which is conditioned upon the employee's remaining in the service of the employer for a specified number of years. This view of the pension benefit is similar, conceptually, to a pure endowment in which the policyholder receives the full face benefit of the policy if he or she lives to the maturity of the policy; however, the beneficiaries receive nothing if the policyholder dies prior to this time period. The consideration of the employee in this case is the reduction in cash wages accepted in lieu of the pension benefit.

In spite of the appeal of the deferred wage theory, it is questionable whether the private pension movement can be explained solely in terms of this concept. Indeed, there is probably no one rationale or theory that fully explains the "reason for being" of private pensions. This conclusion is not surprising in view of the fact that these plans are private, and the demands or reasons that give rise to one plan may be quite different from those leading to the introduction of another plan.

1.5.   RECENT LEGISLATION

Employee benefits in general and pension plans in particular have been the subject of substantial legislative activity in recent years.

After many years of discussion and debate concerning reform of the private pension system, the Employee Retirement Income Security Act of 1974 (ERISA) became law on September 2, 1974. ERISA effected some of the most significant changes ever enacted in the private pension movement. These changes affected virtually all aspects of corporate and self-employed pension plans from a legal, tax, investment, and actuarial viewpoint. In addition, ERISA established new reporting, disclosure, and fiduciary requirements as well as a program of plan termination insurance. Another major feature of ERISA was the establishment of the individual retirement account (IRA) concept, which was initially designed for individuals not covered under a qualified retirement plan.

The Economic Recovery Tax Act of 1981 (ERTA) was one of the biggest tax reduction acts in history. It also included several provisions that affected retirement plans. Most notable were the provisions that greatly expanded IRA opportunities to anyone with personal service income, allowed for voluntary contributions to qualified plans, and increased contribution and deduction limits for both simplified employee pension (SEP) programs and Keogh (H.R. 10) plans. ERTA also made changes that affected stock ownership plans and executive compensation arrangements.

Following on the heels of ERTA came another massive act, the Tax Equity and Fiscal Responsibility Act of 1982 (TEFRA), considered by some to be the biggest revenue-raising bill in history. TEFRA probably touched everyone in some manner and affected retirement plans in many ways. It reduced the maximum limits of pension plan benefits and contributions; brought about parity between corporate plans and plans for self-employed persons; introduced special restrictions on plans that are considered "top heavy," that is, plans that appear to be heavily weighted toward key employees; and provided for federal income tax withholding on pension and annuity payments.

After a one-year hiatus, in 1984 Congress passed two acts with significant implications for qualified retirement plans. The Deficit Reduction Act of 1984 (DEFRA) contained several provisions that substantially modified savings incentives. Cost-of-living adjustments for contribution and benefit limits were frozen for a second time. Estate tax exclusions for distributions from qualified plans and IRAs were repealed. Rules for cash-or-deferred plans, also known as 401(k) plans, were tightened. The Retirement Equity Act of 1984 (REACT) represented an attempt on the part of Congress to provide what was perceived by some as a more equitable distribution of retirement benefits from qualified plans. Young employees and nonworking spouses were the chief benefactors, as REACT required a reduction in the minimum age for mandatory participation, changed the survivor benefit requirements, and allowed for the assignment or alienation of qualified plan benefits in divorce proceedings.

In the most pervasive changes since ERISA, the Tax Reform Act of 1986 imposed new coverage tests and accelerated vesting requirements for qualified plans, changed the rules under which qualified plans can be integrated with social security, lowered limits for retirement benefits that begin before age 65, changed the timing and taxation of plan distributions, and terminated IRA deductions for many qualified plan participants. Substantial changes were also made with respect to employee stock ownership plans and executive compensation. Following the Tax Reform Act of 1986, Congress passed the Omnibus Budget Reconciliation Act of 1987 (OBRA '87) which made significant changes with respect to (1) minimum funding and maximum tax deductions for qualified plans, and (2) plan termination obligations for defined benefit plans.

Under the Technical and Miscellaneous Revenue Act of 1988 (TAMRA), Congress provided the possibility that certain minimum participation requirements enacted in the Tax Reform Act of 1986 may be applied separately with respect to each separate line of business of an employer.   TAMRA also added an additional sanction for highly compensated employees requiring them to include in their gross income for the year in which the minimum participation standard is not met an amount equal to their vested accrued benefit as of the close of that year.

The Omnibus Budget Reconciliation Act of 1989 (OBRA '89) made numerous changes in the statutory provisions that permit a lender to an employee stock ownership plan (ESOP), or ESOP plan sponsor, to exclude 50 percent of the interest from its income for federal tax purposes. OBRA also amended, among other things, provisions pertaining to the Section 404(k) dividend deduction, the ESOP tax-free rollover, and the ESOP estate tax exclusion.

The Omnibus Budget Reconciliation Act of 1990 (OBRA '90) increased Pension Benefit Guaranty Corp. (PBGC) premiums as well as the excise tax on reversions of excess pension plan assets to the employer on termination of a pension plan. However, OBRA '90 presented an opportunity to increase corporate cash flow and possibly to decrease near-term expense through the use of excess pension assets to pay retiree health benefits. The existence of this opportunity depends on the funded status of a pension plan.

Many changes, rulings, and regulations relating to these various pieces of legislation have occurred since their enactment. The legislation and the changes, as well as their impact on retirement plans, will be discussed throughout this book.

QUESTIONS FOR REVIEW

1. Describe the basic economic problems facing the aged.
2. Why have private pension plans grown so rapidly in the last four decades?
3. Explain the alternatives that exist for an employer dealing with superannuated employees. What are the limitations of these alternatives?
4. Briefly describe the principal tax advantages of qualified pension plans.
5. Describe how wage stabilization during World War II affected private pension plans.
6. Explain the role played by the National Labor Relations Board (NLRB) in the development of pension plans.
7. Describe the merits of private pensions as a supplement to social security benefits and individual savings programs.
8. Briefly describe the impact of recent legislation on the design process for private pension plans.

QUESTIONS FOR DISCUSSION

1. Economists have often argued that pension benefits are a form of deferred compensation accepted by employees in lieu of higher present wages. Assume that the employees of a firm ask you how much the pension benefit they earned this year is actually worth in current dollars. In general terms, how would you perform this valuation? What types of assumptions would you need to make? If the employees told you that they would forfeit the entire pension attributable to employer contributions if they were terminated within five years of the time they were originally hired, how would you factor this information into your analysis?

2. For several years it has been argued that one of the primary advantages of a pension plan for employees was that it allowed them to avoid taxation on a portion of their total compensation during the time they were in a high tax bracket and postpone the receipt, and as a consequence the taxation, of this money until after they retire. If, as was usually the case prior to the Tax Reform Act of 1986, the employee expected to be in a lower tax bracket after retirement, the tax savings inherent in this deferral could be substantial. Beginning in 1987, however, it appears the federal income tax system is evolving into a modified form of a flat tax system in which many taxpayers may expect to be taxed at the same rate, regardless of when their money is received. Does this necessarily imply that the tax advantages of private pension plans have ceased to be an important advantage for employees? (Hint: Even if all money received from a pension plan is taxed at the same rate, does the fact that money can accumulate at a before-tax rate of return, instead of an after-tax rate of return, affect the eventual amount of money received by the employee?)

3. The text suggests that a private pension plan allows the burden of retirement security to be spread over a long period of time. Discuss how this specifically applies in the case of investment risk. Assume that there are only two forms of investments for retirement: a risk-free asset with a known rate of return, and a risky asset with a higher expected rate of return. Unfortunately, the risky asset may experience large decreases as well as increases in any particular year. If employees were to invest for their retirement on an individual basis, why might they be willing to choose the risk-free asset, knowing their expected accumulation at retirement will be smaller? In contrast, if employees allowed the employer to invest for their retirement through a defined benefit pension plan (in which the employee's retirement benefit is guaranteed regardless of

the level of the pension assets), would the employer be as likely to choose the lower yielding risk-free asset for the pension plan? (Hint: What is the relevant investment horizon for a pension plan if it is assumed to be an ongoing operation?)

2. Social Security and Medicare

Robert J. Myers[*]

Economic security for retired workers, disabled workers, and survivors of deceased workers in the United States is, in the vast majority of cases, provided through the multiple means of Social Security, private pensions, and individual savings. This is sometimes referred to as a "three-legged stool" or the three pillars of economic-security protection. Still others look upon the situation as Social Security providing the floor of protection, with private sector activities building on top of it and public assistance programs, such as Supplemental Security Income (SSI) providing a net of protection for those whose total retirement income does not attain certain levels or meet minimum subsistence needs.

Although some people may view the Social Security program as one that should provide complete protection, over the years it generally has been agreed that it should only be the foundation of protection.

As described throughout this book, private pension plans have, to a significant extent, been developed to supplement Social Security. This is done in a number of ways, both directly and indirectly. The net result, however, is a broad network of retirement protection. Thus, to properly understand how private pension plans are coordinated with Social Security, it is essential to understand the history and structure of Social Security.

---

[*] Robert J. Myers, FSA, is Professor Emeritus, Temple University and an international consultant on Social Security. This chapter is based on "Social Security and Medicare", *The Handbook on Employee Benefits* (3rd ed) Jerry S. Rosenbloom (ed.) Business One Irwin, Homewood, Ill., 1992. Used with permission of the publisher.

This chapter discusses in detail the retirement, disability, and survivor provisions of the Social Security program and also considers possible future changes. Following this, the Medicare program is described.

The term *Social Security* as used here is the meaning generally accepted in the United States, namely, the cash benefits provisions of the Old-Age, Survivors and Disability Insurance (OASDI) program. International usage of the term *social security* is much broader than this and includes all other types of programs protecting individuals against the economic risks of a modern industrial system, such as unemployment, short-term sickness, work-connected accidents and diseases, and medical care costs.

2.1.   OLD-AGE, SURVIVORS AND DISABILITY INSURANCE PROGRAM

2.1.1.   Persons Covered Under OASDI

OASDI coverage--for both taxes and earnings credits toward benefit rights-- currently applies to somewhat more than 90 percent of the total work force of the United States. About half of those not covered have protection through a special employee retirement system, while the remaining half are either very low-paid intermittent workers or unpaid family workers.

The vast majority of persons covered under OASDI are so affected on a mandatory, or compulsory, basis. Several categories, however, have optional or semioptional coverage. It is important to note that OASDI coverage applies not only to employees, both salaried and wage earner, but also to self-employed persons. Some individuals who are essentially employees are nonetheless classified as self-employed for the sake of convenience in applying coverage.

Compulsory coverage is applicable to all employees in commerce and industry, interpreting these classifications very broadly, except railroad workers, who are covered under a separate program, the Railroad Retirement system. Actually, however, financial and other coordinating provisions exist between these two programs, so that, in reality, railroad workers are really covered under OASDI. Members of the armed forces are covered compulsorily, as are federal civilian employees hired after 1983. Compulsory coverage also applies to lay employees of churches (with certain minor exceptions), to employees of nonprofit charitable and educational institutions, to employees of state and local governments which do not have retirement systems (first effective after July 1, 1991; before then, coverage was elective, on a group basis, by the employing entity) and to

American citizens who work abroad for American corporations.   Self-employed persons of all types (except ministers) also are covered compulsorily unless their earnings are minimal (i.e., less than $400 a year); beginning in 1990, covered self-employment is taken as 92.35 percent of the self-employment net income (such figure being 100 percent minus the OASDI-Hospital Insurance tax rate applicable to employees).

From a geographical standpoint, OASDI applies not only in the 50 states and the District of Columbia but also in all outlying areas (American Samoa, Guam, the Northern Mariana Islands, Puerto Rico, and the Virgin Islands).

Elective coverage applies to a number of categories. Employees of state and local governments who are under a retirement system can have coverage at the option of the employing entity, and only when the current employees vote in favor of coverage. Similar provisions are available for American employees of foreign subsidiaries of American corporations, the latter having the right to opt for coverage. Once that coverage has been elected by a state or local government, it cannot be terminated. Approximately 75 percent of state and local government employees are now covered as a result of this election basis.

Because of the principle of separation of church and state, ministers are covered on the self-employed basis, regardless of their actual status. Furthermore, they have the right to opt out of the system within a limited time after ordination on grounds of religious principles or conscience. Americans employed in the United States by a foreign government or by an international organization are covered compulsorily on the self-employed basis.

2.1.2. Historical Development of Retirement Provisions

When what is now the OASDI program was developed in 1934-35, it was confined entirely to retirement benefits plus lump-sum refund payments to represent the difference, if any, between employee taxes paid, plus an allowance for interest, and retirement benefits received. It was not until the 1939 Act that auxiliary (or dependents) and survivors benefits were added, and not until the 1956 Act that disability benefits were made available. It is likely that only retirement benefits were instituted initially because such type of protection was the most familiar to the general public, especially in light of the relatively few private pension plans then in existence.

The "normal retirement age" (NRA) was originally established at 65. This figure was selected in a purely empirical manner, because it was a middle figure. Age 70 seemed too high, because of the common belief that relatively so few people reached that age, while age 60 seemed too low, because of the large costs that would be involved if that age had been selected. Many of the existing private pension plans at that time had a retirement age of 65, although some in the railroad industry used age 70. Furthermore, labor-force participation data showed that a relatively high proportion of workers continued in employment after age 60. A widely quoted reason why age 65 was selected is that Bismarck chose this age when he established the German national pension program in the 1880s; this, however is not so, because the age actually used originally in Germany was 70. The 1983 Act provided for the NRA to increase from age 65 to age 67 in a deferred, gradual manner. Specifically, the NRA is 65 for those attaining this age before 2003 and first becomes 67 for those attaining this age in 2027.

The initial legislation passed by the House of Representatives did not require eligible persons to retire when age 65 or over in order to receive benefits, although it was recognized that the retirement requirement would be essential to include in the final legislation. The Senate inserted a requirement of general nature that benefits would be payable only upon retirement, and this was included in the final legislation. Over the years, this retirement test, or work clause, has been the subject of much controversy, and it has been considerably liberalized and made more flexible over the years.

Beginning in the 1950s, pressure developed to provide early-retirement benefits, first for spouses and then for insured workers themselves. The minimum early-retirement age was set at 62, again a pragmatic political compromise, rather than being based on any completely logical reasons. The three-year differential, however, did represent about the average difference in age between men and their wives but, of course, as with any averages, the difference actually is larger in many cases. The benefit amounts are reduced when claimed before the NRA, and are increased, although currently to not as great an extent, for delaying retirement beyond the NRA. As the NRA increases beyond age 65, the reduction for claiming benefits at age 62 becomes larger.

2.1.3.   Eligibility Conditions for Retirement Benefits

To be eligible for OASDI retirement benefits, individuals must have a certain amount of covered employment. In general, these conditions were designed to be relatively easy to meet in the early years of operation, thus bringing the program into effectiveness quickly. Eligibility for retirement benefits--termed fully insured status--depends upon having a certain number of "quarters of coverage" (QC), varying with the year of birth or, expressed in another manner, depending upon the year of an individual's attainment of age 62.

Before 1978, a QC was defined simply as a calendar quarter during which the individual was paid $50 or more in wages from covered employment; the self-employed ordinarily received four QCs for each year of coverage at $400 or more of earnings. Beginning in 1978, the number of QCs acquired for each year depends upon the total earnings in the year. For 1978, each full unit of $250 of earnings produced a QC, up to a maximum of four QCs for the year. In subsequent years the requirement has increased, and will continue to increase in the future, in accordance with changes in the general wage level; for 1992, it is $570.

The number of QCs required for fully insured status is determined from the number of years in the period beginning in 1951, or with the year of attainment of age 22, if later, and the year before the year of attainment of age 62, with a minimum requirement of six. As a result, an individual who attained age 62 before 1958 needed only six QCs to be fully insured. A person attaining age 62 in 1990 has a requirement of 39 QCs, while a person attaining age 65 in 1990 needs 36 QCs. The maximum number of QCs that will ever be required for fully insured status is 40, applicable to persons attaining age 62 after 1990. It is important to note that, although the requirement for the number of QCs is determined from 1951, or attainment of age 22, and before attainment of age 62, the QCs to meet the requirement can be obtained at any time (e.g., before 1951, before age 22, and after age 61).

2.1.4.   Beneficiary Categories for Retirement Benefits

Insured workers can receive unreduced retirement benefits in the amount of the Primary Insurance Amount (or PIA), the derivation of which will be discussed next, beginning at the NRA, or actuarially reduced benefits beginning at earlier ages, down to age 62. For retirement at age 62 currently (and until 1999), the benefit is 80 percent of the PIA. As the NRA increases beyond 65, the reduction will become larger (eventually being 30 percent).

Retired workers also can receive supplementary payments for spouses and eligible children. The spouse receives a benefit at the rate of 50 percent of the PIA if claim is first made at the NRA or over, and at a reduced rate if claimed at ages down to 62 (currently, a 25 percent reduction at age 62--i.e., to 37.5 percent of the PIA); as the NRA increases beyond 65, the reduction for age 62 will be larger, eventually being 35 percent. However, if a child under age 16 (or a child aged 16 or over who was disabled before age 22) is present, the spouse receives benefits regardless of age, in an unreduced amount. Divorced spouses, when the marriage had lasted at least 10 years, are eligible for benefits under the same conditions as undivorced spouses.

Children under age 18 (and children aged 18 or over and disabled before age 22, plus children attending high school full-time at age 18) also are eligible for benefits, at a rate of 50 percent of the PIA; prior to legislation in 1981, post-secondary-school students aged 18-21 were eligible for benefits, and spouses with children in their care could receive benefits as long as a child under age 18 was present. Grandchildren and great-grandchildren can qualify as "children" if they are dependent on the individual and if both parents of the child are disabled or deceased.

An overall maximum on total family benefits is applicable as is discussed later. If a person is eligible for more than one type of benefit (e.g., both as a worker and as a spouse), in essence only the largest benefit is payable.

2.1.5.   Computation and Indexing Procedures for Retirement Benefits

As indicated in the previous section, OASDI benefits are based on the PIA. The method of computing the PIA is quite complicated, especially because several different methods are available. The only method dealt with here is that generally applicable to people who reach age 65 after 1981.

The first step in the ongoing permanent method of computing the PIA applicable to persons attaining age 65 in 1982 or after, is to calculate the Average Indexed Monthly Earnings (AIME). The AIME is a career-average earnings formula, but it is determined in such a manner as to closely approximate a final average formula. In a national social insurance plan, it would be inadvisable to use solely an average of the last few years of employment, because that could involve serious manipulation through the cooperation of both the employee and the employer, whereas in a private pension plan, the employer has a close financial interest not to do so. Furthermore, as described later, OASDI benefit computation is not proportionate to years of coverage or proportion of work life in covered employment, as is the case for private pension plans generally.

The first step in computing the AIME is to determine the number of years over which it must be computed. On the whole, such number depends solely on the year in which the individual attains age 62. The general rule is that the computation period equals the number of years beginning with 1951, or the year of attaining age 22, if later, up through the year before attainment of age 62, minus the so-called five dropout years. The latter is provided so that the very lowest five years of earnings can be eliminated. Also, years of high earnings in or after the year of attaining age 62 can be substituted for earlier, lower years.

As an example, persons attaining age 62 in 1990 have a computation period of 34 years (the 39 in 1951-89 minus 5). The maximum period will be 35 years for those attaining age 62 after 1990. For the infrequent case of an individual who had qualified for OASDI disability benefits and who recovered from the disability, the number of computation years for the AIME for retirement benefits is reduced by the number of full years after age 21 and before age 62 during any part of which the person was under a disability.

The AIME is not computed from the actual covered earnings, but rather after indexing them, to make them more current as compared with the wage level at the time of retirement. Specifically, covered earnings for each year before attainment of age 60 are indexed to that age, while all subsequent covered earnings are used in their actual amount. No earnings before 1951 can be utilized, but all earnings subsequently, either before age 22 or after age 61, are considered.

The indexing of the earnings record is accomplished by multiplying the actual earnings of each year before the year that age 60 was attained by the increase in earnings from the particular year to the age-60 year. For example, for persons attaining age 62 in 1990 (i.e., age 60 in 1988), any earnings in 1951 would be converted to indexed earnings by multiplying them by 6.90709, which is the ratio of the nationwide average wage in 1988 to that in 1951. Similarly, the multiplying factor for 1952 earnings is 6.50251, and so on. Once the earnings record for each year in the past has been indexed, the earnings for the number of years required to be averaged are selected to include the highest ones possible; if there are not sufficient years with earnings, then zeroes must be used. Then, the AIME is obtained by dividing the total indexed earnings for such years by 12 times such number of years.

Now, having obtained the AIME, the PIA is computed from a benefit formula. There is a different formula for each annual cohort of persons attaining age 62. For example, for those who reached age 62 in 1979, the formula was 90 percent of the first $180 of AIME, plus 32 percent of the next $905 of AIME, plus 15 percent of the AIME in excess of $1,085. For the 1980 cohort, the corresponding dollar bands are $194, $977, and $1,171, while those for the 1991 cohort are $387, $1,946, and $2,333. These bands adjust automatically according to changes in nationwide average wages.

A different method of computing the PIA for retirement benefits (and also for disability benefits, but not for survivor benefits) is applicable for certain persons who receive pensions based in whole or in part on earnings from employment not covered by OASDI or Railroad Retirement (in the past or in the future, and in other countries as well as in the U.S.). This is done to eliminate the windfall benefits (due to the weighted nature of the benefit formula) that would otherwise arise. Excluded from this provision are the following categories: (1) persons who attain age 62 before 1986; (2) persons who were eligible for such pension before 1986; (3) disabled-worker beneficiaries who became disabled before 1986 (and were entitled to such benefits in at least one month in the year before attaining age 62); (4) persons who have at least 30 years of coverage (as defined hereafter); (5) persons who were employed by the federal government on January 1, 1984, and were then brought into coverage by the 1983 Amendments; and (6) persons who were employed on January 1, 1984, by a nonprofit organization which was not covered on December 31, 1983, and had not been so covered at any time in the past.

Under this method of computation of the PIA, ultimately the percentage factor applicable to the lowest band of earnings will be 40 percent, instead of 90 percent. As a transitional measure, those who become first eligible for OASDI benefits in 1986 have an 80 percent factor, while it is 70 percent for the 1987 cohort, 60 percent for the 1988 cohort, and 50 percent for the 1989 cohort.

For persons who have 21-29 "years of coverage" (as defined hereafter), an alternative phase-in procedure is used (if it produces a larger PIA). The percentage factor applicable to the lowest band of earnings in the PIA formula is 80 percent for 29 years of coverage, 70 percent for 28 years, 60 percent for 27 years, and 50 percent for 26 years.

In any event, under any of the foregoing procedures, the PIA as computed in the regular manner will never be reduced by more than 50 percent of the pension based on noncovered employment (or the pro rata portion thereof based on noncovered employment after 1956 if it is based on both covered and noncovered employment).

Prior to legislation in 1981, if the PIA benefit formula produced a smaller amount than $122 in the initial benefit computation, then this amount was nonetheless payable. However, for persons first becoming eligible after 1981, no such minimum is applicable.

A special minimum applies to the PIA for individuals who have a long period of covered work, but with low earnings. As of December 1991, this minimum is approximately $23.90 times the "years of coverage" in excess of 10, but not in excess of 30; thus, for 30 or more years of coverage, the minimum benefit is $478.20. Before 1991, a "year of coverage" is defined as a year in which earnings are at least 25 percent of the maximum taxable earnings base, while after 1990, a factor of 15 percent is used; for 1979 and after, this base is taken to be what would have prevailed if the ad hoc increases in the base provided by the 1977 Act had not been applicable, and, instead, the automatic increases had occurred. Thus, for this purpose, the 1992 base is taken as $41,400, instead of the actual one of $55,500.

The resulting PIAs then are increased for any automatic adjustments applicable because of annual increases in the consumer price index (CPI)--

or, when the balance of the OASDI Trust Funds is relatively low, by the annual increase in nationwide wages if this is less than the CPI rise--that occur in or after the year of attaining age 62, even though actual retirement is much later. These automatic adjustments are made for benefits for each December. Such CPI increases in the recent past have been 9.9 percent for 1979, 14.3 percent for 1980, 11.2 percent for 1981, 7.4 percent for 1982, 3.5 percent for 1983 and 1984, 3.1 percent for 1985, 1.3 percent for 1986, 4.2 percent for 1987, 4.0 percent for 1988, 4.7 percent for 1989, 5.4 percent for 1990, and 3.7 percent for 1991.

The resulting PIA then is reduced, in the manner described previously, for those who first claim benefits before the NRA. Conversely, retired workers who do not receive benefits for any months after they attain the NRA, essentially because of the earnings test, which will be described later, receive increases that are termed *delayed-retirement credits* (DRC). Such credits for those who attained age 65 in 1982-89 are at the rate of 3 percent per year of delay (actually 0.25 percent per month) for the period between ages 65 and 70. For those who attained age 65 before 1982, the DRC is at a rate of only 1 percent per year. For those who attain the NRA after 1989, such credit is gradually increased from 3.5 percent for the 1990-1991 cases, until it is 8 percent for those attaining the NRA (then 66) in 2009. The DRC applies only to the worker's benefit and not to that for spouses or children.

A Maximum Family Benefit (MFB) is applicable when there are more than two beneficiaries receiving benefits on the same earnings record (i.e., the retired worker and two or more auxiliary beneficiaries). Not considered within the limit established by the MFB are the additional benefits arising from delayed-retirement credits and the benefits payable to divorced spouses. The MFB is determined prior to any reductions because of claiming benefits before the NRA, but after the effect of the earnings test as it applies to any auxiliary beneficiary (e.g., if the spouse has high earnings, any potential benefit payable to her or him would not be considered for purposes of the MFB of the other spouse).

The MFB is determined from the PIA by a complex formula. This formula varies for each annual cohort of persons attaining age 62. The resulting MFB is adjusted for increases in the CPI in the future (in the same manner as is the PIA). For the 1992 cohort, the MFB formula is: 150 percent of the first $495 of PIA, plus 272 percent of the next $219 of PIA, plus 134 percent of the next $217 of PIA, plus 175 percent of PIA in excess of $931. For future cohorts, the dollar figures are changed according to changes in nationwide average wages. The result of this formula is to produce MFBs that are 150 percent of the PIA for the lowest PIAs, with this proportion rising to a peak of 188 percent for middle-range PIAs, and then falling off to 175 percent--and leveling there--for higher PIAs.

2.1.6.   Earnings Test and Other Restrictions on Retirement Benefits

From the inception of the OASDI program, there has been some form of restriction on the payment of benefits to persons who have substantial earnings from employment. This provision is referred to as the "retirement earnings test." It does not apply to nonearned income, such as from investments or pensions. The general underlying principle of this test is that retirement benefits should be paid only to persons who are substantially retired.

The basic feature of the earnings test is that an annual exempt amount applies, so that full benefits are paid if earnings, including those from both covered and noncovered employment, are not in excess thereof. Then, for persons under the NRA (which is age 65 until 2003), for each $2 of excess earnings, $1 in benefits is withheld; the reduction is on a "$1 for $3" basis for those at and above the NRA in 1990 and after. For persons aged 65-69 (at any time in the year), the annual exempt amount is $10,200 for 1992, with the amounts for persons at and above the NRA for subsequent years being automatically determined by the increases in nationwide wages. Beginning with the month of attainment of age 70, the test no longer applies. For persons under age 65, the exempt amount is $7,440 in 1992, with automatic adjustment thereafter.

An alternative test applies for the initial year of retirement, or claim, if it results in more benefits being payable. Under this, full benefits are payable for all months in which the individual did not have substantial services in self-employment and had wages of 1/12 of the annual exempt amount or less. This provision properly takes care of the situation where an individual fully retires during a year, but had sizable earnings in the first part of the year, and thus would have most or all of the benefits withheld if only the annual test had been applicable.

Earnings of the "retired" worker affect, under the earnings test, the total family benefits payable. However, if an auxiliary beneficiary (spouse or child) has earnings, and these are sizable enough to affect the earnings test, any reduction in benefits is applicable only to such individual's benefits.

If an individual receives a pension from service under a government-employee pension plan under which the members were not covered under OASDI on the last day of her or his employment, the OASDI spouse benefit is reduced by two thirds of the amount of such pension. This provision, however, is not applicable to women--or to men who are dependent on their wives--who become eligible for such a pension before December 1982, while for December 1982 through June 1983, the provision applies only to those (both men and women) who cannot prove dependency on their spouse. This general provision results in the same treatment as occurs when both spouses have OASDI benefits based on their own earnings records; and then each receives such benefit, plus the excess, if any, of the spouse's benefit arising from the other spouse's earnings over the benefit based on their own earnings, rather than the full amount of the spouse's benefit.

2.1.7.   Historical Development of Disability Provisions

It was not until the 1956 Act that monthly disability benefits were added to the OASDI program, although the "disability-freeze" provision (in essence, a waiver-of-premium provision), described later, was added in the 1952 Act.[1] It may well be said that long-term disability is merely premature old-age retirement.

The monthly disability benefits initially were available only at ages 50 and over, that is, deferred to that age for those disabled earlier, with no auxiliary benefits for the spouse and dependent children. These limitations were quickly removed, by the 1958 and 1960 Acts.

2.1.8.   Eligibility Conditions for Disability Benefits

To be eligible for disability benefits, individuals must be both fully insured and disability insured.[2] Disability insured status requires 20 QC earned in the 40-quarter period ending with the quarter of disability, except that persons disabled before age 31 also can qualify if they have QC in half of the quarters after age 21.[3] The definition of disability is relatively strict. The disability must be so severe that the individual is unable to engage in any substantial gainful activity, and the impairment must be a medically determinable physical or mental condition that is expected to continue for at least 12 months or to result in prior death. Benefits are first payable after completion of six full calendar months of disability.

2.1.9.   Beneficiary Categories for Disability Benefits

In addition to the disabled worker, the same categories of dependents can receive monthly benefits as in the case of old-age retirement benefits.

---

[1]Actually, it was so written in that legislation as to be inoperative, but then was reenacted in 1954 to be on a permanent, ongoing basis.
[2]Blind persons need be only fully insured.
[3]For those disabled before age 24, the requirement is six QC in the last 12 quarters.

2.1.9.1. Benefit Computation Procedures for Disability Benefits

In all cases, the benefits are based on the Primary Insurance Amount (PIA), computed in the same manner as retirement benefits, except that fewer dropout years than five are allowed in the computation of the Averaged Indexed Monthly Earnings (AIME) for persons disabled before age 47. The disabled worker receives a benefit equal to 100 percent of the PIA, and the auxiliary beneficiaries each receive 50 percent of the PIA, subject to the Maximum Family Benefit.

An overall maximum on total family benefits is applicable, which is lower than that for survivor and retirement benefits--namely, no more than the smaller of (1) 150 percent of the PIA or (2) 85 percent of AIME (but not less than the PIA).

2.1.10. Eligibility Test for Disability Benefits and Other Restrictions on Benefits

The earnings or retirement test applies to the auxiliary beneficiaries of disabled workers, but *not* to the disabled worker beneficiary. However, the earnings of one beneficiary (e.g., the spouse of the disabled worker) do not affect the benefits of the other beneficiaries in the family (e.g., the disabled worker or the children). The test does not apply to disabled worker beneficiaries, because any earnings are considered in connection with whether recovery has occurred, except those during trial work periods (which earnings may possibly lead to removal from the benefit roll later).

OASDI disability benefits are coordinated with disability benefits payable under other governmental programs (including programs of state and local governments), except for needs-tested ones, benefits payable by the Veterans Administration, and government employee plans coordinated with OASDI. The most important of such coordinations is with Workers' Compensation (WC) programs, whose benefits are taken into account in determining the amount of the OASDI disability benefit (except for a few states that provide for their WC benefits to be reduced when OASDI disability benefits are payable--possible only for states that did this before February 19, 1981). The total of the OASDI disability benefit (including any auxiliary benefits payable) and the other disability benefit recognized cannot exceed 80 percent of "average current earnings" (generally based on the highest year of earnings in covered employment in the last six years, but indexed for changes in wage levels following the worker's disablement).

2.1.11. Disability Freeze

In the event that a disability beneficiary recovers, the so-called disability-freeze provision applies. Under this, the period of disability is "blanked out" in the computation of insured status and benefit amounts for subsequent retirement, disability, and survivor benefits.

2.1.12. Historical Development of Survivor Provisions

When what is now the OASDI program was developed in 1934-35, it was confined entirely to retirement benefits (plus lump-sum refund payments to represent the difference, if any, between employee taxes paid, plus an allowance for interest, and retirement benefits received). It was not until the 1939 Act that monthly survivor benefits were added with respect to deaths of both active workers and retirees, in lieu of the refund benefit.

The term "widow" is used here to include also widowers. Until 1983, the latter did not receive OASDI benefits on the same basis as widows, either being required to prove dependence on the deceased female worker or not being eligible at all. Now, because of legislative changes and court decisions, complete equality of treatment by sex prevails for OASDI survivor benefits.

The minimum eligibility age for aged widows was initially established at age 65. This figure was selected in a purely empirical manner, because it was a round figure (see the earlier discussion about retirement benefits as to why this was selected as the minimum retirement age).

Beginning in the 1950s, pressure developed to provide early-retirement benefits, first for widows and spouses and then for insured workers themselves. The minimum early-retirement age was set at 62, again a pragmatic political compromise, rather than a completely logical choice, and was later lowered to 60 for widows. The three-year differential, however, did represent about the average difference in age between men and their wives (but, of course, as with any averages, in many cases the actual difference is larger). The benefit amounts were not reduced for widows when they claimed before age 65 under the original amendatory legislation, but this is no longer the case.

2.1.13. Eligibility Conditions for Survivor Benefits

To be eligible for OASDI survivor benefits, individuals must have either *fully insured status or currently insured status*. The latter requires only 6 QC earned in the 13-quarter period ending with the quarter of death.

2.1.14. Survivor Beneficiary Categories

Two general categories of survivors of insured workers can receive monthly benefits. Aged survivors are widows aged 60 or over (or at ages 50-59 if disabled) and dependent parents aged 62 or over. Young survivors are children under age 18 (or at any age if disabled before age 22), children aged 18 who are full-time students in elementary or secondary educational institutions (i.e., defined just the same as in the case of retirement and disability beneficiaries), and the widowed parent of such children who are under age 16 or disabled. In addition, a death benefit of $255 is payable to widows or, in the absence of a widow, to children eligible for immediate monthly benefits.

The disabled widow receives a benefit at the rate of 71.5 percent of the deceased worker's PIA if claim is first made at ages 50-59. The benefit rate for other widows grades up from 71.5 percent of the PIA if claimed at age 60 to 100 percent if claimed at the Normal Retirement Age, which is age 65 for those attaining age 60 before 2000, grading up to 67 for those attaining age 60 in 2022 and after. Any Delayed-Retirement Credits which the deceased worker had earned also are applicable to the widow's benefit. Widows, regardless of age, caring for an eligible child (under age 16 or disabled) have a benefit of 75 percent of the PIA. Divorced spouses, when the marriage lasted at least 10 years, are eligible for benefits under the same conditions as undivorced spouses.

The benefit rate for eligible children is 75 percent of the PIA. The benefit rate for dependent parents is 82½ percent of the PIA, unless two parents are eligible, in which case it is 75 percent for each one.

The same overall maximum on total family benefits is applicable as is the case for retirement benefits. If a person is eligible for more than one type of benefit, e.g., both as a worker and as a surviving spouse, in essence only the largest benefit is payable.

2.1.15. Benefit Computation Procedures for Survivor Benefits

In all cases, the monthly survivor benefits are based on the PIA, and then are adjusted to reflect the Maximum Family Benefit, both of which are computed in essentially the same manner as is the case for retirement benefits.[4]

---

[4]For individuals who die before age 62, the computation is made as though the individual had attained age 62 in the year of death. In addition, for deferred widow's benefits, an alternative computation based on indexing the deceased's earnings record up to the earlier of age 60 of the worker or age 60 of the widow is used if this produces a more favorable result.

2.1.16. Eligibility Test for Survivor Benefits and Other Restrictions

Marriage (or remarriage) of the survivor beneficiary generally terminates benefit rights. The only exceptions are remarriage of widows after age 60 (or after age 50 for disabled widows) and marriage to another OASDI beneficiary (other than one who is under age 18).

From the inception of the OASDI program, there has been some form of restriction on the payment of benefits to persons who have substantial earnings from employment, the earnings or retirement test. The same test applies to survivor beneficiaries as to retirement benefits. However, the earnings of one beneficiary (e.g., the widowed mother) do not affect the benefits of the other beneficiaries in the family (e.g., the orphaned children).

If a widow receives a pension from service under a government-employee pension plan under which the members were not covered under OASDI on the last day of her employment, the OASDI widow's benefit is reduced by two-thirds of the amount of such pension. This provision, however, is not applicable to women (or men who were dependent on their wives) who became eligible for such a pension before December 1982 or to individuals who became first so eligible from December 1982 through June 1983 and who were dependent on their spouses.

2.1.17. Financing Provisions of OASDI Program

From its inception until the 1983 Act, the OASDI program has been financed entirely by payroll taxes (and interest earnings on the assets of the trust funds), with only minor exceptions, such as the special benefits at a subminimum level for certain persons without insured status who attained age 72 before 1972. Thus, on a permanent ongoing basis, no payments from general revenues were available to the OASDI system; the contributions for covered federal civilian employees and members of the armed forces are properly considered as "employer" taxes.

The 1983 Act introduced two instances of general-revenues financing of the OASDI program. As a one-time matter, the tax rate in 1984 was increased to what had been previously scheduled for 1985 (i.e., for both the employer and employee, from 5.4 percent to 5.7 percent), but the increase for employees was, in essence, rescinded, and the General Fund of the Treasury made up the difference to the OASDI Trust Funds. On an ongoing basis, the General Fund passes on to the trust funds the proceeds of the income taxation of OASDI benefits (first effective for 1984), and, in fact, does so somewhat in advance of actual receipt of such monies.

The payroll taxes for the retirement and survivors benefits go into the OASI Trust Fund, while those for the disability benefits go into the DI Trust

Fund, and all benefit payments and administrative expenses for these provisions are paid therefrom. The balances in the trust fund are invested in federal government obligations of various types, with interest rates at the current market values. The federal government does not guarantee the payments of benefits. If the trust fund were to be depleted, it could not obtain grants, or even loans, from the general treasury. However, a temporary provision (effective only in 1982) permitted the OASI Trust Fund to borrow, repayable with interest, from the DI and HI Trust Fund. A total of $17.5 billion was borrowed ($12.4 billion from HI). The last of such loans were repaid in 1986.

Payroll taxes are levied on earnings up to only a certain annual limit, which is termed the *earnings base*. This base is applicable to the earnings of an individual from each employer in the year, but the person can obtain a refund (on the income tax form) for all employee taxes paid in excess of those on the earnings base. The self-employed pay taxes on their self-employment income on no more than the excess of the earnings base over any wages which they may have had.

Since 1975, the earnings base has been determined by the automatic-adjustment procedure, on the basis of increases in the nationwide average wage. However, for 1979-81, ad hoc increases of a higher amount were legislated; the 1981 base was established at $29,700. The 1982 and subsequent bases were determined under the automatic-adjustment provision. The 1991 base was $53,400, while that for 1992 is $55,500.

The payroll tax rate is a combined one for Old-Age and Survivors Insurance (OASI), Disability Insurance (DI), and Hospital Insurance (HI), but it is allocated among the three trust funds. The employer and employee rates are equal. The self-employed pay the combined employer-employee rate. In 1984-89, they had an allowance for the reduction in income taxes if half of the OASDI-HI tax were to be considered as a business expense (as it is for incorporated employers); such allowance was a uniform reduction in the tax rate--2.7 percentage points in 1984, 2.2 percentage points in 1985, and 2.0 percentage points in 1986-89. After 1989, the direct procedure of considering half of the OASDI-HI taxes as a deduction from income is done. Also, until 1991, the earnings base was the same for OASDI and HI, but in 1991, the base for HI was raised to $125,000, and it is $130,200 in 1992.

The employer and employee rates were 1 percent each in 1937-49, but have gradually increased over the years, until being 7.15 percent in 1986-87 (the latter subdivided 5.2 percent for OASI, 0.5 percent for DI, and 1.45 percent for HI). These rates increased to 7.51 percent in 1988, and are 7.65 percent in 1990 (and after), the later being subdivided 5.6 percent for OASI, 0.6 percent for DI, and 1.45 percent for HI.

2.2.   POSSIBLE FUTURE OASDI DEVELOPMENTS

Advisory groups have, over the years, urged that there should be so-called universal coverage. Following the 1983 Amendments, relatively little remains to be done in this area, except perhaps to cover compulsorily all new hires in state and local government employment (as was done in the federal area).

The minimum retirement age at which unreduced benefits are payable was increased from the present 65 to age 67, phased in over a period of years, by the 1983 Act. This was done in recognition of the significant increase in life expectancy that has occurred in the last 40 years, as well as the likely future increases. If life expectancy increases even more rapidly than currently projected, a further increase in such age would reduce the increased long-range future cost of the program resulting from such improvement.

The earnings test has always been subject to criticism by many persons, who argue that it is a disincentive to continued employment and that "the benefits have been bought and paid for, and therefore should be available at age 65." The 1983 Act, by increasing ultimately (beginning with those who attain age 66 in 2009) the size of the delayed retirement credits (to 8 percent per year) to approximately the actuarial-equivalent level, virtually eliminated the earnings test insofar as the cost aspects thereof are concerned. In other words, when the DRC is at an 8 percent level, the individual receives benefits for delayed retirement having approximately the same value as if benefits were paid without regard to the earnings test beginning at the Normal Retirement Age. Some persons have advocated that the DRC should be at the 8 percent rate as soon as possible.

As to disability benefits, the definition might be tightened, such as by using "medical only" factors (and not vocational ones). Conversely, the definition could be liberalized so as to be on an occupational basis at age 50 and over. Also, the five-month waiting period could be shortened.

The general benefit level was significantly increased in 1969-72 (by about 23 percent in real terms), but financial problems caused this to be partially reversed in subsequent legislation (1974 and 1977). Nonetheless, there will be efforts by many persons to reverse the situation and expand the benefit level.

Over the years, the composition of the OASDI benefit structure-- between individual-equity aspects and social-adequacy ones--tended to shift more toward social adequacy. The 1981 Amendments, however, moved in the other direction (e.g., by phasing out student benefits and the minimum-benefit provision). There may well be efforts in the future to inject more social adequacy into the program--or, conversely, more individual equity.

It frequently has been advocated that people should be allowed to opt out of the OASDI system and provide their own economic security through private-sector mechanisms, using both their own taxes and those of their employer. Although this approach has certain appealing aspects, it has some significant drawbacks. First, it is not possible to duplicate to any close extent the various features of OASDI, most importantly the automatic adjustment of benefits for increases in the CPI.

Second, because the low-cost individuals (young, high-earnings ones) would be the most likely to opt out, there is the question of where the resulting financing shortfalls of the OASDI program would come from, with respect to the high-cost persons remaining in it. Those who make such proposals (or even the more extreme ones, which involve terminating OASDI for all except those currently covered who are near retirement age) do not answer this question. The only source of financing would be from general revenues, and this means more general taxes, which would be paid to a considerable extent by those who have opted out!

Many proposals have been made in the past that part of the cost of OASDI should be met from general revenues. At times, this has been advocated to be done in an indirect manner, such as by moving part of the HI tax rate to OASDI and then partially financing HI from general revenues. The difficulty with this procedure is that no general-revenues monies are available; instead, the General Fund of the Treasury has large deficits. In turn, this would mean either that additional taxes of other types would have to be raised or that the budget deficit would become larger, and inflation would be fueled. Those opposed to general-revenues financing of OASDI, and of HI as well, believe that the financing, instead, should be entirely from direct, visible payroll taxes. Nonetheless, it is likely that there will continue to be pressure for general-revenues financing of OASDI.

According to the latest intermediate-cost estimate for present law, the OASDI Trust Funds will have large annual excesses of income over outgo for the next three decades. As a result, mammoth fund balances will accumulate--amounting to somewhat over $8 trillion in 2025. Under current budgetary procedures, such annual excesses are considered as meeting the budget-deficit targets, and thus they hide the extent of our horrendous general-budget deficits. Further, the presence of such large fund balances could well encourage over-liberalization of the OASDI program now--e.g., by raising benefit levels or by postponing the scheduled increases in the NRA beginning in about a decade.

To prevent these undesirable results from occurring, Senator Daniel Patrick Moynihan proposed that the financing basis of the OASDI program should be returned to a pay-as-you-go basis. This would be done by an immediate reduction in the contribution rates and the introduction of a graded schedule of increases in the contribution rates, beginning in about 20 years.   This proposal produced a vast amount of discussion (and also education of the public).   It will undoubtedly continue to be heard from again in the future, although it is strongly opposed by those who are concerned with the general-budget deficits and seek to hide them through "counting Social Security surpluses."

2.3.   MEDICARE PROGRAM

Health (or medical care) benefits for active and retired workers and their dependents in the United States is, in the vast majority of cases, provided through the multiple means of the Medicare portion of Social Security for persons aged 65 and over and for long-term disabled persons, private employer-sponsored plans, and individual savings.   Still others look upon the situation for persons aged 65 and over and for long-term disabled persons as Medicare providing the floor of protection for certain categories, or, in other cases, providing the basic protection, with public assistance programs, such as Medicaid, providing a safety net of protection for those whose income is not sufficient to purchase the needed medical care not provided through some form of prepaid insurance.

Private health benefit plans supplement Medicare to some extent.   In other instances--essentially for active workers and their families--health benefit protection is provided by the private sector.   The net result, however, is a broad network of health benefit protection.

2.3.1.   Historical Development of Provisions

Beginning in the early 1950s, efforts were made to provide medical care benefits (primarily for hospitalization) for beneficiaries under the OASDI program.   In 1965, such efforts succeeded, and the resulting program is called Medicare.

Initially, Medicare applied only to persons age 65 and over.   In 1972, disabled Social Security beneficiaries who had been on the benefit rolls for at least two years were made eligible, as were virtually all persons in the country who have end-stage renal disease (i.e., chronic kidney disease). Since 1972, relatively few changes in the coverage or benefit provisions have been made.   In 1988, legislation that provided catastrophic-coverage benefits, to be financed largely through a surtax on the income tax of eligible beneficiaries, was enacted.   However, as a result of massive protests from those who would be required to pay the surtax, these provisions were repealed in 1989.

Medicare is really two separate programs. One part, Hospital Insurance (HI),[5] is financed primarily from payroll taxes on workers covered under OASDI, including those under the Railroad Retirement system. Beginning in 1983, all civilian employees of the Federal Government were covered under HI, even though, in general, not covered by OASDI. Also, beginning in April 1986, all newly hired state and local government employees are covered compulsorily (and, at the election of the governmental entity, all employees in service on March 31, 1986, who were not covered under OASDI can be covered for HI). The other part, Supplementary Medical Insurance (SMI), is on an individual voluntary basis and is financed partially by enrollee premiums, with the remainder, currently slightly more than 75 percent, coming from general revenues.

2.3.2.   Persons Protected by HI

All individuals aged 65 and over who are eligible for monthly benefits under OASDI or the Railroad Retirement program also are eligible for HI benefits (as are federal employees and state and local employees who have sufficient earnings credits from their special HI coverage). Persons are eligible for OASDI benefits if they could receive them when the person on whose earnings record they are eligible is deceased or receiving disability or retirement benefits, or could be receiving retirement benefits except for having had substantial earnings. Thus, the HI eligibles include not only insured workers, but also spouses, disabled children (in the rare cases where they are at least age 65), and survivors, such as widowed spouses and dependent parents. As a specific illustration, HI protection is available for an insured worker and spouse, both at least age 65, even though the worker has such high earnings that OASDI cash benefits are not currently payable.

In addition, HI eligibility is available for disabled beneficiaries who have been on the benefit roll for at least two years (beyond a 5-month waiting period). Such disabled eligibles include not only insured workers, but also disabled child beneficiaries aged 18 and over but disabled before age 22, and disabled widowed spouses, age 50-64.

Further, persons under age 65 with end-stage renal disease (ESRD) who require dialysis or renal transplant are eligible for HI benefits if they meet one of a number of requirements. Such requirements for ESRD benefits include being fully or currently insured, being a spouse or a dependent child of an insured worker or of a monthly beneficiary, or being a monthly beneficiary.

---

[5]Sometimes referred to as Part A. Supplementary Medical Insurance is Part B.

Individuals aged 65 and over who are not eligible for HI as a result of their own or some other person's earnings can elect coverage, and then must make premium payments, whereas OASDI eligibles do not. The standard monthly premium rate is $192 for 1992.

2.3.3.   Benefits Provided under HI

The principal benefit provided by the HI program is for hospital services. The full cost for all such services, other than luxury items, is paid by HI during a so-called spell of illness, after an initial deductible has been paid and with daily coinsurance for all hospital days after the 60th one, but with an upper limit on the number of days covered. A spell of illness is a period beginning with the first day of hospitalization and ending when the individual has been out of both hospitals and skilled nursing facilities for 60 consecutive days. The initial deductible is $652 for 1992. The daily coinsurance is $163 for the 61st to 90th days of hospitalization. A nonrenewable lifetime reserve of 60 days is available after the regular 90 days have been used; these lifetime reserve days are subject to daily coinsurance of $326 for 1992. The deductible and coinsurance amounts are adjusted automatically each year after 1992 to reflect past changes in hospital costs.

Benefits also are available for care provided in skilled nursing facilities, following at least three days of hospitalization. Such care is provided only when it is for convalescent or recuperative care, and not for custodial care. The first 20 days of such care in a spell of illness are provided without cost to the individual. The next 80 days, however, are subject to a daily coinsurance payment, which is $81.50 in 1992, and it will be adjusted automatically in the future in the same manner as the hospital cost-sharing amounts. No benefits are available after 100 days of care in a skilled nursing facility for a particular spell of illness.

In addition, an unlimited number of home health service benefits are provided by HI without any payment being required from the beneficiary. Also, hospital care for terminally ill persons is covered if all Medicare benefits other than physician services are waived; certain cost restrictions and coinsurance requirements apply with respect to prescription drugs.

HI benefit protection is provided only within the United States, with the exception of certain emergency services available when in or near Canada. Not covered by HI are those cases where services are performed in a Veterans Administration hospital or where the person is eligible for medical services under a workers' compensation program. Furthermore, Medicare is the secondary payor in cases when: (a) medical care is payable under any liability policy, especially automobile ones; (b) during the first 18 months of treatment for ESRD cases when private group health insurance provides coverage; (c) for persons aged 65 and over (employees and spouses) who are under employer-sponsored group health insurance plans (which is required for all plans of employers with at least 20 employees) unless the employee opts out of it; and (d) for disability beneficiaries under the plan of an employer with at least 100 employees when the beneficiary is either an "active individual" or a family member of an employee.

2.3.4.   Financing of HI

With the exception of the small group of persons who voluntarily elect coverage, the HI program is financed by payroll taxes on workers in employment covered by OASDI. This payroll tax rate is combined with that for OASDI base. The HI tax rate is the same for employers and employees; self-employed persons pay the combined employer-employee tax rate, but have an offset to allow for the effect of business expenses on income taxes as described earlier in connection with OASDI taxes). Such HI tax rate for employees is 1.45 percent in 1990 and all future years. The maximum taxable earnings base for HI was the same as that for OASDI for all years before 1991, but was then raised to $125,000 (versus $53,400 for OASDI); and to $130,200 for 1992 (versus $55,500 for OASDI). It should be noted that long-range actuarial cost estimates indicate that this rate will not provide adequate financing after about a decade from now (or perhaps even sooner).

The vast majority of persons who attained age 65 before 1968, and who were not eligible for HI benefit protection on the basis of an earnings record, were nonetheless given full eligibility for benefits without any charge. The cost for this closed blanketed-in group is met from general revenues rather than from HI payroll taxes.

The HI Trust Fund receives the income of the program from the various sources and makes the required disbursements for benefits and administrative expenses. The assets are invested and earn interest in the same manner as the OASDI Trust Funds.

Although the federal government is responsible for the administration of the HI program, the actual dealing with the various medical facilities is through fiscal intermediaries, such as Blue Cross and insurance companies, which are reimbursed for their expenses on a cost basis. Beginning in 1988, reimbursement for inpatient hospital services is based on uniform sums for each type of case for about 475 diagnosis-related groups.

2.3.5.   Persons Protected under Supplementary Medical Insurance

Individuals aged 65 or over can elect SMI coverage on an individual basis regardless of whether they have OASDI insured status. In addition, disabled OASDI beneficiaries eligible for HI and persons with ESRD eligible under HI can elect SMI coverage. In general, coverage election must be made at about the time of initial eligibility, that is, attainment of age 65 or at the end of the disability-benefit waiting period. Subsequent election during general enrollment periods is possible but with higher premium rates being applicable.   Similarly, individuals can terminate coverage and cease premium payment of their own volition.

2.3.6.   Benefits Provided under SMI

The principal SMI benefit is partial reimbursement for the cost of physician services, although other medical services, such as diagnostic tests, ambulance services, prosthetic devices, physical therapy, medical equipment, and drugs not self-administrable, are covered. Not covered are out-of-hospital drugs, most dental services, most chiropractic services, routine physical and eye examinations, eyeglasses and hearing aids, and services outside of the United States, except those in connection with HI services that are covered in Canada. Just as for HI, there are limits on SMI coverage in Workers' Compensation cases, medical care under liability policies, private group health insurance applicable to ESRD, and employer-sponsored group health insurance for employees and their spouses.

SMI pays 80 percent of "recognized" charges, under a complicated determination basis that usually produces a lower charge than the reasonable and prevailing one, after the individual has paid a calendar-year deductible of $100 for 1991 and after (increased from $75 in 1982-90). Special limits apply on out-of-hospital mental health care costs and on the services of independent physical and occupational therapists. The cost-sharing payments ($100 deductible and 20 percent coinsurance) are waived for certain services--e.g., home health services, pneumococcal vaccine, and certain clinical diagnostic laboratory tests.

2.3.7.   Financing of SMI

The standard monthly premium rate is $29.90 for 1991. The premium is higher for those who fail to enroll as early as they possibly can, with an increase of 10 percent for each full 12 months of delay. The premium is deducted from the OASDI benefits of persons currently receiving them, or is paid by direct submittal in other cases.

The remainder of the cost of the program is met by general revenues. In the aggregate, persons aged 65 and over pay only about 25 percent of the cost, while for disabled persons such proportion is only about 20 percent. As a result, enrollment in SMI is very attractive, and about 95 percent of those eligible to do so actually enroll.

The enrollee premium rate is changed every year, effective for January. In practice, the rate of increase in the premium rate is determined, in part, by the percentage rise in the level of OASDI cash benefits in the previous year under the automatic adjustment provisions, and in part by the percentage rises in the per capita cost of the program. However, for the premium years 1984-90 the premium rate was set at 25 percent of the cost for persons aged 65 or over. The premium rates for 1992-95 have been established by legislation, being $31.80, $36.60, $41.10, and $46.10 respectively.

The SMI Trust Fund was established to receive the enrollee premiums and the payments from general revenues. From this fund are paid the benefits and the accompanying administrative expenses. Although the program is under the general supervision of the federal government, most of the administration is accomplished through so-called "carriers," such as Blue Shield or insurance companies, on an actual cost basis for their administrative expenses.

2.3.8. Possible Future Development of Medicare

Over the years, numerous proposals have been made to modify the Medicare program. Some of these would expand it significantly, while others would curtail it to some extent.

Among the proposals that would expand the program are those to establish some type of national health insurance program, having very comprehensive coverage of medical services applicable to the entire population. Somewhat less broadly, other proposals would extend Medicare coverage to additional categories of OASDI beneficiaries beyond old-age beneficiaries aged 65 and over and disabled beneficiaries on the roll for at least two years--such as to early-retirement cases at ages 62-64 and to all disability beneficiaries.

In another direction, liberalizing proposals have been made to add further services, such as out-of-hospital drugs, physical examinations, and dental services. Still other proposals have been made in the direction of reducing the extent of cost-sharing on the part of the beneficiary by lowering or eliminating the deductible and coinsurance provisions and by eliminating the duration-of-stay limits on HI benefit eligibility.

Proposals have been made to reduce the cost of the Medicare program by increasing the cost-sharing payments made by the beneficiary. For example, the cost-sharing in the first 60 days of hospitalization could be changed from a one-time payment of the initial deductible to some type of daily coinsurance that would foster the incentive to shorten hospital stays. Another proposal is to adjust automatically, from year to year, the SMI annual deductible, which, unlike the HI cost-sharing payments, is a fixed amount, although it has been increased by ad hoc changes from the initial $50 in 1966 to $75 in 1982 and after.

A major risk for persons aged 65 and over that is not covered by Medicare is the cost of long-term custodial nursing-home care. Although many persons recognize the serious nature of this problem, it is currently being met only on a means-test basis by the Medicaid program. Some people believe that the problem should be met on an "insurance" basis under a new Part C of Medicare, but others think that it is not an "insurable" risk and must be handled on a means-test basis (possibly liberalized somewhat).

Proposals have also been made recently to cover compulsorily under HI all state and local government employees (and not merely new hires after March 1986)--as has been done for federal employees.

As to financing aspects, proposals have been made to eliminate the enrollee premiums under SMI and to replace them by complete financing from general revenues or by partial financing from payroll taxes, while at the same time reducing the HI tax rates and making up for this by partial general revenue financing of HI. It also has been proposed that the HI program should be financed partially, or even completely, by general revenues.

Proposals concerning the reimbursement of physicians under SMI have been made to discourage or prevent them from charging the beneficiaries more than the allowable charges. In 1989, legislation was enacted that would eventually restrict such charges so that they could not be more than 15 percent higher than 95 percent of the recognized charges applicable to physicians who take assignment (as well as requiring the physician to submit the bill to the Medicare carrier in all instances). Similarly, various proposals have been made--and some have been enacted--to lower the cost of the HI program as far as reimbursement of hospitals and skilled nursing facilities is concerned, although this would have no effect on the Medicare beneficiary directly.

QUESTIONS FOR REVIEW

1. Explain how quarters of coverage are determined for purposes of the OASDI program.
2. Explain how many quarters of coverage are required for fully insured status under the OASDI program.
3. Outline the beneficiary categories for retirement benefits.
4. Outline the steps involved in computing the average indexed monthly earnings.
5. Describe how the primary insurance amount (PIA) is computed
6. Describe how PIAs are increased for automatic annual adjustments.
7. Describe how PIAs may be increased by delayed retirement credits.
8. Explain the basic features of the earnings test.
9. Explain how the normal retirement age will be adjusted in the future.

QUESTIONS FOR DISCUSSION

1. Describe the drawbacks of allowing people to opt out of Social Security.
2. Explain the federal income taxation provisions with respect to Social Security.

3. Benefit Plan Objectives

It is reasonable to speculate that the first employee benefit plans were established to serve specific purposes -- for example, to avoid "passing the hat" among employees when someone died. For many years, the design of these plans was influenced largely by the insurance industry's attitude toward underwriting, funding, and administration, since these were made available by insurers under the terms and conditions they chose to utilize.

Over the years, many factors have influenced the design of employee benefit plans, and a body of law has emerged that affects these plans in terms of minimum requirements and permissible provisions. The taxation of contributions and benefits has also influenced plan design, and the process of collective bargaining and the interests of organized labor have been a major influence, as has the availability of alternate funding mechanisms. These, and other factors, including a growing degree of sophistication and knowledge of the field, have created an environment in which an employer has a wide degree of choice and flexibility in benefit plan design.

The cost of employee benefits is significant. A well-rounded program (including paid time off) can easily generate a total cost in the vicinity of 30 percent or more of an employer's base payroll. If the cost of statutory benefits is also included, the total cost can easily reach 40 percent of payroll or more. Indeed, some companies have total benefit costs that approach 50 percent of payroll. The amounts accumulated under these plans also are of major importance. For example, the assets accumulated by some companies in their pension plans alone exceed their net worth.

Given the substantial costs involved in employee benefits plans, the importance they have to millions of workers, and the complex legal, tax, and funding environment that exists, it is most important that such plans be designed with particular care, that they be fully supportive of the employer's philosophy, goals, and objectives, and that they at least partially satisfy the perceived needs of the employees. It should also be observed that this concept is of equal importance to small employers and to larger organizations.

The major focus of this text is on the various mechanisms that exist for the delivery of retirement benefits and the ways in which a specific retirement plan might be designed. However, matters that influence the design of a retirement plan also influence the design of other employee benefit plans. Thus, while the primary emphasis of this chapter is on retirement plans, the subject matter is broad enough to apply to all employee benefits.

In this chapter, some of the environmental considerations that can influence plan design are described first. Then employer philosophy and attitudes are discussed. The final portion of the chapter deals with specific employee benefit plan objectives.

3.1.   ENVIRONMENTAL CONSIDERATIONS

Before passage of the Tax Equity and Fiscal Responsibility Act of 1982 (TEFRA), the employer's legal status often influenced plan design. Federal tax law was different as it applied to sole proprietorships, partnerships, Subchapter S corporations, nonprofit organizations, and regular corporations. For example, the defined contribution pension or profit sharing plan generally has been adopted by unincorporated organizations and by Subchapter S corporations because of the deduction limits previously imposed on these organizations. However, these deduction limits and the potential benefits of a defined benefit pension plan have often caused such organizations to incorporate either on a regular basis or as a professional corporation or association. The parity provisions of TEFRA eliminate most of the distinctions in tax law that formerly applied to partnerships and sole proprietorships. However, precedents established by prior practice and on account of prior law may still continue to influence plan design for some organizations.

Section 501(c)(3) organizations need to take special matters into account when considering employee benefits. One such matter is that contributions are not deductible and will not operate to reduce plan costs. Thus, the "out-of-pocket" costs for a given level of employee benefits will be higher for a tax-exempt organization than it would be for a profit making corporation under like circumstances. Also, these organizations have frequently utilized defined contribution concepts because of the availability of tax-deferred annuities under Section 403(b) of the Internal Revenue Code; these arrangements are subject to only some of the nondiscrimination requirements applicable to qualified plans. Another matter that needs to be taken into account is that cash or deferred arrangements (CODAs) under Section 401(k) are not available to these organizations unless adopted before July 2, 1986.

The basic characteristics of the employer and its industry are part of the background for designing an employee benefit program. Is the firm a young, growing organization, or is it relatively mature? Is its history of profits stable and predictable, or have profits been, or are they likely to be, volatile? Does the firm anticipate moderate or significant growth, and what will its need for employees be in the foreseeable future? Is the industry highly competitive? Are profit margins narrow? Is the business cyclical? What are the firm's short- and long-term capital needs? The answers to these questions and others like them can be of great importance in structuring benefit plans that meet employee needs with funding patterns compatible with the employer's objectives and capabilities.

The characteristics of the individuals employed by the employer also play an important role in plan design. The distribution of employees by age, service, sex, and pay can have significant implications in terms of the type of benefit provided, cost levels generated, and similar matters. This distribution can be even more significant under certain funding methods and instruments.

An employer with diversified operations has special considerations when it comes to employee benefit plan design. For example, such an employer needs to consider whether the same benefit program is appropriate for all facets of the business. Factors such as cost, profit margins, competitive need, and geographic differences should be taken into account. Another factor related to this issue is the employer's attitude on the transfer of employees. A uniform program facilitates such transfers, while different plans at different locations may create impediments. Obviously, the employer's basic policy concerning employee transfers, whether encouraged or discouraged, bears on the matter. One approach used by some employers is to establish a basic or "core" program that applies in all areas of the business, with a flexible or varying program of supplemental benefits to accommodate different industry needs.

The communities in which the employer does business can also be an environmental factor in plan design. This is less the case in large, urban areas, but can become quite meaningful when the company is the dominant or a major employer in a discrete geographical area. In this case, the design and structure of an employee benefit plan could reflect the employer's degree of concern over the image it wishes to create in the communities in which it does business. If such a concern exists, it often indicates the need for liberal benefit provisions -- not only by the employer's own industry standards, but by the standards established by different employers involved in the same communities.

The presence or absence of collective bargaining units can be a significant consideration. The demands of labor, both on a local and a national or "pattern" basis, can influence plan design, even for nonbargaining employees. Many employers follow the practice of extending bargained-for benefits to nonbargaining unit employees -- or a practice of making the plans of the nonbargaining unit employees slightly better than those of the bargaining unit employees, to the extent that this does not violate labor laws. Others, however, treat the programs as totally separate, particularly in the context that benefit plans are part of total compensation and that basic salary and wage structures also are quite different between the two groups.

The foregoing is not intended to be an exhaustive discussion of environmental factors that influence plan design. Rather, it is intended to give some indication of items that should be considered. With these in mind, it is appropriate to turn to a discussion of employer philosophy and attitudes.

3.2.   EMPLOYER PHILOSOPHY AND ATTITUDES

Specific objectives for employee benefit plans should be set in the context of the employer's philosophy and attitudes for the management of human resources. The following list of questions and observations, again not all-inclusive, is designed to suggest the nature of some of the items that need to be considered.

1. What is the employer's basic compensation philosophy? Many employers believe benefit plans are part of total compensation and that the cost and benefit structure of these plans should reflect the employer's basic attitude toward other compensation elements. Thus, the employer who has adopted a policy of paying high wages and salaries may very well adopt a liberal benefit program. On the other hand, an employer may choose to establish a benefit program that keeps total compensation costs at an acceptable level while presenting one element of compensation on a more favorable basis. For example, an employer may wish to establish highly competitive wages and salaries but, to keep total compensation costs in line, may provide only modest benefits. Such a compensation strategy, of course, can affect the type of employee attracted and also can influence matters such as turnover rates. It also is possible for an employer to adopt a reverse compensation strategy mix and have a liberal benefit program to go along with a cash compensation program that is not fully competitive. This type of compensation mix often is found in governmental units where cash

compensation is fixed by law and where incentive compensation may not be payable. Here, it is common to find employees with a liberal benefit program.

2. Is the employer's basic attitude toward providing employee benefits one that emphasizes the protection and maintenance of income in the event of economic insecurity? Or is its attitude oriented more toward providing additional current, although tax deferred, compensation? Most employers do not have a clear-cut and total preference for one or the other of these positions; however, one position might be of greater significance than the other. The employer's leaning toward one or the other of these two concepts can find expression in a number of plan decisions. For example, a preference for the income-maintenance approach could suggest the choice of a defined benefit pension plan integrated to the maximum extent with social security benefits,[1] or of a death benefit that provides an income benefit but only to survivors of the employee's immediate family. A compensation-oriented approach, though, might suggest the use of a defined contribution plan as the basic program for providing retirement benefits.

3. Does the employer believe employees should share in the cost of meeting their own economic security needs? Many employers take the position that employees do have such a responsibility, and benefits in the event of medical expense needs, death, disability, and retirement should come from three sources -- the government, the employer, and the employee's own savings. Where desired, employee involvement can be in the form of direct employee contributions, or it can be recognized in indirect ways as, for example, when income-replacement objectives in a noncontributory pension plan are consciously set below what might otherwise be desired levels, or through the use of deductibles, coinsurance, or inside plan limitations in a medical expense plan. Also, an employer can view this issue from the perspective of the total employee benefit program, making some specific plans contributory and some noncontributory, with the overall employee contributions achieving a total level the employer feels is satisfactory.

4. A long-term, advance-funded retirement program involves certain risks. Two of the most important relate to the impact of inflation and investment results. The employer's attitude on who should bear these risks -- the employer or the employees -- can play a significant role in the choice

---

[1] The basic concept of integration is that the benefits of the employer's plan must be dovetailed with social security benefits in such a manner that employees earning over the social security taxable wage base will not receive combined benefits under the two programs proportionately greater than the benefits for employees earning less than this amount. Although the benefit formula under the private plan may favor the higher paid employees, the additional amounts provided for them cannot exceed specific levels set forth in the Internal Revenue Code and supporting regulations. This concept is presented in more detail in Chapters 8 and 14.

between a defined benefit and a defined contribution pension plan.[2] Under the former, these risks are assumed by the employer, although the risk of inflation can be tempered by the choice of a formula that is not pay-related, or by the choice of a career-pay formula, while the employee in effect assumes both of these risks under a defined contribution plan.

5. The selection of specific retirement plan provisions (normal retirement age, early retirement age and subsidies, the treatment of deferred retirement, and the benefit levels provided under all these events) and the amount of postretirement life and medical expense insurance provided can influence the pattern of retirements in any organization. Many employers prefer to encourage employees to retire at or before normal retirement age, and for a variety of reasons, such as keeping promotional channels open. Others prefer to encourage deferred retirements and are reluctant to see skilled workers leave while still capable of making important contributions to the firm's profitability. Still other employers take a neutral position and do not seek to exert any influence on the pattern of retirements in their organizations. In any event, this issue has taken on added significance in view of the 1986 amendments to the Age Discrimination in Employment Act (ADEA), which protect employment rights of all employees age 40 and over. This issue will be influenced by the 1983 social security amendments, which will gradually extend the "normal" retirement age for social security benefits to 67, at the same time reducing the level of benefits available from ages 62 through 66. It will also be influenced by demographic considerations and a general recognition of the fact that the relative size of the work force -- over and under age 65 -- is changing. With these demographic shifts in mind, many employers might choose to encourage employees to remain in the work force beyond age 65.

6. A growing number of employers prefer to structure an employee benefit program on a basis that gives employees a wide choice of plans in which to participate and the extent to which they participate in these plans. This can be accomplished on the basis of before-tax credits in the form of flexible or "cafeteria" benefits, or it can be accomplished by developing various layers of after-tax contributory coverage. Such employers believe this type of flexibility makes the program more meaningful to employees and more efficient, since benefits are delivered only when needed or desired.

---

[2] A defined benefit plan is a pension plan under which the employer provides a determinable benefit, usually related to an employee's service and/or pay. Under this approach, the employer's cost is whatever is necessary to provide the benefit specified. A defined contribution plan is a pension plan under which the employer's contribution is fixed and this contribution is accumulated to provide whatever amount of benefit it can purchase. Thus, an employee's benefit becomes the variable, depending upon factors such as age at entry, retirement age, and investment earnings (or losses). A defined contribution plan can involve a specific contribution or it can take the form of a profit sharing, thrift or savings, or employee stock ownership plan.

Other employers prefer not to become involved in the administrative complexities and cost associated with such flexibility, nor do they wish to absorb any additional costs associated with the adverse selection permitted by such choices. Also, those employers who have a paternalistic attitude might feel many employees would not want to make choices or would not be able to make the right choices.

7. An employer's position concerning the cost levels it can assume can be a major determinant for a plan's benefit levels and the various ancillary benefits that might be included. The assumption of any given level of cost commitment also involves a balancing of employee interests with those of the organization's owners or shareholders. Another aspect relates to the employer's attitude about the need for maintaining controls over future cost levels. A high degree of concern in this area, for example, might lead to the selection of a career-pay or a defined contribution pension plan, to the use of pay-related deductibles in a medical plan, or to nonpay-related death benefits.

8. Whether the plan's benefits should be coordinated with social security benefits is a most important question. The employer's basic philosophy concerning this issue plays an important role in plan design. A great many employers believe that because of the very nature of social security benefits and their relatively larger value for lower paid employees, it would be impossible to achieve an equitable balancing of benefits and costs for employees at all pay levels without integrating pension and disability income plans in some fashion with the benefits provided by social security. Others believe the communications and administrative difficulties associated with integrated plans are such that integration is not desirable.

9. Should an employer provide a benefit program for executives that differs from that provided for its employees in general? Over the years, the majority of benefit programs have been applied across-the-board to all employees, and many employers still believe executives or highly paid employees should be treated the same as all employees. An increasing number of organizations, however, believe the unique needs of executives cannot be met by plans that must meet the nondiscrimination requirements of federal tax law. For example, it may be difficult for a firm to recruit a needed executive in midcareer because of the loss of pension benefits he or she will experience, since a large part of the executive's benefits will be frozen at the pay levels achieved with the prior employer. In such a case, a need may exist for the employer to have a retirement arrangement that restores the benefits such an executive might potentially lose. Similarly, an employer might find it desirable to provide executives with a supplemental pension that applies the basic pension plan formula to the executive's incentive pay, if the basic pension relates to base compensation only. Due to the nondiscrimination requirements described in Chapter 5, special benefits

for executives such as those described cannot be provided through a qualified, nondiscriminatory pension or profit sharing plan. Instead, these benefits must be provided through some form of nonqualified supplemental pension arrangement (these nonqualified arrangements are described in Chapter 26). Many employers also provide executives with additional death benefits, both before and after retirement, as well as with additional disability income protection.

10.   An important question since the passage of the Employee Retirement Income Security Act of 1974 (ERISA) is whether the employer is willing to assume the plan termination obligations imposed upon the employer in the event of the termination of a defined benefit plan before all accrued and vested benefits have been funded. The impact this might have on net worth and on credit ratings and the ability to raise capital has caused a good deal of concern -- particularly among small employers.[3] This potential liability can be avoided if a defined contribution pension plan is adopted and, indeed, over 80 percent of all new tax-qualified plans adopted since the passage of ERISA have been of the defined contribution variety.

3.3.   EMPLOYER OBJECTIVES

With the preceding in mind, it is appropriate to consider specific employer objectives. The following discusses major employer objectives, as well as some of the factors relating to such objectives. Obviously, not all these objectives apply to each employer and, if they do have application, it is likely their relative importance may not be the same for each employer.

3.3.1.   Attraction and Retention of Employees

Most employers recognize they must maintain some form of employee benefit program to attract and retain desirable employees. This is particularly so when the employer must compete with other employers for personnel.

Even so, many employers believe the presence of an adequate benefit program is not a positive influence in their efforts to attract and retain employees -- at least to any significant extent. Rather, these employers reason the absence of such a program could have a negative effect on their recruiting and retention efforts. Put another way, these employers are of the opinion that an inadequate program can hinder their efforts to recruit and

---

[3]The employer's liability on termination of a single-employer plan is quite complex and a detailed discussion of this topic is deferred until Chapter 17. It should be noted that an employer can also be exposed to a liability in the case of a negotiated multiemployer plan.

retain employees, while an overly generous program will not produce a corresponding increase in their ability to attract and hold desirable workers.

While this might be true as a general concept, it is worth noting that some benefit plans might have greater impact than others as far as employees are concerned. Thus, for example, the presence of a generous profit sharing plan might make employment with one employer more attractive than employment with another employer who maintains a more conventional benefit program. In the same vein, employees might find the choice and value of a flexible (or cafeteria) benefit plan of more interest than a plan that offers a standard fare of benefits.

3.3.2. Meeting Competitive Standards

The objective of having competitive employee benefit plans is closely related to the objective of being able to attract and retain good employees. It is, however, somewhat broader in concept and can reflect employers' attitudes concerning their standing in their own industry, as well as in the communities in which they operate. This objective also recognizes that, unlike other forms of compensation, employee benefit plans are highly visible and readily subject to external comparison.

An employer who wishes to have competitive employee benefit plans must establish standards for measuring these plans. Will competitiveness be measured against industry standards, geographic standards, or both? Many employers have a preference for measuring their plans against industry standards. However, it should be recognized that such standards are most appropriate for skilled or professional workers and for management personnel -- those whose capabilities are more related to the employer's own industry. For workers whose capabilities are more readily transferred from one industry to another, a more realistic standard would be the plans maintained by the local companies with which the employer competes on a local basis for human resources. Thus, as a practical matter, most employers seek to compare their plans both on an industry and a geographic basis.

Having identified the standard against which the plans are to be measured, the employer also must decide the relative level of competitiveness to achieve. For example, the employer might decide the objective is to have an employee benefit program that meets the average of the companies that form its comparison base (or it can establish different positions for different plans). The employer also might decide it wishes to be a leader and have a program consistently among the best, or it might wish to rank somewhere between the 50th and 75th percentile. And, of course, the employer might elect to lag somewhat behind other companies because of cost or other considerations.

Even though the comparison base has been identified and the relative ranking within this base established, there remains the important matter of determining the technique to be used to establish the relative standing of the different plans.   One method used quite frequently is to make comparisons of the benefits actually payable to representative employees under different circumstances. For example, the benefit payable under a retirement plan at normal retirement age might be projected for several employees with differing pay, service, and age characteristics. This method is relatively simple in concept, but should be used with caution. First, it shows benefits only and does not necessarily give any true indication of the relative cost of the plans involved.   Also, by isolating a specific benefit, the importance and value of other benefits included in the same plan are not taken into account. For example, a company might be ranked as the highest in terms of benefits payable at normal retirement, but the other companies in the comparison may have much more valuable early retirement or survivor income benefits.   Even if other benefits are illustrated and compared in the same way, the aggregate value of all benefits within the same plan may not be readily ascertainable. This method is also sensitive to the assumptions used in making the illustrations. If retirement benefits are being illustrated, for example, and if future pay increases are not taken into account, the benefit differences attributable to career-pay and final-pay[4] formulas will not be apparent (nor will there be any apparent difference between a final three-year average plan and a final five-year average plan).

Another method used for comparative purposes is to compare actual costs to the employer for different benefit plans. The material used for this purpose usually is information acquired from both published and private surveys about actual employer cost patterns. A major difficulty with this approach is that there is often inconsistent reporting, by different employers, of the information requested. Also, actual contribution patterns do not necessarily reflect the real cost or value of the benefit involved. The cost reported, for example, might be the total annual cost of the plan including employee contributions and reflect the specific characteristics of the employee group involved. In the case of retirement plans, significant differences may exist in annual contributions because of the choice of a particular actuarial method and the combination of actuarial assumptions employed. For example, two employers with identical plans might report significantly different annual costs because of their different choices of assumptions for future investment earnings and growth in pay.

---

[4]A final-pay provision bases benefits on the employee's earnings averaged, for example, over the last three or five years of employment, or over the three or five consecutive years in the 10-year period immediately prior to retirement during which the employee's earnings are the highest. In contrast, a career-pay provision bases benefits on the employee's earnings averaged over the entire career of employment. This concept is presented in detail in Chapter 14.

A third method is to measure plans on a basis that uses uniform actuarial methods and assumptions and focuses on the relative value of the different benefits provided. This technique establishes the value of specific plans, specific benefits within a plan, and the aggregate value of all plans. The method can also establish these relative values on the basis of employer cost only, or on the basis of combined employer and employee cost. By using uniform actuarial methods and assumptions, and by applying these to a database of employees held the same for all employer plans in the study, the actual differences in the value of different benefits are isolated and their relative values established. It should be noted that this technique does not establish actual costs or cost patterns, it simply establishes whether one particular benefit or plan is more valuable than another and the extent to which this is so.

3.3.3. Cost Considerations

Earlier in this chapter, reference was made to an employer's attitude on costs and how this can play a major role in plan design. Since a retirement plan often represents the most significant part of an employer's total benefit program cost, it is particularly important that the employer have specific objectives in this area.

It is important to distinguish between ultimate real cost and estimated annual accruals. With this distinction in mind, an employer may establish specific objectives for actual liabilities assumed under a plan and specific objectives for annual accruals. The employer also may establish objectives in terms of the budgeting pattern to be assumed. For example, does the employer desire an accrual cost that remains level, as a percentage of payroll, or would it be preferable to have a pattern that starts with relatively low accruals, gradually building to higher levels in the future?

The employer's objectives for these cost levels influence the choice of retirement plan formula as well as the inclusion and level of ancillary benefits. These objectives also may influence the decision on whether the plan should be contributory and, if so, the level of employee contributions required.

There are other objectives an employer could have for matters concerning cost. The need for contribution flexibility might be one such objective and, if desired, could influence the choice of actuarial funding method and assumptions and could even lead the employer to adopt a profit sharing plan. Another objective could relate to the employer's willingness to assume the costs associated with future inflation. The extent to which the employer wishes to limit its commitment might dictate the choice of a career-pay formula for a defined benefit plan or even the choice of a defined contribution plan of some type.

The need for a cost-efficient retirement program is an obvious objective. Thus, employers wish to avoid excessive or redundant benefits and to fund the plan in the most efficient manner possible. For this reason, many employers choose to coordinate benefits from all sources, and, for example, integrate their retirement plan benefits with those provided by social security.

It is also possible that an employer may view a retirement plan as a tax shelter for the benefit of key employees. When this is the case, the employer's objective might be to maximize benefits and contributions within the limits permitted by federal tax law.

Other employee benefit plans also involve cost considerations. If postretirement death and medical expense benefits are to be provided, should these liabilities be prefunded, and if so, how? Should inflation-sensitive benefits -- medical expense and pay-related death benefits -- be subjected to some degree of control through plan design? What type of funding mechanism should be utilized to gain greater control over cash flow? Clearly, cost considerations are becoming an increasingly important factor in plan design and in plan funding.

3.3.4.   Compliance with Legal Requirements

Employee benefit plans have almost always been subject to some degree of regulation and other legal requirements. This has become much more the case in the last decade with the advent of ERISA, antidiscrimination laws, and the like. The enactment of the Tax Reform Act of 1986 has had a major impact on the design of plans. Thus, the design and maintenance of employee benefit plans must meet the requirements of federal tax law, antidiscrimination laws, securities laws, labor laws, and state insurance laws. In several areas, state as well as federal laws must be taken into account. Thus, an implicit, if not explicit, objective of any employee benefit plan is that it must comply with these legal requirements.

However, an employer often has a choice in the manner in which compliance is achieved and, in some cases, may avoid compliance requirements by the design of the plan. For this reason, it is desirable that the employer formulate specific objectives in this regard. The following examples should give at least some indication of areas where compliance choices are available.

1. The Age Discrimination in Employment Act (ADEA) prevents discrimination in employment for employees age 40 and over. However, this does not require all benefit plans to treat all employees alike, regardless of

age. It is possible, for example, to reduce life insurance coverage for active employees by reason of age (but only within cost-justified limits). Although it is no longer possible to terminate pension accruals in a defined benefit plan or to discontinue allocations in a defined contribution plan after an active employee has attained age 65, a plan may limit the amount of benefit provided under the plan or the number of years of service or plan participation taken into account. An employer should establish basic objectives on how its over-65, active employees will be treated, and whether compliance with this law should be at or above the minimum level. The employer's decision is, of course, influenced by other objectives and attitudes, such as whether it is desirable to encourage earlier or deferred retirements, its public relations posture, and the like.

2. Federal tax law permits the exclusion from a defined benefit pension plan of employees who have less than one year of service or who are under age 21. Employers may include all employees in their plans or may seek to exclude the maximum number possible, depending upon their attitude on minimum compliance and other objectives.

3. An employer may wish to establish a defined benefit pension plan that includes incentive compensation for executives as part of the compensation base used to determine plan benefits, but may not want to include overtime pay and shift differential paid to other employees. It is unlikely the Internal Revenue Service would approve such a pay definition in a qualified pension plan. Compliance with the nondiscrimination requirements of federal tax law could be satisfied by designing the qualified plan with a nondiscriminatory definition of compensation that relates to base pay only, and by instituting a nonqualified, supplemental executive retirement plan (SERP) that applies the base plan formula to incentive pay.

4. A savings plan can be designed so that some part of both employer and employee contributions can be invested in employer securities. Securities and Exchange Commission (SEC) requirements are such that the plan will have to be registered before employee contributions may be invested in this manner. These requirements can be avoided if employer securities can be purchased only by employer contributions.

3.3.5.   Achieving Optimum Tax Benefits

Federal tax law is such that some advantages exist for distributions from employee benefit plans. This is particularly so in the case of tax-qualified retirement and profit sharing plans. For example: (1) investment income on plan assets is not taxed until it is distributed in the form of a benefit; and (2) certain lump-sum distributions may qualify for favorable tax treatment. Indeed, on the one hand these tax advantages very often are the motivating force behind the adoption of a plan -- particularly in the case of a small employer. Larger employers, on the other hand, are not as apt to give a high priority to achieving optimum tax advantages for plan distributions. Since these plans cover large groups of employees, the employer's objectives more often are oriented toward benefit levels and costs.

If an employer wishes to achieve maximum tax advantages for a retirement program, this can find expression in many areas; for example, the choice of benefit formula, the degree to which the plan is integrated with social security benefits, the level of funding chosen, the funding instrument chosen, the adoption of both a defined benefit and a defined contribution plan, the use of a target benefit plan, and so on.[5]

The desire to maximize tax advantages may also affect other benefits and how they are funded. For example, a preretirement spouse benefit may be included as part of a retirement plan, or it may be funded by a separate group term life insurance program. If funded by life insurance, most of the benefit payments will escape income tax; however, the annual cost of insurance can represent taxable income to the employees under Section 79 of the Internal Revenue Code.[6] If the benefit is provided from retirement plan assets, the payments represent taxable income (except to the extent provided by employee contributions), but there will be no annual cost of insurance to be reported by the employee. The emphasis to be placed on these various tax considerations and the characteristics of the employee group involved influence the choice of how the benefit will be funded.

As mentioned earlier, lump-sum distributions from a pension plan can qualify for favorable tax treatment. This could be very important for highly paid employees, and a desire to achieve maximum tax advantages could lead to the inclusion, in a retirement plan, of a provision that allows such lump-sum distributions. However, since the option also would have to be extended to all employees, consideration needs to be given to possible misuse of this feature by some employees and whether this could defeat overall plan objectives.

---

[5]A target benefit plan is one that combines the concepts of both defined contribution and defined benefit plans. The target benefit plan uses a defined benefit formula to determine an employee's projected pension at normal retirement date. A contribution to provide this benefit is determined. This contribution is not adjusted for future experience. Instead, contributions are accumulated for each employee in an individual account and, depending upon actual investment results, can accumulate to provide a greater or smaller benefit than that originally projected. This approach has the advantage of determining the initial amount to be allocated to each employee on a basis that reflects the employee's age as well as compensation, while at the same time preserving the accumulation aspects of a defined contribution plan. This concept is presented in more detail in Chapter 14.

[6]Life insurance death benefits generally are income tax free. However, if paid in installments, the portion representing interest payments will be taxable.

3.3.6.   Efficiency of Design

The overall cost of employee benefits is quite substantial and, as noted earlier, can amount to one third or more of an employer's payroll costs. For this reason, it is important for an employer to structure its employee benefit program so benefits are provided in the most efficient manner possible and overlapping or redundant benefits are eliminated or, at least, minimized.

One of the most effective ways of doing this is to recognize that while any particular benefit plan has a primary focus (e.g., retirement, death, or disability), all benefit plans and some statutory plans must function in some fashion in the case of an event covered primarily by another plan. For example, the primary plan dealing with retirement is, of course, the employer's retirement plan. However, social security can be a major source of additional retirement income. Supplemental retirement income also can be provided by the employer's savings or profit sharing plan, if such a plan is in existence. The employer's group life insurance and medical expense plans may be the source of additional benefits for a retired employee. Viewing all these plans as a total retirement program can influence the choice of specific benefits and benefit levels. Thus, the existence of significant amounts of postretirement life insurance might suggest that, except for legally required joint and survivor protection, the normal form for payment of retirement benefits exclude any form of death benefit, such as a guarantee that benefits will be paid for a minimum period of time; otherwise, excessive or redundant postretirement death benefits might be provided.

The same approach can be applied to the events of preretirement death and disability. The primary plan in the event of preretirement death is the employer's group life insurance plan. However, additional death benefits may be provided by way of continuation of medical expense coverage for the employee's dependents and, in certain cases, the retirement plan must provide preretirement survivor benefits.[7] Social security can also be a source of substantial survivor benefits, as can a profit sharing or savings plan. In the case of disability, a need exists to coordinate the benefits available from the employer's plan (life insurance, short- and long-term disability income plans, savings and profit sharing plans, and medical expense plans) with those available from social security. Again, efficient plan design suggests the benefits from all these sources be coordinated to insure overall benefits in line with employer objectives.

---

[7] The preretirement survivor benefit requirements for a qualified plan are described in Chapter 6.

3.3.7.   Income-Replacement Ratios

Employer objectives as to income-replacement ratios are critical in the design of disability income and retirement plans.

In the case of disability income plans, the issues are not as complex. The benefit usually is not service related (although some plans are), and it is generally designed to replace a percentage of current pay. There are no restrictions on the ability of a plan to integrate with social security benefits, and it is customary to offset 100 percent of the employee's primary social security disability benefit. In fact, most plans offset 100 percent of the total social security benefit payable, including family benefits. In general, the plan formula recognizes that some part or all of the social security and plan benefits may be income tax free, and that total after-tax income should provide adequate maintenance while at the same time creating an economic incentive for the employee to rehabilitate and return to active work. A typical formula might provide for a total gross before-tax benefit (including social security) of 60 percent of current pay.

Establishing income-replacement objectives for a retirement plan is more complex. Before selecting a specific benefit formula, it is important for an employer to identify the amount of an employee's gross income to be replaced by the retirement plan and under what circumstances.

From the employee's viewpoint, it would be desirable to have a situation where total retirement income permits the full maintenance of the standard of living the employee. enjoyed just prior to retirement.   For most employees, some part of this income consists of social security benefits. Indeed, for employees at lower income levels, a substantial portion of a preretirement gross income will be replaced by social security benefits. For example, the replacement ratios, defined as social security benefits relative to gross pay, exceed 70% for an individual whose final pay is $10,000. At a final pay level of $30,000, social security can replace over 30 percent. Even at $50,000, the replacement ratio is over 25 percent. As is discussed later, the after-tax replacement ratios are even more significant.

An employee's personal savings, including equity in a home, can also be a source of retirement income.   Also, many employers maintain supplemental profit sharing and savings plans that can be a source of additional income.   In the absence of any such plan, however, it must be recognized that many individuals will not be able to save meaningful amounts of money to assist in meeting their retirement needs.

Another   factor   that   should   be   considered   in   setting income-replacement ratios is that some reduction in gross income can take place without causing a significant reduction in a retiree's standard of living. Tax considerations are one reason why this is so. First, a retired employee is no longer paying a social security tax (unless he or she is in receipt of earned income). Moreover, social security benefits are income tax free for many individuals.[8] In addition, the standard deduction for federal taxes is increased for individuals 65 or over. The standard deduction for an unmarried taxpayer who is not a surviving spouse and is age 65 or over is increased by an additional standard deduction of $750. For a married taxpayer who is age 65 or over, the additional standard deduction is $600. Finally, retirement income is not subject to state or local taxes in many jurisdictions.

Another reason why some reduction in gross income can be tolerated is the removal of work-related expenses, such as commuting costs, the expense of maintaining a second car, lunch and clothing costs, and so on.[9] Also, many retired individuals no longer face the costs associated with child rearing (food, clothing, education, and the like) and many will have reduced housing costs because of the completion of mortgage payments and, in some localities, reduced real estate taxes.

With factors such as these in mind, most employers establish income-replacement objectives that generate something less than a 100 percent replacement of full preretirement gross income. Typically, these income-replacement objectives are set with several factors in mind:

1. They usually take the employee's (but not the spouse's) social security benefits into account.
2. The objectives usually are higher for lower paid employees than for higher paid employees.
3. The objectives usually are set for the employee's pay level during the final year of employment or over a three- or five-year average just prior to retirement when the employee's earnings are highest.
4. Full income-replacement objectives are set only for individuals who have completed what the employer considers to be a "career" of employment; individuals who have less than this amount of service with the employer have objectives proportionately reduced.

A few comments are appropriate for each of these points. As indicated earlier, social security benefits can be of great importance to individuals at lower income levels, and they take on added significance since all or a portion of the benefits may be income tax free. Further, the employer has shared in the cost of providing these social security benefits. Thus, even

---

[8]Under the social security amendments of 1983, up to one half of social security benefits will become taxable for single individuals whose income exceeds $25,000 and for married couples, filing a joint return, whose income exceeds $32,000.

[9]While it is difficult to estimate work-related expenses in any definitive way, it is interesting to note that the President's Commission on Pension Policy, in its Interim Report of May 1980, estimated these expenses to be 6 percent of after-tax preretirement income.

though the particular pension formula for the employer's plan may not directly reflect social security benefits, the accrual rates chosen can be designed to produce a net plan benefit that, when added to the employee's primary social security benefit, produces the desired result.[10]

At one time, it was not uncommon for an employer to have a single income-replacement objective for employees at all pay levels. However, it was soon recognized that lower income employees need a higher level of income replacement simply because of minimum income needs. Moreover, it was reasoned that higher paid employees could accept lower income amounts without incurring a major reduction in living standards.

Most defined benefit plans utilize an employee's final average pay to determine benefit amounts. Typically, this is a five-year average, although some plans use a three-year average. It is common for employers who have such a plan to state their income-replacement objectives in terms of the pay base used in the plan. Some employers, however, actually set objectives in terms of the employee's pay in the final year of employment, with the result that the plan benefit, when expressed as a percentage of the final average pay used in the plan, is somewhat higher than the employer's actual objective. It also should be noted that employers who adopt career-pay plans or who adopt defined contribution plans often do so with final-pay income-replacement objectives in mind. Those who use career-pay plans frequently "update" accrued career-pay benefits to reflect current pay levels and to move benefits closer to objectives. Those with defined contribution plans find it more difficult to make such adjustments, but often set contribution levels so that, under reasonable expectations for salary growth and investment return, final-pay objectives might be achieved. Unfortunately, the inherent nature of defined contribution plans is such that, in most situations, these objectives will either be exceeded or not met at all.

Understandably, most employers do not feel an obligation to provide a full level of benefits to short-service employees. Thus, it is common practice to set objectives and design benefit formulas so that proportionately smaller benefits are provided for those individuals who work for an employer for less than what the employer considers to be a reasonable career. The number of years involved, of course, varies from employer to employer and reflects the nature of the employer's business and the degree of maturity it has achieved. However, career periods of from 25 to 35 years are common.

---

[10]It is not customary to take the spouse's social security benefit into account in setting objectives. To do so would be difficult since a direct recognition of this benefit would not be permitted by the Internal Revenue Service, and to approximate its value on an across-the-board basis would result in inequities between employees who have a spouse and those who do not.

TABLE 3-1: Illustrative Income-Replacement
Objectives (employee with 30 years of service)

Final Pay	Retirement Income as a Percentage of Final Pay*
Under $20,000	80-70%
$20,000 to $50,000	75-65
50,000 to 75,000	70-60
75,000 to 100,000	65-55
Over $100,000	60-50

*Including primary social security benefits.

With these factors in mind, Table 3-1 sets forth a typical set of income-replacement objectives. These objectives are merely examples. What is appropriate for one employer may be inappropriate for another and, in any event, what one employer might adopt as objectives necessarily must reflect that employer's own philosophy and environment.

3.3.8. Other Objectives

The foregoing has discussed some of the major employer objectives associated with employee benefit plans. Other employer objectives also play an important role in plan design. Some of these additional objectives are discussed below.

Social Obligations. Many employers feel a strong sense of social responsibility to their employees and to society in general. The adoption of adequate and meaningful employee benefit plans is a form of meeting this responsibility.

Employee Incentives. It would be a rare employer who is not interested in improving employee productivity. Profit sharing plans and plans that involve ownership of employer securities are plans that can create employee incentives and, as a result, improve productivity. Beyond this, employee morale is an important factor that can influence productivity. As noted earlier, the presence of employee benefit plans may not be a positive force in recruiting and retaining employees, and they may not be a positive factor in creating improved morale. However, their absence could be a negative influence and, for this reason, most employers believe a benefit program, along with other positive compensation and personnel practices, is an important factor in maintaining employee morale at a proper level.

Corporate Identification. It may be desirable to have employees identify with overall employer business objectives. This might be accomplished by having employees acquire an ownership interest in the firm. Profit sharing plans, savings plans, and employee stock ownership plans (ESOPs) can achieve this objective. By having all or part of an employee's account invested in employer securities, the employee is made aware of progress of the company and the importance of achieving satisfactory profit results. The employee can also have the opportunity to vote the shares credited to his or her account; and the employer has the additional opportunity of being able to communicate with the employee as a shareholder by sending annual reports, proxy statements, and the like.

Administrative Convenience. Generally, it is desirable that employee benefit plans be designed so that administrative involvement and cost are kept to a reasonable minimum. This objective has become especially important with increasing government regulations and requirements and as design and funding choices become greater and more complex. In this regard, employers should be aware of their own administrative capabilities, as well as those available from external sources. Also, while it is desirable to hold administrative costs to a minimum, these costs are not the most significant element of total plan costs. Thus, good plan design should not be sacrificed for the objective of holding down administrative costs.

QUESTIONS FOR REVIEW

1. Describe some of the environmental factors that should be considered in the pension plan design process.
2. Many employers believe employees should share in the cost of meeting their own economic security needs. This type of employee involvement in a private pension plan may take two alternative forms. Explain.
3. Describe the three techniques that may be used to establish the relative standing of various retirement plans.
4. What are some of the objectives an employer could have for matters concerning the cost of the pension plan?
5. An employer often has a choice in the manner in which compliance with legal requirements for pension plans is achieved. Give four examples of areas where compliance choices are available.
6. What are some of the plan design alternatives available to an employer who wishes to achieve maximum tax advantages for a retirement program?
7. An efficient pension plan design requires the identification of all sources of benefits for a retired employee. What plans should be considered as potential sources of benefits?

8. Why do some employers establish income-replacement objectives that generate something less than 100 percent of full preretirement gross income?

9. Identify the factors that are often considered by employers in setting income-replacement objectives.

10. Describe how retirement plans may be used to provide: (a) employee incentives and (b) corporate identification.

QUESTIONS FOR DISCUSSION

1. Assume that an employer wants to provide a reasonable combined replacement ratio (a ratio that combines both social security and private pension benefits in the numerator) for high-paid employees without providing an excessive replacement ratio for employees at lower income levels. Using the relationship between social security retirement benefits and final pay discussed in Chapter 2, illustrate why it may be necessary for the employer to integrate the pension plan. (The mechanics of the integration procedure will be treated in Chapters 8 and 14.)

2. Provide a numerical example to explain why an executive might experience a loss of pension benefits under a final average defined benefit plan if he or she were to change jobs in midcareer.

3. The age at which unreduced social security retirement benefits may commence is scheduled to gradually increase from 65 to a maximum of 67 after the turn of the century. Assume that you are asked to give advice on how a firm's retirement benefits should be restructured as a result of this change. Discuss how your response will vary depending on the employer's objectives.

4. Defined Contribution versus Defined Benefit Plans

Before discussing specific aspects of retirement plan design, it is important to recognize that an employer has two broad choices in selecting a plan to provide these benefits. One of these, of course, is the defined benefit plan under which the employer provides a determinable benefit, usually related to an employee's service and/or pay. Under this approach, the employer's cost is whatever is necessary to provide the benefit specified. The second approach is the defined contribution plan. Here, the employer's contribution is fixed and this contribution is accumulated to provide whatever amount of benefit it can purchase. Thus, an employee's benefit becomes the variable, depending upon factors such as level of contributions, age at entry, retirement age, and investment earnings (or losses). A defined contribution plan can involve a specific contribution (as in a money purchase pension plan), or it can take the form of a profit sharing, thrift or savings, or employee stock ownership plan (these topics are discussed in Part Three of this Text).

Although only the two polar cases in selecting a pension plan are discussed in this chapter, it is important to note that in recent years some employers have adopted plans that combine the best features of both approaches. These plans, such as target benefit plans, are best understood after the reader is fully cognizant of each of the specific features of a pension plan. Therefore, the discussion of these plans is deferred until Chapter 14.

The choice between a defined benefit or a defined contribution plan to provide or supplement retirement benefits is of great importance, both to employers and employees. Legislative developments in recent years have been a major factor influencing this decision. While a detailed discussion of all these plans is found in subsequent chapters of this text, it is important, at this stage, to provide an overview of the factors involved in making a choice between these two different approaches to providing retirement benefits. This chapter reviews the background and broad considerations involved, as well as the legislative activity that bears on this choice.

4.1.   BACKGROUND

The vast majority of employees covered today by the private pension system in the United States participate in defined benefit plans. There are some notable exceptions. Educational and other nonprofit institutions, for example, have historically favored defined contribution pension arrangements because of the unique tax sanctions granted them under section 403(b) of the Internal Revenue Code. Also, a number of profit-making organizations have opted for deferred profit sharing arrangements to serve as retirement plans. Nevertheless, the defined benefit approach was favored by most employers both small and large -- at least until the passage of the Employee Retirement Income Security Act of 1974 (ERISA).

This preference for defined benefit plans over defined contribution plans has been due to many factors:

1. Most employers have specific income-replacement objectives in mind when establishing a retirement plan. A defined benefit plan can be structured to achieve these objectives. The defined contribution approach, on the other hand, will produce plan benefits that fail to meet or that exceed such objectives as they affect individual employees. This depends on a number of factors such as length of participation, age at retirement, inflation, investment results, and the like.

2. By the same token, most employers wish to take social security benefits into account so that the combined level of benefits from both sources will produce desired results. Defined contribution plans can be integrated with social security benefits by adjusting contribution levels; however, integration of benefits cannot be accomplished as efficiently as is the case under defined benefit plans.

3. The typical defined contribution plan provides that the employee's account balance is payable in the event of death and, frequently, in case of

disability. This, of course, produces additional plan costs or, alternatively, lower retirement benefits if overall costs are held constant. An employer who is interested primarily in providing retirement benefits can use available funds more efficiently for this purpose under a defined benefit plan.

4. Some individuals feel that a more equitable allocation of employer contributions occurs under a defined benefit plan, since the employee's age, past service, and pay may all be taken into account. Others feel just the opposite, that allocations on the basis of pay only produce fairer results. This characteristic of defined contribution plans is one of the reasons they do not lend themselves to achieving consistent income-replacement objectives.

5. A defined benefit plan can be (and often is) structured to provide a benefit that is related to an employee's final pay, thus protecting the employee against the effects of preretirement inflation. Equivalent protection cannot be provided under a defined contribution plan. Thus, in effect, the risk of inflation is assumed by employees, who must rely primarily on investment results to increase the value of their benefits during inflationary periods.

6. This last comment raises another issue in the comparison of defined benefit plans and defined contribution plans. Investment risk and reward are assumed by the employer under the former, by employees under the latter. Risk can be minimized by use of selected investment media. Absent such protection, however, many people feel that it is inappropriate for the average employee to assume such risk with respect to a major component of his or her retirement security.

7. The incremental value from year to year of a younger employee's accrued benefit under a defined benefit plan is relatively small; in the typical final pay plan, the value of accrued benefits for older employees increases each year at relatively substantial rates. By contrast, the increase in the amount of an employee's accrued benefit (his or her account balance) attributable to employer contributions under a defined contribution plan stays relatively constant from year to year as a percentage of pay. One effect of this is that employees who terminate employment at younger ages will typically receive greater benefits under a defined contribution plan than under a defined benefit plan. As a result, termination benefits can be more costly under a defined contribution approach.

The defined contribution approach is, of course, not without its advantages. Deferred profit sharing plans, for example, offer employers maximum flexibility in terms of cost commitment as well as opportunities to increase employee productivity. Through the use of employer securities as a plan investment, greater employee identification with the company and its goals also can be achieved. Additionally, if the employee group covered is relatively young, the defined contribution plan is apt to have greater employee relations value than a defined benefit plan.

4.2.   LEGISLATIVE FACTORS

ERISA has had a significant impact on defined benefit plans. Despite the advantages noted, a defined benefit plan now exposes an employer to significant financial liability if the plan is terminated when there are unfunded liabilities for vested benefits. An employer's net worth is subject to a lien in favor of the Pension Benefit Guaranty Corporation (PBGC) if necessary to meet any liabilities assumed by the PBGC in this event (the specifics of the employer's liability are discussed in Chapter 17). The lien, since it is in the nature of a tax lien, supersedes the liens of any other creditors. The problems of potential employer liabilities were exacerbated by the Multiemployer Pension Plan Amendments Act of 1980, which created substantial liabilities for an employer who wishes to or who must withdraw from a multiemployer plan that has unfunded vested liabilities. Here, the employer is liable for its share of unfunded vested liabilities (generally on the basis of the ratio of the employer's contributions to total contributions).

The vast majority of employees who are not covered by a private retirement program work for smaller companies. Clearly, these small employers, as well as newly formed companies, are apt to be reluctant to adopt a defined benefit plan and the potential liabilities that are imposed by ERISA. Many such employers will find the defined contribution alternative, with no such liabilities, to be a more palatable approach -- despite the possible advantages offered by a defined benefit arrangement.

That this is so would seem to be borne out by Internal Revenue Service (IRS) statistics on the establishment of new plans. Since ERISA, approximately 80 percent of all new plans are defined contribution in nature. To be sure, many of these new plans (e.g., savings plans) supplement existing defined benefit plans. However, this is still a much higher percentage than was the case prior to the passage of ERISA.

Apart from the plan termination provisions of ERISA and their implicit but significant emphasis on defined contribution plans, it is important to note that the federal government -- knowingly or unknowingly -- has emphasized the defined contribution approach in many other ways. For example:

1. Long-standing provisions of the Internal Revenue Code (referred to earlier) permit and encourage the use of tax-deferred annuities (defined contribution plans which are discussed in Chapter 25) for employees of educational and other nonprofit organizations.

2. The basic structure of the Code, as it applied to H.R. 10 or Keogh plans for the self-employed, was strongly oriented toward defined contribution plans. Even though amended to specifically sanction defined benefit plans, the defined contribution approach proved to be the simplest and easiest way to take advantage of this law. Indeed, almost all such plans have utilized the defined contribution approach. This might change as a result of the parity provisions of the Tax Equity and Fiscal Responsibility Act of 1982 (TEFRA), which eliminated most of the distinctions in tax law that formerly applied to different organizations. However, precedents established by prior practice and prior law may still continue to influence plan design for unincorporated organizations.

3. The Individual Retirement Arrangement (IRA) concept (described in Chapter 24) is totally a defined contribution approach.

4. Beginning in 1979, employers were permitted to adopt a simplified employee pension (SEP). A SEP utilizes the IRA concept but has higher contribution limits than an IRA and considerably less paperwork than a conventional retirement plan. Again, the defined contribution approach is mandatory.

5. Employee stock ownership plans (ESOPs), which are defined contribution plans, have also been the subject of special legislation. As will be described in Chapter 11, such plans, unlike defined benefit plans, can be involved with corporate debt financing. In addition, ESOPs have been the subject of special interest legislation -- witness the Regional Rail Reorganization Act of 1973, the Foreign Trade Act of 1974, the Chrysler Corporation Loan Guarantee Act of 1979, the Small Business Employee Ownership Act of 1980, and the Tax Reform Act of 1986. It seems likely that special interest legislation of this type will recur in the future.

6. The Revenue Act of 1978 added section 125 to the Code. This section permits the adoption of cafeteria or flexible benefit plans and provides that an employee can choose between taxable and nontaxable compensation elements without problems of constructive receipt if certain conditions are met. One of these conditions is that deferred compensation plans cannot be one of the choices. However, this section was amended to allow the inclusion of profit sharing and stock bonus plans that meet the requirements of section 401(k) of the Code (described in Chapter 12). Thus, a flexible compensation plan can permit an employee to choose among welfare benefits (e.g., life insurance, disability income, medical expense), cash, deferred profit sharing or savings plan benefits. This legislation encouraged the defined contribution approach. This area is particularly significant since interest in flexible compensation plans is increasing and these plans have become a major factor in the employee benefit planning process.

Some pressures exist to expand flexible compensation legislation so as to include defined benefit pension plans. Even if this does occur, it is still likely that the emphasis on defined contribution plans will remain. There are very real problems involved in trading defined benefits (particularly if they are pay related) for current cash or welfare contributions. It is possible to do this, but it will be necessary to resolve issues of equity and the relative value of choices. In many cases, it will be easier to limit employee elections as to how available dollars can be used -- for example, to a choice of purchasing current benefits or of deferring these dollars under some type of defined contribution program. Indeed, it might be said that flexible compensation plans often apply the defined contribution concept to an employer's entire benefit program.

7. Closely related to flexible compensation plans are the section 401(k) cash/deferred profit sharing or savings plans. A key feature of these plans is that they permit the use of salary reduction arrangements -- an approach that can be very tax effective and that has captured the interest of many employers. Much of the initial interest was in the conversion of existing plans. However, the approach presents attractive advantages and it seems likely that new programs will continue to be enacted. Employers who do not have pension plans may find the combination of tax savings for employees and the possible lesser financial obligations of the defined contribution approach to be an attractive way of establishing a retirement program. This could be particularly true when tied in with an overall flexible compensation program.

8. The plan termination and funding requirements imposed on defined benefit plans by the Omnibus Budget Reconciliation Act of 1987 may foster a much higher level of interest in the relatively unrestricted defined contribution approach.

9. Defined benefit and money purchase pension plans must include both pre- and post-retirement joint and survivor benefits for the benefit of the employee's spouse. These provisions are complex and their administration can be cumbersome. By contrast, other defined contribution plans need not include these joint and survivor provisions if the plan provides that the employee's spouse is the beneficiary for 100% of the employee's account balance and if the employee does not elect an annuity distribution from the plan. These, and other requirements applicable to defined benefit plans (e.g., the anti-cutback rules), have made the design and administration of defined benefit plans much more complex than is the case for defined contribution plans.

4.3.   OTHER FACTORS

As can be seen, there has been a significant amount of direct legislative activity that has enhanced the attractiveness of various defined contribution mechanisms. However, other legislation also may have an indirect effect that will encourage the growth of these plans. Some of the changes made by the 1983 social security amendments are a good example of how indirect legislation can affect the design of private retirement plans.

These amendments gradually change the normal retirement age for social security benefits from 65 to 67. While the earliest age for claiming social security retirement benefits was not increased from 62, the reduction for early benefit commencement will be gradually increased as the normal retirement age increases. Moreover, workers will have an additional incentive to remain in the work force beyond age 65, since delayed retirement credits will be increased and the earnings test has been liberalized (see Chapter 2 for details).

These changes could affect the planning process associated with defined benefit plans. Most of these plans are designed to produce a specific amount of replacement income, together with primary social security benefits, when an employee reaches age 65. The actual income replacement objectives may vary, but they usually reflect the employee's pay level and length of service. While replacement ratios are generally expressed in terms of before-tax income, they are often consciously set with reference to their after-tax value.

The fundamental concept of this planning process revolves around the coordination of two income sources -- the private plan and social security -- usually occurring around the time of the employee's 65th birthday. However, the idea that 65 is a typical retirement age has already begun to diffuse with recent trends toward early retirement. This diffusion will become even greater as the social security normal retirement age is changed, especially since mandatory retirement is no longer possible. What may emerge is a concept that retirement age will become highly subjective for each employee. Actual retirement age may range over a span that begins when employees are in their late 50s and extends until employees reach their early 70s. If retirement becomes spread over such a wide range, it will become increasingly difficult to maintain a plan design structure that is predicated on the majority of employees retiring at age 65 and the coordination of two income sources at this point. Thus, one of the broad but important implications facing employers is the potential need to rethink their approach to plan design and the basic delivery of retirement benefits. Nonintegrated plans and greater use of defined contribution plans are examples of approaches that might be considered. These approaches allow an employer to opt for cost control in lieu of finely tuned benefit levels.

A mandatory private retirement system in the United States is still a long way off -- if, indeed, it ever becomes a reality. Yet the possibility exists that such a system will become law. The President's Commission on Pension Policy, which filed its report in February 1981, recommended that a mandatory minimum pension system be established. More specifically, the Commission recommended that this program be in the form of a defined contribution plan with a minimum employer contribution of 3 percent of compensation. While the Commission did not divulge all of its reasoning in support of this defined contribution recommendation, it is likely that it was perceived as the simplest and most acceptable way of moving into a mandatory system. A mandatory defined benefit program would present a host of issues concerning pay-related benefits, the recognition of prior service, and the imposition of related liabilities.

The prospects of a mandatory private pension system are not clear at this time. Movement in this direction during the next few years is quite unlikely. But, on a long-term basis, there is the distinct possibility that some form of pension coverage will become mandatory. If this should happen, the defined contribution approach is most apt to be used. (Defined benefit equivalents would most likely be permitted -- largely to accommodate existing defined benefit plans -- but a defined contribution plan would be the probable choice for employers installing a plan for the first time.) A mandatory private pension system would have major implications for the expanded growth of defined contribution plans.

4.4.   THE FUTURE

Despite all the foregoing, defined benefit plans are alive and well at this time. They are firmly entrenched in major companies and most of the employees now covered by private pensions participate in defined benefit arrangements. It is unlikely that many of these plans will be shifted -- at least completely -- to defined contribution plans. What might happen, however, is that employers with these plans will hold them at current levels, opting to make benefit improvements via some kind of supplemental defined contribution arrangement (e.g., a salary reduction, section 401(k) savings plan). For employers who do not yet have a pension plan, there has already been and is likely to be greater utilization of one form or another of the defined contribution approaches referred to in this chapter. IRAs, ESOPs, SEPs, flexible compensation and section 401(k) plans are all attractive and viable programs to consider. While defined benefit plans will remain a major component in the U.S. private pension system, the defined contribution plan has begun to take on a more significant role and this role is likely to become greater in the years ahead.

QUESTIONS FOR REVIEW

1. Describe the factors that will determine an employee's retirement benefit under the defined contribution approach.
2. Explain the primary advantages of a defined benefit plan.
3. Explain the primary advantages of a defined contribution plan.
4. Explain the ways in which the federal government emphasized the defined contribution approach.
5. Explain how the 1983 social security amendments might affect utilization of the defined benefit approach.

QUESTIONS FOR DISCUSSION

1. The text states that in the view of some, a more equitable allocation of employer contributions occurs under a defined benefit plan than under a defined contribution plan. Assume that a participant in a defined benefit pension plan, age 25, is currently paid $15,000 per year and will retire at age 65. At that time, he will receive a pension benefit equal to 1 percent of average salary in the last five years times years of service. Compute the present value of the pension benefit accrued from working an additional year, as a percentage of the participant's compensation, at ages 30, 35, 40, 45, 50, 55, 60, and 64. Perform the calculations under two sets of assumptions: (a) the participant has no wage growth and the discount rate is 3 percent, and (b) the participant's wage growth is 7 percent and the discount rate is 10 percent. Graph the change in the present value of accrued benefits from an additional year's work (expressed as a percentage of compensation) against the participant's age under both scenarios. What conclusions can you draw about the allocation of employer contributions under defined benefit plans? (Notice that the discount rate exceeds the wage growth by 3 percent under both scenarios.)
2. Prepare a similar graph to the one in the preceding question for an employee participating in a defined contribution plan providing a contribution of 6 percent of compensation, and compare your results with the previous graphs. What conclusions can you draw about the allocation of employer contributions under a defined contribution plan vis-a-vis those of a defined benefit plan? What implications does this have for the retention of older employees?
3. Assume that you are an employee, age 25, and you are given your choice of participating in the defined benefit plan described in Question 1 or the defined contribution plan in Question 2. Which

one would you prefer? Describe how you made the evaluation and any assumptions required.

PART TWO

Tax and Legal Requirements

While an employer may choose to use a nonqualified approach to providing retirement benefits for certain highly paid executives, the requirements of the Employee Retirement Income Security Act of 1974 (ERISA) are such that a qualified plan is the only effective way to provide these benefits for a large group of employees. Moreover, the tax advantages provided under the Internal Revenue Code for qualified pension and profit sharing plans are most significant -- both to an employer and to its employees.

To obtain these tax benefits, the plan must achieve a qualified status by meeting the requirements of the Internal Revenue Code and appropriate regulations and rulings issued by the commissioner of internal revenue. Chapters 5 and 6 serve as a general guide to the major requirements of federal tax law that a plan must meet if this qualified status is to be obtained.

Chapter 5 discusses those elements of plan design dealing with minimum coverage tests, nondiscrimination rules and permitted disparities. Chapter 6 focuses on the remaining tax law qualification requirements and then concludes with a brief discussion of general provisions included in most plans -- the right to amend or terminate the program, administrative provisions, and the like.

Tax law is clearly the most important law affecting qualified plans. Nevertheless, employers must also be concerned about the effect of other laws. Chapter 7 briefly reviews some of the major laws that need to be considered in this regard. The chapter first discusses the provisions of Title I of ERISA --the labor law provisions dealing with reporting, disclosure, and fiduciary responsibilities. This coverage of labor law provisions also discusses the potential application of other Title I requirements to executive benefit arrangements that cannot meet the tax law standards for a qualified plan. The chapter next treats prohibitions against age and sex discrimination. Securities and Exchange (SEC) requirements are also covered in this chapter since they can be important for plans that permit employees to invest in employer stock. The chapter also includes a limited discussion of collective bargaining issues as well as a brief discussion of unrelated business income.

5. Tax Law Qualification Requirements

While an employer may choose to use a nonqualified approach to providing retirement benefits for certain highly paid executives, the requirements of ERISA are such that a qualified plan is the only effective way to provide these benefits for a large group of employees. Moreover, the tax advantages provided under the Internal Revenue Code for qualified pension and profit sharing plans are most significant -- both to an employer and to its employees. The principal tax advantages of such a plan are:

1. Contributions made by the employer, within the limitations prescribed, are deductible as a business expense.
2. Investment income on these contributions normally is not subject to federal income tax until paid in the form of benefits.
3. An employee is not considered to be in receipt of taxable income until benefits are distributed.
4. A lump-sum distribution to an employee after the employee attains age 59½ will be taxed on a favorable basis if it meets certain requirements.

To obtain these tax benefits, the plan must achieve a qualified status by meeting the requirements of the Internal Revenue Code and appropriate regulations and rulings issued by the commissioner of internal revenue. Chapters 5 and 6, while not intended as an exhaustive treatise on the tax aspects of qualified plans, should serve as a general guide to the major requirements of federal tax law that a plan must meet if this qualified status is to be obtained.

5.1.   KEY CONCEPTS

Although the major emphasis of this chapter pertains to minimum coverage requirements, and nondiscrimination rules, there are a number of key concepts that must be understood before one can implement these qualification requirements. Perhaps the most important concept involves the identification of highly compensated employees (HCEs) as the primary purpose of many of these rules is to ensure that qualified plans do not discriminate in favor of the HCEs of the employer maintaining the plan. Other important concerns in applying these rules deal with when groups of employees must be treated as though they were covered by one sponsor (controlled groups) and when they can be segmented into separate groups for testing purposes (qualified separate lines of business).

The minimum participation rules are also key in that they address two fundamental concerns. First, the provision is intended to promote the nondiscriminatory provision of benefits or features by limiting the extent to which an employer is able to design different benefit formulas for different employees in order to maximize benefit disparities in favor of HCEs. Second, the provision is intended to limit the extent to which a defined benefit plan operates as an individual account for one employee, or a small group of employees, either by currently benefiting only one or a few of the employer's HCEs or by maintaining accrued benefits for only one or a few such employees.

Finally, the amount of plan benefits or contributions, expressed as a percentage of compensation, is generally one of the key factors in determining whether the nondiscrimination provisions have been satisfied. Thus, it is important to know exactly what flexibility is available to the sponsor in defining the term "compensation."

5.1.1.   Determination of HCEs

One of the most important requirements of a qualified plan is that it must be for the exclusive benefit of employees or their beneficiaries. Officers of a corporation and stockholders may participate in the plan if they are bona fide employees. However, a plan cannot be structured so that it discriminates in any fashion in favor of highly compensated employees. An HCE is defined as an employee who is:

1. A 5 percent owner.
2. A person earning over $75,000 (adjusted for inflation) a year in either the current or preceding year.

3. A person earning over $50,000 (adjusted for inflation) a year in either the current or preceding year and is or was in the top 20 percent of all active employees for such year.
4. An officer earning over $45,000 (adjusted for inflation) in either the current or preceding year.

A nonhighly compensated employee (NHCE) is any employee who is not an HCE.

The number of employees that can be considered officers is equal to 10 percent of all employees, or three, whichever is greater. In no case, however, may the total number of officers exceed 50.

If an employee is a family member of a 5 percent owner or one of the top 10 highly paid employees, both will be treated as one person for purposes of the nondiscrimination tests. Family includes the HCE's spouse, lineal ascendants or descendants and spouses of lineal descendants or ascendants.

If an employee (other than a 5 percent owner) earned less than the test amount in the year before the year he or she meets the definition of highly paid employee and was not an officer in that prior year, the employee will not be a member of the highly paid group for the entrance year unless he or she is among the top 100 employees for that year.

5.1.2. Controlled Groups

The minimum coverage rules explained later in this chapter could be easily circumvented if employers were given complete flexibility in splitting employees among a number of subsidiaries. For example, one subsidiary could contain all the HCEs and cover the entire cohort of employees while the second subsidiary would contain the vast majority of the NHCEs and provide no coverage. If the subsidiaries could be tested separately, the plan covering only the employees in the first subsidiary would meet the coverage tests since all employees would be covered.

To minimize the potential for this abuse, ERISA provides that for purposes of applying the coverage and other tests, employees of all corporations who are members of a controlled group of corporations are to be treated as if they were employees of a single employer. A controlled group of corporations consists of any group of a parent-subsidiary controlled group, a brother-sister controlled group, or a combined group. A parent-subsidiary group is one or more chains of corporations connected through stock ownership with a common parent corporation if each corporation is at least 80 percent owned by another corporation in the chain. A brother-sister group is two or more corporations if five or fewer persons own at least 80 percent and more than 50 percent is owned when stock ownership is taken into account only to the extent such ownership is identical with respect to each such corporation. If a common parent of a parent-subsidiary group is also a member of a brother-sister group, all of the corporations in both groups form a combined group.

For purposes of the nondiscrimination tests, all employees of employers who are members of an *affiliated service group* are to be treated as employed by a single employer (except as otherwise provided by regulations). An affiliated service group consists of a service organization and one or more of the following:

1.   any other service organization which is a shareholder or partner in the first organization and which regularly performs services for the first organization or is regularly associated with the first organization in performing services for third persons, and
2.   any other organization if:
     a.   a significant portion of the business of the organization is the performance of services for the first organization, for a service organization described in (1), or for both, of a type historically performed in the service field by employees, *and*
     b.   at least 10 percent of the interests of the organization is held by HCEs

5.1.3.   Qualified Separate Lines of Business

If an employer is treated as operating qualified separate lines of business, the minimum coverage requirements (including the nondiscrimination requirements) and the minimum participation requirements (all three concepts are described later in this chapter) may be applied separately with respect to the employees of each qualified separate line of business. An employer is treated as operating qualified separate lines of business only if all property and service provided by the employer to its customers are provided exclusively by qualified separate lines of business.

A qualified separate line of business is defined as a portion of the employer that is both a *line of business* and a *separate line of business*, and that satisfies certain *statutory* requirements listed below. A *line of business* is a portion of an employer that is identified by the property or service it provides to customers of the employer. The employer is permitted to determine the lines of business it operates by designating the property and service that each of its lines of business provides to customers of the employer.[1]

A *separate line of business* is a line of business that is organized and operated separately from the remainder of the employer according to the following objective criteria:

- the line of business is organized into one or more separate organizational units (e.g., corporations, partnerships, or divisions),
- the line of business constitutes one or more distinct profit centers with the employer, and
- no more than a moderate overlap exists between the employee workforce and management employed by the line of business and those employed by the remainder of the employer[2]

For a separate line of business to be treated as a *qualified* separate line of business, the following three *statutory* requirements must be satisfied:

1. a separate line of business must have at least 50 employees
2. the employer must provide notification that it treats itself as operating qualified separate lines of business for purposes of applying the requirements of the minimum coverage or minimum participation tests separately with respect to employees of the separate lines of business[3]
3. an administrative scrutiny requirement

The administrative scrutiny requirement may be satisfied either by satisfying one of the safe harbors specified in §1.414(r)-5 or requesting and receiving an individual determination.

The employees of a qualified separate line of business consist of all employees who are substantial-service employees with respect to the qualified separate line of business, and all other employees who are assigned to the qualified separate line of business.

5.1.4.   Minimum Participation Requirements

In general, a plan is a qualified plan for a plan year only if it benefits at least the lesser of 50 employees of the employer or 40 percent of the employees of

---

[1]Rules for determining an employer's lines of business are provided in §1.414(r)-2.

[2]Rules for determining an employer's separate lines of business are provided in §1.414(r)-3.

[3]Rules for determining an employer's qualified separate lines of business are provided in §1.414(r)-4(c).

the employer. A plan that satisfies any of the following exceptions passes this requirement automatically for the plan year:[4]

- plans that do not benefit any HCE
- the portion of a multiemployer plan that benefits only employees included in a unit of employees covered by a collective bargaining agreement
- certain underfunded defined benefit plans
- Section 401(k) plans maintained by employers that include certain governmental or tax-exempt entities
- certain acquisitions or dispositions

An additional requirement exists specifically for defined benefit plans.[5] The test applies to the defined benefit plan's prior benefit structure which includes all accrued benefits under the plan as of the *beginning* of the plan year (including benefits rolled over or transferred to the plan). Each defined benefit plan has only one prior benefit structure and it must either:

- provide *meaningful benefits* to a group of employees that includes the lesser of 50 employees or 40 percent of the employer's employees, or
- at least 50 employees and former employees or 40 percent of the employer's employees and former employees have meaningful accrued benefits under the plan.

Whether a plan is providing meaningful benefits, or whether individuals have meaningful accrued benefits under a plan is determined on the basis of all the facts and circumstances. The relevant factors in making this determination include, but are not limited to:

- the level of current benefit accruals
- the comparative rate of accrual under the current benefit formula compared to prior rate of accrual under the plan
- the projected accrued benefit under the current benefit formula compared to accrued benefits as of the close of the immediately preceding plan year
- the length of time the current benefit formula has been in effect
- the number of employees with accrued benefits under the plan
- the length of time the plan has been in effect

---

[4]Technically these exceptions will not apply to a frozen defined benefit plan or top heavy plans (described in Chapter 6).

[5]In addition, a defined benefit plan that benefits former employees (for example, a defined benefit plan that is amended to provide an ad hoc cost-of-living adjustment) must satisfy similar types of numerical tests with respect to its former employees.

5.1.5.   Definition of Compensation

Detailed rules have been developed regarding how compensation may be defined for purposes of applying the Section 415 limits on benefits and contributions described in Chapter 6 (Section "415 compensation") and for using a nondiscriminatory definition of compensation under Section 414(s) (Section "414(s) compensation").

5.1.5.1. Section 415 Compensation

Section 415 compensation is used in determining compliance for the Section 415 limits and for determining which employees are HCEs as described previously.   Except as otherwise provided, Section 415 compensation includes all remuneration listed below and excludes all other forms of remuneration:[6]

- The employee's wages, salary, fees for professional services, and other amounts received for personal services actually rendered in the course of employment to the extent that the amounts are includible in gross income[7]
- Employer-provided accident and health insurance benefits and medical reimbursement plan benefits, but only to the extent includible in the gross income of the employee
- Certain moving expenses paid by an employer
- The value of a nonqualified stock option granted to the employee by the employer (to the extent includible in the gross income of the employee for the taxable year in which it was granted)
- The amount includible in gross income that results when an employee who receives restricted property makes an election to be taxed on it under Section 83(b)

Examples of types of remuneration *not* includible in 415 compensation include:

- Contributions made by the employer to a plan of deferred compensation to the extent that the contributions are not includible in the gross income of the employee
- Certain deferred compensation payments

---

[6]For a self-employed individual (see Chapter 24), compensation means earned income.
[7]This will include commissions paid, compensation for services on the basis of a percentage of profits, commissions on insurance premiums, tips, and bonuses.

- SEP contributions (see Chapter 13) that are excludible from the gross income of the employee
- Amounts realized from the exercise of a nonqualified stock option or when restricted stock or property held by an employee becomes freely transferable or is no longer subject to a substantial risk of forfeiture
- Amounts realized from the sale, exchange, or other disposition of stock acquired under a qualified stock option
- Employer contributions to a tax-sheltered annuity (see Chapter 25) whether or not excludible from the gross income of the employee

Additional definitions of compensation that are treated as 415 compensation include:

- Wages as defined for purposes of federal income tax withholding, or
- Compensation required to be reported in Box 10 on Form W-2, modified at the election of the employer to exclude moving expense reasonably believed to be deductible to the employee.

5.1.5.2. Section 414(s) Compensation

Section 414(s) compensation is used to determine compliance with the general nondiscrimination standards, the average benefit test under the minimum coverage tests (described later in this chapter) and the permitted disparity rules (described in Chapters 8 and 14). It is also used for the ADP and ACP tests described in Chapters 10 and 12.

Section 414(s) compensation may be defined using:

- any of the available definitions of 415 compensation.
- any of the three safe harbor definitions explained below, or
- any reasonable nondiscriminatory definition

5.1.5.2.1.   Safe Harbors

Under the first safe harbor alternative, Section 415 compensation is decreased by all of the following:

- reimbursements or other expense allowances,
- fringe benefits (cash and noncash),
- moving expenses,
- deferred compensation, and

- welfare benefits

The second alternative starts with Section 415 compensation, or Section 415 compensation decreased as provided above, then increased by all salary reduction amounts under cafeteria plans, 401(k) plans, 403(b) annuities (as described in Chapter 25) and deferred compensation plans of state and local government and tax-exempt organizations. The final alternative starts with Section 415 compensation or Section 415 compensation adjusted in any manner provided above, decreased for HCEs through exclusion of additional components of compensation.

5.1.5.2.2.   Any Alternative Nondiscriminatory Definition

In addition to the previous definitions, any definition of compensation satisfies Section 414(s) if the definition of compensation does not by design favor HCEs, is reasonable, and satisfies the nondiscrimination requirement. Reasonable alternative definitions may exclude any type of additional compensation for employees working outside their regularly scheduled tour of duty, bonuses, or any one of the types of compensation excluded under the safe harbor alternative definitions mentioned above. A definition of compensation is not reasonable if it provides that each employee's compensation is a specified portion of the employee's compensation measured for the otherwise applicable determination period under another definition.

An alternative definition of compensation is nondiscriminatory if the average percentage of total compensation included under the alternative definition for an employer's HCEs as a group does not exceed by more than a de minimis amount the average percentage of total compensation included under the alternative definition for the employer's NHCEs as a group.

5.2.   MINIMUM COVERAGE TESTS

The Internal Revenue Code specifies that a qualified retirement plan will have to satisfy one of the following three coverage tests:[8]

1.   The *percentage test* is satisfied if the plan benefits at least 70 percent of the sponsoring employer's NHCEs.

---

[8]Any plan satisfying the percentage test will automatically satisfy the ratio percentage test. Therefore, the ensuing discussion will focus only on the ratio percentage test and the average benefits test.

2.   A plan may qualify under the *ratio percentage test* if the percentage of NHCEs who benefit under the plan is at least 70 percent of the percentage of HCEs who benefit under the plan. For example, if a plan benefits 90 percent of the HCEs, it must benefit 70 percent of 90 percent (63 percent) of the NHCEs.

3.   The *average benefit test* (explained below).

An employee is considered to benefit for a plan year only if he or she receives a contribution or forfeiture, or accrues an increase in the dollar amount of a benefit under the plan for that plan year. There are some exceptions to this rule:

- In the case of the 401(k) or 401(m) plans described in Chapters 10 and 12, any *eligible* employee will be considered to benefit (even if they elect not to make a contribution).

- Plan provisions that implement the Section 415 provisions described in the next chapter are disregarded.

- Employees failing to accrue benefits solely because of a benefit limit under the plan that is uniformly applied to all employees are treated as benefiting under the plan. For example, if a defined benefit plan takes into account only the first 30 years of service for accrual purposes, a participant who has completed more than 30 years of service is still treated as benefiting under the plan.

- An employee is treated as benefiting under a plan even if the current benefit accrual under the plan is offset by the contributions or benefits provided under another plan, assuming the employee has satisfied all other conditions under the plan.

- An employee is treated as benefiting under a defined benefit plan if the employee has attained normal retirement age and fails to accrue a benefit solely because the plan's actuarial adjustment for late commencement of benefits exceeds whatever continued accrual would otherwise be available.

Special coverage rules exist for governmental plans, plans maintained by a church, plans to which no employer contributions have been made after September 2, 1974, collectively bargained plans, plans with no HCEs and employers with no NHCEs.

All of the tests apply on a controlled group basis, unless the employer elects to apply them on a separate line of business basis. Active and former employees must be tested separately for coverage purposes.[9]

---

[9]A plan under which no former employees benefit is treated as satisfying the coverage rules as to former employees. See Reg. Section 1.410(b)-2(c) for more details.

5.2.1.   The Average Benefit Test

Two conditions (the *nondiscriminatory classification test* and the *average benefit percentage test*) must be met for a plan to satisfy the *average benefits test*. First, the plan must benefit a nondiscriminatory class or group of employees. Second, the employer must provide retirement benefits that have an average value for the NHCEs that is at least 70 percent of the average value of retirement benefits for the HCEs.[10]

5.2.1.1. Nondiscriminatory Classification Test

To pass this test, the plan must cover a classification of employees that is both *reasonable* and *nondiscriminatory*. To be considered as reasonable, the classification would have to be "reasonable and established under objective business criteria that identify the category of employee who benefits under the plan." To be considered nondiscriminatory, the classification must meet either an *objective test* or a *facts and circumstances test.*

The objective test is structured in a similar fashion to the ratio percentage test, except that the required "ratio" will be less than 70 percent and therefore easier to satisfy. The degree to which the ratio drops below 70 percent in the objective test is determined by the concentration of NHCEs in the employer's total workforce. For example, if the employer had a total of 1,000 employees consisting of 920 NHCEs and 80 HCEs, the NHCE concentration percentage would be 920/1,000 or 92 percent.

Once the NHCE concentration percentage is known, the next step in this test is to find the appropriate *safe harbor* percentage from Table 5-1. Continuing the example from above, an employer with a NHCE concentration percentage of 92 percent would have a safe harbor percentage of 26 percent. This allows the employer to meet the numerical test with a much smaller percentage of NHCEs covered than would be required under the ratio percentage test. For example, if a plan benefits 90 percent of the HCEs, it must benefit 26 percent of 90 percent (23.4 percent) of the NHCEs under the safe harbor test as opposed to 63 percent under the ratio percentage test. It is important to note that this increased flexibility comes with the additional burdens of proving that the classification is reasonable and passing the average benefit percentage test (tests not required by the

---

[10]A special test applies to a single plan under which both union and nonunion employees are covered by an identical benefit or allocation formula. Such a plan need not meet the average benefit percentage component of the average benefit test if the plan would satisfy the ratio test considering union and nonunion employees together. In other words, the general rule that the portions of the plan treating union employees be treated separately from the portion covering nonunion employees is not relevant in this case.

Table 5-1: Safe Harbor and Unsafe Harbor Percentages

NHCE concentration percentage	Safe harbor percentage	Unsafe harbor percentage	NHCE concentration percentage	Safe harbor percentage	Unsafe harbor percentage
0-60	50.00	40.00	80	35.00	25.00
61	49.25	39.25	81	34.25	24.25
62	48.50	38.50	82	33.50	23.50
63	47.75	37.75	83	32.75	22.75
64	47.00	37.00	84	32.00	22.00
65	46.25	36.25	85	31.25	21.25
66	45.50	35.50	86	30.50	20.50
67	44.75	34.75	87	29.75	20.00
68	44.00	34.00	88	29.00	20.00
69	43.25	33.25	89	28.25	20.00
70	42.50	32.50	90	27.50	20.00
71	41.75	31.75	91	26.75	20.00
72	41.00	31.00	92	26.00	20.00
73	40.25	30.25	93	25.25	20.00
74	39.50	29.50	94	24.50	20.00
75	38.75	28.75	95	23.75	20.00
76	38.00	28.00	96	23.00	20.00
77	37.25	27.25	97	22.25	20.00
78	36.50	26.50	98	21.50	20.00
79	35.75	25.75	99	20.75	20.00

ratio percentage test). Also, employers will receive more flexibility vis-a-vis the ratio percentage test as the NHCE concentration percentage increases.

If a plan fails the safe harbor test, the next step involves the unsafe harbor test. The computation is analogous to that performed for the safe harbor test, with the exception that the smaller percentage in the third column of Table 5-1 is used. The employer with a NHCE concentration percentage of 92 percent would have an unsafe harbor percentage of 20 percent. If the plan benefits 90 percent of the HCEs, it must benefit 20 percent of 90 percent (18 percent) of the NHCEs to avoid failing the unsafe harbor test. Plans that do not pass the unsafe harbor test automatically fail the objective test.

Plans that pass the unsafe harbor test (but fail the safe harbor test) must proceed to a subjective test and demonstrate that the classification does not discriminate in favor of HCEs on the basis of all relevant facts and circumstances. Factors to be considered include the business reason for the classification, employees benefiting under the plan as a percent of all employees, the representation of employees in all salary ranges, the margin by which the plan failed to meet the safe harbor percentage, and the degree to which the average benefit percentage test exceeds 70 percent.

5.2.1.2. Average Benefit Percentage Test

The first step in the average benefit percentage test requires the calculation of an employee benefit percentage for each employee. For purposes of this calculation, employee contributions and employee-provided benefits are disregarded. Employee benefit percentages may be determined on either a contributions or a benefits basis.[11]

If employee benefit percentages are determined on a *contributions* basis for a testing period, each employee's employee benefit percentage is determined as follows:[12]

1. Determine the annual allocation to each employee under all defined contribution plans (including ESOPs)
2. Determine the present value of the accrual to each employee under all defined benefit plans

---

[11]In general, employee benefit percentages for any testing period must be determined on the same basis (contributions or benefits) for all plans in the testing group. An optional rule permits employee benefit percentages to be determined separately with respect to defined benefit plans and defined contribution plans in the testing group. See Reg. Section 1.410(b)-5(e)(3) for details.

[12]For the specific details involved in this calculation see Reg. Sections 1.410(b)-5(d)(5), (d)(7), (e)(7), (e)(8)(ii).

3.   Add these two amounts
4.   Determine the percentage of each employee's compensation contributed to all plans

If employee benefit percentages are determined on a *benefits* basis for a testing period, each employee's employee benefit percentage is determined as follows:[13]

1.   Determine the benefits earned by each employee under all defined benefit plans
2.   Determine the allocation to each employee under all defined contribution plans and convert that allocation into an equivalent annuity benefit
3.   Add these two amounts
4.   Determine the percentage of each employee's compensation represented by this benefit accrual for each employee

The average benefit percentage is determined by dividing the average of the employee benefit percentages for the NHCEs by the average of the employee benefit percentages for the HCEs. All nonexcludable employees of the employer are taken into account for this purpose, even if they are not benefiting under any plan that is taken into account. The average benefit percentage test requires that the plan's average benefit percentage is at least 70 percent.[14]

5.2.2.   Excludable Employees

For purposes of applying the minimum coverage requirements, all employees of the employer, other than those listed below, are taken into account. In general, excludable employees are not taken into account with respect to a plan even if they are benefiting under the plan.[15]

---

[13]For the specific details involved in this calculation see Reg. Sections 1.410(b)-5(d)(6), (d)(7), (e)(7), (e)(8).

[14]With one special exception, the regulations provide that employers must test union and nonunion employees separately. Because union plans always pass coverage, this means that employers need only test nonunion employees.

[15]See Reg. Section 1.410(b)-6(b) for exceptions.

5.2.2.1. Minimum Age and Service

If a plan applies the statutory minimum age and service requirements discussed in Chapter 6 (i.e., age 21 and one year of service) and excludes all employees who do not meet those conditions from benefiting under the plan, then all employees who fail to satisfy those conditions are excludable employees with respect to that plan. If a plan has two or more different tests of minimum age and service eligibility conditions, those employees who fail to satisfy *all* of the different sets of age and service conditions are excludable employees. If a plan does not apply the greatest permissible minimum ages and service conditions, the employer has a choice of excluding either those employees who do not meet the *plan's* minimum age and service requirements or those employees who do not meet the *statutory* minimum age and service requirements.[16]

5.2.2.2. Nonresident Aliens

An employee who is a nonresident alien and who receives no earned income from the employer that constitutes income from sources within the United States is treated as an excludable employee.

5.2.2.3. Collectively Bargained Employees

A collectively bargained employee is an excludable employee with respect to a plan that benefits solely noncollectively bargained employees. If a plan benefits both collectively bargained employees and noncollectively bargained employees for a plan year, the portion of the plan that benefits the collectively bargained employees is treated as a separate plan from the portion of the plan that benefits the noncollectively bargained employees. An employee is not considered included in a unit of employees covered by a collective bargaining agreement for a plan year if more than 2 percent of the employees who are covered pursuant to the agreement are professionals.

---

[16]Sponsors using the second approach must test the portion of the plan benefiting otherwise excludable employees separately.

5.2.2.4. Qualified Separate Lines of Business

If an employer is treated as operating qualified separate lines of business, the employees of other qualified separate lines of business of the employer are treated as excludable employees.

5.2.2.5. Terminating Employees

Sponsors may, but need not, uniformly exclude from testing terminated employees if:

* the employee does not benefit under the plan for the plan year,
* the employee is eligible to participate in the plan,
* the plan has a minimum period of service requirement or a requirement that an employee be employed on the last day of the plan year (last-day requirement) in order for an employee to accrue a benefit or receive an allocation for the plan year,
* the employee fails to accrue a benefit or receive an allocation under the plan solely because of the failure to satisfy the minimum period of service or last-day requirement, and
* the employee terminates employment during the plan year with no more than 500 hours of service, and the employee is not an employee as of the last day of the plan year.

5.2.2.6. Employees of Governmental or Tax-Exempt Entities Precluded from Maintaining a 401(k) Plan

For purposes of testing a 401(k) or 401(m) plan that consists solely of employer matching contributions that are tied to elective contributions under a 401(k) plan, an employer may treat as excludable those employees of governmental or tax-exempt entities who are precluded from being eligible employees under a 401(k) plan, if more than 95 percent of the employees who are not precluded from being eligible employees benefit under the plan.

5.2.3.   Definition of a Plan for Minimum Coverage Purposes

Each single plan is a separate plan for purposes of the minimum coverage tests. For example, the defined contribution portion of a plan is a separate plan from the defined benefit portion of that same plan.[17]

Employers are required to disaggregate certain plans and treat them as two or more plans for coverage testing. They also permit employers to aggregate certain single plans for testing, and specify that certain plans must be aggregated for purposes of the average benefit percentage test.

5.2.3.1. Mandatory Disaggregation

The following describes the rules for certain plans that must be treated as comprising two or more separate plans, each of which is a single plan subject to the minimum coverage rules.[18]

5.2.3.1.1.   Section 401(k) and 401(m) Plans

The portion of a plan that is a 401(k) plan and the portion that is not a 401(k) plan are treated as separate plans for the minimum coverage tests. Similar treatment is provided for 401(m) plan.

5.2.3.1.2.   Employee Stock Ownership Plans

The portion of the plan that is an Employee Stock Ownership Plan (ESOP) and the portion of the plan that is not an ESOP are treated as separate plans for the minimum coverage tests.

5.2.3.1.3.   Plans Benefiting Otherwise Excludable Employees

If an employer applies the minimum coverage tests separately to the portion of a plan that benefits only employees who satisfy age and service conditions

---

[17]However, a defined contribution plan does not comprise separate plans merely because it includes more than one trust, or merely because it provides for separate accounts and permits employees to direct the investment of the amounts allocated to their account. Further, a plan does not comprise separate plans merely because assets are separately invested in individual insurance or annuity contracts for employees.

[18]Special rules apply for plans maintained by more than one employer. See Reg. Section 1.410(b)-7(c)(6) for details.

under the plan that are lower than the statutory minimum age and service requirements, the plan is treated as comprised of separate plans.

5.2.3.1.4.   Plans Benefiting Collectively Bargained Employees

The portion of a plan that benefits collectively bargained employees is treated as a separate plan from the portion of the same plan that benefits noncollectively bargained employees. In addition, the portion of a plan that benefits collectively bargained employees covered under one collective bargaining agreement is treated as a separate plan from the portion of the same plan that benefits collectively bargained employees covered under another collective bargaining agreement.

5.2.3.2.   Permissive Aggregation for the Ratio Percentage Test and the Nondiscriminatory Classification Test

For purposes of applying the ratio percentage test and the nondiscriminatory classification test described previously in this chapter, an employer may generally designate two or more separate plans as a single plan. If an employer treats two or more separate plans as a single plan for these purposes, the plans must be treated as a single plan for all purposes under minimum coverage and nondiscrimination testing.

There are some exceptions to this general rule however. First, an employer may not aggregate portions of a plan that are disaggregated under the rules described previously. Similarly, an employer many not aggregate two or more separate plans that would be disaggregated under those rules if they were portions of the same plan. In addition, in most cases an employer may not aggregate an ESOP with another ESOP.

There is also a prohibition on duplicative aggregation that prevents a plan from being combined with two or more plans to form more than one single plan. For example, an employer that maintains plans A, B, and C may not aggregate plans A and B and plans A and C to form two single plans.

Two or more plans may not be aggregated and treated as a single plan unless they have the same plan year.

5.2.3.3.   Determination of Plans in Testing Group for Average Benefit Percentage Test

For purposes of applying the average benefit percentage test, all plans in the testing group must be taken into account. For this purpose, the plans in the testing group are the plans being tested and all other plans of the employer that could be permissively aggregated with that plan.

5.2.4. Testing Methods

A plan may satisfy the minimum coverage tests for a plan year on a daily, quarterly, or annual basis. Whichever testing option is used for the plan year must also be used for purposes of testing for nondiscrimination for the plan year.[19] The plan provisions and other relevant facts as of the last day of the plan year regarding which employees benefit under the plan are applied to the employees taken into account under the testing option used.

The daily test is satisfied if a plan meets the minimum coverage rules on each day of the plan year, taking into account only those individuals who are employees on that day. The quarterly test requires the plan to satisfy the rules on at least one day in each quarter of the plan year, taking into account only those individuals who are employees on that day.[20] The annual test is satisfied if the plan satisfies the minimum coverage rules as of the last day of the plan year, taking into account all individuals whose are employees on any day during the plan year.

5.3.   NONDISCRIMINATION RULES

Section 401(a)(4) of the Internal Revenue Code provides that a plan is a qualified plan only if the contributions or the benefits provided under the plan do not discriminate in favor of HCEs. In order to satisfy the nondiscrimination requirements under this section, a plan must satisfy each of the following requirements:

- nondiscrimination in amount of contributions or benefits
- nondiscriminatory availability of benefits, rights and features
- nondiscriminatory effect of plan amendments and terminations

A plan may be treated as consisting of two or more component plans for purposes of determining whether the plan satisfies the nondiscrimination rules. If each of the *component* plans of a plan satisfies all of the nondiscrimination and minimum coverage requirements as if it were a

---

[19]The annual testing option must be used in applying the minimum coverage test to a 401(k) or 401(m) plan and in applying the average benefit percentage test.

[20]This does not apply if the plan's eligibility rules or benefit formula operate to cause the four quarterly testing days selected by the employer not to be reasonably representative of the coverage of the plan over the entire plan year.

separate plan, then the *plan* is treated as satisfying the nondiscrimination requirements. A plan may be restructured into component plans, each consisting of all the allocations, accruals, and other benefits, rights and features provided to a selected group of employees in the plan. Any criteria may be used to select the group of employees used for the purpose. The only restriction is that every employee in the plan must be included in one *and only one* component plan.

5.3.1. Nondiscrimination in Amount of Contributions or Benefits

Either the contributions or the benefits provided under the plan must be nondiscriminatory in amount. It need not be shown that *both* the contributions and the benefits provided are nondiscriminatory in amount.

An important concept to keep in mind when analyzing this nondiscrimination requirement is that a limited number of *safe harbors* are provided for both defined contribution and defined benefit plans. Plans that do not satisfy one of these safe harbors may comply with the nondiscrimination requirements by satisfying the *general* test that involves numerical participant-by-participant testing.

5.3.1.1. Defined Contribution Plans

5.3.1.1.1.   Safe Harbors

A defined contribution plan can avoid the general test if it satisfies the *uniformity requirements* and either the *uniform allocation formula* safe harbor or the *uniform points plan* safe harbor. The uniformity requirements consist of the following two-part test:

1.   the same uniform normal retirement age and the same allocation formula must apply to all employees in the plan
2.   all employees in the plan must be subject to the same vesting schedule and the same definition of years of service.[21]

The safe harbor for plans with a uniform allocation formula is satisfied for a plan year if the plan allocates all amounts taken into account in this test

---

[21]For purposes of crediting service, only service with the employer may be taken into account.

(described below for the general test) for the plan year under a formula that allocates the same percentage of plan year compensation or the same dollar amount to every employee in the plan. If the plan qualifies under the Section 401(l) permitted disparity rules described in Chapters 8 and 14, differences in employees' allocation under the plan attributable to the permitted disparities may be ignored.

The safe harbor for a uniform points plan is satisfied if both of the following are met:

1.   The employee's allocation for the plan year equals the product determined by multiplying all amounts allocated (or treated as allocated) to all employees in the plan for the plan year by a fraction. The fraction is defined as the employee's points for the plan year divided by the sum of the points of all employees in the plan for the plan year.
2.   The average of the allocation rates for the HCEs in the plan may not exceed the average of the allocation rates for the NHCEs for the plan year. For this purpose, allocation rates are determined without imputing permitted disparity and without grouping allocation rates (described below).

For purposes of the uniform points plan, an employee's points for the plan year equals the sum of the employee's points for age, service and units of plan year compensation for the plan year. Each employee in the plan must receive the same number of points for each year of age, the same number of points for each year of service and the same number of points for each unit of plan year compensation.[22] A uniform points plan need not grant points for both age and service,[23] but it must grant points for at least one of them in addition to granting points for plan year compensation. This is illustrated in Example 1.

Example 1: Plan A has a single allocation formula that applies to all employees in the plan, and under which each employee's allocation for the plan year equals the product determined by multiplying all amounts taken into account for all employees in the plan for the plan year by a fraction, the numerator of which is the employee's points for the plan year, and the denominator of which is the sum of the points of all employees in the plan for the plan year. Plan A grants each employee 10 points for each year of

---

[22]The unit of plan year compensation used in the allocation formula must be the same for all employees in the plan and must be a single dollar amount that does not exceed $200.
[23]If the plan grants points for years of service, the plan is permitted to limit the number of years of service taken into account to a single maximum number of years of service.

service and 1 point for each $100 of plan year compensation. For the 1994 plan year, the total allocations are $81,200 and the total points for all employees in the plan are 8,120. Each employee's allocation for the 1994 plan year is set forth below:

Employee	Years of Service	Plan Year Compensation	Points	Amount of Allocation	Allocation Rate
H1	20	$200,000	2,200	$22,000	11.0%
H2	10	$200,000	2,100	$21,000	10.5%
H3	30	$100,000	1,300	$13,000	13.0%
H4	3	$100,000	1,030	$10,300	10.3%
N1	10	$40,000	500	$5,000	12.5%
N2	5	$35,000	400	$4,000	11.4%
N3	3	$30,000	330	$3,300	11.0%
N4	1	$25,000	260	$2,600	10.4%
Total	--	--	8,120	$81,200	--

Under these facts, Plan A meets the first test for a uniform points plan. To determine if the second test it met, the average allocation rate for HCEs (11.2 percent) and NHCEs (11.3 percent) is calculated. Because the average of the allocation rates for the HCEs does not exceed the average of the allocation rates for the NHCEs, Plan A satisfies the second test and, thus, the safe harbor for a uniform points plan.

5.3.1.1.2.   General Test

In general, a plan satisfies the general test for nondiscrimination in amount of contributions for a plan year if each *rate group* under the plan satisfies the minimum coverage requirements described earlier in this chapter.[24] A rate group exists under a plan for each HCE in the plan and contains that HCE as well as any other employee in the plan (both HCE and NHCE) that has an allocation rate greater than or equal to the HCE's allocation rate. This concept is illustrated in Example 2.

Example 2: Employer B has only 6 nonexcludable employees, all of whom benefit under Plan C. The HCEs are H1 and H2, the NHCEs are N1 through N4. For the 1994 plan year, H1 and N1 through N3 have an allocation rate of 5.0 percent of compensation. For the same plan year, H2 has an allocation rate of 7.5 percent of compensation and N4 has an allocation rate of 8.0 percent.

---

[24]The permissive aggregation rules are not available to a *rate group* in determining whether it satisfies the minimum coverage requirements.

There are two rate groups in Plan C. Rate group 1 consists of H1 and all those employees who have an allocation rate greater than or equal to H1's allocation rate (H1, H2 and N1 through N4). Rate group 2 consists of H2 and all those employee who have an allocation rate greater than or equal to H2's allocation rate (H2 and N4).

Rate group 1 satisfies the ratio percentage test because the ratio percentage of the rate group is 100 percent (100% of the NHCEs covered divided by 100% of the HCEs covered). Rate group 2 does not satisfy the ratio percentage test because the ratio percentage of the rate group is 50 percent (25% of the NHCEs covered divided by 50% of the HCEs covered). However, rate group 2 does satisfy the nondiscriminatory classification test because the rate group is deemed to satisfy the reasonable classification requirement and the ratio percentage of the rate group is greater than the safe harbor percentage (45.5 percent). If rate group 2 satisfies the average benefit percentage test, then rate group 2 satisfies the minimum coverage tests. In that case, plan E satisfies the requirements of the general test because each rate group satisfies the minimum coverage requirements.

The allocation rate for an employee for a plan year equals the sum of the allocations to the employee's account for the plan year, expressed as either a percentage of the plan year compensation or as a dollar amount. Sponsors may adjust these rates for permitted disparity.

The amounts taken into account in determining allocation rates for a plan year include all employer contributions and forfeitures that are allocated (or treated as allocated) to the account of an employee under the plan for the plan year, other than allocations of earnings, expenses, gains and losses attributable to the balance in an employee's account. Amounts that would be allocated to the account of an employee for the plan year but for the limits of Section 415 are not treated as allocated to the account of the employee.

An employer may treat all employees who have allocation rates within a range of not more than 5 percent above and below a midpoint rate chosen by the employer as having an allocation rate equal to that midpoint rate. As an alternative if allocation rates are determined as a percentage of plan year compensation, an employer may treat all employees who have allocation rates with a range of not more than 0.25 percentage points above and below a midpoint rate chosen by the employer as having an allocation rate equal to that midpoint rate.

In determining whether a rate group satisfies the nondiscriminatory classification test from the minimum coverage rules, the rate group is deemed to satisfy the reasonable classification requirements. Moreover, the facts-and-circumstance requirements do not apply. Instead, the rate group is deemed to satisfy this requirement if the ratio percentage of the rate group is greater than or equal to the lesser of:

- the ratio percentage of the plan, or
- the midpoint between the safe and the unsafe harbor percentage applicable to the plan.

This concept is illustrated by Example 3.

Example 3: Plan D satisfies the minimum coverage requirements by satisfying the nondiscriminatory classification test and the average benefit percentage test. The plan utilizes the facts-and-circumstances requirements to satisfy the nondiscriminatory classification test. The safe and unsafe harbor percentages applicable to the plan are 29 and 20 percent, respectively. The plan has a ratio percentage of 22 percent and rate group 1 under the plan has a ratio percentage of 23 percent.

The rate group is deemed to satisfy the reasonable classification requirement. Even though the ratio percentage of the rate group falls below the safe harbor percentage applicable to the plan, the rate group is deemed to satisfy the facts-and-circumstances requirements because the ratio percentage for the rate group (23 percent) is greater than the lesser of:

- the ratio percentage for the plan as a whole (22 percent), and
- the midpoint between the safe and unsafe harbor percentages (24.5 percent)

The rate group therefore satisfies the nondiscriminatory classification test and, since the plan satisfies the average benefit percentage test, the rate group satisfies the minimum coverage tests.

5.3.1.2. Defined Benefit Plans

Certain defined benefit plans that provide uniform benefits are permitted to satisfy the nondiscrimination requirement by meeting one of the five safe harbor tests described below. Four of these safe harbors are design-based and do not require the determination and comparison of actual benefits under the plan. If none of the safe harbors are satisfied, a general test requiring the determination of individual benefit accrual rates must be satisfied.

5.3.1.2.1.   Safe Harbors

A defined benefit plan can avoid the general test if it satisfies the *uniformity requirements* and safe harbors for any of the following types of plans:[25]

- unit credit plans,
- unit credit fractional accrual plans, and
- flat benefit plans (two alternatives).

The uniformity requirements consist of the following five-part test:

1. The same benefit formula must apply to all employees in the plan.
2. With respect to an employee with a given number of years of service at any age after normal retirement age, the annual benefit commencing at the employee's age must be the same percentage of average annual compensation or the same dollar amount that would be payable commencing at normal retirement age to an employee who had the same number of years of service at normal retirement age.
3. Each subsidized optional form of benefit under the plan must be available to substantially all employees in the plan.
4. All employees in the plan must be subject to the same vesting schedule and the same definition of years of service for all purposes under the plan.
5. The plan must be a noncontributory defined benefit plan.

A plan will satisfy the safe harbor for *unit credit plans* if it satisfies the 133 1/3 percent accrual rule described in Chapter 6 and an employee's accrued benefit under the plan as of any plan year is determined by applying the plan's benefit formula to the employee's years of service and (if applicable) average annual compensation, both determined as of that plan year.

The safe harbor for *unit credit plans using the fractional accrual rule* is satisfied if each of the following requirements are met:

1. The plan satisfies the fractional accrual rule described in Chapter 6.
2. An employee's accrued benefit under the plan as of any plan year before the employee reaches normal retirement age is determined by multiplying the employee's fractional rule benefit by a fraction, the numerator of which is the employee's years of service determined as of

---

[25]There is also a safe harbor provided for plans that are funded exclusively through the purchase of individual insurance contracts. See Reg. Section 1.401(a)(4)-3(b)(7) for details.

the plan year, and the denominator of which is the employee's projected years of service as of normal retirement age.

3.   No employee accrues normal retirement or post-normal retirement benefits at a rate that is more than 1/3 larger than the rate of any other employee, ignoring employees with more than 33 years of projected service at normal retirement age.[26]

The implementation of this safe harbor is illustrated by Example 4.

Example 4: Plan E, which has never permitted employee contributions, provides a normal retirement benefit equal to 4 percent of average annual compensation times each year of service up to 10 and 1 percent of average annual compensation times each year of service in excess of 10 and not in excess of 30. Plan E further provides that an employees' accrued benefit as of any plan year equals the employee's fractional rule benefit multiplied by a fraction, the numerator of which is the employee's years of service as of the plan year, and the denominator of which is the employee's projected years of service as of normal retirement age. The greatest benefit that an employee could accrue in any plan year is 4 percent of average annual compensation. Among employees with 33 or fewer years of projected service at normal retirement age, the lowest benefit that an employee could accrue in a plan year is 1.82 percent of average annual compensation (60 percent divided by 33 equals 1.82 percent). Plan E fails to meet the safe harbor for unit credit plans using the *fractional accrual rule* because 4 is more than 1/3 larger than 1.82 percent.

A plan satisfies the safe harbor for *flat benefit plans* for a plan year if it satisfies each of the following requirements:

1.   The plan satisfies the fractional rule.
2.   An employee's accrued benefit under the plan as of any plan year before the employee reaches normal retirement age is determined by multiplying the employee's fractional rule benefit by a fraction, the numerator of which is the employee's years of service determined as of the plan year, and the denominator of which is the employee's projected years of service as of normal retirement age.
3.   The normal retirement benefit under the plan is a flat benefit.

---

[26]In addition, in the case of a Section 401(l) plan, an employee is treated as accruing benefits at a rate equal to the excess benefit percentage in the case of an excess plan, or at a rate equal to the gross benefit percentage in the case of an offset plan.

4.   The plan requires a minimum of 25 years of service at normal retirement age for an employee to receive the unreduced flat benefit, determined without regard to Section 415.

If a flat benefit plan does not satisfy the flat benefit safe harbor solely because it does not meet the 25-year rule, it may qualify under the *alternative flat benefit safe harbor.* This safe harbor requires that the average of the normal accrual rates for all NHCEs is at least 70 percent of the average of the normal accrual rates for all HCEs.

5.3.1.2.2.   General Tests

In general, a plan satisfies the general test for nondiscrimination in amount or contributions for a plan year if each *rate group* under the plan satisfies the minimum coverage requirement described earlier in this chapter.   For purposes of a defined benefit plan, a rate group exists under a plan for each HCE in the plan and contains that HCE as well as any other employee in the plan (both HCE and NHCE) that have a normal accrual rate greater than or equal to the HCE's normal accrual rate, and that also have a most valuable accrual rate greater than or equal to the HCE's most valuable accrual rate.[27] The concept of a normal accrual rate and a most valuable accrual rate are described after Example 5 illustrates the numerical concepts involved in the general test for defined benefit plans.

Example 5: Employer F has 100 nonexcludable NHCEs (N1 through N100) and 10 nonexcludable HCEs (H1 through H10).   Employer F maintains Plan G, a defined benefit plan that benefits all of these nonexcludable employees.   Assume that Plan G is not eligible to use the alternative test explained in the footnote.   The normal and most valuable accrual rates for employees in the 1994 plan year are:

---

[27]An alternative test exists in the case of a plan that determines the qualified joint and survivor annuity at each age as a uniform percentage of each employee's normal retirement benefit.   In essence, this will allow testing solely on the basis of most valuable accrual rates.   See Reg. Section 1.401(a)(4)-3(c)(2) for details.

Employee	Normal Accrual Rate	Most Valuable Accrual Rate
N1 through N10	1.0	1.40
N11 through N50	1.5	3.00
N51 through N75	2.0	2.65
N76 through N100	2.3	2.80
H1 through H5	1.5	2.00
H6 through H10	2.0	2.65

There are ten rate groups in Plan G because there are ten HCEs in the plan. Rate group 1 consists of H1 and all employees who have a normal accrual rate greater than or equal to H1's normal accrual rate *and* who also have a most valuable accrual rate greater than or equal to H1's most valuable accrual rate. This will include H1 through H10 and N11 through N100. Rate group 1 satisfies the ratio percentage test because the ratio percentage of the rate group is 90 percent (90% of the NHCEs covered divided by 100% of the HCEs covered). Rate groups 2 through 5 (established from the accruals of H2 through H5) are identical to rate group 1 and similarly pass the minimum coverage tests.

Rate group 6 consists of H6 and all employees who have a normal accrual rate greater than or equal to H6's normal accrual rate *and* who also have a most valuable accrual rate greater than or equal to H6's most valuable accrual rate. This will include H6 through H10 and N51 through N100. Rate group 1 satisfies the ratio percentage test because the ratio percentage of the rate group is 100 percent (50% of the NHCEs covered divided by 50% of the HCEs covered). Rate groups 7 through 10 (established from the accruals of H7 through H10) are identical to rate group 6 and similarly pass the minimum coverage tests.

Plan G satisfies the general test because each rate group under the plan satisfies the minimum coverage test.

The normal accrual rate for an employee generally can be described as the yearly rate at which the employee's normal retirement benefit under the plan accrues. This rate is determined for the plan year under either the annual method, the accrued-to-date method or the projected method after normalizing the employee's normal retirement benefit to the employee's testing age. The most valuable accrual rate for an employee can be described as the yearly rate at which the employee's most valuable optional form of benefit under the plan accrues. This rate is determined after normalizing the qualified joint and survivor annuity at each age under the plan to the employee's testing age and then comparing the normalized qualified joint and survivor annuity for each of these ages to determine which is the most valuable. If the plan provides a qualified Social Security supplement,[28] the most valuable accrual rate also takes it into account in conjunction with the qualified joint and survivor annuity at each age under the plan.

Under the *annual* method, the normal accrual rate for an employee is the percentage amount determined from the following steps:

1. Determine the employee's normalized accrued benefit as if the employee's benefit under the plan had been frozen as of the last day of the plan year.
2. Determine the employee's normalized accrued benefit as if the employee's benefit under the plan had been frozen as of the last day of the prior plan year.
3. Subtract the answer from step two from the answer in step one.
4. Divide the answer from step three by the employee's testing compensation.

The most valuable accrual rate for an employee under this method is determined by the following steps:

1. Determine the normalized qualified joint and survivor annuity, and the normalized qualified Social Security supplement (if any) payable in conjunction with the qualified joint and survivor annuity, at each age payment of these benefits to the employee could commence under the plan. Calculate each qualified joint and survivor annuity and each qualified Social Security supplement as if the employee's benefits under the plan had been frozen as of the last day of the plan year.
2. Determine the normalized qualified joint and survivor annuity, and the normalized qualified Social Security supplement (if any) payable in conjunction with the qualified joint and survivor annuity, at each age payment of these benefits to the employee could commence under the plan. Calculate each qualified joint and survivor annuity and each qualified Social Security supplement as if the employee's benefits under the plan had been frozen as of the last day of the *prior* plan year.
3. Subtract the normalized qualified joint and survivor annuity determined for each age in step two from the normalized qualified joint and survivor annuity determined for each age in step one.
4. Subtract the normalized qualified Social Security supplement determined for each age in step two from the normalized qualified Social Security supplement determined for each age in step one.

---

[28] A qualified Social Security supplement is defined as a Social Security supplement that meets accrual, vesting and joint and survivor rules just as if it were part of the accrued benefit. It must also be available under the same eligibility requirements as early retirement benefits.

5.   Add the answer for each age in step three with the answer in step four for the same age.
6.   Divide the answer for each age in step five by the employee's testing compensation.
7.   The largest rate found in the answer to step six is the employee's most valuable accrual rate for the plan year.

Under the *accrued-to-date method*, the normal accrual rate is determined from the following steps:

1.   Determine the employee's normalized accrued benefit as if the employees' benefit under the plan had been frozen as of the last day of the plan year.
2.   Divide the answer from step one by the employee's testing service.
3.   Divide the answer from step two by the employee's testing compensation.

The most valuable accrual rate for an employee under this method is determined under the following steps:

1.   Determine the normalized qualified joint and survivor annuity, and the normalized qualified Social Security supplement (if any) payable in conjunction with the qualified joint and survivor annuity, at each age payment of these benefits to the employee could commence under the plan. Calculate each qualified joint and survivor annuity and each qualified Social Security supplement as if the employee's benefits under the plan had been frozen as of the last day of the plan year.
2.   Add the normalized qualified joint and survivor annuity for each age to the normalized qualified Social Security supplement for each age.
3.   Divide the answer for each age in step two by the employee's testing service.
4.   Divide the answer for each age in step three by the employee's testing compensation.
5.   The largest rate found in the answer to step four is the employee's most valuable accrual rate for the plan year.

Under the *projected method*, the normal accrual rate is determined under the following steps:[29]

---

[29]For employees who terminate before the end of the plan year, accrual rates are calculated under the accrued-to-date method. Also, the projected method may not be used for a plan year if the pattern of accrual under the plan discriminates in favor of highly compensated employees.

1. Determine the employee's normalized accrued benefit as if the employee's benefit under the plan had been frozen as of the employee's testing age.
2. Divide the answer in step one by the testing service the employee would have as of the employee's testing age.
3. Divide the answer in step two by the employee's testing compensation as of the employee's testing age.

The most valuable accrual rate under this method is determined under the following steps:

1. Determine the normalized qualified joint and survivor annuity, and the normalized qualified Social Security supplement (if any) payable in conjunction with the qualified joint and survivor annuity, at each age payment of these benefits to the employee could commence under the plan. Calculate each qualified joint and survivor annuity and each qualified Social Security supplement as if the employee's benefits under the plan had been frozen as of the age payment of the qualified joint and survivor annuity and the qualified Social Security supplement (if any) to the employee would commence under the plan.
2. Add the normalized qualified joint and survivor annuity for each age to the normalized qualified Social Security supplement for the same age.
3. Divide the answer for each age in step two by the testing service the employee would have as of that age.
4. Divide the answer for each age in step three by the employee's testing compensation as of that age.
5. The largest rate found in the answer to step four is the employee's most valuable accrual rate for the plan year.

5.3.2. Nondiscriminatory Availability of Benefits, Rights and Features

A benefit, right, or feature provided under a plan is made available to employees in the plan in a nondiscriminatory manner only if the benefit, right, or feature separately satisfies the *current availability* and *effective availability* requirements. The benefits, rights, and features subject to the nondiscriminatory availability rule are all optional forms of benefit, ancillary benefits, and other rights and features available to any employee under the plan. In general, each benefit, right, and feature provided under a plan is *separately* subject to the requirements regardless of whether it is actuarially equivalent to any other benefit, right or feature provided under the plan.

5.3.2.1. Current Availability

The group of employees in the plan to whom a benefit, right, or feature is currently available during the plan year must satisfy either the ratio percentage test or the nondiscriminatory classification test. In determining whether the group of employees satisfies these tests, an employee is treated as benefiting only if the benefit, right, or feature is currently available to the employee under the plan.

Whether a benefit, right, or feature is currently available to an employee generally is determined based on the current facts and circumstances with respect to the employee (e.g., current compensation, current accrued benefit, current position, or current net worth). The fact that an employee may satisfy a precondition to receipt of the benefit, right, or feature in the future generally does not cause the benefit, right, or feature to be currently available.

5.3.2.2. Effective Availability

Based on all facts and circumstances, the group of employees to whom the benefit, right, or feature is effectively available must not substantially favor HCEs. This requirement must be met even if the benefit, right, or feature is, or has been, currently available to a group of employees that satisfies the current availability requirement.

5.3.3.   Plan Amendments and Plan Terminations

If a *plan amendment* or series of plan amendments discriminates significantly in favor of HCEs, the plan will not satisfy the nondiscrimination requirements. For this purpose, a plan amendment includes the establishment or termination of a plan and any changes in the benefit, right, or features under the plan.

Whether a plan amendment or series of plan amendments discriminates significantly in favor of HCEs is determined based on all relevant facts and circumstances. These include, for example, the relative numbers of HCEs and NHCEs affected by the plan amendment, the relative accrued benefits of HCEs and NHCEs before and after the plan amendments, any additional benefit provided to highly and NHCEs under other plans, the relative length of service of highly and NHCEs, the length of time the plans and the benefit, right, or feature being amended have been in effect, and the turnover of employees prior to the plan amendment. In the case of a plan amendment that creates past service credits, the relevant facts and circumstances also include the benefits former employees would have received had the plan, as amended, been in effect throughout the period for which past service credits are granted.

A plan must also provide that the annual payment to certain employees are restricted to an amount under a straight life annuity that is the actuarial equivalent of the accrued benefit and other benefits to which the employee is entitled under the plans (other than a qualified Social Security supplement) and the amount of the payments that the employee is entitled to receive under a Social Security supplement.[30] A plan may limit the group to whom these restrictions apply to only the 25 HCEs and former HCEs with the greatest compensation in the current or any prior year.

QUESTIONS FOR REVIEW

1. Describe the principal tax advantages for a qualified plan.
2. Who is a highly compensated employee? Explain.
3. Describe when common ownership results in a controlled group of corporations or businesses.
4. Explain the importance of a qualified separate line of business in testing for qualification.
5. Describe the minimum participation requirements.
6. Are employers allowed to adopt any definition of compensation for purposes of defining benefits and/or contributions for a qualified retirement plan? Explain.
7. Describe the steps involved in satisfying the average benefit test for minimum coverage requirements.
8. What employees may be excluded in applying the minimum coverage requirements?
9. What is a rate group? How does it apply to the general test for the nondiscrimination requirements?
10. What is a most valuable accrual rate? How does it relate to the identification of a rate group?

QUESTIONS FOR DISCUSSION

1. If the average benefit test may be satisfied with fewer nonhighly compensated employees covered than that required under the ratio

---

[30]These restrictions will not apply if the funding ratio of the plan (measured on a current liability basis as defined in Chapter 16) exceeds 110 percent after payment of all benefits to the employee, the value of the benefit payable to the employee is less than one percent of the value of current liability before distribution, or the benefit is less than $3,500.

percentage test, why would employers even bother testing under the latter method?

2.   Prepare a flowchart for testing a plan for nondiscrimination.

3.   Explain why it is important to identify the highly compensated employees in reference to pension plan qualification.

6. Tax Law Qualification Requirements (Continued)

Chapter 5 discussed those elements of plan design dealing with minimum coverage tests, nondiscrimination rules and permitted disparities. In this chapter, attention is focused on the remaining tax law qualification requirements. The chapter concludes with a brief discussion of general provisions included in most plans -- the right to amend or terminate the program, administrative provisions, and the like.

6.1. SECTION 415 LIMITATIONS ON BENEFITS AND CONTRIBUTIONS

ERISA imposed limits on the benefits and contributions that can be provided under qualified plans. For a defined benefit plan, the annual employer-provided benefit for an employee cannot exceed a stipulated dollar amount or, if lesser, 100 percent of the first $200,000, adjusted for inflation (as explained later in this chapter) of the employee's average annual pay for the three consecutive years of highest pay.[1]

The dollar limit was initially established at $75,000 to be adjusted annually to reflect increases in the Consumer Price Index. By 1982, this

---

[1]If an employee has never been covered by a defined contribution plan, an annual pension of up to $10,000 can be paid even if it exceeds 100 percent of pay.

limit had reached $136,425. Under changes made by TEFRA, however, this limit was rolled back to $90,000, beginning in 1983. It is adjusted for future increases in the Consumer Price Index, reaching a level of $108,963 in 1991. These limits do not apply to employee-provided benefits and need not be adjusted for preretirement ancillary benefits such as death or disability benefits. The maximum permissible benefit will be reduced if payments begin before the social security retirement age and will be increased if they begin after that age.[2] The reduction will be 5/9 of one percent for the first 36 months of early retirement plus 5/12 of one percent for each additional month of early retirement after age 62. The reduction for ages before age 62 will be based on actuarial factors using the plan's interest rate (but not less than 5 percent) for early retirement. The dollar limit is reduced proportionately if the employee completes fewer than 10 years of participation before retirement; the percentage limit is reduced proportionately if the employee completes fewer than 10 years of service before retirement. The limits also must be reduced for the value of any pension-related, postretirement death benefits; however, a reduction will not be required if payments are made on a qualified joint and survivor basis (even if the percentage continued is 100 percent) and the joint annuitant is the employee's spouse.

In the case of a defined contribution plan, the limitation is expressed in terms of the maximum annual addition that may be made to the employee's account. This maximum annual addition is limited to the lesser of 25 percent of the first $200,000 (adjusted for inflation) of annual pay or a stipulated dollar amount. This dollar amount was originally set at $25,000 also to be adjusted annually to reflect increases in the Consumer Price Index. This limit had reached $45,475 in 1982, but was rolled back by TEFRA to $30,000, beginning in 1983. The Tax Reform Act of 1986 redefined the defined contribution dollar limit as the greater of $30,000 or 25 percent of the dollar limit for defined benefit plans. Thus, there will be no further increase in the defined contribution dollar limit until the defined benefit dollar limit reaches $120,000. The annual addition is defined to include employer contributions, the employee's own contributions, and forfeitures.[3]

---

[2]Effective for distributions made after December 31, 1986, certain transitional rules exist to protect a participant whose previously accrued benefit under a defined benefit plan would otherwise be reduced by the actuarial reduction for benefits beginning before the social security retirement age.

[3]For years beginning before January 1, 1987, the term annual addition meant the sum of employer contributions, nondeductible employee contributions in excess of 6 percent of the participant's compensation (or 50 percent of employee contributions, if less), and forfeitures. This distinction is important for purposes of the combined limits (described later) because of its cumulative nature.

If a participant is covered by both a defined benefit plan and a defined contribution plan maintained by the same employer, then a special expanded annual limit applies. The defined benefit plan projected annual benefit and the defined contribution plan annual addition are converted into fractions, added, and then tested against a 1.0 limit. The *defined benefit fraction* is the participant's projected annual benefit (as of the close of the limitation year) divided by the lesser of 125 percent of the defined benefit dollar limit or 140 percent of the average high compensation. The numerator for the *defined contribution fraction* is the sum of the annual additions of a participant's account (as of the close of the limitation year). The denominator is the sum for the current year and each prior year of the participant's service with the employer of the lesser of 125 percent of the defined contribution dollar limit or 140 percent of compensation eligible under the defined contribution percentage limit.

The application of this combined limit might best be illustrated by the following example, which, for the sake of simplicity, ignores the cumulative aspects of the limit. Under the employer's profit sharing plan, a highly compensated employee will receive a contribution of 12.5 percent of annual pay in 1992. If the employee's compensation was $80,000, the defined contribution fraction would be:

$$.125 \times \$80,000 \div \min[1.25 \times \$30,000; 1.4 \times .25 \times \$80,000] = .3571$$

Therefore, the maximum defined benefit fraction would be:

$$1 - .3571 = .6428$$

Computing the maximum numerator for the defined benefit fraction:

$$.6428 \times \min[1.25 \times \$90,000; 1.4 \times 1.0 \times \$80,000] = \$72,000$$

or 90 percent ($72,000 ÷ $80,000) of the otherwise allowable limit.

If, instead, the employee earned $150,000, the defined contribution fraction is:

$$.125 \times \$150,000 \div \min[1.25 \times \$30,000; 1.4 \times .25 \times \$150,000] = .5$$

Therefore, the maximum defined benefit fraction must be .5 (which is again obtained by subtracting the defined contribution fraction from 1.0) and the numerator in the defined benefit fraction is:

$$.5 \times \min[1.25 \times \$90,000; 1.4 \times 1.0 \times \$150,000] = \$56,250$$

or 62.5 percent ($56,250 ÷ $90,000) of the otherwise allowable limit.

Where the limits are applicable, the employer may establish an excess benefit plan to restore the benefits or contributions lost by reason of the application of the limit. Such a plan is not subject to the provisions of ERISA.

If an employee is participating in the plans of another incorporated or unincorporated business under common control (only a 51 percent interest is necessary for this purpose), the plans of all such businesses must be aggregated for purposes of applying the limitations on benefits and contributions.

These limits must be applied on the basis of a limitation year that is the calendar year, unless a different 12-month period is elected by the employer. This could be of significance where a noncalendar year plan does not have a limitation year that parallels the plan year. For example, assume the plan year for an employer's profit sharing plan ends on January 31, and that on that date an employee was credited with $1,000 or 10 percent of compensation during the plan year. If the employee terminates employment at the end of February and the employee's compensation for the two months of the current calendar year was $2,000, and if the limitation year is the calendar year, the addition to the employee's account for such calendar year would be 50 percent of compensation (the $1,000 allocation divided by the $2,000 of compensation received). This would exceed the allowable contribution limit and could cause disqualification of the plan.

6.2.   SECTION 401(A)(17) COMPENSATION CAP

Section 401(a)(17) of the Internal Revenue Code provides an annual compensation limit for each employee under a qualified plan. The limit applies to a plan in two ways. First, a plan may not base contributions or benefits on compensation in excess of the annual limit. Second, the amount of an employee's annual compensation that may be taken into account in applying certain specified nondiscrimination rules under the Code is subject to the annual limitation. As described in Chapter 5, an employee's compensation in excess of the annual limit is disregarded in applying the nondiscrimination rules for determining the allocation rates for defined contribution plans and the accrual rate for defined benefit plans.

The amount of the annual limit is $200,000 adjusted annually for calendar years after 1989 for increases in the cost of living. The limit for the 1991 plan year was $222,200. It is important to note that any increase in the annual limit applies only to compensation taken into account for the year of the increase and subsequent years and does not apply to compensation for prior years that are used in determining an employee's benefit.

6.3.   DETERMINATION OF SERVICE

An employee's length of service is an important factor in determining his or her rights and benefits under a pension plan. First, length of service may establish the employee's initial eligibility to participate in the plan, and may establish eligibility for death and disability benefits and the right to retire early. Length of service also establishes vesting rights in the event of termination of employment and, in most situations, service is a major factor in the plan's benefit formula, thus establishing the amount of the employee's benefit.

The law establishes specific requirements for the determination of service in three key areas: (1) initial eligibility to participate, (2) vesting, and (3) the right to a benefit accrual. The law does not mandate how service is to be determined for other purposes (e.g., the right to retire early) but for administrative convenience most plans determine service in the same manner for all purposes.

The basic concept of the law is that an employee must be given credit for a year of service for any computation period during which the employee works 1,000 hours. (A computation period is a 12-month period and may be established as a plan year, calendar year, or an employment year; however, in the case of service used for eligibility purposes, the initial 12-month period must begin with date of employment.) The employee also must be given a ratable benefit accrual, if participation has commenced, for any computation period in which he or she is credited with at least 1,000 hours of service.

If an employee completes fewer than 1,000 hours of service within a computation period, credit need not be given for a year of service and the employee need not be given any benefit accrual for the period in question. However, if the employee has completed at least 501 hours of service in the computation period, this will prevent the employee from incurring a "break in service." Whether the employee has incurred a break in service is significant in terms of eligibility and vesting of benefits.

Additional requirements of the law for the determination of service are as follows:

1. Service must include periods of employment with any corporation that is a member of a controlled group of corporations (i.e., where there is 80 percent control). Similar principles apply for service in an unincorporated business under common control.

2. Service with a predecessor employer must be taken into account for eligibility and vesting purposes if the employer maintains the plan of the predecessor. If the employer maintains a plan that is not the plan of the predecessor, service with the predecessor will have to be considered to the extent prescribed in regulations.

3. In the case of service used to determine initial eligibility to participate in the plan, the initial computation period must begin with the employee's date of employment. The employer has the choice of converting the computation period to a plan or calendar-year basis after the first 12 months of employment, provided the beginning of such new computation period overlaps with the first employment year.

4. For vesting purposes, certain periods of service may be excluded. Specifically, the plan may exclude service prior to age 18. Service need not include any period during which the employee did not elect to contribute under a plan requiring employee contributions. It may also exclude service prior to the adoption of the plan (or predecessor plan). Years of service before a one-year break in service may also be excluded but only if the number of consecutive one-year breaks in service equals or exceeds the greater of five or the number of prebreak years of service, *and* the participant did not have any nonforfeitable right to the accrued benefit.

5. A special rule for maternity or paternity absences exists. This rule applies to an individual who is absent from work by reason of the pregnancy of the individual, the birth of a child of the individual, the placement of a child with an individual in connection with adoption, or for purposes of caring for such child for a period beginning immediately following birth or placement. The law requires that, for purposes of determining whether a one-year break in service has occurred, the plan treat as hours of service the lesser of the hours that otherwise would have been credited to the individual or 501 hours. If a participant would be prevented from incurring a one-year break in service solely because the period of absence is treated as hours of service, the hours of service are credited only in the year in which the absence from work begins; otherwise hours are credited in the year immediately following.

The following describes specific ways in which service may be calculated under the law.

6.3.1. Hour of Service

The first issue involved in calculating service is determining what constitutes an hour of service. The regulation defines an hour of service as an hour for which an employee is paid, or entitled to payment, for the performance of duties for the employer; and an hour for which the employee is paid, or entitled to payment, by the employer on account of a period of time during which no duties are performed (irrespective of whether the employment relationship has terminated) due to vacation, holiday, illness, incapacity (including disability), layoff, jury duty, military duty, or leave of absence; and each hour for which back pay, irrespective of damages, is either awarded or agreed to by the employer. However, a plan need not credit an employee with more than 501 hours of service for any single, continuous period during which the employee performs no duties, or for any period of nonworking service for which payment is made under workers' compensation, unemployment compensation, or state disability laws.

Depending upon the compliance method selected, all or some of these hours of service will have to be taken into account. (Under the elapsed time method of compliance, the hours-of-service concept is not relevant, since total service is measured from date of employment to date of severance.)

6.3.2. Compliance Methods

An employer has three methods to choose from in crediting employees with hours of service. The same method may be used for all purposes or, under the decoupling provisions of the regulations, a different compliance method may be used within the same plan for eligibility, vesting, and benefit accrual purposes. Also, if discrimination does not result, a different method may be used for different classes of employees (a particularly helpful factor when distinguishing between part-time and full-time employees). Finally, the regulations permit the use of one compliance method for pre-ERISA service and another for post-ERISA service (again, an important factor in view of the lack, in many instances, of adequate pre-ERISA employment records).

The first method is the standard-hours-counting method under which all hours for which compensation is paid must be taken into account. While this method is, in one sense, the simplest to describe, many employers find it difficult to administer -- particularly in the case of exempt employees who often do not keep a record of actual hours worked.

The second method involves the use of equivalencies. Under this method, four alternatives exist. The first uses hours worked where service is determined only on the basis of actual hours worked, including overtime and excluding all other nonworked hours for which compensation is received, such as vacations, holidays, and so forth. The second alternative involves only regular hours worked. Under this alternative, service is determined on the basis of actual hours worked, excluding overtime, and excluding all other nonworked hours for which compensation is received. The third alternative concerns a time period selected for the plan -- day, by shift, weekly, semimonthly, or monthly -- and an employee is credited with an imputed number of hours for the time period involved as long as he or she is credited with at least one hour of service during such time period. The fourth alternative involves the employee's earnings and here, hours of service are related to the earnings received by the employee during the period involved.

The third method is called the elapsed-time method. Under this method, service is measured from the employee's date of employment to date of severance.

An employer who wishes to use an equivalency in lieu of counting hours must pay a "premium." In the case of time-period equivalencies, this premium is measured in terms of the number of hours that must be credited for the time period selected. In essence, the hours credited will exceed a normal work schedule for the period involved to build in a credit for overtime or additional hours that might have been worked. The specific hours that must be credited under each of the time-period equivalencies are as follows:

> **One day -- 10 hours.**
> **One week -- 45 hours.**
> **Half-month -- 95 hours.**
> **One month -- 190 hours.**
> **Shift -- actual hours included in the shift.**

Under the daily time-period equivalency, for example, an employee must be credited with 10 hours for each day in which he or she is credited with one hour of service. Thus, after five such days, the employee will have been credited with 50 hours of service. This, of course, means that under the time-period equivalencies, an employee will be credited with 1,000 hours of service in a much shorter period of time (in the average situation) than would be the case under the actual hours-counting method.

The premium for using the other equivalencies is measured by reducing the 1,000-hour standard for a full year of service and the 501-hour standard for applying the break-in-service rules. The reductions for the different equivalencies are shown in Table 6-1. As indicated by this table, for example, under the hours-worked equivalency an employee will only have to be credited with 870 hours (instead of 1,000 hours) to be credited with one year of service, and need only be credited with 435 hours of service in a computation period (instead of 501 hours) to avoid having a break in service.

**TABLE 6-1: Adjustments in Hours of Service
Required for Crediting a Year of Service and for
Break-in-Service Rules under Certain Equivalencies**

Equivalency	Year of Service	Break in Service
Hours worked	870	435
Regular hours worked	750	375
Earnings		
Hourly-rated employees	870	435
Other employees	750	375

Under the elapsed-time method, service credit for eligibility and vesting must begin with the employee's date of hire (except for permissible statutory exclusions such as service prior to the effective date of the plan). For bene-fit-accrual purposes, service must be credited starting with the date the employee begins participation in the plan. Service must continue to be credited, for all purposes for which the elapsed-time method is used, until the employee's date of severance. In the case of quitting, discharge, retirement, or death, the employee's severance date will be immediate. In the case of absence from active employment for other reasons such as layoff, leave of absence, and disability, the employee's severance date will be 12 months after the beginning of the absence. After the employee's severance date, the plan need not credit service. However, there are two exceptions to this rule. The first exception is if the employee is reemployed within 12 months after quitting, discharge, or retirement, the plan must grant service credit for the period of the employee's severance (but only for eligibility and vesting purposes and not for benefit accruals). The second exception is if an employee quits, is discharged, or retires during a layoff, disability, or leave of absence, and is reemployed within 12 months after the absence began, the plan must grant service credit for the period of severance (again, for eligibility and vesting, but not for benefit accruals). Also, under the elapsed-time method, a one-year period of severance is treated the same as a one-year break in service.

6.4.   NONDIVERSION/EXCLUSIVE BENEFIT RULES

The trust must specifically provide that it is impossible for the employer to divert or recapture contributions before the satisfaction of all plan liabilities -- with certain exceptions, funds contributed must be used for the exclusive benefit of employees or their beneficiaries. One exception to this rule may occur at termination of a pension plan if any funds then remain because of "actuarial error" and all fixed and contingent obligations of the plan have been satisfied. In this event, such excess funds may be returned to the employer. A second exception makes it possible to establish or amend a plan on a conditional basis so that employer contributions are returnable within one year from the denial of qualification if the plan is not approved by the Internal Revenue Service. It is also possible for an employer to make a contribution on the basis that it will be allowed as a deduction; if this is done, the contribution, to the extent it is disallowed, may be returned within one year from the disallowance. Further, contributions made on the basis of a mistake in fact can be returned to the employer within one year from the time they were made.

6.5.   PERMANENCY

The plan must be a permanent one. While the employer may reserve the right to amend or terminate the plan at any time, it is expected that the plan will be established on a permanent basis. Thus, if a plan is terminated for any reason other than business necessity within a few years after it has been in force, this will be considered as evidence that the plan, from its inception, was not a bona fide one for the benefit of employees. This, of course, could result in adverse tax consequences.

In the profit sharing area, as described in Chapter 9, it is not necessary that the employer make contributions in accordance with a definite predetermined formula. However, merely making a single or an occasional contribution will not be sufficient to create a permanent and continuing plan. The regulations require that "substantial and recurring" contributions must be made.

6.6.   ELIGIBILITY REQUIREMENTS

In the generally accepted sense, eligibility requirements are those conditions an employee must meet to become a participant in the plan. In noncontributory plans, an employee who meets the eligibility requirements automatically becomes a participant when first eligible. In contributory plans, the employee usually has the option of participating and must take some affirmative action before becoming a participant. Thus, the employee must usually sign an application for participation under which the employee agrees to make contributions and also designates a beneficiary.

Eligibility requirements fall into two broad categories -- those that defer an employee's participation until some stipulated conditions are met, and those that exclude an employee from participation on a permanent basis (or, at least, until the employee has had some change in employment classification). An example of an eligibility requirement that defers participation would be a requirement that the employee must attain some minimum age before becoming eligible. On the other hand, a provision that excludes hourly employees is illustrative of a requirement that may exclude certain employees from ever participating in the plan.

Those eligibility requirements that defer participation often are included for administrative cost considerations. Inclusion of employees who are still in what might be termed the high-turnover stage of their employment will involve the creation and maintenance of records and, depending on the funding instrument involved, could create additional and unnecessary costs for the employer. For example, an employee who terminates employment shortly after becoming a participant under an individual policy plan creates a cost to the employer measured in terms of the difference between the premiums paid for the employee's coverage and the cash surrender value (including any dividends) that is available from the insurer under the employee's insurance or annuity contract (these funding instruments are described in Chapter 21). However, care must be exercised so that the eligibility requirements are not too stringent. The positive psychological effect of the plan may be lost if a number of employees find that they are not yet eligible to participate. The selection of appropriate eligibility requirements balances these factors so that within the employer's objectives as many employees as possible are eligible, while financial losses and administrative difficulties are kept to a minimum.

Those eligibility requirements that may permanently exclude employees from participation must obviously be made in light of the minimum coverage and nondiscrimination requirements discussed in Chapter 5. To the extent that flexibility is provided to the employer, the decisions with respect to this aspect of eligibility requirements for employees are generally dictated by the employer's objectives, by bargaining agreements, or by cost considerations. For example, if a bargaining unit is negotiating for a pension plan, coverage is generally confined to employees represented by the bargaining unit.

The most common eligibility requirements involve the use of a minimum age and/or a minimum period of service. In the broad sense, other eligibility requirements also may be considered, such as the use of employment classifications.

One further point is that eligibility requirements that defer participation also might affect the employee's benefit and the ultimate cost of the plan, since, for example, they could limit the time during which credited service may be accrued. Many plans, however, and particularly those negotiated by collective bargaining units, give credit for total service or give credit for all service up to some maximum such as 30 years.

With the above discussion as general background, it is now appropriate to consider certain specific eligibility requirements in greater detail.

6.6.1.   Years of Service and Minimum Age

In most situations, it is possible to demonstrate that an employer's highest rate of turnover occurs among employees who have been with the firm for a relatively short period of time. It is generally desirable that any minimum service and age requirements of the plan be set to provide that only those persons who have been employed beyond this period will be eligible.

Under federal tax law, however, eligibility cannot be delayed beyond the time an employee reaches age 21 and completes one year of service. Thus, the maximum service requirement that may be used is one year, and the highest minimum age that may be used is age 21.[4] Further, the use of entry dates cannot delay the participation of an employee more than six months. Thus, if it is desired to use the most stringent minimum age and service requirements possible, the plan should permit entry at least every six months. The use of an annual entry date will be permissible only when the minimum age and/or service requirements are at least six months less than those permissible under the law (age 20½ or six months of service).

An exception to the one-year service requirement is available if the plan provides full and immediate vesting (an infrequent situation in a defined benefit pension plan). Here, a two-year service requirement, along with a minimum age requirement of 21, will be permissible for plans that do not have a cash or deferred arrangement. For these plans, a year of service preceding a one-year break in service need not be considered in determining whether an employee is eligible to participate.

6.7.   SEVERANCE OF EMPLOYMENT BENEFITS

The right of an employee to the benefits attributable to employer contributions under a pension plan in the event of termination of employment prior to retirement has been the subject of considerable discussion for many years. A major accomplishment of ERISA was to require that an employee achieve such rights, or a vested interest, after some reasonable period of service.

The Internal Revenue Code requires that the employee's rights to that portion of his or her accrued benefit attributable to his or her own

---

[4]The minimum age is increased from 21 to 26 in the case of a plan maintained exclusively for employees of an educational institution that provides that each participant having at least one year of service has full 100 percent vesting.

contributions be fully vested at all times. This does not require a minimum benefit equal to the amount the employee has contributed. In a defined contribution plan, for example, there may have been investment losses that result in the value of the employee's contribution being less than the amount actually contributed by the employee. In such a situation, the plan would not have to return to the employee an amount greater than the value of the employee's contributions after taking investment losses into account.

In any event, accrued benefits attributable to employer contributions must vest when the employee reaches normal retirement age. Otherwise, they must vest at least as rapidly as provided by one of two alternative standards. The first standard requires that all accrued benefits must be 100 percent vested after five years of service. The second standard permits graded vesting, with 20 percent of accrued benefits vesting after three years of service and that percentage increasing in 20 percent multiples each year until 100 percent vesting is achieved after seven years. Of course, more liberal vesting schedules than required will be acceptable.

6.7.1.   Determination of Accrued Benefit

The Code also stipulates minimum standards to be followed in determining an employee's accrued benefit for purposes of applying a vesting schedule. A plan will be acceptable if it meets any one of three rules:

1. *The 3 percent rule.* The employee's accrued benefit must be at least equal to 3 percent of the projected normal retirement benefit for each year of participation, to a maximum of 100 percent after 33 1/3 years of participation.

2. *The 133 1/3 percent rule.* The accrued benefit may be the employee's actual benefit earned to date under the plan, provided any future rate of benefit accrual is not more than 133 1/3 percent of the any prior year's benefit accrual rate.

3. *The fractional rule.* The employee's accrued benefit is not less than the projected normal retirement benefit prorated for years of plan participation.

Most plans are expected to be able to satisfy either or both the 133 1/3 percent rule and the fractional rule. However, any plan that permits the accrual of benefits for more than 33 1/3 years will not be able to satisfy the 3 percent method.

If a defined benefit plan requires employee contributions, the accrued benefit attributable to employer contributions is determined by subtracting the life annuity value of the employee's contributions. In making this calculation, the employee's contributions are accumulated with interest compounded annually at the applicable rate, and are multiplied by a factor of 10 percent -- for example, if the employee's contributions with interest amount to $5,000, the annual annuity attributable to the employee's contributions will be $500.[5] The applicable interest rate for pre-ERISA years is the plan rate; it is 5 percent for subsequent years through 1987 and, beginning in 1988, it will be 120 percent of the midterm applicable federal rate as in effect for the first of the plan year. This amount will be subtracted from the total accrued benefit to determine the accrued benefit attributable to employer contributions. The Internal Revenue Service has the authority to revise the factor from time to time.

An employee's accrued benefit is established on a pure life annuity basis only, and does not have to include any ancillary benefits such as death or disability benefits.

6.7.2. Other Vesting Requirements

The Internal Revenue Code also establishes a number of other requirements concerning the vesting and payment of an employee's benefits.

1. If an employee is less than 50 percent vested and withdraws his or her contributions, any benefits attributable to employer contributions may be canceled, but any such employee must be permitted to "buy back" the forfeited benefits upon repayment of the withdrawn contributions plus, if a defined benefit plan, compound interest. If the employee's vested interest is 50 percent or more, withdrawal of employee contributions cannot result in a cancellation of benefits attributable to employer contributions.

2. Except as provided above, an employee's vested interest cannot be forfeited under any circumstances (other than death), even if termination of employment is due to dishonesty.[6]

3. An automatic cash-out of an employee's entire interest is permitted upon termination of employment where the value of this benefit does not exceed $3,500. Under such circumstances and for purposes of determining the employee's accrued benefit, the plan may disregard service for which the employee has received such a payment. If the amount exceeds $3,500 the same will hold true but only if the employee agreed in writing to the cash payment.[7] In any event, if the plan wishes to disregard such service, a

---

[5]The 10 percent factor applies if normal retirement age is 65 and normal retirement benefits are provided as straight life annuities. Other circumstances are controlled by Revenue Ruling 76-47.

[6]Plans can provide that nonforfeitable accrued benefits derived from employer contributions will not be paid if the participant dies -- except to the extent that a QPS or QJS annuity is payable. A description of these annuities is provided later in this chapter.

[7]To be considered made on account of termination of participation in the plan, the distribution (whether voluntary or involuntary) must be made no later than the close of the second plan year following the year in which the termination occurs.

terminating employee who has received a cash-out and is later reemployed must be permitted to "buy back" the accrued benefit by repaying the cash payment with compound interest (currently 5 percent per year). (In the case of a defined contribution plan, such a buy-back is required only before the employee has incurred five consecutive one-year breaks in service, and interest need not be paid.)

4. Any employee who terminates employment must be given written notification of his or her rights, the amount of his or her accrued benefits, the portion (if any) that is vested, and the applicable payment provisions.

5. A terminated employee's vested benefit cannot be decreased by reason of increases in social security benefits that take place after the date of termination of employment.

6. If the plan allows an active employee to elect early retirement after attaining a stated age and completing a specified period of service, a terminated employee who has completed the service requirement must have the right to receive vested benefits after reaching the early retirement age specified. However, the benefit for the terminated employee can be reduced actuarially even though the active employee might have the advantage of subsidized early retirement benefits.

7. Any plan amendment cannot decrease the vested percentage of an employee's accrued benefit. Also, if the vesting schedule is changed, any participant with at least three years of service must be given the election to remain under the preamendment vesting schedule (for both pre- and postamendment benefit accruals).

8. The accrued benefit of a participant may not be decreased by an amendment of the plan.[8] This includes plan amendments that have the effect of eliminating or reducing an early retirement benefit or a retirement-type subsidy or eliminating or reducing the value of an optional form of benefit with respect to benefits attributable to service before the amendment. In the case of a retirement-type subsidy, this applies only with respect to a participant who satisfies the preamendment condition for the subsidy, either before or after the amendment.

6.8.   MANDATORY DEATH BENEFITS

The two death benefits required by the law are: (1) in the case of a vested participant who retires under the plan, the accrued benefit must be provided in the form of a qualified joint and survivor (QJS) annuity, and (2) in the

---

[8]Technically, there are two very limited exceptions to this rule. Amendments described in IRC section 412(c)(8) and ERISA section 4281 are permissible.

case of a vested participant who dies before the annuity starting date and who has a surviving spouse, a qualified preretirement survivor (QPS) annuity must be provided to the surviving spouse. However, the plan may provide that the annuity payment will be reduced to reflect the additional cost of the survivorship provision. The only plans that may be exempted from these new requirements are defined contribution plans that are not subject to the minimum funding standards and certain employee stock ownership plan (ESOP) benefits. For a defined contribution plan to be exempt, it must meet the following requirements: (a) the plan must provide that the participant's nonforfeitable accrued benefit is payable in full to the surviving spouse on the death of the participant, and (b) the participant does not elect a payment or benefit in the form of a life annuity. The ESOP exemption is described in Chapter 11.

The law defines a QJS annuity as an annuity for the life of the participant with a survivor annuity for the life of the spouse that is not less than 50 percent of (and is not greater than 100 percent of) the amount of the annuity that is payable during the joint lives of the participant and the spouse. The QJS must also be the actuarial equivalent of a single annuity for the life of the participant.

In general, the QPS annuity provides a survivor annuity for the life of the spouse in an amount not less than the amount that would be payable as a survivor annuity under the QJS annuity (or the actuarial equivalent thereof). In the case of a participant who dies after the date on which the participant attained the earliest retirement age, it is assumed that he or she had retired with an immediate QJS annuity on the day before the date of death. In the case of a participant who dies on or before the day on which the earliest retirement age would have been attained, it is assumed that he or she had separated from service on the date of death, survived to the earliest retirement age, retired with an immediate QJS annuity at the earliest retirement age, and died the next day. A plan may not delay the commencement of QPS annuity payments beyond the month in which the participant would have attained the earliest retirement age under the plan. In the case of a defined contribution plan, the term QPS annuity means an annuity for the life of the surviving spouse, the actuarial equivalent of which is not less than 50 percent of the account balance of the participant as of the date of death.

The law also provides detailed notification requirements for QJS and QPS annuities. The rules for QJS annuities require that each plan provide to each participant a written explanation of:

1.   The terms and conditions of the QJS annuity.
2.   The participant's right to make, and the effect of, an election to waive the joint and survivor annuity form of benefit.

3.   The rights of the participant's spouse.
4.   The right to make, and the effect of, a revocation of an election.

This explanation must be provided within a reasonable period of time before the annuity starting date.

The rules for QPS annuities require a qualified plan to provide to each participant a written explanation with respect to the QPS annuity comparable to that required for the QJS annuities. This explanation must be provided within the applicable period defined as the later of:

1.   The period beginning with the first day of the plan year in which the participant attains age 32 and ending with the close of the plan year preceding the plan year in which the participant attains age 35.
2.   A reasonable period after the individual becomes a participant.
3.   A reasonable period after the plan ceases to fully subsidize the costs of the annuity.
4.   A reasonable period after the survivor benefit requirements become applicable with respect to a participant.
5.   A reasonable period after separation from service in case of a participant who separates before attaining age 35.

The law requires that each participant may elect at any time during the applicable election period[9] to waive the QJS annuity form of benefit or the QPS annuity form of benefit (or both), and may revoke any such election at any time during the applicable election period. Moreover, the spouse must consent to the election. This requirement is satisfied if the spouse of the participant consents in writing to such election, and the spouse's consent acknowledges the effect of such election and is witnessed by a plan representative or a notary public, or it is established to the satisfaction of a plan representative that this consent cannot be obtained because there is no spouse, or because the spouse cannot be located. It should be noted, however, that these rules do not apply where the plan fully subsidizes the costs of the benefits.[10] The law defines this as a situation under which the failure to waive the benefit by a participant would not result in a decrease in

---

[9]The applicable election period is defined as the 90-day period ending on the annuity starting date in the case of an election to waive the QJS annuity form of benefit, or the period that begins on the first day of the plan year in which the participant attains age 35 and ends on the date of the participant's death in the case of an election to waive the QPS annuity.

[10]A plan may take into account, in any equitable manner, the increased costs of providing a QJS or QPS annuity. The cost may be placed on the participant or beneficiary by reducing the benefit otherwise provided. A plan may, however, fully subsidize the cost of the QJS annuity, QPS annuity, or both.

any plan benefit with respect to the participant and would not result in increased contributions for the participant.

The law permits that survivor annuities need not be provided if the participant and spouse were married less than 1 year. In general, the QJS and QPS annuities will not be required to be provided unless the participant and spouse had been married through the one-year period ending on the earliest of the participant's annuity starting date, or the date of the participant's death. However, if a participant marries within one year before the annuity starting date, and the participant and the participant's spouse have been married for at least a one-year period ending on or before the date of the participant's death, the participant and spouse must be treated as having been married throughout the one-year period ending on the participant's annuity starting date.

6.9.   TOP-HEAVY PLANS

One of the most dramatic changes made by TEFRA was the introduction of the concept of top-heavy plans and the imposition of complex rules upon such plans beginning in 1984. These rules are applicable to qualified plans and:

1.   Require the plan to meet one of two accelerated vesting schedules.
2.   Call for minimum contribution and/or benefit levels for nonkey employees.
3.   Reduce maximum contribution/benefit limits for key employees if an employer maintains both a top-heavy defined benefit plan and a top-heavy defined contribution plan.

This portion of the chapter first discusses the definition of a top-heavy plan. It next discusses the definition of a key employee. The remaining material considers the qualification rules that apply to top-heavy plans and the implications of these rules.

6.9.1.   Top-Heavy Plans Defined

A defined contribution plan is top-heavy in a plan year if, as of the determination date (generally, the last day of the preceding plan year), either: (1)the sum of the account balances of all key employees participating in the plan is more than 60 percent of the sum of the account balances of all covered employees; or (2) the plan is part of a top-heavy group, as explained below.

A defined benefit plan is top-heavy in a plan year if, as of the determination date, either: (1) the present value of the accumulated accrued benefits of all key employees participating in the plan is more than 60 percent of the present value of the accumulated accrued benefits of all covered employees; or (2) the plan is part of a top-heavy group.

A top-heavy group is the combination of two or more plans and, under the law, it may be either required or permissible to aggregate two or more plans to determine top-heaviness. It is required to aggregate into a group (1) all plans covering a key employee and (2) any plan upon which a key-employee plan depends for qualification under the coverage and discrimination requirements of the Code. It is permissible for an employer to expand the group by aggregating other plans as long as the resulting group continues to satisfy the coverage and discrimination rules.

The 60 percent test applies to the top-heavy group. If the group is top-heavy, then each plan is also deemed to be top-heavy. However, a plan included solely at the employer's election is not necessarily considered top-heavy. In applying the top-heavy group rules, all plans of all employers who are part of the same controlled group are treated as a single plan.

In determining the present value of accrued benefits and account balances, the employer may count both employer and employee contributions. Accumulated deductible employee contributions, however, must be disregarded.[11] Also, the employer must count any amount distributed to or for a participant under the plan within the five-year period ending on the current determination date.

Rollover contributions and similar transfers to a plan made after 1983 will not be part of the top-heavy plan computation, unless they are made to a plan maintained by the same, or an affiliated, employer. Presumably, rollovers made before 1983 will have to be considered.

6.9.2.   Key Employees Defined

Key employees are defined as: (1) all officers[12] (up to a maximum of 50) with an annual compensation greater than 50 percent of the annual dollar limitation for defined benefit plans in effect for the plan year; (2) the 10 employees who own the largest interest in the employer with an annual

[11]A federal income tax deduction was available for qualified voluntary employee contributions prior to 1987.

[12]If the employer has between 30 and 500 employees, the number of officers included will never have to be greater than 10 percent of all employees. Also, Regulation 1.416-1, T-13 states that the determination of whether a person is an officer will be based on all the facts and circumstances. Thus, not all individuals with the title of officer will be deemed officers for this purpose.

compensation greater than 100 percent of the maximum dollar limits for the annual addition to defined contribution plans; (3) an employee who owns more than a 5 percent interest in the employer; and (4) an employee who owns more than a 1 percent interest in the employer and whose annual compensation is more than $150,000. An employee who falls into more than one category, of course, is counted only once.

An employee is considered to be a key employee if the employee falls into one of the above classifications at any time during the current plan year or the four preceding plan years. Thus, the group of key employees may be larger than the actual operating group of key employees for any period of time.

If an employer has more officers than are required to be counted, the officers to be considered are those with the highest compensation.

In determining stock ownership, an employee is treated as owning stock even if it is owned by other members of his or her family or certain partnerships, estates, trusts, or corporations in which the employee has an interest. The rules for determining ownership in noncorporate entities are similar to those for determining corporate ownership.

6.9.3. Qualification Rules

A top-heavy plan must meet certain additional requirements if it is to be qualified under the Code. Moreover, the IRS currently requires all plans (except governmental plans and certain plans covering only employees who are members of a collective bargaining unit), even if they are not top-heavy, to include provisions that will automatically take effect if that event should occur. These additional requirements are as follows.

6.9.3.1. Vesting

A top-heavy plan must meet one of two alternative "fast" vesting schedules for all accrued benefits. The two vesting schedules are: (1)100 percent vesting after three years of service; and (2) graded vesting of at least 20 percent after two years of service, 40 percent after three, 60 percent after four, 80 percent after five, and 100 percent after six years.

6.9.3.2. Minimum Benefits for Nonkey Employees

A top-heavy plan must provide a minimum benefit or contribution for all nonkey employee participants. Social security benefits or contributions may not be applied toward these minimums. For each year (maximum of 10) in which a defined benefit plan is top-heavy, each nonkey employee participant must accrue an employer-provided benefit of at least 2 percent of compensation (generally defined as the average of the five consecutive highest years of pay). For each year in which a defined contribution plan is top-heavy, an employer must contribute at least 3 percent of compensation for each nonkey employee participant; however, in no case does an employer have to contribute more than the percentage contributed for key employees.   Reallocated forfeitures and any amounts contributed on account of salary reduction arrangements (see Chapter 12) are counted as employer contributions under defined contribution plans. When a nonkey employee participates in both a defined benefit and a defined contribution plan, the employer does not have to provide minimum benefits under both plans.

6.9.3.3. Limitations on Contributions and Benefits

In the case of any top-heavy plan, the aggregate Section 415 dollar limit described earlier in this chapter is reduced to 100 percent. The dollar limit can be increased back to 125 percent, however, if the plans meet the "concentration test" and provide an extra minimum benefit for nonkey employees. The concentration test is satisfied if the present value of the key employees' accrued benefits (or account balances) is not more than 90 percent of the total value for all covered employees. The extra minimum benefits to be provided for each nonkey employee are: (1) for defined benefit plans, a benefit accrual of one percent of compensation for each year of service during which the plan is top-heavy, up to a maximum of 10 years; and (2) for defined contribution plans, a contribution of 1 percent of compensation for each year of service during which the plan is top-heavy.

6.10.   DISTRIBUTION RULES

Internal Revenue Code Sections 401(a)(14) and 401(a)(9) provide specific guidance on when benefit payments to a participant must begin and whether a participant may defer payment of benefits indefinitely. Unless otherwise requested by the employee, benefit payments must commence within 60 days of the latest of the following three events: the plan year in which the employee terminates employment, the completion of 10 years of participation, or the attainment of age 65 or the normal retirement date specified in the plan.

Qualified retirement plans must provide that *even if the participant remains in employment,* either the entire interest of the participant be distributed to the participant not later than the required beginning date, or the participant's interest be paid out in installments that start on or before the required beginning date. The required beginning date is April 1 following the calendar year in which the participant reaches age 70½. The installments must be paid over

- the life of the participant,
- the lives of the participant and the participant's designated beneficiary, or
- a period not extending beyond the life expectancy of the participant or the joint life expectancies of the participant and the participant's designated beneficiary.

The tax consequences of providing insufficient distributions are described in Chapter 23.

6.11.   LEASED EMPLOYEES

A leased employee is an individual who performs services for another person under an arrangement between the recipient and a third person who is otherwise treated as the individual's employer. The services performed by an individual for the recipient must be of a type that is historically performed by employees.

The leased employee is treated as the recipient's employee if the leased employee has performed services for the recipient pursuant to an agreement with the leasing organization on a substantially full-time basis for a period of at least one year and the services are of a type historically performed by employees in the recipient's business field.[13] Once this occurs, the leased employee's years of service for the recipient include the entire period for which he or she performed service for the recipient.

If the leasing organization maintains a qualified retirement plan, contributions or benefits for the leased employee are treated as if provided by the recipient to the extent the contributions or benefits are attributable to service perform by the leased employee for the recipient.

Under safe harbor rules, the employee leasing rules will not apply to any leased employee if the employee is covered by a plan which is

---

[13]Internal Revenue Code Section 414(n)(5) describes certain conditions under which the leased employee will not be treated as an employee of the recipient.

maintained by the leasing organization if, with respect to such employee, the plan is a money purchase pension plan with a nonintegrated employer contribution rate of at least 10 percent of compensation, and provides for immediate participation and for full and immediate vesting. Also, to be a safe harbor plan, the leasing organization must cover 100 percent of its employees other than (1) employees who perform substantially all of their services for the leasing organization (rather than for recipients), and (2) employees whose total compensation from the leasing organization is less than $1,000 during the plan year and during each of the three preceding plan years.

In addition, the safe harbor plan cannot be used (that is, the leased employees must be treated as recipient's employees) if more than 20 percent of the recipient's nonhighly compensated workforce are leased employees. The term "nonhighly compensated workforce" is defined to mean the number of persons (other than highly compensated employees) who are (1) employees of the recipient (other than leased employees) and have performed for the recipient (or for the recipient and related persons) on a substantially full-time basis for a period of one year, and (2) leased employees with respect to the recipient. For purposes of this 20-percent rule, the term "leased employee" includes any person who performs services for the recipient both as a nonemployee and as an employee, and who would be a leased employee if all such services were performed as a nonemployee.

6.12.   OTHER REQUIREMENTS

6.12.1. Must Be in Writing

A qualified plan must be in writing and must set forth all the provisions necessary for qualification. This is normally accomplished by means of a trust agreement, a plan instrument, or both. In group pension programs, the plan provisions are sometimes contained in the group contract and, in this event, neither a trust agreement nor a separate plan instrument is necessary.

A trust agreement is generally required for trust fund plans and for plans using individual insurance or annuity contracts along with a conversion fund.[14] This allows the employer to make irrevocable

---

[14]A trust agreement is not necessary for plan assets held in insurance policies or nontransferable annuities, or for assets held by insurance companies, and for funds held in custodial accounts. However, a plan instrument of some type still would be required so that the plan provisions can be set forth in writing.

contributions on a basis that permits the employee to defer including these contributions as taxable income until they are distributed. If a group pension contract is employed, an intervening trust usually is not necessary, since the same results can be achieved through the group contract itself; that is, the contract can be written so that employer contributions are irrevocably made without the employees being considered in receipt of these contributions until they are distributed.

6.12.2. Communication to Employees

The plan must also be communicated to employees. An announcement letter or booklet is frequently used for this purpose. If employees are not given a copy of the actual plan, they should be told that a copy is available for inspection at convenient locations.

6.12.3. Definitely Determinable Benefits

A qualified pension plan must provide definitely determinable benefits. A defined contribution pension plan meets this requirement, since the employer's contribution formula is definite and, for this reason, benefits are considered actuarially determinable. Also, variable annuity plans or plans under which the benefit varies with a cost-of-living index will be acceptable.

Because of the definitely determinable benefit requirement, any amounts forfeited by terminating employees may not be used to increase benefits for the remaining participants under a defined benefit pension plan. Instead, these forfeitures must be used to reduce employer contributions next due. Moreover, a defined benefit plan will not be considered to provide definitely determinable benefits unless actuarial assumptions are specified in the plan whenever any benefit under the plan is to be determined using those assumptions. The assumptions must be specified in the plan in a way that precludes employer discretion. For defined contribution plans, forfeitures can be applied to increase benefits or to reduce contributions.

The definitely determinable benefit requirement does not apply to qualified profit sharing plans. Here, there is a requirement that the plan must provide for participation in the profits of the employer by the employees or their beneficiaries. While it is not required that there be a definite formula for determining the amount to be contributed to the profit sharing plan, it is required that there be a definite predetermined formula for allocating contributions among participants and for distributing funds after a fixed number of years, the attainment of a stated age, or upon the happening of some event such as layoff, illness, disability, retirement, death, or severance of employment.

6.12.4. Trust

If a trust is used, it must be one organized or created in the United States and maintained at all times as a domestic trust. The earnings of a trust created outside of the United States will be taxable, although if the trust would otherwise qualify, the employer will be allowed to take appropriate deductions for its contributions and the beneficiaries of the trust will be allowed the same tax treatment for distributions as if the trust had been qualified.[15]

6.12.5. Increases in Social Security

Any increase in social security benefits that takes place after retirement or after termination of employment cannot operate to reduce an employee's benefits.

6.13.   GENERAL PLAN PROVISIONS

Chapter 5 and the preceding portion of this chapter have dealt with the major plan provisions an employer must consider when establishing a pension plan. There are, of course, a number of other provisions that are a part of any plan and that relate generally to the rights and duties of the interested parties and to the administrative aspects of the program. The following discusses, very briefly, the most significant of these general provisions.

6.13.1. Employer's Right to Amend or Terminate the Plan

While a pension plan is established on an indefinite and presumably permanent basis, an essential plan provision is one that gives the employer the unilateral right to amend or terminate the program at any time. As will be seen, however, the rights reserved to the employer under such a clause are limited to some extent by federal law.

---

[15]Special rules exist concerning the taxation of distributions .

The right-to-amend clause is usually straightforward and reserves the right of the employer to make plan amendments without the consent of employees or their beneficiaries. However, as explained below, if a plan is to maintain its qualified status, an amendment may not reduce benefits related to contributions made prior to the amendment, deprive any employee of the employee's then accrued vested interest, nor permit the employer to recover any funds previously contributed to the plan. Thus, the amendment clause normally restricts the employer's rights to this extent unless the amendment itself is required to make the plan conform to federal or state laws. Also, as previously noted, if an amendment changes the plan's vesting schedule, any participant with at least three years of service must be given the election to remain under the preamendment vesting schedule.

The typical right-to-terminate clause gives the employer the unilateral right to terminate the plan (or to discontinue contributions) for any reason and at any time. However, for a plan to achieve a qualified status under federal tax law, it must be permanent and, while the Internal Revenue Service will approve a plan with such a termination provision, restrictions are imposed on the employer's right to terminate the program. Thus, if an employer terminates the plan for reasons other than "business necessity" within a few years of its inception, the plan may lose its qualified status for all prior open tax years, since this action will be considered by the Service as evidence that the plan, from its inception, was not a bona fide program for the exclusive benefit of employees in general. If business necessity exists, the employer may terminate the plan without adverse tax consequences. Valid reasons for a plan termination include financial incapacity, bankruptcy, insolvency, change of ownership, and so on.

The termination-of-plan clause must make provision for the distribution of plan assets if the plan is terminated or contributions are discontinued. Since federal tax law prohibits the return of any funds to the employer on plan termination (other than excess amounts remaining because of "actuarial error" after satisfaction of all plan liabilities), the plan assets must be applied for the benefit of the employees or their beneficiaries in a specified order of priorities.[16]

The Internal Revenue Service requires the inclusion of a provision that limits the benefits payable to certain highly paid employees in the event of plan termination. The provision limits benefits payable to the 25 highest paid employees of the employer at the inception of the plan whose anticipated individual annual retirement benefit from employer contributions will exceed $1,500. An employee could be within this group even though not a participant when the plan was established. This limitation on benefits applies if the plan is terminated within 10 years after

---

[16]This topic is described in detail in Chapter 17.

its effective date. (It also will apply to any benefits that become payable with respect to this group during the first 10 plan years even though the plan has not been terminated if, when the distribution is made, the "full current costs" of the plan have not been met.) Under Regulation 1.401-4(c)(7), the limitation is the greater of:

1. A dollar amount equal to the present value of the maximum termination benefit guaranteed by the PBGC (described in Chapter 23).[17]

2. The greater of $20,000 or 20 percent of the first $50,000 of annual compensation times the number of years between plan establishment and termination.

6.13.2. Anti-Cutback Rules

A qualified retirement plan may not be amended to eliminate or reduce a benefit that has already accrued unless the Internal Revenue Service approves a request to amend the plan or the elimination or reduction satisfies certain requirements.[18] However, a plan may (subject to certain notice requirements) be amended to eliminate or reduce benefits with respect to benefits not yet accrued.

6.13.3. Miscellaneous Provisions

The plan must also contain a number of provisions relating to the broad administration of the program, many of these provisions being dictated by the funding instrument employed to provide benefits. The following list, while by no means all-inclusive, indicates some of the provisions that must be considered.

6.13.3.1. Mergers and Consolidations

A plan must provide that the value of an employee's accrued benefit cannot be diminished in any way by any merger or consolidation with, or transfer of assets or liabilities to or from, any other plan.

---

[17]For purposes of the 25 highest paid employees, the amount of the PBGC guarantee depends on whether the employee is a substantial owner. A substantial owner is an individual who owns the entire interest in an unincorporated trade or business, is a more-than-10 percent partner, or owns (directly or indirectly) more than 10 percent in value of either the voting stock of a corporation or all classes of stock.

[18]See Reg. Section 1.411(d)-4 for details.

6.13.3.2.   Small Benefits

Many plans include a provision that permits payment of the employee's retirement benefit in a lump sum if its value is less than $3,500. However, an involuntary cash-out may not be made after a participant's annuity starting date unless the participant and spouse consent in writing to the distribution. If the participant dies, the surviving spouse must consent to a cash-out after the annuity starting date. Obviously, the payment of small amounts on a periodic basis is of little value to the retired employee, and the administrative problems involved in maintaining the necessary records and making the small payments could be significant. Thus, payment of the benefit in a lump sum is generally desirable for all concerned.

6.13.3.3.   Assignment of Benefits

The Code requires that the plan prohibit the assignment or alienation of benefits, with three exceptions: an employee may be permitted to assign up to 10 percent of any benefit payment, an employee may use his or her vested interest as collateral for a loan from the plan (if such loan is not a prohibited transaction), and a payment may be made to an alternate payee pursuant to a qualified domestic relations order (QDRO).

A QDRO is a domestic relations order that satisfies all the following requirements:

1. It must create or recognize the existence of an alternate payee's right to, or assign to an alternate payee the right to, receive all or a portion of the benefit payable with respect to a participant under a plan. An alternate payee is a spouse, former spouse, child, or other dependent of a participant who is recognized by a domestic relations order as having a right to receive all, or a part of, the benefits payable under a plan.

2. It must clearly specify certain facts about the participant's benefits. The order must clearly specify the name and the last known mailing address of the participant and the name and mailing address of each alternate payee covered by the order; the amount or percentage of the participant's benefit to be paid by the plan to each such alternate payee, or the manner in which such amount or percentage is to be determined; the number of payments or period to which such order applies; and each plan to which such order applies.

3. It must not alter the amount or form of the benefits. The QDRO may not require a plan to provide:

•   any type or form of benefit, or any option, not otherwise provided under the plan;

- (actuarially) increased benefits; or
- the payment of benefits to an alternate payee that are required to be paid to another alternate payee under another order previously determined to be a QDRO.

In the case of any payment before a participant has separated from service, a QDRO may require that payment be made to an alternate payee on or after the date on which the participant attains the early retirement age[19] as if the participant had retired on the date on which payment is to begin under the order. In this case, the amount of the payment is determined by taking into account the present value of the benefits actually accrued and not the present value of an employer subsidy for early retirement. The QDRO must be limited to a form that may be paid under the plan to the participant.

6.13.3.4.   ERISA-Required Provisions

In addition to some of the provisions already mentioned, ERISA requires that several other items be covered in the plan. For example, the plan must provide for named fiduciaries as well as a procedure for establishing and carrying out the plan's funding policy. The plan also should describe clearly any procedure for the allocation of fiduciary and administrative duties and responsibilities, and should stipulate the basis on which payments will be made to and from the plan.

QUESTIONS FOR REVIEW

1. Describe the dollar limits for defined benefit and defined contribution pension plans. Under what conditions must these limits be reduced?
2. Describe a qualified joint and survivor annuity (QJS).
3. Describe the payments that must be provided under a qualified preretirement survivor annuity (QPS) if (a) a participant dies after reaching the earliest retirement age, and (b) a participant dies on or before the date of attaining the earliest retirement age.
4. Describe the vesting requirements for accrued benefits attributable to (a) the employee's contributions and (b) the employer's contributions.

---

[19]This has been defined as the earlier of (1) the earliest date benefits are payable under the plan or (2) the later of the date the participant attains age 50 or the date on which the participant could obtain a distribution from the plan if the participant separated from service.

5.   Does an employer have complete flexibility in determining the minimum benefit amount that must be credited to a participant who terminates from the plan in a vested status? Explain.

6.   How is top-heaviness determined for a qualified pension plan? What are the consequences of such a status?

7.   Describe the restrictions that can be placed on the amount of compensation that can be taken into account in determining benefits and/or contributions under a qualified retirement plan.

8.   The law establishes specific regulations for the determination of service in what key areas?

9.   When will an employee incur a break in service? Why is this significant?

10.   Explain (a) how hours of service are generally related to the calculation of service for plan participants, (b) the break-in-service rules for maternity or paternity absences, and (c) the compliance methods available for counting hours of service.

QUESTIONS FOR DISCUSSION

1.   An employer maintains two plans. Plan A covers key employees, while Plan B covers nonkey employees. Both plans independently satisfy the coverage and nondiscriminatory requirements of the IRS Code. (a) Must the employer aggregate the two plans to determine top-heaviness? (b) May the employer aggregate the two plans to determine top-heaviness? (c) Why would an employer want to aggregate the two plans if this option is available?

2.   Assume that a calendar year defined contribution plan has a one-year minimum service requirement. An employee is hired on January 1, 1984, at $90,000 with increases of $10,000 each January 1. By 1987, the annual additions for the employee amount to $72,500. If the same employer establishes a defined benefit pension plan that covers this employee, what is the maximum annual benefit that can be provided to this employee from the second plan?

7. Other Legal Requirements

Tax law is clearly the most important law affecting qualified plans. Nevertheless, employers must also be concerned about the effect of other laws. This chapter briefly reviews some of the major laws that need to be considered in this regard.

The chapter first discusses the provisions of Title I of ERISA --the labor law provisions dealing with reporting, disclosure, and fiduciary responsibilities. This coverage of labor law provisions also discusses the potential application of other Title I requirements to executive benefit arrangements that cannot meet the tax law standards for a qualified plan.[1] The chapter next treats prohibitions against age and sex discrimination. Securities and Exchange (SEC) requirements are also covered in this chapter since they can be important for plans that permit employees to invest in employer stock. The chapter also includes a limited discussion of collective bargaining issues as well as a brief discussion of unrelated business income.

7.1. ERISA -- TITLE I

The labor law provisions of ERISA, which are contained in Title I of this Act, include many provisions which are virtually identical to the tax law provisions that were passed at the same time. Thus, for example, Title I has minimum participation, funding and vesting requirements, as well as joint

---

[1]The provisions of Title IV of ERISA that deal with plan termination insurance and the Pension Benefit Guaranty Corporation (PBGC), because of their complexity and the fact that they are applicable to defined benefit plans only, are treated separately in Chapter 17.

and survivor protection for the spouses of employees. For the most part, however, jurisdiction and administration of these provisions has been assigned to the IRS under the tax provisions -- a notable exception being that the Department of Labor (DOL) was given jurisdiction over the determination of service for eligibility, vesting and benefit accrual purposes.

Title I, however, contains important provisions concerning two key areas -- reporting and disclosure, and fiduciary requirements. Except for some restrictions on prohibited transactions, there is no counterpart for these provisions in the tax law.

The following first discusses reporting and disclosure, and then provides an overview of the fiduciary provisions of the law. There is also discussion of executive benefit plans which are not tax-qualified and which could come within the purview of other Title I provisions if certain conditions are not observed.

7.1.1.   Reporting and Disclosure

A major aspect of Title I concerns the disclosure of information -- to participants and their beneficiaries and to the government. These requirements generally apply to most tax-qualified plans, regardless of the number of participants involved. There are, however, a limited number of exemptions. They do not, for example, apply to unfunded excess benefit plans -- plans which are maintained to provide employees with benefits they would otherwise have received but which were not provided under the qualified plan because of Section 415 limitations. Also, if an unfunded plan is maintained for the exclusive benefit of a "select group of management or highly compensated employees," the only disclosure requirement is that the DOL be notified of the existence of the plan and the number of employees that it covers.

Otherwise, the disclosure and reporting provisions require that certain items be automatically filed with the government, others must automatically be given to employees, and still others must be reasonably available to employees on request. Items that must be filed with the government include:

- The plan's summary plan description (SPD) -- the booklet, folder, or binder that describes the plan and is given to employees.
- Any summary of material modifications (SMM) -- a summary of any plan amendment or change in information that is required to be included in the SPD after the initial SPD has been issued.
- The plan's annual financial report. (Filed using Form 5500 or one of its variations.)

Items that must be automatically distributed to employees include:

- The plan's SPD.
- Any SMMs.
- A summary annual report (SAR) -- a summary of the plan's annual financial report.
- A statement of benefits for all employees who terminate employment.
- A written explanation to any employee or beneficiary whose claim for benefits is denied.[2]

The foregoing lists items that must be given to employees on an automatic basis. There are other items which must be given to them on request and/or made available for examination at the principal office of the plan administrator and at other locations convenient for participants. These items include:

- Supporting plan documents.
- The complete application made to the IRS for determination of the plan's tax-qualified status.
- The complete copy of the plan's annual financial report.
- A personal benefits statement (on written request only and required to be furnished only once a year).
- A plan termination report (IRS Form 5310) should the plan be terminated.

The locations at which documents must be made available include any distinct physical location where business is performed and in which at least 50 participants work. Plan materials need not be kept at each location as long as they can be provided there within 10 working days after a request for disclosure. The employer may charge for reproduction of all materials requested unless the material falls in a category where it must be furnished automatically. Any item distributed automatically by mail must be sent by a class of mail that ensures timely delivery.

7.1.1.1. Summary Plan Description.

The SPD must be given to new employees within 90 days after becoming participants and to beneficiaries within 90 days after they start receiving benefits. For new plans, the initial SPD must be given to participants within

---

[2]There are many other items that must be automatically furnished to employees under other provisions of the law.

120 days after establishment of the plan and must be filed with the DOL at the same time. New, complete SPDs must be filed and distributed at least every ten years. If there have been material changes since the last SPD was issued; however, the employer must file and distribute a new SPD every five years.

The SPD must be in permanent form and must be current regarding all aspects of the plan and the information required by Title I. It must include the following information:

- The plan name and the type of plan (e.g., profit sharing).
- The type of plan administration (e.g., trusteed).
- The name (or position title) and address of the person designated as agent for the service of legal process, as well as a statement that legal process also may be served on a plan trustee or the plan administrator.
- The name, address and telephone number of the plan administrator.
- The name and address of the employer (or employee organization) that maintains the plan.
- The name and/or title, and business address of each trustee.
- The employer's identification number assigned by the IRS and the plan number assigned by the plan sponsor.
- In the case of a collectively bargained plan maintained by at least one employer and one employee organization, or in the case of a plan maintained by two or more employers, the name and address of the most significant employer or organization plus either of the following: (1) a statement that a complete list of sponsors may be obtained on written request and is available for review; or (2) a statement that, on written request, participants may receive information about whether a particular employer or organization is a sponsor and, if so, the sponsor's address.
- If a collective bargaining agreement controls any duties, rights, or benefits under a plan, a statement that the plan is maintained in accordance with the agreement and that a copy of the agreement may be obtained on written request and is available for examination.
- Plan requirements as to eligibility for participation and benefits (e.g., age, service, retirement age).
- A description of the provisions for nonforfeitable benefits.
- Information about vesting, forfeiture of benefits, credited service, breaks in service, and so forth.
- A description of any joint and survivor benefits and any action necessary to elect or reject them.
- Circumstances that may result in disqualification, ineligibility, denial, loss, forfeiture, or suspension of benefits.

- A statement of the extent to which a pension plan is insured by the Pension Benefit Guaranty Corporation (PBGC), where more information about this insurance is available (usually from the administrator), and the name and address of the PBGC. A summary of the pension benefit guaranty provisions of Title IV of ERISA is included in the SPD content regulations. An SPD incorporating this language will be in compliance. In addition, SPDs for any pension plans that are not insured (e.g., profit sharing plans) must note the reason for lack of insurance.
- The source of contributions to the plan, the method by which contributions are determined, and the identity of any organization through which the plan is funded or benefits are provided.
- A description and explanation of plan benefits.
- The date of the end of the plan year for purposes of maintaining the plan's fiscal records.
- The procedures to be followed in presenting claims for benefits under the plan and the remedies available under the plan for the redress of claims that are denied in whole or in part.
- A statement of participants' rights under Title I. This must appear as a consolidated statement; no information may be omitted. (The regulations contain suggested language which, if used, will assure compliance.)

When different classes of participants are covered with different benefits under the same plan, prominent notice must appear on the first page of the text listing the various classes for whom different SPDs have been prepared.

All this information must be "written in a manner calculated to be understood by the average plan participant" and should be "sufficiently accurate and comprehensive" to inform employees and beneficiaries of their rights and obligations under the plan. The explanations provided by legal plan texts and insurance contracts ordinarily will not meet these standards. The DOL regulations recommend the use of simple sentences, clarifying examples, clear and liberal cross-references, and a table of contents in the SPD. The use of type is important; varying sizes and styles of type may not be used when they may mislead employees.

If a plan covers 500 or more people who are literate only in a language other than English, or if 10% or more of the participants working at a "distinct physical place of business" are literate only in a non-English language (25% or more where the plan covers fewer than 100 participants), the SPD must include a prominent notice in the familiar language offering assistance -- which may be oral -- in understanding the plan.

Retired and terminated vested participants, as well as beneficiaries receiving benefits, come under Title I's definition of participants. Thus, they must be furnished automatically with copies of SPDs and SMMs; irrelevant plan amendments, however, need not be communicated although copies must be available upon request.

7.1.1.2. Annual Report

A plan's annual financial report is filed on Form 5500 (or one of its variations). This form must be filed with the IRS within seven months after the close of each plan year. For employers who have received extensions from the IRS for income tax filings, identical extensions are automatically granted for the plan's annual financial report.

The annual report is designed to require a complete disclosure of all financial information relevant to the operation of the plan. Thus, for example, it includes items such as a statement of assets and liabilities presented by category and valued at current value, changes in assets and liabilities during the year, and a statement of receipts and disbursements. It requests details, where applicable, for transactions with parties in interest, loans and leases in default or uncollectable, and on certain reportable transactions (e.g., transactions involving in excess of 3% of the current value of plan assets). The report also requires information on plan changes made during the reporting period, and on employees included or excluded from participation.

Certain financial statements in the report have to be certified by an independent qualified public accountant. Insurance companies and banks are required, within 120 days after the end of the plan year, to furnish any information necessary for the plan administrator to complete the annual report.

Plans that are fully insured are granted limited exemptions. These plans do not have to complete the financial information sections of the form, nor need they engage an accountant for audit or include an accountant's opinion. Plans with fewer than 100 participants can file using simplified versions of Form 5500.

7.1.1.3. Summary Annual Report

An SAR must be automatically distributed to plan participants within two months after the filing date for Form 5500. The SAR is a simplified summary of the full annual report and may use language prescribed in current DOL regulations.

7.1.1.4.   Summary of Material Modification

When a material modification is made to a plan, a summary description of that change, written in clear language, must be distributed automatically to all affected participants and beneficiaries. The SMM must also be filed with the DOL. The SMM must be furnished within 210 days after the end of the plan year in which the change is adopted.

7.1.1.5.   Plan Documents

Plan documents include the text of the actual plan itself, and any collective bargaining agreement, trust agreement, contract or other document under which the plan is established or operated.   Plan participants and beneficiaries are entitled to receive copies of these documents within 30 days of making written request. The DOL may request copies of these documents at any time.

7.1.1.6.   Benefit Statements for Terminating Employees

Each participant who terminates service with a vested right in his or her plan benefits should receive a clear statement of these benefits and the percentage that is vested. The statement should include the nature, amount and form of the benefit. Any participant who has had a break in service of one year is automatically entitled to receive a benefits statement. Statements must be given to vested participants within 210 days after the end of the plan year in which they terminate service.

The tax law provisions also require a statement be given to employees who terminate or incur a one-year break in service without a vested interest, thus clearly communicating that any such individual is not entitled to receive benefits under the plan.

7.1.1.7.   Personal Benefits Statement

Plan participants and beneficiaries may request in writing a statement of their own benefits, but not more often than once in any 12-month period. The statement should include the total benefits accrued and the portion, if any, that is vested or, if benefits are not vested, the earliest date on which they will become vested.

7.1.1.8.   Claim Denials

Anyone denied a claim under any plan is entitled to a written statement giving the reasons for the denial, usually within 90 days. This explanation should be a clear, comprehensible statement of the specific reasons for the denial of the claim. The explanation also must include a description of any material or information necessary for the claimant to improve the claim and the reasons why this additional material is needed. Also in the explanation should be a full description of the plan's appeal procedure. The claimant must be given at least 60 days thereafter in which to appeal the claim, and is entitled to a final decision in writing within 60 days of the appeal (120 days in special circumstances).

7.1.1.9.   Joint and Survivor Notifications

Under pension plans and some defined contribution plans, each participant must be informed, individually and in writing, of the right to elect or reject both pre- and post-retirement survivor benefits.

Timing for notification as to post-retirement survivor benefits is nine months before the earliest retirement date under the plan. Notification for pre-retirement survivor benefits must be provided between the first day of the plan year in which the participant becomes age 32 and the end of the plan year in which he or she becomes 35. If an employee is over age 32 when hired, notification must be provided within three years after that employee becomes a plan participant. If a vested participant terminates employment before age 32, notice must be provided within one year after the termination date.

The notifications must include enough information about the potential financial impact on the individual's own benefit for the participant to make an informed decision.   Contents of the notification are specified by regulations.

7.1.1.10.   Rollover Notifications

When a distribution from a qualified plan is eligible to be rolled over into an IRA or another employer's qualified plan, the plan administrator, within 60 days after the distribution, must send a notice to the participant or beneficiary explaining how taxes can be reduced or deferred (i.e., rollover or income averaging). If the plan administrator does not determine whether a distribution qualifies for rollover treatment, the notice must also explain how the participant or beneficiary can determine its eligibility.

7.1.1.11.   Enforcement

ERISA provides for a number of penalties for violation of the disclosure requirements. Among the penalties are the following:

- If a plan administrator does not fill a participant's or beneficiary's request within 30 days, the plan administrator may be personally liable to the individual who made the request for a fine of up to $100 per day.
- Willful violation of any of the reporting and disclosure provisions may incur a criminal penalty of up to a $5,000 fine and/or one year in prison for an individual, and up to a $100,000 fine for a corporation.
- Civil actions may be brought against the plan administrator by participants or beneficiaries to obtain information to which they are entitled under their plan, to enforce their rights under the plan, or to clarify their rights to future benefits under the plan.
- Civil action may also be brought by the secretary of labor, by a participant, beneficiary, or by another fiduciary against an individual who breaches his or her fiduciary duty.

It is expected that random audits will be performed continually, and that a team of investigators will follow up on all discrepancies found and all complaints filed by plan participants or beneficiaries. Records are now required to be kept for a period of six years after the documents are due for filing, even for those plans that are exempt from filing.

7.1.2.   Fiduciary Requirements

Fiduciary provisions are set forth in Part Four of Title I of ERISA, although the definition of fiduciary is found in Part One of ERISA, Section 3(21). The following provides a brief overview of these provisions.

7.1.2.1.   Definition of Fiduciary

A person (or corporation) will be considered a fiduciary under ERISA if that person exercises any discretionary authority or control over the management of the plan, any authority or control over assets held under the plan or the disposition of plan assets, renders investment advice for direct or indirect compensation (or has any authority or responsibility to do so), or has any discretionary authority or responsibility in the administration of the plan.

Clearly, the trustee of a plan is a fiduciary. So also are officers and directors of a corporation who have responsibility for certain fiduciary functions -- e.g., the appointment and retention of trustees or investment managers. On the other hand, individuals whose duties are purely ministerial (e.g., applying rules of eligibility and vesting) are clearly not fiduciaries.

7.1.2.2.   Fiduciary Responsibilities

A fiduciary is required to discharge all duties solely in the interest of participants and beneficiaries and for the exclusive purpose of providing plan benefits and defraying reasonable administrative expenses. In addition, a fiduciary is charged with using the care, skill, prudence, and diligence that a prudent person who is familiar with such matters would use under the circumstances then prevailing -- a standard that has come to be called the *prudent expert* rule. A fiduciary is also responsible for diversifying investments so as to minimize the risk of large losses unless it is clearly prudent not to diversify.[3] Finally, the fiduciary must conform with the documents governing the plan and must invest only in assets subject to the jurisdiction of U.S. courts.

7.1.2.3.   Prohibited Transactions

Both labor law (Title I of ERISA) and the IRC prohibit certain transactions between the plan and "disqualified persons."[4] A disqualified person is broadly defined to include any plan fiduciary, a person providing service to the plan, any employer or employee organization whose employees or members are covered by the plan, a direct or indirect owner of 50 percent or more of the business interest of the employer, a relative of any of the above, an officer, director and certain HCEs, or a person having 10 percent or more of the ownership interest in any of the above. Under ERISA, an employer is also considered to be a party in interest; an employee, however, is not considered to be a disqualified person.

The following transactions between the plan and a party in interest or a disqualified person are prohibited:

---

[3]Investments in employer securities in accordance with the prohibited transaction rules are also permitted under the diversity requirement; however, they must comply with the prudence and "exclusive benefit of employees" standards.

[4]The IRC refers to transactions between the plan and disqualified persons. ERISA refers to transactions between the plan and "parties in interest." For the most part, IRC and ERISA provisions are similar, although the penalties for engaging in a prohibited transaction differ.

- the sale, exchange or leasing of property
- lending money or extending credit (including funding the plan by contributing debt securities)
- furnishing goods, services or facilities
- a transfer to or the use of plan assets
- the acquisition of qualifying employer securities and real property in excess of allowable limits

These prohibitions apply even to "arm's length" transactions and even though the plan is fully protected.

Under ERISA, a fiduciary will be personally liable for any breach or violation of responsibilities, and will be liable to restore any profits made though the use of plan assets. Under the IRC, an excise tax of 5 percent of the amount involved in a prohibited transaction may be levied on the disqualified person who engages in the transaction. If the situation is not corrected within the time allowed (90 days unless extended by the IRS), a further excise tax of 100 percent of the amount involved may be imposed. Engaging in a prohibited transaction will not cause the plan to be disqualified, however.

As noted above, the prohibited transaction rules limit the investment of plan assets in qualifying employer securities and real property. Qualifying employer securities include stock; marketable obligations, e.g., bonds and notes, are also considered to be qualifying employer securities if certain requirements are met. Qualifying employer real property is real property that is dispersed geographically, is suitable for more than one use and had been leased to the employer.

In general, defined benefit and money purchase plans cannot invest more than 10 percent of the fair market value of plan assets in employer securities. Deferred profit sharing plans (including savings plans and CODAs) that specifically so provide may invest without limit in employer securities or real property; if the plan does not so specify, however, a 10 percent limit will apply. Stock bonus plan are primarily invested in employer securities, of course.

Even though investment in employer securities and real property is permitted under the prohibited transaction rules (and under the fiduciary requirements for diversity), investments of this type must still satisfy the overriding requirement that they be for the exclusive benefit of employees. Moreover, they must also satisfy the fiduciary requirement of prudence.

7.1.2.4.   Fiduciary Liabilities

Apart from excise taxes that might be imposed because of a prohibited transaction under the tax law, a fiduciary will be personally liable for any breach or violation of responsibilities, and will be liable to restore any profits made through the use of plan assets.

A fiduciary may also be liable for the violations of a cofiduciary if the fiduciary knowingly participates in or conceals a violation, has knowledge of a violation, or by the fiduciary's own violation enables the cofiduciary to commit a violation. If a plan uses separate trusts, however, a trustee of one trust is not responsible for the actions of the other trustees. Also, a fiduciary will not be responsible for the acts of a duly appointed investment manager (except to the extent that the fiduciary did not act prudently in selecting or continuing the use of the investment manager). A trustee also is not responsible for following the direction of named fiduciaries in making investment decisions if the plan so provides.

7.1.2.5.   Delegation of Authority

Non-investment activities can be delegated by a fiduciary if the plan so permits and the procedure for doing so is clearly spelled out; however, fiduciaries remain responsible, under the prudent expert rule, for persons delegated those responsibilities. Similarly, they remain responsible for the acts of their agents in performing ministerial duties.

7.1.2.6.   Earmarked Investments

The law permits a defined contribution plan to be established on a basis that allows "earmarked investments" --i.e., employees are allowed to direct the investment of their own accounts. Under these plans, sponsors and other plan fiduciaries might be exempt from liability for investment returns that result from participant choices, provided that participants are given the opportunity to exercise control over the assets in their individual accounts and can choose from a broad range of categories.

The DOL has issued proposed regulations that provide statutory relief from fiduciary liability under these plans if certain requirements are met. Failure to comply with these requirements does not necessarily mean that the fiduciaries will be liable for investment performance; it simply means that this regulatory protection is not available.

To ensure that participants have control over their assets and the opportunity to diversify their holdings, the proposed regulations:

- Require the plan to provide participants with reasonable opportunities to give investment instructions to the plan fiduciary, who is obligated to comply with these instructions.
- Require that a plan offer at least three "diversified categories of investment" -- with materially different risk and return characteristics -- that collectively allow participants to construct a portfolio with risk and return characteristics within the full range normally appropriate for a plan participant.
- Establish specific rules regarding participant transfer elections; sponsors must allow at least quarterly elections for transfers in or out of the three diversified investment options that must, as a minimum, be offered under the plan, and more frequent transfers may be required if appropriate in light of the volatility of a particular investment.

Look-through investment vehicles, such as mutual funds or bank commingled funds and guaranteed investment contracts qualify as diversified categories of investment because the underlying assets are diversified. Employer stock, however, does not qualify as a diversified category of investment although some liability protection is provided if the stock is publicly traded and if certain other conditions are met.

7.1.2.7.   Miscellaneous Requirements

Plan provisions that purport to relieve a fiduciary of responsibilities are void and of no effect. However, a plan, employer, union, or fiduciary may purchase insurance to cover the fiduciary's liability but if the plan purchases this insurance, the insurer must have subrogation rights against the fiduciary. An employer or union may also agree to indemnify a fiduciary against personal liability.

If convicted of certain specified crimes, a person cannot serve as a plan administrator, fiduciary, officer, trustee, custodian, counsel, agent, employee, or consultant for five years after conviction (or the end of imprisonment, if later). This prohibition will not apply if citizenship rights have been restored or if approved by the United States Board of Parole.

All fiduciaries and persons who handle plan funds or other plan assets are to be bonded for 10% of the aggregate amount handled, with minimum and maximum dollar amounts specified.

A plan must be established and maintained pursuant to a written instrument that specifically provides for one or more named fiduciaries. Each plan must provide a procedure for establishing and carrying out a funding policy and method to achieve plan objectives, and must describe any procedure for allocating operational and administrative responsibilities.

There must also be a provision that sets forth the amendment procedure and identifies the persons who have authority to amend. The plan must also specify the basis on which payments are made to and from the plan.

7.1.3.   Non-Qualified Plans

As noted earlier, Title I of ERISA contains a number of provisions that parallel the tax law requirements that apply to qualified plans. For the most part, these labor law provisions do not come into play insofar as qualified plans are concerned and, with the exception of determining service for eligibility to participate, vesting and benefit accruals, the tax law provisions are controlling.

It must be remembered, however, that ERISA defines "pension plan" in very broad terms -- on a basis that encompasses any plan, fund or program maintained by an employer to the extent that by its express terms or as a result of surrounding circumstances provides retirement income to employees or results in a deferral of income for periods extending to termination of employment or beyond.

Thus, any plan of deferred compensation, to the extent it does not meet the tax law requirements for a qualified plan, comes under the purview of Title I and, unless exempted, must comply with various requirements such as minimum participation, funding and vesting, joint and survivor provisions, and the like. If a plan is not tax-qualified, and if it must be funded and vested, the tax consequences could be undesirable -- with employees being in constructive receipt of the value of vested benefits. Thus, most employers prefer to design programs that qualify for one of the available exemptions.

One specific exemption is granted for "excess benefit" plans -- plans that provide employees with contributions and/or benefits which would otherwise have been provided to them under the qualified plan were it not for the limitations of Section 415. This exemption is total for excess benefit plans that are unfunded; if funded, the exemption is partial and compliance is required only for reporting, disclosure and fiduciary rules.[5]

Another exemption applies to plans which are "unfunded and ... maintained by an employer primarily for the purpose of providing deferred compensation for a select group of management or highly compensated employees." However, these plans are still subject to the reporting and disclosure requirements of Title I.[6] Although ERISA has been in effect since the mid-1970s, this phrase has never been clarified by the DOL. Thus,

---

[5]A partial exemption from disclosure and reporting has been provided by the DOL for these plans. In essence, all that is required is that the DOL be notified of the existence of any such plan and the number of individuals it covers.

[6]The partial exemption from disclosure and reporting also applies to these plans.

there is some uncertainty as to how it may be applied. The concern, of course, is that if the group covered does not come within this exemption, the entire plan could become subject to all Title I provisions.

Despite this uncertainty, many employers have established supplemental executive benefit programs that rely on this exemption. Many of them are limited to "restoration " plans that simply restore benefits lost under qualified plans due to restrictions other than Section 415 -- e.g., the limitation on pay that can be used to determine contributions and benefits or the annual limit on elective deferrals. Other plans are much broader in scope, encompassing all forms of deferred compensation and providing benefits for executives that are clearly in addition to those contemplated by broad-based programs. Executive benefit programs are covered at length in Chapter 26.

7.2.   UNRELATED BUSINESS INCOME

While the investment income of a qualified trust established in conjunction with a qualified plan is generally exempt from tax, all or part of this income could be subject to tax if it is considered to be unrelated business income.

Unrelated business income is the gross income derived from any unrelated trade or business regularly carried on by the trust, less allowable deductions directly connected with the carrying on of such trade or business, with certain exclusions. An unrelated trade or business is any trade or business carried on by the trust.

Only income resulting from the *direct* operation of the unrelated trade or business is subject to tax. Thus, for example, if the trust owns all of the stock of a corporation but the corporation directly operates the business, the stock dividends received by the trust will not be subject to tax.

The following income is not considered to be unrelated business income: dividends, interest, annuities, royalties, most rents from real property and gains from the sale or exchange of noninventory property, except if such income is attributable to debt-financed property.

7.3.   AGE/SEX DISCRIMINATION

Discrimination on the basis of age is prohibited by the Age Discrimination in Employment Act (ADEA), as amended; discrimination on the basis of sex (or sex-related conditions such as pregnancy) is prohibited by Title VII of the Civil Rights Act of 1964, as amended.

In the case of age discrimination (which protects employees age 40 and older), the major requirements are as follows:

- An employee cannot be excluded from participation because of age. Use of a minimum age of up to 21, as permitted under ERISA and the tax law, is acceptable; use of any maximum age is prohibited.
- An employee cannot be required to contribute more or at higher levels because of having attained an age that is 40 or more, nor can employer contributions and/or employer-provided benefits be increased or decreased by reason of age.   It is permissible, however, for both employee and employer contributions and for employer-provided benefits to change with respect to length of service where this is clearly not age-related.[7]
- An employee cannot be made to retire upon attaining any specified age such as the plan's normal retirement age.[8]
- As long as a participating employee remains employed, he or she must be eligible to continue full participation in the plan.   In the case of a defined contribution plan, this means that the employee must continue to share in employer contributions (assuming the employee makes any mandatory contributions or elective deferrals that are required as a condition of receiving such contributions).   In the case of a defined benefit plan, the employee must continue to accrue benefits with respect to actual pay changes up to the time of retirement; the employee must also continue to accrue benefits with respect to service until the plan maximum, if any, on service has been reached. These requirements exist even though the employee has reached age 70 1/2 and is receiving plan distributions while actively employed because of the minimum distribution rules.

The prohibitions against sex discrimination are similar:

- Different employee and/or employer contributions cannot be made or required on account of the employee's sex.
- Benefits provided cannot be different by reason of the employee's sex.
- There can be no distinction in any plan eligibility requirements -- for initial participation, rights to certain options or benefits, treatment of leaves of absence, etc. -- on account of sex.
- If annuity or lifetime installment benefits are offered by the plan, there can be no distinction in annuity or installment costs and/or benefits on

---

[7]In the case of a defined benefit pension plan, any increase in employer-provided benefits on account of length of service would have to comply with the benefit accrual rules that limit the extent to which a plan can be "back-loaded."

[8]There is a limited exception for "bona fide" executives whose annual employer-provided benefit from all sources is $44,000 or more. For these individuals, an employer can enforce mandatory retirement at age 65.

account of sex -- these costs and benefits must be based on unisex mortality tables.

7.4.   SECURITIES AND EXCHANGE (SEC) REQUIREMENTS

Various securities law requirements affect employee benefit and executive compensation plans.   The following is a brief discussion of registration requirements and insider trading restrictions.

7.4.1.   Offering Registration

In general, an offer to sell securities must either be registered with the SEC or conform to an available exemption from registration. If an offering must be registered with the SEC, a prospectus must generally be prepared for distribution to potential purchasers.

For purposes of this registration requirement, employee benefit plans can be divided into two groups: (1) those under which *employee* contributions are invested in employer stock; and (2) all other plans. Aftertax contributions are always considered employee contributions for this purpose. Elective deferrals, however, are treated differently depending upon whether they are made by way of salary reduction or by foregoing a year-end profit sharing contribution or bonus. The former type of elective deferral is considered to be an employee contribution, notwithstanding the fact that for tax purposes, it is considered to be an employer contribution. The latter type is treated by the SEC, as well as by tax law, as an employer contribution.

A plan that does not involve the investment of employee contributions in employer stock does not have to be registered with the SEC -- e.g., an ESOP funded entirely with employer contributions.   However, any employee benefit plan in which employee contributions may be invested in employer stock is considered an offering to sell securities. Thus, such a plan must be registered with the SEC (and a prospectus prepared) or it must fit within an exemption. In many cases, no exemption is available for plans of publicly traded companies and such plans must be registered. A special type of registration, using the format of Form S-8, is available.[9]

---

[9]Plans of private companies may be exempt under Rule 701. This rule permits an employer to grant up to $5 million worth of stock annually to employees without registration. This rule also requires that employees be given a copy of the plan document and that they receive adequate disclosure of material information. Further, the SEC must be notified within 30 days after sales total $100,000 and annually thereafter.

In lieu of using a prospectus, an employer can meet its disclosure requirements through a variety of documents, including SPDs; however, the typical SPD will not be sufficient, by itself, to meet the SEC disclosure requirements -- e.g., that there be a three-year history of financial data on investment alternatives.

It should also be noted that a prospectus (or equivalent information) must be given to employees before they are eligible to participate in the plan.

Plans that are registered with the SEC must file annual reports with the Commission, using Form 11-K; this requirement, however, does not apply (except for the initial filing) to plans with fewer than 300 participants.

7.4.2.   Insider Trading Restrictions

Section 16(b) of the Securities Exchange Act prohibits an "insider" from buying and selling, or selling and buying, company stock in a publicly traded company within a six-month period.[10] Insiders who violate this six-month trading restriction are required to turn over all profits made on the transaction to the company. Insiders with respect to a publicly traded company include its directors, any employee owning more than 10% of the company's stock, and certain officers.

Insiders are required to report changes in their ownership of company equity securities (i.e., nonexempt purchases and sales of stock) within ten days after the close of the calendar month in which the change occurs. Reportable transactions include all plan contributions (employee and employer) invested in company stock as well as any purchases/sales an insider makes by switching account balances to or from an employer stock fund. Insiders will also have to report stock they acquire in an ESOP. In a defined contribution plan, *each* allocation of company stock to an insider is considered a "purchase" unless it is covered by an exemption. Without such an exemption, an insider who also sold company stock in the preceding six months -- or sells stock in the six months following the purchase -- must return any profits to the company. Further, sales that can be "matched" with a purchase are not limited to transactions within the same plan; *any* sale the insider makes could trigger the liability. Since allocations are typically made on a monthly basis, these purchases, unless exempted, could mean that insiders would have to refrain from selling any company stock until they terminate employment.

SEC rules offer a number of conditional exemptions for participant-directed investments in company stock. Basically, these exemptions address

---

[10]The insider trading rules do not apply to privately traded companies.

three types of transactions -- ongoing purchases/sales through payroll contributions, purchases/sales that insiders make by switching account balances to and/or from a company stock fund, and sales related to plan distributions. A detailed discussion of these exemptions, however, is beyond the scope of this text.

7.5.   COLLECTIVE BARGAINING REQUIREMENTS

It has long been recognized that employee benefits are mandatory subjects of collective bargaining under the National Labor Relations Act (NLRA). Thus, employers may not refuse to discuss providing employee benefits to employees who are represented by a collective bargaining unit, and must negotiate in good faith concerning their demands.

In many situations, plans negotiated for union employees will be unilateral plans that cover only individuals who work for the employer. Typically, the negotiation process involves design issues such as eligibility, contribution levels, vesting provisions, and so forth, with funding of the benefits being left under employer control. On occasion, however, a union's proposal may be for coverage under a joint labor-management trust fund --a multi-employer or Taft-Hartley plan, as they are sometimes called. The law requires that these latter plans have equal labor and management representation on the board of trustees. For the most part, multi-employer plans have been limited to defined benefit pension plans and health and welfare programs.

QUESTIONS FOR REVIEW

1.   What are disclosure items that must be automatically furnished to the government under Title I of ERISA?
2.   What information must be included in an SPD?
3.   Describe the claim denial procedure that must be included in an employee benefit plan.
4.   Are the directors of a corporation fiduciaries under Title I of ERISA? Why or why not?
5.   Under what circumstances do the provisions of Title I of ERISA apply to nonqualified plans maintained for executives?
6.   Describe the requirements of ADEA that apply under defined benefit plans when an employee continues employment beyond his or her normal retirement date.

7.   Under what circumstances do SEC requirements apply to qualified profit sharing and savings plans.

QUESTIONS FOR DISCUSSION

1.   An employee can become fully vested in his or her accrued benefits after five years of service and well before he or she has attained age 32. Once vested, the employee must be automatically protected by the joint and survivor provisions of the law. Nevertheless, the law does not require that the employee be notified of the joint and survivor benefits and rights until he or she has attained age 32. Explain why notification is not required before age 32 even though the employee could be entitled to the benefit.

2.   Explain the rationale for the DOL's position, in proposed regulations, concerning the granting of safe harbors for plans that permit earmarked investments (where employees choose the funds in which their contributions will be invested), and the conditions under which these safe harbors will apply.

3.   Do SEC requirements concerning the disclosure of information to eligible employees (when employee contributions may be used to purchase employer stock) supplant the SPD disclosure requirements of Title I of ERISA? Why or why not?

PART THREE

Defined
Contribution Plans

Even though the vast majority of individuals are covered by defined benefit plans, there is no question that since the passage of ERISA, employers have favored the use of defined contribution plans -- whether in the form of a basic retirement program or as some type of supplemental arrangement.

This part reviews the major types of defined contribution plans that may be utilized by an employer. Money purchase plans, where the employer makes a fixed contribution each year, are covered in Chapter 8. Deferred profit sharing plans, where the employer's contribution is determined by a profit sharing formula or is made on a discretionary basis, are the subject of Chapter 9.

Technically, the Internal Revenue Code does not recognize savings plans as a specific type of plan; thus, they are usually designed and qualified as profit sharing plans. Although they fit in this category, they differ in many ways from conventional profit sharing arrangements and, for this reason, are discussed separately in Chapter 10.

Employee stock ownership plans (ESOPs), which are designed to invest primarily in employer securities, have proven to be of great interest to many employers -- particularly when used in conjunction with corporate financing. Chapter 11 describes ESOPs and their unique characteristics, as well as the many special tax law provisions that apply to these plans.

The ability to choose between having compensation paid currently in cash or deferred to some future time is an important tax advantage that can be attached to profit sharing, savings and stock bonus plans, but only if special provisions of the tax law are met. These plans (known as CODAs), and their technical requirements, are treated in Chapter 12.

Simplified employee pensions (SEPs) are the subject of the final chapter of this part -- Chapter 13. SEPs were authorized by Congress in an effort to encourage the adoption of private pension plans by small employers; these plans can be established with a minimum of paperwork and regulatory compliance.

8. Money Purchase Pension Plans

Pension plans are either *defined benefit* or *defined contribution* in nature. The vast majority of employees in the United States are covered by defined benefit plans, reflecting the fact that most large employers and almost all union-negotiated plans have utilized this approach. Since the passage of ERISA, however, there has been a growing interest in the defined contribution concept -- in fact, approximately 80 percent of all new plans established since the mid-1970s utilize the defined contribution approach. To be sure, many of these defined contribution plans have been supplemental in nature -- and most have been profit sharing or stock bonus programs, including so-called savings plans and CODAs (cash or deferred arrangements).[1] Even so, some of these plans have been true pension arrangements that use defined contribution concepts; these latter plans are called *money purchase* pension plans.

A defined benefit plan provides a fixed amount of pension benefit. The amount of each employee's benefit usually depends on length of service and pay level -- for example, a pension of 1 percent of pay for each year of service. In collectively bargained plans, however, pay often is not taken into account; the monthly pension is typically a fixed dollar amount (such as $20) for each year of service. In any event, a defined benefit plan promises a fixed

---

[1]Technically, the tax law only provides for pension, profit sharing and stock bonus plans. Savings plans are not a recognized form of plan, as such, and are usually qualified as profit sharing plans. CODAs, under the tax law, are not plans at all -- they are arrangements that are attached to an underlying profit sharing or stock bonus plan. Nevertheless, common usage refers to both savings plans and CODAs as though they were separate types of plans.

level of benefit and the employer contributes whatever is necessary to provide this amount.

By contrast, the defined contribution or money purchase pension approach focuses on contribution levels. The employer's contribution is fixed as a percent of pay or as a flat dollar amount.[2] This contribution, along with any amounts contributed by the employee, is accumulated and invested on the employee's behalf. The amount of pension an employee receives will thus vary depending on such factors as length of plan participation, the level of contributions and investment gains and losses.

This chapter begins with a review of the general characteristics of money purchase pension plans. It then treats the contribution structure of these plans. The chapter concludes with a discussion of the additional or different tax law requirements that apply to these plans.

8.1.   GENERAL CHARACTERISTICS

In a sense, money purchase pension plans are hybrids. Because they are pension plans, they are treated for many purposes in much the same fashion as defined benefit plans. They are, for example, subject to the minimum funding and joint and survivor requirements of the tax law that apply to defined benefit arrangements. In other areas, however, the tax law treats money purchase plans as defined contribution arrangements. Thus, individual accounts must be maintained for employees, the plans are subject to the annual addition limits of Section 415 of the IRC, and they are not subject to the plan termination provisions of Title IV of ERISA.

Despite the fact that they are treated differently for different tax law purposes, a money purchase plan is fundamentally a defined contribution plan. For this reason, it has many of the same basic characteristics that are found in all defined contribution plans -- particularly when contrasted with defined benefit arrangements.

One example of this concerns the allocation of employer contributions. The amount an employer contributes for each employee under a money purchase plan is usually expressed as a percent of the employee's current pay (for the year involved), with the result that each employee, regardless of age, receives the same percentage of pay contribution. By contrast, the allocation of employer contributions under a final-pay defined benefit plan is such that age and prior service are also taken into account. Thus, the amount of aggregate employer contribution that is allocated to younger employees usually is much higher under a money purchase plan than it is

---

[2]This fixed contribution requirement is a characteristic of money purchase plans that distinguishes them from other defined contribution arrangements where the employer's contribution is a variable that is related to profits or is made on a discretionary basis.

under a defined benefit plan. Some employers feel that this is an equitable allocation of their contributions. Others, however, feel that it is fairer to allocate contributions in such a way that older (and usually longer service) employees receive proportionately greater amounts. Regardless of how an employer might feel about this issue, the fact remains that this type of allocation pattern can produce higher levels of severance benefits for employees who terminate at younger ages with a vested interest and, to this extent, higher plan costs.

Another example concerns the way in which money purchase plans respond to inflation. In essence, the retirement benefits that might be provided to an employee are the result of contributions that are based on the employee's career average compensation. There will be some reflection of inflation that takes place during his or her pre-retirement years, in that current and future contributions will take the accumulated effects of inflation into account. And, if the employee's account balance is invested in equity-type investments, some inflation protection may be provided by investment results.[3] Also, because of the very nature of the employer's commitment, no post-retirement inflation protection is provided under a money purchase plan. By contrast, the typical final-pay defined benefit plan provides for an initial level of income that reflects inflation up to the time of retirement. Further, a great many employers provide for "ad hoc" increases for their retirees, from time to time, under defined benefit arrangements.

A related comparison concerns investment risk. Under defined contribution plans, including money purchase plans, the employee receives the benefit of all positive investment returns; the employee also bears the risk of all unfavorable results. Under a defined benefit plan investment risk and reward is borne by the employer.

Some of the more specific or typical characteristics of money purchase plans are as follows:

- In establishing the plan, the employer agrees to make a fixed contribution each year for each eligible employee. This contribution is usually expressed as a percent of pay, although it may be a flat dollar amount. This constitutes a definite commitment on the part of the employer and the contribution must be made each year, regardless of profits, and cannot be varied except by plan amendment.
- The plan may require employees to make contributions in order to participate. If so, these contributions can be made only from aftertax

---

[3]Most employees, however, tend to elect relatively conservative investments (fixed income or guaranteed interest funds) when choices are made available to them, with the result that significant inflation protection may not be provided from this source -- at least in many situations.

income -- salary reduction or elective deferral contributions cannot be made under a money purchase plan. When employees do contribute:

* the contribution rate is fixed (unlike the typical savings plan where the employee can choose from among different levels of participation).

* the employer's contribution rate is often set with reference to what employees are contributing -- for example, at two times the employee contribution rate.

- Regardless of whether employees are required to make mandatory contributions in order to participate, they may be permitted to make voluntary contributions -- those which do not attract any type of employer contribution.

- Forfeitures which arise when partially vested or nonvested employees terminate employment may be used to reduce employer contributions or may be reallocated among the remaining plan participants; the customary practice in money purchase plans is to use these contributions to reduce the employer contributions next due.[4]

- Both employer and employee contributions are transferred to a trustee (or an insurance company under a group annuity type of contract) where they are invested on behalf of the employees.

- As with other types of defined contribution plans, employees are frequently given a choice of several investment funds in which to invest their account balances.

- Individual accounts are established for participating employees. Each account is credited with employer and employee contributions, reallocated forfeitures (if applicable), and its proportionate share of investment gains and losses.

- An employee's benefit, at any given time, is whatever can be provided by his or her vested account balance at that time. If the employee retires, the employee will have the option of receiving this account balance in a lump sum or in the form of monthly installments -- usually over a period equal to the employee's life expectancy or the joint life expectancy of the employee and his or her beneficiary.

- The employee's account balance (even if not otherwise vested) is usually payable in full in the event of the employee's death.

- Unlike conventional profit sharing and savings plans, a money purchase plan generally cannot make distributions until the employee has severed employment. Thus, in-service withdrawals are not permitted.

---

[4]Prior to the Tax Reform Act of 1986 (TRA 86), forfeitures could only be used to reduce employer contributions under money purchase plans.

- While it is possible for a money purchase plan to provide for loans to employees, this practice is unusual. In general, money purchase plans focus on their role as retirement vehicles; permitting loans could be viewed as being inconsistent with this fundamental purpose.

8.2.   CONTRIBUTION STRUCTURE

As previously noted, money purchase plans do not provide a fixed benefit for employees. Instead, the employer contributions (and any employee contributions), together with investment income, are applied to provide as much in the way of pension benefits as is possible. Since the cost of a given amount of benefit varies by entry age and retirement age, the benefits of any employee will depend on these factors as well as on contribution levels and investment results.

In the past, the employee's sex was also a factor in determining the amount of retirement benefit that could be provided under a money purchase plan. If a male and female employee were the same age and had exactly the same amount accumulated under such a plan, the male employee would receive a higher lifetime pension than the female employee. This was because the female employee was expected to live longer and, in anticipation of this, the same initial amount was expected to be paid over a longer period of time. Because of this difference in life expectancies, the actuarial value of the pension, in both cases, was considered to be the same. In 1983, however, the Supreme Court ruled (in *Arizona Governing Committee* v. *Norris*) that life annuities under an employer-sponsored defined contribution plan must be provided on a uniform basis.[5]

Defined contribution plans are often contributory. In this case, the employer's contribution is usually a match or multiple of the employee's contribution. For example, the plan could call for the employer and employee each to contribute 5 percent of the employee's compensation; or the employee's contribution could be set at 3% of compensation with the employer contributing 6%.

It should be noted that defined contribution plans have several inherent limitations when viewed from the perspective of providing retirement income. First, an employee who joins the plan at an older age will have only a short period of time to accumulate funds, with the result that the employee's benefit often will be inadequate. Table 8-1 indicates the results

---

[5]It should be noted that employees can buy annuities from insurance companies on the open market (i.e., apart from the qualified plan). At this time, insurers are not required to offer such annuities on a unisex basis, although legislation that would require this has been proposed. Even though not required to do so, however, many insurers provide for unisex premiums.

that could flow under a money purchase plan and the disparity in benefits that could be produced. This table assumes that the compensation shown for each employee will continue until normal retirement; that the contribution made by the employer each year is 10 percent of the employee's pay; that this contribution will accumulate at 6 percent compound interest until retirement; and that the fund accumulated at retirement will be applied under representative annuity purchase rates to provide a monthly pension benefit.

Table 8-1: Illustration of Money Purchase Formula Without Earnings Projection

Age at Entry	Normal Retirement Age	Pay	Contribution	Fund at Retirement	Monthly Benefit	Benefit as a Percent of Pay
30	65	12,000	1,200	141,745	1,274	127
40	65	14,000	1,400	81,419	732	63
45	65	9,500	950	37,043	333	42
53	65	30,000	3,000	53,646	482	19
55	65	12,000	1,200	16,766	151	15

As Table 8-1 shows, younger employees have a much longer time to accumulate funds and receive a proportionately larger benefit. Moreover, the money purchase plan has an additional weakness since, because of the effect of compound interest, greater weight is given to the employee's lower compensation at the younger ages than will be given to the higher compensation the employee receives when he or she is older.

An additional comment about the potential disadvantages of money purchase plans has to do with its ability to respond to growth in an employee's earnings -- particularly during periods of inflation. Table 8-1 projected benefits for employees on the assumption that earnings would remain constant. This is not a realistic assumption since, in all probability, most employees will receive a number of pay increases over their working careers. Thus, it is important to illustrate and compare the results depicted in Table 8-1 with what would be the case if all assumptions remain the same except for future pay growth. This comparison for the same group of employees is set forth in Table 8-2, which assumes that earnings will grow at the rate of 4% a year. As can be seen, the potential benefit, as a percent of final pay, is considerably lower when future earnings growth is taken into account.

Another observation about the deficiencies of a money purchase plan is that the employee's benefit under this approach can only be estimated. This lack of certainty as to benefits could prove to be an unsatisfactory employee relations feature of such a plan. Also, the variation in benefit levels for different employees makes it difficult, if not impossible, to design a contribution formula that produces benefit levels uniformly responsive to employer objectives. As a final observation, a money purchase plan is a career pay plan; however, unlike the practice for career-pay defined benefit plans, it is relatively uncommon for an employer to "up-date" accrued benefits to take inflation into account.

Table 8-2: Illustration of Money Purchase Formula
With and Without Projection of Pay

	Pay		Fund at Retirement		Monthly Benefit		Benefit as Percent of	
				With	Flat	With	Entry	Final
Age at Entry	At Entry	Final	Flat Pay	Projected Pay	Pay	Projected Pay	Pay	Pay
30	12,000	45,532	141,745	237,864	1,274	2139	127.4	56.4
40	14,000	35,886	81,419	120,652	732	1,085	62.7	36.3
45	9,500	20,015	37,043	51,156	333	460	42.1	27.6
53	30,000	46,184	53,646	65,375	482	588	19.3	15.3
55	12,000	17,080	16,766	19,754	151	178	15.1	12.5

8.3.   TAX LAW PROVISIONS

Money purchase plans are subject to almost all of the tax law provisions that generally apply to qualified plans. The following is a brief discussion of the major tax law provisions that are different as they apply to money purchase plans. In some instances, the discussion is in terms of how money purchase plans are treated differently from other types of defined contribution plans.

8.3.1.   Nondiscrimination in Contributions and Benefits

If a money purchase plan involves after-tax employee and matching employer contributions, an actual contribution percentage (ACP) test will have to be satisfied each year in accordance with the terms of Section 401(m) of the IRC.[6] The ACP test also applies to voluntary aftertax

---

[6]The complete details of this test are discussed in Chapter 12 since the ACP test is similar to the actual deferral percentage (ADP) test applicable to elective deferrals under CODAs and, quite often, the two tests must both be made for the same plan. Further, there is a limitation on the

employee contributions even when there is no employer match. This test limits the participation of HCEs so that their average contribution percentages cannot exceed the average contribution percentages of the NHCEs by more than a stipulated amount. In general, the ACP for HCEs cannot be more than 125% of the ACP for the NHCEs. An alternative limitation permits the ACP for HCEs to be as much as two times the ACP for NHCEs, but not more than two percentage points higher. If the portion of the plan that is subject to this test meets its requirements each year, this portion will satisfy the nondiscrimination in contributions and benefits requirements of Section 401(a)(4) of the IRC.

If the ACP test is not applicable to employer contributions (e.g., there are no mandatory employee contributions), this portion of the plan must satisfy the nondiscrimination requirements of Section 401(a)(4) of the IRC. The regulations prescribe two safe harbors that can be met in order to satisfy these requirements. The first safe harbor is for plans with a uniform contribution formula -- where contributions equal the same percentage of pay or the same dollar amount for every covered employee -- and will apply to most money purchase plans. To use this safe harbor, the same vesting schedule and definition of years of service must apply to all participants. Also, if the plan integrates with Social Security benefits by providing a higher contribution percentage for pay above a specified level than for pay below that level, the plan will be deemed to satisfy this safe harbor if the plan meets the permitted disparity requirements of Section 401(l).[7]

The second safe harbor applies to nonintegrated "uniform points plans" (other than ESOPs) which allocate contributions based on a formula weighted for age and/or service and units of pay that do not exceed $200. This safe harbor is available to such plans if the average of the allocation rates for HCEs does not exceed the average of the allocation rates for the NHCEs.

If neither of these safe harbors is met, the general testing requirements of Section 401(a)(4) will be applicable.[8]

8.3.2.   Integration with Social Security

Section 401(l) of the IRC permits most qualified plans to "integrate" or coordinate contributions and/or benefits with the benefits provided by Social Security. In essence, this provision of the law provides for a limited form of discrimination in that it permits plans to provide higher

---

use of the alternative limitation under these tests which applies when both tests apply to the same plan.

[7] These permitted disparity requirements are discussed in the following section of this Chapter.

[8] These requirements are discussed in Chapter 5.

contributions or benefits for higher paid employees so as to compensate for the fact that the relative value of Social Security decreases as pay goes up.

Thus, a money purchase plan can have two employer contribution levels -- one for pay up to a specified amount and another higher contribution for pay in excess of that amount. Section 401(l) requires that the difference between these two employer contribution levels cannot exceed a certain amount -- called the permitted disparity.

The point at which the contribution percentage changes is called the plan's "integration level." The law permits the use of an integration level in any plan year of any amount up to the Social Security taxable wage base at the beginning of that year.

When a plan's integration level equals the Social Security taxable wage base or is set at a level which is at or below 20 percent of this taxable wage base, the contribution percentage for pay above this amount may exceed the contribution percentage for pay below this amount by the lesser of: (1) 5.7 percent; and (2) the percentage applicable to pay below the wage base. In other words, when the contribution percentage applicable to pay below the integration level is equal to or less than 5.7 percent, the contribution percentage for pay above the integration level cannot be more than twice the lower contribution percentage; if the lower percentage is greater than 5.7 percent, the higher percentage cannot be more than the lower percentage plus 5.7 percent.

Thus, for example, if the lower contribution percentage is 4 percent, the higher percentage cannot exceed 8 percent; if the lower percentage is 6 percent, the higher percentage cannot exceed 11.7 percent. Table 8-3 shows illustrative maximums for plans that are integrated at the Social Security wage base or at or below 20 percent of this amount.

Table 8-3: Defined Contribution Plan Integration Limits
(If Integration Level is at Social Security Taxable Wage
Base or at or below 20 Percent of this Amount)

If lower contribution percentage is:	Upper contribution percentage cannot exceed:
1.0%	2.0%
2.0	4.0
3.0	6.0
4.0	8.0
5.0	10.0
5.7	11.4
6.0	11.7
7.0	12.7
8.0	13.7

If a plan's integration level is between 20 percent and 100 percent of the Social Security taxable wage base, the 5.7 percent standard in these rules is reduced. If the plan's integration level is more than 80 percent of the Social Security taxable wage base, it is reduced to 5.4 percent; if the integration level is between 20 percent and 80 percent of the wage base, it is reduced to 4.3 percent.

It should be noted that if a money purchase plan is part of an arrangement which involves an ESOP or a CODA, neither of these portions of the program -- the ESOP or the CODA -- may be integrated. Also, if a plan fails to meet the specific requirements of Section 401(l), it may still be able to qualify if it can pass the nondiscrimination tests of Section 401(a)(4) of the IRC.

8.3.3.   Section 415 Limitations

As noted earlier, a money purchase plan is considered to be a defined contribution plan for purposes of the limitations of Section 415. Thus, the annual additions to an employee's account (employer and employee contributions plus any reallocated forfeitures) cannot exceed the lesser of: (1) $30,000 (indexed to increase with changes in the CPI when the defined benefit plan dollar limitation reaches $120,000); or (2) 25 percent of compensation. Further, the combined Section 415 limitation can become applicable if the employer also maintains a defined benefit plan.[9]

8.3.4.   Joint and Survivor Requirements

The joint and survivor requirements (both pre- and post-retirement) that apply to defined benefit plans apply equally as well to money purchase plans. It should be noted that other forms of defined contribution plans are exempted from these requirements if the employee's spouse is beneficiary for 100 percent of the employee's account balance and if the employee does not elect an annuity distribution. This exemption, however, is not available to money purchase plans.

8.3.5.   Before-Tax Contributions

The CODA feature of Section 401(k) of the IRC, which permit employees to make elective deferrals and thus make before-tax contributions, is not

---

[9]The Section 415 limitations are discussed in Chapter 6.

available to money purchase plans. These elective deferral contributions can be made only in conjunction with profit sharing and stock bonus plans and savings plans that are qualified as profit sharing plans. If a savings plan is qualified as a money purchase pension plan, as is occasionally the case, the elective deferral option will not be available (nor will the plan be able to permit in-service withdrawals).

8.3.6.   Forfeitures

The amounts forfeited when an employee terminates employment with less than full vesting can be applied in two ways under a money purchase plan. These amounts can be used to reduce employer contributions or they can be reallocated among the remaining employees.

8.3.7.   Employer Securities

Defined benefit plans are generally prohibited from having more than 10 percent of their assets invested in qualifying employer securities. Profit sharing and stock bonus plans, on the other hand, are permitted to invest up to 100 percent of their assets in qualifying employer securities if the plans so provide. Money purchase plans, even though they are defined contribution plans, are subject to the same 10 percent limitation that applies to defined benefit plans.[10]

8.3.8.   In-Service Distributions

As noted in earlier discussion, a money purchase plan, since it is a pension plan, is not permitted to make distributions to employees on an in-service basis. In general, these plans can make distributions only in the event of termination of employment (including retirement, death and disability). They may also make distributions upon termination of the plan. In this regard, they differ significantly from other types of defined contribution arrangements which are qualified as profit sharing or stock bonus plans.

---

[10]A limited grandfathering provision was provided for money purchase plans in existence on September 2, 1974 and which then provided for investing more than 10 percent of their assets in employer securities.

8.3.9. Minimum Funding Standards

Because a money purchase plan is, in fact, a pension plan, it is subject to the minimum funding requirements of the IRC. While an actuarial valuation is not required, the plan must maintain a minimum funding standard account. The operation of this account is much simpler than is the case with a defined benefit plan since, for example, there is no amortization of liabilities or funding gains and losses. Nevertheless, the account must be maintained and will be charged each year with the amount of the contribution that is required to be made under the plan. In effect, there is no flexibility in meeting this requirement and, in normal circumstances (absent a funding waiver), the required contribution must be made in full each year. As a result, the money purchase plan can be viewed as being the most rigid of all plans in terms of funding flexibility.

8.3.10. Deduction Limits

There are no specific deduction limits, as such, for money purchase plans. The general concept that the amount contributed must represent reasonable compensation applies, of course, and there is a practical limit in that Section 415 stipulates that the maximum annual addition to an employee's account cannot exceed 25 percent of pay. Also, if another plan or plans exist, there would be a maximum combined deductible limit for all plans of 25 percent of covered payroll.

QUESTIONS FOR REVIEW

1. What characteristic of a money purchase plan distinguishes it from other defined contribution plans?
2. What are the factors that ultimately influence the amount of retirement benefit an employee might receive under a money purchase pension plan?
3. Describe the ACP test that applies to a money purchase plan that requires employee contributions.
4. Describe the Section 415 limitations that apply to money purchase plans.
5. What limitations apply to the investment of plan assets in employer securities under a money purchase plan?
6. What deduction limits apply to a money purchase plan? Alone and in conjunction with another qualified plan?

7.   Are money purchase plans subject to the minimum funding standards of the tax law? Why or why not?

QUESTIONS FOR DISCUSSION

1.   Describe the permitted disparity limitations that apply to a money purchase plan that is integrated with Social Security benefits.

2.   The text states that money purchase plans are, in a sense, hybrids. Describe the ways in which money purchase plans are sometimes treated in much the same fashion as defined benefit pension plans, and the ways in which they are sometimes treated as defined contribution plans.   What reasons exist for these differences in treatment?

3.   Evaluate the efficiency of a money purchase plan as an employer's primary vehicle for providing retirement benefits.

9. Profit Sharing Plans

Profit sharing plans constitute an important component in the overall structure of employee benefit programs in the United States. The requirements imposed by ERISA as to minimum funding and employer liabilities for plan terminations have resulted in a growing interest in individual-account retirement programs. Profit sharing and thrift plans have considerable appeal in this regard since they embody the individual account concept without imposing any fixed commitment on employers to provide any specific level of benefits. Thus, one can expect to see greater use of profit sharing plans in lieu of pension plans or of a basic pension benefit plus a supplemental savings or profit sharing program.

9.1. DEFINITION OF PROFIT SHARING

Many definitions of profit sharing have been suggested. One broad concept is that profit sharing is a plan in which the company's contributions are based upon business profits, regardless of whether the benefit payments are made in cash, are deferred, or are a combination of the two. This definition suggests three basic profit sharing plan approaches, which may be defined as follows: (1) current (cash) -- profits are paid directly to employees in cash, check, or stock as soon as profits are determined (for example, monthly, quarterly, semiannually, or annually); (2) deferred -- profits are credited to employee accounts to be paid at retirement or other stated dates or circumstances (for example, disability, death, severance, or under withdrawal provisions); and (3) combination -- part of the profit is paid out currently in cash and part is deferred. This can take place under one plan with both current and deferred features or under two separate plans -- one cash and the other deferred, covering, by and large, the same employee groups.

The definition of a profit sharing plan as set forth in federal income tax regulations is as follows:

> A profit sharing plan is a plan established and maintained by an employer to provide for the participation in his profits by his employees or their beneficiaries. The plan must provide a definite predetermined formula for allocating the contributions made to the plan among the participants and for distributing the funds accumulated under the plan after a fixed number of years, the attainment of a stated age, or upon the prior occurrence of some event such as layoff, illness, disability, retirement, death, or severance of employment.[1]

Qualification of profit sharing plans for tax exemption under Section 401 of the Internal Revenue Code, then, is restricted to deferred or combination type plans. Current or cash profit sharing plans, therefore, are not treated in this chapter. Also, combination cash or deferred plans, because of the unique requirements of federal tax law that apply to such plans, are treated separately in Chapter 12. Thus, this chapter relates only to tax-qualified deferred profit sharing plans.

9.2.   QUALIFICATION REQUIREMENTS

The qualification requirements for profit sharing plans are, for the most part, identical to those applicable to pension plans -- a detailed discussion of which can be found in Chapters 5 and 6. However, it is appropriate in this chapter to discuss these requirements in terms of their application specifically to profit sharing plans. This discussion relates only to plans that are not top heavy. The special requirements applicable to top-heavy plans are covered in Chapter 6.

9.2.1.   Coverage Requirements

To qualify, a profit sharing plan must be for the exclusive benefit of employees or their beneficiaries. Therefore, a plan will not qualify if the coverage requirements result in discrimination in favor of the highly compensated employees--i.e., the plan must meet the coverage requirements of Section 410(b) of the IRC. Restriction of coverage by type of employment (for example, salaried employees, hourly employees, sales representatives) is permitted, provided that such coverage requirements do not result in the prohibited discrimination.

---

[1]Reg. 1.401(b)(1)(ii).

Relatively few profit sharing plans impose a minimum age requirement, but practically all profit sharing plans specify a service requirement as a condition for participation in the plan. The Code permits the use of a minimum age of up to 21 and a service requirement of up to one year (two years if the plan provides for full and immediate vesting and is not a cash or deferred arrangement).

Apart from the requirements of the Code, eligibility requirements under profit sharing plans generally tend to be less restrictive than those usually found under pension plans. One reason for this is that profit sharing plans often are established to provide a direct incentive for employees to increase productivity and reduce operating costs. If this is the primary objective of the plan, it is only logical that few restrictions on participation be imposed. Another reason is that liberal eligibility requirements may produce relatively favorable results for key employees since the nonvested accumulations of terminating employees may be reallocated among remaining participants.

9.2.2.   Contribution Requirements

The Internal Revenue Code does not require, as a condition for qualification, that a profit sharing plan include a definite predetermined contribution formula. And, for plan years beginning after December 31, 1985, it is no longer necessary that contributions be based on profits. In the absence of such a formula, however, the regulations require that "substantial and recurring" contributions must be made if the requirement of plan permanency is to be met.

Contributions under a profit sharing plan may be made on a discretionary basis (for example, as determined annually by the board of directors of the company) or in accordance with a definite predetermined formula. The discretionary approach offers the advantage of contribution flexibility. The board of directors can adjust contributions in view of the firm's current financial position and capital needs. Also, the discretionary basis precludes the possibility that contribution payments will exceed the maximum amount currently deductible for federal income tax purposes (to be discussed later in this chapter). If the amount of contribution is discretionary, the plan often imposes certain minimums and maximums. For example, the plan may provide that contributions cannot exceed 15 percent of profits, but it is discretionary up to that limit, or 10 to 30 percent of profits -- the percentage to be determined by a board of directors, or as discretionary, but as approximately 25 percent of profits before taxes.

There are advantages in using a definite predetermined formula. A definite formula promotes increased employee morale and feelings of security. Without a definite formula, employees may feel that they cannot count on a share of what they have helped to produce.

Whether a definite formula or a discretionary contribution approach is used, management still must determine the extent to which employees are to directly or indirectly share in the firm's profits. In arriving at this decision, management must take into account such factors as the objectives of the plan, the nature of the firm's business, the pattern of profits, and the age and service composition of the employee group. Obviously, a good deal more thought must be given to this matter if a definite contribution formula is used.

The contribution commitment under definite formula plans generally is expressed as a fixed percentage or a sliding scale of percentages of profits. The specified percentages usually are applied to profits before taxes, although the base of after-tax profits is also permitted. The sliding scale formulas provide for higher percentage contributions for higher levels of profits. A percentage of compensation formula also can be used.

Whether a definite formula or discretionary basis is used, the plan usually specifies some limitation on the amount of annual contribution payable. One reason is to give priority to a minimum rate of return on capital for stockholders. Limitations on contribution payments can be expressed in several different ways. For example, the plan may provide that no contribution will be made in years in which dividend payments are less than a specified amount, or unless aggregate profits exceed a stated amount, or if profits are less than a given percentage of the firm's capital funds. Many plans also impose the limitation that contributions in any one year cannot exceed the maximum amount deductible for federal income tax purposes.

9.2.3. Employee Contributions

It is conceptually illogical to *require* employee contributions under profit sharing plans. Furthermore, in those plans that require employee contributions, the employer's contribution usually is based on the amount of the employee's contribution. For these reasons, contributory plans are generally referred to as thrift or savings plans to distinguish them from the traditional profit sharing plans. For a complete discussion of these plans, see Chapters 10 and 12.

Even though employee contributions usually are not required under profit sharing plans, it is quite common to permit them on a "voluntary" basis, with employees being given this option regardless of the level of employer contributions involved. When allowed, these voluntary contributions may be made as "elective deferrals" under Section 401(k) of the IRC or as contributions from after-tax income. If made as elective deferrals, the plan must meet the ADP test requirements of Section 401(k); if made as after-tax contributions, the plan must meet the ACP test of Section 401(m).

9.2.4.   Allocations To Employee Accounts

It was noted above that the Internal Revenue Service does not require a plan to include a definite contribution formula as a condition for qualification. However, it is necessary that the plan include a definite allocation formula to become qualified. Since contributions to the plan are generally based on profits, a method or formula is needed to determine the amount to be credited to each participant's account.

The employer must decide the basis upon which the contributions to the plan are to be divided among the various participants. The allocation of contributions to the account of each participant is usually made on the basis of compensation or a combination of compensation and service. If compensation is used, then allocations are made on the basis of the proportion of each participant's compensation to the total compensation of all participants. For example, if employee A earns $10,000 a year and the total annual compensation for all participants is $200,000, A will be credited with 5 percent of the employer's total annual contributions. Under a formula that reflects both compensation and service, a unit of credit might, for example, be given for each year of service and an additional unit for each $100 of compensation. With 20 years of service, employee A would have 20 units of service and 100 units for compensation of $10,000 a year. Employee A's share of contributions will be determined, therefore, by the fraction of 120 over the total number of units similarly calculated for all participants.

The Internal Revenue Service requires a definite allocation formula in qualified plans so that it may determine whether contributions are shared in a nondiscriminatory manner. The plan must also meet the nondiscrimination requirements of Section 401(a)(4) of the IRC. In general, these requirements will be passed if the plan allocates contributions on the basis of a uniform percentage of pay, and if the same vesting schedule and years of service definition apply to all participants. (For purposes of this requirement, an integrated allocation formula that meets the permitted disparity requirements of Section 401(1) will be considered to have a uniform percentage allocation formula.) If the allocation formula is weighted for age and/or service and for units of pay that do not exceed $200, the plan will meet the nondiscrimination requirements if the average of the allocation rates for HCEs does not exceed the average of the allocation rates for the NHCEs. Otherwise, the plan will have to meet the testing requirements of Section 401(a)(4). The most popular allocation formulas are those based on compensation, although many plans use a combination of compensation and years of service.

The allocation formula is used to determine the employee's share of contributions for accounting or record-keeping purposes. The contribution dollars are not segregated on behalf of each participant. Contributions are received, administered, and invested by the trustee as unallocated assets. The balance in each participant's account represents the participant's share at that moment of the assets of the fund. An exception is the case where the trust permits each participant's account to be invested in "earmarked" investments. Whether the participant is currently entitled to all or a part of the money credited to his or her account depends upon the provisions of the plan.

Finally, it should be noted that the allocation of employer contributions is subject to the contribution and benefit limitations of the IRC. These limits are described in Chapter 6.

Under many profit sharing plans, there may be some forfeited amounts when employees terminate with less than full vesting. These forfeitures may be used to reduce employer contributions. More typically, in profit sharing plans, they are reallocated among remaining participants. These reallocations generally are based on the pay of each remaining participant in relation to the total of pay of all remaining participants. The IRS will not permit reallocations on the basis of the account balances of the remaining participants if such a procedure would produce discrimination in favor of HCEs. However, the investment income of a profit sharing plan may be allocated on the basis of account balances. Thus, it is possible to have different allocation formulas for contributions, forfeitures, and investment income.

9.2.5.   Integration with Social Security

As mentioned earlier, profit sharing plans seldom are integrated with social security benefits. However, these plans can be integrated with social security benefits, subject to IRC requirements for defined contribution plans plus the further restriction that the integrated portion cannot be withdrawn.[2] Also all or any portion of a plan that consists of a CODA may not be integrated. It should be noted that the maximum deductible amount that can be allocated to each participant's account in any one year pertains to the aggregate of employer contributions and forfeitures of nonvested accumulations during the year. In nonintegrated profit sharing plans, the

---

[2]The IRC requirements for integrated defined contribution plans are described in Chapter 8.

maximum deductible annual contribution is 15 percent of compensation. Furthermore, if the plan is not integrated, forfeitures may be reallocated among remaining participants without reducing the 15 percent maximum. Lastly, if an employer has integrated both its pension and profit sharing plans covering any of the same employees, the integration under both plans cannot exceed 100 percent of the integration capability of a single plan. The objective of this requirement is to avoid the discrimination in favor of HCEs that would otherwise result.

9.2.6. Provision for Distributions

As indicated earlier, the definition of profit sharing in the regulations permits distributions "after a fixed number of years, the attainment of a stated age, or upon the prior occurrence of some event such as layoff, illness, disability, retirement, death, or severance of employment."

The primary objective of many deferred profit sharing plans is to permit the employee to build up an equity in the fund to enhance his or her economic security after retirement. The law requires that the accumulations credited to the employee's account vest in full at normal retirement age, regardless of the employee's length of service. Most plans also fully vest the amounts credited to the employee upon death, while a lesser but still significant number of plans provide full and immediate vesting upon the occurrence of total and permanent disability.

Whether an employee is entitled to a distribution from the fund upon voluntary termination of employment or upon being laid off depends upon the vesting provisions of the plan. Of course, if the plan is contributory, the employee is always entitled, at a minimum, to a return of the benefit attributable to his or her contributions upon death, total and permanent disability, or severance of employment.

The value of employer-provided contributions under a deferred profit sharing plan also must vest upon severance of employment in accordance with the requirements of the Code. Thus, the plan must satisfy one of the two alternative vesting schedules.[3]

Some plans also permit participants to withdraw a portion of their vested benefits in the plan prior to separation of employment.[4] The regulations permit distributions from a qualified profit sharing plan "after a fixed number of years." The Internal Revenue Service has interpreted this to mean that accumulations cannot be distributed in less than two years. In

---

[3]See Chapter 6 for a full discussion of these minimum vesting requirements.

[4]Contributions made on an elective deferral basis are subject to the withdrawal restrictions described in Chapter 12.

other words, if contributions have been credited to an employee's account for three years, he or she can withdraw an amount equal to the first year's contribution and the investment income credited in that year (assuming that the plan permits such withdrawals). The right to withdraw may be restricted to employee contributions, or it may apply to the vested portion of accumulations attributable to employer contributions. Of course, the participant must report the withdrawn amount as taxable income in the year in which it is received (except to the extent it is considered to be a return of the employee's own contributions), and such amount will be taxable as ordinary income. Moreover, an additional tax of 10 percent of the taxable portion of the distribution could be assessed on distributions before the participant reaches age $59\frac{1}{2}$. Although a withdrawal provision may be desirable in a plan, care should be exercised, since a provision that is too liberal could result in defeating the long-term savings objective of the plan. Since the withdrawals are now prevalent in savings plans (and more complex), they are discussed at greater length in Chapter 10.

Loan provisions also are found in some deferred profit sharing plans. Under a loan provision, a participant generally is entitled to borrow up to a specified percentage (50 percent, for example) of the vested portion of his or her account (including any employee contributions). The loan provision has an advantage over a withdrawal provision in that repayment of the loan will permit achievement of the objective of a long-term program geared toward retirement. However, some employers may prefer the withdrawal provision, since such a provision might help in avoiding possible employee dissatisfaction that could result from the feeling that they must pay interest on the use of their "own" money. The loan provision is also advantageous in that, if IRS requirements are met, the sums borrowed are not subject to federal income tax. However, the interest payments are no longer deductible for federal income tax purposes. The law requires that loans be available to all participants on a reasonably equivalent basis and that a loan not be made available to HCEs in a percentage greater than that made available to other employees. The law also requires that the loan bear a reasonable rate of interest, be adequately secured, and be made only by the plan (and not by a third party, such as a bank, with the employee's account balance as security). If the loan provision meets the requirements of the Department of Labor (DOL) and the IRS, the loan will be exempted from the prohibited transactions provisions of ERISA and the IRC. If a loan is made and is not exempted, this could constitute a prohibited transaction and could be in violation of the legal requirement that a plan prohibit assignments and alienations; this could result in a plan disqualification.

A loan to an employee will be treated as a taxable distribution unless certain requirements are met. These requirements involve the amount of the loan (or accumulated loans) and the time period for repayment. The maximum amounts that can be borrowed without being considered a distribution depend upon the amount of the employee's vested interest in his or her account balance. If it is: (1) $10,000 or less, the entire vested interest is available; (2) between $10,000 and $20,000, $10,000 is available; (3) between $20,000 and $100,000, 50 percent of the vested interest is available; or (4) $100,000 or more, $50,000 is available. The $50,000 limitation on loans from qualified plans is reduced by the excess of the highest outstanding loan balance during the preceding one-year period over the outstanding balance on the date a new loan is made.[5]

As to the time period for repayment, the loan, by its terms, must be repaid within five years; substantially level amortization of the loan is required, with payments made at least quarterly. If the loan is used to acquire a dwelling unit (which is to be used as a principal residence of the participant) and meets the amount limitation, the five-year time limit does not apply.

9.2.7.   Investment Options

It is possible for the assets of a profit sharing plan to be invested in a single fund, with all employees sharing proportionately in the investment gains and losses of that fund. And, in fact, some plans are designed and operated in this fashion. Most plans, however, allow employees to direct the investment of their accounts and to choose from among several different investment options. These options typically include two or more of the following: a guaranteed interest contract or arrangement, a corporate bond or fixed income fund, a government bond fund, one or more equity funds (with varying degrees of risk), and an employer stock fund. Larger employers might have even more funds to choose from and might include, for example, a real estate fund. Some employers make these choices available by arranging for choice between several of the funds offered by an investment company.

A major reason for permitting these choices is to limit the employer's fiduciary responsibility. Statutory relief from this liability can be obtained by complying with proposed regulations issued by the DOL. In general, these regulations require that a plan offer at least three diversified categories of investment with materially different risk and return characteristics, and that participants have the right to change investments at

---

[5]The Department of Labor has taken the position that a loan cannot exceed 50% of the employee's vested account balance. Because of this conflict between the DOL and the IRS, most plans limit this loan to 50% of the vested account balance and ignore the $10,000 minimum.

least quarterly -- more often if needed because of the volatility of a particular fund. Regulatory liability protection can be afforded to employer stock if the shares are publicly traded in a recognized market and if the plan also offers the three required options; however, all purchases, sales, voting and related share activities must be implemented confidentially through a fiduciary who is independent of the employer. It should be noted that failure to comply with the DOL regulations does not mean that fiduciaries are automatically liable -- it simply means that the regulatory safe harbor for liability attributable to participants' investment choices is not available. Also, compliance does not relieve the employer from responsibility for ensuring that the investments are prudent and properly diversified.

It should also be noted that if employer stock is an investment and can be purchased with employee contributions, the requirements of the SEC will have to be met. These requirements are discussed in Chapter 7.

A plan can also be written to permit employees to invest part of their account balances in life and health insurance. When this is done, and when a participant is investing funds that have accumulated for less than two years, additional IRS requirements must be met. These requirements are that such amounts, when used to purchase life or health insurance, must be "incidental." The IRS has defined incidental as follows:

1.   If only ordinary life insurance contracts are purchased, the aggregate premiums in the case of each participant must be less than one half the total contributions and forfeitures allocated to his or her account.
2.   If only accident and health insurance contracts are purchased, the payments for premiums may not exceed 25 percent of the funds allocated to the employee's account.
3.   If both ordinary life and accident and health insurance contracts are purchased, the amount spent for the accident and health premiums plus one half of the amount spent for the ordinary life insurance premiums may not, together, exceed 25 percent of the funds allocated to the employee's account.

In addition, the purchase of an ordinary life insurance contract will be incidental only if the plan requires the trustee to convert the entire value of the life insurance contract at or before retirement into cash, or to provide periodic income so that no portion of such value may be used to continue life insurance protection beyond retirement, or to distribute the contract to the participant.

9.2.8.   Other Requirements

Qualified profit sharing plans, like qualified pension plans, must meet the requirements of the IRC. Thus, they must be in writing, permanent, communicated to employees, and must preclude diversion or recapture by the employer of contributions to the plan. A qualified profit sharing plan must treat service as required by ERISA, must permit employees to buy back their benefits under stated conditions, and must include a number of other features such as a prohibition against assignments (with the exception of certain specified events), the protection of an employee's benefits in the event of plan merger or consolidation, and the payment of benefits by prescribed times. The plan must also comply with the top-heavy provisions of the law.

The requirement that a qualified pension plan provide definitely determinable benefits obviously does not apply in the case of qualified profit sharing plans. Also, certain other provisions of ERISA are not applicable to qualified profit sharing plans -- for example, the minimum funding standards and the plan termination insurance requirements.

9.3.   LIMITS ON DEDUCTIBILITY OF EMPLOYER CONTRIBUTIONS

The limits on the deductibility of employer contributions to a profit sharing plan are set forth in Section 404 of the IRC.

For profit sharing plans, the maximum deductible contribution is equal to 15 percent of the compensation paid or otherwise accrued during the employer's taxable year to all covered employees.[6] Carryover provisions apply in profit sharing plans when the contribution in one taxable year is greater than the deductible limit for such taxable year. This type of carry-over is called a "contribution carryover." Thus, if a contribution is made in a given year in excess of the allowable deduction for such year, the employer will be allowed to take a deduction for such excess payment in a succeeding taxable year if it does not bring the deduction for the succeeding year to over 15 percent of the participating payroll for such succeeding year. However, any excess contribution is subject to a 10 percent penalty tax.

---

[6]If the contribution to the profit sharing plan is less than this amount, the difference between the amount actually paid in and the 15 percent limit (called a "credit carryover") can be contributed and deducted in succeeding years, but only if the carryover was accumulated before 1987. However, the credit carryover contribution in any later year cannot exceed 15 percent of the compensation paid or otherwise accrued during such later year. Also, there is an overall annual limitation when a credit carryover is involved. This overall limit is 25 percent of current covered payroll.

If both a pension plan (defined benefit or money purchase) and a profit sharing plan exist, with overlapping payrolls, the total amount deductible in any taxable year under both plans cannot exceed 25 percent of the compensation paid or accrued to covered employees for that year.[7] When excess payments are made in any taxable year, the excess may be carried forward to succeeding taxable years, subject to the limitation that the total amount deducted for such succeeding taxable year (including the deduction for the current contribution) cannot exceed 25 percent of the compensation paid or accrued for such subsequent year.

The 25 percent limitation does not eliminate the requirement that a currently deductible profit sharing contribution must not exceed 15 percent of the payroll of the participating employees and that a currently deductible pension contribution must not exceed the amount that would have been the limit had only a pension plan been in effect.

9.4.   TAXATION OF DISTRIBUTIONS

The taxation of distributions from a qualified profit sharing plan is identical to the tax treatment of distributions from a qualified pension plan, discussed in detail in Chapter 23. However, the tax treatment of distributions of securities of the employer should be mentioned here because investing a portion of trust assets in the securities of the employer is a common practice under profit sharing plans. Securities of the employer include stocks, bonds, and debentures issued by the employer's parent or subsidiary corporations. If a total distribution (defined in Chapter 23) of the employee's account is made under conditions qualifying for favorable tax treatment, the value of the securities of the employer for the purpose of determining the employee's gain is the lower of the cost to the trust or the fair market value of the securities. In other words, the employee is not taxed at the time of distribution on the unrealized appreciation unless he or she so elects.[8] However, the unrealized appreciation is taxed as ordinary income when sold. If the employee elects to defer taxation of this amount, this value then becomes the employee's cost basis should the securities be sold at a later date. If the securities of the employer are included in a distribution not subject to favorable tax treatment, only the portion of the securities

---

[7]This 25 percent limit will be increased to the extent larger contributions are required by the Code's minimum funding standards, as described in Chapter 16.

[8]Even though not subject to regular tax in the year of distribution, the net unrealized appreciation would be taken into account for purposes of the excess distribution tax. See Chapter 23.

attributable to employee contributions can be valued on the basis of cost to the trust.

9.5.   TERMINATION OF PLAN

Although a qualified profit sharing plan must be permanent, the Internal Revenue Service does permit inclusion of a provision giving the employer the right to amend or terminate the plan. However, if the vesting schedule is changed, any participant with at least three years of service must be given the election to remain under the preamendment vesting schedule. If the plan is terminated for reasons other than "business necessity" within a few years after its inception, this action will be considered by the Service as evidence that the plan, from its inception, was not a bona fide program for the exclusive benefit of employees in general. If business necessity exists, the employer may terminate the plan without adverse tax consequences.

If a plan is terminated, all assets in the fund are vested immediately in plan participants. Since all plan assets are allocated to specific participants, no problem exists regarding any order of priorities in the distribution of the fund. Each participant is entitled to the balance in his or her account.

Upon termination of the plan, the trustees will determine, in accordance with plan provisions, a method of distributing the plan assets. The participants' shares may be distributed in a lump sum, distributed in installments over a period of years, or used to purchase immediate or deferred annuities (either fixed or variable), or the assets may be distributed in kind.

QUESTIONS FOR REVIEW

1. What are the typical participation requirements found in a profit sharing plan? Explain.
2. What might explain why profit sharing plan participation requirements are generally less restrictive than those found in pension plans?
3. What contribution requirements are imposed by the IRC on profit sharing plans?
4. What advantages can be ascribed to a definite predetermined contribution formula for a profit sharing plan?
5. Describe a common approach for allocating employer contributions that recognizes both compensation and length of service.
6. What usually happens to forfeited amounts of nonvested contributions in a profit sharing plan? Explain.

7. Is a profit sharing plan obligated to permit participants to withdraw a portion of their vested benefits prior to separation from employment? Explain.
8. Explain a typical loan provision that may be included in a profit sharing plan.
9. Can a qualified profit sharing plan be terminated? Explain.
10. What is meant by an incidental insurance benefit under a profit sharing plan?

QUESTIONS FOR DISCUSSION

1. Discuss the conditions under which an employer may desire to establish a profit sharing plan.
2. Assume that an employer has had a profit sharing plan for several years and that the reaction of the employees toward the plan has been unsatisfactory. Discuss the plan design flexibility available for a profit sharing plan that may be utilized by the employer to improve the employees' reaction without increasing the employer's annual cost.
3. Assume that a publicly held firm decides to sponsor a profit sharing plan that will incorporate a definite predetermined contribution formula. Discuss how you would establish such a formula, keeping in mind the need to be equitable to stockholders, bondholders, and employees.

10. Savings Plans

Savings plans have become an increasingly popular form of employee benefit. Having started with the large petroleum companies, they have spread gradually to many corporations in a number of other industries. Most of the major companies in manufacturing and service industries now have such plans for their employees.

Unlike other employee benefit plans, which usually are designed with a specific purpose or objective in mind, savings plans generally meet a number of objectives and provide for the payment of benefits under several different contingencies. From an employer's viewpoint, they offer most of the advantages of profit sharing plans, but at a considerably lower cost. As a result, many employers have instituted savings plans to provide relatively low-cost supplemental benefits in the event of the retirement, death, or disability of an employee, as well as to provide meaningful benefits during active employment. Further they may be used to provide employees with some protection against the erosive effects of post-retirement inflation. It generally is recognized, however, that because of relatively lower contribution levels, savings plans do not have the same incentive value for employees as do profit sharing plans.

Under federal tax law, a savings plan may achieve a qualified status and, as a result, the employer and employees may obtain the favorable tax benefits that flow from having such a plan. For this purpose, savings plans generally are designed to meet the qualification requirements applicable to profit sharing plans.[1] Thus, with the exception of employee and employer contribution patterns, savings plans possess most of the general

---

[1] A contributory money purchase pension plan also could be regarded as a savings plan, particularly if it is supplemental in nature. However, such plans are relatively uncommon since they would not permit employees to withdraw funds prior to termination of employment. The discussion in this chapter relates only to savings plans that are tax qualified as profit sharing plans.

characteristics of deferred profit sharing plans.   The significant characteristics of savings plans are as follows:

1. Employee participation in the plan is voluntary and, to participate, an employee must agree to make contributions.

2. An employee usually has the option of determining the level of his or her contributions -- that is, the employee may choose to make contributions at the minimum or maximum level set by the plan or at permitted intermediate levels.

3. Employer contributions usually match or are equal to some fraction of the contributions made by employees up to a specified level. (Employer contributions sometimes are made in full or in part by means of a profit sharing formula or on a discretionary basis; however, in most savings plans the employer contributes a fixed percentage of employee contributions.)

4. Both employer and employee contributions generally are made to a trust fund.

5. Assets of the trust are usually invested in one or more investment funds, with the employee frequently having the option of choosing how his or her own contributions (and sometimes the employer contributions on the employee's behalf) will be invested. In some plans, employer contributions are invested automatically in securities of the employer, with the employee having an investment option only for his or her own contributions.

6. An employee's account is generally paid to the employee (or on behalf of the employee) in the event of retirement, death, disability, or termination of employment. Benefits on termination of employment are, of course, limited to the employee's vested interest. However, savings plans usually have relatively liberal vesting provisions.

7. Most savings plans permit an employee, during active employment, to withdraw the value of employee contributions as well as all or part of the employee's vested interest in employer contributions. Such withdrawals, however, are often subject to some form of penalty (such as a period of suspended participation). Some plans limit withdrawals to those made for specific financial needs such as those associated with illness, the purchase of a home, college education, and the like.[2]

The balance of this chapter discusses the various objectives that may be met by savings plans, as well as their basic features.

---

[2] Withdrawals could be subject to an additional 10 percent tax if considered to be an early distribution.

10.1.   SAVINGS PLAN OBJECTIVES

As noted earlier, a savings plan may serve a number of different objectives. It is important, when designing such a plan, to establish those objectives that are of paramount importance to the employer. This is necessary since the design of the plan will be influenced by the objectives it is to serve. For example, if a major objective of a particular plan is to provide supplemental retirement income, it is quite likely that withdrawal privileges, if permitted at all, will be relatively restricted; otherwise, an employee could defeat the employer's basic objective by making substantial withdrawals from his or her account prior to retirement.

Savings plans usually serve one or more of the following objectives:

1.   To attract and retain employees.
2.   To provide deferred compensation on an advantageous tax basis.
3.   To encourage employee thrift and savings.
4.   To provide benefits to supplement other employee benefit plans in the event of illness, disability, death, retirement, or termination of employment.
5.   To accumulate funds for other purposes.
6.   To foster a greater sense of company identification through the purchase of company securities.

Each of these objectives and its influence on plan design is discussed below.

10.1.1. Attracting and Retaining Employees

Generally speaking, most employee benefit plans serve the broad purpose of attracting and retaining employees. In that sense, then, savings plans are the same as other benefit programs. However, savings plans (and profit sharing plans) have a somewhat greater appeal to younger employees, since they offer immediate and tangible benefits during the early years of employment. For this reason, savings plans can be particularly effective in attracting new employees.

Where this is a primary objective of a savings plan, it generally would indicate that the plan should be designed with minimum eligibility requirements, a definite formula for determining employer contributions, relatively generous benefits, and liberal vesting requirements.

10.1.2. Deferred Compensation

As noted earlier, a savings plan, if it meets the necessary requirements, may be considered a qualified plan under federal tax law. Employer contributions made on behalf of the employee are not taxable (even though the employee has a vested right to such contributions) until they are distributed. Moreover, investment income earned on both employer and employee contributions qualifies for the same deferred tax treatment. Distributions to an employee may be taxed at a relatively low rate, particularly when they begin after age 59½. For these reasons, a significant objective of many savings plans is to provide tax-deferred compensation.

Where deferred compensation is a key objective, the plan generally is designed to permit maximum employer and employee contributions.

10.1.3. Employee Savings

Even though they are called savings plans, the specific objective of encouraging employees to save is not always a primary consideration in the establishment of such a plan. Nevertheless, many employers believe that employees should plan on meeting at least part of their own economic security needs without relying fully on government and employer-provided benefits. A savings plan is a most efficient vehicle in meeting such an objective.

A savings plan to further such an objective is generally designed with liberal eligibility requirements and with maximum flexibility in terms of the levels at which an employee may contribute. The plan also may permit employees to contribute additional amounts (without a matching employer contribution) up to the maximum permitted by federal tax law. Also, to overcome any reluctance on the part of an employee to tie up savings until some future event such as retirement, death, or termination of employment, the plan probably should permit loans and, possibly, withdrawals during active employment -- at least to the extent of the employee's own after-tax contributions.

10.1.4. Supplemental Benefits

The vested portion of an employee's account under a savings plan is paid to the employee (or on behalf of the employee) in the event of retirement, death, disability, or termination of employment. As a result, a savings plan can provide meaningful benefits to supplement an employer's other benefit plans that deal with these contingencies. It is common for an employer to adopt a savings plan for the specific purpose of supplementing another such plan, rather than making direct improvements in the plan itself. For example, an employer might feel that the level of benefits provided under its pension plan is not adequate. Rather than improving the benefit formula under its retirement plan, the employer might seek to remedy the inadequacy of the retirement plan by instituting a savings plan. The two plans together could meet the employer's objectives in terms of total retirement income and, at the same time, create the additional advantages that could accrue from the savings plan itself.

If supplementing other employee benefit plans is an important objective of a savings plan, this will have a material influence on the design of the plan as it relates to employer contributions. Also, this objective generally suggests that employees be given limited, if any, withdrawal privileges during active employment, since to do otherwise could defeat a major plan objective.

10.1.5. Company Identification

It is quite possible, in the case of a publicly held corporation, that a major objective of instituting a savings plan might be to promote a greater sense of company identification by having employees become corporate shareholders. While this also may be accomplished with other plans, a savings plan under which part of the assets is invested in employer securities can assist in achieving this employer objective. On occasion, the assets of a savings plan of a privately held firm are invested in the same fashion; however, this is relatively uncommon.

If assets are to be invested in employer securities, a common plan provision is to require that all employer contributions be invested in this manner, while employees have the option of having their own contributions invested in fixed income or equity investments. Employees are sometimes given the option of having their own contributions invested in employer securities. Some plans, rather than mandating that employer contributions be invested in employer securities, give the employee complete investment options for both employer and employee contributions.

10.2. BASIC FEATURES

The preceding discussion has touched generally upon the basic features of savings plans. The balance of this chapter discusses each of the following major plan provisions in greater detail: eligibility requirements, employee contributions, employer contributions, allocation to employee accounts, investment of funds, vesting, withdrawals and loans, and the distribution of benefits.   This material relates primarily to plans where employee contributions are made on an after-tax basis.   Savings plans where employees contribute by way of salary reduction -- so-called Section 401(k) plans or CODAs -- are discussed in Chapter 12.   Also, this chapter deals only with plans that are not top heavy. The special requirements applicable to top-heavy plans are discussed in Chapter 6.

10.2.1. Eligibility Requirements

Savings plans are subject to the same requirements of the IRC as are pension and profit sharing plans. Typically, an employee will be required to meet some minimum service requirement and to have attained some minimum age before being given the opportunity to join the plan. Under tax law, the service requirement cannot exceed one year (two years if the plan provides for full and immediate vesting), and the minimum age cannot be higher than 21.

It is also possible to use other eligibility requirements such as an employment classification. Such requirements, however, are relatively rare in savings plans.

If a savings plan is to be considered a qualified plan under federal tax law, it must not discriminate in favor of HCEs.   Thus, the eligibility requirements chosen must not result in discrimination in favor of this group and the plan must meet the coverage requirements of Section 410(b) of the IRC.

10.2.2. Nondiscrimination Requirements

The same nondiscrimination tests that apply to elective deferrals under cash or deferred arrangements (CODAs) are applied to employee after-tax contributions and employer matching contributions to a savings plan. Although these tests are described in considerable detail in Chapter 12, the following description provides a brief summary of the operation of the average contribution percentage (ACP) test in general and the specific manner in which it is applied to a savings plan.

The actual contribution percentage for HCEs cannot exceed the greater of (1) 125 percent of the actual contribution percentage for all other eligible employees, or (2) the lesser of 200 percent of the actual contribution percentage for all other eligible employees, or such contribution percentage plus two percentage points. The actual contribution percentage for a group of employees is the average of the contribution ratios computed separately for each individual employee in the group. The contribution ratio for an individual is the sum of the employer matching and employee contributions made on behalf of each employee, expressed as a percentage of the employee's compensation for the year.

10.2.3. Employee Contributions

As noted earlier, most savings plans are contributory.   Thus, an eligible employee must agree to make contributions to participate.   While it is possible to have a single employee contribution rate, it is customary to permit an employee to elect to contribute at any one of several different levels. Thus, for example, the plan may permit an employee to contribute 1, 2, or 3 percent of compensation. Another common provision is to permit the employee contribution rate to be any whole percentage of from 1 to 6 percent. Employee contributions also can be established as flat dollar amounts or by the use of earnings brackets.

Many savings plans permit supplemental employee contributions to be made.   Any such contributions would become part of the employee's account and, until distributed, investment income on such contributions would not be subject to federal income tax. Employee contributions (both basic and supplemental) are considered for the contribution test referred to above and as part of the maximum annual addition that may be made on an employee's behalf under federal tax law.

Permitting an employee to elect the level at which he or she wishes to participate is generally desirable, since each employee can select the pattern best fitted to individual needs. This flexibility is continued by permitting the employee to change contribution rates from time to time after becoming a participant. Thus, for example, an employee who initially contributed at a rate of 3 percent might, after participating for a year or so and finding that personal circumstances have changed, reduce the contribution rate to 2 percent or increase it to 6 percent, assuming that these rates are permitted by the plan. By the same token, the employee is usually granted the privilege of suspending contributions for some period of time.

The right to change contribution rates or to suspend contributions usually may be exercised, after reasonable notice, at various times during the plan year. Some plans restrict these rights so that they may be exercised only at the beginning of each quarter; others are more flexible and permit change at the beginning of any pay period following the required notice. For administrative reasons, most plans do impose some form of limitation on the number of times such changes might be made. For example, the right to change or suspend contributions, might be limited so that the right can be exercised only once in any 12-month period. Also, for administrative reasons, most plans require that if an employee suspends contributions this must be done for a minimum period, such as six months or one year.

Consistent with these requirements, most savings plans do not impose any penalty on employees who do not elect to participate when first eligible. Any such employee is usually permitted to join the plan on any subsequent entry date.

10.2.4. Employer Contributions

Under federal tax law, savings plans are generally designed to be profit sharing plans. As a practical matter, however, most such plans contemplate that employer contributions will be made on a fixed basis related to employee contributions.[3]

The basic approach used by most savings plans is to provide for an employer contribution equal to some percentage of the employee's contribution. Typical employer contribution schedules would call for an employer contribution of 25 or 50 percent of the employee's contribution.[4] One variation of this basic approach is to increase the employer's contribution as the employee's length of participation increases. The plan, for example, could provide for an employer contribution rate of 50 percent during the first 10 years of the employee's participation, 75 percent during the next 10 years, and 100 percent for participation in excess of 20 years. However, this type of plan may have difficulty satisfying the nondiscrimination tests described earlier, particularly if there is a substantial correlation between service and pay level.

Another variation in determining employer contribution levels is to provide for a basic contribution related to employee contributions, such as that described, plus a supplemental contribution related to current profits. Such a supplemental contribution might be made in accordance with a predetermined formula, or it could be made on a discretionary basis. It is also possible to design a plan so that the entire employer contribution is determined on a current profit basis; such a provision, however, is relatively uncommon in savings plans.

As is the case with profit sharing plans, forfeitures that arise when participating employees terminate without full vesting may be reallocated among employees or may be used to reduce employer contributions. While the majority of profit sharing plans reallocate such forfeitures among

---

[3] The IRC does not recognize savings plans as a separate category of deferred compensation plans. Since savings plans possess many of the characteristics of profit sharing plans, they have generally been considered in that category.

[4] This would apply only for the employee's basic contribution. A corresponding employer contribution is not made for supplemental employee contributions.

employees, the common provision in savings plans is to use them to reduce employer contributions.

10.2.5. Allocations to Employee Accounts

An individual account is maintained for each participating employee under a savings plan. An employee's account is credited with the employee's own contributions, including any supplemental contributions, along with employer contributions made on the employee's behalf. The employee's account is also credited with its proportionate share of the investment income (or loss) of the trust fund. In this regard, the employee's account might be subdivided to reflect the different investment funds available under the plan and the different investment results that these funds might have achieved.

If the plan so provides, the employee's account is also credited with the employee's share of any forfeitures that might arise. When this is the case, forfeitures are usually allocated among employees based on the compensation of each participating employee in relation to the total compensation of all participating employees.

10.2.6. Investment of Funds

Although individual accounts are maintained for each participating employee for record-keeping purposes, contributions and actual trust funds are not segregated on behalf of each individual participant. Such contributions are turned over to a trustee (or trustees) and/or insurance company who invests these contributions for the benefit of the participating employees.

Some savings plans are structured so that all contributions are held and invested as a single investment fund. This is particularly so when the size of the fund is relatively small. Under such an arrangement, the employee has no choice as to how his or her account will be invested.

Most savings plans provide for two or more investment funds and give the employee a choice as to the investment of account values. For example, the plan might provide for two funds, one consisting of a guaranteed interest contract or fixed income securities and the other consisting of equity-type investments. The employee would then be permitted to have all of the account values invested in either fund or to have part of such values invested in each fund.

Other investment variations are possible, of course. Some savings plans also give employees the opportunity of investing in more than one equity-type fund, each having a varying degree of potential risk and return. Also, if employer securities are involved, a separate fund usually is established for this purpose.[5] A further investment variation is to give an employee the opportunity to direct that a portion of the account be invested in life insurance. Insurance company contracts providing a guarantee of principal and interest are becoming increasingly popular as an employee investment option.

A number of plans give an employee additional investment opportunity, as the employee approaches retirement age, by permitting the employee to transfer all or part of his or her account to an account not subject to market value fluctuations. Such a provision enables an employee to exercise some degree of control over the timing of the liquidation of account values and protects the employee from being forced to accept the market conditions that might exist at the time of retirement.

One reason for permitting these investment choices is to limit the employer's fiduciary liability for poor investment performance. Statutory relief from this liability can be obtained by complying with proposed regulations issued by the DOL. In general, these regulations require that a plan offer at least three diversified categories of investment with materially different risk and return characteristics, and that participants have the right to change investments at least quarterly -- more often if needed because of the volatility of a particular fund. Regulatory liability protection can be afforded to employer stock if the shares are publicly traded in a recognized market and if the plan also offers the three required options; however, all purchases, sales, voting and related share activities must be implemented confidentially through a fiduciary who is independent of the employer. It should be noted that failure to comply with the DOL regulations does not mean that fiduciaries are automatically liable -- it simply means that the regulatory safe harbor for liability attributable to participants' investment choices is not available. Also, compliance does not relieve the employer from responsibility for ensuring that the investments are prudent and properly diversified.

Regardless of the number of investment funds involved, there remains the further question of the investment powers of the trustee. Under some plans, the trustee is granted full authority for the investment of the fund; under others, the trustee is subject to control that ranges from broad directives to the approval of each investment. In some situations, the employer might retain investment counsel to be responsible for the

---

[5]If the employee has the option of having his or her own employee contributions invested in employer securities, it will be necessary to register the plan with the Securities and Exchange Commission; it is then necessary that requirements of the SEC be observed, with particular reference to any descriptive or enrollment material given to employees. Also, it will be necessary that employees be given a prospectus. SEC requirements are discussed in Chapter 7.

investment of plan assets, with the trustee acting primarily as a custodian. In making investments, the trustee might maintain an individually managed portfolio or might utilize one or more common trust funds.[6]

If an employee is given investment options, usually some restrictions are imposed upon the employee's right to make and change investment elections. Generally speaking, if more than one fund is available, the employee will be limited in terms of the percentages of the account that can be so invested. For example, the plan may permit the employee to invest 100 percent of account values in either of two available funds -- 50 percent in each fund, or 25 percent in one fund and 75 percent in the other. Another similar restriction would be that the employee can exercise investment options only in multiples of 10 percent.

An employee is generally permitted to change investment elections only as of a date that the funds are being valued. Some savings plans are valued quarterly, with the result that there are only four times a year that an employee could make such a change. Other plans are valued only once a year.[7] Even if a plan is valued more frequently than quarterly, the employee's right to make changes might still be restricted to a limited number of valuation dates during the year.

10.2.7. Vesting

All savings plans provide that 100 percent of the value of an employee's account is paid to the employee (or on behalf of the employee) in the event of retirement, disability, or death. For this purpose, retirement is usually defined as retirement in accordance with the employer's retirement plan. The definition of disability is more varied, but frequently is the same as that applicable to the employer's disability income plan.

A few savings plans also provide for 100 percent vesting in the event of severance of employment. However, most plans require that the employee must have completed some period of service before being entitled to full vesting of the value of employer contributions.[8] While plans vary considerably as to the degree of service or participation required for vesting, the general pattern is that full vesting is achieved after a relatively short time. Savings plans frequently develop more liberal vesting provisions than

---

[6] The manner in which investment responsibilities are handled can have a significant effect on the fiduciary responsibilities of the parties involved. These fiduciary responsibilities are discussed in Chapter 7.

[7] Internal Revenue Service regulations require that the assets of a profit sharing plan be valued at least once a year at fair market value; also, a plan with only annual valuations will not qualify for the regulatory safe harbor from fiduciary liability under DOL regulations.

[8] The value attributable to the employee's own contributions is, of course, always vested.

those found in profit sharing plans intended as the basic plan for retirement income. A typical vesting provision might provide that an employee will be vested at the rate of 20 percent for each year of service (or participation), so that full vesting is achieved after five years. In any event, a savings plan must meet the requirements of federal tax law and satisfy one of the alternative vesting schedules described in Chapter 6.

10.2.8. Withdrawals and Loans

A most valuable aspect of a savings plan is that it can be designed to permit the distribution of benefits during active employment. Such a distribution may be made by permitting employees either to make withdrawals or to make loans.

Withdrawal Provisions. When a savings plan has been designed to be a profit sharing plan under federal tax law, it is possible to make distributions to employees after a fixed number of years. This provision has been interpreted by the Internal Revenue Service to be a period of at least two years. Thus, it is possible to permit the withdrawal of funds that have been held in the fund for at least two years. Federal tax law also permits funds to be distributed from a profit sharing plan upon the happening of an event such as a hardship or, as interpreted by the IRS, upon the completion of five years of plan participation. It should be pointed out that withdrawals are permitted on a relatively flexible basis for the value of after-tax employee contributions and employer contributions that are not used for an ADP test. This is unlike the restrictions on withdrawals that apply to elective deferrals and employer contributions used for ADP testing; these latter restrictions are described in Chapter 12.

Withdrawal provisions vary widely and reflect the desires and objectives of individual employers. For example, some plans permit withdrawal rights only for the value of employee contributions. Others permit withdrawal of the value of vested employer contributions, but only after the value of employee contributions has been withdrawn. Some plans limit the right of withdrawal so that only 50 or 100 percent of the value of the employee's contributions may be withdrawn and, if a right to withdraw employer contributions also is granted, a similar percentage restriction also might apply.

Another common approach to the design of withdrawal provisions is much more flexible, and allows withdrawals to be made at any time after the employee has completed at least five years of plan participation. A more restrictive approach, found in some plans, is to permit withdrawals only in the event of hardship -- e.g., for the purchase of a new home, college education, and the like. The definitions of hardship used for this purpose in a savings plan without elective deferrals can be much more liberal than the definitions used in a CODA.

Withdrawals are usually permitted only on a date the fund is otherwise being valued (often at the end of each quarter). Also, despite other provisions, there usually is a requirement that the minimum amount withdrawn be at least some dollar amount, such as $300. Further, once a withdrawal has been made, the employee is usually not permitted to make a second withdrawal until some period of time has expired. A typical provision would be to restrict withdrawals to not more than one in any 12-month period.

It is common practice to impose a penalty on any employee who makes a withdrawal. One such penalty would be to suspend an employee's participation in a plan for a period of time following withdrawal. The suspension operates as a penalty, since it automatically results in the employees forgoing some amount of future employer contributions.[9]

Loans. A less popular but still common provision permits an employee to utilize the value of his or her account during active employment by making a loan from the plan. Under a loan provision, an employee is usually allowed to borrow up to a specified percentage (such as 50 percent) of the vested portion of the employee's account.

A loan to an employee will be treated as a taxable distribution unless certain requirements are met. These requirements involve the amount of the loan (or accumulated loans) and the time period for repayment. The maximum amounts that can be borrowed without being considered a distribution depend upon the amount of the employee's vested interest in his or her account balance. If it is: (1) $10,000 or less, the entire vested interest is available; (2) between $10,000 and $20,000, $10,000 is available; (3) between $20,000 and $100,000, 50 percent of the vested interest is available; or (4) $100,000 or more, $50,000 is available.[10] The $50,000 limitation on loans from qualified plans is reduced by the excess of the highest outstanding loan balance during the preceding one-year period over the outstanding balance on the date a new loan is made.

As to the time period for repayment, the loan, by its terms, must be repaid within five years; substantially level amortization of the loan is required, with payments made at least quarterly. However, if the loan is used to acquire a dwelling unit (which is to be used as a principal residence

---

[9]As mentioned earlier in this chapter, withdrawals may be subject to federal income tax. Moreover, a 10 percent penalty tax may apply to distributions made before the participant's death, disability, or attainment of age 59½. See Chapter 23 for a detailed discussion.

[10]The DOL has taken the position that a loan cannot exceed 50% of the employee's vested account balance. Because of this conflict between the DOL and the IRS, most plans limit the loan to 50% of the vested account balance and ignore the $10,000 minimum.

of the participant) and meets the amount limitation, the five-year time limit does not apply.

The loan provision must be available to all participants on a reasonably equivalent basis and must not be made available to HCEs in a percentage greater than that made available to other employees. The law also requires that the loan bear a reasonable rate of interest, be adequately secured, and be made only by the plan (and not by a third party, such as a bank, with the employee's account balance as security). If the loan provision meets the requirements of the DOL and the IRS, the loan will be exempted from the prohibited transactions provisions of ERISA and the IRC. If a loan is made and is not exempted, this could constitute a prohibited transaction and could be in violation of the legal requirement that a plan prohibit assignments and alienations; this could result in a plan disqualification.

10.2.9. Distribution of Benefits

Most savings plans provide that the value of an employee's account be distributed in the form of a cash payment. Usually, there is also a provision that allows an employee to elect to have a distribution in the form of installments over a period of time or to have all or part of the account applied to the purchase of an annuity contract. If the possibility exists that the benefit could be paid out in the form of a life annuity, federal tax law requirements with respect to joint and survivor annuities for married employees could apply.

When any part of the employee's account is invested in employer securities, it is customary to provide that this portion will be distributed in the form of securities rather than in cash. This could produce a tax advantage to an employee who receives a distribution of such securities purchased by employer contributions upon severance of employment or after age 59½ and under circumstances when the entire value of his or her account is distributed within one year. Under such circumstances, the value of the securities is the lower of their cost to the trust or their fair market value. Thus, if the employee so elects, he or she would not be taxed, at the time of distribution, on any unrealized appreciation that has taken place since the time the securities were acquired by the trust.[11] If the employee should subsequently sell the securities, the gain would then be taxable. If securities purchased by employee contributions are distributed, deferral of the tax on any unrealized appreciation is available without the requirement

---

[11]Even though not subject to regular tax in the year of distribution, the net unrealized appreciation would be taken into account for purposes of the excess distribution tax. See Chapter 23.

that the employee receive the distribution upon severance of employment or after age 59½, or that it be part of a total distribution within one year.

QUESTIONS FOR REVIEW

1. Explain the significant characteristics of savings plans.
2. Explain the basic objectives of savings plans.
3. What eligibility requirements typically are found in savings plans? Explain.
4. How is flexibility incorporated into a savings plan with respect to employee contributions?
5. What approaches are used for determining the extent of an employer's contribution to a savings plan?
6. How are savings plan assets invested? Explain.
7. Explain vesting as it pertains to savings plans. How do the vesting requirements compare with those typically found in profit sharing plans?
8. Explain the approaches that are used in providing withdrawal benefits.
9. Does the federal tax law impose any restrictions on loan provisions in a savings plan? Explain.
10. What alternative ways may benefits be distributed in a savings plan?

QUESTIONS FOR DISCUSSION

1. Discuss the conditions under which an employer may desire to establish a savings plan.
2. Assume that an employer has had a savings plan for several years and that the reaction of the employees toward the plan has been unsatisfactory. Discuss the plan design flexibility available for a savings plan that may be utilized by the employer to improve the employee's reaction without increasing the employer's annual cost.
3. Discuss how the new nondiscrimination requirements for matching contributions and nondeductible employee contributions are likely to affect plan design for savings plans.

11. Employee Stock Ownership Plans

Employee stock ownership plans (ESOPs) have existed for many years. However, it was not until the 1970s that these plans began to grow in popularity. Much of the interest in these plans in recent years was attributable to the "tax credit" ESOP where the plan was financed with an employer tax credit and, typically, where there was no additional employer contribution. The tax credit for these plans expired on January 1, 1987, however, so that no additional funding of these plans is now taking place. Nevertheless, these plans continue to exist in terms of their accrued benefits and many have been modified or incorporated into other qualified plan arrangements -- e.g., savings plans or CODAs.

The ongoing interest in ESOPs is largely attributable to the so-called "leveraged" ESOP where the plan is used in conjunction with debt financing. As a result of the Tax Reform Acts of 1984 and 1986, leveraged ESOPs offer several significant tax advantages not available to other types of qualified plans. In exchange for these privileges, however, they must meet a unique set of qualification rules. This chapter begins with an overview of the leveraged ESOP and its potential advantages and disadvantages. The chapter then focuses on ESOP qualification requirements and tax benefits.

11.1.   OVERVIEW

11.1.1. Basic Concepts

Under a leveraged ESOP, a trust is created and the trustee acquires funds through a loan. The loan may be made directly by the lending institution to the trustee. In this event, the loan is usually guaranteed by the employer since the trust cannot generate income (other than investment income) on its own. Alternatively, the employer can make the loan from the lending institution and immediately loan the same amount to the trustee in what is termed a "back-to-back" arrangement. The trustee then uses these funds to purchase employer stock, usually directly from the employer.

The stock purchased by the trustee is held in a plan suspense account and is pledged as collateral for the loan. The employer then makes contributions to the plan for the benefit of employees. The plan uses these contributions to repay the loan, including interest. As the loan is repaid, shares of stock are released from the suspense account and are allocated to the individual accounts of eligible employees. In most situations, the number of shares released is determined under what is termed the "fractional" method. This method reflects the ratio of the amount of the current principal and interest payment to the total current and future principal and interest payments. A second method relates only to current and future principal payments and may be used if the loan duration is less than 10 years.

This type of loan under an ESOP is exempt from the prohibited transactions provisions of ERISA provided the loan is made primarily for the benefit of participants in the plan and the interest is not in excess of a reasonable rate. In this regard, the regulations note that these loans "will be subject to special scrutiny by the Department of Labor and the Internal Revenue Service to ensure that they are primarily for the benefit of plan participants and beneficiaries."[1] Also, ESOPs are exempt from the diversity requirements of the fiduciary provisions of ERISA; they are not, however, exempt from the prudency requirements nor are they exempt from the requirement that fiduciaries must act solely for the exclusive benefit of employees and their beneficiaries.

---

[1]DOL Reg. 54.49975-7(b)(2).

11.1.2. Advantages and Disadvantages

Advocates of the ESOP often claim that since employer contributions are tax-deductible, the debt created in conjunction with the ESOP is retired with pre-tax dollars and, as a result, the ESOP is a tax-efficient way to raise capital (as contrasted with conventional debt and equity financing). This claim is, at best, an oversimplification. Technically, the trust and not the employer has incurred the debt with the employer having contingent liability as the guarantor of the loan. The debt is retired by the trust with contributions being made by the employer. The employer is entitled to a deduction only because its contributions are being made to a qualified plan for the benefit of employees. Thus, while the debt is being retired indirectly with pre-tax dollars, it must be understood clearly that the way in which it is being done is a charge to earnings. This could result in lower net income and lower earnings per share. There could also be a dilution in share value as well as cash flow implications.   Also, it must be remembered that employer contributions (and resulting expense) will often continue under the ESOP long after the debt has been retired. In short, careful analysis is necessary to fully evaluate the financial implications of a leveraged ESOP -- and additional analysis is necessary with respect to its role as an employee benefit. Nevertheless, significant advantages (including tax advantages) do exist for these plans and they can serve many useful purposes.

An ESOP, of course, can be considered for many good reasons. First and foremost, it can be a very effective employee benefit plan that is capable of satisfying several important employer objectives.   It can also be an effective device for converting a public company to a private organization, for disposing of a corporate division (the selling corporation would establish a new corporation that, in turn, would establish an ESOP for the purpose of raising capital and purchasing the division), and for providing estate liquidity to a major shareholder.

Many employers will find leveraged ESOPs attractive because they can put relatively large blocks of stock into presumably friendly hands. While this could be an advantage in case of a takeover attempt, a leveraged ESOP must still exist primarily for employee benefit purposes and takeover protection can only be incidental.

Utilizing a leveraged ESOP gives the employer the advantage of avoiding some of the expenses and complexities of selling stock to the public and/or existing shareholders.   Also, the plan may create a proprietary interest on the part of employees and can supplement existing compensation and benefit plans.

From an employer's viewpoint, there is the potential disadvantage that no portion of the stock held in the unallocated suspense account can revert to the employer if the trust is terminated prematurely. Also, there may be some risk of disqualification because of failure to meet the "exclusive benefit" requirements of the law. Another potential drawback to the employer is that an ESOP could be an inefficient compensation tool if the stock appreciates in value because the company forgoes a tax deduction for capital appreciation on shares that under a typical nonleveraged plan would have been made in future years. This same aspect, however, can produce an advantage to employees, particularly to HCEs, since this appreciation in the value of stock will not be a part of the employee's annual addition under Section 415.

For employees, an ESOP is much the same as a profit sharing plan, but with greater assurance of employer contributions. There is a potential disadvantage to employees, however, in that their financial security may be too closely tied to the fortunes of the employer.

As will be seen in the next portion of this chapter, there are many tax advantages -- both for employers and employees -- that are associated with ESOPs. These advantages can be quite valuable and place ESOPs in a unique category in terms of qualified plan benefits.

Like any other employee benefit plan, careful consideration should be given to the employer's objectives and the plan's relative advantages and disadvantages before it is adopted. Even though financial aspects may be the driving force behind a plan's adoption, it must always be remembered that an ESOP is still an employee benefit plan and should thus fit in with the employer's overall human resource philosophy and objectives.

11.2.   TAX LAW PROVISIONS

At the outset, it should be recognized that an ESOP is a qualified plan; as such, it must meet the general requirements applicable to all qualified plans. These requirements are described in Chapters 5 and 6. In addition, ESOPs must meet a number of special requirements. Moreover, there are other unique provisions of the tax law that apply only to ESOPs. The major ESOP tax law provisions are described in the following section.

11.2.1. ESOP Defined

In a broad sense, an ESOP could be defined as any type of qualified employee benefit plan (including profit sharing and savings) that invests some or all of its assets in employer securities. The definition of an ESOP contained in the law, however, is much narrower in scope. Specifically, the IRC defines an ESOP as a qualified stock bonus plan or a combination qualified stock bonus plan and defined contribution (money purchase) plan designed to invest primarily in employer securities.[2] IRS regulations, in turn, define a stock bonus plan as a plan established and maintained by an employer to provide benefits similar to those of a profit sharing plan except that the contributions by the employer are not necessarily dependent upon profits and the benefits are distributable in the stock of the employer company. (Cash distributions are permitted; however, the employee must have the right to demand a distribution in the form of employer securities.) The plan must formally state that it is an ESOP and that assets are to be invested primarily in employer securities.

11.2.2. Employer Securities Requirements

Plan assets may be invested only in "qualifying employer securities." In general, this includes both common and convertible preferred stock that are publicly tradable. In the case of stock which is not readily tradable on an established securities market, the term means common stock having a combination of voting power and dividend rights equal to or greater than: (1) that class of the employer's common stock having the greatest voting power; and (2) that class of the employer's stock having the greatest dividend rights.

Some of the other requirements concerning employer securities are described in the following material.

11.2.2.1.   Voting Rights

Participants must be given the right to vote shares that have been allocated to their accounts. In the case of a closely held company, voting rights generally have to be given only with respect to major issues: mergers, consolidations, recapitalization, reclassification, liquidation, dissolution or sale of substantially all of the firm's assets. However, if the shares of the closely held company were acquired with the proceeds of a loan where the lender was able to exclude 50 percent of interest from income (see subsequent discussion of this provision), all voting on allocated shares must be given to participants. The voting requirements for closely held companies can be satisfied by providing each participant with one vote, regardless of the number of shares actually allocated, and voting all shares held by the plan (whether or not allocated) in proportion to the vote.

---

[2]The phrase "designed to invest primarily in employer securities" has never been defined by the government, but most practitioners believe that this requirement will be met if more than 50 percent of the plan's assets are so invested, when viewed over the life of the plan.

11.2.2.2.   Rights of First Refusal

Stock may be made subject to a right of first refusal in favor of the employer, the ESOP, or both. However, the stock must be publicly traded at the time the right may be exercised. Also, the selling price and other terms under the right must not be less favorable to the seller than the greater of the value of the stock or the purchase price and other terms offered by a buyer, other than the employer or ESOP, making a good faith offer to purchase the security. The right of first refusal must lapse no later than 14 days after the stockholder gives written notice that an offer by a third party to purchase the stock has been received.

11.2.2.3.   Put Options

A put option is not required for publicly traded stock. Otherwise, such an option is required and, under this option, the employee will have the right to require the employer to repurchase the stock. This put option must be exercisable only by the employee (or his or her donee, the employee's estate, or a distributee from the employee's estate).

The put option may not bind the plan, but it may grant the plan the option to assume the rights and obligations of the employer at the time it is exercised. The put must be exercisable for at least 60 days following the distribution of the stock and, if not exercised, for a second period of at least 60 days in the plan year following the distribution. The price must be determined under a fair valuation formula.

If an employer is required to repurchase employer stock that is distributed to the employee as part of a total distribution of the entire amount of the employee's account within one taxable year, the payment may be made in substantially equal periodic payments over a period not exceeding five years. The payments may not be made less frequently than annually and must begin no later than 30 days after the option is exercised. In addition, the employer must provide adequate security and pay reasonable interest on the unpaid amount. If the employer is required to repurchase the stock as part of an installment distribution, it must pay for the stock in full within 30 days after the option is exercised. A separate put option exists for each installment.

11.2.2.4.   Valuation of Securities

Stocks must be valued at fair market value, which presents no difficulty if stock is regularly traded in a recognized market. If the stock is closely held or not publicly traded, an acceptable procedure must be developed for appraising and determining the fair market value of the stock. Generally, determination of fair market value must be on at least an annual basis and independently arrived at by a person who customarily makes such appraisals and who is independent of any party to a transaction involving a right of first refusal or a put option.

11.2.2.5.   Nondiscrimination Testing/Integration with Social Security

An ESOP cannot be combined with other plans in applying the coverage and nondiscrimination requirements of the IRC, except for the purposes of the average benefits test.[3] Similarly, the portion of a plan that is an ESOP and the portion that is not must be treated as separate plans.

The contributions (and allocations) made for employees under an ESOP may *not* be integrated with social security benefits.

11.2.2.6.   Diversification Requirement

Employees who are at least age 55 and who have completed at least 10 years of participation must be given the opportunity to diversify their investments by transferring from the employer stock fund to one or more of three other investment funds.[4] The right to diversify need be granted only for a 90-day window period following the close of the plan year in which the employee first becomes eligible to diversify and following the close of each of the next five plan years. This right is limited to shares acquired after 1986, and is further limited to 25 percent of such shares until the last window period, when up to 50 percent of such shares may be eligible for diversification.

11.2.2.7.   Section 415

An employee's annual addition limit under Section 415 is determined on the basis of the employer's contributions to the plan and not on the value of the stock at the time it is allocated to the employee's account. Also, stock dividends, since they are considered to be investment income, are not charged to the annual addition limit when they are added to the employee's account.

---

[3] See the discussion of these requirements in Chapter 5.
[4] Alternatively, amounts subject to the right of diversification may be distributed from the plan.

If no more than one third of the deductible employer contribution for the year is allocated to HCEs, repayments of interest on the loan and reallocated forfeitures derived from leveraged shares also will not be part of the annual addition.

11.2.2.8.   Distribution Requirements

As noted earlier, an ESOP is generally required to make distributions to employees in the form of employer securities. Cash payments may be established in a plan as the normal form of distribution but the participant must have the right to elect to receive stock. (This requirement does not apply to the extent the participant has elected to diversify his or her account balance.)

Like all qualified plans, an ESOP cannot force distribution of a participant's account (if more than $3,500) until the later of age 62 or the plan's normal retirement age, and must observe the minimum distribution rule requirements. Unlike other qualified plans, ESOPs are required to permit accelerated distributions for stock acquired after 1986 when participants terminate employment. Unless otherwise requested by the participant, ESOPs must distribute such stock by the end of the year following: (1) the year in which the participant dies, retires or becomes disabled; or (2) the fifth plan year following the year of termination for any other reason. (Longer periods are allowed if the participant's account balance exceeds $500,000 [indexed].) The employer may delay distribution of stock acquired under a loan until the plan year following the plan year in which the loan has been repaid in full.

11.2.2.9.   Joint and Survivor Requirements

As noted in Chapter 8, money purchase pension plans are generally subject to the qualified joint and survivor rules. A money purchase plan that is part of an ESOP, however, will be exempt from these rules to the same extent as other defined contribution plans if: (1) the participant's account balance is payable in full to his or her spouse unless the spouse consents in writing to the designation of another beneficiary; and (2) the participant does not elect benefits in the form of a life annuity.

11.2.2.10. Stock Dividends

As a general rule, a corporation will not be allowed a tax deduction for dividends paid to shareholders. These dividends are normally paid out of aftertax income. If dividends are passed through or paid in cash to employees on a current basis under an ESOP, however, the employer will be able to claim a tax deduction for the dividends so paid.[5] This particular feature has attracted the attention of many employers who are considering the possibility of establishing an ESOP for a conventional employer stock fund under a CODA.

Cash dividends are also deductible if they are used to repay an ESOP loan where the shares on which the dividends were paid were acquired with the proceeds of such loan. If the dividends are for allocated shares, participants must receive an allocation of employer securities with a fair market value equal to or greater than the amount of such dividends.

11.2.2.11. Deductibility of Employer Contributions

In the case of a nonleveraged ESOP, the normal deduction limits apply to employer contributions -- i.e., 15 percent of covered compensation in the case of a stock bonus plan. Under a leveraged ESOP, however, the employer may contribute and deduct up to 25 percent of covered payroll on an annual basis for principal repayments on the loan. In addition, contributions made for the entire amount of loan interest will also be deductible.

11.2.2.12. Interest Exclusion

One half of the interest paid on an ESOP loan may be excluded from a qualified lender's taxable income under limited circumstances. The qualified lender must be a bank, insurance company, investment company, or other commercial lender. The exclusion is not available unless the ESOP owns more than 50 percent of each class of outstanding stock or more than 50 percent of the total value of all outstanding stock of the employer, the loan term does not exceed 15 years, and voting rights on all allocated shares are passed through to participants.

---

[5]Dividends so paid to employees will be taxable; however, they will not be subject to the 10 percent early distribution tax.

11.2.2.13.   Deferral of Gain on Stock Sales to ESOPs

A shareholder of a closely held company may be able to sell stock to the ESOP and to defer recognition of the gain on such sale if certain conditions are met. One such condition is that immediately after the sale, the ESOP must own at least 30 percent of the total value of outstanding employer securities or 30 percent of each class of outstanding stock. Also, the employer stock must have been held by the selling shareholder for more than one year and must not have been received as a distribution from a qualified plan or pursuant to stock options.

To qualify for the deferral, the selling shareholder must reinvest the entire proceeds in either debt securities or stock of another domestic corporation that does not have passive investment income in excess of 25 percent of its gross receipts for the preceding taxable year. Also, 50 percent of the new corporation's assets must be used in the active conduct of a trade or business. This reinvestment must occur within a period beginning three months before and ending 12 months after the sale to the ESOP.

The selling shareholder (and family members) and any other person owning more than 25 percent of any class of the employer securities will not be able to participate in the ESOP if this option is exercised.

QUESTIONS FOR REVIEW

1.   Describe a "back-to-back" loan that is sometimes entered into under a leveraged ESOP.
2.   Identify the potential advantages that might accrue to an employer who adopts a leveraged ESOP.
3.   Describe the potential advantages and disadvantages that might to accrue to employees under a leveraged ESOP.
4.   What types of securities meet the definition of "qualifying employer securities" in the case of a company whose stock is not readily tradable on an established securities market?
5.   What voting rights must be given to employees when the stock of an ESOP is the stock of a closely held company?
6.   Under what circumstances may stock held under an ESOP be made subject to a "right of first refusal"?
7.   Under what circumstances must stock held under an ESOP be subject to a "put" option?
8.   Describe the diversification requirement that must be included in an ESOP.
9.   Under what circumstances may an employer be allowed a tax deduction for stock dividends paid with respect to stock held under an ESOP?

QUESTIONS FOR DISCUSSION

1. ESOP loans are exempted from some of the fiduciary requirements of ERISA. Which fiduciary requirements continue to apply to these loans and from which requirements are they exempted, and what rationale exists for granting these exemptions?
2. ESOP advocates often claim that a leveraged loan allows the employer to retire debt with pre-tax dollars. Explain why this is an oversimplification of the financial aspects of a leveraged ESOP.
3. Describe the special tax advantages that have been granted to leveraged ESOPs and why these plans have received more favorable tax treatment than other qualified plans.

12. Cash or Deferred Plans

Conventional deferred profit sharing plans, along with savings and employee stock ownership plans, are discussed in Chapters 9, 10 and 11. This chapter deals with a variation of these plans -- one where the employee is given a choice of receiving an amount in the form of currently taxable compensation (for federal tax purposes) or of deferring this amount to be taxed at a future time. More specifically, the employee has the choice of receiving an employer contribution in cash or having it deferred under the plan, and/or the choice of making his or her own contribution to a plan from before-tax income, thus avoiding any federal tax on this amount until it is received in the form of a plan distribution.

Cash or deferred arrangements (CODAs) are not an entirely new concept. They have existed since the 1950s. However, they were beset with legislative and regulatory doubt during the middle 1970s. The Revenue Act of 1978, along with proposed regulations issued by the Internal Revenue Service in 1981, has opened the way for these plans. Their growth, since 1981, has been significant.

This chapter reviews the legislative history of these plans, the technical requirements they must meet, some special considerations that must be taken into account and their relative advantages and disadvantages -- both to employers and employees. General matters of plan design and tax qualification that apply equally to CODAs as well as to other tax-qualified plans are not discussed in this chapter since they are covered elsewhere.

12.1.   LEGISLATIVE HISTORY OF CODAs

Before 1972, the Internal Revenue Service provided guidelines for qualifying cash option CODAs in a series of revenue rulings. In essence, more than half of the total participation in the plan had to be from the lowest paid two thirds of all eligible employees. If this requirement was met, employees who elected to defer were not considered to be in constructive receipt of the amounts involved even though they had the option to take cash. Salary reduction plans satisfying these requirements were also eligible for the same favorable tax treatment.

In December 1972, the Internal Revenue Service issued proposed regulations stating that any compensation that an employee could receive as cash would be subject to current taxation even if deferred as a contribution to the employer's qualified plan. Although primarily directed at salary reduction plans, the proposed regulations also applied to cash option profit sharing plans.

As the gestation period for ERISA was coming to an end, Congress became increasingly aware of the need to devote additional time to the study of the CODA concept. As a result, ERISA included a section providing that the existing tax status for CODAs was to be frozen until the end of 1976. Plans in existence on June 27, 1974, were permitted to retain their tax-favored status; however, contributions to CODAs established after that date were to be treated as employee contributions and, as a result, were currently taxable.

Unable to meet its self-imposed deadline, Congress extended the moratorium on CODAs twice; the second time the deadline was extended until the end of 1979.

The Revenue Act of 1978 enacted permanent provisions governing CODAs by adding Section 401(k) to the Internal Revenue Code, effective for plan years beginning after December 31, 1979. In essence, CODAs are now permitted, as long as certain requirements are met.

This legislation, in itself, did not result in any significant activity in the adoption of new CODAs. It was not until 1982, after the Internal Revenue Service issued proposed regulations in late 1981, that employers began to respond to the benefit-planning opportunities created by this new legislation. By providing some interpretive guidelines for Section 401(k), and by specifically sanctioning "salary reduction" plans, the Service opened the way for the adoption of new plans and for the conversion of existing, conventional plans. For example, many employers converted existing after-tax savings plans to CODAs to take advantage of the Section 401(k) tax shelter on employee contributions.

The Tax Reform Act of 1984 provided some subtle modifications to Section 401(k). Among other things, it made it clear that CODA could not be integrated. The 1984 legislation also extended cash or deferred treatment to pre-ERISA money purchase plans, although contributions were limited to the levels existing on June 27, 1974.

The changes imposed by the Tax Reform Act of 1986 were much more substantive. In addition to reducing the limit on elective deferrals, this legislation provided a new definition of highly compensated employees, restricted the ADP test, established a new test for after-tax and matching employer contributions, imposed an additional tax on early distributions, and reduced the employer's flexibility in designing eligibility requirements for these arrangements.

12.2.   TECHNICAL REQUIREMENTS

Section 401(k) states that a qualified CODA is any arrangement that:

1. Is part of a profit sharing or stock bonus plan, a pre-ERISA money purchase plan, or a rural electric cooperative plan[1] that meets the requirements of Section 401(a) of the Code.
2. Allows covered employees to elect to have the employer make contributions to a trust under the plan on behalf of the employees, or directly to the employees in cash.
3. Subjects amounts held by the trust that are attributable to employer contributions made pursuant to an employee's election to certain specified withdrawal limitations.
4. Provides that accrued benefits derived from such contributions are nonforfeitable.
5. Does not require, as a condition of participation in the arrangement, that an employee complete a period of service with the employer maintaining the plan in excess of one year.

As a tax-qualified plan, a CODA must meet all of the nondiscriminatory requirements generally applicable to such plans. The special requirements for CODAs are covered in the following material. Before discussing these requirements, however, it is important to understand the difference between elective and nonelective contributions. Elective contributions are amounts that an employee could have received in cash but elected to defer.

---

[1]For purposes of IRC Section 401(k), the term rural electric cooperative plan means any pension plan that is a defined contribution plan and that is established and maintained by a rural electric cooperative or a national association of such cooperatives. For further details see IRC Section 457(d)(9)(B).

Nonelective contributions are employer contributions that are automatically deferred under the plan.

12.2.1. Type of Plan

As noted, a CODA may be part of a profit sharing or stock bonus plan. This, of course, includes savings plans. The only qualified, defined contribution plan that cannot be established as a CODA is a post-ERISA money purchase or defined contribution pension plan.[2]

As a practical matter, most CODAs fall into one of two categories -- either cash or deferred profit sharing plans or savings plans. CODAs can also be subdivided into plans that involve employer contributions only, both employer and employee contributions, and employee contributions only. Plans involving only employee contributions are not expected to be used to a great extent, largely because of the difficulty these plans will experience in satisfying the special tests which are described later.

12.2.2. Individual Limitations

There is a limitation on exclusion for elective deferrals for any taxable year. This limit was initially set at $7,000 and is indexed to changes in the Consumer Price Index (CPI). Any excess amounts are included in the employee's gross income. This limitation applies to the aggregate elective deferral made in a taxable year to all CODAs and simplified employee pensions (SEPs).

A second limit, effective in 1989, caps the amount of pay that can be taken into account for most qualified plan purposes, including the determination of contributions and benefits, at $200,000. This limit is also indexed to changes in the CPI.

12.2.3. Nondiscrimination in Coverage and Contributions

A CODA will not be qualified unless the employees eligible to benefit under the arrangement satisfy the coverage provisions described in Chapter 5 and the contributions under the plan are deemed to be nondiscriminatory. To satisfy the nondiscrimination in contributions requirement, an actual deferral percentage (ADP) test must be met; if after-tax employee

---

[2] CODAs are not available to tax-exempt organizations unless adopted before July 2, 1986, or to states or local governments unless adopted before May 6, 1986.

contributions and/or employer matching contributions are involved, an actual contributions percentage (ACP) test must also be met.

The ADP test is a mathematical test that must be satisfied by the close of each plan year. The first step in applying this test is to determine the actual deferral percentage for each eligible employee. This is done by dividing the amount of contribution deferred at the employee's election (plus, at the election of the employer, any matching or nonelective contributions that satisfy the CODA withdrawal limitations and nonforfeitability requirements) by the amount of the employee's compensation. This percentage is determined for all eligible employees, whether or not they are actually participating. Thus, the ADP for a nonparticipating but eligible employee is zero. For purposes of this test, the compensation used must meet one of the four acceptable definitions of compensation found in the regulations. (It should be noted that the plan may use another nondiscriminatory definition of compensation for purposes of determining plan contributions; for testing, however, one of the definitions that is acceptable to the IRS must be employed.) These four definitions are as follows:

- Wages subject to withholding,
- W-2 wages (reported on Box 10),
- "Section 415 compensation" -- generally, W-2 compensation less income associated with certain stock transactions and deductible moving expenses, and
- "Modified Section 415 compensation" -- which includes only some of the items in the traditional definition.

These four definitions may be modified by an employer to include or exclude certain items of compensation. Elective deferrals (under a CODA, tax-sheltered annuity or a flexible benefit plan), for example, may be included; items that may be excluded are expense reimbursements or allowances, cash or noncash fringe benefits, moving expenses, deferred compensation and welfare benefits.

The next step is to divide the eligible employees into two groups -- the highly compensated employees and all other eligible employees. For each of these groups, the actual deferral percentages are mathematically averaged. If the average ADP for the HCEs does not exceed the average ADP for the NHCEs by more than the allowable percentage, the test is satisfied for the year. The basic test is that the ADP for HCEs cannot be more than 125% of the ADP for NHCEs. An *alternative* limitation can produce a higher ADP for the HCEs in many situations. This alternative limitation permits the ADP for HCEs to be as much as two times the ADP for the NHCEs, but not more than two percentage points higher. The allowable percentages are set forth in Table 12-1.

TABLE 12-1: Allowable ADP Percentages for Highly Compensated Employees

If Average Deferral among Nonhighly Compensated Employees (ADP_{NHCE}) Is	Then Average Deferral Percentage among Highly Compensated Employees May Not Exceed:
Less than 2 percent	2 times ADP_{NHCE}
At least 2 percent but less than 8 percent	ADP_{NHCE} plus 2 percent
8 percent or more	1.25 times ADP_{NHCE}

Table 12-2 shows the permissible ADPs for HCEs at various levels, assuming whichever of the above tests permits the highest result.

TABLE 12-2 Permissible ADPs for HCEs

If the ADP for NHCEs is	Then the ADP for HCEs May Not Exceed
1%	3%
2	4
3	5
4	6
5	7
6	8
7	9
8	10
9	11¼
10	12½

It should be noted that the ADP test determines a maximum average deferral percentage for the HCEs. It does not necessarily indicate the maximum deferral percentage for an individual in this group. As long as the average deferral for the highly compensated employees is less than or equal to the maximum allowed, it will be permissible for an individual in this group to defer an amount in excess of that limitation.

If any highly compensated employee is a participant under two or more CODAs of the employer, all such CODAs will be treated as one CODA for purposes of determining the employee's actual deferral percentage.

A similar test, known as the average contribution percentage (ACP) test applies to any after-tax employee contributions and any employer matching contributions. (Note that if employer contributions are fully vested and subject to withdrawal restrictions, the employer may elect to have these contributions -- called qualified nonelective contributions [QNECs] -- used as part of the ADP test.) If a plan must meet both the ADP and ACP tests, there is a restriction on the multiple use of the alternative limitation -- in other words, one of these tests must be met using the basic or 125% test. An aggregate limit test is available for plans that can pass each test only by using the alternative limitation. The first step in this test is to add up the ADP and ACP for HCEs to arrive at the "aggregate HCE percentage." Then, the larger of the ADP or ACP for the NHCEs is multiplied by 1.25. Next, the smaller of the ADP or the ACP for NHCEs is multiplied by two. The resulting product is compared with the sum of two plus the smaller of the NHCE ADP or ACP. Whichever of the two results is smaller is added to the result produced from the 125% test. If the resulting sum equals or exceeds the aggregate HCE percentage, the aggregate limit test is passed. This test can also be run in a different way by reversing the items just described. Thus, the smaller of the NHCE ADP or ACP is multiplied by 1.25, and it is the larger of the NHCE ADP or ACP that is multiplied by or added to two. The employer may choose whichever way produces the most favorable result.

There are several ways in which an employer can minimize or eliminate the possibility that a plan will not meet the ADP and ACP tests. The following lists some of the techniques that might be used for this purpose.

1. The plan can be designed so that it is in automatic compliance. For example, the employer might make an automatic 5 percent contribution for all employees that satisfies the CODA withdrawal limitations and nonforfeitability requirements. Employees may then be given the option of contributing up to 1.0 percent of pay by way of salary reduction. The plan will always satisfy the ADP test since the ADP for the HCEs will never exceed the 1.25% basic test.

2. The plan also could be designed to encourage maximum participation from the NHCEs. This could be done under a savings plan, for example, by providing for higher levels of employer contributions with respect to lower pay levels or with reference to lower rates of contribution.

3. Limits may be placed on the maximum amounts that might be deferred or contributed.

4. A mandatory minimum deferral or contribution may be required from all participating employees.

5. The plan could include a provision allowing the employer to adjust prospective deferrals or after-tax contributions (either upward or downward) if the plan is in danger of failing to meet the tests.

6. The employer may make additional contributions at the end of the plan year to the extent necessary to satisfy the applicable test. (Such contributions, of course, would have to satisfy the CODA withdrawal limitations and nonforfeitability requirements if they are to be used in the ADP test.)

7. Contributions for a plan year could be determined in advance of the plan year and, once established on a basis that satisfies the test, requirements could be fixed on an irrevocable basis (except, possibly, that NHCEs could be given the option of increasing their contributions).

12.2.4. Treatment of Excess Deferrals and Contributions

Excess deferrals may arise if the amount deferred by an employee exceeds the allowable elective deferral limit for the year in question. Excess contributions may arise as a result of a plan's failure to meet the ADP, ACP or aggregate limit test.

Excess deferrals due to the elective deferral limit may be allocated among the plans under which the deferrals were made by March 1 following the close of the taxable year, and the plan may distribute the allocated amount back to the employee by April 15. Although such a distribution will be includable in the employee's taxable income for the year to which the excess deferral relates, it will not be subject to the 10 percent excise tax that might otherwise apply to distributions prior to age 59½; however, even though distributed, this amount will generally have to be taken into account by the employer when applying the ADP test for the year. Any income on the excess deferral will be treated as earned and received in the taxable year in which the excess deferral was made. Any excess deferral not distributed by this date (April 15 of the following year) will remain in the plan, subject to all regular withdrawal restrictions. Moreover, the amount will again be treated as taxable income when it is later distributed.

If excess contributions arise because of the ADP, ACP or aggregate limit tests, there are several ways in which the problem can be addressed. The first, of course, is for the employer to make additional contributions to the extent necessary to satisfy the test requirements. If it is the ADP test that has been failed, the employer can "recharacterize" the excess deferrals as after-tax employee contributions; in this event, however, they will then be subject to the ACP test requirements. The third method is to refund the excess contributions using the "leveling" method prescribed in the regulations (whereby the HCE or HCEs with the highest rate of deferrals are reduced first and to the extent necessary to satisfy the test). For purposes of the law, an excess attributable to a failure of the ADP test is called an "excess contribution." An excess due to failure of the ACP test is called an "excess aggregate contribution."

If contributions are to be returned, there are two critical dates to keep in mind. The first such date is 2½ months after the end of the plan year in which the excess occurred. If excess or excess aggregate contributions are returned by that time, the amount generally will be considered as income on the earliest date that amounts deferred for the plan year being tested would otherwise have been received in cash. A return of after-tax contributions, of course, would not be taxable; however, other returned amounts, including investment income on both after-tax and elective deferrals, will be taxable. The amounts distributed will not attract the 10 percent excise tax that might otherwise apply to early distributions.

The second critical date that relates to the return of excess contributions is the last day of the plan year following the plan year in which the excess occurred. If the required amounts are distributed after the first critical date and before the second critical date, the amount returned is taken into income in the year of distribution. In addition, the employer is subject to a 10 percent penalty tax on the amount of principal involved (but not investment earnings).

If excess contributions are not returned by the second critical date, the consequences could be serious. If the excess is an excess contribution, the CODA portion of the plan could lose its qualified status for the years in question, with the result that *all* employees could be taxed on amounts they could have received in cash. If the excess is an excess aggregate contribution, the entire plan could lose its qualified status for the years in question; this could entail a loss of deductions, the taxation of plan investment income, and the taxation of all employees to the extent of their vested account balances.

12.2.5. Nonforfeitability Requirements

The value of all elective and any after-tax employee contributions to a CODA must be fully vested at all times. The value of employer contributions must vest in accordance with one of ERISA's prescribed vesting standards. It should be noted, however, that the vested amount of elective contributions cannot be considered for this purpose. Thus, the vesting of employer contributions must be accomplished independently.

As mentioned previously, if employer contributions are fully vested from the outset (and if they are subject to withdrawal restrictions) they may be taken into account when applying the ADP test.

12.2.6. Limitations on Withdrawals

A common provision in many profit sharing and savings plans is one that permits an employee to make a withdrawal of some part of the vested account balance while still actively employed. Sometimes, this withdrawal right is limited to hardship situations; more often than not, however, a withdrawal can be made for any reason, and is typically subject to some period of suspension from plan participation.

In the case of a CODA, the ability to make in-service withdrawals is severely limited. The value of elective contributions may be distributable only upon death, disability, separation from service, the termination of the plan (provided no successor plan other than an ESOP or a SEP is established), or certain sales of businesses by the employer.

Distributions of elective contributions will be permitted after the employee has attained age 59½ or before this age in the case of a hardship. For hardship withdrawals, however, the amount available is limited to the elective contributions themselves; investment income on such contributions can be included only to the extent earned prior to December 31, 1988 (for calendar year plans). Also, it should be noted that if employer contributions have been included in the ADP test, the withdrawal restrictions on these amounts are even greater; any such contributions and any investment income earned on such contributions is withdrawable for hardship only to the extent made or earned before the end of the last plan year ending before July 1, 1989.

Limiting the withdrawal of elective contributions to hardship cases only can be of significance to many employers, since it could have a negative effect on the participation of lower paid employees, thus creating problems in meeting the ADP and ACP tests. The regulations define hardship in a very narrow way. Specifically, these regulations require that the hardship be caused by immediate and heavy financial needs of the employee. Further, they require that the withdrawal must be necessary to satisfy the financial need.

The regulations permit each of these conditions to be met on a "facts and circumstances" basis, but also provide for the use of safe harbors. For determining "immediate and heavy financial need," the following events are acceptable:

- The incurring of certain medical expenses by the employee, the employee's spouse or certain dependents of the employee, as defined in Section 152 of the IRC, or the need for "up-front" funds to obtain certain medical services for these individuals.
- The purchase (excluding mortgage payments) of a principal residence for the employee.

- Payment of tuition and related educational fees for the next 12 months of post-secondary education for the employee or the employee's spouse or dependents.
- The need to prevent the eviction of the employee from his or her principal residence, or foreclosure on the mortgage of the employee's principal residence.

The regulatory safe harbor for the second requirement ("necessary to satisfy the financial need") includes four conditions. First, the distribution must not exceed the amount of the need. Second, the employee must have obtained all distributions (other than hardship distributions) and all nontaxable loans currently available under all plans maintained by the employer. Third, the plan (and other plans maintained by the employer) must provide that the employee's elective and after-tax contributions will be suspended for at least 12 months after receipt of the distribution. Fourth, the plan and all other employer plans must limit the employee's elective contributions for the immediately following calendar year to no more than the excess, if any, of that year's elective contribution limit over the amount electively contributed in the year of the distribution.

A plan may use a "facts and circumstances" approach, may rely on the safe harbors, or use a combination of both in designing and administering a hardship withdrawal provision.

It should be noted that some amounts might still be available for nonhardship, in-service withdrawals. As already noted, employer contributions may be withdrawn (unless they are designated to be part of the ADP test). Also, the value of any after-tax employee contributions may be withdrawn, as may the value of any contributions (employer and employee) made to a plan before it became a CODA. Finally, even elective contributions may be withdrawn on a nonhardship basis after the employee attains age 59½.

12.2.7. Separate Accounting

The proposed regulations state that all amounts held by a plan that has a CODA will be subject to the CODA nonforfeitability and withdrawal requirements unless a separate account is maintained for benefits specifically subject to these requirements. Included are amounts contributed for plan years before 1980, contributions not subject to a deferral election, and contributions made for years when the CODA is not qualified.

12.2.8. Loans

Because of the restrictions on the in-service withdrawal of elective contributions, many employers have included loan provisions in their CODA programs. The legal requirements for loans are the same for CODAs as they are for profit sharing plans. Since these requirements were discussed at length in Chapter 9, they are not repeated here.

12.3.   OTHER CONSIDERATIONS

The preceding has dealt with the requirements of federal tax law for the qualification of CODAs and the income tax treatment of elective contributions. There are, however, other issues that must be addressed. The following section discusses the status of elective contributions for purposes of social security, other employer-sponsored plans, and state and local taxes. It also discusses the deduction limits for 401(k) contributions, the treatment of excess deferrals, and the effect of such contributions on deduction limits.

12.3.1. Social Security

Originally, elective contributions to a CODA were not considered to be wages for purposes of social security. Thus, they were not subject to social security (FICA) tax, nor were they taken into account when calculating social security benefits.

This was changed by the 1983 social security amendments. Elective contributions are now considered as wages for social security (and federal unemployment insurance) purposes. Thus, FICA taxes will be paid on such amounts (if they are under the taxable wage base) and they will be taken into account when calculating an employee's social security benefits.

12.3.2. Other Employer-Sponsored Plans

A matter of some concern to employers was the question of whether an employee's elective contributions could be considered as part of the compensation base for purposes of other tax-qualified plans. This uncertainty was resolved in 1983 when the Internal Revenue Service ruled that the inclusion (or exclusion) of elective contributions under a CODA as compensation in a defined benefit pension plan does not cause the pension plan to be discriminatory.

Employers also maintain other pay-related employee benefit plans. These include short- and long-term disability income plans, group term life insurance, survivor income benefits, and, in some cases, health care plans. There appear to be no legal reasons why pay, for the purpose of determining benefits under these plans, cannot be defined to include elective contributions made under a CODA. If such contributions are to be included, care should be taken to make sure that necessary plan and/or insurance contract amendments are made so that compensation is properly defined.

A CODA will not be qualified if any other benefit (other than the employer's matching contribution) provided by the employer is conditioned, either directly or indirectly, on the employee electing to have the employer make or not make contributions under the arrangement in lieu of receiving cash.

12.3.3. State and Local Taxes

The treatment of elective contributions under state and local tax laws is not completely uniform. For years, many states followed principles of federal tax law in the treatment of employee benefits. This practice was also followed by many local governments that impose some form of income tax.

With the increased use of individual retirement accounts (IRAs) in recent years, and with the publicity that CODAs have received, there has been growing concern among state and local tax authorities over the potential loss of tax revenue. As a result, the question of state and local taxation of elective contributions has become an important issue.

At this time, most state and local authorities have indicated that they will follow federal tax law. However, a few have announced that elective contributions will be taxable and subject to employer withholding. It seems reasonable to expect that other state and local authorities might adopt this latter position.

12.3.4. Deduction Limits

Section 404 of the Code imposes limits on the amount an employer can deduct for contributions made to qualified plans. For profit sharing plans, this limit is expressed as 15 percent of the payroll of the employees covered. If the employer has both a defined benefit plan and a defined contribution plan, the combined limit is 25 percent of the covered payroll.

Elective contributions affect the maximum deduction in two ways. First, they will reduce the amount of the covered payroll to which the percentage limitations apply, thus reducing the dollar amount available as a maximum deduction. Second, they are considered to be employer contributions and thus reduce the amount otherwise available for the employer to contribute and deduct.

As a practical matter, the effect of CODAs on these limits should not be of great concern to most employers. For those who maintain liberal plans, however, the level of elective contributions permitted might have to be limited in order to preserve deductions for regular employer contributions.

12.4.   ADVANTAGES AND DISADVANTAGES OF CODAs

The advantages of CODAs are significant, although most of these accrue to employees rather than employers. Nevertheless, the advantages to employers are important.

From an employer's viewpoint, CODAs have all the advantages normally associated with any employee benefit plan. Thus, they should be of material value in the attraction and retention of employees, in improving employee morale, in achieving a better sense of corporate identification (when employer securities are involved), and so forth. In addition, they can serve specific corporate objectives such as increasing the level of participation in an existing plan that has had conventional after-tax employee contributions. For some employers, converting a conventional savings plan to a CODA, and thus increasing take-home pay for participating employees, could minimize pressures for additional cash compensation.

From the viewpoint of employees, the first and foremost advantage involves taxes. If a conventional savings plan is converted to a CODA, the participating employees can realize an immediate increase in take-home pay. But of more importance is the fact that contributions are accumulating under a tax shelter. This means that an employee can receive investment income on amounts that otherwise would have been paid in taxes. Over a period of years, the cumulative effect of this can be quite substantial. Finally, when amounts are distributed and subject to tax, the actual amount of tax paid might be considerably less than would otherwise have been the case. Installment distributions could be taxed at a lower effective tax rate (due to lower levels of taxable income, extra tax exemptions, and indexed tax brackets). And lump-sum distributions also may qualify for favorable five-year averaging tax treatment.

Employees also have the flexibility of determining, on a year-to-year basis, whether to take amounts in cash or to defer these amounts under the plan. Since employee needs and goals change from time to time, this element of flexibility could be quite important.

The disadvantages of CODAs also should be recognized. From the employer's viewpoint, these plans involve complex and costly administration. Also, the employer must be prepared to deal with employee relations and other problems that can occur in any year that the plan fails to satisfy the ADP and ACP tests. These plans also will involve more communications efforts than are associated with conventional employee benefit plans.

From the viewpoint of employees, the disadvantages of CODAs are not as great. In fact, the only significant disadvantage is that elective contributions are subject to the previously mentioned withdrawal limitations and the possible application of the early distribution tax (described in Chapter 23). This could be of major importance to some employees, particularly those at lower pay levels, and could be a barrier to their participation in the plan.

12.5.   THE FUTURE

Despite the uncertainties that currently surround CODAs, they have already become an important part of the employee benefit planning process.

Many organizations already have established CODAs or have converted existing plans to CODAs. Many others are actively moving in this same direction. There is every reason to believe that the growth of these plans will continue, although perhaps at a slower pace than that expected during the early 1980s.

CODAs are an interesting and tax-efficient way of providing employee benefits. They are consistent with the growing concept that employee benefit plans need to be flexible and need to address the varying needs of employees at different times during their careers. There seems little doubt that, barring legislative or regulatory interference, they will be a major factor in the employee benefit planning process of the future.

QUESTIONS FOR REVIEW

1. What requirements must be satisfied by a CODA for it to be qualified under the IRC?
2. Explain the steps involved in the ADP test.
3. May contributions (expressed as a percentage of compensation) for the higher paid employees under a qualified CODA be larger than contributions for their lower paid counterparts? Explain.

4. Explain the vesting requirements for contributions to a qualified CODA.

5. Describe the impact of CODA deferrals on social security taxes and benefits.

6. May elective contributions to a CODA be considered as part of the compensation base for purposes of other tax-qualified plans? Explain.

7. Describe how elective contributions to a CODA will affect the employer's deduction limits.

8. Explain the advantages and limitations of a CODA from the viewpoint of employees.

9. Explain the disadvantages of a CODA from the viewpoint of the employer.

QUESTIONS FOR DISCUSSION

1. Discuss the conditions under which an employer may desire to establish a CODA.

2. Assume that an employer has had a CODA for several years and that the reaction of the employees toward the plan has been unsatisfactory. Discuss the plan design flexibility available for a CODA that may be utilized by the employer to improve the employees' reaction without increasing the employer's annual cost.

3. Discuss how the dollar limit on elective contributions is likely to affect plan design for CODAs.

13. Simplified Employee Pensions

Congress, in an attempt to encourage the adoption of private pension plans, created the concept of simplified employee pensions (SEPs). In effect, SEPs are individual retirement accounts (IRAs) with higher contribution limits than those normally applicable to these arrangements. Further, they allow an employer to adopt a retirement program with a minimum of paperwork and regulatory compliance.

This chapter provides a brief overview of the tax law provisions applicable to SEPs. It also includes a discussion of the eligibility requirements applicable to these plans, the deductibility of contributions, and the use of salary reduction arrangements.

13.1. GENERAL TAX LAW REQUIREMENTS

Employers (whether incorporated or not) were permitted to establish SEPs beginning in 1979. At that time, tax-deductible contributions of up to 15 percent of total compensation or $7,500, whichever was less, could be made. The Economic Recovery Tax Act of 1981 (ERTA) raised the $7,500 limit on contributions to $15,000 for the years 1982 and 1983. The Tax Equity and Fiscal Responsibility Act of 1982 (TEFRA) increased the limits beginning in 1984 to the lesser of 15 percent of pay or $30,000. This dollar limit, since it is related to the Section 415 limit on annual additions to a defined contribution plan, is indexed to increase with changes in the Consumer Price Index (CPI); however, the $30,000 defined contribution annual addition limit will not be increased until the defined benefit limit reaches $120,000.

The general authority for SEPs is found in Sections 408(j) and (k) of the IRC which provide for an increase in the normal IRA limit if certain requirements are met. Thus, a SEP is treated, under the law, as an IRA with higher limits.

For the employer, a SEP is a written plan utilizing individual retirement accounts or annuities to provide retirement benefits for employees. The program must be defined contribution in nature; the defined benefit approach is not permitted for these plans. The SEP must be a formally adopted program having the following characteristics:

- It must be in writing and must specify the requirements for receiving a contribution. Further, it must specify how each eligible employee's contribution will be computed.
- The employer must make contributions to the SEP for any employee who has received any compensation for service during the current calendar year, is at least 21 years of age, has worked for the employer during any three of the last five calendar years, and has received at least $300 (indexed) in compensation from the employer for the year.
- Employer contributions may not discriminate in favor of any HCE.
- Each employee must be fully vested in his or her account balance at all times.
- The program may not restrict the employee's rights to withdraw funds contributed to his or her SEP at any time -- i.e., the program must give unrestricted withdrawal rights to the employees.
- The employer may not require that an employee leave some or all of the contributions in the SEP as a condition for receiving future employer contributions.
- SEPs are subject to the Section 415 limitations on annual additions; however, if the SEP utilizes a cash or deferred arrangement (discussed later in this chapter), the employee's contribution need not be considered as part of the annual addition.
- The top-heavy provisions of the law also apply to SEPs; however, a special provision allows employers to elect to measure aggregate employer contributions, instead of aggregate account balances, to test if the SEP has exceeded the 60 percent limit.
- Since they are IRAs, SEPs cannot permit employees to make loans.

13.2.   ELIGIBILITY

For an IRA funded by employer contributions to be treated as a SEP, the employer must contribute to the SEP for all eligible employees. As long as the employee satisfies the eligibility criteria mentioned above, he or she must receive a contribution. The employer does not have to make a contribution, however, for: (1) members of a collective bargaining unit if retirement benefits were the subject of good faith bargaining; and (2) certain nonresident aliens with no United States source income.

Controlled group rules apply to SEPs, and if the employer is a member of a controlled group, SEP contributions must be made for all eligible employees of each one of the businesses that comprise the group.

13.3.   CONTRIBUTIONS

Employer contributions to a SEP must bear a uniform relationship to total compensation not in excess of $200,000 (indexed to the CPI). However, employer contributions under a SEP may be integrated with social security benefits under the same rules that apply to defined contribution plans (described in Chapter 8).

During any calendar year, an employer's contribution to a SEP, as long as it is made in a nondiscriminatory fashion, may be in any amount up to 15 percent of the employee's compensation but not in excess of the annual addition limit for Section 415 purposes -- currently $30,000. If the employer contribution to the SEP in any calendar year is less than the normal IRA limit of $2,000, the employee may contribute the difference up to $2,000. The employee contribution may be made either to the SEP or an IRA of his or her own choice.

Like a regular IRA, contributions made up to April 15 of the following calendar year are treated as being made on the last day of the prior calendar year if they are made on account of that year. For example, the XYZ Company has a SEP that provides for a contribution of 15 percent of an employee's compensation during each calendar year. In 1991, employee A earns $20,000 and the maximum permissible contribution under the tax law is $3,000 (.15 x $20,000). The XYZ Company makes a $1,500 contribution for A on December 31, 1991 and contributes the remaining $1,500 on March 15, 1992. The entire $3,000 contribution is treated as being made on December 31, 1991.

As noted earlier, only the first $200,000 (indexed) of compensation is taken into account for plan purposes, including the requirement that contributions be made on a uniform and nondiscriminatory basis. For example, assume that A is a highly compensated employee earning more than $200,000 and that a maximum contribution of $30,000 is made on his behalf. In this situation, the applicable percentage of compensation that must be contributed for other employees will be 15 percent. This is determined by dividing the $30,000 contribution made for A by the $200,000 maximum. Since A is considered to have received a 15 percent contribution, all other eligible employees must receive the same percentage contribution.

It should also be noted that in the case of self-employed individuals (proprietors and partners), the 15 percent contribution limitation will be on the basis of "earned income" as that term is defined in the law. This means that the contribution will be determined with reference to earned income after having subtracted the amount of the contribution. The result is that the 15 percent contribution limit, as it is applied to these individuals, is 13.0435 percent of net income before subtracting the amount of the contribution. For example, assume that the sole proprietor of the business has taxable income, before making the SEP contribution, of $100,000. The maximum contribution for this individual will be $13,043.50. This amount, subtracted from the $100,000, leaves earned income of $86,956.50. The 15 percent contribution limit, when applied to this lower amount of earned income, produces the maximum contribution of $13,043.50.

Employers may cut off all contributions to employees at the maximum contribution limit or at some lower figure. Although this could cause contributions to be discriminatory, they will not discriminate in favor of highly compensated employees since contributions for this group represent a smaller percentage of their earnings.

13.4.   DEDUCTIONS

The employer's contributions are deducted in the tax year that begins in the calendar year during which the contributions are made or treated as being made. The deduction may not exceed 15 percent of compensation paid to employees during that calendar year. If the employer contributes more than the amount deductible, the employer can carry over the excess deduction to succeeding taxable years; however, a 10 percent excise tax will be levied on any contribution made to the extent it is not deductible.

If both a qualified profit sharing plan and a SEP exist, the maximum deduction permitted for contributions to the qualified profit sharing plan is reduced by the amount of the allowable deduction for contributions to the SEP.

13.5.   SALARY REDUCTION AGREEMENTS

In the case of a SEP maintained by an employer with 25 or fewer employees throughout the entire preceding year, an employee may elect to have the employer make payments as elective contributions to the SEP on behalf of the employee, or to the employee directly in cash. At least 50 percent of the employees must elect a salary reduction, and the average deferral percentage (ADP) for *each* highly compensated employee may not exceed 125 percent of the average deferral percentage of all non-highly compensated employees.

The definition of excess contributions and the rules for their distribution are similar to those described in Chapter 12 for cash or deferred arrangements.

QUESTIONS FOR REVIEW

1. What annual limitations apply to the maximum amount that may be contributed by or on behalf of an employee under a SEP?
2. For whom must employers make contributions under a SEP?
3. Explain how the limitation on compensation that may be taken into account under a SEP can also affect the percentage of pay that must be contributed for NHCEs.
4. What is the deduction limit for employer contributions made to a SEP?
5. Under what circumstances may salary reduction agreements be used in conjunction with a SEP?

QUESTIONS FOR DISCUSSION

1. Evaluate the relative advantages and disadvantages of a conventional deferred profit sharing plan and a SEP in terms of their application to a self-employed individual as a means of establishing a formal program for accumulating "retirement" funds.
2. SEPs are, under the law, treated as IRAs with higher limits. What justification exists for permitting higher limit IRAs for some individuals and not for others?

PART FOUR

Design Considerations for Defined Benefit Plans

An employer adopting a qualified defined benefit pension plan must make a number of decisions as to the basic features to be included in the plan. The employer must, for example, determine what benefits the participants will receive upon retirement, death, or disability; how and when these benefits will be paid; and whether or not employees will contribute toward the cost of these benefits.

Some of the basic features involving the tax law requirements have already been discussed in Part Two. Chapter 14 discusses the various factors that bear on an employer's decisions concerning the design of the more prominent features to be included in a defined benefit pension plan. The features discussed in this chapter include retirement ages, employee contributions, retirement, death, and disability benefits. This chapter then discusses the plan design approaches used to counteract the effect of preretirement inflation and approaches used to offset postretirement inflation.

Chapter 15 considers some of the important implications of funding defined benefit plans and acquaints the reader with the factors affecting the ultimate cost of these plans, apart from specific plan provisions and benefits. What is still needed, however, is some actuarial technique to determine how the estimated costs of the plan are to be spread over future years. These techniques, referred to as actuarial cost methods, are described in Chapter 16 in conjunction with the relevant constraints imposed by the government through minimum required contributions and maximum deductible contributions.

Although the minimum required contributions described in Chapter 16 are designed to reduce the likelihood that pension assets would be insufficient to cover promised benefits in the case of a plan termination, such events are still quite common in troubled industries. The Pension Benefit Guaranty Corporation (PBGC) is a federal government agency that was created to insure these promises, subject to specific limitations. Chapter 17 discusses the government's plan termination insurance program for single-employer defined benefit pension plans.

14. Defined Benefit Plan Features

An employer adopting a qualified defined benefit pension plan must make a number of decisions as to the basic features to be included in the plan. The employer must, for example, determine what benefits the participants will receive upon retirement, death, or disability; how and when these benefits will be paid; and whether or not employees will contribute toward the cost of these benefits.

Legal requirements, of course, play a major role in plan design. The requirements of the Internal Revenue Code and appropriate regulations are of vital importance if the employer wishes to obtain the favorable tax benefits that flow from having a "qualified" plan. While the requirements for qualification were discussed at length in Chapters 5 and 6, it should be emphasized at this point that such a plan must not discriminate in any way (i.e., in benefits, contributions, or coverage) in favor of the highly compensated employees (HCEs). Thus, the organization, if it is to have a qualified plan, cannot pick and choose the employees to be covered nor can it determine their benefits in a selective manner. Instead, the employer must adopt a plan that treats employees fairly and equitably and that does not produce discrimination in favor of the highly compensated employees.

As was pointed out in Chapter 3, the design of a pension plan for a particular employer should reflect a thorough evaluation of the objectives and circumstances of that employer. It often happens that an employer will adopt a "package" plan only to find, at a later date, that this plan is deficient in some respect. Unfortunately, the remedy to this type of problem frequently involves considerable expense and effort on the part of all concerned.

Some of the basic features involving the tax law requirements have already been discussed in Chapters 5 and 6. This chapter discusses the various factors that bear on an employer's decisions concerning the design of the more prominent features to be included in a defined benefit pension plan. While much of this material applies equally well to defined contribution plans, it is oriented specifically toward qualified defined benefit pension plans. The features discussed in this chapter include retirement ages, employee contributions, retirement, death, and disability benefits. This chapter then discusses the plan design approaches used to counteract the effect of preretirement inflation and approaches used to offset postretirement inflation.

14.1.   EMPLOYEE CONTRIBUTIONS

A major question the employer must resolve is whether employees will be required to make contributions toward the cost of plan benefits. Sound arguments may be presented for both contributory and noncontributory plans, although the ability of the employer or employees to pay is often the controlling factor. In any event, the trend is clearly in the direction of noncontributory plans, at least in the case of defined benefit plans.

Arguments advanced in favor of contributory plans include the following:

1.   From a philosophical viewpoint, employees are responsible for meeting part of their own economic security needs.
2.   If employees contribute, it will mean a smaller employer contribution to provide the same overall plan benefits.
3.   If employers do not want to use employee contributions to reduce their own contribution, then by making the plan contributory, the overall plan benefits will be larger.
4.   Something for nothing is too often taken for granted, and the deductions from current earnings will continually remind employees that the employer is assuming a large share of providing the plan benefits. (It would seem that this argument could be minimized by an effective method of repeatedly publicizing the plan and its value to employees.)
5.   Employees are encouraged to save. The contributory plan also provides an employee with additional funds in the event of termination of employment.

The proponents of a noncontributory plan hold that the contributory plan has the following disadvantages:

1.   Employer contributions represent dollars that have not been taxed. On the other hand, dollars received by the employee as earnings that are then contributed under the plan are dollars that have been taxed to the employee. Hence, dollar for dollar, employer contributions provide more than those of an employee.

2.   Deductions from earnings are a source of constant irritation to employees.

3.   The employer might be forced to increase salaries to compensate for the additional deductions.

4.   The number of participants required for a qualified plan (or required by the insurer under certain funding instruments) might not enroll.

5.   Some employees may refuse to participate, in which case the employer will still have a problem when these employees reach retirement age.

6.   Additional records must be kept by the employer, thereby increasing administrative work and costs.

If the employer decides that employees should make contributions, the next decision will be the amount employees should contribute. While employee contributions may be related to the cost of benefits, generally it is much more satisfactory to relate these contributions to earnings. In this way, an employee's contributions are geared to the ability to make them. Furthermore, in most plans it is impossible to predict exactly what the cost of an employee's pension will be until actual retirement.   Hence, any contributions made by the employee and related to cost necessarily are estimated and do not have an exact relationship.

Contributory plans usually require that an employee, before becoming a participant, must sign a request for participation agreeing to make the required contributions and authorizing the employer to withhold contributions from earnings. If an employee fails to make such an election when first eligible, it is customary to impose some form of penalty. In plans using a unit credit formula,[1] for example, past service benefits as well as the future service benefits[2] that would otherwise have accrued might be forfeited until the employee joins the plan. If the plan employs a flat percentage of earnings formula,[3] the benefits might be reduced by multiplying the benefit the

---

[1]A unit credit formula gives specific recognition for service as well as earnings. Under such a formula, an employee receives a benefit credit equal to a percentage of earnings for each year that he or she is a participant under the plan.

[2]Past and future benefits are defined relative to the date of plan inception. This concept is discussed in detail later in this chapter.

[3]This type of formula does not take an employee's service into account, except in those plans that require that the employee must have completed a minimum period of service by normal retirement date and that provide for a proportionately reduced benefit if his or her service is less than the required number of years. Some percentage of earnings, usually ranging from 25 to 50 percent, is selected as the measure of the pension benefit.

late entrant would otherwise have received by a fraction, the numerator being the years of actual contribution and the denominator the number of years the employee could have contributed. A few plans are even more severe and provide that if an employee does not join when first eligible, the right to participate will be forfeited for all time. Another approach used by some employers is to give employees the option of participating if they are employed when the plan becomes effective, but to require participation as a condition of employment for all future employees.

Another provision to be considered in contributory plans is the right of an employee to suspend or discontinue contributions. Many plans do not give an employee either of these privileges. Others permit a temporary suspension (for a year or so) without affecting benefits, and some permit a complete discontinuance at any time. Still others permit only a complete discontinuance. If discontinuance of contributions is permitted, further questions exist, such as whether the employee is permitted to rejoin the plan and, if so, what benefits the employee will then be entitled to receive.

14.2.   RETIREMENT AGES

14.2.1. Normal Retirement Age

The normal retirement age in most plans is 65. The choice of this age has been influenced not only by the fact that this was the age at which full Social Security benefits commence but also that retiring employees before age 65 with full benefits often produces prohibitive costs. Federal law defines normal retirement age to be the age specified in the plan, but no later than age 65 or the fifth anniversary of the participant's date of initial plan participation, whichever is the last to occur. Occasionally, an earlier age such as 60 will be chosen as the normal retirement age although, to a great extent, this practice has been confined to public, quasi-public, and charitable institutions. Also, where an employee's occupation is such that his or her working career is shorter than in most other occupations, and when this does not result in prohibited age discrimination, a plan may provide for a normal retirement age lower than 65. It should be noted, however, that there has been a growing interest (both with management and employees) in retiring earlier than age 65 -- frequently by means of some form of subsidized early retirement benefit. On the other hand, the 1983 Social Security amendments gradually change the "normal" retirement age for collecting unreduced Social Security benefits from 65 to 67. It remains to be seen whether this will influence the choice of normal retirement age under private plans, assuming ERISA and the Code are amended to permit this action.

14.2.2. Early Retirement Age

Most plans provide that an employee may choose early retirement on a reduced pension, although a few plans limit this feature to cases of total and permanent disability. If an early retirement provision is included, it is customary to establish some requirements an employee must fulfill before being allowed to elect early retirement.

A typical requirement for early retirement would be that the employee must have attained at least age 55 and completed at least 10 years of service or participation in the plan. Requirements such as these limit the option to situations where the employee is actually retiring, as opposed to changing jobs. They also tend to create a situation in which the employee will receive a reasonable benefit.

The benefit payable at early retirement typically is lower than the normal retirement benefit for two reasons. First, the full benefit will not have accrued by the employee's early retirement date. Second, the benefit, because it is starting several years earlier than anticipated, will be paid over a longer period of time. Thus, an actuarial reduction factor usually is applied to the value of the employee's accrued benefit to determine the amount of early retirement benefit.

Determining the value of the employee's accrued benefit is relatively simple under an allocated funding instrument.[4] In a pension plan funded entirely by individual insurance policies, for example, the value of the accrued benefit generally is the cash surrender value of the employee's insurance or annuity contract at the time of retirement. In this type of plan, the actuarial reduction is accomplished by the use of the settlement option rates contained in the contract. The employee's benefit is generally that amount that may be provided by applying the cash surrender value under the option at the employee's attained age on his or her retirement date.

In plans using an unallocated funding instrument, and where the benefit formula reflects the employee's service, the benefit is generally measured in terms of the employee's accrued benefit to the date of retirement. If the plan uses another type of formula, however, the determination of the value of the employee's accrued benefit is more difficult. One often-used approach is to multiply the value of the employee's projected benefit at

---

[4]Funding instruments are classified on the basis of whether contributions are allocated to provide benefits to specific employees or whether contributions are accumulated in an unallocated fund to provide benefits for employees.

normal retirement date by a fraction, the numerator being the years of participation or service the employee has completed at early retirement date and the denominator the years of participation or service the employee would have completed at normal retirement date.

In any event, an employee's accrued benefit at early retirement must meet the accrued benefit requirements of federal tax law that apply to vested benefits (discussed in Chapter 6).

The reduction factor applied to the value of the employee's accrued benefit might be something as simple as a reduction of one half of 1 percent for each month by which early retirement precedes normal retirement; or, as sometimes is the case, an actuarial reduction factor is determined from a table included in the plan or group contract.

As noted earlier, there has been a growing interest in recent years in the possibility of retiring earlier than age 65. While some plans actually establish a normal retirement age earlier than age 65, a greater number encourage early retirement by not applying a full actuarial reduction if certain conditions are met. One approach, for example, is to provide for no actuarial reduction at all if the employee retires after attaining some age (such as 60) and after completing some period of service (such as 30 years). A similar approach would be to apply no reduction factor (or a minimum factor) if early retirement occurs when the employee's age and service total to some number such as 90 — for example, an employee who is age 62 and who has completed 28 years of service would satisfy this requirement. Still another approach would be to apply some simple factor, such as one fourth of 1 percent for each month by which early retirement precedes normal retirement, that is considerably less than the reduction that would otherwise be called for by full actuarial reduction factors. Approaches such as these will, of course, increase the cost of the pension plan; however, employees generally find such a provision to be attractive, and quite frequently the employer finds its overall interests are best served by a provision that encourages early retirement.

14.2.3. Late Retirement Age

Plans must also include a provision allowing an employee to defer retirement. This feature could also be important to the employer, since it permits a greater degree of flexibility in scheduling the actual retirement of a key employee when there is a problem in obtaining or training a replacement.

The Federal Age Discrimination Law and state laws protecting employment rights are discussed in Chapter 7. In general, these laws require employees to continue accruing benefits without regard to any maximum age limit.

14.3.   RETIREMENT BENEFITS

The formula selected for determining an employee's retirement benefit is a vital provision in a pension plan.   The employer's financial capacity and general philosophy concerning the desired level of retirement benefits, as well as the employer's specific objectives as to the distribution of benefits among employees, all play an important role in selecting such a formula.

Many employers believe that a plan should be designed to provide a higher paid career employee with an income after retirement that, together with primary Social Security benefits, will be about 50 to 55 percent of earnings just before retirement.   For lower paid employees, the percentage generally is set at a higher level -- perhaps as much as 80 to 85 percent.   For employees considered to be less than career employees (usually those employees with fewer than 25 or 30 years of service with the employer), these percentages would be proportionately smaller.   From the employer's viewpoint, the benefit formula selected should in no event result in a plan that produces unacceptable costs so as to endanger the continuation of the plan if corporate earnings are decreased or if current tax advantages are reduced.

Basically, there are two types of benefit formulas for the employer to consider.   The first is called a defined contribution or a money purchase formula.   Under this type of formula, contribution rates are fixed, and an employee's benefit varies depending upon such factors as the amount of the contributions made, investment earnings on plan assets, and the employee's entry age and retirement age.[5]

The second type is called a defined benefit or an annuity purchase formula.   Here, a definite benefit is established for each employee, and contributions are determined to be whatever is necessary to produce the desired benefit results.   Defined benefit formulas may be subdivided into several different classifications.[6]

14.3.1. Determination of Compensation

Since the amount of benefit under most formulas is based on an employee's compensation, it is important, before discussing specific formulas, to have a

---

[5]This chapter is concerned only with defined benefit pension plans.   Defined contribution plans, such as money purchase pension plans, profit sharing and thrift and savings plans, are discussed in Chapters 8 through 13.

[6]It has been said that a third type of benefit formula is emerging, one in which the employee's benefit will vary depending upon the performance of the common stock market or upon changes in a cost-of-living index.   Actually, this is not so, since variable benefit plans involve either a defined contribution or a defined benefit formula.

clear idea of the various considerations involved in selecting the compensation base to which the benefit formula will be applied. Such items as overtime pay, holiday pay, sick pay, bonuses, and commissions must specifically be excluded or included. The definition chosen must not discriminate in favor of HCEs (i.e., it must satisfy the requirements detailed in Chapter 5).

The question of whether plan benefits should be based on the average of the earnings paid over the entire period of the employee's participation in the plan or on an average of the employee's earnings during some shorter period of time that is near the employee's normal retirement age is crucial to proper plan design. The latter type of provision, often called a *final-pay provision*, would base benefits on the employee's earnings averaged, for example, over the last three or five years of employment, or over the three or five consecutive years in the 10-year period immediately prior to retirement during which the employee's earnings are the highest.

The advantage of a final-pay plan is that it relates benefits to the employee's earnings and standard of living during a period just preceding retirement. As a result, the employee's initial benefit keeps pace with any preretirement inflationary trends. Moreover, a final-pay plan is more likely to meet employer objectives as to benefit levels than is a *career-pay plan*. This type of plan, however, is usually more expensive than one that bases benefits on career average earnings. Many employers believe it is best to use a career average earnings plan and to make periodic adjustments in the benefit formula when economic trends justify such an action.

While a final-pay plan has the disadvantage of committing an employer to increased costs during an extended inflationary period, it should be remembered that in many situations the employer's capacity to absorb these increases also may be increased. Moreover, a final-pay plan generally produces more favorable results for key employees than the career average approach.

A final point to be noted concerns the requirement of federal tax law that an employee's normal retirement benefit can never be less than the highest early retirement benefit that he or she could have received. Thus, any salary reductions that occur after an employee first becomes eligible to retire early cannot have the effect of reducing the employee's normal retirement benefit.

14.3.2. Defined Benefit Formulas

Broadly speaking, there are four basic defined benefit formulas. These include: (1) a flat amount formula, which provides a flat benefit unrelated to an employee's earnings or service; (2) a flat percentage of earnings formula, which provides a benefit related to the employee's earnings but which does not reflect service; (3) a flat amount per year of service formula, which reflects an employee's service but not earnings; and (4) a percentage of earnings per year of service formula, which reflects both an employee's earnings and service. Defined benefit formulas also may be integrated with Social Security benefits; as discussed in Chapter 5.

14.3.2.1.   Flat Amount Formula

As indicated above, this type of formula provides for a flat benefit that treats all employees alike, regardless of their service, age, or earnings. For example, the benefit might be $100 or $150 a month. The flat amount formula, since it is considered to produce inequitable results, seldom is used by itself. On occasion, this formula is used in conjunction with some other type of formula; for example, a plan may provide a flat benefit of $150 a month for a covered employee, plus a percentage of his or her earnings in excess of the current Social Security taxable wage base.

While the employee's length of service is not reflected directly in this type of formula, service is in effect recognized since most plans require that an employee, upon attaining the normal retirement age specified by the plan, must have been employed for some period of time, such as 25 years. Plans that include such a requirement provide for a proportionately reduced benefit if the employee has accumulated fewer than the required number of years, thus creating, in effect, a formula weighted for service.

14.3.2.2.   Flat Percentage of Earnings Formula

This type of formula is sometimes used today, particularly in plans that cover salaried or clerical employees. Some percentage of earnings, usually ranging from 25 to 50 percent, is selected as the measure of the pension benefit. It may be used with either career average or final average earnings, although it is used most frequently in final-pay plans.

This type of formula does not take an employee's service into account, except in those plans that require that the employee must have completed a minimum period of service by normal retirement date and that provide for a proportionately reduced benefit if his or her service is less than the required number of years.

14.3.2.3.   Flat Amount per Year of Service Formula

This type of formula is often found in negotiated plans.   It provides a flat dollar amount for each year of service accumulated by the employee.   Thus, in a plan that provides for a benefit of $10 a month for each year of service, an employee with 27 years of employment would receive a monthly pension of $270.

This type of formula frequently requires that an employee must have worked for a minimum number of hours during a plan year to receive a full benefit credit for such year.   Minimums often used for this purpose are 1,600 and 1,800 hours.   An employee who works fewer than the required number of hours in a given year usually receives some proportionate credit for the actual hours worked.   Federal tax law requires that a proportionate credit be given if the employee is credited with at least 1,000 hours of service in the 12-month computation period used by the plan.

Some plans limit benefits to service performed after the plan was made effective, although in most cases credit is given for service prior to the inception of the plan.   When this is done, credit may or may not be given for service needed to meet any eligibility requirements of the plan.   Also, it is not uncommon to include a provision that limits the total service that may be credited for benefit purposes to a period such as 30 years.

14.3.2.4.   Percentage of Earnings per Year of Service Formula

A formula that gives specific recognition for service as well as earnings is considered by many pension practitioners to produce the most equitable results in terms of a benefit formula that provides benefits for employees in relation to their value or contributions to the firm.   A formula producing this result is often called a unit credit or past and future service formula. Under such a formula, an employee receives a benefit credit equal to a percentage of earnings for each year that he or she is a participant under the plan.   This benefit credit is called the employee's future service or current service benefit.   The percentage of earnings credited varies from plan to plan, but a typical percentage would be 1 percent or 1.25 percent.   It may be used with either career average or final earnings, and works particularly well with career average plans.

Many plans also include a "past service" benefit for employees who enter the plan on its effective date.   In a plan that bases future service benefits on career average earnings, the past service benefit is usually expressed as a fixed percentage of the employee's earnings on the effective date of the plan multiplied by the employee's years of past service.   In determining past service benefits, however, it is customary to exclude service that would have been required to join the plan had it always been in effect. It is also possible to limit the total years of past service credited. For example, past service could be limited to a given number of years (such as 10), to service completed after a certain calendar year (such as the year in which the firm was acquired by the current ownership interests), to service completed after attaining a certain age (such as 21), or to a combination of these factors. The percentage applied to earnings to determine past service benefits is usually a lower rate than is applied for future service benefits. The reason for this is that the earnings of an employee on the effective date of the plan generally are higher than the average of the employee's earnings over the period of his or her past service. Rather than determine the employee's actual average earnings during his or her past service, which is often difficult or even impossible because of the lack of records, a rough approximation is made by reducing the percentage applicable to the employee's higher earnings at the time the plan is established.

If the plan bases benefits on final earnings, a distinction is usually not made between past and future service benefits. Here, the employee's total service (subject to any limitations such as a maximum service credit provision or excluding service needed to meet eligibility requirements) is applied to the percentage of final earnings to determine the total retirement benefit.

14.3.2.5.   Variable Benefit Formulas

Variable benefit plans are designed to protect against the effects of inflation on a retired employee's pension benefit. They take either of two general forms: (a) the benefit varies to reflect changes in the value of a specific portfolio of common stocks and similar investments, or (b) the benefit varies to reflect changes in a recognized cost-of-living index such as that published by the Bureau of Labor Statistics. In either case, the plan attempts to adjust benefits to keep an employee's purchasing power on a relatively level basis. These plans are discussed in detail later in this chapter.

14.3.3. Permitted Disparities

A plan will not be discriminatory merely because it uses a benefit formula that provides a larger percentage of benefits for earnings in excess of some amount such as the Social Security taxable wage base than it does for earnings under this amount.[7] However, if the benefit formula is in any way integrated with Social Security benefits, certain requirements are imposed to prevent discrimination in favor of the HCEs. The basic concept of these requirements is that the benefits from the employer's plan must be dovetailed with Social Security benefits in such a manner that employees earning over the taxable base will not receive combined benefits under the two programs that are proportionately greater than the combined benefits for employees earning under this amount.

Before describing the provisions of the disparities permitted under Internal Revenue Code Section 401(l), it is important to establish the relationship between the discussion in this section and the nondiscrimination requirements in Chapter 5. If a plan satisfies the Section 401(l) requirements, permitted disparities in employer-provided contributions or benefits are disregarded in determining whether the plan satisfies any of the safe harbors previously described. However, even if disparities in employer-provided contributions or benefits under a plan are permitted under Section 401(l), the plan may still fail to satisfy the *nondiscrimination* requirements for other reasons. On the other hand, even if disparities in employer-provided contribution or benefits under a plan are not permitted under Section 401(l) and thus may not be disregarded for purposes of the nondiscrimination tests, the plan may still be found to be nondiscriminatory under the nondiscrimination tests, including the rules for imputing permitted disparity.[8]

Before proceeding with a discussion of the permitted disparity rules, it will be useful to provide some definitions:

- integration level: the dollar amount specified in an excess plan at or below which the rate of employer-provided contributions or benefits under the plan is less than the rate of employer provided contributions or benefits under the plan above such dollar amount
- offset level: the dollar limit specified in the plan for the amount of each employee's final average compensation taken into account in determining the offset under an offset plan
- covered compensation: the average (without indexing) of the taxable wage bases in effect for an employee for each year during the 35-year

---

[7]For plan years beginning before January 1, 1989, a qualified plan is also able to exclude individuals who earn less than the maximum taxable wage for social security purposes.

[8]Section 401(l) treatment is not available for certain plans including plans where participants are not covered by either Social Security or Railroad Retirement, ESOPs, 401(k) and 401(m) plans, and SEPs.

period ending with the year in which Social Security retirement age is attained.[9]

There are two alternative methods of meeting the Section 401(l) requirements for a defined benefit plan. This can be accomplished through a defined benefit excess plan under which the rate at which employer-provided benefits are determined with respect to *average annual compensation* above the integration level under the plan is greater than the rate at which employer-provided benefits are determined with respect to average annual compensation at or below the integration level (expressed as a percentage of such average annual compensation). Alternatively, a defined benefit plan can be structured as an offset plan in which each employee's employer-provided benefit is reduced or offset by a specified parentage of the employee's *final average compensation* up to the offset level under the plan.

Average annual compensation is calculated as an average over a period of at least three consecutive years, and can exclude years before the final ten years of service. For purposes of permitted disparity calculations, *final average compensation* is the average of the employee's annual compensation from the employer for the three consecutive year period ending with or within the plan year. Compensation for any year in excess of the taxable wage base in effect at the beginning of that year must not be taken into account in determining final average compensation.

14.3.3.1. Maximum Excess Allowance

In the case of a defined benefit excess plan, the disparity between the excess benefit percentage and the base benefit percentage may not exceed the maximum excess allowance defined as the lesser of:

- the base benefit percentage or
- 0.75 percent (reduced for any integration level or retirement age modifications as explained below).

The plan must use the same base benefit percentage and the same excess benefit percentage for all employees with the same number of years of service.

Example 1 provides an illustration of a plan that exceeds the maximum excess allowance.

---

[9]The taxable wage base for future years are assumed to be the same as the amount currently applicable.

Example 1 Plan J is a defined benefit excess plan that provides a normal retirement benefit of 0.5 percent of average annual compensation up to the integration level, plus 1.25 percent of average annual compensation in excess of the integration level, for each year of service up to 35. The disparity provided under the plan exceeds the maximum excess allowance because the excess benefit percentage (1.25 percent) exceeds the base benefit percentage of 0.5 percent by more than the base benefit percentage.

14.3.3.2.   Maximum Offset Allowance

In the case of a defined benefit offset plan, the disparity (as determined by the offset percentage) may not exceed the maximum offset allowance defined as the lesser of:

- 0.75 percent (reduced for any integration level or retirement age modifications as explained below) or
- one-half of the *gross benefit percentage*, multiplied by a fraction (not to exceed one) equal to the employee's average annual compensation divided by the employee's final average compensation up to the offset level.

The plan must use the same gross benefit percentage and the same offset percentage for all employees with the same number of years of service.

Examples 2 and 3 illustrate the maximum offset allowance. Both examples assume that the plan is noncontributory and is the only plan ever maintained by the employer. The plans use a normal retirement age of 65 and contain no provision that would require a reduction in the 0.75 percent factor. The plans use each employee's *covered compensation* as the offset level and in the first example the plan provides that an employee's final average compensation is limited to the employee's average annual compensation. Each example discusses the benefit appropriate to an employee who has a Social Security retirement age of 65.

Example 2 Plan K is an offset plan that provides a normal retirement benefit equal to 2 percent of average annual compensation, minus 0.75 percent of final average compensation up to the offset level, for each year of service up to 35. The disparity provided under the plan is within limits because the offset percentage of 0.75 percent does not exceed the maximum offset allowance equal to the lesser of 0.75 percent or one-half of the gross benefit percentage (1 percent).

Example 3 Plan L is an offset plan that provides a normal retirement benefit of 1 percent of average annual compensation, minus 0.5 percent of final average compensation up to the offset level, for each year of service up to 35. The plan determines an employee's average annual compensation using an averaging period comprising five consecutive 12-month periods ending with the plan year. The plan does not provide that an employee's final average compensation is limited to the employee's average annual compensation.

Employee M has average annual compensation of $20,000, final average compensation of $25,000, and covered compensation of $32,000. The maximum offset allowance applicable to Employee A for the plan year is one-half of the gross benefit percentage multiplied by the ratio, not to exceed one, of Employee M's average annual compensation divided by the final average compensation (up to the offset level). Thus, the maximum offset allowance is 0.4 percent (1/2 × 1 percent × $20,000/$25,000). Therefore, the plan must reduce Employee M's offset percentage to 0.4 percent.

14.3.3.3.   Integration and Offset Levels

The integration level in a defined benefit excess plan or the offset level in a defined benefit offset plan must satisfy one of the following:[10]

1. the integration or offset level for each employee is the employee's covered compensation
2. the integration or offset level for each employee is a uniform percentage (greater than 100 percent) of each employee's *covered compensation*[11]
3. the integration or offset level for all employees is a single dollar amount that does not exceed the greater of $10,000 or one-half of the covered compensation of an individual who attains Social Security retirement age in the calendar year in which the plan year begins.
4. the integration or offset level for all employees is a single dollar amount that is greater than the third integration or offset level, the plan satisfies specified demographic requirements[12] and the 0.75 percent factor in the

---

[10]Modifications apply in the case of a short plan year.

[11]In the case of a defined benefit excess plan, the integration level may not exceed the taxable wage base in effect for the plan year and in the case of an offset plan, the offset level may not exceed the employee's final average compensation.

[12]These demographic tests are described in Reg. Section 1.401(l)-3(d)(8). An additional alternative is available that does not require the use of the demographic tests; however, it may provide for a larger reduction to the 0.75 percent factor. See Reg. Section 1.401(l)-3(d)(6) for details.

maximum excess allowance or the maximum offset allowance is adjusted if the integration or offset level exceeds the covered compensation.

If the integration or offset level specified under the plan exceeds an employee's covered compensation , the 0.75 percent factor in the maximum excess allowance or maximum offset allowance must be reduced. Precise details for computing the reduction are provided in Reg. Section 1.401(l)-3(d)(9).

14.3.3.4.   Benefits Commencing at Ages Other Than Social Security Retirement Age

The 0.75 percent factor in the maximum excess allowance and the maximum offset allowance applies to a benefit commencing at the employee's Social Security retirement age.   In general, if a benefit payable to an employee under a defined benefit excess plan or a defined benefit offset plan commences at an age before then, the factor *is* reduced.[13] If the benefit commences at a later date, the factor *may be* increased.   Precise details for computing the modifications are provided in Reg. Section 1.401(l)-3(e)(2).

14.3.3.5.   Benefits, Rights and Features

In the case of a defined benefit excess plan, each benefit, right, or feature provided under the plan with respect to employer-provided benefits attributable to average annual compensation above the integration level (the "excess benefit, right, or feature") must also be provided on the same terms with respect to employer-provided benefits attributable to average annual compensation up to the integration level (the "base benefit, right, or feature"). Alternatively, an excess benefit, right, or feature may be provided on different terms than the base benefit, right, or feature if the terms used to determine it produce an inherently equal or greater value than that produced under the terms used to determine the excess benefit, right, or feature.
    In the case of an offset plan, each benefit, right, or feature provided under the plan with respect to employer-provided benefits before application of the offset (the "gross benefit, right, or feature") must also be provided on the same terms as those used to determine the offset applied to the gross benefit, right, or feature. Alternatively, a gross benefit, right, or feature may be provided on different terms from those used to determine

---

[13]Exceptions exist for certain disability benefits.

the offset applied to the gross benefit, right, or feature if the terms used to determine it produce an equal or greater value than that produced under the terms used to determine the offset applied to the gross benefit, right, or feature. In addition, if benefits commence before an employee's normal retirement age, the gross benefit percentage must be reduced by a number of percentage points no less than the reduction applied to the offset percentage.

For purposes of applying the maximum excess allowance and the maximum offset allowance, no reduction is made in the 0.75 percent factor solely because the plan provides disparity in death benefits that are unrelated to retirement benefits and are payable before an employee's Social Security retirement age.

Benefits attributable to employee contributions to a defined benefit plan are not taken into account in determining whether the maximum disparity is violated. This means that the base benefit percentage and the excess benefit percentage under a defined benefit excess plan are reduced to the extent that benefits are attributable to employee contributions. Similarly, the gross benefit percentage under a defined benefit offset plan is reduced to the extent the benefit is attributable to employee contributions.[14]

14.3.3.6.   Overall Permitted Disparity Limits

The maximum excess allowance and maximum offset allowance explained above limit the disparity that can be provided *for a plan year*. The *overall* permitted disparity rules described in this section apply to limit:
1.   the disparity provided for a plan year if an employee benefits under more than one plan maintained by the employer (the "annual overall permitted disparity limit"), and
2.   the disparity provided for an employee's total years of service (the "cumulative overall permitted disparity limit").

14.3.3.6.1. Annual Overall Permitted Disparity Limit

If an employee benefits under more than one plan, the annual overall permitted disparity limit is satisfied if the sum of the employee's annual disparity fractions does not exceed one. The annual disparity fractions are defined as the disparity provided under the plan divided by either the

---

[14]The mechanism for determining the employer-provided benefit in a contributory defined benefit plan is explained in Reg. Section 1.401(a)(4)-6(b).

maximum excess allowance (for excess plans) or the maximum offset allowance (for offset plans). The annual disparity fraction for an employee benefiting under a plan that imputes permitted disparity under the nondiscrimination requirements is defined as equal to one.

14.3.3.6.2. Cumulative Permitted Disparity Limit

The cumulative permitted disparity limit is satisfied if the sum of the employee's total annual disparity fractions does not exceed 35.   This requirement is automatically deemed to be satisfied for employees who do not benefit under a defined benefit plan after 1991.

14.3.4. Minimum Benefits

Closely related to the choice of an adequate benefit formula is the question of whether provision for a minimum pension should be included in the plan.

A minimum pension provision is generally a desirable feature of any pension plan.   It is often possible for a benefit formula to produce a very small pension benefit as applied to certain employees.   The use of a minimum pension can result in the payment of at least a minimum amount to these employees, while at the same time avoiding the embarrassment and ill will that might otherwise be generated in these situations.   Apart from these considerations, if the plan is insured, the insurer may insist on the inclusion of a minimum pension provision as a part of its general underwriting requirements -- particularly in the case of a plan funded with individual policies.

14.3.5. Target Benefit Plans

Many of the favorable aspects of the defined contribution pension plans described in Chapter 8 have caused growing interest in the so-called target benefit plan -- one that combines the concepts of both defined contribution and defined benefit plans. A target benefit plan is a money purchase plan under which contributions to an employee's account are determined with respect to the amounts necessary to fund the employee's stated retirement benefit under the plan. Target benefit plans will generally be tested under the general method for defined contribution plans (described in Chapter 5) on a benefits basis by converting allocations to equivalent benefits, or alternatively, will be tested under a special safe harbor.

The final regulations contain detailed mechanics for determining required contributions under the safe harbor design. In general, required contributions are determined by amortizing the excess of the present value of the stated benefit over the *theoretical reserve* on a level basis to normal retirement age. The theoretical reserve can be thought of as prior years' required contributions adjusted with interest.

14.4. DEATH BENEFITS

An employer-provided death benefit is an optional benefit under a pension plan; however, a great many plans include such a benefit.[15]   Broadly speaking, such a death benefit may take one of two forms -- the first consists of life insurance provided under some form of individual policy or group life insurance contract issued by an insurer, and the second consists of cash distributions from plan assets.   Death benefits also may be classified as being payable in the event of death either before or after retirement.

Death benefits provided under individual policy plans and death benefits provided from plan assets are considered a part of the plan and, as such, are subject to the requirement of the Internal Revenue Service that the death benefit must be "incidental." In a defined benefit plan using life insurance, the incidental test is satisfied if the benefit does not exceed 100 times the expected monthly pension benefit or, if greater, the reserve for the pension benefit. The incidental test is not violated if the death benefit does not exceed the sum of the reserve of the life insurance policy and the amount held for the employee in the conversion fund.   Also, as long as less than 50 percent of the employer's contributions for an employee have been used to purchase life insurance, the face amount of the life insurance plus the employee's share of the conversion fund may be paid as the death benefit under a defined benefit plan without violating the incidental death benefit rules.

A plan may provide both a lump-sum preretirement death benefit and a QPS annuity, as long as the incidental death benefits rule is not violated. A plan under which the only preretirement death benefit is a QPS annuity satisfies the incidental death benefits rule. However, a QPS annuity is considered an integral part of a preretirement death benefit.   Thus, for defined benefit plans, the QPS annuity must be considered with other

---

[15]In the case of a married participant, a qualified retirement plan is required to provide a death benefit to the participant's surviving spouse unless an election and consent to waive such benefits have been made. See Chapter 6 for details.

preretirement benefits to determine whether the benefits provided are incidental.   A plan that provides a lump-sum preretirement death benefit equal to 100 times the monthly annuity amount and a QPS annuity violates the incidental death benefits rule.[16]

According to Revenue Ruling 85-15, however, there are several amendments that would enable a plan with a lump-sum preretirement death benefit to satisfy the incidental death benefits requirement.   For example, the plans could offset the (otherwise) incidental preretirement death benefit by the value of the QPS.   In this regard, if life insurance contracts are purchased by the plan to provide the lump-sum preretirement death benefit, the proceeds could be paid to the plan's trust with the trust providing the QPS to the surviving spouse and the excess, if any, of the lump-sum preretirement death benefit over the value of the QPS annuity to the participant's beneficiary (who could also be the surviving spouse).

14.5.   DISABILITY BENEFITS

In the pension area, disability benefits, even in insured plans, generally have been provided on a self-insured basis; that is, the benefits are paid in some form directly from plan assets, and the employer's experience in this regard is reflected in the cost level of the plan.

A number of pension plans, particularly those funded with individual policies, provide for full vesting if an employee becomes totally and permanently disabled.   Other plans treat such a disability as an early retirement if the employee has completed some minimum period of service or participation in the plan and has attained some minimum age. Unfortunately, the disability benefits provided under such provisions are either nonexistent or inadequate for disabilities occurring at younger ages.

Some group pension and trust fund plans, however -- particularly those that have been union negotiated -- provide for a separate and distinct benefit in the event of total and permanent disability.   The benefit provided under such plans sometimes is a specified dollar amount, a specified percentage of earnings, or an amount equal to the employee's accrued or projected pension credits (with or without actuarial reduction).   Often, the disability benefit under the plan is integrated with benefits available under government plans such as worker's compensation or Social Security benefits. Frequently, the plan provides that the disability benefit will terminate when

---

[16]Rev. Rul. 85-15. Since the lump-sum preretirement death benefit already equals the maximum amount considered "incidental," the addition of a preretirement survivor annuity would cause the plan's total preretirement death benefit to violate Internal Revenue Service regulations.

the employee reaches normal retirement age, at which time the accrued normal pension benefit will be payable.[17]

Most plans will continue to accumulate pension credits during disability and while long-term disability benefits are being paid.   If the pension benefit is based on the participant's salary, additional credits are often frozen at the level of the pre-disability salary.

14.6.   THE IMPACT OF INFLATION ON PENSIONER INCOME[18]

Everyone, in one way or another, bears the burden of inflation. For many individuals, this burden can be lightened or even eliminated by improvements in pay, investment opportunities, changes in lifestyle, and the like. One segment of the population, however -- pensioners who are living on a fixed income -- has limited opportunity to counteract the effects of inflation and, as a result, can suffer to a greater extent than those who are still actively employed or those who have accumulated independent wealth.

The rate of inflation slowed down to a considerable extent during the 1980s. Even so, the general expectations that inflation will continue, at least to some extent, and that the number of years employees will spend in retirement will increase (as a result of recent trends in early retirement and increases in life expectancy), make it important to consider the needs of the retired population. It is also significant that the size of this population is increasing not only in numbers, but also as a percentage of the total population; according to some projections, by the turn of the century there will be one person over age 65 for every two workers under that age.

Inflation affects pensioners not only in the period following retirement, but also during the period of active employment while their pensions are being accrued. The following discusses, first, the plan design approaches used to counteract the effect of preretirement inflation and, second, approaches used to offset postretirement inflation. Although the primary focus relates to retirement income levels, the material concludes with a brief discussion of postretirement death and medical expense benefits often provided by employers for their pensioners.

---

[17]It would seem such a provision is consistent with the Age Discrimination in Employment Act, as amended in 1986.   However, the Department of Labor and the Equal Employment Opportunity Commission have indicated, in their opinion, such a provision might be in violation of the law concerning disabilities occurring after age 60 -- where the continuation of some disability income benefit might have to be provided for some period after age 65.

[18]The material in this section is based on material prepared by Towers, Perrin. All rights reserved.

14.6.1. Preretirement Inflation

As noted earlier, employer commitments to provide private plan retirement benefits vary from none at all to a replacement of a substantial part of an employee's pay determined at or shortly before retirement.

If an employer's plan provides a specific amount of retirement benefit, the amount of this benefit is expressed either as a dollar amount or in relation to the employee's pay. If pay-related, the benefit may be determined as a percentage of pay averaged over the employee's career or over a relatively short period such as three or five years -- often the high three- or five-year average during the last 10 years of employment.

Dollar amount plans (e.g., plans that provide a benefit such as $15 per month per year of service) do not directly reflect inflation because they are not pay related. However, these plans are typically union negotiated and, in practice, the dollar amount is increased periodically via the collective bargaining process. Thus, in fact, these plans tend to provide initial retirement benefits that allow for preretirement inflationary trends. Of course, the extent to which this is so for any specific pensioner will depend upon the time of actual retirement and the dollar level then in effect for benefits under the plan.

Those plans that base benefits on final pay provide a retiring employee with an initial benefit that reflects inflation that has taken place prior to retirement. In fact, the majority of the nonnegotiated defined benefit plans in effect today use some form of final-pay base to determine benefits and thus recognize most of the inflation that takes place prior to retirement. The use of a five-year average for this purpose has been quite common. Because most of these plans are noncontributory, the cost of accommodating preretirement inflation is being borne primarily by employers. This cost becomes dramatically evident in inflationary periods as total pension plan costs rise, relative to payroll costs, because of pay movement in excess of that anticipated.

Some employers have chosen to develop benefit and cost commitments on the basis of career-pay plans. These plans, of course, reflect some part of the inflation that takes place prior to retirement. However, unless the rates of accrual are set unusually high, or the employer has updated the benefits that have accrued for employees, or the plan also has a minimum benefit formula based on final pay, the initial level of benefit provided for a pensioner will not fully reflect the inflation that has taken place during a working career. In many situations, employers periodically update career-pay plans by recalculating accrued benefits on the basis of then current pay. Although the career-pay approach, with periodic updates, provides less assurance to employees than the final-pay approach concerning the adequacy of their benefits, there are definite advantages to the employer.

First, the employer retains control over the timing and extent to which the cost of inflation is assumed. Second, the employer also receives credit for making periodic benefit improvements.

14.6.2. Postretirement Inflation

The techniques utilized to adjust benefits for employees who have already retired may be automatic or nonautomatic. The automatic adjustments provide for increases, at stated intervals, that are related to some form of index such as the CPI or to rates of return on an investment fund. The nonautomatic increases are provided on an irregular basis, at the employer's discretion, with the amount of increase determined in a variety of ways. The following discusses and evaluates these different techniques.

14.6.2.1.   Automatic Adjustments

Four basic forms of automatic adjustment techniques have been used for making postretirement benefit changes:

1.   Equity pensions.
2.   Cost-of-living formulas.
3.   Wage-related formulas.
4.   Specified percentage formulas.

14.6.2.1.1. Equity Pensions

An equity pension, often called a variable annuity, provides retirement income that varies in dollar amounts to reflect the investment results of an underlying fund of common stocks. The equity feature (usually affecting only a portion of the retirement income amount) may operate during the years of active employment as well as during the postretirement payout period. In either case, the assumption is that stock price movement will vary with the movement of all other prices and, hence, reflect the general level of inflation. Proponents of the equity pension approach argue that active employees and pensioners have some assurance their retirement income will fluctuate with the general level of economic activity. Until the late 1960s and early 1970s, calculations of stock market performance indicated that only in a few periods would the pensioner have been better off with fixed-dollar retirement income. Also, from the employer's standpoint, the cost of equity pensions can be predicted beforehand. This is because the risk of potential investment gains and losses has been shifted to plan participants. Another potential advantage to the employer is that equity pensions may eliminate or reduce the need for other pension benefit liberalizations. Finally, an equity pension plan, at least during a rising market (such as the one experienced from late 1982 until mid-1987), could prove to be popular with employees, particularly where preretirement accruals are geared to stock performance.

Despite these points, equity pensions have some disadvantages:

1.   Employees and/or pensioners are required to assume the risk of investment loss as well as the reward of investment gain. It is questionable whether individuals at lower income levels should be asked to assume this risk/reward situation for an item that constitutes an important part of their economic security.

2.   The downward fluctuations in pension payments, which invariably occur from time to time, may cause hardship for pensioners. Recognizing this problem, employers may limit the amount of annual downward (or upward) adjustment through use of a securities fluctuation reserve.

3.   Equity pensions are more complicated than fixed-dollar pensions and are often more difficult to explain than other methods of adjusting pensions. This could be particularly important in a situation where the employer's fund fails to perform as well as recognized equity indexes.

4.   If the objective is to have an employee's retirement income vary directly with cost- or standard-of-living changes, equity pensions may not be appropriate in the timing and magnitude of the pension fluctuations. At best, equity pensions are only an indirect means of relating retirement income to economic trends. At worst, and particularly over the short term, equity pensions may result in decreasing pension amounts during periods of rampant inflation.

5.   From the employer's viewpoint, the equity pension approach may, in fact, produce additional or unnecessary costs. If the value of equities increases faster than the cost of living, benefits will be greater than may be needed to maintain the original income-replacement ratios of pensioners. At the same time, the excess investment return that causes this result will not be available to reduce employer costs. On the other hand, if the cost of living outpaces the performance of the equity market, the employer may very well feel the need to assume the additional cost of providing some form of supplemental benefit for pensioners. Thus, the employer reaps none of the gain of superior investment performance and might become involved in the cost of

underwriting this performance when it falls short of cost-of-living changes.

The difficulties encountered in the late 1970s, when relatively high rates of inflation occurred during periods of depressed stock values, have caused many companies to move from the equity pension concept to some other form of pension adjustment technique. At this time, equity pensions are used primarily by colleges and universities.

14.6.2.1.2. Cost-of-Living Formulas

A direct approach to automatic pension adjustments involves linking retirement income amounts by formula to upward (and in some cases, downward) changes in a cost-of-living or price index such as the CPI. Under these plans, pension amounts increase periodically, subject to limits, if the increase in the price index equals or exceeds a predetermined level. The major advantages of this approach are that employees have advance assurance their retirement income will be adjusted periodically to help preserve their purchasing power and that the CPI, used almost exclusively in such plans, is well known and at least partially understood by most employees. Consequently, the employer has a good chance of avoiding criticism that the pension adjustment technique is faulty.

The following are possible disadvantages:

1. The employer assumes a largely undeterminable future liability tied to a government index over which it has no control. (However, the adjustment formula may be designed to provide ceilings on the amount of the increase in benefits and thus the maximum additional costs that are assumed.)

2. No allowance is made for any rising standard of living that may be experienced by active employees.

3. The CPI may, in fact, overstate rates of inflation and the presumed needs of pensioners, thus resulting in additional and unnecessary costs.

4. The tax law requires that any automatic increases be given to vested terminations -- individuals for whom the employer may feel little or no continuing obligation.

5. If the pension plan provides for subsidized early retirement benefits, the cost of this subsidization very possibly will increase because the assurance of protection against inflation will most likely cause an increase in the incidence of early retirement.

6.   Providing automatic cost-of-living adjustments for pensioners could create pressure to follow the same approach (i.e., automatic cost-of-living adjustments for wages) for active employees.

The cost implications of providing automatic cost-of-living increases for pensioners can be quite significant. The actual cost increases associated with such a benefit will, of course, vary from plan to plan and can range from about 8 to 20 percent for each 1 percent annual increase in benefits. Paradoxically, the greater the degree of funding achieved by a plan, the greater the percentage increase in plan costs when pensioner benefits are increased (as would be true whenever any of the benefits of such a plan are increased). Also, the greater the proportion of females covered by the plan, the greater the cost of pensioner increases. Assuming that a plan is approximately 50 percent funded and that the majority of pensioners are male, one rule of thumb is that pension costs will increase by about 10 percent for each 1 percent annual increase in pensioner benefits. Increases in accrued benefit liabilities would generally follow the same increase pattern. The extent of the increase in accrued benefit liabilities would be different for each plan and would be most significant where existing pensioner liabilities are small compared to total plan liabilities and where females form a substantial portion of all plan participants.

Cost-of-living formulas are frequently found in the public sector (e.g., the federal civil service and military retirement systems, and various state and municipal plans), but are still relatively rare in the private sector. Although there is growing interest in this approach, many employers are wary of its cost implications, particularly if the feature is not needed to provide retirement benefits that are competitive either on the basis of industry or geography.

14.6.2.1.3. Wage-Related Formulas

This method involves the automatic fluctuation of retirement income payments in response to changes in some designated wage index. This permits pensioners to benefit from standard-of-living improvements enjoyed by active employees. The index could be one of a general nature, such as the Bureau of Labor Statistics' index of the average wage for industrial workers, or a more specialized one, such as the average wage paid by the individual employer. The former alternative normally would seem most appropriate as a measure of general standard-of-living variations, but it might have limited application to a specific employee group. The latter could have a significant impact on pension plan costs if an employer maintains a liberal salary or wage increase policy. Some governmental units sponsor plans with wage-related formulas for pension adjustments; however, this type of plan is relatively uncommon, particularly in the private sector.

14.6.2.1.4. Specified Percentage Formulas

Under this approach, a predetermined percentage formula governs the amount of annual increase in retirement income. Unlike cost-of-living or wage-related plans, the company, in a sense, estimates future economic trends and commits itself to a specific increase on this estimation. For example, the pension may be increased automatically by 1.5 percent a year on the assumption that this increase will offset, at least partially, upward trends in prices. When compared with cost-of-living and wage-related formulas, a specified percentage formula permits a more reliable prediction of plan costs. The primary disadvantage is that no assurance exists that the retirement income increases will actually reflect shifts in the cost of living, particularly over the short run. It is only by coincidence that such a plan would respond precisely to inflation and fulfill employee needs. This approach is not commonly employed except in some state and municipal pension plans.

14.6.2.2. Nonautomatic Adjustments

The most popular method of coping with postretirement inflation, and the one that has been adopted by a majority of large, well-known organizations, has been the nonautomatic or discretionary form of adjustment made at irregular intervals and with varying ways of determining the amount of increase provided. Reasons for adopting a discretionary rather than an automatic approach to pension increases include the following:

1. Because the rate of inflation is uncertain, an organization should not commit itself to a predetermined or formula method.
2. Discretionary adjustments have a predictable cost because they remain under the employer's control, both as to timing and amount.
3. Both the scope and level of Social Security benefits may eliminate or reduce substantially the need for future retirement income improvements.
4. The employer receives credit for making a plan improvement each time benefits are increased.

One obvious disadvantage of the discretionary approach is the lack of assurance for pensioners that retirement income levels will continue to meet their needs. Another possible disadvantage is that this technique offers no possibility of prefunding the cost of the increases or having employees share in this cost during their active employment.

The discretionary adjustment techniques most frequently used are either fixed percentage, or flat-dollar formulas, or a combination of the two.

A *flat percentage* increase may be applied uniformly to the retirement income of all pensioners. Alternatively, graded percentages may be used with variations based on a pensioner's age group, years of service prior to retirement, or the number of years since retirement date or the last pensioner increase. In a few instances, the pension increase may be limited to a defined "subsistence" income group -- that is, a percentage increase is applied only if a pensioner's total income from the company's plan and Social Security falls below certain dollar amounts. The percentage increase may be at least indirectly contingent on changes in the CPI. Frequently, the increase is subject to a stated dollar minimum and/or maximum; for example, the minimum monthly increase might be $10, with the maximum established at $75 or $100. The usual rationale for having a maximum is that the need for additional income is not as acute for pensioners who are receiving substantial pension payments. However, the higher the level of total pension income, the greater will be the loss of purchasing power because of inflation. This, of course, is because of the effect of automatic Social Security increases and the significance they have for pensioners at lower income levels.

A *flat-dollar* increase may be applied uniformly or on a variable basis. The latter approach is often used for nonunion, salaried pensioners to provide them with the same level of benefit increases provided for union pensioners.

The choice of formula and the level of percentage or dollar amount chosen depend upon a number of factors including the cost and funding implications involved, the original level of pension provided, actual CPI movement, changes in Social Security benefits, the timing and form of the last pensioner increase (if any), competitive practices, and the cost and level of other benefits (death and medical expense) being provided.

It also should be noted that nonautomatic adjustments have been negotiated for retired members of a collective bargaining unit. Although these increases are not a mandatory subject of collective bargaining, there is nothing to prevent voluntary negotiations on this issue. Contracts negotiated in recent years between the United Auto Workers and the major automobile manufacturers are examples of this type of negotiation.

These discretionary adjustments are sometimes made part of the underlying formal plan. At other times, particularly when the formula will not meet Internal Revenue Service requirements for a qualified pension plan, discretionary adjustments are provided as a separate, nonqualified benefit. Even so, such nonqualified benefits are still subject to the labor provisions of ERISA unless they qualify for the exemptions provided.

Although the nonqualified approach has the advantage of permitting flexibility in the design of the formula, it has potential funding disadvantages; for example, the liability for the increase must be funded on a current disbursement basis over the remaining lifetimes of the pensioners, and there is no ability to vary this funding level from year to year without affecting the benefits payable to pensioners. (However, the possibility of some overall funding flexibility is available if the funded position of the underlying formal plan is such that its funding level can be reduced to reflect payments being made under the nonqualified supplement.) Although the same rate of funding probably is desirable if the benefit is funded as part of the formal plan, the flexibility does exist for amortizing this additional liability over as much as a 30-year period.

14.6.3. Supplemental Benefits

Many employers provide some form of death and/or medical expense benefit for their pensioners. Often the benefits are provided at no cost to the pensioner or on the basis of only a modest contribution. Although these benefits do not provide a form of direct income, they do assist pensioners in meeting their economic security needs and, in so doing, reduce the amounts pensioners would otherwise have to spend to obtain this protection. Employer practices in this regard vary to a considerable extent. The following very briefly discusses the benefits most frequently provided.

14.6.3.1.   Death Benefits

Group life insurance is almost always provided for active employees. Often, some basic amount of coverage is provided at no cost to the employee, with optional amounts available on a contributory basis. In other situations, the entire amount of group life insurance is available only on a basis that requires employee contributions.

Very few major employers completely discontinue noncontributory group life insurance at retirement; on the other hand, very few continue the full amount of such coverage throughout retirement. Typically, the coverage is reduced either all at once or in equal installments over a 5- or 10- year period. The ultimate amount of insurance provided is often a flat amount such as $5,000, or an amount equal to 25 or 50 percent of the pensioner's final pay before retirement. In the case of early retirement, it is common to continue the full coverage until the pensioner reaches age 65, at which time the scheduled reductions begin.

In situations where the full amount of group life insurance requires employee contributions, the pattern of postretirement reductions and coverage is similar to that described above. However, when the coverage is provided by a combination of noncontributory and contributory coverage, the contributory coverage is almost always terminated at retirement (although, in the case of early retirement, full coverage might be made available to the pensioner until age 65 if he or she continues to make any required contributions).

Survivor benefits are another form of postretirement death benefit for pensioners. Typically, the benefit is in the form of continuing all or part of the pensioner's income to a designated survivor. Survivor benefits may be provided at no cost to the pensioner, at full cost to the pensioner, or on a basis where the cost is shared by both the employer and the pensioner.

Most employers do not assume the full cost of providing postretirement survivor benefits. Those that do often provide the benefit only for the pensioner's spouse. In this event, the benefit is usually in the form of continuing 25 or 50 percent of the pensioner's income to the spouse for his or her lifetime.

If the pensioner is paying all or part of the cost of the postretirement survivor benefit, the typical method of making the benefit available is through the use of the optional payment provisions of the pension plan. Thus, the form of payment could guarantee that the benefit would be paid for a minimum number of years or, as is more often the case, the benefit could be payable on a joint-and-survivor basis with all or part of the pensioner's benefit being continued to the spouse. (The Code requires that the automatic payment form for a married pensioner, subject to a right of revocation, be a life annuity with at least 50 percent of the pensioner's benefit continued after death to the pensioner's spouse. However, the full cost of this benefit can be passed on to the pensioner.) The cost of providing such postretirement benefits is met by reducing the amount of benefit otherwise payable to the pensioner. If the pensioner is paying all of the cost, the reduction will be the full amount necessary to create a benefit that is the actuarial equivalent of the amount payable to the pensioner as a life annuity; those employers who assume part of the cost do so by subsidizing the amount by which the pensioner's benefit is reduced -- that is, the amount of the reduction is not a full actuarial equivalent.

14.6.3.2.   Medical Expense Benefits

Currently, many of the employers who provide retirement benefits also provide some form of postretirement coverage for medical expenses. According to Employee Benefit Research Institute tabulations of the August 1988 Current Population Survey, 43 percent of those aged 40 and over had retiree health coverage through their own or their spouse's current or former employer.[19] It is quite possible that this will be modified in the future though as a result of the Financial Accounting Standards Board's Statement No. 106, "Employers' Accounting for Postretirement Benefits Other Than Pensions."[20]

In the case of early retirement, it is common to provide a pensioner and spouse with the full level of coverage provided for active employees. When the pensioner or spouse reaches age 65, adjustments are made. Some employers terminate the coverage; others continue coverage, sometimes with lesser benefits, and in some fashion recognize that the pensioner or spouse has become eligible for medicare. The two most common approaches are to: (1) "carve out" medical payments from the employer's plan; or (2) supplement medicare benefits by paying all or part of the deductibles and coinsurance features of medicare or, possibly, by paying for certain items not covered by medicare such as prescription drugs and private duty nursing. Some employers also pay the pensioner's premium cost for Part B coverage under medicare.

Medical coverage provided for pensioners after age 65 is frequently but not always noncontributory. If contributions are required from active employees and if full coverage is continued from early retirement to age 65, it is customary to continue collecting contributions from the pensioner, at least for coverage prior to age 65.

QUESTIONS FOR REVIEW

1. Describe the advantages and disadvantages of a final-pay pension plan.
2. For what purpose is a target benefit plan treated as a defined benefit pension plan? For what purposes is it treated as a defined contribution pension plan?

---

[19]This includes both private and public employers. See Jennifer Davis, "Retiree Health Benefits: Issues of Structure, Financing, and Coverage," *EBRI Issue Brief* (Washington, D.C.: Employee Benefit Research Institute, March 1991).

[20]In December 1990, the Financial Accounting Standards Board approved Statement No. 106 that will require companies to eventually record a liability for retiree health benefits on their balance sheet to comply with generally accepted accounting standards.

3. Explain the four basic defined benefit formulas.
4. Describe how defined benefit pension plans may be integrated with social security.
5. Describe how preretirement inflation would be treated in (a) dollar amount plans and (b) career-pay plans.
6. From the employer's viewpoint, what advantages are offered by a career-pay approach with periodic updates?
7. Describe the potential advantages and disadvantages of an equity pension.
8. Describe how wage-related formulas may be used to treat the impact of postretirement inflation on pensioner income.
9. Describe the advantages and disadvantages associated with the use of a specified percentage formula.
10. Why might an employer adopt a discretionary rather than an automatic approach to pension increases?

QUESTIONS FOR DISCUSSION

1. Summarize the general theory behind the nondiscrimination requirements for integrated pension plans.
2. Assume that you have been asked to prepare a report to determine if the current system of benefit adjustments for private pension plans could be replaced by automatic benefit increases tied to specific price indicators. What are the major points that need to be covered in such a report?
3. An employer asks you to comment on a new concept of providing pension adjustments for retirees. Under this concept, employees are provided with an option to receive benefits in the form of an increasing annuity. Describe the plan design considerations of such an approach and its relative advantages and limitations.

15. Cost and Funding Considerations

A pension plan, in its simplest form, is a promise by the employer to pay a periodic benefit (usually for life) to employees who meet the requirements set forth in the plan. For a given pension benefit, the amount of annual benefit payments under the plan depends upon the number of retired workers. The number of retired workers, in turn, depends upon the rate at which already retired workers die and the rate at which new employees are added to the retirement rolls. Since the average life expectancy for a 65-year-old is about 15 years, it is quite likely that for some time after the plan is established, more new members are added to the retired employee group than are removed from the group as a result of death. Therefore, under a typical plan, the aggregate annual benefit payout should increase for a substantial number of years after the inception of the plan. The annual benefit payout continues to increase until a point is reached at which the size of the retired employee group tends to stabilize; that is, the point at which the number of retired workers dying is about equal to the number of new additions to the retired group.

However, when the employer funds the plan, the pattern of the annual contributions under the plan will differ from the benefit payout pattern because, as indicated earlier, the benefit payout pattern for a given level of pension benefit is dependent upon the number of retired workers eligible for benefits during each year and will be the same regardless of the manner in which contributions are made.

The objective of this chapter is to consider some of the important implications of funding and to acquaint the reader with the factors affecting the ultimate cost of a pension plan, apart from specific plan provisions and benefits. Particular reference is made to the various actuarial assumptions and cost methods that can be used in determining the incidence and amount of pension costs. The discussion later in this chapter assumes a fixed set of plan specifications and also assumes, for the purpose of simplicity, that the plan is noncontributory.

15.1.   ESTIMATED COST VERSUS ULTIMATE COST

The only way to determine the true cost of a pension plan would be to wait until the last retired employee has died, add up all the benefit payments and administrative expenses that have been paid since the inception of the plan, and subtract the investment earnings. The ultimate cost of the plan could then be stated as the benefits paid plus administrative expenses less investment earnings over the total life of the plan.

However, no business firm would ever establish a pension plan if the cost of the plan were completely uncertain until the plan is terminated at some date in the distant future. The obvious solution is that although the specific ultimate cost is unknown, actuaries are able to estimate the ultimate cost of the plan with reasonable accuracy and thus arrive at a level of estimated plan contributions. To do this, assumptions must be made regarding the factors that affect the plan's ultimate cost. In subsequent years, adjustments in the estimated amounts of contributions required may have to be made, based on comparisons between the actual experience under the plan and the assumed experience. Experience more favorable than expected permits a reduction in future contributions. Conversely, adverse experience under the plan requires an increase in future contributions.

The point that pension cost projections are estimates and not actual cost figures cannot be overstressed. A moment's reflection regarding the nature of a pension plan should make this point quite clear. Assume, for example, that a pension plan provides employees with a retirement benefit only after attainment of age 65 and completion of a minimum of 5 years of service with the employer. It is obvious that not all current employees of the firm will be entitled to a retirement benefit under the plan. Some employees may die and others may quit, be laid off, or become disabled prior to age 65. Other employees may defer their retirement beyond age 65; and, also, the number of years that retired workers will live cannot be predicted with certainty. Furthermore, in the case of funded plans, the rate of investment income to be earned in the future on accumulated assets in the pension fund can only be estimated.

But, how does the pension actuary make an estimate of the ultimate cost of a pension plan? The first step is to make estimates of the various components of the ultimate cost; that is, estimates of the benefits paid, the expenses, and the investment return expected. The estimate of benefits paid depends on three things: the benefit provisions of the pension plan; the characteristics of the participants in the plan (age, sex, salary, and length of service); and the actuarial assumptions used to predict the amount of future benefit payments. The benefit provisions and characteristics of plan participants are unique to the plan being valued, while the actuarial assumptions are determined by the pension actuary valuing the plan. Selection of the appropriate actuarial assumptions for predicting future benefit payments along with actuarial assumptions as to expenses and investment return are discussed in the next section of this chapter.

Once an estimate of the ultimate cost of the plan is determined, the next step is to determine the contributions required to pay for the estimated cost in an orderly manner. One of several actuarial cost methods will be used to allocate the costs to the various years and will be discussed in the next chapter.

15.2.   CHOICE OF ASSUMPTIONS

Two important points should be made regarding the choice of assumptions for the calculation of estimated pension costs.

First, the flexibility available in choosing a particular set of actuarial assumptions depends in large part upon the funding instrument involved.[1] The greatest flexibility is available under trust fund plans and under unallocated group pension contracts such as a group deposit administration contract. If the employer has competent advice, the assumptions used will be reasonable for the type of plan and the characteristics of the employee group covered. Fully insured individual policy plans and group permanent and group deferred annuity instruments offer the employer the least choice in cost assumptions, since the insurance company effectively establishes the assumptions to be used by its premium rates.

Second, the choice of a particular set of assumptions does not normally alter the ultimate cost of the plan. The choice of assumptions will affect the cost allocated to a given year, but the ultimate cost is primarily dependent on actual experience over the life of the pension plan. Obviously, the ages at which employees retire or the rate at which they die or leave their jobs is not necessarily the same as the assumptions in these areas made by the pension actuary. The relative magnitude of actuarial gains and losses under the plan will vary, given different original assumptions, but the end result will be an approximately similar ultimate cost picture except to the extent

---

[1]Funding instruments are described in Chapters 20 and 21.

that investment earnings are affected by the incidence of contributions produced by the funding assumptions chosen. This conclusion does not apply fully in the case of plans funded with individual policies. In the case of individual contracts, there is a certain degree of pooling of experience among the whole class of business. For example, the mortality or expense experience under a particular plan is not directly reflected in the insurance company's dividends paid to that group, since the dividend scale for individual policies is determined by the experience for that class of business as a whole. There is also an element of pooling in some group plans.

15.3. COST ASSUMPTIONS

As discussed above, one approach in considering the factors affecting the cost of a pension plan is to relate these factors to the formula for determining the ultimate cost of the plan; that is, benefits paid plus administrative expenses less investment earnings.

15.3.1. Benefits Paid

Number of Employees Retiring. The amount of benefits paid under a plan depends upon several factors. The first factor is the number of workers who will ultimately be entitled to receive benefits under the plan. The number of employees who will be eligible for benefits will depend on four factors: (1) mortality rates among active employees, (2) rates and duration of disabilities among active employees under a plan that offers a disability benefit, (3) layoffs and voluntary terminations of employment, and (4) rates of retirement at different ages. Let us now turn to a consideration of each of these cost factors.

Mortality. The higher the rate of mortality among active employees, the lower will be the cost of retirement benefits under the plan. However, if a participant is entitled to a preretirement death benefit, this will increase the cost of the plan, as additional benefits are being provided.

Mortality among active employees can be an important cost-reducing factor in those plans providing little or no death benefit beyond the mandated death benefits described in Chapter 14. This is particularly true for small plans, where a few deaths can have a significant impact on the cost of the plan.

Actuaries generally use the same mortality table in projecting mortality among both active and retired employees.

Several mortality tables are available for pension cost calculations. Projections have also been developed to reflect the probable continuing improvements in mortality. Thus, as improvements in mortality occur, or are expected to occur, the actuary often uses a group annuity mortality table with the projection that he or she believes to be appropriate for the given case. Mortality gains or losses will develop from year to year, and the actuary can keep abreast of the experience through subsequent modifications of the mortality assumption.

The question is often raised whether a mortality assumption should be used in calculating the amount of contributions to be paid into a conversion fund under combination plans -- particularly those plans covering a small group of employees.[2] Pension practitioners seem to be divided in their opinions on this point. Some planners prefer to use a mortality assumption in these cases, while others believe that the size of the covered group generally involved in plans of this type is too small to permit the expectations to be realized. If the expected mortality among a small group of employees does not materialize, the employer will be faced with the need for additional contributions in future years. Those favoring the use of a mortality assumption in these situations argue that its use results in a lower initial contribution requirement, which might be best suited to the current financial needs of some employers, and that any actuarial losses due to the use of such an assumption may be offset by actuarial gains due to severance of employment. Furthermore, it is argued that if the expected mortality is realized, the use of a mortality assumption produces a more realistic projection of future costs. Although there is merit in the latter position, the pension planner should clearly point out to the employer the full implications of using a mortality assumption with relatively small groups.

Rate and Duration of Disability. If a pension plan offers a disability benefit, cost projections for that plan should include a disability assumption. The plan actuary must establish two sets of probabilities in evaluating the cost of providing a disability benefit. First, a rate of occurrence (frequency) of disabilities of the nature entitling the disabled employee to a benefit under the plan must be estimated. The rates of disability will vary with the plan's definition of disability, the age and sex composition of the covered employee group, the nature of the employment, and the general level of economic activity. At the inception of a plan, the disability experience projected for a particular plan may be based on insurance company data, or on the actual experience of the employer, or on the experience of a large

---

[2]A combination plan is an arrangement under which two funding instruments are used, with a portion of the contributions placed in a trust fund (or a conversion fund held by an insurer) and the balance paid to an insurance company as contributions under a group annuity contract or as premiums on individual life insurance or annuity contracts. The entire pension for each participant is generally paid by the insurance company, with transfers from the trust fund or conversion fund being made as required.

company in the same or a comparable industry. Ultimately, the plan's own experience may be used as a yardstick.

Having determined the probable incidence of disability, the actuary must then project the duration of the disability. The duration of the disability will be affected by reemployment opportunities, which in turn are related to the nature of the employment and general economic conditions. The duration of the benefit period also will be affected by the mortality rates among disabled workers.

It can be seen, then, that the ability to project future disability rates is a difficult task. The actuary must keep a careful check on the actual disability experience evolving under the plan.

Turnover. Employees who voluntarily quit or who are laid off represent a cost-reducing factor to a pension fund, assuming the absence of full vesting. Separate assumptions may be made regarding mortality, disability, and turnover; or, as is quite common, the plan actuary may use one set of termination rates covering all causes of termination of employment among nonretired workers.

TABLE 15--1: Present Value of $1 of Monthly Benefit Beginning at Age 65

Male Age	(1) No Turnover	(2) Scale A	(3) Scale B	Ratio (2) ÷ (1)	Ratio (3) ÷ (1)
25	$ 8.78	$ 4.86	$ 2.64	55%	30%
35	15.85	13.03	10.67	82	67
45	28.87	28.22	27.59	98	96

Table 15-1 shows the effect on costs using three different turnover assumptions. The yearly withdrawal rates under Scale A and Scale B are as follows:

Male Age	Scale A	Scale B
25	5.00%	10.00%
35	2.50	5.00
45	0.75	1.50
50	0	0

As indicated in these examples, most turnover tables assume a greater withdrawal rate at the younger ages than at the older ages, which normally would be the case.

The problems of developing accurate turnover rates for a specific plan are obvious. Future withdrawal rates vary among employers and industries and with changing economic conditions. The age composition of the covered group has a significant impact on turnover rates. It is generally recognized that turnover rates for younger workers are very high. Turnover rates also vary depending on the length of service of employees. Furthermore, working conditions and the personnel policies and benefit programs of a particular employer may affect turnover rates in that firm. Lastly, economic recessions or periods of prosperity may significantly alter turnover rates. During periods of recession, employees will be less likely to quit, while the rate of layoffs will probably increase. The opposite situation generally prevails during periods of economic prosperity.

The concept of turnover is broader for multiemployer plans than it is for single-employer pension funds. In the former, the employee's coverage is terminated only if he or she fails to be reemployed by a participating employer within a specified time period, usually one or two years. In the skilled trades, withdrawal from the industry is less likely than separation from an individual employer. One of the basic assumptions justifying the existence of a multiemployer pension arrangement is the high degree of job mobility of the covered employees. But it is also assumed that there is a tendency for employees to be reemployed within the scope of coverage of the plan.

It is not surprising, therefore, that two actuaries may recommend considerably different withdrawal rates for the same plan. The choice of turnover assumption must rest, in the final analysis, on the sound judgment of the actuary. This judgment is based on the characteristics of the employee group, the factors discussed above, and the actuary's overall experience in pension cost projections. Turnover tables developed to guide pension consultants are of assistance for initial cost calculations, and adjustments in assumed turnover rates can be made as the actual experience under the plan evolves.

The question arises whether a turnover assumption should be used in calculating the level of annual contributions to be made under a plan using an unallocated funding instrument (including the conversion fund under a combination plan) when the plan covers a relatively small number of employees. The arguments for and against the use of a turnover assumption in these cases are somewhat similar to the arguments set forth earlier regarding the advisability of a mortality assumption under these plans. There is one more argument against use of a turnover assumption, and that is the fact that turnover is even less predictable than mortality for relatively small groups of employees. However, those pension planners who take the opposite stand say that there will obviously be some turnover in a plan (where there may be no mortality) and to ignore it is not to be realistic.

Rate of Retirement. In estimating the cost of pension benefits, one must make an assumption regarding the ages at which individuals will retire under the plan.

For those plans that allow retirement at ages other than the normal retirement age, it would be appropriate to make an assumption about the percentage of people retiring at each age (just as the turnover assumption varies by age). However, for practical reasons, most actuaries assume that all employees retire at one age.

The higher the retirement age, the lower will be the cost of a given amount of retirement benefit. For example, if an employee decides to work to age 65 rather than retiring at age 62, there is an additional three-year period during which the employee may die, with the resulting possibility that the employee will never receive retirement benefits. More importantly, the requirement of retiring at 65 will reduce the length of the benefit period. In most plans, offsetting these two factors is the fact that the individual will continue to accrue benefits and hence will be entitled to a larger basic pension.

An actuary generally will use a retirement age assumption lower than the normal retirement age specified in the plan when the plan provides some form of subsidized early retirement benefit (i.e., an early retirement benefit that is greater than the actuarial equivalent of the normal retirement benefit) and when it is expected that many employees will, in fact, retire early.

It is not unusual to find that some employees defer retirement beyond the normal retirement age. Thus, it may be logical to assume in cost estimates that the actual average retirement age is higher than the normal retirement age. This will tend to lower the estimated costs for the plan. Although not typical, some plans provide actuarially equivalent (larger) benefits to persons deferring retirement beyond normal retirement age. In these plans, no discount should be reflected in the cost calculations for postponed retirements.

Length of Benefit Period.   In addition to the number of employees retiring, the amount of benefit paid under the plan is affected by the length of time that retired workers receive their pension benefits (or the length of time payments will be continued under the normal form to a beneficiary of the retired worker after his or her death). The length of the benefit period depends upon the longevity of retired workers and the normal annuity form. Therefore, an assumption must be made regarding mortality among retired lives. As indicated earlier, the mortality table used for retired lives is generally identical to the table used for active lives, except in the case of individual policy plans.

Benefit Formula.   The last factor affecting the total amount paid under the plan is the amount of pension paid to each retired worker. It goes without saying that the higher the benefit level, the greater will be the cost of the plan.

However, projecting benefit levels is more difficult under some benefit formulas than under others. The least difficult formula is one that provides a flat benefit for all retired workers, for example, a $100-a-month benefit. On the other hand, if the benefit formula calls for a pension benefit related to compensation, cost projections may include an assumption regarding expected future increases in the salaries of covered employees. For example, if a plan provides a pension benefit of 1 percent of salary per year of covered service, future increases in salary will increase benefit levels and, therefore, the cost of the plan.

The decision on the size of the salary progression assumption is an extremely important one, because of its dramatic impact on the level of projected costs. Other things being equal, the use of a salary progression assumption substantially increases cost estimates, but the absence of such an assumption may significantly understate future plan costs. The substantial impact on a cost estimate that results from use of a salary progression can be illustrated as follows: if a salary progression in the future is at the rate of 5 percent a year, the employee hired at age 20 for $10,000 a year would be receiving about $90,000 a year at age 65.

Also, in the case of negotiated plans providing a flat benefit per year of service, there is generally no advance provision for future increases in the unit benefit amount, and, in fact, current IRS regulations do not allow an assumption of future increases. It is generally recognized that benefit levels will be increased periodically due to inflationary pressures, but recognition is not given to this fact in cost projections until increases are actually negotiated.

15.3.2. Expenses

The expenses of administering the pension plan must be added to the benefits paid in arriving at the ultimate cost of the plan. The expense assumption used depends on the type of administration and the funding instrument involved. Under individual policy plans and some group pension contracts, the insurance company includes a loading for expenses in the gross premiums charged for purchased benefits. The expense loading is largest under individual policy plans and decreases considerably under group pension contracts. Additionally, some administrative fees necessitated by ERISA may be charged separately from the gross insurance premium.

In the case of trust fund plans, the employer may pay the actuarial, legal, administrative, and investment expenses associated with the plan separately from the contribution payments to the plan. Nevertheless, these expenses must be added to the amount of benefit payment in arriving at the ultimate cost of the plan, even though they are not included in the actual cost estimates.

Possible differences in the handling of expenses, then, must be recognized in comparisons of cost projections involving different funding instruments.

15.3.3. Investment Return

The investment income earned on the accumulated assets of a funded pension plan reduces the ultimate cost of the plan. Thus, the higher the investment return assumption, other things being equal, the lower will be the projected cost of the plan. For example, under one mortality table and assuming a 5 percent loading factor, the single-premium sum required for a 45-year-old to purchase a pure life annuity of $1 a month beginning at age 65 is $30.27 using a 6 percent investment return assumption, as compared with a single premium of $23.48 using a 7 percent investment return assumption. Thus, in this example, an increase of 1 percent in the investment return rate assumption results in a reduction of about 22 percent in the estimated cost of the plan. For a given plan, the impact of a change in the investment return assumption on the estimated cost of the plan depends on the age distribution of participants and their relative benefit credits.

The investment return assumption used should recognize the total anticipated rate of return including investment income, dividends, and realized and unrealized capital appreciation (or depreciation). Therefore, selection of an appropriate investment return assumption should take into account the size of the fund, the anticipated investment policy of the plan trustees, current and projected long-term rates of return, and any other factors that might affect the future pattern of investment earnings of the fund. The choice of an appropriate rate of investment return is particularly difficult if a sizable portion of the assets is invested in common stocks, since these investments are subject to significant fluctuations in value. In addition to having an impact on the selection of an investment return assumption, investments in equities raises the rather difficult issue of when to recognize unrealized capital gains or losses.

For a number of reasons, current market values of securities have seldom been used in actuarial valuations. Two of the most important reasons are: (1) market values will generally be relatively high in periods of high corporate earnings, thereby reducing the apparent need for contributions (and also the tax deductible limits) at times when the employer may be best able to make large contributions toward the pension fund (in periods of low corporate earnings the reverse will often be true, with required contributions and tax deductible limits increased at a time when the employer's capacity to contribute is at a minimum); and (2) because of market value fluctuations, to measure a plan's unfunded liabilities on any given date by the current market values of the fund's equities could produce a very irregular funding pattern -- the antithesis of the orderly procedure, which is an essential characteristic of a satisfactory pension funding program.[3]

In spite of the above objections, current market values are used in some situations. In fact, the Internal Revenue Code requires that the value of a defined benefit plan's assets shall be determined by any reasonable actuarial valuation method that takes into account fair market value.[4] Generally, the IRS has taken the position that this condition is satisfied if the asset valuation method generates an asset value that is between 80 and 120 percent of fair market value.[5] Obviously, fair market value alone would be an acceptable method. Market values also often are used in valuing the conversion fund under a combination plan.

A number of approaches have been developed to overcome the drawbacks noted above to the use of current market value. For example, to minimize the effects of short-term market fluctuations, a moving average (e.g., a five-year average) of market values may be used. Another method used to minimize such fluctuations is to recognize appreciation annually, based on an expected long-range growth rate (e.g., 3 percent) applied to the cost (adjusted for appreciation previously so recognized) of common stocks. When this method is used, the total cost and recognized appreciation (or depreciation) usually are required to be within a specified percentage (e.g., 80 percent) of the market value.

15.4.   SUMMARY

Historically, pension actuaries have used actuarial assumptions considered reasonable "in the aggregate" while each assumption might not be "individually realistic." For example, when making cost estimates where the benefit is related to final five-year average earnings, a zero percent salary increase assumption might be used, but the corresponding understatement in costs is offset by a conservative (low) investment return assumption.

However, actuaries are now required to use actuarial assumptions that are individually realistic. As can be seen from the above discussion, the

---

[3]William F. Marples, *Actuarial Aspects of Pension Security* (Homewood, Ill.: Richard D. Irwin, 1965), p. 107.

[4]Money purchase plans must base assets solely on the basis of fair market value.

[5]For multiemployer plans, the valuation of assets rules do not apply to bonds (or other evidences of indebtedness) if a plan administrator makes a special election to value these instruments on an amortized basis.

choice of actuarial assumptions has a significant impact on the estimated costs of a pension plan. It must be repeated, however, that the choice of a particular set of assumptions generally has little effect on the ultimate cost of the plan. As with the choice of an actuarial cost method discussed in the next chapter, the choice of assumptions can have an impact on the incidence of plan costs. As gains or losses arise in the future the annual contribution account will be affected, even though the ultimate cost of the plan is unchanged.

QUESTIONS FOR REVIEW

1. Can cost uncertainties be eliminated by using a fully insured individual policy approach? Explain.
2. What factors enter into the determination of the number of employees who will be eligible for benefits under a pension plan?
3. Describe how the type of benefit formula used may present difficulties in projecting the costs of a pension plan.
4. How does administrative expense relate to ultimate pension plan costs? What are some of the major administrative costs?
5. Does the federal law require the use of current market value in the valuation of securities used to fund pension plans? Explain.
6. Describe the approaches used to overcome the drawbacks of using current market value in the valuation of pension plan assets held in the form of securities.
7. Does the choice of an actuarial cost method affect the ultimate cost of a pension plan? Explain.
8. Explain how the investment rate assumption affects the ultimate cost of a pension plan.

QUESTIONS FOR DISCUSSION

1. Assume that you are asked to set assumptions for a new defined benefit pension plan. Describe the procedure you would follow.
2. How often should the assumptions established in Question 1 be updated?

16. Budgeting Pension Costs

16.1.   BUDGETING PENSION COSTS

The discussion in Chapter 15 set forth the various factors that affect the ultimate cost of a pension plan and how the choice of actuarial assumptions can significantly affect the estimated costs. What is still needed, however, is some actuarial technique to determine how the estimated costs of the plan are to be spread over future years. These techniques are referred to as actuarial cost methods. More specifically, an actuarial cost method is a particular technique for establishing the amounts and incidence of the normal costs and supplemental costs pertaining to the benefits (or benefits and expenses) of a pension plan.[1]

Two approaches have been used to finance pension plans in the past. Before describing the different actuarial cost methods, it might be helpful to review the current disbursement approach and the terminal funding approach. Though basically no longer permitted by the Internal Revenue Code for qualified plans, knowledge of these two approaches should provide a better basis for understanding advance funding required by law, a discussion of which follows later.

---

[1]The terminology pertaining to the actuarial aspects of pension planning reflects, wherever possible, the thinking of the Committee on Pension and Profit Sharing Terminology, sponsored jointly by the American Risk and Insurance Association and the Pension Research Council, University of Pennsylvania.

16.1.1. Current Disbursement Approach

Under the current disbursement approach, the employer pays each retired worker's monthly pension as each payment becomes due. There is no accumulation of pension funds in an irrevocable trust or through a contract with an insurance company.

An illustration of the current disbursement approach would be a supplemental executive retirement plan (described in Chapter 26) under which the employer promises all employees with at least 10 years of service a lifetime pension of $100 a month beginning at age 65. If no employees are eligible for benefits during the first two years after the plan is established, the employer would not make any pension plan payments during that period. The employer's pension outlay of $100 a month begins with the retirement of the first eligible employee; the outlay increases by that amount as each new retired worker is added to the pension rolls and decreases by $100 a month as each retired worker dies. These monthly pension outlays are provided out of current operating income and, in effect, are treated as a part of wage costs.

16.1.2. Terminal Funding

Under the terminal funding approach, the employer sets aside for each employee, on the date the latter retires, a lump-sum amount sufficient to provide the monthly pension benefit promised under the plan. The lump-sum amount needed to provide the promised benefit is a function of the amount of benefit assumptions as to the expected benefit period, and the rate of investment return expected to be earned on the investment of this principal sum. For example, assuming mortality rates will occur in accordance with a recent group annuity mortality table (for males) and assuming the rate of investment return will be 6 percent, the sum needed to provide $100 a month for life to a male, age 65, is $11,122.[2]

If the mortality and investment return assumptions prove to be accurate, the principal plus investment earnings will be sufficient, on the average, to provide the $100-a-month benefit.

---

[2]An expense assumption is ignored in the above calculation, since the authors are interested solely in illustrating the concept of terminal funding. In practice, the expenses of administering the benefit would be taken into account in the single-premium rate charged by an insurance company or in determining the amount to be set aside in a trust fund under noninsured plans, if expenses associated with the plan are paid from the trust fund. Normally, the expenses under trust fund plans are paid directly by the employer and, therefore, no expense allowance is required.

The employer, therefore, sets aside the appropriate single-premium sum as each employee retires. Like the current disbursement approach, terminal funding does not require the employer to make any contributions on behalf of employees who are still actively at work.

The benefits can be funded through the purchase of single-premium annuities from insurance companies, or the employer can transfer the estimated single-premium sums to a trust fund.

The reader should not confuse the concept of terminal funding with the practice of split funding that is prevalent in the pension field. The term split funding, as it is commonly used in pension planning, refers to the use of two different funding agencies in administering the assets of a pension plan. For example, a plan may provide that contributions on behalf of active employees are to be administered by a corporate trustee. When an employee retires, the trust agreement may require the corporate trustee to withdraw from the trust fund and transfer to an insurance company the single-premium sum needed to purchase a life annuity equal to the monthly pension earned by the employee under the terms of the pension plan. This type of plan is considered to be an advance funded plan unless the employer is paying to the corporate trustee an annual sum exactly equal to the amount of single premiums needed to provide the benefits for workers retiring each year -- a highly unlikely situation.

16.1.3. Advance Funding

Under advance funding, the employer (and the employee, under contributory plans) sets aside funds on some systematic basis prior to the employee's retirement date. Thus, periodic contributions are made on behalf of the group of active employees during their working years. This does not mean that each dollar of contributions is necessarily earmarked for specific employees. As will be noted in subsequent chapters, contributions are not allocated to specific employees under certain funding instruments; for example, trust fund and group deposit administration plans. Thus, it is true that in some plans using unallocated funding instruments, contributions in the early years may only be sufficient to provide lifetime benefits to the first group of employees retiring under the plan. However, if contributions are continued on an advance funding basis, the accumulated assets in the pension fund will soon exceed the aggregate single-premium sums needed to provide benefits to those workers who are already retired. This excess of pension assets, then, represents the advance funding of benefits that have been accrued or credited to the active (nonretired) employees.

Pension plans operating on an advance funded basis are invariably qualified with the Internal Revenue Service. An employer is generally not willing to make advance contributions to an irrevocable trust fund unless it receives the tax advantages of a qualified plan.

The relatively even distribution of annual pension outlays under advance funding produces a more equitable allocation of the firm's cash flow over the years. The pension is being provided to employees for the year of service rendered to the firm. Thus, it would seem that the funds available to the owners of the firm (e.g., stockholder dividends) should be reduced by pension contributions in an amount approximately equal to the present value of benefits accruing under the plan. It is true that credit for past service, offered at the inception of the plan, creates a problem. Since the plan was not in existence during those past service years, it is highly improbable that previous generations of owners would be willing to retroactively refund a portion of the funds they received from the firm. The next best solution seems to be to amortize past service cost in the first 20 or 25 years after the inception of the plan. ERISA originally required that for new plans, past service costs must be amortized over no more than 30 years. The amortization period was reduced substantially as a result of the Omnibus Budget Reconciliation Act of 1987.[3]

The accumulation of assets in a pension fund resulting from the advance funding of benefits serves as a buffer during periods of financial stress. During a period of low earnings or operating losses, an employer may find it advisable to reduce or eliminate pension contributions for a year or even a longer period. This can be done in those cases where the pension fund is of sufficient size that a temporary reduction of contributions does not violate the minimum funding requirements imposed by ERISA. It should be noted that this financing flexibility does not necessitate any reduction or termination of pension benefits.

Under advance funding, then, the plan actuary uses a set of assumptions and an actuarial cost method in estimating the annual cost of a plan. Annual contribution payments usually are based on these estimated annual costs. However, it should be noted that actual annual contribution payments need not be identical to the estimated annual costs generated by a given actuarial cost method, nor is it likely that they be identical to the accounting expenses described in Chapter 22.[4] As will be noted in later chapters, the employer has some flexibility in the timing of contribution payments under unallocated funding instruments.

---

[3]This concept is explained in detail in Section 16.4 of this chapter.

[4]Moreover, the valuation of liabilities described in this chapter will most likely differ from those in Chapter 22 and those used for plan termination insurance purposes (Chapter 17).

There are several different actuarial cost methods, each producing different patterns of annual costs under the plan. Having different actuarial cost methods to calculate annual pension costs is analogous to having different methods for determining the annual amount of depreciation of plant and equipment to charge against operations. The depreciation methods that can be used may produce different annual charges, but the total value of the building and equipment to be depreciated is constant regardless of the depreciation formula used. Similarly, the various actuarial cost methods will produce different levels of annual cost, but the choice of a particular actuarial cost method will not affect the ultimate cost of the plan. One important exception to the latter conclusion is the fact that if an actuarial cost method is chosen that produces higher initial contributions than other methods, then the asset accumulation will be greater (assuming a positive rate of return) in the early years of the plan, thereby producing greater investment income. An increase in investment income will decrease the ultimate cost of the plan.[5]

If the choice of actuarial cost method usually has little effect on the ultimate cost of a pension plan (after taking into consideration interest, and so on), what factors determine which method will be used in calculating the amount and incidence of pension contributions? The answer to this question will become more apparent after the following discussion of the specific cost methods. However, the reader may find it helpful to keep in mind that the choice of a specific actuarial cost method is influenced to a great degree by the degree of flexibility in annual contribution payments desired by the employer and available under the particular funding instrument used.

16.2.   ACTUARIAL COST METHODS

Actuarial cost methods can be broadly classified into (1) accrued benefit, and (2) projected benefit cost methods.[6]

As further explained below, the class into which a particular cost method falls depends upon whether, for cost determination purposes, an employee's benefits under the pension plan are deemed to "accrue" in direct relation to years of service or are viewed as a single "projected" total.

---

[5]More precisely, the timing of contribution payments has additional cost implications if federal income tax rates change; or if alternative uses of capital vary over time; or if investment return rates vary over the life of the plan.

[6]Parts of the material in this section were drawn from Joseph J. Melone, "Actuarial Cost Methods -- New Pension Terminology," *Journal of Insurance* 30, no. 3 (September 1963), pp. 456-64.

Most actuarial cost methods break down the total actuarial cost into the normal cost and the supplemental cost of the plan. The normal cost of the plan is the amount of annual cost, determined in accordance with a particular actuarial cost method, attributable to the given year of the plan's operation.

Most plans provide credit for service rendered prior to the inception date of the plan. If the normal cost under the particular cost method is calculated on the assumption that annual costs have been paid or accrued from the earliest date of credited service (when in fact they have not), the plan starts out with a supplemental liability. At the inception of the plan, the supplemental liability (also known as the actuarial accrued liability, the accrued liability, or the past service liability) arises from the fact that credit for past service is granted, or part of the total benefit is imputed, to years prior to the inception of this plan. The annual contribution normally will be equal to the normal cost of the plan plus at least enough of a contribution to amortize the supplemental liability over a specified period of time.[7] If it is desired to fund this supplemental liability in a more rapid manner (10 years is generally the minimum period over which it can be funded on a deductible basis), larger annual contributions will be required. The portion of the annual cost applied toward the reduction of the supplemental liability is referred to as the plan's supplemental cost. As the plan continues in operation, the size of the supplemental liability normally will change. In addition to normal changes in the supplemental liability that may occur as a result of the actuarial method being used, these changes in the size of the supplemental liability may result from variations in benefit formulas, deviations of actual from expected experience, and changes in the actuarial assumptions or in the actuarial cost method used in subsequent normal cost calculations. Offsetting any increase in the supplemental liability will be any unanticipated increase in the size of pension fund assets. The unfunded supplemental liability, then, is the difference between the supplemental liability and any assets that may have accumulated under the plan as a result of prior contributions.

16.2.1. Accrued Benefit Cost Method

An accrued benefit cost method is one under which the actuarial costs are based directly upon benefits accrued to the date of cost determination, such benefits being determined either by the terms of the plan or by some assumed allocation of total prospective benefits to years of service. To

---

[7]The minimum amortization amount will depend upon when the supplemental liability was created and may also depend upon the funding status of the plan. See Section 16.4 of this chapter for a detailed explanation.

determine the actuarial cost of the plan for a given year, the method assumes that a precisely determinable unit of benefit is associated with that year of a participant's credited service.

This method of calculating the actuarial costs of pension plans is sometimes referred to as the single-premium, unit credit, unit cost, or step-rate method.

The accrued benefit method is limited to those plans that provide a unit benefit type of formula based on career average compensation (for example, a percentage of each year's compensation), or a specified dollar amount for each year of credited service.[8] Under these benefit formulas, a precisely determinable unit of benefit is associated with each year of a participant's credited service.

Although best adapted to those plans that use a unit benefit type of formula, the accrued benefit cost method also can be used when the plan provides a composite benefit based on the participant's total period of credited service. For example, the plan may provide a $100 monthly pension benefit at age 65 after 25 years of service, or the plan may use a benefit formula based on final average compensation. In these instances, the accrued benefit method requires that a portion of the prospective benefit be imputed to each year of credited service. This requires some arbitrary basis of allocating total prospective benefits to particular years of service. When used for plans of this type, it is usually referred to as the projected unit credit method.

The first step in the calculation of the normal cost under the accrued benefit cost method is to determine the present value of each participant's benefit credited during the year for which costs are being calculated. The cost per dollar of benefit is a function of the participant's age and sex and of the mortality, interest, and other assumptions used. Thus, the normal cost per dollar of benefit under the accrued benefit cost method increases with the age of the participant, assuming that all other assumptions are held constant. For example, using a recent group annuity mortality table, a 6 percent interest assumption and a 5 percent loading, the normal cost per $1 of monthly benefit beginning at age 65 for a male employee at various ages would be as follows:

---

[8]Because of sharply increasing costs, regulations do not permit use of the accrued benefit cost method for minimum funding requirements for final average plans.

Age	Normal Cost
25	$ 9.24
30	12.41
35	16.69
40	22.48
45	30.39
50	41.45
55	57.31
60	80.70

If the benefit formula is related to salary, increases in compensation would also increase the normal cost for a given participant.

The normal cost of the plan as a whole is simply the sum of the separate normal costs for the benefits credited for each participant during that particular year. Although the normal cost for a given participant increases over time under the accrued benefit cost method, the normal cost for the plan as a whole generally does not increase as rapidly, or may even remain fairly constant or decrease. The reason for this is that some older employees will die or terminate, and they will probably be replaced by much younger workers. If the distribution of current service benefit credits by age and sex remains constant, the total normal cost of the plan will remain constant.

At the inception of the plan, the supplemental liability under the accrued benefit cost method arises from the fact that either past service credits have been granted or a part of the benefits of the plan is imputed to past service. The supplemental liability at the inception of the plan under the accrued benefit cost method is simply the present value of the accrued past service benefits credited as of that date. Using the single-premium rates indicated above, the supplemental liability for a male employee, age 40, at the inception date of the plan, would be $22.48 per $1 a month of past-service benefit payable beginning at age 65. If the benefit formula provides a $10-a-month benefit per year of service and the employee has 10 years of credited past service, the supplemental liability for that individual would be $2,248.00 ($22.48 × $100 past-service benefit). The supplemental liability for the plan as a whole at the inception would be the sum of the supplemental liabilities for each of the covered employees.

It should now be clear why the accrued benefit method is readily adaptable to unit benefit formula plans. Also, this method generally is used under group deferred annuity plans, since a unit of benefit usually is purchased for each year of credited future service under these contracts. The employer has some flexibility in funding the supplemental liability.

16.2.2. Projected Benefit Cost Methods

Rather than costing the benefits credited during a specific period, one can project the total benefits that will be credited by retirement date and spread the costs for these benefits evenly over some future period. These costing techniques are referred to as projected benefit cost methods. More specifically, a projected benefit cost method is one under which the actuarial costs are based upon total prospective benefits, whether or not they are attributed to any specific periods of service. The actuarial cost determination assumes regular future accruals of normal cost, generally a level amount or percentage of earnings, whose actuarial present value is equal to the present value of prospective benefits less the value of plan assets and unfunded supplemental liabilities. From the preceding definition one can see that projected benefit cost methods differ from accrued benefit cost methods in two important respects. First, the normal cost accrual under a projected benefit cost method is related to the total prospective benefit, rather than the benefit for a particular year. The projected benefit methods generally are used when the plan provides a composite benefit based upon the participant's total period of credited service, such as $100 per month or 30 percent of average earnings for the last five years of service. These latter formulas do not allocate benefits to any particular year. However, it may be necessary, in the case of early retirement or termination of service with vested rights, to allocate the total potential benefit to actual years of service or to define the accrued benefit in terms of the amount purchasable by the accrued level annual cost. A projected benefit cost method can be, and is, used with benefit formulas that do allocate units of benefit to particular years of service. When so used, the normal cost accruals are still calculated on the basis of total projected benefits rather than annual units of benefit. For example, if a plan provides a retirement benefit of $10 a month per year of service, the normal cost computation is based on a projected monthly retirement benefit of $10 times the expected number of years of credited service as of normal retirement age. If the employee is age 35 upon entry into the plan and the normal retirement age is 65, then the total projected benefit is $300 a month.

A second distinguishing characteristic of projected benefit cost methods is that these techniques are generally applied with the objective of generating a normal cost that is a level amount or percentage of earnings for either the individual participants or the participants as a group. Therefore, these methods can be characterized as level cost methods. A cost method is characterized as level if it is based on an actuarial formula designed to produce a constant year-to-year accrual of normal cost (either in amount or as a percentage of payroll or other index) if (a) the experience conforms with the actuarial assumptions, (b) there are no changes in the plan, and (c) certain characteristics of the employee group remain unchanged.

However, the actual experience of the plan seldom conforms precisely with the actuarial assumptions used, and it is likely that there will be changes in the composition of the group for which cost accruals are assumed.   Nevertheless, these methods are characterized as level cost methods, since the theoretical objective of most of these methods is to produce a level normal cost. By contrast, the accrued benefit cost method theoretically should produce increasing annual costs until the plan matures. However, as noted earlier, changes in the composition of the group may, in practice, result in fairly level normal costs under the accrued benefit cost method.

Projected benefit cost methods may be subdivided into (1) individual level cost methods and (2) aggregate level cost methods.

16.2.2.1.   Individual Level Cost Methods

This individual subcategory of projected benefit cost methods is characterized by the assumed allocation of the actuarial cost for each individual employee, generally as a level amount or percentage of earnings, over all or a part of the employee's period of service or period of coverage under the plan, or some other appropriate period uniformly applied. Under individual cost methods, the total actuarial cost is generally separable as to the various participants; that is, costs are calculated individually for each employee or are calculated by group methods in such a way as to produce essentially the same total result as though individually calculated.[9]

The individual level cost methods may be further subdivided as to whether or not a supplemental liability is created.

---

[9]It should be noted, however, that this does not mean that it is possible, at any given time, to identify a participant's "share" in the plan assets. For example, a turnover assumption reduces the normal cost attributable to each participant. However, this normal cost figure is too low for the participant who does not terminate and eventually retires under the plan. Likewise, this normal cost figure is excessive for those participants who subsequently terminate with no vested benefits. For the plan as a whole, however, this normal cost figure may be entirely appropriate. This point should be kept clearly in mind, particularly in those sections of the chapter illustrating the calculations of normal costs under the various actuarial cost methods in terms of an individual participant. The authors recognize the weakness of this approach, but feel that the basic nature of each method is illustrated more clearly through use of individual participant examples.

16.2.2.1.1. Without Supplemental Liability

As indicated above, projected benefit cost methods have as their objective the spreading of the costs of total projected benefits evenly over some future period. One logical period over which costs can be spread is the period from the attained age of the employee at the time he or she entered the plan to normal retirement age under the plan.

The normal cost accruals are determined by distributing the present value of an individual's total projected benefits as a level amount or percentage of earnings over his or her assumed future period of coverage under the plan. Total projected benefits include past-service benefits, if any, as well as future-service benefits to be credited by retirement age. Thus, no unfunded supplemental liability is created under this cost method at the inception of the plan, since the present value of future benefits is exactly equal to the present value of future normal cost accruals. Thereafter, there is still no supplemental liability if contribution payments have been made equal to the normal costs that have accrued in prior years. It must be reemphasized that a supplemental liability may be created for other reasons. The point to be made here is that this actuarial cost method, other things being equal, does not of itself generate a supplemental liability.

This actuarial cost method requires, then, a projection of total benefits distributed by age at inception of coverage, and calculation of the normal cost based on a set of level premium deferred annuity rates.[10]

The latter may be determined by dividing the present value of an annuity at normal retirement age by the present value of a temporary annuity running to normal retirement age. For example, assume that the total projected benefit for a participant age 35 at the inception date of the plan is $200 a month beginning at age 65. The normal cost for this participant's benefit would be equal to the present value at age 35 of an annuity of $200 a month beginning at age 65, divided by the present value of a temporary annuity due of $1 for 30 years.

If there is no change in the projected benefits of any employee and the covered group remains constant, the normal cost under the plan will remain constant (subject to adjustment to the extent that actual experience deviates from the assumptions employed). Obviously, this will not prove to be the

---

[10]Regardless of which actuarial cost method is used, there is the question of whether to include in the cost calculations employees who have not yet met the plan participation requirements. One view is that a certain percentage of the currently noneligible employees will eventually qualify for participation in the plan and, therefore, the cost calculations should recognize this fact. Some actuaries, however, project costs only for those employees who are actually eligible for participation in the plan. The latter approach generally produces lower cost estimates. Either approach can be justified, but the reader should recognize that differences in cost projections may be due, at least in part, to the approach used.

case in most plans. For example, if the benefit formula is related to compensation, employees will be entitled to larger projected benefits as they receive salary increases. Where salary scales have not been used in the original cost calculations, the increase in projected benefits due to salary increases is spread evenly over the period from the year in which compensation is increased to the year in which the employee reaches normal retirement age. This, of course, results in an increase in annual contributions for the plan as a whole. Also, new employees will become eligible for participation in the plan, and some currently covered workers will terminate their participation under the plan. Since the age and sex distribution and the benefit levels of new employees are not likely to be identical to those of terminated participants, there are bound to be variations in the annual contributions for the plan as a whole.

The reader will recognize that the individual level cost method without supplemental liability is, in effect, the actuarial cost method used under fully insured individual policy and group permanent plans.[11] Indeed, this cost method is analogous to the level premium concept used in individual life insurance premium calculations. For this reason, this actuarial cost method is sometimes referred to as the individual level premium method or the attained age level contribution method.

16.2.2.1.2. With Supplemental Liability

This cost method is similar to the previous method except that the assumption is made, for the initial group of participants, that the period over which costs are spread begins with the first year they could have joined the plan had it always been in effect. For an employee who enters after the inception date of the plan, the normal cost under this method is the same as would be generated by the previous method.[12]

This follows since that employee's entry year coincides with the year in which participation began. In the case of the initial group of participants, a supplemental liability is automatically created because of the assumption that normal cost payments have been made prior to the inception date of the plan.

Using the example cited above, assume that an employee is entitled to a total projected benefit at age 65 of $200 a month. The employee is age 35 at the inception of the plan, but would have been eligible at age 30 had the plan been in effect. Under the individual level cost method with supplemental liability, the normal cost for this participant's benefit would be

---

[11]See Chapter 21 for a detailed explanation of these plans.
[12]This statement assumes that the normal cost is calculated in a consistent manner for both the original group and subsequent entrants.

equal to the present value at age 30 (rather than age 35, as is the case under the previous cost method) of an annuity of $200 a month beginning at age 65, divided by the present value of a temporary annuity due of $1 for 35 years (rather than 30 years). In the above example, the numerator is smaller and the denominator larger than the corresponding values calculated under the individual cost method without a supplemental liability. The result, of course, is that the normal costs are lower under the individual cost method with a supplemental liability. However, since the normal costs have not been paid for the prior years, there is a supplemental liability on behalf of this employee. Unlike the accrued benefit cost method, the initial supplemental liability under the individual cost method does not bear a precise relationship to past service benefits.

The difference between the two individual level cost methods can be made clear by reference to a situation in the individual life insurance field. Let us assume that an individual, age 25, purchased a 10-year convertible term life insurance contract. At age 30, the insured decides to convert the policy to an ordinary life insurance policy. If the conversion is made as of issue age (25), the ordinary life premium for age 25 can be viewed conceptually as the annual normal cost under the individual level cost method with supplemental liability. The sum of the annual premiums from issue date (age 25) to conversion date (age 30), improved at the assumed rate of interest and adjusted to reflect the insurance cost, would be analogous to the supplemental liability under this method. If the conversion were made as of attained age, the annual premium for age 30, adjusted to reflect the insurance cost, would be analogous to the annual cost required under the individual cost method without supplemental liability.

In valuations after the first year of the plan, the normal cost and supplemental liability would be calculated in the same manner as at the plan's inception. However, the annual contribution would be a payment of the normal cost and some payment toward the unfunded supplemental liability (the supplemental liability less any assets that have accumulated). The normal cost calculation would be affected by any changes in assumptions or plan provisions, while the calculation of the unfunded supplemental liability would be affected not only by changes in assumptions or plan provisions, but also by any actuarial gains or losses since the plan actually started. The individual level cost method with a supplemental liability also is referred to as the entry age normal method.

16.2.2.2.   Aggregate Level Cost Methods

The distinguishing characteristic of aggregate level cost methods is that the normal cost accruals are calculated for the plan as a whole without identifying any part of such cost accruals with the projected benefits of specific individuals. The cost accruals are expressed as a percentage of compensation or as a specified dollar amount.

The normal cost accrual rate under an aggregate method can be determined by dividing the present value of future benefits for all participants by the present value of the estimated future compensation for the group of participants. This accrual rate is then multiplied by the total annual earnings to determine the initial normal cost of the plan. If the normal cost accrual rate is to be expressed in terms of a dollar amount, then the present value of $1 per employee for each year of future service must be computed. Since there is no assumption that any normal costs have been accrued prior to the inception date of the plan, the above method does not create a supplemental liability.

In the determination of cost accruals after the inception of the plan under the above method, recognition must be given to the plan assets that presumably have been accumulated to offset prior normal cost accruals. Thus, for those years subsequent to the establishment of the plan, the accrual rate is determined by dividing the present value of aggregate future benefits, less any plan assets, by the present value of future compensation.

The normal cost accrual can be calculated under an aggregate method to produce a supplemental liability. This can be done in many ways, but the most clearly understood approach to creating a supplemental liability under the aggregate method is to exclude past service benefits in the projection of aggregate future benefits. This decreases the numerator of the fraction, thereby producing a smaller normal cost accrual rate. Or the actuary may simply use a supplemental liability generated by one of the individual cost methods. However the supplemental liability is calculated, the unfunded supplemental liability must be subtracted (along with plan assets) from the present value of aggregate future benefits in the calculation of subsequent accrual rates.

The aggregate level cost method without supplemental liability is also referred to as the percentage of payroll, the aggregate, or the remaining cost method. When there is a supplemental liability in connection with this method, it is sometimes referred to as the attained age normal or entry age normal method with initial supplemental liability.

16.2.3. Amortization of Supplemental Liability

The actuarial cost methods that create a supplemental liability offer the employer greater flexibility in annual contribution payments than is available under the cost methods without supplemental liability. Under the former cost methods, the employer has the alternative of funding the initial supplemental liability at a pace consistent with its financial objectives and, of course, applicable law in addition to the annual normal costs under the plan. In most cases, the employer makes some contribution toward the amortization of the supplemental liability. The length of the period over which the supplemental liability should be funded varies with the circumstances surrounding each plan and is heavily influenced by the minimum funding standards and the full funding limitation described in Sections 16.4 and 16.5 of this chapter, respectively.

16.3.   DEFINED CONTRIBUTION PLANS

The discussion thus far in this chapter has been concerned primarily with the role of actuarial assumptions and actuarial cost methods in calculating the annual cost of a plan. The question arises as to the degree to which this discussion is pertinent in the case of defined contribution (money purchase) plans. In these plans, the employer's contribution commitment is fixed and is usually expressed as a specified percentage of the compensation of covered employees. Thus, it would seem that there is little need for actuarial assumptions and cost methods to determine annual costs under these plans. To allow the employer to estimate future costs or benefits under the plan, projections are required based on appropriate actuarial assumptions and a specific actuarial cost method. In estimating ultimate costs under a defined contribution plan, the actuary could use either the accrued benefit method or a projected benefit cost method, depending on how benefits are defined. Also, under traditional defined contribution plans, the annual contribution on behalf of each employee is viewed as a single-premium payment for a unit of deferred annuity to begin upon attainment of normal retirement age. Indeed, some of the defined contribution plans are funded through group deferred annuity contracts. Thus, the age of the employee and mortality and interest assumptions determine the amount of benefit being credited each year. The amount of benefit credited each year for a given employee will vary with the size of the contribution payment and the number of years to retirement age.

A variation of the traditional defined contribution plan is found in some negotiated plans that have both a fixed contribution and a fixed benefit. Negotiated multiemployer plans are established on this basis. The union negotiates a fixed pension contribution rate with all participating employers, and the rate is usually expressed in terms of cents per hour worked or unit of production, or as a percentage of the compensation of covered employees. The contributions are paid into a single trust fund, and a uniform benefit schedule applicable to all covered employees is established. Actuarial assumptions and an actuarial cost method are needed to determine the level of benefits that can be supported by the fixed contribution commitment. In these plans, an additional assumption must be made in actuarial computations that was not mentioned earlier in the chapter; that is, the expected level of future contributions. Since the contribution commitment is usually related to compensation or hours worked, changes in levels of economic activity affect the contribution income of the plan. The actuary, therefore, must project the future flow of contribution income to determine an appropriate benefit formula for the plan.

The cost method normally used in actuarial computations for fixed contribution-fixed benefit plans is the projected benefit cost method with a supplemental liability. One reason is that this method tends to produce annual normal costs that may be expected to remain fairly stable as a percentage of payroll or in terms of cents per hour, if the actuarial assumptions are in fact realized; and this is consistent with the contribution commitment under these plans, which is normally expressed as a percentage of payroll or in cents per hour of work. Another reason is the existence of a supplemental liability, which permits some flexibility in annual contribution income. As indicated above, changes in levels of employment will result in fluctuations in the annual aggregate contribution income of the plan, which may not match fluctuations in the amount of benefits credited. During periods of prosperity, the excess of actual over expected contribution income can be applied toward amortizing the supplemental liability at a rate faster than anticipated; likewise, periods of recession result in extensions of the period over which the supplemental liability is to be amortized. Of course, in both cases, the amortization periods must be in line with the minimums and maximums permitted under federal law.

16.4.   MINIMUM FUNDING STANDARDS

The basic minimum funding standard required by the Code is that a pension plan having supplemental liabilities must amortize such liabilities over a specified period of time in addition to the funding of normal cost.

The requirement for amortizing supplemental liability applies only to defined benefit plans, since a defined contribution plan cannot technically have a supplemental liability. For defined contribution plans, the minimum contribution is the amount indicated by the plan formula. The requirements also apply to negotiated plans that have both a fixed contribution rate and a fixed benefit. Such plans may use the "shortfall" method described later in this chapter.

In meeting the minimum funding standards, the liabilities of a pension plan must be calculated on the basis of actuarial assumptions and actuarial cost methods that are reasonable and that offer the actuary's best estimate of anticipated experience under the plan. Each individual assumption must be reasonable or must, in the aggregate, result in a total contribution equal to that which would be determined if each of the assumptions were reasonable.

For plans in existence on January 1, 1974, the maximum amortization period for supplemental liability is 40 years; for single-employer plans established after January 1, 1974, the maximum amortization period is 30 years. Moreover, experience gains and losses for single-employer plans must be amortized over a 5-year period. The shorter amortization period for gains and losses was designed to stimulate the use of realistic actuarial assumptions. Changes in supplemental liabilities associated with changes in actuarial assumptions must be amortized over a period not longer than 10 years.

An amortization period may be extended by the Internal Revenue Service for up to ten years if the employer shows the extension would provide adequate protection for participants and their beneficiaries. Such potential extensions are advantageous for those cases where a substantial risk exists that unless such an extension were granted, a pension plan would be terminated, or greatly reduced employee benefit levels or reduced employee compensation would result.

The Treasury Department can also allow some flexibility in employers meeting the minimum funding standards of the Code. In those circumstances where an employer would incur *temporary* substantial business hardships and if strict enforcement of the minimum funding standards would adversely affect plan participants, the secretary of the treasury may waive for a particular year payment of all or a part of a plan's normal cost and the additional liabilities to be funded during that year. The law provides that no more than three waivers may be granted a plan within a consecutive 15-year period; the amount waived, plus interest, must be amortized not less rapidly than ratably over 5 years.

There are certain exemptions from the mandated minimum funding standards. Generally, the minimum funding standards apply to pension plans (as opposed to profit sharing and stock bonus plans) of private employers in interstate commerce, plans of employee organizations with members in interstate commerce, and plans that seek a qualified status under the tax laws. Exempt plans include government plans and church plans, unless they elect to comply with the requirements of the Code. Fully insured pension plans (funded exclusively through individual or group permanent insurance contracts) are exempt from the minimum funding rules as long as all premiums are paid when due and no policy loans are allowed. Additionally, plans that are also exempt are arrangements designed to provide deferred compensation to highly compensated employees, plans that provide supplemental benefits on an unfunded, nonqualified basis, and those plans to which the employer does not contribute.

16.4.1. Funding Standard Account

All pension plans subject to the minimum funding requirements must establish a "funding standard account" that provides a comparison between actual contributions and those required under the minimum funding requirements. A determination of experience gains and losses and a valuation of a plan's liability must be made at least once every year.[13] The basic purpose of the funding standard account is to provide some flexibility in funding through allowing contributions greater than the required minimum, accumulated with interest, to reduce the minimum contributions required in future years.

16.4.1.1.   Operation of the Account

For each plan year, the funding standard account is charged with the normal cost for the year and with the minimum amortization payment required for initial supplemental liabilities, increases in plan liabilities, experience losses, the net loss resulting from changes in actuarial assumptions, waived contributions for each year, and adjustments for interest in the preceding items to the end of the plan year.[14] The account is credited in each plan year for employer contributions made for that year, with amortized portions of decreases in plan liabilities, experience gains, the net gain resulting from changes in actuarial assumptions, amounts of any waived contributions, and adjustments for interest in the preceding items to the end of the plan year.[15] If the contributions to the plan, adjusted as indicated above, meet the minimum funding standards, the funding standard account will show a zero balance. If the funding standard account has a positive balance at the end of the year, such balance will be credited with interest in future years (at the rate used to determine plan costs). Therefore, the need for future contributions to meet the minimum funding standards will be reduced to the extent of the positive balance plus the interest credited.

---

[13]Under certain circumstances, the IRS may require an actuarial valuation more frequently. Internal Revenue Code Section 412(c)(9).

[14]Plan sponsors are able to change their funding methods with the (sometimes automatic) approval of the IRS. See Revenue Proceeding 85-29 and IRS Notice 90-63.

[15]In certain situations, the account will also be credited with a full funding limitation credit. See Prop. Reg. Sec. 1.412(c)(6)-1(g).

If, however, the funding standard account shows a deficit balance, called the accumulated funding deficiency (minimum contributions in essence have not been made), the account will be charged with interest at the rate used to determine plan costs. Moreover, the plan will be subject to an excise tax of 10 percent of the accumulated funding deficiency (100 percent if not corrected or paid off within 90 days after notice of a deficiency by the secretary of the treasury). All members of the employer's controlled group are liable for payment of the minimum contribution and excise tax, with a lien on the employer's assets imposed for a deficiency in excess of $1 million. In addition to the excise tax, the employer may be subject to civil action in the courts for failure to meet the minimum funding standards.

Minimum funding contributions must be made on a quarterly basis with the final payment due 8½ months after the close of the plan year.[16] Interest on unpaid quarterly installments is charged in the funding standard account at a rate equal to the larger of 175 percent of the Federal mid-term rate or the rate of interest used to determine costs by the plan.

16.4.1.2.   Deficit Reduction Contributions for Underfunded Plans

The Omnibus Budget Reconciliation Act of 1987 established additional minimum funding requirements for plans covering more than 100 participants and that are not at least 100 percent funded for current liabilities.[17] The additional contribution is based on an 18-year amortization of the 1988 unfunded current liability, additional payments for any benefit improvements, and a payment toward current benefits for "unpredictable contingent events" (such as a plant shutdown) that have taken place. In general, the current liability is the plan's liability determined on a plan termination basis. Specifically, it is the present value of accrued benefits projected to the end of the current plan year, but excluding the value of unpredictable contingent events that have not occurred. The present value of this liability is calculated using the plan's valuation interest rate, provided that it is between 90 percent and 110 percent of the weighted average of rates of interest on 30-year Treasury securities during the four-year period ending on the last day of the prior plan year. Furthermore, the interest rate should be consistent with current insurance company annuity rates. The IRS may, by regulation, extend this range downward if 90 percent of the weighted average is unreasonably high, but to no lower than 80 percent of

---

[16]This deadline does not extend the time limit for making a contribution for tax *deduction* purposes. That time limit is described later in this chapter.

[17]The additional contributions are phased in for plans with between 100 and 150 participants. All defined benefit plans must be aggregated to determine the number of participants in applying this exception.

the weighted average. Also, the unfunded liability is calculated by subtracting the actuarial value of assets; any credit balance in the funding standard account must first be subtracted from the actuarial value of assets.

When a plan has an unfunded current liability, the charges to the funding standard account are increased by the excess, if any, of the deficit reduction contribution over the net total of the following funding standard account amortization charges and credits:

- Charge for the initial unfunded accrued liability
- Charges for plan changes
- Credits for plan changes

This increase is limited by the amount necessary to increase the actuarial value of assets, net of the credit balances, to the current liability.

The deficit reduction contribution is equal to the sum of the unfunded old liability amount and the unfunded new liability amount. The unfunded old liability amount equals an 18-year amortization, beginning in 1989, of the unfunded current liability, if any, at the beginning of the 1988 plan year (called the unfunded old liability) based on the plan provisions in effect on October 16, 1987.

The unfunded new liability amount equals a specific percentage of the unfunded new liability. The unfunded new liability equals the excess, if any, of the unfunded current liability over the unamortized portion of the unfunded old liability, and without regard to the liability for unpredictable contingent events. The percentage of the unfunded new liability recognized depends on the funded current liability percentage, defined as the ratio of the plan's actuarial value of assets, net of the credit balance, to its current liability. If this ratio is 35 percent or less, the percentage of the unfunded new liability recognized is 30 percent. For every percentage point by which the funded current liability percentage exceeds 35 percent, the percentage of unfunded new liability recognized declines by .25 percent. Thus, if the funded current liability percentage equals 99 percent, then the percentage recognized equals 14 percent:

$$30\% - .25 \times (99\% - 35\%) = 14\%.$$

16.4.2. Alternative Minimum Funding Standard

A pension plan using a funding method that requires contributions in all years not less than those required under the "entry age normal funding method" can elect compliance under the alternative minimum funding standard. Under this standard, the minimum annual contribution to the pension plan would be the lesser of the normal cost determined for the plan or the normal cost determined under the accrued benefit cost method plus the excess, if any, of the actuarial value of the accrued benefits over the fair market value of the assets. All assets, under this standard, are valued at their actual market value on the date of valuation without benefit of averaging or amortization, while the actuarial value of accrued benefits is calculated based on assumptions appropriate for a terminating plan; for example, rates published by the Pension Benefit Guaranty Corporation (PBGC). Adherence to this standard would assure that the pension plan would have assets, valued at market, at least equal to the actuarial value of all accrued benefits, whether vested or not. The rationale for this alternative approach is that a pension plan should not be required to hold assets in excess of those needed to meet accrued benefits.

A pension plan using this approach must set up an alternative minimum funding standard account. Such an account is charged each year with the lesser of the normal cost of the plan or the normal cost determined under the accrued benefit cost method plus the excess of the actuarial value of accrued benefits over plan assets (not less than zero) and will be credited with contributions. All entries are adjusted for interest to the end of a plan year. There is no carryover of contributions over the required minimum from one year to the next, since any excess contributions simply become a part of the plan assets for the following year's comparison of assets and liabilities. Conversely, as with the regular funding standard account, any deficiency of contributions is carried over from year to year, with interest, and the excise tax described earlier is payable on the cumulative funding deficiency.

A pension plan electing the alternative funding standard must maintain both an alternate funding standard account and the basic funding standard account. The basic funding standard account is charged and credited under the normal rules, but an excise tax will not be levied on any deficiency in that account if there is no deficiency in the alternate account. A pension plan making this choice is required to maintain both accounts, since the minimum required contribution in a particular plan year is the lesser of the contributions called for by the basic and alternate standards. If a plan switches from the alternate standard back to the basic standard, the excess of the deficiency in the standard account over the deficiency in the alternate standard account must be amortized over five years.

16.4.3. Shortfall Method

A negotiated plan that has both a defined contribution rate and a defined benefit may elect to determine entries to the funding standard account under the shortfall method. Under the shortfall method, the net charge to the funding standard account for a year is based on the fixed contribution rate for the year times the actual number of units of service or production during the year; that is, hours worked or tons of coal mined. The difference between the net charge so computed and the amount that would otherwise have been computed under the funding standard account is the shortfall gain or loss that must be amortized over future years. In general, the shortfall gain or loss is amortized over the 15 years following the year in which it arose. For plans maintained by more than one employer, the start of the amortization period may be deferred up to five years after the shortfall gain or loss arose, but the amortization period still ends 15 years after the gain or loss arose. If the shortfall method is adopted after 1980 (or if it is decided to abandon use of the shortfall method after it is once used) it requires prior approval from the secretary of the treasury.

16.5.   DEDUCTIBILITY OF EMPLOYER CONTRIBUTIONS

16.5.1. Basic Requirements

Apart from the specific provisions of the Internal Revenue Code dealing with the deductibility of employer contributions to a qualified plan, it is first required that if such a contribution is to be deductible, it must otherwise satisfy the conditions of an ordinary and necessary business expense under Code Sections 162 (relating to trade or business expenses) or 212 (relating to expenses for the production of income). Also, a deduction will not be allowed for any portion of the contribution for any employee that, together with other deductions allowed for compensation for such employee, exceeds a reasonable allowance for services the employee actually has rendered.

The employer's contributions to a qualified plan are generally deductible under Section 404(a) of the Internal Revenue Code. Expenses such as actuary's and trustee's fees that are not provided for by contributions under the plan are deductible under Sections 162 or 212 to the extent they are ordinary and necessary expenses.

Employer contributions are generally deductible only in the year in which paid. However, an employer will be deemed to have made a contribution during a taxable year if it is in fact paid by the time prescribed for filing the employer's return for such taxable year (including extensions) and if the employer claims the contribution as a deduction for such year. It is important, however, that the plan be in existence by the close of the employer's taxable year in the case of deductions claimed for the first plan year that begins in such taxable year.

16.5.2. Limits on Tax-Deductible Contributions to a Defined Benefit Plan

Basically, two provisions determine the maximum amount an employer can contribute and take as a deduction to a qualified pension plan in any one taxable year. The first of these rules permits a deduction for a contribution that will provide, for all employees participating in the plan, the unfunded cost of their past and current service credits distributed as a level amount or as a level percentage of compensation over the remaining future service of each such employee. If this rule is followed, and if the remaining unfunded cost for any three individuals is more than 50 percent of the total unfunded cost, the unfunded cost attributable to such individuals must be distributed over a period of at least five taxable years. Contributions under individual policy pension plans are typically claimed under this rule.

The second rule, while occasionally used with individual policy plans, is used primarily in group pension and trust fund plans.[18] This rule permits the employer to deduct the normal cost of the plan plus the amount necessary to amortize any past service or other supplementary pension or annuity credits in equal annual installments over a 10-year period.

The maximum tax deductible limit will never be less than the amount necessary to satisfy the Code's minimum funding standards. By the same token, the maximum tax-deductible limit cannot exceed the amount needed to bring the plan to its full funding limit. The full funding limit is defined as the lesser of 100 percent of the plan's actuarial accrued liability (including normal cost) or 150 percent of the plan's current liability, reduced by the lesser of the market value of plan assets or their actuarial value.

If amounts contributed in any taxable year are in excess of the amounts allowed as a deduction for that year, the excess may be carried forward and deducted in succeeding taxable years, in order of time, to the extent that the amount carried forward to any such succeeding taxable year does not exceed the deductible limit for such succeeding taxable year. However, a 10 percent excise tax is imposed on nondeductible contributions by an employer to a qualified plan. For purposes of the excise tax, nondeductible contributions are defined as the sum of the amount of the employer's contribution that exceeds the amount deductible under Section 404 and any excess amount

---

[18]These funding instruments are discussed in Chapters 20 and 21.

contributed in the preceding tax year that has not been returned to the employer or applied as a deductible contribution in the current year.

16.5.3. Overstatement of Pension Liabilities

An excise tax will be imposed on an underpayment of taxes that results from an overstatement of pension liabilities. A 20 percent penalty tax is imposed on the underpayment of tax if the actuarial determination of pension liabilities is between 200 and 399 percent of the amount determined to be correct. If the actuarial determination is 400 percent or more of the correct amount, the penalty tax is increased to 40 percent. If the tax benefit is $1,000 or less, no excise tax will be imposed.

16.5.4. Special Limits for Combined Plans

If both a defined benefit pension plan and a defined contribution plan exist, with overlapping payrolls, the total amount deductible in any taxable year under both plans cannot exceed 25 percent of the compensation paid or accrued to covered employees for that year.[19] When excess payments are made in any taxable year, the excess may be carried forward to succeeding taxable years, subject to the limitation that the total amount deducted for such succeeding taxable year (including the deduction for the current contribution) cannot exceed 25 percent of the compensation paid or accrued for such subsequent year.

The 25 percent limitation does not eliminate the requirements that a currently deductible profit sharing contribution must not exceed 15 percent of the payroll of the participating employees and that a currently deductible pension contribution must not exceed the amount that would have been the limit had only a pension plan been in effect.

16.5.5. Non-Deductibility of Contributions to Provide Benefits in Excess of Section 415 Limits

No deduction is allowed for the portion of a contribution to a defined benefit plan to fund a benefit for any participant in excess of the Section 415 annual benefit limitation for the year (see Chapter 6 for details). In calculating the contribution to a defined benefit plan, anticipated cost-of-

---

[19]This 25 percent limit will be increased to the extent larger contributions are required by the Code's minimum funding standards for the defined benefit plan.

living increases in the allowable annual retirement benefit *cannot* be taken into account before the year in which the increase becomes effective.

QUESTIONS FOR REVIEW

1. Define the following terms: (a) normal cost, (b) supplemental cost, and (c) past service liability.
2. Explain the steps in the calculation of (a) the normal cost and (b) the supplemental liability at plan inception under the accrued benefit cost method.
3. How does a projected benefit cost method differ from an accrued benefit cost method?
4. Distinguish between the individual level and aggregate level cost methods.
5. How does an employer amortize a supplemental liability? Over what time period can this be done, according to ERISA?
6. What are the amortization periods for unfunded supplemental liabilities for single-employer plans? In what situations will variance from the standards be permitted?
7. What are the exemptions from the mandated minimum funding standards?
8. What are the annual charges and credits in the funding standard account?
9. What is the impact of (a) a positive balance and (b) a negative balance for the funding standard account at the end of the year?
10. What alternate minimum funding standard exists for plans that use the entry age normal method?

QUESTIONS FOR DISCUSSION

1. Discuss why an employer might prefer to use an accrued benefit cost method instead of a projected benefit cost method, and vice versa.
2. Discuss why an employer might prefer to use an aggregate level cost method instead of an individual level cost method.
3. Discuss the factors that might influence an employer's choice of an amortization period for the supplemental liability.

17. Plan Termination Insurance

The Pension Benefit Guaranty Corporation (PBGC) is a federal government agency created under Title IV of the Employee Retirement Income Security Act (ERISA). In general, the purposes of the PBGC are to encourage the continuation and maintenance of voluntary private pension plans for the benefit of their participants, provide for the timely and uninterrupted payment of pension benefits to the participants and beneficiaries under all insured plans, and minimize over the long run the premiums charged for the insurance coverage. The PBGC administers two insurance programs: one for single-employer and one for multiemployer pension plans. This chapter deals exclusively with single-employer plans.[1]

In 1974, the ERISA established a plan termination insurance program for the majority of defined benefit pension plans in the United States to ensure that pensioners' rights would be protected (up to a maximum amount per month) in the event of a pension plan terminating with unfunded liabilities. In 1986, one of the major defects associated with the original design was corrected when the Single Employer Pension Plan Amendments Act (SEPPAA) changed the insured event from that of, in essence, any plan termination to a termination accompanied by a specified event for the plan sponsor.

This change effectively limited the insurable event to an insufficient termination due to bankruptcy by the sponsor, thereby virtually eliminating

---

[1]ERISA, and more significantly the Multiemployer Pension Plan Amendments Act (MEPPAA) of 1980, had major effects upon the Pension Benefit Guaranty Corporation's jurisdiction over multiemployer pension plans, employer liabilities, and the administrative practices of trustees. The complex law has many implications for almost all aspects of multiemployer plans, especially concerning plan termination insurance and employer liabilities.

the opportunity of an ongoing sponsor to exchange the unfunded vested liabilities of the plan for 30 percent of its net worth (an option existing under the original provisions of ERISA). However, it did nothing to change the premium structure from a flat dollar amount per participant. Congress redressed this shortcoming in part by enacting a *variable rate premium* structure in 1987 that relates the sponsor's annual premium to the plan's underfunding (as measured on a termination basis). Although this change factors the plan's potential severity into the determination of the annual premium, it is not the same as a *risk-related premium* structure that would characterize the insurance if it were to base annual premiums not only on the potential severity but also the probability of an insured event taking place (i.e., bankruptcy of a sponsor with an underfunded plan). The new premium system also differs from what would likely evolve in a free market approach in that it includes a maximum charge per participant.

17.1. PLANS COVERED

The PBGC's single-employer plan termination insurance provisions apply to virtually all defined benefit pension plans. The following material examines the specific plans covered and then describes the type of pension benefits protected by this insurance program.

Subject to specific exceptions, ERISA Section 4021(a) requires mandatory coverage of employee pension benefit plans that either affect interstate commerce (and in the case of nonqualified plans, have for five years met the standards for qualified plans) or that are qualified under the Internal Revenue Code. The following plans are specifically excluded from coverage:

1. Individual account plans (e.g., money purchase pension plans, profit sharing plans, thrift and savings plans, and stock bonus plans).
2. Government plans.
3. Certain church plans other than those that have voluntarily opted for coverage.
4. Certain plans established by fraternal societies to which no employer contributions are made.
5. Plans that do not provide for employer contributions after September 2, 1974.
6. Nonqualified deferred compensation plans established for select groups of management or highly compensated employees.
7. Plans established outside of the United States for nonresident aliens.
8. So-called excess benefit plans established and maintained primarily to pay benefits or accrue contributions for a limited group of highly paid employees in excess of the Section 415 limits.

9. Plans established and maintained exclusively for "substantial owners," meaning proprietors, partners with a greater than 10 percent interest in the capital profits of a partnership, or shareholders of a corporation owning, directly or indirectly, more than 10 percent in value of either the voting stock or of all the stock of the corporation.

10. Plans of international organizations exempt from tax under the International Organization Immunities Act.

11. Plans maintained only to comply with workers' compensation, unemployment compensation, or disability insurance laws.

12. Plans established and maintained by labor organizations as described in Section 501(c)(5) of the Internal Revenue Code that do not provide for employer contributions after September 2, 1974.

13. Plans that are defined benefit plans to the extent that they are treated as individual account plans.[2]

14. Any plan established and maintained by professional service employers, provided that there are not, at any time after September 2, 1974, more than 25 active participants in the plan.

For purposes of the last category, a professional service employer means any proprietorship, partnership. corporation, or other association or organization owned or controlled by professional individuals or by executors or administrators of professional individuals, the principal business of which is the performance of professional services.

17.2.   PLAN TERMINATION DEFINED

The termination of a pension plan should be a clearly identifiable event. Otherwise, it may be difficult to assess if a termination has occurred and, if so, when. Establishing the exact date of termination is important to all parties concerned -- the plan sponsor, the plan participants and beneficiaries, and the PBGC. A plan termination can be voluntary or involuntary. However, the PBGC will not proceed with a voluntary termination of a plan if it would violate the terms and conditions of an existing collective bargaining agreement.[3]

During the first 10 years of the PBGC's existence, the insured event for single-employer plan termination insurance was simply the termination of the defined benefit pension plan. This event is generally within the control

---

[2]However if the assets under a terminating cash balance plan are insufficient to meet the benefit obligation under the plan, the Pension Benefit Guaranty Corporation will assume the unfunded benefits on the same terms as those applicable to traditional defined benefit plans.

[3]It should be noted that this will not limit the PBGC's authority to proceed with an involuntary termination as described later in this chapter.

of the sponsor and, coupled with the fact that the sponsor's liability to the PBGC was at that time limited to 30 percent of its net worth, several underfunded plans were terminated even though the sponsor continued in existence and in some cases even attempted to establish a new pension plan immediately after the original plan was terminated. As the financial condition of the PBGC continued to deteriorate in the first half of the 1980s, several attempts were made to legislatively amend the definition of the insured event. SEPPAA radically changed these provisions in an attempt to preserve the financial integrity of the system. The following section describes the new circumstances under which the single-employer plan termination insurance applies.

17.2.1. Voluntary Plan Termination

A single-employer plan may be terminated voluntarily only in a standard termination or a distress termination. Disclosure of the appropriate information is provided through a series of PBGC forms known as the Standard Termination Filing and Distress Termination Filing forms.

17.2.1.1.   Standard Termination

A single-employer plan may terminate under a standard termination if, among other things, the plan is sufficient for benefit liabilities (determined as of the termination date) when the final distribution of assets occurs.

Provided the PBGC has not issued a notice of noncompliance and the plan is sufficient for benefit liabilities when the final distribution occurs, the plan administrator must distribute the plan's assets in accordance with the requirements for allocation of assets under ERISA Section 4044 (described below).

17.2.1.2.   Distress Termination

After receiving the appropriate information, the PBGC must then determine whether the necessary distress criteria have been satisfied. Basically, these criteria are met if each person who is a contributing sponsor or a member of the sponsor's controlled group meets the requirements of any of the following:
1.   Liquidation in bankruptcy or insolvency proceedings.

2. Reorganization in bankruptcy or insolvency proceedings.[4]
3. Termination required to enable payment of debts while staying in business or to avoid unreasonably burdensome pension costs caused by a declining work force.

If the PBGC determines that the requirements for a distress termination are met, it will either determine (1) that the plan is sufficient for guaranteed benefits or that it is unable to make a determination on the basis of the available information, or (2) that the plan is sufficient for benefit liabilities or that it is unable to make a determination on the basis of the available information. The plan administrator will be notified of the decision and one of the following types of terminations will be carried out:[5]

1. In any case in which the PBGC determines that the plan is sufficient for benefit liabilities, the plan administrator must distribute the plan's assets in the same manner as described for a standard termination.
2. In any case in which the PBGC determines that the plan is sufficient for guaranteed benefits, but is unable to determine that the plan is sufficient for benefit liabilities, the plan administrator must distribute the plan's assets in the same manner as described for a standard termination.
3. In any case in which the PBGC determines that it is unable to determine that the plan is sufficient for guaranteed benefits, PBGC will commence proceedings as though an involuntary termination (described below) were taking place.

The plan administrator must meet certain requirements during the interim period from the time the PBGC is notified to the time a sufficiency determination is made. Essentially the administrator must:
1. Refrain from distributing assets or taking any other actions to carry out the proposed termination.
2. Pay benefits attributable to employer contributions, other than death benefits, only in the form of an annuity.
3. Not use plan assets to purchase irrevocable commitments to provide benefits from an insurer.
4. Continue to pay all benefit liabilities under the plan, but, commencing on the proposed termination date, limit the payment of benefits under

---

[4]For this requirement to be met, a bankruptcy court must determine that, unless the plan is terminated, the sponsor will be unable to pay all its debts pursuant to a plan of reorganization and will be unable to continue in business outside the Chapter 11 reorganization process.
[5]ERISA Section 4041(c)(3).

the plan to those benefits guaranteed by the PBGC or to which assets are required to be allocated under Section 4044 (described below).

When two organizations merge, the resulting single plan does not result in a termination if the new merged organization assumes responsibility for the plan. Also, under ERISA, a pension plan may not be merged or consolidated with another pension plan, or have its assets transferred to another plan, unless each participant in the prior plan is credited in the successor plan with a benefit at least as great as that which he or she would have received had the old plan terminated.[6]

17.2.2. Involuntary Plan Termination

The PBGC may institute termination proceedings in a U.S. district court in the jurisdiction where the employer does business if it finds that (a) the plan does not comply with the minimum funding standards of the Internal Revenue Code; (b) the plan is unable to pay benefits when due; (c) within the preceding 24 months, and for a reason other than death, a distribution of $10,000 or more has been made to a participant who is the substantial owner of the sponsoring firm and that following the distribution there are unfunded liabilities; or (d) the eventual loss to the PBGC for the plan may be expected to increase unreasonably if the plan is not terminated. Moreover, the PBGC is required to institute proceedings to terminate a single-employer plan whenever it determines that the plan does not have assets available to pay benefits that are currently due under the terms of the plan. The PBGC may decide not to seek involuntary termination, even if one of the conditions for action has occurred, if it deems that it would be in the best interests of those involved not to force termination of the plan.

17.2.3. Reportable Events

The administrator of any covered pension plan is required to report to the PBGC certain events that may indicate possible termination of a pension plan. These reportable events are:

- inability of the plan to pay benefits when due;
- a failure to meet the minimum funding standards;
- determination that a complete or partial plan termination for tax purposes has occurred;

---

[6]IRC Sec. 401(a)(12)

- a merger or consolidation of the plan with another plan;
- loss of qualified status under the Internal Revenue Code;
- a plan amendment that decreases the benefits of the participants;
- if the unfunded vested benefit is at least $250,000, a decrease in active participants of more than 20 percent of the number at the beginning of the plan year, or 25 percent of the number at the beginning of the previous plan year;
- a distribution of $10,000 or more within a 24-month period to a substantial owner, for reasons other than death, that creates or increases unfunded vested liabilities;
- whenever the Department of Labor determines a plan has failed to meet any of the requirements contained in ERISA Title I;
- if the Department of Labor prescribes an alternative method of compliance for a particular plan or a specific limited group of plans.;
- when a contributing sponsor in a controlled group files for bankruptcy, becomes insolvent, or is in the process of complete liquidation or dissolution;
- whenever as a result of a transfer of assets, a new contribution sponsor emerges which is not a member of the controlled group of the previous contribution sponsor, the contributing sponsor leaves the controlled group, or the contribution sponsor becomes a member of a different controlled group; and
- any other event the PBGC designates as reportable.[7]

17.2.4. Date of Termination

For purposes of Title IV of ERISA, the termination date of a single-employer plan is one of the following:

1. In the case of a plan terminated in a standard termination, the termination date proposed in the notice of intent to terminate.
2. In the case of a plan terminated in a distress termination, the date established by the plan administrator and agreed to by the PBGC.
3. In the case of an involuntary termination, the date established by the PBGC and agreed to by the plan administrator.
4. In the case of distress or involuntary termination in any case in which no agreement is reached between the plan administrator and the PBGC, the date established by the court.

---

[7]ERISA Sec. 4043 and PBGC regulations [29 CFP Part 2615].

The date on which the termination of a plan becomes effective is significant for a number of reasons. It not only establishes the date the PBGC assumes legal obligation for the plan's benefits, but also establishes the date for the determination of the employer's possible contingent liability for unfunded benefits (described below). The effective termination date also is important to the participant. It fixes the date on which benefit accruals cease, vesting schedule position is determined, and when the phase-in of insurance coverage stops.

17.2.5. Restoration of Plan

If it appears that the pension plan could be continued, even though plan termination proceedings have begun, the PBGC may halt the proceedings and take whatever action is necessary to restore the plan.[8]

17.3. BENEFITS GUARANTEED

Even though a plan is covered by the PBGC's single-employer plan termination insurance, there is no assurance that all accrued pension benefits will be paid after the plan's termination. The individual participant (or beneficiary) must first meet three prerequisites before the benefit is guaranteed by the PBGC. Assuming the prerequisites are met, the individual may still be subject to specific limitations on the amount of the benefit covered.

17.3.1. Prerequisites for PBGC Guarantees

Subject to the various limits described below, the PBGC guarantees the payment of all nonforfeitable benefits that qualify as a pension benefit other than those accelerated by plan termination. A benefit that becomes nonforfeitable solely because of plan termination is not subject to ERISA benefit guarantees; however a benefit won't fail to satisfy the PBGC requirement merely because a participant is required to submit a written application, retire, or complete a mandatory waiting period as a condition for receiving pension payments.

There are two additional exceptions to the general rule on forfeitability. First, guaranteed benefits paid to survivor beneficiaries are not deemed to be forfeitable for purposes of the PBGC guarantee merely because the plan provides for termination of benefit payments should the beneficiary remarry

---

[8]ERISA Section 4047.

or attain a specific age. Second, disability benefits will not be deemed forfeitable solely because they end on a participant's recovery.

For a payment to qualify as a pension benefit, it must be payable as an annuity or as one or more payments related to an annuity, Further, the benefit must be payable either to a participant who permanently leaves or has left covered employment or to a surviving beneficiary. It is also necessary for the pension benefit payment to provide a substantially level income to the recipient, although the leveling could be accomplished in conjunction with Social Security payments. Under certain circumstances, the PBGC will also guarantee annuities payable for total disability[9] and benefits payable in a single installment.[10]

The final requirement for protection under the PBGC guarantee is that the participant or beneficiary be entitled to the benefit. This prerequisite is satisfied if any of the following are satisfied:

1. The benefit was in pay status on the date of plan termination.
2. The benefit payable at normal retirement age is an optional benefit under the plan and the participant elected the optional form of payment before the plan termination date.
3. The participant is actually eligible to receive benefits and could have received them before the plan terminated.
4. The benefit would be payable on the participant's retirement absent a contrary election.
5. The PBGC determines the participant is entitled to the benefit based on the particular circumstances.

17.3.2. Limitation on Amount of Monthly Benefits

There is a limit on the amount of monthly guaranteed benefits insured by the PBGC. The amount is adjusted annually to reflect changes in the social security taxable wage base. The original limit was $750 per month, but for plans terminated in 1991 the limit increased to $2,250.00 per month. The limit is in terms of a single life annuity commencing at age 65, and without a refund feature. If the benefit is payable at a lower age, it is reduced by actuarial factors denoted by the PBGC. The benefit is not actuarially increased when the participant retires at an age later than 65.

---

[9]PBGC Regulation Section 2613.7.

[10]The benefit will not be paid in a single installment, but the PBGC will guarantee the alternative benefit, if any, in the plan that provides for the payment of equal periodic installments for the life of the recipient. PBGC Regulation Section 2613.8.

The guaranteed monthly benefit of a participant cannot be greater than his or her average gross monthly income during the five consecutive years of highest earnings (or, if the period is shorter, the time during which he or she was an active participant in the plan).

17.3.3. New or Amended Plans and Benefits

To prevent possible abuses, the insurance covers guaranteed benefits, provided those benefits have been in effect under the provisions of the plan for 60 months or longer at the time of plan termination.[11] If benefits are attributable to a plan amendment or to a new plan adopted, the benefits attributable to that amendment or new plan are guaranteed only to the extent of the greater of 20 percent of the amount of such increased or new benefit multiplied by the number of years (up to five) that the plan or amendment has been in effect, or $20 per month multiplied by the number of years (up to five) that the plan or amendment has been in effect.

17.3.4. Payments in Excess of Unfunded Guaranteed Benefits

Participants, beneficiaries, and alternate payees under a single-employer plan will be paid a percentage of their unfunded benefit liabilities in excess of PBGC-guaranteed benefits equal to a percentage recovered by the PBGC on the total claim.[12] Amounts will be allocated to participants in accordance with the ERISA Sec 4044 asset allocation rules. Generally, the recovery percentage will be determined from past PBGC experience. In the case of large amounts (i.e., unfunded benefit liabilities in excess of guaranteed benefits of at least $20 million) data from the particular termination will be used in determining the recovery percentage.

Specifically, the amount is determined by multiplying (1) the "outstanding amount of benefit liabilities" by (2) the applicable "recovery ratio." The "outstanding amount of benefit liabilities" is (1) the value of the benefit liabilities under the plan less (2) the value of the benefit liabilities which would be so determined by only taking into account benefits which are guaranteed or to which assets of the plan are allocated under ERISA Sec. 4044.[13]

In the case of a terminated plan in which the outstanding amount of benefit liabilities is less than $20,000,000, the "recovery ratio" is the average

---

[11]ERISA Section 4022(b)(8).
[12]ERISA Section 4022(c).
[13]ERISA Section 4001(a).

ratio, with respect to "prior plan terminations" under the plan sponsor liability rules of:[14]

The value of the recovery of the PBGC under the plan
sponsor liability rules for the prior plan terminations
The amount of unfunded benefit liabilities under the plan
as of the termination date of the prior plan terminations.

In the case of a terminated plan for which the outstanding benefit liabilities exceed $20,000,000, the term "recovery ratio" is the ratio of:

The value of the recoveries of the PBGC under the
plan sponsor liability rules for the terminated plan
The amount of unfunded benefit liabilities under the
plan as of the termination date

For purposes of the above ratios, the "amount of unfunded benefit liabilities" is (1) the value of benefit liabilities under the plan less (2) the current value of the assets of the plan.

Determinations under these rules are to be made by the PBGC. A determination will be binding unless shown by clear and convincing evidence to be unreasonable.

17.4.   ALLOCATION OF ASSETS ON PLAN TERMINATION

17.4.1. Priority Categories

Plan assets must be allocated to the benefit categories applicable on plan termination under ERISA Section 4044. This prevents employers from establishing new benefit levels, terminating plans, and allocating existing plan assets to such benefit resulting in the subordination of insured to uninsured benefits. On termination, the assets of a plan must be allocated in the following order of priorities:[15]

---

[14]A "prior plan termination" is a termination of which (1) the PBGC has determined the value of recoveries under the plan sponsor liability rules and (2) notices of intent to terminate were provided after December 31, 1987, and within the five fiscal years of the federal government ending before the year in which the date of the notice of intent to terminate the plan of which the recovery ratio is being determined was provided .

[15]ERISA Sec. 4044.

1. Employees' voluntary contributions.
2. Employees' mandatory contributions.
3. Annuity payments in pay status at least three years before the termination of the plan (including annuity payments that would have been in pay status for at least three years if the employee had retired then) based on the provisions of the plan in effect during the five years before termination of the plan under which the benefit would be the least.
4. All other insured benefits. This includes benefits that would be insured except for the special limitation with respect to a "substantial owner"; also, the aggregate benefit limitation for individuals does not apply.
5. All other vested, but uninsured, benefits.
6. All other benefits under the plan.

An allocation within a priority category that cannot be covered in full is settled on a pro rata basis, except that subpriorities within a priority category may be provided for by the plan. If there are any assets remaining after satisfaction of all liabilities for accrued benefits, they may be paid to the employer if provided for by the plan provisions.

17.4.2. Reversion of Residual Assets to the Employer

In general, the funds in a qualified pension plan may not be used for purposes other than the exclusive benefit of employees or their beneficiaries prior to the termination of the plan and the satisfaction of all liabilities. However, with the exception of pension plan assets attributable to employee contributions, employers may recapture any residual assets of a terminated single-employer defined benefit pension plan if the following conditions are satisfied:

1. All liabilities of the plan to participants and their beneficiaries have been satisfied.
2. The distribution does not contravene any provision of law.
3. The plan provides for such a distribution in these circumstances.

Residual assets are equal to the plan funds remaining after satisfaction of all liabilities.[16]

The PBGC, Treasury Department, and the Department of Labor have issued the following joint implementation guidelines on asset reversions:

---

[16]Restrictions on reversions from recently amended plans are specified in ERISA Section 4044(d)(2). The allocation of residual assets attributable to employee contributions is described in ERISA Section 4044(d)(3).

1. An employer may not recover any surplus assets until it has fully vested all participants' benefits and has purchased and distributed annuity contracts.

2. If employees are offered lump-sum payments in lieu of future pensions, the amount of the lump-sum distribution must fairly reflect the value of the pension to the individual.

3. An employer that terminates a sufficiently funded defined benefit pension plan may establish a new defined benefit plan covering the same group of employees, granting past service credit for the period during which an employee was covered by the terminated plan. This is known as a termination/reestablishment and the successor plan is exempt from the five-year phase-in of benefit guarantees that applies to newly established plans.

4. Spinoff/terminations[17] will not be recognized and any attempt to recover surplus assets will be treated as a diversion of assets for a purpose other than the exclusive benefit of employees and beneficiaries unless the employees receive timely notice of the event and the following conditions are satisfied:

    a. The benefits of all employees must be fully vested and nonforfeitable as of the date of the termination. This also applies to the benefits covered by the ongoing plan.

    b. All accrued benefits must be provided for by the purchase of annuity contracts.

5. In the case of a spinoff/termination and a termination/reestablishment, attempts to recover surplus assets will be treated as a diversion of assets for a purpose other than the exclusive benefit of employees and beneficiaries unless the funding method for the ongoing plans is to be changed by modifying the amortization bases.[18]

6. An employer may not engage in either a termination-reestablishment or spinoff/termination transaction, involving reversion of assets, any earlier than 15 years following any such transaction.

Amounts recovered under a reversion are subject to a 50% excise tax.[19] This penalty is reduced to 20% if (1) 25% of the otherwise recoverable reversion

---

[17]Under a spinoff/termination, the active participants (and their liabilities) are spun off from the original defined benefit plan. Assets are then transferred from the original plan to the new plan in an amount at least equal to the active participants' liabilities. The original plan, which at this point covers only retired and terminated employees, is then terminated and annuities are used to satisfy the plan's obligations.

[18]The modification must be in accordance with IRC Section 412(b)(4). Details of the modification are provided in PBGC News Rel. 84-23.

[19]Prior to the Omnibus Budget Reconciliation Act of 1990, the tax rate had been 15 percent. In addition to the increased penalty, this legislation allowed employers to use surplus pension assets to prefund retiree health plans through 401(h) accounts.

is transferred to another qualified retirement plan that covers at least 95% of the active participants of the terminated plan, (2) 20% of the otherwise recoverable reversion is used to provide pro rata increases in the benefits accrued by participants under the terminated plan, or (3) the employer is in Chapter 7 bankruptcy liquidation.

If the employer adopts a plan amendment increasing terminated defined benefit plan benefits, the 25% cushion is reduced dollar for dollar by the present value of the increase. These benefit increases must satisfy the generally applicable qualification requirements, such as the nondiscrimination rules described in Chapter 5.

Compliance with the 20% pro-rata increase option requires that increased benefits must be provided to all qualified participants. This includes active participants, participants and beneficiaries receiving benefits on the termination date, and other participants who retain rights under the plan and who terminate employment (or plan eligibility) during a period starting 3 years before the termination date and ending on the final asset distribution date.[20] Beneficiaries of this last group also are eligible if they have a vested plan benefit. Employees who stop working before the plan termination date and receive a lump sum distribution are not entitled to benefit increases.

17.5.   LIABILITIES ON PLAN TERMINATION

17.5.1. Distributee Liability-Recapture

When a plan terminates, the termination trustee is authorized to recover for the benefit of the pension plan certain payments received by a participant within the three-year period prior to plan termination. The "recoverable amount" is the sum of all payments made to the participant in excess of $10,000 made during any consecutive 12-month period within three years before termination or, if lesser, the amount he or she would have received as a monthly benefit under a single-life annuity commencing at age 65.[21] Payments to a disabled participant and payments made after or on account of the death of a participant are not subject to recovery. PBGC can totally or partially waive any amount otherwise entitled to be recaptured whenever recapture would result in substantial economic hardship to a participant or his or her beneficiaries.

---

[20]The assets allocated to increase the benefit of non-active participants cannot exceed 40% of the total.
[21]ERISA Sec. 4045.

17.5.2. Employer Liability

During the legislative process leading up to the enactment of ERISA, concern was expressed that in the absence of appropriate safeguards under an insurance system, an employer might establish or amend a plan to provide substantial benefits with the realization that its funding may be inadequate to pay the benefits called for. Such an employer might, it was argued, rely on the insurance as the backup that enables it to be more generous in promised pension benefits to meet labor demands than would be the case if it knew that the benefit would have to be paid for entirely out of the assets of the employer. On the other hand, it was clear that the imposition of heavy obligations on employers would discourage provisions for adequate pension plans.

To deal with these competing considerations, it was determined to impose on the employer a limited liability to reimburse the insurance system for a portion of the payment that must be made by the PBGC in satisfaction of its obligation if the employer plan fails. Unfortunately, the limited liability was much 'smaller than the amount of unfunded benefit for many sponsors and several plans in this category were terminated to take advantage of this so-called pension put.

SEPPAA substantially modified the computation of the sponsors liability on termination. The Omnibus Budget Reconciliation Act of 1987 made further modifications the following year. Currently, in any case in which a single-employer plan is terminated in a distress termination or an involuntary termination is instituted by the PBGC, any person who is, on the termination date, a contributing sponsor of the plan or a member of such a contributing sponsor's controlled group will incur a liability under Section 4062 of ERISA. This liability consists of two components:

1. The liability to the PBGC.
2. The liability to the Section 4042 trustee (described below).

Although special rules pertain to the case in which it is discovered that the plan is unable to pay guaranteed benefits after the authorized commencement of termination,[22] the following section defines the rules generally applying to the two components of the sponsor's liability and the required means of payment.

---

[22]ERISA Sections 4062(b)(1)(B).

17.5.2.1.   Liability to the PBGC

The liability to the PBGC consists of the total amount of the unfunded benefit liabilities (as of the termination date) to all participants and beneficiaries under the plan, together with interest (at a reasonable rate) calculated from the termination date in accordance with regulations prescribed by the PBGC.

The total amount of the liability is paid to the PBGC, which pays out a portion of unfunded benefit liabilities in excess of the unfunded guaranteed benefits based on the total value of the PBGC's recovery with respect to the total liability of the employer. Amounts paid to participants are allocated in accordance with Section 4044.

The liability to the PBGC is generally due as of the termination date. The PBGC and any person liable for payment may also agree to alternative arrangements for the satisfaction of liability.

17.5.2.2.   Liability to the Section 4042 Trustee

The liability to a Section 4042 trustee for the sponsoring employer and each member of its controlled group consists of the outstanding balance (accumulated with interest from the termination date) of:

1.   The accumulated funding deficiency of the plan, modified to include the amount of any increase that would result if all pending applications for waiver of the minimum funding standard account and for extension of the amortization period were denied and if no additional contributions were made.
2.   The amount of waived funding deficiencies.
3.   The amount of decreases in the minimum funding standard account.

17.5.2.3.   Determination of Net Worth

In general, the collective net worth, for purposes of determining the liability to the PBGC, consists of the sum of the individual net worths of all persons who have individual net worths greater than zero, and are contributing sponsors of the terminated plan or members of their controlled groups. The net worth of a person is determined on whatever basis best reflects, in the determination of the PBGC, the current status of the person's operations and prospects at the time chosen for determining the net worth of the person. The net worth is increased by the amount of any transfers of assets made by the pension that are determined by the PBGC to be improper under the circumstance. Determinations of net worth are made as of a day chosen by PBGC during the 120-day period ending with the termination date. Net worth is computed without regard to termination liabilities.

17.5.2.4.   Liability of Substantial and Multiple Employers

A liability applies to all employers, other than multiemployer plans terminating after April 29, 1980, who maintain a plan under which more than one employer makes contributions. The liability also attaches to all employers who, at any time within the five plan years preceding the date of plan termination, made contributions under the plan. The liability is allocated among the employers in the ratio of their required contributions for the last five years prior to termination, except that the 30 percent of net worth exposure applies separately as to each corporation.

If the withdrawing employer prefers, a bond may be furnished to the PBGC in an amount not exceeding 150 percent of its liability. The bond must be issued by a corporate surety acceptable on federal bonds on the authority granted by the secretary of the treasury.

17.5.2.5.   PBGC Lien for Employer Liability

To the extent an employer liability is not satisfied and the amount does not exceed 30 percent of the collective net worth of the sponsor and its controlled group, the amount of the liability (including interest) is a lien in favor of the PBGC upon all property and rights to property, whether real or personal, belonging to the employer. The lien is in the nature of a tax lien that supersedes the liens of other creditors of the corporation.

17.6.   PREMIUMS

Although Congress corrected several of the major design flaws in the single-employer plan termination insurance system with the passage of SEPPAA, there were still lingering doubts concerning the equity of a premium structure based solely on a flat-rate premium per participant. Therefore, Congress mandated that the PBGC prepare a study on several issues relating to the premium structure. On the basis of their findings, the PBGC proposed a variable-rate premium structure that added an additional premium charge based on the difference between the plan liabilities and the plan assets. This basic concept was incorporated into the Omnibus Budget

Reconciliation Act of 1987 and later modified by the Omnibus Budget Reconciliation Act of 1990.

For plan years beginning after 1990, the single-employer flat-rate per-participant premium is $19. An additional premium of $9 per $1,000 of unfunded vested benefits, with a maximum per-participant additional premium of $53, is also required of underfunded plans.[23] The contributing sponsor or plan administrator must pay the premiums imposed by the PBGC. If the contributing sponsor of any plan is a member of a controlled group, each member is jointly and severally liable for any premiums.

17.7.   SECURITY RULES FOR UNDERFUNDED PLANS

If a single-employer defined benefit plan adopts an amendment which increases current liability under the plan and the funded current liability percentage of the plan in the year in which the amendment takes effect is less than 60 percent (including the amount of the unfunded current liability[24] under the plan attributable to the plan amendment), the contributing sponsor and members of the controlled group must provide security (e.g., a bond) to the plan. The amount of the security required is the excess over $10 million of the lesser of:

1.   the amount of additional plan assets which would be necessary to increase the funded current liability percentage under the plan to 60 percent, including the amount of the unfunded current liability under the plan attributable to the plan amendment, or
2.   the amount of the increase in current liability under the plan attributable to the plan amendment.

QUESTIONS FOR REVIEW

1.   In general, what types of pension plans are covered by plan termination insurance?
2.   What classes of pension plans are specifically excluded from plan termination insurance coverage?
3.   How is the PBGC kept apprised of events affecting plan solvency or operations that may justify an involuntary termination?
4.   Explain the significance of the date of termination for a pension plan.

---

[23]For purposes of determining the value of vested benefits, the interest rate is equal to 80 percent of the yield per annum on 30-year Treasury securities for the month preceding the month in which the plan year begins.

[24]In computing unfunded current liability, the unamortized portion of the unfunded old liability amount as of the close of the plan year is not taken into account.

5. Explain the definition of a basic benefit with respect to: (a) early retirement incentives and (b) death and disability benefits.
6. Explain how insurance coverage is phased in for benefits that have been in effect for less than five years.
7. Why is it necessary to establish priority classes for pension benefits at the time of termination?
8. Is the trustee authorized to recapture benefit payments already made prior to the occurrence of the plan termination? Explain.
9. Must the sponsor of a terminated plan reimburse the PBGC for any loss that it incurs in meeting the benefit obligations of the terminated plan?
10. What condition must be satisfied before a plan sponsor is able to recapture excess assets from a pension plan?

QUESTIONS FOR DISCUSSION

1. Discuss the public policy issues involved in the termination of overfunded defined benefit pension plans.
2. In 1987, the PBGC adopted a new variable rate premium structure that would include a premium component based on the amount of a defined benefit pension plan's unfunded vested benefits. Discuss the relative merits of this approach.
3. Many people have suggested that the PBGC should switch to a risk-related premium structure in which the premium a sponsor pays for plan termination insurance is based on the relative likelihood that the plan will terminate as well as the potential magnitude of the claim. Discuss the relative merits of this approach.

PART FIVE

Operational and Administrative Aspects

Chapter 18 describes the essential elements of an investment policy and provides a brief introduction to the major factors to be considered in the asset allocation decision. Chapter 19 concludes the discussion of investment objectives by considering the various tactics available to achieve these objectives. The most popular classes of assets used for pension plan investments are described, the process of selecting an investment manager is explained, and the relative advantages and limitations of passive management of pension assets are explored.

A qualified plan must use a funding instrument (trusts, custodial accounts, or group contracts) to hold and accumulate plan assets. Chapter 20 deals with trust fund plans while insurance and annuity products are discussed in Chapter 21.

Accounting procedures for pension plans consist of three components, each of which is controlled by a separate Financial Accounting Standards Board (FASB) Statement. Chapter 22 focuses primarily on the consequences of sponsoring a single-employer pension plan on the employer's financial statements. A brief discussion of the evolution of pension accounting standards is presented first, and then the FASB statements are described in detail and their impact on pension plan sponsors is analyzed.

Although the same general taxation principles apply to retirement plan distributions regardless of the contingency that gives rise to them, Chapter 23 discusses the tax aspects of a distribution in terms of the contingency that has brought it about. Thus, this chapter briefly explores the tax situation of an employee during employment (including in-service distributions of the employee's account), as well as the tax situation when distributions are made because of the employee's retirement, death, severance of employment, or disability. In certain instances, penalty taxes are imposed *in addition to federal income taxes* on distributions that: exceed certain amounts, commence too early, or commence too late. The last three sections of this chapter provide a discussion of these penalty taxes.

18. Investment of Pension Plan Assets

The next four chapters focus exclusively on the investment of plan assets for defined benefit pension plans. Chapters 18 and 19 describe the management of pension plan assets while Chapters 20 and 21 explain the basic types of funding instruments used by pension plans. Although investment of pension plan assets is also important in individual account plans (i.e., money purchase, profit sharing, thrift and savings, and cash or deferred arrangements -- CODAs), a fundamental difference exists in that the investment risk is borne directly by the employees covered by these plans. As a result of this difference, sponsors of individual account plans typically provide participants with a choice of investment vehicles. Alternative funds provided under individual account plans generally include company stock, diversified funds, equity funds, fixed income funds, guaranteed investment contracts (GICs), and a money market fund.

By contrast, the investment risk under a defined benefit pension plan is borne almost entirely by the plan sponsor. It should be noted that active and retired employees may have at least an indirect interest in the performance of the plan assets, however. As discussed in Chapter 14, many defined benefit pension plans grant ad hoc increases every few years to counter the effects of inflation. To the extent that these increases depend upon a particular "cushion" of plan assets, the sponsor's investment performance may indeed have an impact on the participants. The participants may also have a stake in the adequacy of plan assets if a plan is terminated with unfunded liabilities.

18.1.   INVESTMENT POLICY

An investment policy prescribes an acceptable course of action to the fund's investment managers. It communicates a risk policy in that it states the degree of investment risk that the sponsor is willing to assume.

18.1.1.   Determining Investment Objectives

By contrast to an investment policy, an investment objective is a desired result of the investment process. Before such objectives can be established, the various risk-return characteristics of the alternative investments must be recognized.

18.1.1.1.   Types of Risk

Modern portfolio theory (described later in this chapter) defines risk in terms of the volatility of an investment (or portfolio of investments) in relation to the market. However, it is useful to consider the individual components of this aggregate concept:[1]

1.   Purchasing power risk.
2.   Business risk.
3.   Interest rate risk.
4.   Market risk.
5.   Specific risk.

Purchasing power risk reflects the relationship between the nominal rate of return on an investment and the increase in the rate of inflation. Business risk involves the prospect that the corporation issuing the security may suffer a decline in earnings power that would adversely affect its ability to pay interest, principal, or dividends. Interest rate risk comprises the well-known inverse relationship between interest rates and (long-term) bond prices; that is, when interest rates increase, the value of long-term bonds will fall.

The final two types of risk are usually used exclusively to explain stock price behavior. Market risk can be thought of as an individual stock's reaction to a change in the "market." In general, most stock prices will increase if the stock market increases appreciably and decrease if the market

---

[1]Jerome B. Cohen, Edward D. Zinbarg, and Arthur Zeikel, *Investment Analysis and Portfolio Management*, 5th ed. (Homewood, Ill.: Richard D. Irwin, 1987), pp. 6-11.

decreases appreciably; however, the price of one stock may change half as fast as the market, on average, while another may change twice as fast. This relationship is quantified later in the chapter by a measure known as "beta."

Obviously, market risk cannot account for the entire fluctuation of a stock's price. For example, if a biotechnology firm suddenly patents an unexpected cure for cancer, there would most likely be a rapid increase in its stock price in expectation of the future profit stream. In contrast, if the product developed by this firm later resulted in a massive product liability award for which the firm was not adequately insured, the stock price would most likely fall. These factors, intrinsic to the firm, are known as specific risks.

18.1.1.2.   Characteristics of Investments

There are four primary characteristics of pension plan investments that need to be considered:

1.   Tax advantages.
2.   Liquidity.
3.   Stability in value.
4.   Ability to preserve purchasing power.

The tax aspect of the investment is important due to the tax-exempt status of the pension fund, mentioned in Chapter 5. Because investment income of qualified pension plans is tax-exempt, certain types of investments may not be as attractive to pension funds as they would be for other types of funds. For example, the price of municipal bonds is likely to be bid up by individual investors in the highest marginal tax rates until they reach a point where their before-tax rates of return are below those that can be realized on corporate bonds or U.S. government bonds of a similar maturity.

Liquidity refers to the ability to convert an investment to cash within a short time period with little, if any, loss in principal. This may be an important attribute for at least a portion of the pension plan assets in case the plan has to weather a short period of time when the plan sponsor is unable to make contributions (or contributions are less than the amount of the benefit payments for the year) and at the same time the securities markets are depressed. If the plan did not possess an adequate degree of liquidity, the sponsor would have to sell securities at an inopportune time, perhaps resulting in the realization of capital losses.

Stability in value is closely akin to liquidity in that it emphasizes investments with minimal fluctuations in value. Achieving maximum stability in value is not particularly difficult -- one need only limit investments to U.S. Treasury bills and money market instruments. However, the opportunity cost of forgone higher investment returns in riskier assets may be prohibitive. Instead, the objective of the sponsor should be to construct a portfolio that will maximize investment income for the desired level of risk.

The ability to preserve purchasing power is important because many defined benefit pension plans attempt to provide at least a partial offset against inflation for their retirees.

18.1.1.3.   Historical Returns Achieved by the Various Classes

Although there have been several empirical studies of the historical risk-return trade-off exhibited by the major classes of investments, the seminal work is that of Ibbotson and Sinquefield.[2] More recently Ibbotson Associates, Inc. has statistically analyzed a 65-year time series of the major classes of investments and found, as expected, that the riskiest investments also generated the highest yields.[3] Common stocks provided the highest annual return with a mean of 10.3 percent.[4] However, investors purchasing common stocks paid a price in terms of the volatility of their investment. Over the past few decades, the S&P 500-stock average experienced one-year losses of as high as 26 percent (in 1974). Long-term bonds issued by the government had a significantly lower return (4.7 percent). U.S. Treasury bills were obviously the safest investment in terms of annual volatility; however, they only generated a return of 3.7 percent.

These figures cannot be viewed in isolation, and it is important to consider how they fared after the effects of inflation had been removed. During this period, the compound inflation rate was 3.1 percent, an amount that should be subtracted from the nominal rate of return to find the real rate of return produced by an investment. For example, the real rate of return of common stocks during this period was 7.2 percent, while U.S. Treasury bills generated a real rate of return of only 0.6 percent.

---

[2]Roger G. Ibbotson and Rex A. Sinquefield, *Stocks, Bonds, Bills and Inflation: Historical Returns 1926-1978* (Charlottesville, Va.: The Financial Analysts Research Foundation, 1979).

[3]Karen Slater, "Long-Haul Investing: Riding Out the Risk in Stocks," *The Wall Street Journal*, December 16, 1991, p. C1.

[4]Technically, the returns reported in this chapter are geometric average returns (sometimes referred to as compound annual returns). The figure can be obtained by multiplying (1+ rate of return) for each of the n years in the time series and then taking the nth root of the product. It should be noted that this is not the same as computing an arithmetic average, which is obtained by simply adding the rates of return for each of the n years in the time series and then dividing by n. Unless the rate of return is constant over the n-year time series, the geometric average will be less than the arithmetic average.

18.1.2. Guidelines for Investment Managers

After the investment objectives have been developed, they need to be expressed in a manner that is useful to the investment manager. Often, this expression takes the form of a guideline statement. The guideline statement should cover such questions as:[5]

1. How much risk is the plan sponsor prepared to take to achieve a specific benchmark rate of return?
2. What is the time period for measurement of performance relative to objectives?
3. What is the sponsor's preference in terms of asset mix, especially as it relates to stocks?
4. What is the liability outlook for the plan and what should the fund's investment strategy be in light of this outlook?
5. What are the sponsor's cash flow or liquidity requirements?
6. How much discretion is the manager permitted regarding foreign investment, private placements, options, financial futures, and so on?

Another matter that needs to be discussed at an early stage is exactly what constitutes an acceptable level of turnover. If the sponsor has decided that extensive turnover activity does not add value to the portfolio performance, guidelines to limit this activity should be established. If the sponsor has come to the conclusion that turnover expenses should be virtually eliminated, a tactic known as passive investment should be considered.[6]

18.1.3. Performance Measurement

The primary purpose of performance measurement is to "obtain information on which to base decisions in regard to investment objectives, portfolio strategy, and manager selection. In addition, performance measurement should improve communications with managers by creating a standard format for discussion."[7]

Effective performance measurement requires four steps:[8]

---

[5]Martin D. Sass, "How (Not) to Manage Your Pension Fund Manager," FE Manual, August 1985, pp. 38-39.
[6]See Chapter 19 for a detailed discussion of this topic.
[7]Sidney Cottle, "Pension Asset Management -- Measuring Performance," *Financial Executive,* September 1981, p.24.
[8]Ibid, p.25.

1. *Definition.* Establishment of investment objectives and, to the extent practical, clearly formulated portfolio strategy.
2. *Input.* Availability of reliable and timely data. Incorrect and tardy data will render the most sophisticated system ineffective.
3. *Processing.* Use of appropriate statistical methods to produce relevant measurements. The complex interaction of objectives, strategies, and managers' tactics cannot be understood if inappropriate statistical methods are used. A meaningful summary will make possible analysis of the investment process at the necessary depth.
4. *Output.* Analysis of the process and results presented in a useful format. Presentation should relate realized performance to objectives and preestablished standards. Enough material should be available to understand and analyze the process. Exhibits should be designed to highlight weaknesses in the investment process and to suggest possible improvements.

Four important caveats must be kept in mind in choosing a performance measurement system:[9]

1. There is a danger that a hastily chosen system, poorly related to real needs, can rapidly degenerate into a mechanistic, pointless exercise.
2. The system should fit the investment objectives and not the reverse.
3. Measuring the process may alter it.
4. To save time and cost, it is important that overmeasurement be avoided.

18.1.3.1. Performance Measurement Methodology

Before any performance is measured, it is necessary to agree upon the correct definition for the return that is measured. Two alternative definitions, internal rate of return and time-weighted rate of return, have been used in the investment community for over 20 years. It is quite likely that the two rates of return will vary considerably. Therefore, it is critical that the sponsor understand the differences.

The internal rate of return (or dollar-weighted rate of return) is the rate that accumulates all of the cash flows of a portfolio, including all outlays, to exactly the market value of the ending balance.

The internal rate of return is valuable in that it allows the sponsor to determine whether the investment is achieving the rate of return assumed for actuarial calculations; however, it is largely ineffective as a means of

---

[9]Cottle, "Pension Asset Management," p.25.

evaluating investment managers because it is contaminated by the effects of the timing of investments and withdrawals -- a factor over which the investment manager presumably has no control. In response to this limitation of the internal rate of return approach, the Bank Administration Institute published a study in 1968 that suggested a different performance measurement technique known as the time-weighted rate of return. This value is computed by:[10]

> dividing the interval under study into subintervals whose boundaries are the dates of cash flows into and out of the fund and by computing the internal rate of return for each subinterval. The time-weighted rate of return is the [geometric] average for the rates for these subintervals, with each rate having a weight proportional to the length of time in its corresponding subinterval.

18.1.3.2.   Assessing Risk

Having correctly measured the time-weighted returns, it is necessary to evaluate the risk-adjusted performance of investment managers. Although some investment managers still report their performance by comparing their equity portfolio return with a common stock index (such as the Standard & Poor's 500 Stock Average [S&P 500] index) and their bond portfolio results with a bond index (such as the Shearson Lehman Brothers government and corporate bond index) without any adjustment for their portfolio's risk, there is a growing realization that return cannot be meaningfully evaluated without simultaneously considering the risk of the investment. Portfolio risks are commonly measured in one or more of three ways:[11]

1.   Total variability in absolute terms.
2.   Total variability in relative terms.
3.   Market-related variability.

Absolute risk can be measured in one of two ways. The most common is to compute the standard deviation of the periodic returns. Another method is to rank in order the returns over a particular period and to divide the distribution into percentiles. The range from the 25th to the 75th percentile, referred to as the semi-interquartile range in several measurement systems, is then used as a measure of the portfolio's absolute risk.

---

[10]*Measuring the Investment Performance of Pension Funds for the Purpose of Inter-Fund Comparison* (Park Ridge, Ill.: Bank Administration Institute, 1968).
[11]Cottle, "Pension Asset Management," p.28.

Relative risk measurements start with one of the two absolute risk measurements for the portfolio in question and then divide it by a similar measure for the market during the same time period. For example, if the absolute risk measure for an equity portfolio was its standard deviation based on quarterly returns for the last five years, the denominator for the relative risk measure might be the standard deviation of the S&P 500 based on quarterly returns for the last five years.

Although relative risk measurement is an improvement over absolute risk measurement in that it factors in the activity of the market over the measurement period, at present the state of the art for adjusting returns for risk is to use the capital asset pricing model (CAPM).[12] The CAPM uses standard statistical techniques (simple linear regression) to analyze the relationship between the periodic returns of the portfolio and those of the market (e.g., the S&P 500). Although several modifications of the basic regression analysis exist, most applications will begin by subtracting out a risk-free rate of return (e.g., the Treasury bill rate) from both the portfolio and market returns.

For those not familiar with regression analysis, this technique can be thought of as simply plotting the periodic returns of the portfolio (on the vertical axis) against the periodic returns of the market (on the horizontal axis). A minimum number of data points are required for the statistical procedure to operate with a desired degree of confidence. The number of observations plotted depends upon the type of returns measured -- five years of data are typically used in the case of quarterly returns, while three years of data are typically considered to be sufficient if monthly information is used. The straight line that provides the "best fit" for the observations is drawn on the graph and two features of this line are noted. The first is the point at which the line crosses the vertical axis and zero on the horizontal axis. This is referred to as the portfolio's "alpha" value, and can be thought of as the amount of return produced by the portfolio, on average, independent of the return on the market. The second feature is the slope of the line measured as the change in vertical movement per unit of change in the horizontal movement. This is referred to as the portfolio's "beta" value, and represents the average return on the portfolio per 1 percent return on the market. For example, if the portfolio's beta is 1.25, then a 2 percent

---

[12]It should be noted that this theory is based on a number of very restrictive assumptions: investors are risk-averse individuals who maximize the expected utility of their end-of-period wealth; investors make their investment decisions based on a single-period horizon; transaction costs are low enough to ignore; taxes do not affect the choice of buying one asset versus another; all individuals can borrow and lend unlimited amounts of money at a single-period riskless rate of interest; and all individuals agree on the nature of the return and risk associated with each investment. However, extensions of the CAPM have solved many of these problems.

increase (decrease) in the market would be expected to be associated with a 2.5 percent (1.25×2) increase (decrease) in the portfolio, on average.

18.1.3.3.   Assessing Performance

Once the portfolio's beta has been computed, it is possible to use the CAPM to provide a risk-adjusted measure of the portfolio's performance. The CAPM asserts that the predicted risk-adjusted rate of return for the portfolio (R_p) will be equal to the risk-free rate (R_f) plus a risk premium that is equal to the amount of risk, beta (β), times a market risk premium that is equal to the difference between the market rate of return (R_m) and the risk-free rate:

$$R_p = R_f + (R_m - R_f) \times \beta.$$

To illustrate this concept, assume that an investment manager's portfolio has a beta of 1.25, the risk-free rate of return is 6 percent, and the market rate of return is 10 percent. If the portfolio yielded a rate of return of 11.5 percent, what is the risk-adjusted rate of return? The answer is found by first finding the predicted risk-adjusted rate of return for the portfolio. This is accomplished by simply substituting the values in the equation above:

$$R_p = .06 + (.1 - .06) \times 1.25 = .11 .$$

This predicted value is then subtracted from the portfolio's actual value to produce a risk-adjusted rate of return of a positive 0.5 percent (11.5 - 11). The risk-adjusted rate of return can be used to measure risk-adjusted performance and to compare portfolios with different risk levels developed by actual portfolio decisions.

18.2.   ALLOCATION OF FUND ASSETS

The asset allocation decision is a process that determines the best portfolio composition among the various major types of assets (stocks, bonds, etc.). This decision takes into account the sponsor's investment objective and, as a result, reflects the level of risk desired by the sponsor.

18.2.1. Major Factors to Be Considered

In addition to the type of plan (i.e., defined benefit versus individual account), there are three considerations that must be assessed in setting investment objectives:

1.   Characteristics of the sponsor and its industry.
2.   Demographics of the work force and maturity of the plan.
3.   Possibility of plan termination.

Characteristics of the sponsor and its industry must be considered in determining policy. For example, a sponsor with thin profit margins, high labor costs, and in a highly cyclical industry has less tolerance for variability in pension costs than does a company with relatively large profit margins, low labor costs, and a less cyclical earnings pattern. Whether the industry as a whole is growing, stagnant, or declining also will affect the degree of conservatism built into the investment strategy.

Demographics is also important because a rapidly growing company with a young work force has less concern for cash flow and investment liquidity than does a company with a more mature work force and many pensioners. A sponsor in the first category would be more likely to have the ability to withstand several years of capital losses on the pension plan portfolio without impeding benefit payments.[13]

The possibility of plan termination is important for companies with some risk of plan shutdown, merger, acquisition, or other corporate reorganization because the investment policy must take into account the possibility that the Pension Benefit Guaranty Corporation (PBGC) will take over the plan and value the plan assets at the time of termination at the current market value. If a plan termination occurs during a business recession and the PBGC steps in, the claim against the sponsoring company will be larger.

QUESTIONS FOR REVIEW

1.   Describe the major types of investment risk.

---

[13]This statement only considers the cash flow aspects of the plan. As described in Chapter 16. many of the actuarial cost methods used to determine the minimum funding standard for a defined benefit pension plan will amortize investment gains and losses over a maximum of 5 years. Therefore, if the sponsor desires to control volatility of the contribution stream from year to year, it is important that pension plan investments do not experience a large decline in value. Moreover, with the advent of FASB 87, there are now several accounting consequences of pension plan asset allocation that must take into consideration the goals of the plan.

2. Describe why an investment's relative liquidity may be important to a pension plan's investment manager.

3. What have historical studies demonstrated with respect to the risk-return characteristics of the major classes of investments?

4. What types of questions should the investment manager's guideline statement cover?

5. Describe the steps involved in effective performance measurement.

6. Explain how the internal rate of return and the time-weighted rate of return are calculated.

7. Which of the two rates of return mentioned in the previous question should be used for performance measurement? Explain.

8. Explain the importance of the alpha and beta values produced by the capital asset pricing model (CAPM).

9. Explain the importance of the risk-adjusted rate of return.

10. Explain the factors that should be considered in the allocation of pension fund assets.

QUESTIONS FOR DISCUSSION

1. If common stocks are assumed to produce a higher long-term rate of return than bonds, discuss why many defined benefit pension plan portfolios contain a significant percentage of bonds.

2. Discuss how the beta value produced by the capital asset pricing model could be used to construct an investment portfolio suited to the employer's objectives.

3. Discuss why performance measurement based exclusively on rate of return may lead to nonoptimal investment strategies.

19. Investment Objectives: Tactics

Chapter 18 described the essential elements of an investment policy and provided a brief introduction to the major factors to be considered in the asset allocation decision. This chapter concludes the discussion of investment objectives by considering the various tactics available to achieve these objectives. The most popular classes of assets used for pension plan investments are described, the process of selecting an investment manager is explained, and the relative advantages and limitations of passive management of pension assets are explored. The trust fund mechanism for holding and accumulating assets is discussed in Chapter 20, and special insurance and annuity products are discussed in Chapter 21.

19.1. CLASSES OF ASSETS

Retirement plan assets are estimated to be more than $1.8 trillion for the 1,000 largest U.S. plans. The largest 200 defined benefit and defined contribution funds held the following assets in their portfolios in 1990:[1]

---

[1]"Special Report: The Top 1,000 Funds," *Pensions & Investments,* January 21, 1991, p. 1, ff.

Asset category	Defined Benefit	Defined Contribution
Stocks	43.4%	16.1%
Fixed Income	39.3%	15.3%
Cash	7.4%	9.4%
Real estate equity	4.9%	0.0%
GICs/BICs	1.1%	34.7%
Annuities	0.4%	0.0%
Mortgages	1.5%	0.0%
Company Stock	0.0%	22.6%
Other	2.0%	1.9%

Annuities are discussed in Chapter 21. The other major classes, as well as mutual funds and financial futures, are discussed below.

19.1.1. Money Market Instruments

As discussed in Chapter 18, pension plans will typically have a need to retain at least a portion of their assets in vehicles that will be readily convertible to cash. The exact portion will depend upon the specifics of the plan design (e.g., loan features and employee's ability to select lump-sum distributions) and the demographics of the plan participants. This portion of the portfolio should be invested in assets that have a low default risk, a short maturity, and are readily marketable. There are five major categories of this type of investment alternative: U.S. Treasury bills and notes, federal agency issues, certificates of deposit, commercial paper, and money market mutual funds.

U.S. Treasury Bills and Notes. Treasury bills have maturities at issue ranging from 91 to 360 days, while Treasury notes have initial maturities ranging from 1 to 5 years. There is no default risk on these investments. In other words, the probability that either interest or principal payments will be skipped is zero.

Federal Agency Issues. The Treasury is not the only federal agency to issue marketable obligations. Other agencies issue short-term obligations that range in maturity from one month to over 10 years. These instruments will typically yield slightly more than Treasury obligations with a similar maturity.

Certificates of Deposit. These certificates are issued by commercial banks and have a fixed maturity, generally in the range of 90 days to one year. The ability to sell a certificate of deposit prior to maturity usually depends upon its denomination. If it is over $100,000, it can usually be sold in a secondary market; if it is under that amount, banks will usually assess a penalty if they buy it back early. The default risk for these certificates depends upon the issuing bank, but it is usually quite small. Therefore, their yield is generally only slightly higher than similar maturities in the previous two categories.

Commercial Paper. This is typically an unsecured short-term note of a large corporation. This investment offers maturities that range up to 270 days, but the marketability is somewhat limited if an early sale is required. The default risk depends upon the credit standing of the issuer, but commensurately higher yield is available.

Money Market Mutual Funds. These funds invest in the money market instruments described above. As a result, investors achieve a yield almost as high as that paid by the direct investments themselves and at the same time benefit from the diversification of any default risk over a much larger population of investments. In addition, these funds allow the pension plan to maintain complete liquidity with respect to this portion of their portfolio.

19.1.2. Bonds

The use of bonds in pension plan portfolios can typically be attributed to one of two reasons. First, if the sponsor realizes that (to a large extent) the pension plan's obligations are fixed dollar obligations that will be paid out several years in the future, there may be a desire to purchase assets that will generate a cash flow similar to the benefit payments. This technique is referred to as dedication or immunization and is described in detail later in this chapter. Second, the investment manager may be willing to purchase assets with a longer maturity than the money market instruments described above. This assumption of interest rate risk is presumably compensated by a higher yield than that available from shorter maturities.

Bonds are simply long-term debt claims entitling the holder to periodic interest and full repayment of principal by the issuer. For purposes of this discussion, the universe of bonds will be dichotomized into corporate bonds and government bonds.

Corporate Bonds. There are several characteristics of corporate bonds that are important to pension plan investment managers. For example, there are different degrees by which the promises of future cash flow are secured. Under a mortgage bond, a corporation pledges certain real assets as security for the bond. In contrast, a debenture is a long-term bond that is not secured by a pledge of any specific property. However, it is secured by any property not otherwise pledged.

The ability of the issuing corporation to call in the bond for redemption prior to the stated maturity date is known as a call provision. Although the issuer must typically pay some type of penalty (known as a call premium) for exercising this right, the holder of a bond with a call provision must be cognizant of the fact that the amount received (call premium plus principal) may be less than the value of the bond if the call had not been exercised. This will typically be the case in times of declining interest rates.

The marketability of corporate bonds is usually not an issue. However, if the investment manager sells them prior to the maturity date, the price received will be subject to both the business risk and interest rate risk described in Chapter 18. Investment managers must also be concerned with business risk, even if there is an intention to hold the bonds until maturity.

Government Bonds. As mentioned in Chapter 18, pension plans will limit their investments in government bonds to those that generate taxable investment income. Hence, municipal bonds are not candidates for inclusion in a pension plan portfolio. Federal government bonds are possible candidates and they are evaluated in a manner similar to the corporate bonds. The major exception is that the default risk is nonexistent and, as a result, the yield would be expected to be lower than that available on corporate bonds of similar maturities.

The field of government bonds has expanded to include mortgage-related securities. Government National Mortgage Association (GNMA) pass-through certificates have an interest in a pool of single-family residential mortgages that are insured by the Federal Housing Authority or the Veteran's Administration. The timely payment of principal and interest on these securities is guaranteed by the U.S. government. The Federal Home Loan Mortgage Corporation (FHLMC) issues another mortgage-backed security, known as Freddie Mac. Although this instrument is not guaranteed by the U.S. government, it is unconditionally guaranteed by the FHLMC.

19.1.3. Common Stocks

Although there is no definitive manner of categorizing common stocks, it is customary to speak of them in the following terms:[2]

1. *Blue chip stocks.* These are stocks issued by major companies with long and unbroken records of earnings and dividend payments. They should appeal primarily to pension plans seeking safety and stability.

2. *Growth stocks.* These are stocks issued by companies whose sales, earnings, and share of the market are expanding faster than either the general economy or the industry average. They represent a higher risk, but the prospects for capital appreciation should produce a correspondingly higher total return. Because they pay relatively small dividends, they may not be attractive to pension plans with cash flow problems.

---

[2]Jerome B. Cohen, Edward D. Zinbarg, and Arthur Zeikel, *Investment Analysis and Portfolio Management,* 5th ed. (Homewood, Ill.: Richard D. Irwin, 1987), pp. 21-29.

3. *Income stocks.* These are stocks that pay higher than average dividend returns. They were attractive to pension plans that bought stock for current income. However, they have taken on new importance for nontax-exempt investors since the Tax Reform Act of 1986 phased out the advantages of capital gains treatment. It remains to be seen whether the price of these stocks will be bid up to prohibitive levels.

4. *Cyclical stocks.* These are stocks issued by companies whose earnings fluctuate with the business cycle and are accentuated by it.

5. *Defensive stocks.* These are stocks issued by recession-resistant companies. This may be an important consideration for pension plans that cannot afford major capital losses.

6. *Interest-sensitive stocks.* These are stocks whose prices tend to drop when interest rates rise, and vice versa.

19.1.4. Mutual Funds

For plans with assets too small to be handled by an investment manager, mutual funds may be the only choice, other than a common trust fund. Larger plans may also choose mutual funds as a relatively inexpensive way of diversifying their portfolios.[3]

Pension plans have been choosing mutual funds more frequently in recent years for the following reasons:[4]

1. Greater liquidity through ease of entry and exit.
2. Greater degree of diversification.
3. Easier means of portfolio specialization.
4. Daily update of holdings through newspaper listings.
5. Ease of meeting asset allocation or market timing goals.
6. Ease of checking past performance through published studies and indexes.

19.1.5. Real Estate

The enormous number of real estate investments available in today's market makes a comprehensive treatment of this topic beyond the scope of this

---

[3]See the passive versus active management section later in this chapter for more detail.

[4]Jay M. Dade, "Mutual Funds Today: Strength through Diversity," *Pension World,* December 1986, pp. 34-36.

book.[5] However, certain basic characteristics of this market provide insight as to its overall place in a pension plan portfolio. First, real estate investments (particularly ownership interests) appear to offer an adequate inflation hedge under most scenarios. Second, real estate investing does not operate in the same efficient market as stocks and bonds. Instead of having several thousand individuals bidding on the price of a homogeneous asset each day, a real estate property may be on the market for months before any offer is made. A third point, closely related to the second, is the relative lack of marketability for many real estate investments. This feature alone would prevent most pension plans from investing the preponderance of their assets in real estate. A final point deals with the volatility of real estate investments. Although it is difficult to develop reliable estimates in the absence of an active market, the consensus opinion appears to be that the volatility of real estate investments has been significantly below that of common stocks.

19.1.6. Futures

A futures contract is an agreement to make or take delivery of a specified commodity (e.g., the S&P 500 index) at a specified date at an agreed-upon price. No money changes hands until the delivery date; however, a deposit is required that may be invested in Treasury securities in the interim. The account is settled each day. This means that if a pension plan made a contract to sell the S&P 500 in the future and the index declined that day, money is deposited into the pension plan's account; however, money would be withdrawn from the account if the index had increased.

Although this may appear to be a highly speculative investment when viewed in isolation, many pension plans have started to use this technique in conjunction with an existing portfolio of equities. This may serve as a useful hedge against losses in the equity portfolio. A particular type of hedging, known as portfolio insurance, is described later in this chapter.

19.1.7. Guaranteed Investment Contracts

Some insurance companies have developed contracts for special lump-sum arrangements designed to attract pension or profit sharing funds. These contracts, often called guaranteed investment contracts, guaranteed interest

---

[5]For an excellent discussion of this topic, see *Investment Policy Guidebook for Corporate Pension Plan Trustees*, Appendix A (Brookfield, Wis.: International Foundation of Employee Benefit Plans, 1984).

contracts, guaranteed income contracts, guaranteed return contracts, or just GICs, have proven extremely popular in recent years. In 1991, GICs were estimated to account for 65%-70% of all 401(k) investments.[6]

The market for GICs appears to be large for a number of reasons. Primarily, GICs often provide a rate of return in excess of rates obtainable from most fixed income securities. GICs historically provided the contract holder with a combination of protection against loss of principal if interest rates increased generally from the time of purchase either by receiving payment of principal at book value in a lump sum under some contracts, or over a period of time under others. They also provided a call on higher guaranteed interest rates during extended payout option periods if interest rates declined from the time of purchase to the time of payout.

However, GIC customers have recently found themselves in a dilemma, since several of the insurance companies that market GICs have shaky portfolios because of investments in real estate and highly leveraged transactions. The uncertainty over these products escalated during the first half of 1991 when the California Insurance Department estimated that pension plans that purchased Executive Life Insurance Co. GICs would receive 81 cents on the dollar.[7]   Mutual Benefit Life's rehabilitation, although it reported only $769 million in GIC liabilities in 1990, followed closely on the heels of the failure of Executive Life.[8]

Many variations exist among the GICs offered. However, two basic types of contracts are used, the so-called bullet contract and the extended guarantee contract. The bullet type of GIC receives a single deposit from a plan sponsor, holds the funds for a specified period at a specified interest rate, and pays the funds at a maturity. Under the extended guarantee type of GIC, the insurance company accepts deposits from the plan sponsor over a period of several years and credits them with the agreed-upon interest rates. Most GIC fund options have market value adjustment clauses that permit early withdrawals at the lesser of book or market value.

Pension fund sponsors are learning that a guarantee is only as good as the insurance company behind it. Turmoil in the insurance industry - brought on by carrier insolvencies, rating downgrades, and problem investments - has shaken the guaranteed investment marketplace and forced investors to review investment policies and attitudes toward carriers.

Some 23% of the corporate benefits executives responding to a poll conducted by the International Foundation of Employee Benefit Plans (IFEBP) said that their organization has changed or plans to change its

---

[6]Fran Hawthorne, "The Foolproof Investment That Wasn't," *Institutional Investor*, July 1991, pp. 65-68

[7]Joanne Wojcik, "Executive Life Sale Won't Derail Lawsuits," *Business Insurance*, August 12, 1991, p.1

[8]Judy Greenwald, "Panic Rattles GIC Industry," *Business Insurance*, July 22, 1991, p. 68.

policies related to sponsorship of GICs because of recent insurance company failures. Despite concerns over GIC provider solvency, 85% of the respondents said that they were satisfied that their defined contribution plan fiduciaries were fulfilling their responsibilities regarding GIC providers. A total of 82% said that their organization periodically evaluates the financial condition of its GIC providers. [9]

In light of the recent problems for some insurance companies, plan sponsors may consider new strategies. Preferring true collateral to an implicit guarantee, many plan sponsors are adding more "synthetic" GICs to their 401(k) plans. These hybrids are backed by a pool of securities placed in a separate account controlled by the plan sponsor. It is estimated that $6.5 billion will be placed in synthetic GICs in 1991. The instruments come in various forms but usually involve a separate account portfolio of high-quality securities, backing the guarantee.[10]

GICs are a viable, attractive investment option. The notion of a guarantee is tempting and likely to continue to draw participant-directed money into such investments. There is no reason why a properly managed GIC portfolio should not live up to its guarantee. By being aware of the risks to which such portfolios are vulnerable - credit risk, concentration risk, and reinvestment risk - it is possible to structure a portfolio that will meet investors' expectations and make good on that guarantee. In selecting GICs, portfolio managers who want the flexibility of benefit-responsive contracts may have to accept a lower yield in exchange for the liquidity.

In evaluating GICs, particular attention should be paid to some of the following plan characteristics:

1. The level of guaranteed interest rate return.
2. Whether the contract is on a participating or nonparticipating basis.
3. The length of the period over which payment of the specified interest rate is guaranteed.
4. The right of the contract holders to liquidate their contracts for cash, should cash be needed, before the maturity date.
5. Whether any penalties or risk of loss exist on cash-out or termination of a contract at or after maturity, if there is an upward movement in interest rates from the time of purchase to the time of cash-out or maturity.
6. The optional methods of obtaining maturity values and the level of expenses charged against the earnings.

---

[9]"Survey Finds 23 Percent Changing GIC Policies," *National Underwriter* (Life/Health/Financial Services). Sep 30, 1991, p. 21.
[10] Fred Williams, "GICs Awash in Change," *Pensions & Investments*, Aug 19, 1991, p. 3.

7.   The attractiveness of guaranteed annuity purchase rates provided under the optional methods of settlement and the time period of such guarantees.

GICs were practically the exclusive preserve of insurance companies until 1987 when banks and savings and loans entered the market with their own form of bank investment contracts (BICs). BICs are a form of bank deposit that are technically different from GICs but operate similarly. The difference between bank investment contracts (BICs) and insurance companies' GICs is the assurance that a plan sponsor will get its principal and interest returned to the pension fund at the end of the guarantee period. A potential advantage of BICs was that they were guaranteed by the Federal Deposit Insurance Corporation (FDIC) for up to $100,000 per participant.[11]

A survey of the BIC industry, commissioned by the American Council of Life Insurance, found the volume of outstanding BICs to be about $13.6 billion at the end of the first quarter of 1990. The BIC industry was concentrated in about a dozen banks at that time, with 5 issuing 64% of the total and another 5 issuing 14%. The average BIC contract was $10 million-$30 million for larger banks and $1 million-$13 million for smaller banks.[12]

The life insurance industry, whose GICs are not federally insured, contends that federal insurance coverage gives banks an unfair competitive advantage and represents an additional danger to a banking system already threatened by a shaky savings and loan industry. Banks counter that the danger is minimal and that FDIC coverage encourages competition on investment contracts and improves security for participants in defined contribution plans, whose sponsors are encouraged to diversify beyond insurer GICs.

19.2.   SELECTING AN INVESTMENT MANAGER

The process of selecting an investment manager obviously differs from sponsor to sponsor; however, the following five steps are typical of the procedure employed by many sponsors.[13]

---

[11]In November of 1991, Congress approved banking reform legislation that eliminated FDIC coverage for BICs that allow withdrawals and deposits without penalty. However, the bill included a grandfather clause that preserves FDIC overage of $100,000 per individual per institution for existing BICs.

[12] Fred Williams, "An About-Face for FDIC," *Pensions & Investments*. (Oct 1, 1990), p. 59.

[13]*Investment Policy Guidebook*, pp. 103-6.

19.2.1. Review of Investment Firms

The first step is to initiate a search to screen initial candidates. This procedure is generally conducted by an individual within the plan sponsor's firm, perhaps with the aid of outside consultants. Plan sponsors can obtain outside consulting services from a number of sources, including brokerage firms, actuarial and accounting organizations, and pension consulting firms.

Although many sponsors may be inclined to perform the investment firm review solely on an in-house basis, there are several potential advantages of a consultant that should be considered. First, since the consultants have continuing exposure to the investment firms, they will probably have a better understanding of which investment firms could best serve the sponsor's objectives. Second, consultants have much more experience in the evaluation process. They are less likely to ask the investment firms vague questions that yield little, if any, useful information and they are less inclined to have their decisions swayed by ingenious presentations. On a more positive side, they can pinpoint the specific information needed from investment management candidates, frame the questionnaire, and help organize the subsequent interviews. Third, consultants can help construct the initial list, so that firms may be screened efficiently without the search team having to waste time and effort.

Regardless of whether the plan sponsor is being aided by a consultant, there is an obvious need to obtain information on investment firms at this stage. Fortunately, several sources exist for this purpose. Included among these are top management and members of the board of directors, counterparts at other companies, pension fund actuaries, accountants and attorneys, specialized magazines, and senior officers of brokerage companies.

19.2.2. Send Detailed Questionnaires

After the original list has been reduced to a manageable size (perhaps with the aid of a consultant), a detailed questionnaire should be sent to the remaining investment firms. The questionnaire should be carefully designed to elicit specific information on several topics, including:

1.   Portfolio strategies and tactics.
2.   Ownership as well as employee compensation.
3.   Decision-making procedures.
4.   List of current clients and specific people to contact for references.
5.   Names of accounts lost as well as those gained in recent years.
6.   Historic performance of each class of assets managed.

7.   Explanation of exactly how the firm's performance statistics have been computed.

19.2.3. Conduct Interviews

After the questionnaires have been reviewed and the references have been thoroughly checked, interviews should be conducted (in the presence of the sponsor's consultant, if one is used). Whether it is better to hold the initial interview at the sponsor's location or to visit the offices of candidates is debatable; however, it is argued that the latter produces a more realistic impression of the investment firm.

It is important that specific guidelines for the presentations be formulated in advance. For example, the "canned presentations" should be limited within some specific time frame. Moreover, questions should be designed to elicit specific information on:

- Research procedures.
- Decision-making routine.
- Strategies and tactics employed.
- Control disciplines.
- Transaction guidelines.
- Levels of salaries and other incentives for employees.
- Key personnel.
- Investment performance statistics and the degree of performance variation among accounts.

19.2.4. Final Evaluation

Before an attempt is made to analyze the information obtained from the interviews, it may be useful to review sample portfolios of the investment firms to assess whether a firm actually utilizes the methods described by its literature and representatives. At this time, the written questionnaires are often reviewed to check for inconsistencies with oral statements made during the interviews. Using the assembled information, the list of investment firms is condensed to a small group of finalists (e.g., less than five) and the information is given to the sponsor's top management.

The management of the sponsor will then meet with senior officers and relevant portfolio personnel of the finalist firms, and the decision on which firm(s) to retain to manage the pension assets is made.

19.2.5. Post-Selection Activity

A substantial amount of activity remains after the decisions have been made. For example, legal agreements should be reviewed, all fees and other costs should be determined, and the initiation date for performance measurement should be established.

The selection of the investment firm is not the final step in this process. Indeed, it is just the first iteration of a continuing operation. Portfolio review and evaluation using the performance measurement techniques described in Chapter 18 must be performed periodically. This will be facilitated by having the mechanics of fund and reporting systems worked out as soon as possible.

19.3.   PASSIVE VERSUS ACTIVE MANAGEMENT

A passive investment strategy is characterized by a broadly diversified buy and hold portfolio aimed at replicating the return on some broad market index at minimum cost. The costs of highly trained professionals can be minimized and the transactions costs are relatively low due to the reduced amount of trading. In contrast, active investment strategies attempt to outperform the market either by selecting assets whose returns, on average, exceed those of the market, or by timing the movement of funds into and out of the market in an attempt to capitalize on swings in the prices of the assets.

Proponents of the passive strategy argue that as the stock market becomes increasingly efficient, it is more difficult for investment managers to consistently outperform the market. If actively managed funds do indeed encounter difficulties producing a gross rate of return superior to that of the market, it will obviously be even more difficult to produce a superior return on a net basis (after the effects of fees and transactions costs have been accounted for).

There are various degrees to which passive investing may be implemented. The three most popular forms -- index funds, dedication and immunization techniques, and portfolio insurance -- are described below.

19.3.1. Index Funds

Index funds represent the ultimate form of passive investing. An equity index fund replicates a particular index such as the S&P 500 and is designed to generate a beta of 1.0 (i.e., the rate of return on the fund is expected to be equal to that of the S&P 500). These funds are based on the efficient market hypothesis (EMH) that states that the securities markets are efficient in the processing of information. In other words, the prices of securities observed at any time are based on a correct evaluation of all information available at the time.

If this hypothesis were true, the value of an investment manager's services would be far less than the current level of compensation enjoyed by these professionals. However, a number of published studies have reported contrary evidence indicating at least a lack of complete efficiency in the market. Anomalous results have been found in the so-called weekend, small firms, and January effects.[14]

Regardless of the merits of the EMH, more than a quarter of all institutional tax-exempt funds are indexed or managed under a similar type of passive investment strategy.[15] Some sponsors will use index funds as an investment for the core of their portfolio and allow active management of the remaining amount of the assets. This tactic possesses the advantage of freeing the investment managers from having to deal with the core portfolio and, instead, allowing them to focus their time on their specialty areas. Moreover, given a relative sense of security for the core investment, investment managers are able to pursue a higher risk strategy on their subset of the plan's assets in hopes of above-average returns.

19.3.2. Dedication and Immunization Techniques

Another form of passive investment of pension plan assets makes use of the bond market and has been variously referred to as dedication, immunization, and contingent immunization.[16] This technique attempts to construct a bond portfolio such that its cash flow can be used to fund specific plan liabilities; for example, to pay benefits to a group of retirees.

The typical dedication program will start by modeling the expected schedule of liabilities under a particular subset of the plan. The benefits related to the retired population are often chosen due to the fact that the benefits are already determined (i.e., there is no uncertainty regarding career or final average salary) and the time horizon will be shorter than the

---

[14]R. Rogalski, "New Findings Regarding Day-of-the-Week Returns over Trading and Non-trading Periods: A Note," *Journal of Finance*, December 1984; M. Reinganun, "Abnormal Returns in Small Firm Portfolios," *Financial Analysts Journal*, March/April 1981; and D. Keim, "Size Related Anomalies and Stock Market Seasonality: Further Empirical Evidence," *Journal of Financial Economics* 12 (1983).

[15]Ed Christman, "Passive Portfolios Contain 26.8 Percent of Tax Exempt Assets," *Pensions & Investment Age,* May 19, 1986, p.2.

[16]Martin L. Leibowitz, "The Dedicated Bond Portfolio in Pension Funds -- Part I: Motivations and Basics," *Financial Analysts Journal*, January-February 1986, pp. 68-75.

liabilities associated with the active employee population. The model will produce a monotonically decreasing payout schedule over time, most likely reaching a negligible amount by the end of 30 years (the maximum maturity for most types of bonds). A computer program will then search for an optimal combination of acceptable bonds that will produce a cash flow over this period to meet the liability payout schedule.

Perhaps the easiest way to visualize this is to assume that all payouts will be met through principal payments (when the bonds mature) or coupon payments. This would certainly minimize the administrative complexity of the program since, if principal and coupon payments are exactly equal to the payouts each year, there would be no need to reinvest the proceeds. However, this may not produce the optimal combination of bonds in that another combination of maturities (one that assumes some proceeds need to be reinvested for a period of time before they are used to satisfy plan liabilities) may produce a lower total cost to the sponsor. It should be realized that this is a riskier undertaking, however, since the eventual cost to the sponsor may increase if the assumed rates at which these proceeds may be reinvested proves to be too optimistic.[17]

In contrast to the cash-matching nature of dedication, an immunization program attempts to construct a portfolio of bonds whose market value equals the present value of the selected subset of liabilities and, even if the interest rate changes, whose value will always be at least as great as the value of the liabilities.[18] Although the feasibility of this approach may not be intuitively obvious, it depends upon the capital gains on the assets offsetting the decrease in reinvestment income when interest rates fall. This balancing is accomplished through a concept known as "duration," which provides a measure of the portfolio's sensitivity to interest rate changes.[19]

As opposed to the relatively simple administrative requirements involved in a dedicated portfolio, an immunized portfolio will require subsequent rebalancing. Moreover, although immunization provides more flexibility in constructing the bond portfolio (and should therefore result in a lower cost to the sponsor), it is possible for the assumptions used in the

---

[17]Other risks that may exist in either type of dedication include call vulnerability, quality, type of issue, and diversification across type and individual issues. See Leibowitz, "Dedicated Bond Portfolio, Part I," pp. 73-74.

[18]Martin L. Leibowitz, "The Dedicated Bond Portfolio in Pension Funds -- Part II: Immunization, Horizon Matching and Contingent Procedures," *Financial Analysts Journal*, March- April 1986, pp. 47-57.

[19]The duration measure can be thought of as the average life of the liabilities when weighted by the present value of their respective cash flows. Technically, the duration match of assets and liabilities is not a sufficient condition for an "immunized" portfolio. In addition, certain second-order conditions must be satisfied. See Michael R. Granito, *Bond Portfolio Immunization* (Lexington, Mass.: Lexington Books, 1984) for more detail.

immunization model to be violated and, as a result, the sponsor may experience a shortfall from this approach.

Largely in response to the limitations of the immunization approach, a hybrid technique known as horizon matching has been recently introduced. In essence, this approach splits the liabilities into two portions. The first portion consists of all liabilities that occur up to a certain horizon (three to five years) and is handled through a dedicated portfolio. The second portion consists of liabilities beyond the horizon and is treated through immunization. Although this tactic will give up some of the cost savings of a full immunization approach, the restructuring will mitigate the effects of failing to satisfy the assumptions of the immunization approach.[20]

A major disadvantage of the immunization approaches is that the sponsor gives up the opportunity to produce additional income through active management of the bond portfolio. This is overcome, to a certain extent, through a device known as contingent immunization. Basically, this approach assumes the sponsor is willing to accept a minimum rate of return on the bond portfolio a percentage point or two below the current market rate. This differential provides a safety margin for the investment manager to adopt an active management strategy. If the safety margin is exhausted through market losses, the portfolio will be in a position such that it can be immunized at the minimum rate of return.

19.3.3. Portfolio Insurance

Portfolio insurance is a device used to protect the value of the portfolio in the event of a significant market decline without giving up the potential to benefit from rising markets.[21] Although numerous variations of this approach exist, it is basically implemented through one of two approaches: dynamic hedging or transactions in the financial futures markets.

It should be noted at the outset that there is nothing intrinsically unique about a device that reduces the risk of a pension plan portfolio. Indeed, this decision is often made implicitly in the asset allocation stage. An investment manager could easily decrease the riskiness of the portfolio by 50 percent by lowering the active asset allocation from 100 percent to 50 percent (and leaving the remainder in a risk-free asset such as T bills). However, this strategy would automatically result in a proportionate decrease in the portfolio's expected return. In contrast, portfolio insurance offers a combination of financial instruments that will -- at least in theory --

---

[20]Specifically, this is designed to dampen the effect of yield curve reshaping.
[21]Hayne E. Leland, "Who Should Buy Portfolio Insurance?" *Journal of Finance* 35 (May 1980), pp. 581-94.

truncate the distribution of possible rates of return at some prespecified minimum floor return (e.g., no more than a 15 percent decline during the next year). There is obviously a cost associated with such a "guarantee"; although in the case of portfolio insurance, it can be conceptualized as a constant cost (as opposed to a cost that is proportional to the rate of return the portfolio would have otherwise produced) in the region above the minimum floor return.[22]

Portfolio insurance may be created by dynamic hedging strategies that periodically adjust a portfolio's asset allocation between active and risk-free assets. Based on the level and term of protection desired, an initial active allocation is established. It is then adjusted in response to changes in portfolio values and the passage of time. Portfolio insurance is not a market-timing technique; there is no attempt to forecast returns. In rising markets, an increasing percentage of the portfolio is allocated to active assets; in declining markets, an increasing percentage is allocated to reserve assets. Under extreme conditions, the portfolio may be allocated entirely to either active or reserve assets.[23]

Alternatively, portfolio insurance may be implemented by indirectly changing asset allocations through the financial futures markets. As the market declines, more financial futures are sold short against the equity assets insured. The profit generated from these sales is presumed to offset the losses on the pension plan assets. Conversely, as the market rises, these contracts can be removed.

QUESTIONS FOR REVIEW

1. Describe the various forms of money market instruments.
2. Explain why a pension plan investment manager might invest pension assets in bonds instead of money market instruments. What are the additional risks associated with this decision?
3. Explain why pension plans have been choosing mutual funds more frequently in recent years.

---

[22]This cost does not materialize directly; instead, it can be thought of as the opportunity cost of having a portion of the pension plan assets in risk-free assets at the time of a market increase. The cost will obviously be positively associated with the degree of protection desired. In other words, a "guarantee" that the portfolio will not decline by more than 15 percent in one year will require less activity than one that permits no decline at all in the same time period. Perhaps less obvious is that the cost should decline as the term of protection is lengthened. For more information, the mathematically inclined reader should see Simon Benninga and Marshall Blume, "On the Optimality of Portfolio Insurance," *Journal of Finance* 40 (December 1985), pp. 1341-52.

[23]John R. Meneghetti, "Portfolio Insurance: Finding the Right Balance," *Pension World*, September 1986, p.36.

4. What type of information should be elicited in questionnaires sent to prospective investment managers?
5. Explain why a passive investment strategy may be attractive to a pension plan sponsor.
6. Describe the basic objectives behind the use of dedication or immunization techniques for pension plan portfolios.

QUESTIONS FOR DISCUSSION

1. Discuss how you would assess the cost of a portfolio insurance strategy.
2. Discuss how FASB 87 might influence an employer's decision to utilize dedication or immunization techniques.
3. Discuss how an employer should decide between active and passive investment strategies.

20. Trust Fund Plans

A qualified plan must use a funding instrument (trusts, custodial accounts, or group contracts) to hold and accumulate plan assets. This chapter deals with trust fund plans while insurance products are discussed in the next chapter. The trust fund arrangement was the first of the existing funding instruments to be used to fund private pension benefits. In addition to being the oldest of the funding instruments, trust fund plans currently account for the bulk of the employees covered and the assets held by private plans. The trust fund approach is used extensively in the case of multiemployer plans, although the increased flexibility now available under group pension contracts has resulted in greater life insurance company competition for multiemployer plan business.

This chapter is concerned with those plans in which all or a substantial portion of the plan assets are accumulated and invested by the trustee. In other words, the discussion in this chapter does not pertain to plans in which a trustee is used but benefits are funded entirely through insurance company contracts (for example, a fully insured individual policy plan).

20.1. GENERAL CHARACTERISTICS

A trust fund plan is an arrangement under which employer and employee contributions, if any, are deposited with a trustee who is responsible for the administration and investment of these moneys and the income earned on accumulated assets of the fund, and who normally is responsible for the direct payment of benefits to eligible participants under the plan. If the trust fund arrangement is used in combination with an insured funding instrument, benefit payments to participants are generally made by the insurance company, with transfers from the trust fund made as required. The trustee is usually a corporate trustee (trust company). Individuals can also serve as trustees of the plan, although this practice has become less frequent because of the fiduciary requirements of ERISA.

20.1.1. Trust Agreement

The duties and responsibilities of the trustee are set forth in a trust agreement executed by the employer and the trustee. In the case of a negotiated multiemployer plan, the trust agreement is executed by individuals representing the unions and an equal number of individuals representing the employers, and these persons often compose the board of trustees responsible for the administration of the plan. The board of trustees may retain the task of investing plan assets, or it may choose to delegate this duty to a corporate trustee. In the latter case, a trust agreement setting forth the duties and responsibilities of the corporate trustee is executed by the board of trustees and the corporate trustee.

A typical trust agreement between an employer and a corporate trustee contains provisions regarding the irrevocability and nondiversion of trust assets; the investment powers of the trustee; the allocation of fiduciary responsibilities; the payment of legal, trustee, and other fees relative to the plan; periodic reports to the employer to be prepared by the trustee; the records and accounts to be maintained by the trustee; the conditions for removal or resignation of the trustee and the appointment of a new trustee; the payment of benefits under the plan; and the rights and duties of the trustee in case of amendment or termination of the plan.

The trust agreement, then, is concerned primarily with the receipt, investment, and disbursement of funds under a pension plan. The plan provisions may be incorporated in the trust agreement or they can be set forth in a separate plan document. The use of two separate documents is prevalent in trust fund plans and is almost always the approach used in multiemployer plans. The advantage of a separate plan document is that amendments to the plan can be made without the need to involve the trustee in frequent amendments to the trust agreement.

20.1.2. Administrative Duties of Trustee

The bulk of the record-keeping associated with a pension plan is normally performed by the employer under single-employer trust fund plans. If the plan is contributory, the employer generally retains responsibility for maintaining a record of employee contributions. In this case, total contributions are paid to the trustee without reference to any division of employer and employee contributions. The employer normally also assumes responsibility for the maintenance of records of earnings and credited service for each participant. In some cases, the record-keeping function is performed by the consulting actuary for the plan or a third-party administrator.

Most corporate trustees are able to relieve the employer of the burden of maintaining the necessary records associated with the plans. Corporate trustees sometimes maintain records in the case of profit sharing plans or defined contribution pension plans and, to a more limited extent, for multiemployer plans. If the trustee performs any record-keeping function, a service charge, in addition to the trustee's investment fee, is levied on an account basis, as explained later in this chapter. The advantages of specialization and the economies of size permit corporate trustees who handle a substantial volume of pension business to perform these services for a reasonable fee. The employer must decide whether it is more economical in its case to maintain these records itself or to have this service provided by the trustee or by a consulting actuary or service organization.

In the case of a negotiated multiemployer plan, the board of trustees, rather than the individual employers, is generally responsible for the maintenance of plan records. The record-keeping function is usually performed by a pension fund office created by the board of trustees. If a corporate trustee is retained to manage the assets of the fund, the plan trustees may delegate the task of record-keeping to the corporate trustee. In recent years, there has been a significant increase in the number of professional plan administrators. The function of a professional administrator is to keep all the specific records of service and earnings for individual members of the plan and to handle all routine administrative transactions.

Whether or not the corporate trustee performs the record-keeping function, it never makes any benefit distributions from the fund without authorization from the employer or retirement committee. In the case of a single-employer trust fund plan, the employer generally appoints a plan or retirement committee, usually composed of officers of the company. It is the responsibility of this committee to determine a participant's eligibility for benefits under the plan. Under multiemployer plans, authorization of benefit payments is the responsibility of the board of trustees or a committee of its members appointed by the board; but in some cases, this function is delegated to a professional administrator.

Apart from the administrative aspects of trust fund plans, a corporate trustee is always responsible for maintaining accurate and detailed records of all investments, receipts, disbursements, and other transactions involving the trust assets. In addition, the trustee is required to submit an annual statement regarding these trust transactions to the plan or retirement committee, usually within 90 days of the close of the plan's fiscal year. The trust agreement may require that statements be rendered to the committee more frequently than annually; for example, quarterly or monthly. Also, in some cases, the trustee assumes responsibility for the filing of forms for the trust as required by tax regulations.

Additionally, the trustee must make annual reports under the provisions of the Employee Retirement Income Security Act (ERISA) and the basic information must be made available in summary form to all participants and beneficiaries.

20.1.3. Investment Powers of Trustee

For very large pension plans, it is common to use investment advisors or multiple investment managers with the corporate trustee serving as custodian. For most other pension plans, the primary function of a trustee is the investment management of trust assets. The trustee invests the trust assets (including contributions and investment income) in accordance with the provisions of the trust agreement, the investment policy desired by the employer or retirement committee, and the fiduciary standards imposed by ERISA and by general trust laws. The investment power granted to a trustee by the trust agreement varies among plans; it may range from approval by the investment committee of every action affecting the fund's assets, to full discretion in investment affairs. Furthermore, the corporate trustee does maintain personal contact with the employer, and therefore the latter may influence, directly or indirectly, investment decisions. If the trust agreement fails to specify the investment powers of the trustee, the trustee is restricted to investments that are legal for trust funds in the state in which the trust is established and the federal statute governing fiduciary investments.

The trustee, until the enactment of ERISA, could invest all trust assets in the securities of the employer. Essentially, ERISA restricts investment of pension plan assets in an employer's securities to 10 percent of the fund value. The limit does not apply to profit sharing or thrift plans that explicitly permit larger investments in employer securities. Nor does it apply to stock bonus plans or employee stock ownership plans (ESOPs) that are typically invested primarily in employer securities. Loans to the employer made from plan assets, except for ESOPs, have generally been forbidden by ERISA even though adequate security for the loan and a reasonable rate of return exist. The law considers as a possible prohibited transaction a loan or extension of credit between the qualified plan and a party in interest such as the employer.[1]

---

[1]For a discussion of this aspect of trust investments, see Chapter 7.

The trustee is required to maintain a separate accounting and an actual segregation of the assets of each trust. In other words, the assets of a trust generally cannot be commingled with the assets of other trusts or with the general assets of the trustee. Thus, under these circumstances, there is no pooling of the investment experience of a number of trusts. If the investment experience has been exceptionally favorable for a particular trust, the full benefit of that experience is credited to the trust account. On the other hand, the trust must bear the full impact of adverse investment income and capital loss experience. Therefore, a relatively small trust fund plan would be subject to the danger of inadequate diversification of its investment portfolio. To meet this problem, corporate trustees have established collective investment funds. A collective investment fund permits the commingling of assets of all participating trusts. Although originally established to meet the needs of smaller trusts, corporate trustees have obtained permission to allow pension trusts of any size to participate in collective investment funds established specifically for qualified pension plans. A trust participating in a commingled fund for investment purposes buys units or shares of the fund.[2] Dividends are paid on each unit, each dividend being a proportionate share of the total income earned by the commingled fund. These units fluctuate in value as the value of the assets of the commingled fund fluctuates.

The principal advantage of a collective investment fund is that it permits any trust to enjoy the investment advantages normally available only to the very large funds. These potential advantages have been described as follows.[3]

1. Higher rate of return on fixed income investments. Commingled investment permits purchases in amounts large enough to take advantage of private placements and special offerings of securities, which generally carry higher yields than regular market offerings; and in mortgages, leaseback arrangements or other interests in real property.

2. Increased growth potential through selective stock holding. Commingled investment permits such funds to achieve a degree of selective diversification in equities that would be impossible to attain through individual investment, except in sizable funds.

3. Maximum liquidity of funds for cash requirements. Commingled investment permits redemption of units at the end of any month, at the current market value of units, so that money required for payouts is made available through use of current cash flow rather than having to sell investments, as might have to be done in a separate fund.

---

[2]Bank of New York, *Trusteed Employee Benefit Plans* (New York: Bank of New York, 1966), p. 10.
[3]*Ibid.*, pp. 10-11.

4. Dollar averaging on investment purchases. Current cash flow from incoming contributions, spaced as they are at intervals throughout a given year, has the effect of dollar averaging on investment purchases, which generally works to the advantage of all participating trusts.

5. Lower investment brokerage fees. A collective investment fund can purchase stocks in round lots and in amounts that entail lower brokerage commissions.[4]

Most corporate trustees believe collective investment funds offer significant advantages to the larger plans as well as to smaller plans. In one large urban bank, approximately 55 percent of all its pension trust accounts participate in the bank's commingled pension trust. However, there is an element of inflexibility in the use of a collective investment fund that should be noted; that is, the inability to transfer specific fund assets to another funding agency. Units can be liquidated, but during a period of depressed security prices the employer may prefer to transfer trust assets in kind, with the expectation that market prices will be higher at some future date.

Participation in a commingled pension trust is restricted to qualified plans. Participation by a nonqualified trust could result in loss of the qualified tax status of the entire collective investment fund.

Some corporate trustees have established many collective investment funds, with each fund designed to provide an investment medium having certain principal characteristics and objectives. For example, one fund may emphasize investments in bonds, notes, debentures, and other fixed income obligations. A second fund may be invested principally in private placements, mortgages, or other interests in real property. A third fund may be invested in a selection of quality common stocks with the objective of growth of principal and income over the long term. In addition, a special equity fund may be available for those trusts interested in pursuing a more aggressive investment policy. The multiple collective investment funds offer the employer considerable flexibility in the proportion of trust assets to be invested in each of the classes of investments.

Investment flexibility has been an attractive feature of the trust arrangement for many employers. During the past several decades, many employers have expressed a preference for investment of a relatively large proportion of pension assets in common stocks. Insured plans were not able to offer this investment flexibility until the development of separate account funding.

---

[4]A small trust fund plan can also obtain the advantages of commingling through investments in mutual fund shares.

20.2.   BENEFIT STRUCTURE

20.2.1. RETIREMENT BENEFITS

The trust fund arrangement offers maximum flexibility in the design of a retirement benefit formula. Since funds are not allocated, even for retired employees, any type of benefit formula can be utilized under a trust fund plan. As is true in the case of several of the insurance products described in the next chapter (deposit administration and immediate participation guarantee plans), retirement benefits based on final earnings can be provided without difficulty under trust fund plans.   Likewise, benefit formulas that provide for the integration of social security benefits can be accommodated readily under the trust fund arrangement.

It is true that the more complex the benefit formula, the more difficult is the task of the actuary in projecting costs and calculating contribution payments under the plan. The fact remains, however, that the trust fund instrument does not of itself present any obstacles to the use of the most complex of benefit formulas. For example, even those few plans that have a provision for adjustments of retired employees' benefits in accordance with a designated cost-of-living index can be provided under this funding instrument. The actuary can include in the cost calculations an assumption regarding future price level changes, which admittedly is not readily predictable with a great degree of accuracy. However, actuarial gains and losses because of variations of actual from expected price levels can be reflected in subsequent valuations and determinations of contribution payments. Trust fund plans can also provide a retirement benefit that varies with the market value of the assets supporting the pension benefits of retired workers (variable annuities).

Defined contribution formulas can also be used in trust fund pension plans. A pension plan generally provides a lifetime annuity benefit to retired employees. The law requires the plan to provide a joint and one-half survivor annuity for an employee and his or her spouse unless there is an election to the contrary. Therefore, under a defined contribution pension plan formula, at some point in time the accumulations on behalf of each participant must be expressed in terms of a lifetime monthly benefit (except in cases where lump-sum distributions are made). The monthly benefit may be calculated as each annual contribution is received, or annual contributions may be accumulated to retirement date and the determination of the level of monthly benefits may be made at that time.

In the case of some negotiated plans, particularly multiemployer plans, the employer's financial commitment is expressed as some specified cents per hour worked or as a fixed percentage of compensation. However, these plans generally are not traditional defined contribution plans in that they also provide a defined benefit. The trust fund instrument can accommodate these plans without any difficulty.

Early retirement benefits can be, and frequently are, provided under trust fund plans. The amount of early retirement benefit may be the actuarial equivalent of the participant's accrued normal retirement benefit, or, if the employer desires, a more liberal early retirement benefit may be provided. The additional cost under the latter alternative can be anticipated in computations of contribution payments required under the plan.

20.2.2. Death Benefits

An increasing proportion of the larger trust fund plans provide preretirement death benefits. Preretirement death benefits seldom have been provided under small-sized trust fund plans. The law requires all qualified plans to include an option providing at least a 50 percent joint and survivor annuity. As described in Chapter 6, if a participant dies before the annuity starting date and has a surviving spouse, the automatic benefit must be in the form of a qualified preretirement survivor (QPS) annuity to the surviving spouse.

The availability of postretirement death benefits depends on the normal annuity form under the plan. A pure life annuity has been the typical normal annuity form under trust fund plans or a modified refund annuity in the case of contributory plans. Once again, however, the law provides that the joint and one-half survivor annuity be the normal annuity form for a participant and his or her spouse unless an election is made to the contrary. The level of benefits under a joint and one-half survivor annuity can be greater than the actuarial equivalent of the previous normal annuity form. If the cost of this increase in benefit is not passed on to the participants and is assumed by the employer, it can be projected in the actuary's calculations of the periodic contributions required under the plan. These benefits can be provided without difficulty under trust fund plans.

20.2.3. Disability Benefits

Some trust fund plans provide disability benefits. Responsibility for determining whether a participant is eligible for disability benefits usually rests with a retirement committee appointed by the employer. In the case of a multiemployer plan, this function is assumed by the board of trustees or a committee composed of board members. The trustee begins payment of disability benefits on receipt of certification by the retirement committee of a participant's eligibility for benefits. The retirement committee also assumes responsibility for reviewing approved disability claims to determine whether continuance of disability exists.

Several reasons exist for the prevalence of disability benefits under trust fund plans. First, union leaders strongly favor provision of disability benefits under pension plans, and a substantial proportion of negotiated plans utilize the trust fund approach. Second, disability benefits provide employers with a desirable personnel management tool if control over the determination of disability rests with the employer. A disability pension can be used as a graceful, and often relatively economical, method of retiring unproductive employees. Third, the reluctance of insurance companies (at least until recent years) to insure long-term disability benefits encouraged the self-insuring of these benefits under trust fund plans.[5] However, in recent years, the use of insured group long-term disability plans has increased.

20.2.4. Vested Benefits

The rights of trust fund plan participants to benefits derived from employer contributions, as is true under other funding instruments, depend upon the vesting provisions of the plan. The vesting provisions in the plan must be at least as generous as those required under the law. If the actuarial value of the employee's vested benefit is less than $3,500, the employer may cash out the benefit. This reduces the administrative expense of keeping records of terminated employees. Additionally, if the terminating employee agrees, a vested benefit in excess of $3,500 may be cashed out under certain conditions. The value of the vested benefit may be transferred to an individual retirement account (IRA) or, with the consent of the employer, to the pension plan of the employee's next employer if the new employer also consents. Of course, terminating employees are always entitled to the benefit attributable to their own contributions. Under defined benefit trust fund plans, the availability of vested benefits may be deferred until the terminating employee reaches normal retirement age. If the plan is contributory, entitlement to the vested benefit has generally been conditioned on the terminating employee leaving his or her own contributions in the plan; withdrawal of the contributions results, in these cases, in the forfeiture of the portion of the vested benefit attributable to

---

[5]It should be noted that under deposit administration and immediate participation guarantee plans, disability benefits, when provided, generally are self-insured by the employer in that these benefits are paid directly by the employer or charged directly to the unallocated account.

employer contributions. The law permits employees to withdraw their own contributions without having vested benefits canceled unless an employee is less than 50 percent vested. In those cases, an employer can cancel vested benefits if an employee withdraws his or her own contributions. The plan must contain a payback provision allowing employees to restore their benefits by repaying prior distributions with interest.

Since contributions to a trust fund are not allocated to specific participants under the plan (with the possible exception of a traditional defined contribution plan), vesting is always expressed in terms of benefits rather than contributions. A terminating employee's vested benefits represent a deferred claim against the assets of the trust fund. This claim is conditioned on (1) the terminating employee living to retirement age (except for his or her own contributions), (2) the employee making application for the benefit in accordance with plan provisions, and (3) the adequacy of the trust fund to provide the vested benefit and the protection afforded by the Pension Benefit Guaranty Corporation for defined benefit plans. In case of termination of the plan, the priority, if any, of vested benefits is dependent on plan provisions subject to the requirements of the law.

20.3. CONTRIBUTIONS

The annual contribution payments under a defined benefit trust fund plan are determined by periodic actuarial valuations by the plan actuary who must be an enrolled actuary under the law. The plan actuary calculates the amount of contributions to be made to the trust fund on the basis of: (1) a given set of actuarial assumptions, (2) a particular actuarial cost method, and (3) the census data for the group of employees covered under the plan. It is the task of the actuary, as strongly reinforced by the law, to choose a set of actuarial assumptions and techniques that, based on his or her judgment and experience, appear to be reasonable for the particular plan. This obligation is imposed on all enrolled actuaries who provide actuarial services for plans covered under the law, whether such actuaries are acting in a consulting capacity or working for insurance companies. Generally, the actuary will choose assumptions more conservative than the experience actually expected under the plan, to provide a margin for contingencies. It is also the responsibility of the actuary to choose an appropriate actuarial cost method to be used in calculations of contribution payments. Since the choice of an actuarial cost method has a significant impact on the incidence of contribution payments, it is important that the employer have a clear understanding of the factors involved in the final selection of a cost method.

Under defined benefit trust fund plans, the employer has some input in decisions regarding the choice of actuarial assumptions and the cost method to be used in calculations of contribution payments. Thus, the employer has maximum flexibility under a trust fund plan in directing the timing of contribution payments as long as such contributions meet the minimum funding standards of the law.

Of course, this does not mean the ultimate cost of the plan is necessarily lower under trust fund plans. The actuarial gains from turnover and mortality under allocated funding instruments eventually are recognized in the form of employer credits against premiums due in future years. Also, lower levels of contributions in the initial years of the plan must be offset by higher contribution levels in subsequent years. Actuarial assumptions and cost methods do not affect the ultimate cost of the plan, except to the extent that they influence levels of funding and, therefore, the amount of investment income earned on plan assets. The fact remains that the employer has greater control over the incidence of contribution payments under trust fund plans because of the way in which actuarial assumptions and methods are established and the unallocated nature of the funding instrument. This flexibility is also available, to almost the same degree, under most group pension contracts.

In addition to the contribution payments necessary to provide the benefits to participants of the plan, the employer must make some provision for the expense associated with trust fund plans. The major expenses under trust fund plans are trustee, consulting actuary, and legal fees, as well as record-keeping and other administrative expenses. Investment fees of corporate trustees usually are expressed as a percentage of the trust corpus -- the percentage being graded downward with the size of the fund.

The trustee imposes additional charges if it maintains plan records, makes pension payments to retired employees, or holds insurance and annuity contracts. Because of the additional reporting and other administrative requirements of ERISA, additional fees for the additional services are probably necessary. If the employer performs the administrative functions associated with the plan, the cost of performing these duties should be recognized in determining the true cost of a trust fund plan.

With reference to legal and actuarial fees, it is virtually impossible to quote any figures that can be viewed as typical charges under trust fund plans since fees for these services vary so widely among plans. The legal services required for the plan are normally performed by the attorney who handles all other legal work for the employer, and therefore are usually incorporated into the overall legal retainer paid by the employer. A consulting actuary's fee varies with the type and amount of service rendered. The actuary may perform preliminary cost studies or special projects on a fixed-fee basis, but most of his or her services to the plan are billed on an hourly or daily rate basis. The fees for legal and actuarial services can be paid by the trustee out of trust assets or they can be paid directly by the employer. The latter approach is the procedure followed in most cases.

No guarantees are available under trust fund plans.[6] The trustee cannot guarantee a minimum rate of investment income, nor can it guarantee plan assets against capital losses. Likewise, the mortality risk cannot be transferred to the trustee. The absence of guarantees is consistent with the legal nature of trust arrangements. A trustee's obligation is limited to the management of trust assets in a reasonable and prudent manner and in accordance with the duties set forth in the trust agreement and state and federal law. The adequacy of the fund to provide the benefits promised under the plan is the responsibility of the employer. The high degree of responsibility imposed on the employer under a trust fund plan is consistent with the maximum degree of flexibility available to the employer under this funding instrument. Guarantees must be minimized or eliminated if an employer desires maximum contribution flexibility and complete and immediate reflection of plan experience. Therefore, in choosing a funding instrument, the employer should consider the extent to which guarantees and flexibility are desired.

Many large employers have chosen funding instruments that offer a high degree of flexibility and immediate reflection of plan experience. In the case of a trust fund plan, the actual experience of the plan is reflected immediately in the status of the fund. For example, if investment experience has been favorable, the fund receives the full benefit of the favorable experience. Likewise, the full impact of adverse investment experience is borne by the individual trust. However, the investment risk can be spread to some extent through the use of a commingled investment fund. The use of a collective investment fund reduces a plan's investment risk as a result of the greater investment diversification available; but it still does not offer a guarantee of principal or a minimum rate of return. The employer cannot shift the mortality risk under trust fund plans. If the plan covers a large number of employees, the employer may be willing to assume the mortality risk. The mortality risk becomes a more significant consideration as the size of the group covered decreases. Deviations of actual from expected experience for other factors (for example, turnover, disability rates, and actual retirement ages) also are immediately reflected in the status of the trust fund.

---

[6]In order to compete with the guaranteed investment contracts (GICs) offered by insurance companies, many sophisticated techniques are being used to try to match maturities of investments with the time that specific amounts are needed to pay benefits. These include such approaches as immunization and dedicated portfolio techniques, which are discussed in Chapter 19.

Under trust fund plans, actuarial valuations are performed periodically (usually annually, but no less frequently than every three years for regulatory purposes) to determine the adequacy of the fund. If the actual experience evolving under the plan indicates the current level of funding is inadequate, actuarial assumptions can be revised to produce higher levels of contributions in future years. Since the liabilities under a pension plan evolve over a long period of time, adequate provision for these liabilities can be made if frequent actuarial valuations are performed and if the employer is willing and able to make the necessary contributions.

20.4.   TERMINATION OF PLAN

In the event of termination of a trust fund plan, the disposition of plan assets is determined in accordance with the provisions of the law.

Situations sometimes arise in which an employer desires to switch funding agencies without any intention of terminating the plan. A transfer of assets to another trustee or to an insurance company can be effected without difficulty under trust fund plans. The trust agreement contains no prohibitions against transfer of plans assets (assuming that such transfers are made in accordance with the requirements of the Internal Revenue Service). The trustee may impose a minor charge for the administrative duties associated with a termination of the trust. Of course, losses may be sustained if assets must be liquidated over a relatively short period of time. In some cases, transfers of securities and other assets may be permitted rather than requiring liquidation of investments, unless the assets are held in a commingled trust, in which case transfers of securities generally are not permitted. The freedom to transfer plan assets and the flexibility it offers in case of mergers or other circumstances is viewed by some employers as an important advantage of trust fund plans.

20.5.   SPLIT FUNDING

The trust fund arrangement can be used in conjunction with individual insurance and annuity contracts as one approach in funding pension benefits. This approach is generally referred to as a combination plan. Group pension contracts also can be used in combination with the trust fund arrangement. These latter arrangements are usually referred to as split-funded plans (although the term combination plan can be applied to describe any plan utilizing two or more funding instruments).

Split-funded plans generally utilize group deposit administration or immediate participation guarantee or modified immediate participation guarantee contracts. The decision of the employer to split-fund its pension plan is usually motivated by a desire to obtain, at least in part, the advantages of an insurer's guarantees and a possibly favorable investment opportunity. For example, the trust agreement may provide that the trustee administer all assets held on behalf of active employees and that an immediate annuity be purchased as each employee retires. Likewise, an insurer may enjoy relatively high yields on direct placement and mortgage investments, and therefore the employer may decide to invest a portion of plan assets in a deposit administration contract, an immediate participation guarantee contract, or a guaranteed investment contract.

QUESTIONS FOR REVIEW

1. What is a trust fund plan?
2. Describe the provisions that are generally found in a trust agreement.
3. Describe the typical administrative duties and investment powers of a trustee.
4. How does the federal law restrict the trustee's investment powers?
5. What is a collective investment fund?
6. What advantages does a collective investment fund have over an individually managed fund?
7. It has been said that any benefit formula can be used in conjunction with trust fund plans. Explain.
8. What are the major expenses of a trust fund plan in addition to the contributions needed to pay plan benefits?

QUESTIONS FOR DISCUSSION

1. Discuss how the investment risks assumed under a trust fund plan should be treated by the employer.
2. Discuss how the mortality risks assumed under a trust fund plan should be treated by the employer.

21. Special Insurance and Annuity Products

21.1. INTRODUCTION

Originally, the majority of pension plan assets were placed with insurance companies and were protected by strong guarantees as to investment and mortality experience. Beginning with group deferred annuity contracts in the early 1920s, insurance products were designed specifically for use in pension plans. These contracts provided that a single premium would be paid to purchase a contract on each employee promising to pay (at normal retirement age) the equivalent of his or her accrued benefit for that year. Although all investment and mortality risks were transferred from the employer to the insurance company once the contracts were purchased,[1] it was difficult to provide a substantial degree of flexibility in plan design features such as past service benefits and supplemental benefits, since the price of funding a dollar's worth of monthly retirement income increases prohibitively as the employee approaches normal retirement age.

The limited flexibility of this contract, as opposed to the virtually unlimited freedom offered by the trust fund approach provided by banks,

---

[1] The rates were typically guaranteed for the first five years' purchases of deferred annuities.

eventually led the insurance industry to develop an unallocated[2] form of instrument known as a deposit administration contract. The chief advantage of this contract was the fact that virtually any type of benefit formula or actuarial cost method could be utilized under this approach. Although deposit administration contracts also insulated the sponsor from fluctuations in mortality and investment experience to a large extent, the dividend formula provided that the sponsor's actual cost would be influenced to some degree by the actual experience under the pension plan. This was particularly true as the insurance industry started to move from a situation in which the average rate of return for the insurance company's entire portfolio of pension assets was used to accumulate the book value of the sponsor's assets to a concept known as the new-money or investment-year method, in which the interest rate credited on the sponsor's assets is a function of the year they were deposited with the insurance company.

Although the deposit administration contract improved the plan design flexibility features of an insured plan, there was still a certain amount of discontent among plan sponsors due to the delay in the receipt of plan dividends and the use of contingency funds to smooth out experience over time. In response, the insurance industry developed a new product in the 1950s known as an immediate participation guarantee contract; it determines plan costs based on the sponsor's direct experience with respect to mortality and investment experience, while still providing annuity guarantees to the retirees under the plan.

In time, some sponsors began to question the need for locking up funds for annuity purchases and many were disenchanted with the restrictions or implicit penalties imposed on the withdrawal of funds in immediate participation guarantee contracts. The insurance industry again responded to this demand by offering guaranteed investment contracts which offer a unique type of investment guarantee. No guarantees are provided with respect to mortality, however, and the insurance company provides no assurance that sufficient funds will be available to pay the accrued benefits of participants. In summary, the evolutionary process has made insurance companies another form of investment manager.

The major development in the group pension field in the last decade is the substantial increase in flexibility under insurance contracts. Insurers are now in a position to tailor the contract to the specific needs of the employer. Employer demands for greater flexibility in investment policy and in the timing of contribution payments have led to a strong preference for the unallocated type of contract in the group pension market. This demand for

---

[2]Funding instruments are classified on the basis of whether contributions are allocated to provide benefits to specific employees prior to retirement or whether contributions are accumulated in an unallocated fund to provide benefits for employees when they retire.

greater flexibility has extended to the small employer market, and insurers have accommodated this demand by making unallocated contracts available to relatively small firms. The result has been a dramatic decline in the relative importance of the group deferred annuity contract to the point where it is almost completely obsolete.

While there are some deposit administration and immediate participation guarantee contracts still active at most insurers, many policyholders have opted to convert their funds into more modern funding vehicles. A growing number of court cases challenging the viability of these contracts is perhaps the major issue confronting these contracts today. Generally, these suits call into question the insurer's fiduciary standard under the Employee Retirement Income Security Act (ERISA) in making certain interest credits or fund adjustments on contract termination.

21.2. GROUP DEFERRED ANNUITY CONTRACTS

The group annuity contract, unlike individual insurance and group permanent contracts, was devised specifically to meet the funding needs of pension plans, the first such contract being issued in 1921. The volume of these contracts grew very rapidly in the following two decades, and they constituted by far the most prevalent group insured funding instrument prior to the growth of deposit administration plans in the 1950s. However, they are rarely used today.

Group annuity contracts provide for the funding of benefits through the purchase of units of single-premium deferred annuities for each participant. However, some insurance companies offer level premium deferred annuities on a group underwriting basis.

Unlike group life insurance, group annuity contracts are subject to very little statutory regulation regarding eligible groups or minimum number of covered lives. However, insurance companies do impose, as a matter of underwriting policy, certain requirements for these contracts. Most insurers require a minimum number of eligible employees (10, for example) for an employer to be eligible for a group annuity contract. If the plan is contributory, at least 75 percent of the eligible employees must participate in the plan, 100 percent participation being required in the case of noncontributory plans. These underwriting requirements are not imposed so much to minimize adverse selection as to produce a sufficient-sized case to justify the insurer expenses incurred in setting up the plan. A minimum annual premium per participant or for the plan as a whole also is imposed to assure the above objective. Also, the insurer may impose an administrative charge if the total premium in a contract year is less than a specified amount.

21.3. GROUP DEPOSIT ADMINISTRATION CONTRACTS

The deposit administration contract, which first appeared in the 1920s, evolved from the basic group deferred annuity contract. For this reason, it is often referred to as a deposit administration group annuity contract. The deposit administration contract was developed to overcome certain of the inflexibilities associated with the group deferred annuity contract. Although originally developed as a result of interinsurer competition, the growth in popularity of the deposit administration plan began in the early 1950s largely in response to the increased competition from the trust fund arrangement, which offers a great deal of flexibility in plan design, timing of employer contributions, and investment alternatives. Because of the other more flexible funding instruments currently available and discussed later in this chapter, group deposit administration contracts are not as popular today.

The distinguishing characteristic of deposit administration contracts, as contrasted with group deferred annuity contracts, is that employer contributions are not allocated to specific employees until retirement date. Stated differently, the actual purchase of annuities (which includes a charge for expenses) does not take place until an employee retires.

One major advantage of deposit administration contracts is the flexibility available in designing the plan's benefit provisions. Whereas group deferred annuity contracts are limited largely to unit benefit formulas, any type of retirement benefit formula can be employed without difficulty under a deposit administration contract. For example, deposit administration contracts may be used without difficulty in plans that base benefits on final average earnings. The fact that benefits cannot be precisely determined until the employee actually retires presents no problem under these contracts since annuities are not purchased until the date of retirement. Likewise, minimum retirement benefits and the most complex integrated benefit formulas can be handled readily under deposit administration plans. Furthermore, the availability of equity funding permits the use of variable annuity benefits. The absence of annuity purchases until retirement date permits considerable flexibility in the establishment of early and late retirement benefit provisions. For example, early retirement benefits may be provided on a more liberal basis than the actuarial equivalent of normal retirement benefits (subject to Internal Revenue Service limitations), while additional benefits may be permitted for service rendered after the normal retirement date. Moreover, such auxiliary plan benefits as pre-retirement spousal and disability benefits - which by nature do not lend themselves to the deferred annuity approach - are readily accommodated by the deposit administration contract.

Contributions are credited to an unallocated fund that, under a conventional deposit administration contract, is variously referred to as the deposit fund, active life fund, deposit account, or purchase payment fund. However, the dramatic growth of separate account funding[3] (which many insurance companies make available under their deposit administration contracts) has led to changes in contract terminology. For example, instead of deposit account, some insurers now use the terms general investment portfolio account or fixed dollar account, since contributions credited to the deposit account are invested in the insurer's general investment portfolio, which in turn is composed principally of fixed income securities. The insurer offering a separate account facility must append some appropriate term to distinguish this account (or accounts, if more than one is established) from its general investment account. A variety of terms have been used to identify the separate account; for example, equity account, separate account, or variable contract account.

The main thrust of the separate accounts development, from the policyholder's point of view, is the broadened choice of investments between fixed dollar and equity securities. Therefore, fixed dollar account and equity account are the terms that are used when discussing the features of deposit administration contracts from the policyholder's viewpoint. The terms general investment account and separate account are used when discussing investment alternatives under these plans from the insurer's point of view.

A fixed dollar account, maintained for each policyholder, represents a record of the portion of plan funds held to be invested primarily in fixed income obligations. An equity account, also maintained for each policy holder, represents a record of the portion of plan funds held to be invested primarily in common stocks. The policyholder has complete discretion as to the proportion of plan contributions to be credited to each of these accounts. If the employer so desires, 100 percent of contributions (assuming state regulatory requirements are met) can be credited to the fixed dollar account or to the equity account, although the usual decision is to allocate some portion to each of the accounts.

The contributions credited to the fixed dollar account become part of the general assets of the insurance company for investment purposes. If the insurer has established a separate account for fixed dollar investments, plan contributions can be allocated to the general investment account or the fixed dollar separate account in accordance with policyholder instructions. The fixed dollar account is credited with the rate of interest guaranteed in the contract. Also, dividends due under the contract are credited to the

---

[3]The assets held in separate accounts are not commingled with the general assets of the insurer and are exempt from state statutory investment restrictions normally applied to life insurance companies.

fixed dollar account. As pensions become payable to retiring employees, annuities may be provided by allocations from either the fixed dollar or the equity account, although generally annuities are provided by allocations from the fixed dollar account. When an annuity is established, a certificate is issued to the retired employee describing the benefits.

The contributions credited to the policyholder's equity account are invested in one or more of the insurer's separate accounts provided under the contract. While equity account accounting procedures differ among insurance companies, the following approach is illustrative of the general concepts involved in separate account funding. Each policyholder's share of the separate account is determined on a participation unit (or variable unit) basis. The policyholder's equity account provides a cumulative record of the number of participation units credited to the account and the number of units allocated or withdrawn from the account. The balance of participation units credited to the account multiplied by the current participation unit value equals the amount of equity account assets held on behalf of the policyholder at any given point in time. The participation unit value is adjusted periodically, usually each business day, to reflect investment results under the separate account. The insurer offers no guarantee as to principal or interest on moneys credited to the equity account.

The policyholder generally has some flexibility in transferring funds between the fixed dollar account and the equity account. Generally, advance written notice to the insurer (e.g., 15 business days) is required. The advance notice requirement serves to minimize the potential problem of an undue amount of switching activity that might arise from attempts to play the market. Also, the insurer generally reserves the right to limit the amount or the percentage permitted to be transferred from the fixed dollar account to the equity account either on a per policyholder basis or on a book of business approach. For example, the total of the amounts transferred in any month may not exceed $1 million for all policyholders, or each policyholder may transfer up to 20 percent of the fixed account in any one year. The objective of this provision is to minimize potential financial antiselection and liquidity problems arising from such transfers. Likewise, the insurer has the right -- which it might exercise under some conditions, as when the stock markets are unstable -- to limit transfers in a given month from the equity account according to the restrictions described above.

If the policyholder decides to place future contributions with a new funding agency such as another insurance company or a bank, the policyholder may either: (1) permit the fixed dollar and equity accounts to be used to purchase annuities until exhausted or (2) elect a transfer date for the transfer of funds credited to the fixed dollar and equity accounts. If the policyholder has elected to transfer the funds in its accounts, purchase of annuities will cease as of a specified date such as the 15th business day after the insurer receives such request. Transfer payments begin on the transfer date and are usually made on a monthly basis. The minimum amount that can be transferred monthly from the fixed income account is specified in the contract; for example, 1 percent of the amount of the account on the date annuity purchases cease, or the balance of the account, if less, with insurer permission required to transfer amounts in excess of the minimum monthly amount. Thus, the insurer reserves the right to spread transfer payments over a period of time. In other words, if the contract provides that monthly transfer payments will not be less than 1 percent of the amount of the account on the date purchases cease, the insurer has the right to stretch transfer payments over a 15- or 20-year or more period, depending on the interest rate being credited to the account. In practice, the agreed-upon transfer schedules generally are considerably shorter than the maximum permissible contractual period. The insurer generally permits lump-sum transfers, on a market value basis, although for very large accounts the insurer may reserve the right to spread payments over a period of time. With reference to the equity account, the contract generally provides that the sum transferable is the contract fund balance valued on a market value basis. Also, the maximum payout period is generally shorter than the period applicable to the fixed dollar account. For example, the contract might provide that monthly transfer payments from the equity account will not be less than (1) the greater of $1 million worth of participation units or 5 percent of the amount of the account on the date annuity purchases cease, or (2) the balance of the account, if less. In this latter case, the maximum period over which insurer transfer payments can be made is 20 months. The difference in treatment of transfers from each account is due to the differences in liquidity and marketability between fixed dollar and equity securities.

In the case of transfers to another funding agency, the insurer usually reserves the right to withhold some amount of the fund (usually up to 5 percent, the specific percentage to be determined by the insurer) to cover expenses not yet recovered and to offset possible financial antiselection (although transfers on a market value basis minimize the latter problem).

An administration charge is normally levied when annual premiums are less than a specified amount. For example, one insurer imposes an annual administration charge under its fixed dollar contracts equal to $800 less 2 percent of any amount of annual contributions paid in excess of $25,000 but not in excess of $65,000. Thus, there is no charge if the previous year's contributions were at least $65,000. If equity funding is utilized under the contract, the annual charge is somewhat higher (e.g., $1,100 less 2 percent of the amount by which the previous year's contributions exceeded $25,000 but not $80,000). The charge for the first contract year is based on the appropriate expense formula, but using as a base the contributions anticipated in the first contract year. The contract administration charge is generally allocated from the fixed dollar account.

In the intervening decades since their introduction, group annuity contracts following the basic deposit administration concept have been offered in considerable variety, including immediate participation guarantee (IPG) and guaranteed investment contracts (GICs) - varying from product to product in both the degree of insurer guarantee and the degree of contractholder discretion as to contributions, investment, and the mobility of funds. Some such contracts were, in fact, group annuity contracts in name only, functioning solely as investment vehicles, with the purchase of annuities a seldom-used contractholder's option. Most GICs and many separate account contracts are, in practice, investment-only contracts. A major variant of the deposit administration theme, the group immediate participation guarantee contract, is described later in this chapter.

21.4.   SEPARATE ACCOUNT FUNDING

Historically, life insurance companies have invested the bulk of their assets in fixed dollar investments. The laws in most states restrict the investments of life insurance companies' general account assets in common stocks to some specified percentage (e.g., 5 percent) of the total assets of the company. This restriction is imposed because of the fixed dollar obligations and contractual guarantees provided in traditional life insurance and annuity contracts and, also, because of the relatively small surplus maintained by life insurance companies.

However, with the advent of separate accounts in 1962, insurers could offer group clients a wide range of investment choices. The assets held in separate accounts are not commingled with the general assets of the insurer and are exempt from state statutory investment restrictions normally applied to life insurance companies.

There is much variety in the manner in which separate accounts are operated by the various insurance companies. Some insurers offer accounts only on a commingled basis; others also offer accounts maintained solely for a single customer. Initially, separate accounts were invested primarily in common stocks, but other forms are now available; further major developments in the nature and form of the separate accounts available as the types of underlying investments in these accounts are broadened can be expected. For example, some insurers have established separate accounts invested primarily in mortgages, including equity participations; others have established commingled separate accounts invested primarily in the ownership of income-producing real property; and other accounts are invested in publicly traded bonds, short-term securities, direct placements and, most recently, foreign securities. One or more separate accounts may be used under the same group pension contract.

Separate accounts were developed for two reasons: (1) to compete with trust fund plans in making equity investments available to employers for funding fixed dollar plans, and (2) to fund variable annuity plans. In the first case, many employers believe the long-term rate of return on equities will be greater than the return on fixed income investments and the increased return will serve to reduce their cost of providing the fixed benefits promised under the plan. In the second case, equity-based variable annuities by definition require the assets supporting these annuities generally be fully invested in equity securities.

The insurer does not guarantee principal or interest for plan assets held in a separate account. The income and gains or losses, realized or unrealized, on separate account investments are credited to or charged against the separate account without regard to the other income, gains, or losses of the insurance company.

Separate accounts are subject to regulation by the Securities and Exchange Commission (SEC). However, exemptions from certain provisions of the acts administered by the SEC have been accorded to qualified retirement plans over the years. First, exemptions under the Securities Act of 1933 and the Investment Company Act of 1940 were provided by Rule 156 and Rule 3(c)3 for noncontributory, qualified plans covering at least 25 lives at the time the contract is issued. Later, Rule 6(e)1 extended the exemption to contributory plans, provided that certain conditions were satisfied regarding employee contributions allocated to separate accounts. Lastly, the Investment Company Amendments Act of 1970 exempts from the 1940 Act separate accounts used exclusively to fund qualified plans, and from most provisions of the 1933 Act and the Securities Exchange Act of 1934 separate accounts interests issued in connection with qualified plans (except for H.R. 10 and IRA plans). Separate accounts are also subject to state regulatory requirements. A 1980 change to the Securities Acts extended the exceptions to plans of governmental units even though not qualified. SEC Rule 180 (December 1981) provides an exception to the registration requirements of the 1933 Act for certain financially sophisticated H.R. 10 plans.

21.5. GROUP IMMEDIATE PARTICIPATION GUARANTEE CONTRACTS

The deposit administration contract went a long way toward providing employers with the desired degree of flexibility not available under the traditional group annuity contract. In addition, the deposit administration contract offers certain interest and annuity rate guarantees. However, the insurance company is able to provide these guarantees only because it accumulates a contingency reserve and because it has control, through dividend computations, over the rate at which actuarial gains pertaining to guaranteed items are credited to the employer. Some employers object to these features of deposit administration plans. These employers prefer an immediate reflection of the actual experience under their plans and are willing to give up the guarantees of the deposit administration plan to get it. Thus, insurance companies developed the immediate participation guarantee (IPG) contract, the first contract of this type being issued in 1950.[4] In an IPG plan, the employer's account is credited with the contributions received during the contract period plus its share of actual investment income for the year according to the investment year method. There is generally no guarantee of principal or a minimum rate of interest under these contracts. The account is charged with all the expenses associated with the particular contract. As issued by many insurance companies, these contracts provide that all benefits, including annuity payments, are charged directly against the account as they are paid. In other words, annuities are not actually purchased for participants at retirement date, as is the practice under deposit administration plans. Some insurance companies do segregate from the account the gross premium for the annuities of retired workers in order to provide annuity guarantees. However, in these latter cases, the premium amount remains in the policyholder's contract funds. The result is similar to that achieved by insurers that only charge to the account the annuity payments actually made. There is no charge to the account for an allocation toward building up a contingency reserve. Also, since no dividend as such is paid, all the record-keeping pertaining to a particular contract can be maintained in one account. Thus, the employer can be quickly apprised of the experience to date under the plan.

If annuity premiums are segregated from, or within, the account at retirement date, the insurer does perform periodic valuations to be certain the credit balance in the account is at least sufficient to provide the promised annuity payments to retired workers. If the credit balance approaches the amount of reserve required to provide the benefits of already retired employees, annuities are actually purchased for the retired workers.

The IPG contract also specifies a schedule of guaranteed annuity gross premium rates. However, since annuities are not actually purchased at retirement date, these guaranteed annuity rates are only of significance if the plan or contract is terminated.

---

[4]This type of contract is also referred to as a pension administration contract.

All the aspects of flexibility in contribution timing and plan design discussed under deposit administration plans are equally applicable to IPG contracts. The further reduction in insurer guarantees and the immediate reflection of actual experience under the plan bring the IPG contracts one step closer to trust fund arrangements.

Some insurance companies have developed a contract that possesses characteristics of both deposit administration and IPG contracts; it is usually referred to as a modified immediate participation guarantee contract or a direct-rated deposit administration contract. The major characteristic of this latter contract is that the unallocated account is maintained on an immediate participation basis, but single-premium immediate annuities are actually purchased for each participant on retirement.

Equity funding and variable annuity benefits generally are available under IPG contracts. The features of equity funding are basically similar to those discussed under deposit administration contracts.

There is another variation on the immediate participation guarantee concept that became prevalent in the late 70s and early 80s. There is no generic name for this product variation, as insurers increasingly moved to a brand name for this product concept. Essentially the insurer provides a one-year guarantee to the policyholder based on expectations of what the new money concept will generate for investment returns in the forthcoming year, rather than providing direct experience of the investment year method system in arrears. The policyholder receives a new one-year interest guarantee each year. Usually there are also more liberal contract features than in an immediate participation guarantee contract.

21.6. ANNUITY SEPARATE ACCOUNT

Within the past five years, a fundamentally new type of group annuity contract arrived in the marketplace - the annuity separate account contract which provides for the establishment of fixed-dollar annuity guarantees whose underlying reserves are invested, not in the insurer's general account, but in one or more of the insurer's market valued separate accounts.

Annuity separate account contracts have been written primarily on the deposit administration pattern, with unallocated funds and annuities at retirement, but have also been enlisted for single-premium annuitization with both immediate and deferred annuities.

Although the participation aspect of an annuity separate account contract is highly comparable to the IPG with regard to mortality experience, and to separate account unit valuation as to investment results, it is unique in combining the two in a way that for the first time allows plan sponsors to direct the investment of assets supporting their already annuitized pensions.

21.7.   SINGLE-PURCHASE ANNUITY CONTRACTS

Group single-premium annuity contracts have been designed to provide annuities for participants in an uninsured pension or profit sharing plan that has terminated.[5]

In addition, the high level of interest rates, increasing government regulations of defined benefit pension plans, and financial accounting standards have contributed to the termination of defined benefit pension plans in favor of defined contribution plans. In recent years, the accelerating pace of corporate mergers and takeovers has led to considerable interest in single-purchase group annuity arrangements. Apparently, there is sometimes concern among the officers of the corporation being absorbed that pension assets will be used by the new management for subsequent acquisitions or the rate of funding will be reduced to a point at which the security of their pension benefits will be impaired, though this should not be as much of a problem since the enactment of ERISA. If annuities are purchased, the funds are unavailable to the new management and the purchased annuity benefits are guaranteed by the insurance company.

During the late 1980s in particular, before the enactment of stronger federal constraints on plan asset reversions to employers, single-premium contracts were used as the vehicle for meeting federal prerequisites. An employer terminating a pension plan in order to recover excess funding was required to purchase annuity guarantees for all the given plan's accrued-but-uninsured benefits as a pre-condition of such reversion.

Under a single-purchase contract, immediate annuities are provided for present pensioners and deferred annuities for those who are below retirement age. This type of contract almost always is nonparticipating. Since single-purchase situations invariably involve substantial sums of money, a great deal of competition exists among insurers for this type of business. These contracts are generally available for single purchases of $50,000 or more.

This type of contract also may be used by plans that have not terminated but wish to purchase annuities for a block of retired persons to take advantage of favorable rate guarantees and possibly favorable corporate balance sheet affects.

---

[5]For a detailed discussion of what happens when a pension plan terminates, see Chapter 17.

21.8.   FULLY INSURED PLAN

Under individual policy plans, the cash value under the contract as of the retirement date of the employee can be used as the single-premium sum needed to provide the annuity benefit. Thus, in theory, any permanent life insurance or any annuity contract can be used to fund a pension benefit. However, under a fully insured plan, the policy cash values at retirement must be sufficient to provide the full benefit, since no other source of funds is contemplated under the plan. To generate sufficient cash values under ordinary life policies, the face amount of the policy must be considerably in excess of 100 times the monthly retirement benefit or more than the requirement in a defined contribution plan that no more than 50 percent of the premium be used for life insurance -- the maximum permitted under qualified plans. Thus, retirement income or retirement annuity contracts typically were used, since they were designed specifically by insurers to provide the proper ratio of insurance to income and to generate the cash values needed to provide a specified monthly income as of a given retirement age. Some insurers offer a variation of the conventional fully insured plans by funding pension benefits with ordinary life insurance and a fixed dollar or guaranteed annuity. The cash value of the whole life policy together with the annuity provides the retirement benefit. The preretirement benefit consists of the face amount of the whole life policy plus the death benefit under the annuity (greater of cash value or total premiums paid).

The retirement annuity contract is an individual deferred annuity contract and is expressed in units of a $10-a-month annuity benefit payable beginning at a specified age, usually the normal retirement age under the plan. The retirement income policy is expressed in terms of $1,000 of face value of life insurance for each $10-a-month annuity benefit on some stipulated annuity form.

Many insurance companies in the pension market issue a variation of the retirement annuity frequently referred to as a flexible purchase payment annuity. Although the contract provides for a schedule of payments, it is flexible; that is, payments can be decreased, increased, or skipped as circumstances may require as long as the amount of any purchase payment made is at least some minimum such as $15. The right to suspend or resume contributions at any time is commonly referred to as a "stop and go" feature. At retirement, the termination value of the contract may be taken as a lump-sum cash payment or it can be converted to a guaranteed income for the life of the annuitant plus the life of his or her spouse, if desired, at rates currently guaranteed in the contract. If the participant dies before retirement, the beneficiary receives an amount equal to the total purchase payments made or the guaranteed termination value of the contract, whichever is greater. As discussed in Chapter 6, if a participant dies before the annuity starting date and has a surviving spouse, the automatic benefit must be in the form of a qualified preretirement survivor (QPS) annuity to the surviving spouse. Because of the flexibilities inherent in this type of contract, it has largely replaced the more traditional retirement income and retirement annuity contracts for the funding of smaller defined contribution pension plans.

Individual policy plans require that separate contracts be issued on the life of every covered employee. In many cases, a trust agreement is executed between the employer and the trustee, and the trustee serves as custodian of the individual contracts. The trustee normally applies for the insurance or annuity contracts and pays the premiums due. The insured employee, of course, must sign the application for the contract. Legal ownership of the contracts is vested in the trustee, either through the use of an ownership clause or by attachment of an appropriate rider to each of the contracts. Generally, the use of a trustee is required under the Internal Revenue Code. There are exceptions if a nontransferable retirement income, annuity, or a life insurance contract that provides incidental life insurance is used. These requirements are imposed to preclude the possibility of the employer recovering funds that must be irrevocably committed to the plan.

The use of a trustee under individual policy plans has resulted in the use of the term pension trust to describe these plans. This terminology is unfortunate, since plans employing funding instruments other than individual policies quite often use a trust agreement. In the case of a noninsured plan, for example, a trust agreement is a necessary condition for qualification of the plan. Thus, the term pension trust should not be used unless the plan has a trustee. Indeed, it would probably be best if the term disappeared entirely from pension terminology.

21.9.   COMBINATION PLANS

21.9.1. General Characteristics

The term combination plan can be used to describe any funding arrangement that employs two or more different funding instruments. However, the term is generally used in practice to describe those plans that use a combination of individual contracts and an unallocated conversion fund. The conversion fund is also sometimes referred to as the auxiliary fund or the side fund. The objective of the combination plan is to retain, in part, the guarantees and life insurance benefits associated with individual contracts, while at the same time obtaining a degree of the flexibility inherent in unallocated funding instruments.

The mechanics of the plan involve the purchase of a whole life insurance contract (or its equivalent) on the life of each participant, frequently with a face amount usually equal to 100 times the monthly expected pension benefit. Although almost any type of cash value policy can be used (including some of the newer forms such as universal life policies that provide interest-sensitive investment returns), the general practice is to purchase ordinary life contracts. Some insurance companies use an endowment-type contract that provides a relatively small fixed cash value as of age 65 regardless of the issue date of the contract; for example, $400 per $1,000 of face value. Standardization of the amount of cash value available at retirement simplifies the calculation of the amounts required in the conversion fund. Ordinary life contracts or endowment contracts generate the lowest scale of cash values of the various whole life and endowment contracts, and therefore a significant portion of the funding may be provided through the conversion fund. Thus, ordinary life contracts are favored since the flexibility inherent in the conversion fund often is a prime factor in the employer's decision to use a combination plan. On the average, the cash values of the ordinary life contract will equal about 35 percent of the net single-premium sum required at normal retirement age to provide the monthly pension benefit, the remaining 65 percent being provided out of the conversion fund. The exact proportion of the cash value to the principal sum required at retirement will, of course, vary somewhat with the age at issue, the individual insurance company employed, and the length of time that the contract is in force as of the retirement date, unless endowment-type contracts are used.

The combination plan may require the use of a trustee. If the conversion fund is administered by a corporate trustee, the latter party normally also serves as the trustee to own the ordinary life insurance contracts. The conversion fund often is held and administered by the life insurance company that issues the insurance contracts. In this case, the trustee is generally an individual -- often one of the officers of the firm. Only one trust agreement is required, regardless of whether the conversion fund is administered by a corporate trustee or an insurance company.

Evidence of insurability may be required for the insurance contracts issued under a combination plan. However, most insurers are willing to issue these contracts up to some limit on a guaranteed issue basis, subject to certain underwriting restrictions.

21.9.2. Contributions

The periodic contributions required under a combination plan are composed of premium payments for the life insurance contracts and contributions to the conversion fund. The premium rates for purchased ordinary contracts are guaranteed and level in amount, subject to reduction through dividends. Of course, if an employee's benefits are increased, additional amounts of life insurance will have to be purchased at the rates in effect at the time the contract is actually purchased. In addition to the guarantee of premium rates, the issued contracts also carry an insurer guarantee of the annuity rates applicable at the employee's retirement date. The guaranteed annuity rates apply to the sums withdrawn at the retirement date from the conversion fund, as well as to the cash values accumulated under the life insurance contract as of that date. The extent of the annuity rate guarantee applicable to the moneys from the conversion fund normally is expressed as some multiple of the face amount of insurance; for example, at the rate of $10 to $30 of monthly income for each $1,000 of face amount. Some insurers impose a conversion charge, usually expressed as a percentage of the difference between the principal sum required at retirement age to provide the pension and the cash value of the policy as of that date. This charge is generally 2 or 2.5 percent, although a higher effective percentage may be imposed where the insurance benefit is less than 100 times the monthly benefit. The higher charge is required in the latter cases to offset the reduced amount of loading available to the insurer because of the relatively lower amounts of insurance.

If the conversion fund is held by an insurance company in a fixed dollar account, the insurer guarantees that the fund will be credited with a minimum rate of interest and that there will be no capital depreciation. In addition, most insurers pay interest in excess of the guaranteed rate, as conditions permit. The conversion fund can be administered by a trustee, if the employer desires, in which case there is no guarantee of principal or interest.

The amount of annual contribution to the conversion fund depends on the actuarial assumptions and the actuarial cost method used. Since the assets in the conversion fund are not allocated to specific employees, the employer can discount in advance for expected mortality and turnover. In practice, a mortality assumption frequently is used, but seldom is there a discount for turnover. Some flexibility also exists in its choice of a reasonable interest assumption for the conversion fund. Thus, different estimates of the amount of contribution required for the conversion fund can be generated depending upon the choice of assumptions. It should be noted however that the enrolled actuary has final control for the assumptions used to determine the amount of the conversion fund contribution.

Some flexibility also exists in the choice of an actuarial cost method to be used in calculating contribution requirements under a combination plan as long as the minimum funding standards are met. For example, an individual level cost method with supplemental liability can be used. As discussed in Chapter 16, this method generates a low annual normal cost. Employers are free to fund the supplemental liability as they see fit, subject to the limitations imposed by the Internal Revenue Code. During periods of financial difficulty, the employer may reduce contributions to the conversion fund, again within the limitations imposed by the Internal Revenue Code. Thus, the combination plan provides considerably greater flexibility as to the timing of contribution payments than is available under a fully insured plan. Furthermore, the employer has a great deal of investment flexibility with reference to the conversion fund. If the fund is administered by a trustee, the assets can be fully invested in common stocks, if such an investment policy is desired. Of course, investments must be made in accordance with the prudent expert rule established in the law. Also, in the past several years, most major life insurance companies have developed many different types of investment products in which conversion fund assets can be invested.

However, since contributions to the conversion fund do not constitute premiums as such, responsibility for the adequacy of the fund rests with the employer. If the actuarial assumptions prove to be erroneous, the assets in the conversion fund may not be adequate to provide the promised benefits. Also, it must be remembered that the choice of actuarial cost method has little effect on the ultimate cost of the plan. Lower contributions in the early years must be offset by a higher level of contribution payments in future years. Nevertheless, the flexibility in the timing of contribution payments under combination plans is offered as an important advantage of this funding arrangement over fully insured individual policy plans.

The calculation of the amounts of required periodic contributions for the conversion fund generally is performed by the insurance company, although some companies provide this service only if they hold the conversion fund. If the employer desires, a consulting actuary can be retained to perform this service. In any event, the actuarial valuation must be performed by an enrolled actuary who has the professional, educational, and experience qualifications required by law.

QUESTIONS FOR REVIEW

1. Explain why many cash value life insurance policies cannot be used by themselves to fund pension benefits.
2. Distinguish between retirement income and retirement annuity contracts.
3. What are the advantages of using a combination plan?
4. Why are ordinary life contracts favored for use with combination plans?
5. How is the annual contribution to the conversion fund in a combination plan determined?
6. Compare deposit administration contracts with group deferred annuity contracts with respect to the allocation of employer contributions.
7. What flexibility does an employer have with respect to annual contributions under a deposit administration plan?
8. Contrast the deposit administration contract with a group immediate participation guarantee (IPG) contract with respect to insurance company guarantees.

QUESTIONS FOR DISCUSSION

1. Discuss how an employer would decide between an insured funding arrangement and a self-insured, or trust fund, arrangement.
2. Discuss how an employer would decide among the various alternative insured funding arrangements.
3. Discuss how an insurance company would price the various guarantees it offers employers through its contracts.

22. Employers' Accounting for Pensions

Accounting procedures for pension plans consist of three components, each of which is controlled by a separate Financial Accounting Standards Board (FASB) Statement. FASB Statement No. 35, *Accounting and Reporting by Defined Benefit Pension Plans* (FASB 35), establishes standards for financial accounting and reporting for the annual financial statement of a defined benefit pension plan. FASB Statement No. 87, *Employers' Accounting for Pensions* (FASB 87), establishes standards for financial reporting and accounting for an employer that offers pension benefits to its employees.[1] Closely related to FASB 87, FASB Statement No. 88, *Employers' Accounting for Settlements and Curtailment of Defined Benefit Pension Plans and for Termination Benefits* (FASB 88), establishes standards for an employer's accounting for settlement of defined benefit pension obligations, for curtailment of a defined benefit pension plan, and for termination benefits.

This chapter focuses primarily on the consequences of sponsoring a single-employer pension plan on the employer's financial statements. Therefore, the major emphasis is on FASB 87[2] and 88. A brief discussion of the evolution of pension accounting standards is presented first, and then

---

[1] In FASB parlance, pension benefits are defined as periodic (usually monthly) payments made pursuant to the terms of the pension plan to a person who has retired from employment or to that person's beneficiary.

[2] Although they are beyond the scope of this chapter, FASB 87 also contains provisions treating multiemployer plans, non-U.S. pension plans, and business combinations.

the FASB statements are described in detail and their impact on pension plan sponsors is analyzed.

22.1.   THE EVOLUTION OF PENSION ACCOUNTING STANDARDS

Although various accounting conventions were applied to pension plans prior to 1966,[3] this was an era in which the accounting profession exercised little control over pension accounting while the government exercised considerable control over pension funding. As a result, pension accounting during this time has been characterized as essentially a discretionary system that typically resulted in the amount of pension expense recorded for a year being equal to the employer's pension contribution.

Since 1966, employer pension accounting has been governed by Accounting Principles Board Opinion No. 8, *Accounting for the Cost of Pension Plans* (APB 8). This pronouncement eliminated the previous discretionary method of accounting for pension costs and replaced it with a methodology that established a range of minimum and maximum annual costs based on a number of approved actuarial cost methods. For a variety of reasons, however, the appropriateness of this standard has been questioned since the passage of ERISA in 1974. In that year, the FASB added two pension projects to its agenda: one to cover accounting principles for the pension plan itself and another to cover accounting by employers for pensions.

As a result of these projects, FASB 35 and FASB Statement No. 36, *Disclosure of Pension Information* (FASB 36), were issued in 1980. FASB 35 established rules governing the measurement and reporting of plan assets and plan obligations by the plan itself. Under this pronouncement, plan assets must typically be measured at market value, while plan liabilities (both vested and nonvested) must be measured on a basis that ignores future salary progression. FASB 36, which established rules governing how the employing firm must disclose plan assets and liabilities on its financial statements, required a measurement procedure compatible with FASB 35. Although FASB 36 was heralded by some financial analysts as a significant improvement in disclosure, it was intended to serve only as a stopgap measure until the more contentious issues raised in response to the perceived limitations for APB 8 could be resolved.

---

[3]For an interesting historical analysis of the evolving relationship between the employer contributions and the charge for pension expense, see E. L. Hicks and C. L. Trowbridge, *Employer Accounting for Pensions: An Analysis of the Financial Accounting Standards Board's Preliminary Views and Exposure Draft* (Homewood, Ill.: Richard D. Irwin for the Pension Research Council, 1985), pp. 16-18.

22.2.   FASB 87

Even with the modifications imposed by FASB 36, the APB 8 approach to pension accounting was criticized for the following reasons:

1.   Pension costs were not comparable from one company to another.
2.   Pension costs were not consistent from period to period for the same company.
3.   Significant pension obligations and assets were not recognized in the body of the financial statements (although FASB 36 did require footnote disclosure in the balance sheet).

The Board had four basic objectives in the preparation of FASB 87. The first objective was to provide a measure of pension cost that better reflects the terms of the plan and recognizes the cost of the employee's pension over his or her service with the employer. As shown in Chapter 16, many of the actuarial cost methods chosen for funding purposes allocate pension contributions as a percentage of payroll. Of the actuarial cost methods acceptable for minimum funding purposes, only the accrued benefit cost method determines an amount that is based directly upon benefits accrued to the valuation date. Second, the Board wanted to provide a more comparable measure of pension cost. Not only were pension plan sponsors able to choose from a number of acceptable actuarial cost methods, but, prior to 1987, they were also given a degree of flexibility in choosing the amortization period for supplemental liabilities (in essence, anywhere from 10 to 30 years). Third, they desired to have disclosures that would allow users to understand the effect of the employer's undertaking. Previous pension accounting standards allowed the sponsor to record one net amount for the pension expense. It was believed that disclosure of the individual components of this amount would significantly assist users in understanding the economic events that have occurred. In theory, those disclosures also would make it easier to understand why the reported amount changed from period to period, especially when a large cost is offset by a large revenue to produce a relatively small net reported amount. Finally, as mentioned above, there was a desire to improve reporting of financial position. This relates primarily to the inclusion of underfunded pension liabilities on the balance sheet of the sponsor.

The new accounting requirements mandated by FASB 87 was phased in with a two-step process. The income statement (expense) provisions must be applied for years beginning after December 15, 1986, while the balance sheet (liability) provisions must be applied for years beginning after December 15, 1988.

22.2.1. Scope

FASB 87 definitely excludes postretirement health care and life insurance benefits. Although these benefits were originally part of the Board's project on accounting for pension benefits, it has since been spun off into a separate endeavor and is currently controlled by FASB Statement No. 106, "Employers' Accounting for Postretirement Benefits Other Than Pensions"

22.2.2. Use of Reasonable Approximations

FASB 87 is intended to specify accounting objectives and results, rather than specific computational means of obtaining those results. Pension plan sponsors are allowed to use shortcuts if they will not result in material differences from the results of a detailed application.

22.2.3. Single-Employer Defined Benefit Pension Plans

The most significant elements of FASB 87 involve an employer's accounting for a single-employer defined benefit pension plan. After describing the basic elements of pension accounting, this section first explains the recognition procedures for the net periodic pension cost and then for the pension liabilities and assets. Certain details concerning measurement procedures are demonstrated and the new disclosure requirements are presented. Finally, certain miscellaneous provisions are presented.

22.2.3.1.   Basic Elements of Pension Accounting

It is important to note that FASB 87 does not apply to the government constraints on minimum or maximum (deductible) funding. Although the accrued benefit cost method (or projected unit credit method in FASB parlance) mandated for use in computing the net periodic pension cost is one of the acceptable actuarial cost methods under the Internal Revenue Code Section 412, it is highly likely that the FASB 87 net periodic pension cost will differ substantially from the ERISA minimum funding amount. Furthermore, it is important to understand that FASB 87 incorporates two different definitions of the sponsor's pension liability. The *projected benefit obligation* is the amount used to measure pension cost and is defined as the actuarial present value of all benefits attributed by the plan's benefit formula to employee service rendered prior to that date, assuming future salary levels if the formula is based on future compensation.[4] In contrast, the *accumulated benefit obligation* is used for balance sheet recognition. It is determined in the same manner as the projected benefit obligation but without salary assumptions. Therefore, for those plans with nonpay-related pension benefit formulas, the projected benefit obligation and the accumulated benefit obligation are the same.

22.2.3.2.   Recognition of Net Periodic Pension Cost

Under FASB 87, the net periodic pension cost is made up of six components:

1. Service cost.
2. Interest cost.
3. Actual return on plan assets, if any.
4. Amortization of unrecognized prior service cost, if any.
5. Gain or loss to the extent recognized.
6. Amortization of the unrecognized net asset or obligation existing at the date of the initial application of FASB 87.

Service cost is the actuarial present value of benefits attributed by the pension benefit formula to employee service during that period.[5] Interest cost is the increase in the projected benefit obligation due to the passage of time. This can be thought of simply as the accrual of interest on a present value or discounted amount. The actual return on plan assets is based on the fair value of plan assets at the beginning and the end of the period, adjusted for contributions and benefit payments.[6]

The prior service cost component for accounting purposes is conceptually similar to the amortization of supplemental liability described in Chapter 16; however the allocation procedure does not result in a level dollar amount assigned to each year in the amortization period. Under FASB 87, the cost of retroactive benefits is the increase in the projected benefit obligation at the date of the amendment. This cost is then amortized by assigning an equal amount to each future period of service of each employee active at the date of the amendment who is expected to

---

[4]Turnover and mortality also are assumed.

[5]There are obvious similarities between this component of net periodic pension cost under FASB 87 and the normal cost under the accrued benefit cost method described in Chapter 16.

[6]While the return is titled actual for disclosure purposes, FASB 87 states that the difference between the actual and expected return on plan assets must be accounted for as a part of the gain or loss component of pension expense. The net result of this treatment is that the expected return on plan assets is used to calculate pension cost for the period.

receive benefits under the plan. Once determined, the amortization period does not change for that amendment.

The basic notion represented by this new amortization procedure can be illustrated by the following simple example. Assume that a defined benefit pension plan is amended on January 1, 1988, generating an unrecognized prior service cost of $100,000. At that time, the employer has three employees who are expected to receive benefits under the plan. Employee A is expected to leave after one year, employee B after two years, and employee C after three years. The expected years of service in 1988 from this employee population would be equal to three (one year from all three employees), in 1989 there would only be two expected years of service (since employee A would already have left), and in 1990 there would only be one expected year of service. Summing these figures gives an aggregate expected years of future service of six (three from 1988, plus two from 1989, plus one from 1990).

The amortization rate for each year is determined by taking the ratio of expected years of service for that year and dividing it by six (the aggregate expected years of service). The amortization rate for the year is then multiplied by the increase in the projected benefit obligation resulting from the plan amendment to determine the amortization for the year. In this example, the 1988 amortization amount would be $100,000 \times (3 \div 6) = $50,000. The amount in 1989 would be $100,000 \times (2 \div 6) = $33,333; in 1990 the amount would be $100,000 \times (1 \div 6) = $16,667.

In certain cases, the amortization of prior service cost must be accelerated. A history of regular plan amendments may indicate that the period during which the employer expects to realize benefits (through employee goodwill, etc.) for an amendment is shorter than the remaining service period. This is likely to transpire in collective bargaining agreements with flat dollar plans in which the dollar amount is renegotiated upward every several years.[7]

The fifth component of net periodic pension cost (gain or loss) results from changes in either the projected benefit obligation or plan assets. These changes result either from experience different from that assumed or from changes in assumptions. Gains and losses include both realized and unrealized gains and losses. Asset gains and losses are equal to the difference between the actual return on assets during a period and the expected return on assets for that period. The expected return on plan assets is determined from the expected long-term rate of return on plan

---

[7]It is also possible for a plan amendment to decrease the projected benefit obligation. In that case, the reduction must be used to reduce any existing unrecognized prior service cost, and the excess, if any, must be amortized on the same basis as the cost of benefit increases.

assets and the market-related value of plan assets.[8] Amortization of unrecognized net gain or loss is included as a component of net pension cost if, at the beginning of the year, the unrecognized net gain or loss (excluding asset gains and losses not yet reflected in market-related value) exceeds a so-called corridor amount.   This corridor was designed to minimize the volatility in pension expense that would otherwise result from application of the new accounting convention and is defined as 10 percent of the greater of the projected benefit obligation or the market-related value of plan assets. The amortization for the year will be equal to the amount of unrecognized gain or loss in excess of the corridor divided by the average remaining service period of active employees expected to receive benefits under the plan.

In addition to the amortization of the unrecognized net gain or loss from previous periods, the overall gain or loss component of net periodic pension cost also consists of the difference between the actual return on plan assets and the expected return on plan assets.

The final component of net periodic pension cost is the amortization of the unrecognized net asset or obligation existing at the date of initial application of FASB 87. At the time the plan sponsor first applies FASB 87, the projected benefit obligation and the fair market value of plan assets must be determined.[9] The difference between these two amounts is then amortized on a straight line basis over the average remaining service period of employees expected to receive benefits under the plan. There are two exceptions to this general rule, though. First, if the average remaining service period is less than 15 years, the employer may elect to use a 15-year period. Second, if all, or almost all, of a plan's participants are inactive, the employer must use the inactive participant's average remaining life expectancy period instead.

22.2.3.3.   Recognition of Liabilities and Assets

Under FASB 87, a balance sheet entry will be made if there is a discrepancy between net periodic pension cost and employer contributions. Specifically, a liability (unfunded accrued pension cost) is recognized if net periodic pension cost exceeds employer contributions, and an asset (prepaid pension cost) is recognized if net periodic pension cost is less than employer

---

[8]The market-related value of assets must be either fair value or a calculated value that recognizes change in fair value in a systematic and rational manner over not more than five years.

[9]Technically, this amount will be increased by any previously recognized unfunded accrued pension cost and reduced by any previously recognized prepaid pension cost. These terms are defined in the next paragraph.

contributions. Moreover, a balance sheet entry will be made if the firm sponsors an "underfunded" plan. If the accumulated benefit obligation is greater than plan assets, employers must recognize a liability (including unfunded accrued pension cost) equal to the unfunded accumulated benefit obligation. It should be noted, however, that the treatment is not symmetrical: FASB 87 does not permit recognition of a net asset if plan assets are greater than the accumulated benefit obligation.

If an additional liability is recognized, an equal amount is recognized on the balance sheet as an intangible asset, provided that the asset recognized does not exceed the amount of unrecognized prior service cost. In the case where the additional liability is greater than the unrecognized prior service cost, then the excess is reported as a reduction of equity, net of any tax benefits.

22.2.3.4.   Measurement of Cost and Obligations

FASB 87 provides much more guidance than its predecessors with respect to the interest rate assumptions chosen by the plan sponsor. In essence, the interest rate assumption used for funding calculations actually has two separate elements in the pension accounting context. The first is the assumed discount rate, which must reflect the rates at which the pension benefit could be effectively settled. FASB 87 states that it is appropriate to consider rates used to price annuity contracts that could be used to settle the pension obligation (including the rates used by the PBGC to value the liabilities of terminating pension plans). Rates of return on high-quality, fixed income investments currently available and expected to be available during the period to maturity of the pension benefits also may be considered.

The second assumption deals with the expected long-term rate of return on plan assets and is not necessarily equal to the discount rate assumption. FASB 87 states that this assumption must reflect the average rate of earnings expected on the funds invested or to be invested to provide for the benefits included in the projected benefit obligation. This will necessitate an assumption as to the rate of return available for reinvestment as well as for the current assets.

22.2.3.5.   Disclosures

An employer sponsoring a defined benefit pension plan must disclose the following:[10]

1.   A description of the plan including employee groups covered, type of benefit formula, funding policy, type of assets held, significant nonbenefit liabilities, if any, and the nature and effect of significant matters affecting comparability of information for all periods presented.
2.   The amount of net periodic pension cost for the period, showing separately the service cost component, the interest cost component, the actual return on assets for the period, and the net total of other components.
3.   A schedule reconciling the unfunded status of the plan with amounts reported in the employer's statement of financial position, showing separately:
    a.   The fair value of plan assets.
    b.   The projected benefit obligation, identifying the accumulated benefit obligation and the vested benefit obligation.
    c.   The amount of unrecognized prior service cost.
    d.   The amount of unrecognized net gain or loss (including asset gains and losses not yet reflected in market-related value).
    e.   The amount of any remaining unrecognized net obligation or net asset existing at the date of initial application of FASB 87.
    f.   The amount of any additional liability recognized as a result of underfunded accumulated benefit obligation.
4.   The amount of net pension asset or liability recognized in the statement of financial position (the net result of combining (a) through (f).
5.   The weighted-average assumed discount rate and rate of compensation increase (if applicable) used to measure the projected benefit obligation and the weighted-average expected long-term rate of return on plan assets.
6.   If applicable, the amounts and types of securities of the employer and related parties included in plan assets, and the approximate amount of annual benefits of employees and retirees covered by annuity contracts issued by the employer and related parties. Also, if applicable, the alternative amortization methods used to amortize prior service cost and gains or losses and the existence and nature of commitment beyond the written terms of the plan.

---

[10]FASB 87, ¶54.

22.2.3.6.   Employers with Two or More Plans

If an employer sponsors more than one defined benefit pension plan, all provisions of FASB 87 apply to each plan separately. Moreover, unless an employer has a right to use the assets of one plan to pay benefits of another, the excess assets of an overfunded plan cannot offset the additional liability for unfunded accumulated benefit obligations of another plan sponsored by the same company.

22.2.3.7.   Contracts with Insurance Companies

Benefits covered by annuity contracts are excluded from the projected benefit obligation and accumulated benefit obligation. If the benefits are covered by nonparticipating annuity contracts, the cost of the contract determines the service cost component of net periodic pension cost for that period. If participating annuity contracts are used, the excess premium (over that available from a nonparticipating annuity contract) must be recognized as an asset and amortized systematically over the expected dividend period under the contract.

22.2.4. Defined Contribution Plans

Under FASB 87, the net periodic pension cost for the typical defined contribution plan will be the contribution called for in that period. However, if a plan calls for contributions for periods after an individual retires or terminates, the estimated costs must be accrued during the employee's service period. An employer that sponsors one or more defined contribution plans must disclose the following separately from its defined benefit plan disclosures:

1.   A description of the plan(s), including employee groups covered, the basis for determining contributions, and the nature and effect of significant matters affecting comparability of information for all periods presented.
2.   The amount of cost recognized during the period.

22.3.   FASB 88

FASB 88 defines one event (a settlement) that requires immediate recognition of previously unrecognized gains and losses and another event (a curtailment) that requires immediate recognition of previously unrecognized prior service cost. It also changes the method of computing gains or losses recognized on asset reversions and specifies special transition rules for companies that have undergone previous asset reversions. Companies were required to adopt FASB 87 and 88 simultaneously.

22.3.1. Definitions

Before discussing the mechanics behind these new accounting procedures, it is important to note the Board's interpretation of the following terms.

Settlement. A settlement is defined as a transaction that is an irrevocable action, relieves the employer of primary responsibility for a projected benefit obligation, and eliminates significant risks related to the obligation and the assets used to effect the settlement. Examples of settlements include making lump-sum cash payments to plan participants in exchange for their rights to receive specified pension benefits, and purchasing nonparticipating annuity contracts to cover vested benefits. For an example of a transaction that would *not* qualify as a settlement, assume that a sponsor invests in a portfolio of high-quality, fixed income securities with principal and interest payment dates similar to the estimated payment dates of benefits. Note that in this case, the decision can be reversed, and such a strategy does not relieve the employer of primary responsibility for an obligation, nor does it eliminate significant risks related to the obligation.

Annuity Contract. If the substance of a participating annuity contract is such that the employer remains subject to most of the risks and rewards associated with the obligation covered or the assets transferred to the insurance company, the purchase of the contract does not constitute a settlement.

Curtailment. A curtailment is an event that significantly reduces the expected years of future service of present employees or eliminates for a significant number of employees the accrual of defined benefits for some or all of their future services. Examples of a curtailment include the termination of employees' services earlier than expected (e.g., closing a facility) and termination or suspension of a plan so that employees do not earn additional defined benefits for future services.

22.3.2. Accounting for Settlement of the Pension Obligation

The maximum gain or loss in this case is the unrecognized net gain or loss plus any remaining unrecognized net asset existing at the date of initial application of FASB 87.[11] The entire maximum amount is recognized in earnings only if the entire projected benefit obligation is settled. However, if only part of the projected benefit obligation is settled, the employer will recognize in earnings a pro rata portion of the maximum amount equal to the percentage reduction in the projected benefit obligation.

If a participating annuity contract is purchased, the maximum gain is reduced by the cost of the participation right. Also, a provision is included to allow flexibility for employers who annually purchase annuities as a funding vehicle. If the cost of all settlements in a year is less than or equal to the sum of the service cost and interest cost components of net periodic pension cost for the plan for the year, gain or loss recognition is permitted but not required for those settlements. However, the accounting policy adopted must be applied consistently from year to year.

22.3.3. Accounting for a Plan Curtailment

Under FASB 88, the unrecognized prior service cost associated with years of service no longer expected to be rendered as the result of a curtailment is treated as a loss. This includes the cost of retroactive plan amendments and any remaining unrecognized net obligation existing at the date of initial application of FASB 87.

It should be noted that the projected benefit obligation may be decreased or increased by a curtailment. To the extent that such a gain exceeds any unrecognized net loss (or the entire gain, if an unrecognized net gain exists), it is a curtailment gain. To the extent that such a loss exceeds any unrecognized net gain (or the entire loss, if any unrecognized net loss exists), it is a curtailment loss. Any remaining unrecognized net asset existing at the date of initial application of FASB 87 is treated as an unrecognized net gain and is combined with the unrecognized net gain or loss arising subsequent to transition to FASB 87.

22.3.4. Special Transition Rules for a Reversion

Employers that entered into a reversion before the effective date of FASB 88 must recognize a gain as the cumulative effect of a change in accounting principle at the time of initial application of FASB 87. The amount of gain recognized is the lesser of:

---

[11]This will include any net gain or loss first measured at the time of settlement. This may happen if the insurance company uses an interest rate assumption for determining the annuity purchase price that differs from the discount rate assumed by the employer.

1. The unamortized amount related to the asset reversion.
2. Any unrecognized net asset for the plan (or the successor plan) existing at the time of transition.

QUESTIONS FOR REVIEW

1. Describe the accounting conventions used for pension plans prior to FASB 87.
2. What were the limitations of the pre-FASB 87 accounting conventions for pension plans?
3. Explain the scope of FASB 87.
4. Explain the difference between accumulated benefit obligation and projected benefit obligation.
5. Identify the six components of pension expense under FASB 87.
6. Under what circumstances must a pension plan sponsor recognize a pension liability on its balance sheet?
7. What types of interest rate assumptions are required under FASB 87?
8. Describe how contracts with insurance companies are handled under FASB 87.
9. Describe the FASB 88 accounting treatment for settlement of pension obligations.
10. Describe the FASB 88 accounting treatment for plan curtailments.

QUESTIONS FOR DISCUSSION

1. Discuss the likely impact of FASB 87 on funding levels for defined benefit pension plans.
2. Discuss the likely impact of FASB 87 on asset allocation decisions for defined benefit pension plans.
3. Assume an employer has an overfunded defined benefit pension plan and is currently considering the merits of terminating the plan and replacing it with a defined contribution pension plan. Discuss how FASB 88 might influence the employer's decision.

23. Taxation of Distributions

Unquestionably, a major advantage of a qualified pension or profit sharing plan is that an employer's contributions, although currently deductible, will not be considered as taxable income to an employee until they are distributed. Moreover, when a distribution does represent taxable income to the employee or a beneficiary, it may be received under favorable tax circumstances.

Broadly speaking, distributions from a qualified plan are taxable in accordance with the annuity rules of Section 72 of the Internal Revenue Code. If a lump-sum distribution is made, however, a special five-year income-averaging device will apply if certain conditions are met.[1] Although these general principles apply regardless of the contingency that gives rise to the distribution, this chapter discusses the tax aspects of a distribution in terms of the contingency that has brought it about. Thus, this chapter briefly explores the tax situation of an employee during employment (including in-service distributions of the employee's account), as well as the tax situation when distributions are made because of the employee's retirement, death, severance of employment, or disability.

With a view toward achieving some degree of simplicity, the discussion has been confined to the federal taxation of typical forms of distribution under plans that have a qualified status when the distributions are made. In certain instances, penalty taxes are imposed *in addition to federal income taxes* on distributions that:

---

[1] A special transitional rule applies to individuals who reached age 50 before January 1, 1986. Such an employee may elect 10-year averaging under pre-1986 tax rates. This issue will be discussed later in this chapter.

- exceed certain amounts,
- commence too early, or
- commence too late.

The last three sections of this chapter provide a discussion of these penalty taxes.

For a complete treatment of the taxation of distributions from a qualified retirement plan, the discussion of tax-free rollovers to an individual retirement account or another qualified retirement plan in Chapter 24 should be consulted. In addition, Chapter 9 discusses the requirements that must be met to prevent a loan from a qualified pension plan to be treated as a taxable distribution.

23.1.   TAXATION DURING EMPLOYMENT

Even though employer contributions may be vested fully in an employee under a qualified plan, the employee will not have to report these contributions as taxable income until such time as they are distributed. Thus, employer contributions made on behalf of an employee generally will not be considered as taxable income to the employee during the period of employment.

If the plan includes a life insurance benefit for employees, however, the employee is considered to have received a distribution each year equal to the portion of the employer's contribution (or the portion of the trust earnings) that has been applied during such year to provide the pure insurance in force on the employee's life.[2] The pure insurance is considered to be the excess, if any, of the face amount of the employee's life insurance contract over its cash value. The amount that the employee must include as taxable income for each year is the one-year term insurance rate for the employee's attained age multiplied by the amount of pure insurance involved. This insurance cost often is called the PS 58 cost because the original Treasury Department ruling on the subject was so numbered.

Since the term insurance rate increases each year with the employee's increasing age, this factor tends to increase the amount the employee has to include as taxable income each year. An offsetting factor, however, is the increasing cash value of the contract, which reduces the amount of pure insurance in effect each year. For plans that employ some form of whole life

---

[2]Note that the amount applied during any year to provide life insurance often covers a period extending into the following year. The employee, however, will not be permitted to apportion this insurance cost between the two years and will be required to include this amount as taxable income in the year in which it is applied, even though the period of protection extends into the subsequent year.

insurance or its equivalent, the insurance cost will tend to rise each year, the reduction in the amount of pure insurance being insufficient to offset the increase in the term insurance rate caused by the employee's advancing age. If the plan is funded with retirement income contracts, the yearly increase in cash value is more substantial and, ultimately, the cash value will exceed the face amount of the contract. Under this type of contract, the insurance cost (after the first few years) will tend to decrease and will ultimately disappear.

Normally, the term insurance rates employed to determine the cost of the employee's insurance coverage are the rates contained in PS 58 (reissued as Revenue Ruling 55-747, as amplified by Revenue Ruling 66-1105). However, the insurer's own rates may be used if they are lower than the rates set forth in these rulings. If an employee is insurable only on an extra premium basis and the employer contributes the extra premium necessary to obtain full coverage (and follows the same practice for all employees in similar circumstances), the employee's insurance cost will be determined on the basis of the standard rates, and the extra premium paid because of the rating need not be taken into account.[3]

If employees are making contributions, the plan may provide that an employee's contribution will first be applied toward the cost of insurance coverage. This provision makes it possible to reduce or eliminate having any portion of the employer's contribution considered as taxable income to the employee during employment.

If the death benefit being provided is outside the qualified plan by a nondiscriminatory group term life insurance contract issued to the employer rather than to the trustee of the pension trust, the employee is not required to consider any part of the premium paid by the employer as taxable income, except to the extent that the employee's coverage exceeds $50,000. However, if the trustee of a qualified trust purchases the group term life insurance instead of the employer, the value of the insurance attributable to employer contributions will be considered as taxable income to the covered employees, regardless of the amounts of coverage involved.

23.2.   DETERMINATION OF COST BASIS

Before discussing the taxation of benefits, it is important to have a clear idea of the elements that constitute an employee's cost basis (or "investment in

---

[3] If the contract is issued on a graded or graduated death benefit basis, that is, a standard premium is paid but there is a reduction in the amount of insurance due to the extra mortality risk involved, the employee's insurance cost will be lower since less insurance protection is being provided.

the contract"), if any, since the employee's cost basis is an important factor in the taxation of distributions under the plan.

Briefly, Section 72 of the Internal Revenue Code provides that an employee's cost basis includes:

1.   The aggregate of any amounts the employee contributed while employed.
2.   The aggregate of the prior insurance costs the employee has reported *on that policy* as taxable income.   (If the employee has made contributions and the plan provides that employee contributions will first be used to pay any cost of insurance, the employee's reportable income for any year is the excess, if any, of the insurance cost of protection over the amount of the employee's contribution for the year, and not the full cost of insurance protection.)
3.   Other contributions made by the employer that already have been taxed to the employee. An example could be where the employer has maintained a nonqualified plan that was later qualified.
4.   Loans from the qualified retirement plan to the participant that were treated as taxable distributions.

There also is provision for the inclusion of other items in an employee's cost basis, such as contributions made by the employer after 1950 but before 1963 while the employee was a resident of a foreign country. For the most part, however, the items listed above will constitute an employee's cost basis in the typical situation.

23.3.   TAXATION OF IN-SERVICE DISTRIBUTIONS

When an employee receives an in-service cash distribution of the entire value of his or her account, the amount of the distribution that exceeds the employee's cost basis will be taxable in the year of distribution as ordinary income. In addition, it may be subject to the early and excess distribution taxes discussed later in this chapter. A distribution that occurs after age 59½ may be eligible for special averaging treatment if it meets the requirements for a qualifying lump sum distribution, as discussed in the next section.

If the in-service distribution represents only a part of the employee's account, it will still be taxed as ordinary income, with a pro rata tax-free recovery of the employee's cost basis. The amount of the distribution that is considered a recovery of cost basis is determined by multiplying the distribution amount by a fraction. The numerator is the employee's total costs basis; the denominator is the present value of the employee's vested account balance. If the value of the employee's total vested account balance is $100,000 and the corresponding cost basis is $30,000, the fraction is 3/10. If the employee's partial distribution is $10,000, 3/10 of this amount or $3,000 would be considered as a tax-free recovery of cost basis; $7,000 would be taxed as ordinary income. It should be noted that this result occurs no matter how the plan *describes* the withdrawal. Thus, even though the plan permits only a withdrawal of after-tax employee contributions, and an employee perceives that only his own money is being returned, the distribution will be taxed in this manner.

The Tax Reform Act of 1986 provided some relief for defined contribution (and some defined benefit plans[4]) by permitting them to categorize the portion of the employee's account balance attributable to after-tax contributions as a *separate account* for purposes of the basis recovery rules.[5] In effect, this permits employers to make distributions only from the account or separate contract that consists solely of after-tax employee contributions plus earnings. Thus, while the pro rata distribution rule still applies, calculations are based on the ratio of after-tax employee contributions to the value of the separate contract that consists of these contributions and earnings thereon. To use this approach, the plan must maintain adequate separate accounts by keeping separate records of after-tax contributions and earnings and by allocating earnings, gains, losses and other credits between the separate account and other portions of the plan on a reasonable and consistent basis.[6]

23.4.   TAXATION OF RETIREMENT BENEFITS

This section examines the taxation of retirement benefits received in the form of lump-sum distributions as well as distributions in the form of periodic payments.

---

[4]A defined benefit plan is to be treated as a defined contribution plan for this purpose to the extent that a separate account is maintained for employee contributions to which is credited actual earnings and losses. Crediting employee contributions with a specified rate of earnings will not be sufficient to create a separate account. Notice 87-13. Q&A-14. Except for plans permitting unmatched voluntary contributions allocated to a separate account, it is unlikely that most contributory defined benefit plans will satisfy this requirement.

[5]Internal Revenue Code Section 72(d).

[6]For examples of the advantages of this treatment see Labh S. Hira, "Planning for Nonannuity Distributions from Contributory Plans," *TAXES--The Tax Magazine* August 1987, pp. 514-8.

23.4.1. Qualifying Lump-Sum Distributions

A lump-sum distribution is a distribution from a qualified retirement plan of the balance to the credit of an employee made within one taxable year of the recipient. The distribution must be made on account of the employee's death, attainment of age 59½, or separation from service.[7] It should be noted that a distribution to the employee in the form of annuity payments after retirement will not prevent the employee's *beneficiary* from receiving a lump-sum distribution.

23.4.1.1.   Distributions to a Retired Employee

If an employee's benefit is paid from a qualified plan in the form of a lump-sum benefit at retirement, the employee's cost basis will be recovered free of income tax. The excess of the distribution over the employee's cost basis will qualify for favorable tax treatment if the following conditions are met:

1.   The distribution is made after the employee attains age 59½.
2.   The distribution represents the full amount then credited to the employee's account and the entire distribution is received within one of the employee's taxable years.

If these conditions are met, the taxable distribution may qualify for favorable tax treatment. It should be noted, however, that even though a provision exists for the favorable taxation of a lump-sum distribution to an employee who is age 59½ or over, a qualified retirement plan may not make distributions to an employee prior to his or her severance of employment.

An employee who has been a participant for at least five years may elect to treat such a lump-sum distribution under a five-year averaging rule; however, this election can be made only once by the participant. Under this rule, one first determines the *total taxable amount* which is the amount of the distribution that is includable in income, excluding the unrealized appreciation on employer securities (if elected by the employee).[8] The tax on the total taxable amount is determined by taking one fifth of the distribution and calculating the ordinary income tax on this portion using single-taxpayer rates and assuming no other income, exemptions, or

---

[7]The separation of service provision is not available for self-employed individuals. They are able to qualify on the basis of disability however.

[8]If the employee makes this election, the unrealized appreciation will be taxed when the employer securities are sold. Even if such an election is made, however, the net unrealized appreciation will be taken into account for purposes of the excess distribution tax described later in the chapter.

deductions. The actual tax is then determined by multiplying this amount by five. There is a minimum distribution allowance equal to the lesser of $10,000 or 50 percent of the total taxable amount, reduced by 20 percent of the amount by which the total taxable amount exceeds $20,000. If available, the minimum distribution allowance is subtracted from the total taxable distribution before calculating the tax.

A special transition rule exists for individuals who attained age 50 before January 1, 1986. Qualifying lump-sum distributions made to these individuals can continue to utilize the capital gains provisions in effect prior to the Tax Reform Act of 1986 and have the entire pre-1974 portion of the lump-sum distribution taxed as a long-term capital gain with a maximum rate of 20 percent. In addition, five-year averaging can be used on all or on the remaining portion of the lump-sum distributions and can apply to lump-sum distributions received prior to age 59½. An eligible individual making such an election may also elect to choose 10-year (as opposed to 5-year) averaging. If 10-year averaging is chosen, however, the individual must use the tax rates in effect for the 1986 tax year. Not more than one election may be made under these transition provisions with respect to an employee, and five-year averaging is lost for any other distribution.

For purposes of determining whether there has been a qualifying lump-sum distribution, all plans of the same type (e.g., defined benefit or defined contribution) and all plans within a given category (pension, profit sharing, or stock bonus) are aggregated and treated as a single plan. Because only similar types of plans are required to be aggregated for this purpose, it is possible to have a distribution from a profit sharing plan qualify as a lump-sum distribution even though the employee has an interest in a pension plan sponsored by the employer.

The value of any annuity contract distributed (including contracts distributed during the preceding five years), even though this amount is not taxable currently, must be taken into account in determining the marginal tax rate on the amount of the distribution that is being taxed under the five-year averaging rule. Community property laws are disregarded.

23.4.1.2. Distributions to an Alternate Payee

Any alternate payee who is the spouse or former spouse of the participant is treated as the distributee of any distribution or payment made to him or her under a QDRO. For purposes of computing the tax on lump-sum distributions, the balance to the credit of an employee does not include any amount payable under a QDRO.

23.4.2. Distributions in the Form of Periodic Payments

23.4.2.1.   Distributions to a Retired Employee

If a retiring employee receives the distribution in the form of periodic payments, these payments will be taxed to the employee as ordinary income in accordance with the annuity rules of Section 72 of the Internal Revenue Code.

Thus, in a plan where the employee has no cost basis, periodic payments will be subject to tax as ordinary income when received; otherwise the regular annuity rules of Section 72 apply.[9] First, an exclusion ratio is determined for the employee. The exclusion ratio is the ratio of the employee's cost basis (investment in the contract) to the employee's "expected return." The resulting percentage represents the portion of each income payment that is excluded from taxable income.

For example, assume that a male employee retiring at age 65 is entitled to an annual income of $10,000 for life (with no death benefit payable in the event of his death after retirement) and that the employee has a cost basis of $50,000. The first step would be to determine the employee's expected return. This would be done by obtaining his life expectancy under the tables included in the regulations and multiplying this figure by the amount of the annual payment. In this example, the employee's life expectancy under these tables would be 20. Multiplying 20 by the annual payment of $10,000 produces an expected return of $200,000. The next step would be to divide the employee's cost basis ($50,000) by his expected return ($200,000), which yields an exclusion ratio of 25 percent. Consequently, $2,500 of each year's payment (25 percent of $10,000) would be excluded from the employee's taxable income, and the balance of $7,500 would be subject to tax as ordinary income.

The total amount excluded under the exclusion ratio is limited to the investment in the contract. If the annuitant dies before his or her entire basis is recovered, the unrecovered amount may be claimed as a deduction in the annuitant's final taxable year.[10]

---

[9]For annuities whose starting date was before July 1, 1986, the exclusion ratio approach did not apply to any employee annuity under which employee contributions were recoverable within three years of the annuity starting date. Instead, all payments are excluded from taxable income until the payments received equal the employee's cost basis. Thereafter, the payments are taxed as ordinary income when received.

[10]For annuity starting dates before January 1, 1987, the exclusion ratio, once established, will apply to all future payments regardless of the length of time the employee actually lives and receives payments. If the employee lives longer than the average life expectancy assumed in the

If payments are made to the employee for a period certain or with a refund feature, the cost basis will be adjusted, when determining the employee's exclusion ratio, to reflect the value of the refund or period certain feature. In the example described above, if the retirement benefit of $10,000 was payable for life with a guarantee that payments would be made for at least 10 years, it would be necessary to reduce the employee's cost basis of $50,000. Under the tables included in the regulations, the value of the 10-year guarantee for a male, age 65, is 6 percent. Consequently, the $50,000 would be reduced by 6 percent ($3,000) and the employee's adjusted cost basis would be $47,000. His exclusion ratio would then be determined in the regular fashion.

If retirement payments are being made under some form of joint and survivor annuity, the expected return, rather than the cost basis, would be adjusted to reflect the value of the survivorship feature.

23.4.2.2.   Distributions to an Alternate Payee

Any alternate payee who is the spouse or former spouse of the participant is treated as the distributee of any distribution or payment made under a QDRO.[11] Under IRS regulations to be issued, the investment in the contract must be allocated on a pro rata basis between the present value of such distribution or payment and the present value of all other benefits payable with respect to the participant to which the QDRO relates.

23.5.   TAXATION OF DEATH BENEFITS

23.5.1. Lump-Sum Distributions

A lump-sum distribution to the employee's beneficiary from a qualified plan made on account of the employee's death after age 59½ (either before or after severance of employment), will entitle the beneficiary to the favorable tax treatment previously described if the distribution represents the full amount then credited to the employee's account and if it is received within one taxable year of the beneficiary.

---

tables included in the regulations, a portion of each payment will continue to be received free of income tax, even though by that time the employee's cost basis will have been recovered.

[11]For payments prior to October 22, 1986, this treatment also applied to alternate payees other than a spouse or former spouse.

In determining the net amount of gain subject to tax, the beneficiary's cost basis will be the same as the employee's (i.e., the aggregate of the employee's contributions and any amounts, such as insurance costs, on which the employee has previously been taxed) plus, unless otherwise used, the employee death benefit exclusion provided by Section 101(b) of the Internal Revenue Code up to a maximum of $5,000. It should be noted that in the case of a lump-sum distribution that otherwise qualifies for the favorable tax treatment, this exclusion under Section 101(b) applies regardless of whether the employee's rights were forfeitable or nonforfeitable.[12]

If any portion of the distribution consists of life insurance proceeds and the employee either paid the insurance cost or reported this cost as taxable income, the pure insurance, that is, the difference between the face amount of the contract and its cash value, will pass to the beneficiary free of income tax under Section 101(a) of the Internal Revenue Code. The beneficiary will only have to treat the cash value of the contract, plus any other cash distributions from the plan, as income subject to tax.

The following example illustrates how the death benefit under a typical retirement income contract would be taxed if the employee died before retirement and the face amount of the contract were paid to the beneficiary in a lump sum.

Face amount of contract	$25,000
Cash value of contract	11,000
Amount of pure insurance excludable under Section 101(a)	$14,000
Cash value of contract	$11,000
Amount excludable under Section 101(b) (assuming not otherwise utilized)	5,000
Balance subject to income tax	$6,000
Beneficiary's cost basis (aggregate of prior insurance costs which employee reported as taxable income)	940
Balance taxable to beneficiary	$ 5,060

---

[12]Briefly, Section 101(b) permits a beneficiary to exclude from gross income any payments made by the employer of a deceased employee up to a maximum of $5,000. Except as noted, this exclusion is available only to the extent the employee's rights to the amounts were forfeitable immediately prior to death.

The beneficiary would, therefore, receive $19,940 of the total distribution free of income tax, and only $5,060 would be considered as being taxable.

The regulations provide that if the employee did not pay the insurance cost of his or her contract, or did not report the cost of insurance as taxable income, the portion of the insurance proceeds consisting of pure insurance will be considered as taxable income to the beneficiary.

When an employee dies after retirement and after having received periodic payments, a lump-sum death payment to the employee's beneficiary, if it meets the requirements previously noted, will qualify for the favorable tax treatment described. The beneficiary's cost basis, however, will be reduced by any amount that the employee had recovered free from income tax.

23.5.2. Distribution in the Form of Periodic Payments

23.5.2.1.   Death before Retirement

If death occurs before retirement and the plan provides for the distribution of the employee's death benefit over a period of years (including payments based upon the life expectancy of the beneficiary), these payments will be taxed in accordance with the annuity rules of Section 72 of the Internal Revenue Code.

The beneficiary's cost basis will consist of the amount that would have been the employee's cost basis had the employee lived and received the payments, plus, if applicable, the exclusion allowed under Section 101(b) of the Internal Revenue Code up to the maximum of $5,000. While the question of whether the employee's rights were forfeitable is immaterial for the application of Section 101(b) to a lump-sum distribution from a qualified plan on death, the same is not so when the distribution is in the form of periodic payments. Here, the exclusion under Section 101(b) is applicable only to amounts to which the employee's rights were forfeitable immediately prior to death.

If any part of the periodic payments arises from pure life insurance, the proceeds are divided into two parts:

1.   The cash value of the contract immediately before death.
2.   The pure insurance (the excess of the face amount of the contract over its cash value).

That portion of each periodic payment attributable to the cash value of the contract will be taxed to the beneficiary under the annuity rules. The balance of each payment that is attributable to the pure insurance element will be treated as insurance proceeds under Section 101(d) of the Internal Revenue Code.

To illustrate, if the face amount of the employee's contract were $25,000 and the proceeds were paid to the beneficiary in 10 annual payments of $3,000 each, the following would be the manner in which the payments would be taxed to the beneficiary, assuming that the contract had a cash value at death of $11,000, that the employee had forfeitable interests to the extent of $5,000, and that the aggregate of the insurance costs that the employee previously reported as taxable income was $940.

The portion of each annual payment of $3,000 attributable to the cash value is $1,320 (11/25 of $3,000). The beneficiary's cost basis for this portion would be $5,940 (the $5,000 exclusion under Section 101(b) plus the aggregate insurance costs of $940). The expected return under this portion would be $13,200 (the annual payment of $1,320 multiplied by the 10 years of payments). An exclusion ratio would be determined by dividing the cost basis ($5,940) by the expected return ($13,200). This produces an exclusion ratio of 45 percent, which would be applied to the portion of each annual payment attributable to the cash value of the contract. As a result, $594 (45 percent of $1,320) would be excluded from income each year, and the balance of $726 would be taxed to the beneficiary as ordinary income.

The portion of each annual payment of $3,000 attributable to the pure insurance is $1,680 (14/25 of $3,000). Of this amount, $1,400 (1/10 of $14,000) is excludable from gross income as Section 101 proceeds, and only the balance of $280 would be taxable as ordinary income to the beneficiary. A beneficiary of the employee would include $1,006 ($280 plus $726) as ordinary income each year, and $1,994 of each annual payment would be received free of income tax.

23.5.2.2. Death after Retirement

The taxation of payments to the beneficiary of an employee who dies after retirement and after periodic payments have begun depends upon whether the employee had a cost basis (and if so, whether it had been recovered by the employee), as well as upon the method of payment involved. If the employee had no cost basis, each payment would be considered as taxable income to the beneficiary as received. However, where the payments are being continued under a joint and survivor annuity form, the exclusion ratio established when the annuity became effective would apply until the unrecovered investment in the contract is eliminated.[13]

23.5.2.3.   Tax on Excess Accumulations

Because payments to beneficiaries are exempt from the tax on excess distributions described later in this chapter, an equivalent estate tax is imposed on excess retirement accumulations.

23.6.   TAXATION OF SEVERANCE-OF-EMPLOYMENT BENEFITS

For the most part, the discussion in this chapter on the taxation of distributions at retirement is equally applicable to the taxation of distributions on severance of employment. If the distribution is in the form of periodic payments, the taxation of payments to the employee will be governed by the annuity rules after taking the employee's cost basis, if any, into account. So, also, a lump-sum distribution, provided that the necessary conditions are met, may qualify for the favorable tax treatment described. However, a penalty tax on early distributions may apply as explained later in this chapter.

If the distribution is in the form of a life insurance contract, its cash value less the employee's cost basis, if any, will be considered as taxable income in the year in which the employee receives the contract, even though the contract is not then surrendered for its cash value. The distribution may qualify for favorable treatment if all necessary conditions are met. On the other hand, the employee may avoid any current tax liability by transferring this amount, within 60 days, to a qualified individual retirement savings plan (described in Chapter 24). The employee also may avoid any current tax liability by making an irrevocable election, within 60 days of the distribution, to convert the contract to a nontransferable annuity that contains no element of life insurance.[14] If the employee would otherwise receive a cash

---

[13]This assumes an annuity starting date after December 31, 1986; otherwise, the tax treatment described in footnote 6 would be operative.

[14]The regulations spell out what is meant by nontransferable, and the language of the regulations has been used as a guide by many insurers in endorsing their contracts. Such an endorsement might read approximately as follows:

> This contract is not transferable except to the ABC Insurance Company. It may not be sold, assigned, discounted, or pledged as collateral for a loan or as security for the performance of an obligation or for any other purposes to any person other than this Company; provided, however, that notwithstanding the foregoing, the owner may designate a beneficiary to receive the proceeds payable upon death, and may elect a joint and survivor annuity.

distribution but has the option under the plan of electing, within 60 days, to receive a nontransferable annuity in lieu of the cash payment, he or she may also avoid current tax liability by making a timely exercise of this option.

If current tax liability is avoided by such an election, the employee will not pay any tax until payments are made from the annuity contract. At that time, the payments will be considered as ordinary income under the annuity rules.

If the distribution is in the form of an annuity contract, the tax situation will be governed by the date of issue of the contract. If issued after December 31, 1962, the distribution will be treated exactly the same as the distribution of a life insurance contract unless the annuity is endorsed or rewritten on a nontransferable basis within the 60 days allowed. If issued before January 1, 1963, the employee will not have to include any amount as taxable income until payments are actually received. At that time, payments will be considered as ordinary income under the annuity rules.

23.7.   TAXATION OF DISABILITY BENEFITS

Many qualified pension plans provide for a monthly benefit if an employee becomes totally and permanently disabled. Typically, the benefit is payable for life (subject to the continuance of the disability), but only for a disability that occurs after the employee has attained some minimum age such as 50 or 55, or has completed some minimum period of service such as 10 years. The benefit may or may not be related to the employee's accrued or projected pension. Frequently, the amount of the benefit will be adjusted if disability continues until the employee attains the normal retirement age specified in the plan.

Generally speaking, disability benefits of this type will be taxed to the employee in accordance with the annuity rules of Section 72 of the Internal Revenue Code; however, such disability benefits may qualify for the retirement income tax credit provided for in the Code.[15]

23.8.   TAX ON EXCESS DISTRIBUTIONS

The Tax Reform Act of 1986 imposed a tax equal to 15 percent of the individual's "excess distributions," although the amount of the tax is reduced

---

[15]For tax years beginning after 1983, the tax credit for the elderly is expanded to include individuals under age 65 who are permanently and totally disabled and who retire on a disability and receive disability income from a private or public employer. See Internal Revenue Code Sections 22(b)-(e) for details.

by the amount (if any) of the 10 percent additional tax on early distributions attributable to such excess distributions. The term excess distributions means the aggregate amount of the retirement distributions (including qualified pension plans, individual retirement plans, and tax-deferred annuities) with respect to an individual during a calendar year to the extent such amount exceeds the greater of $150,000 or $112,500 adjusted at the same time and in the same manner as the dollar limitations under Section 415 for defined benefit pension plans. If a distribution qualifies for favorable tax treatment, however, up to five times the normal limit (i.e., up to the greater of $750,000 or $562,500 as indexed) can be paid without imposition of the excise tax.

The following distributions will not be taken into account:

1. Any retirement distribution with respect to an individual made after his or her death.[16]
2. Any retirement distribution with respect to an individual payable to an alternate payee pursuant to a QDRO if includable in income of the alternate payee.
3. Any retirement distribution with respect to an individual that is attributable to the employee's investment in the contract
4. Any retirement distribution to the extent not included in gross income by reason of a rollover contribution (described in Chapter 24).

If, during any calendar year, retirement distributions with respect to any individual are received by the individual and at least one other person, all distributions will be aggregated for purposes of determining the amount of the excess distributions.

The tax will not apply to benefits accrued before August 1, 1986, if the employee elected grandfather protection on tax returns for 1987 or 1988. The election was available only if the accrued benefit as of August 1, 1986, exceeded $562,500.

23.9.   TAX ON EARLY DISTRIBUTIONS

The Tax Reform Act of 1986 added an additional 10 percent tax on any taxable amounts received before age 59½ from a qualified retirement plan. The additional tax does not apply in the case of death, disability, or early

---

[16]However, there is a corresponding estate tax of an individual dying with "excess retirement accumulations." The details for calculating this amount are provided in IRC Section 4981(d).

retirement under plan provisions after age 55. Exceptions are also granted for:

1.   Distributions that are part of a series of substantially equal periodic payments made for the life (or life expectancy) of the employee or the joint lives (or joint life expectancies) of the employee and his or her beneficiary.
2.   Distributions used to pay medical expenses to the extent the expenses exceed 7.5 percent of adjusted gross income.
3.   Certain distributions made before January 1, 1990, from an ESOP.
4.   Payments to alternate payees pursuant to a qualified domestic relations order (QDRO).

23.10. TAX ON LATE DISTRIBUTIONS

Chapter 6 described the requirement that participants must commence benefit payments by April 1 of the calendar year following the calendar year in which they reach age 70½. The penalty for failure to make a required distribution of (at least) the correct amount is a nondeductible excise tax of 50 percent of the difference between the minimum required amount and the actual distribution. This tax is imposed on the payee.

If the participant's benefit is determined from an individual account, the minimum amount that must be paid each year is determined by dividing the account balance[17] by the applicable life expectancy. The applicable life expectancy is the life expectancy of the employee, or the joint life expectancies of the employee and the employee's designated beneficiary, if any. The life expectancy of the employee and/or the employee's spouse can be recalculated annually.[18]

If the participant's benefit is determined by the annuity distribution from a defined benefit plan, the annuity must be paid for one of the following durations:

• the life of the participant
• the lives of the participant and the participant's designated beneficiary
• a period certain not extending beyond the life expectancy of the participant or the joint life expectancy of the participant and the participant's designated beneficiary.

---

[17]Technically this is the account balance as of the plan's last valuation date in the calendar year immediately preceding the calendar year for which the distribution is made.

[18]However, the life expectancy of a beneficiary other than a spouse cannot be recalculated.

QUESTIONS FOR REVIEW

1. What factors are included in determining an employee's cost basis in a pension plan?
2. Under what condition will a lump-sum distribution qualify for favorable tax treatment?
3. What is the five-year averaging rule?
4. How are the pension distributions in the form of periodic payments taxed when the employee has no cost basis in the plan?
5. How will the answer to the previous question change if the employee has a cost basis in the plan?
6. How are death benefits taxed for income tax purposes when paid in the form of a lump-sum distribution?
7. How are death benefits payable in the form of periodic payments taxed for income tax purposes if death takes place before retirement?
8. How will the answer to the previous question change if death takes place after retirement?
9. How are severance-of-employment benefits taxed?
10. Explain the taxation of disability benefits.

QUESTIONS FOR DISCUSSION

1. Discuss how the Tax Reform Act of 1986 changes are likely to influence employees' choices between receiving retirement distributions as a lump sum versus periodic payments.
2. Discuss the likely effect of the new excess distribution excise tax on plan design.
3. Discuss the likely effect of the new early distribution penalty tax on plan design.

PART SIX

Miscellaneous
Considerations

The first five parts of this book have primarily dealt with retirement plans and issues for corporate employees. Part Six focuses on other important issues in retirement planning; namely, plans for the self-employed and individuals not covered by a qualified retirement plan or whose income is below a certain level (Chapter 24), plans for employees of certain nonprofit, educational or religious organizations (Chapter 25), and plans for executives who may have special retirement needs beyond those provided by qualified retirement plans (Chapter 26).

24. Plans For the Self-Employed and Individual Retirement Arrangements

Previous chapters in this book have covered retirement plans for employees of incorporated businesses. The focus in this chapter is on two different groups: (1) self employed individuals and (2) individuals not participating in a qualified retirement plan or those whose income is below a certain level. Tax-favored retirement plans have been provided in the law for those groups; namely, Keogh (HR-10) plans for the self-employed and individual retirement accounts (IRAs) for those not covered by a qualified retirement plan or whose income is below a certain level.

24.1. PLANS FOR THE SELF EMPLOYED

For many years, corporate employees had been able to enjoy the tax benefits of qualified pension and profit sharing plans, while self employed individuals (such as partners and proprietors) were denied these tax benefits even though they were permitted to establish tax-favored plans for their employees. For approximately 11 years, Congress considered a number of different bills in an effort to remove this tax inequity; the culmination of these efforts occurred in 1962 with the passage of the "Self-Employed Individuals Tax Retirement Act," more popularly known as Keogh or H.R. 10.

This law permitted a self-employed individual to establish a qualified pension or profit-sharing plan but with many restrictions and limitations when compared with the choices available to corporate employees. Because of these restrictions and limitations of Keogh plans, many unincorporated businesses incorporated primarily for the tax savings possible under corporate retirement plans. Over the years since 1962, several pieces of legislation liberalized some of the limitations of Keogh plans, and in 1982, the Tax Equity and Fiscal Responsibility Act of 1982 (TEFRA) essentially established a level playing field for the retirement plans of incorporated and unincorporated businesses.

Since most of the provisions of Keogh plans now parallel those of corporate plans and have been discussed previously in detail throughout this book, the remainder of this section of the chapter will concentrate on the few differences that remain.

24.1.1. Plan Provisions

Before discussing Keogh arrangements as they relate to actual plan provisions, it is important to recognize that the law distinguishes between self-employed individuals and owner-employees. While all owner-employees are self-employed individuals, not all self-employed individuals are owner-employees. The distinction is in the amount of proprietary interest held by the individual. An owner-employee is a self-employed individual who owns the entire interest in an unincorporated business (a sole proprietor) or a partner who owns more than 10 percent of the capital or profit interest of the partnership. Thus, a partner owning 10 percent or less of the capital or profit interest of a partnership is not an owner-employee, even though he or she is a self-employed individual. This distinction is important, since some provisions of the law are more restrictive for self-employed individuals who also are owner-employees.

24.1.2. Eligibility

If an owner-employee wishes to establish and participate in a Keogh plan, he or she must cover all full-time employees who are at least 21 years of age and have one year of service with the employer. A two-year waiting period can be used if the plan provides 100 percent vesting after the two-year period.

Keogh plans also may be established for individuals who are self-employed on a part-time basis as long as they have earned income.

In addition, Keogh plans must meet the same nondiscrimination requirements as other qualified plans, for example the top-heavy rules, affiliated service rules and leased employees. These rules (discussed in detail in Chapters 5 and 6) can be especially important for owner-employees under Keogh plans.

24.1.3. Contributions and Benefits

Keogh plans can be established either on a defined benefit or a defined contribution basis. If a defined benefit Keogh plan is used, the same limit applies as for a defined benefit corporate pension plan, that is, the amount necessary to fund the lesser of 100 percent of the participant's highest three consecutive years of earnings or $90,000 (indexed annually for inflation).

For defined contribution Keogh plans, the maximum annual contribution is the lesser of 25 percent of earned income or $30,000. This limit is indexed but will not be effective until the defined benefit limit reaches $120,000. Earned income refers to the individual's net earnings from self employment that takes into account employer contributions to qualified retirement plans including Keogh plans.

For example, assume George Jones is a proprietor with two employees each earning $20,000 per year. Mr. Jones's gross profit for the year is $150,000 and all business expenses, other than Keogh contributions, are $50,000. The Keogh contribution rate is 10 percent. Therefore, the Keogh contribution for each employee would be $2,000. George Jones's Keogh contribution would be determined as follows:

Gross profit	$150,000
Minus business expenses	-$50,000
Net Income	$100,000

The formula for determining George Jones's Keogh contribution is:

$$\frac{\text{Keogh Contribution Rate (Net Income - Other Employee Contributions)}}{1 + \text{Keogh Contribution Rate}}$$

In this case,

$$\frac{.10\ (\$100,000 - \$4,000)}{1.10} = \frac{\$9,600}{1.10} = \$8,727.27$$

Thus, George Jones's Keogh contribution would be $8,727.27.

In summary, the Keogh plan contributions for George Jones's firm would be as follows:

Net income		$100,000.00
Minus Keogh Plan Contributions		
Employee 1	$2,000.00	
Employee 2	$2,000.00	
George Jones	$8,727.27	
Total Keogh Contributions		-$12,727.27
George Jones's Earned Income		$ 87,272.73

24.1.4. Taxation of Distributions

As far as regular employees are concerned, distributions will be taxed in exactly the same fashion as distributions made from a qualified plan established by a corporate employer.[1] Lump-sum distributions to self-employed individuals are not permitted except for disability as defined in the Code. Death benefits will still be included in the self-employed's gross estate for federal estate tax purposes even though paid to a named personal beneficiary.

24.1.5. Retirement and Severance Benefits

Generally speaking, distributions in the form of periodic payments will be taxed as ordinary income in accordance with the annuity rules of Section 72 of the Internal Revenue Code (IRC). The self-employed's cost basis for this purpose will be the sum of the amounts which he or she was not able to deduct.

24.1.6. Death Benefits

If a life insurance benefit is provided by the plan, the beneficiary of a plan participant may consider the pure insurance portion of the benefit (i.e., the excess of the face amount over the cash value of the contract) as income tax-

---

[1]For a complete discussion of this subject, see Chapter 23.

free life insurance proceeds. The cash value of the contract, however, as well as any other form of cash distribution under the plan, is considered taxable income to the beneficiary. The beneficiary's cost basis is the same as the plan participant's cost basis at the time of his or her death. The tax treatment of the distribution is the same as that described for distributions to the plan participant.

24.1.7. Loans

Loans from Keogh plans are generally permitted on the same basis as for qualified retirement plans. However, plan loans are not permitted to self-employed individuals who are owner employees. Owner employees are considered as previously mentioned sole proprietors and partners owning more than 10 percent of either the capital or profit interest in a partnership. Also excluded is any stockholder employee in a Subchapter S corporation.

24.1.8. Rollovers

Tax-free rollovers from a Keogh plan to another Keogh plan, to an employer-sponsored retirement plan, or to an individual retirement arrangement (IRA) are permitted. However, self-employed individuals may not make a rollover from a Keogh plan to a qualified corporate plan.

24.2.   INDIVIDUAL RETIREMENT ARRANGEMENTS

Despite the rapid growth of the private pension system, more than 40 million American workers were not covered by qualified pension or profit sharing plans at the beginning of 1974. Congress, in recognition of this fact, included provisions in ERISA that would enable such individuals to establish their own retirement plans on a tax-deferred basis beginning in 1975. An eligible individual could make tax-deductible contributions (up to prescribed limits) under such a plan, and the investment income earned on the contributions generally would be currently sheltered from income tax. Such contributions and investment income would be taxed as ordinary income as they were received or made available. The law was later extended to provide that if a married individual had a spouse who received no compensation and neither party was an active participant in a qualified plan, a separate individual retirement account could be set up for each individual. With the enactment of the Economic Recovery Tax Act of 1981 (ERTA) and the Tax Equity and Fiscal Responsibility Act of 1982 (TEFRA), IRAs became available to just about everyone; however, the Tax Reform Act of 1986 (TRA '86) reduced the number of taxpayers that are eligible to make IRA contributions on a tax-deductible basis.

Some employers (both incorporated and unincorporated) also are utilizing or sponsoring individual retirement savings plans or simplified employee pension (SEP) plans, discussed in Chapter 13, in lieu of the more traditional qualified plans because, under present law, the requirements that must be met by a qualified pension plan are considerably more complex than the requirements applicable to IRA or SEP accounts.

The material in this section of the chapter discusses eligibility to participate in an individual retirement savings plan, the deductible contribution limits, and how such plans may be funded. Also discussed are requirements relative to distributions and rollover provisions.

24.2.1. Eligibility And Contribution Limits

24.2.1.1. Eligibility

Before an individual is eligible to establish an individual retirement savings plan he or she must have earned income from personal services--investment income does not qualify for such a plan.[2] If an individual and spouse both have compensation or self-employment income during a taxable year, each spouse may establish an individual retirement savings plan. Community property laws do not apply to such plans. If an individual is married and otherwise eligible for an IRA and has a nonworking spouse, two IRAs may be established, but subject to certain limitations to be discussed in the next section.

In any event, an individual will cease to be eligible to make contributions to an individual retirement savings plan on and after the taxable year in which the individual attains age 70½.

24.2.1.2. Amount of Deductible and Nondeductible Contributions

As mentioned previously, TRA '86 disallowed tax-deductible IRA contributions for many taxpayers. A person may still make an IRA

---

[2]All alimony and separate maintenance paid under a divorce or separation instrument and includable in gross income is a compensation substitute for IRA purposes.

contribution each taxable year of $2,000 or 100 percent of income, whichever is less. However, beginning in 1987, if either the taxpayer or his or her spouse is an active participant [3] in an employer-maintained plan for any part of a plan year ending with or within the taxable year, the $2,000 figure is reduced (but not below zero) based on adjusted gross income (AGI), calculated without regard to any IRA contributions, in the following manner:[4]

1. In the case of a taxpayer filing a joint return, the maximum deductible amount is equal to $2,000 -.2 × (AGI - $40,000).
2. In the case of a married individual filing a separate return, the maximum deductible amount is equal to $2,000 - .2 × (AGI).
3. In the case of any other taxpayer, the maximum deductible amount is equal to $2,000 - .2 × (AGI -$25,000).

More specifically, what the above formulas illustrate are the varying situations under which IRA deductions are permitted. For example, an employee covered by an employer's qualified plan may still make a full $2,000 IRA deduction if his or her income is $25,000 or under ($40,000 for married couples filing a joint income tax return). For employed individuals earning $25,000-$35,000 ($40,000-$50,000, for couples filing joint income tax returns) covered by their employers retirement plan IRA contributions will be proportionately reduced and phased out entirely at $35,000 (or $50,000 for joint income tax filers). Note that married filing separate returns are extremely limited in making deductible IRA contributions.

Employees covered by their employers' retirement plan earning over $35,000 ($50,000 for joint filers) are not eligible to make tax deductible IRA contributions.

Whether or not a spouse is an active plan participant is not taken into consideration in the case of a married individual filing a separate return for the taxable year.

Nondeductible contributions also may be made to an IRA if they are designated as such on the taxpayer's return. Although these contributions will be made from after-tax income, they will benefit from tax-sheltered investment income during the time they remain in the IRA. Nondeductible contributions cannot exceed the difference between $2,000 ($2,250 in the case of a spousal IRA, described below) and the deductible contribution made for that year. Taxpayers may elect to treat contributions as

---

[3]The determination of whether an individual is an active participant is made without regard to whether the individual's rights under the plan are nonforfeitable.

[4]No dollar limitation will be reduced below $200 until the limitation is completely phased out.

nondeductible even though they are eligible to make deductible contributions.

If an individual and spouse both have compensation, then each spouse may establish a separate IRA if each is eligible up to the lesser of 100 percent of income or $2,000. An otherwise eligible individual also may set up an IRA for a nonworking spouse or a spouse who elects to be treated as having no compensation for the year for purposes of the IRA maximum deduction amount. Under a spousal IRA plan of this type the spouses must file a joint income tax return, no more than $2,000 can be contributed to the account of either spouse, and the maximum tax deduction (after application of the AGI test described above) is limited to the lesser of 100 percent of earned income, or $2,250. Contributions to spousal accounts are not permitted after the elder spouse reaches age 70½. If the employee-spouse is younger, he or she can continue only his or her own IRA after the other spouse reaches age 70½. Since the deduction is against gross income, it may be taken even though the individual does not itemize deductions. If the individual's employer makes the contribution directly to the plan on behalf of the individual, it must still be reported and taken as a deduction against gross income. This contribution will be subject to FICA (Social Security tax) and FUTA (Federal Unemployment Tax Act) but not to withholding taxes.

The contribution must be made in cash before the due date for the individual's filing of the federal income tax return for the taxable year in which the deduction is claimed. Thus, the contribution of existing property (e.g., an insurance policy) will not be permitted.

Any excess contribution is subject to a nondeductible 6 percent excise tax in addition to current taxation. The excise tax continues to be applied each year until the excess contribution is withdrawn from the IRA. For example, if an individual makes an excess contribution of $100 to an IRA in 1991, an excise tax of $6 is imposed for 1991 and for each year thereafter until the excess contribution is withdrawn.

Because of the restrictions on distributions from an IRA (discussed in a later section of this chapter) the question arises whether the withdrawal of an excess contribution is itself a taxable event. If the excess contribution is withdrawn before the tax return filing date for the year for which the contribution was made, the withdrawn amount is not included in taxable income, and the 10 percent premature distribution tax is not applied.

Any excess contributions not taken as a distribution may be eliminated in later years by contributing less than the maximum allowable deduction in such years. For example, if an individual contributed $2,100 in one year, the situation can be remedied by contributing only $1,900 the following year. If excess contributions are not eliminated through these steps, the excess amounts will be subject to a cumulative 6 percent excise tax each year until they are eliminated.

24.2.2. Funding

An individual may establish an individual retirement savings plan by making contributions to one or more of the following:

1. An individual retirement account.
2. An individual retirement annuity.
3. A U.S. retirement bond (permitted prior to May 1, 1982).

The following material discusses each of these approaches in greater detail, as well as the restrictions of the Internal Revenue Code for prohibited transactions and unrelated business income.

24.2.2.1.   Individual Retirement Account

This type of plan entails the establishment of a trust or a custodial account and is by far the most popular type of IRA account. The trustee or custodian may be a bank, another person, or an organization that demonstrates to the satisfaction of the Internal Revenue Service that the IRA will be administered in accordance with the law.

The only restriction on investments in such an IRA is that the assets cannot be invested in life insurance contracts except for endowment contracts with incidental life insurance features, and ERTA effectively eliminates investments in collectibles such as antiques, works of art, stamps, coins, and the like.[5] Most IRAs are invested in assets such as bank-pooled funds, savings accounts, certificates of deposit, savings and loan association accounts, mutual fund shares, face-amount certificates, and insured credit union accounts. A self-directed IRA retirement arrangement can also be established. Under this approach a corporate trustee is selected and fees charged for the services provided. The individual is free to make the investment decisions, within the constraints outlined below, for his or her IRA.

The key requirements of an individual retirement account are as follows:

---

[5]Under TRA '86, an exception to the prohibition against investments in collectibles is made for investments in legal tender gold and silver coins minted by the United States.

1. The annual contribution must be made in cash and cannot exceed $2,000, or $2,250 if a nonworking spouse is included.
2. The entire value of the account must be nonforfeitable.
3. No part of the funds may be invested in life insurance contracts or collectibles, other than legal tender gold and silver coins minted by the United States.
4. The assets in the account cannot be commingled with any other property (except the assets of other qualified trusts).
5. Distributions must be made in accordance with the restrictions imposed by the law.

The Internal Revenue Service (IRS) has issued prototype trust and custodial agreements (Forms 5305 and 5305A). If these prototypes are used, the plan is considered as automatically approved by the IRS. If the trustee or custodian wishes to utilize its own agreement, it may do this and submit the agreement to the IRS for approval on Form 5306. An individual who utilizes such approved plans does not need to submit his or her individual plan for IRS approval.

24.2.2.2.   Individual Retirement Annuity

Under this type of plan, the individual's contribution is invested through the device of purchasing a flexible premium annuity IRA from a legally licensed life insurance company.

The annuity contract must involve flexible premiums and may be participating or nonparticipating. Also, the annuity may be fixed or variable. The key requirements of a flexible premium annuity plan are as follows:

1. The annual premium cannot be fixed and cannot exceed $2,000, or $2,250 for a spousal IRA.
2. The contract must be nontransferable.
3. The individual's interest in the contract must be nonforfeitable.
4. Dividends must be used before the end of the next year to purchase additional benefits or to reduce future premiums.
5. Distributions must be made in accordance with the restrictions imposed by law.

An insurance company may utilize a prototype plan or use special editions of its standard contracts that contain the specific requirements of the law. By using IRS Form 5306, the insurance company may secure IRS approval of its prototype plan or modified contracts. Any individual who uses such an approved arrangement need not submit his or her individual plan for IRS approval.

24.2.2.3.   Selection of Funding Arrangement

No restrictions exist on the number of individual retirement savings plans an individual may establish; however, the aggregate contributions made to all plans in a given year cannot exceed the allowable contribution limits. Also, as a practical matter, the combination of the maximum permissible contribution and the minimum contribution requirements of the institutions offering such plans effectively limits the number of plans that can be operated at the same time.

Selection of the appropriate funding arrangement involves many of the same considerations taken into account in the selection of a funding instrument for a qualified pension plan. Thus, the individual must give consideration to potential investment return as well as investment risk. The expenses associated with the particular funding arrangement also must be taken into account as must benefit security and services provided.

24.2.3.   Prohibited Transactions

Individual retirement savings plans are subject to the prohibited transactions provisions of ERISA. If the individual engages in a prohibited transaction, the plan will be disqualified as of the first day of the taxable year in which the transaction occurred. The individual must then include the fair market value of the assets of the plan (determined as of the first day of such year) in ordinary income. In addition, if the individual has not attained age $59\frac{1}{2}$ (or is not disabled), an additional 10 percent tax will be levied since this is treated as a premature distribution. Generally speaking, fiduciaries and parties in interest are prohibited from engaging in the following:

1. Selling, exchanging, or leasing property.
2. Lending money or extending credit.
3. Furnishing goods, services, or facilities.
4. Transferring to or using plan assets.

There are, of course, exceptions to the prohibited transaction rules. One of the more significant exceptions permits a financial institution to provide ancillary services where this is done without interference with the interests of the participants and beneficiaries, where not more than reasonable compensation is charged, and where adequate internal safeguards exist to prevent providing services in an excessive or unreasonable manner.

Except for the individual (and his or her beneficiary), a party in interest who engages in a prohibited transaction will be subject to an excise tax of 5 percent of the amount involved. If the situation is not corrected within the time allowed (90 days unless extended by the IRS), a further excise tax of 100 percent of the amount involved will be levied.

24.2.4. Unrelated Business Income

An individual retirement savings plan is subject to federal income tax on any unrelated business income that arises from the conduct of any trade or business that is not substantially related to the exempt purpose of the plan. If a plan develops such unrelated business income, the plan will not be disqualified; however, such income will be subject to tax.

24.2.5. Distributions

The law contains very specific provisions that relate to distributions from individual retirement savings plans. In general, these provisions are designed to support the basic purpose of such plans--that they should provide retirement income. Thus, premature and lump-sum distributions are discouraged. On the other hand, the individual is expected to begin receiving payments by age 70½ and is encouraged to draw down benefits over his or her remaining lifetime (or the joint lifetimes of the individual and his or her spouse).

The following material discusses the law's basic limitations on payments, the taxation of distributions, and the treatment of premature distributions.

24.2.5.1.   Limitation on Distributions

Except in the event of the individual's death or disability, distribution from an individual retirement savings plan may not be made prior to age 59½ without incurring additional tax liability. For purposes of the law, an individual is considered to be disabled "if he is unable to engage in any substantial gainful activity by reason of any medically determinable physical or mental impairment which can be expected to result in death or to be of long-continued and indefinite character."

In any case, distribution must commence prior to April 1 of the year after the year in which the individual attains age 70½. Distribution may be in the form of a lump sum or in periodic payments not to exceed the life expectancy of the individual or the joint life expectancy of the individual and a designated beneficiary.[6] If an individual entitled to benefits dies before the entire interest is distributed, the required distribution to the beneficiary depends upon whether distributions to the IRA owner had already started by the date he or she died. If they have, the remaining portion of the interest is distributed at least as rapidly as under the method of distribution being used at the date of death. If they have not, the entire interest of the employee will be distributed within five years after the death of the employee. However, there is an exception to the five-year rule for certain amounts payable over the life of the beneficiary. If any portion of the employee's interest is payable to (or for the benefit of) a designated beneficiary, such portion may be distributed over the life of such designated beneficiary (or over a period not extending beyond the life expectancy of such beneficiary) if such distributions begin no later than one year after the date of the IRA owner's death. If the designated beneficiary is the surviving spouse of the IRA owner, additional flexibility exists. In this case, distributions do not have to begin prior to the time the IRA owner would have attained age 70½.

If plan assets are not distributed at least as rapidly as described above, an excise tax will be levied. This excise tax will be 50 percent of the "excess accumulation." The excess accumulation is the difference between the amount that was distributed during the year and the amount that should have been distributed under the rules described above.

24.2.5.2.   Taxation of Distributions

Distributions from an individual retirement savings plan (whether to the individual or his or her beneficiary) are taxable under IRC Section 72 (i.e., if nondeductible contributions have been made, a portion of each distribution is treated as a return of basis.) Lump-sum distributions do not qualify for long-term capital gains treatment nor do they qualify for the special five-year averaging treatment made available to corporate qualified plans.

As described in Chapter 23, a portion of an IRA distribution may be subject to a 15 percent excise tax. This results if the aggregate taxable distribution to an individual in any year for all tax-favored plans--IRAs as

---

[6]The life expectancy of an individual, or the joint life expectancy of the individual and beneficiary, may be recomputed as frequently as once a year. For distributions to an individual and a designated beneficiary other than the individual's spouse, IRS regulations will provide a method of taking into account changes in the individual's life expectancy, but not that of the beneficiary.

well as pensions, savings and stock bonus plans, CODAs, and tax-sheltered annuities--exceeds the greater of $150,000 or $112,500 (indexed to the CPI beginning in 1988).

For estate tax purposes, the entire value of a lump-sum distribution is included in the decedent's gross estate.

24.2.5.3.   Premature Distributions

If an individual is not disabled and receives a taxable distribution from an individual retirement savings plan before attaining age 59½, it is considered to be a premature distribution. The amount of the premature distribution must be included in the individual's gross income in the year of receipt. There will also be an additional nondeductible tax of 10 percent of the amount of the premature distribution.

If an individual has an individual retirement annuity and borrows any money under or by use of that annuity contract, the annuity will lose its tax-exempt status as of the first day of the taxable year in which the transaction occurred. The fair market value of such annuity (as of the first day of such taxable year) will have to be included in the individual's gross income for such year. If the individual has not attained age 59½ or is not disabled at such time, this also will be considered to be a premature distribution and the additional tax of 10 percent of the amount involved will be levied.

If an individual has an individual retirement account and uses all or any portion of the account as security for a loan, the portion so used will be treated and taxed as a distribution. Again, if the individual has not attained age 59½ or is not disabled, the 10 percent additional tax also will be levied.

24.2.5.4.   Rollovers

Under certain conditions, the law permits the transfer of assets, called rollovers, on a tax-free basis from one plan to another. Such rollovers can occur from one IRA to another or to or from qualified retirement plans.[7]

The law allows the rollover from one IRA to another as long as the full amount taken from one IRA is transferred to the new IRA within 60 days. Only one such rollover can occur every 12 months.

For rollovers to or from qualified retirement plans or 403(b) annuities, certain conditions must be met. The rollover must be in a lump sum of the participant's entire account, consist of only employer contributions or

---

[7]See Jerry S. Rosenbloom and G. V. Hallman, *Employee Benefits Planning* (3rd ed.) Prentice Hall, Englewood Cliffs, N.J., 1991, pp. 369-370.

deductible voluntary employee contributions (allowed prior to TRA '86) and the rollover is made because the employee has reached age 59½, has died or become disabled, has separated from the service of the employer or the plan has terminated.

Partial lump-sum rollovers from qualified plans and 403(b) annuities may be permitted provided the amount involved is at least 50 percent of the participant's entire account and must be because of disability, separation from service, or made to the beneficiary of a death benefit at the death of a spouse.

24.2.6. Employer-Sponsored IRAs

Although the IRA is viewed primarily as a device for facilitating individual retirement savings, an employer--including a self-employed person--may sponsor an IRA for some or all employees. A labor union also may sponsor an IRA plan for its members. No requirement exists that the employer-sponsored IRAs be available to all employees or be nondiscriminatory in benefits. The contributions to the IRA may be made as additional compensation or by payroll deduction. Any amount contributed by an employer to an IRA is taxable to the employee as additional compensation income. The employee is then eligible for the IRA tax deduction up to the $2,000 limitation. The amounts contributed are additional compensation and subject to FICA (Social Security) and FUTA (Federal Unemployment Tax Act) taxes. No federal income tax withholding is required if the employer believes the employee will be entitled to the offsetting IRA tax deduction.

An employer-sponsored IRA may use separate IRA trusts or annuity plans for each employee, or a single account may be used. However, the single account must provide a separate accounting for each participant's interest. Either a commingled trust fund or a nontrusteed group annuity contract with individual certificates may be used. In an employer-sponsored IRA, the prohibited transaction rules apply to transactions between the employer or other disqualified person and the IRA itself. Such prohibited transactions are subject to the ERISA penalties. The entire IRA plan or trust will not be disqualified as a result of a prohibited transaction involving an individual participant. If the individual participant engages in a prohibited transaction with the employer-sponsored IRA, only his or her individual portion of the IRA becomes disqualified, much as if he or she maintained the IRA separately.

An employer sponsoring an IRA may request a determination letter from the IRS. Furthermore, the same reporting, disclosure, and fiduciary requirements applicable to qualified plans under ERISA may apply to an employer sponsoring an IRA plan, if the employer endorses the IRA.[8] The participation, funding, and vesting rules of ERISA do not, however, apply. The funding and vesting rules are really irrelevant since the IRA plan may be funded only through the permitted IRA funding vehicles previously discussed, and each participant always is 100 percent vested. If an employer makes no actual contribution to employee IRAs, but merely provides certain facilities such as payroll deduction or checkoff, or allows the actual sponsor (e.g., an insurer or labor union) to publicize the program among employees, the reporting and disclosure requirements will not apply to the employer.

24.2.7. Reporting and Disclosure

An individual having an IRA is not subject to any reporting and disclosure requirements except in years in which a rollover has occurred, or one of the penalty taxes is payable. An employer sponsoring an IRA may be subject to the reporting, disclosure, and fiduciary requirements described above.

QUESTIONS FOR REVIEW

1. Describe the type of tax-favored retirement plans available to self-employed individuals.
2. Distinguish between a self-employed individual and an owner-employee.
3. Describe the contribution deduction limits available for defined benefit and defined contribution Keogh plans.
4. Can an individual be covered by a corporate qualified pension plan and also by an IRA? Explain the consequences with respect to the deductibility of the IRA contribution.
5. What is a prohibited transaction under ERISA? Explain when this concept can be relevant for IRAs.
6. Are there any restrictions on the period of time over which distributions from an IRA can be made? Explain.
7. Describe a premature distribution from an IRA and explain the tax penalties that could result from a premature distribution.
8. What are the conditions that must be met before an individual retirement account plan rollover will qualify as a tax-free rollover?
9. Is it possible for a person to receive a lump-sum distribution from a qualified pension or profit-sharing plan and transfer the funds tax free

---

[8]The criteria for an employer endorsement are found in DOL Regulation Section 2510.3-2.

to an individual retirement savings plan? If so, what are the federal income tax results?

10. May any individual retirement savings plan be used to transfer property from one type of qualified pension plan to another? Explain.

QUESTIONS FOR DISCUSSION

1. Discuss how retirement plans for the self-employed compare with qualified corporate retirement plans.
2. The new IRA deduction limitation will undoubtedly decrease the participation of employees in this arrangement. Discuss how this is likely to affect plan design for qualified plans.
3. Discuss the various approaches to funding IRA plans.

25. Section 403(b) Plans

25.1. INTRODUCTION

A tax-favored retirement mechanism exists for employees of public schools and certain other nonprofit tax-exempt organizations. Such arrangements known as 403(b) annuities allow thousands of eligible organizations the opportunity to provide defined contribution retirement plans to their employees. Two approaches either separately or in combination are possible. Under the first approach, often called the organization's basic retirement plan, employer contributions usually are established as a fixed percentage of each participating employee's salary -- typically between 5 and 10 percent. In addition, the plans often require the employee to contribute up to 5 percent from his or her salary. Many plans also permit employees to make their contributions on a tax-deferred basis through a salary reduction agreement with their employer.

A second but related use of 403(b) annuities establishes a vehicle for voluntary employee tax-deferred savings within the limits established by law. Often referred to as a tax deferred annuity (TDA) or supplemental retirement annuity (SRA), this type of 403(b) arrangement is intended as a voluntary tax-deferred savings plan, usually to supplement an institution's basic retirement plan and generally does not involve employer contributions. Under an SRA, once the employee decides how much to contribute (within permitted limits), a salary reduction agreement for that amount is entered into with the employer. The amount by which the employee's salary is reduced is then contributed by the employer to the SRA on behalf of the employee. Although the savings under an SRA are intended for retirement purposes, some or all of the accumulated funds in these programs can be made available to employees prior to retirement in the event of financial hardships as defined by Internal Revenue Service (IRS) regulations and under other specified circumstances.

The remainder of this chapter reviews the key features and legal requirements of Section 403(b) plans.

25.2.   REQUIREMENTS OF A 403(b) PLAN

25.2.1. The Present Statute

To qualify for the favorable tax treatment provided in the law, plans must comply with the statutory requirements of Section 403(b) of the Internal Revenue Code (IRC) as amended, which now provides, in part, that:

> If an annuity contract is purchased for an employee by an employer described in Section 501(c)(3)...or for an employee...who performs services for an educational institution (as defined in Section 151(e)(4)), by an employer which is a State, a political subdivision of a State, or an agency or instrumentality of any one or more of the foregoing...the employee's rights under the contract are nonforfeitable, except for failure to pay future premiums, and except in the case of a contract purchased by a church, such contract is purchased under a plan which meets the nondiscrimination requirements...then amounts contributed by such employer for such annuity contract...shall be excluded from the gross income of the employee for the taxable year to the extent that the aggregate of such amounts does not exceed the exclusion allowance for such a taxable year.[1]

The Employee Retirement Income Security Act (ERISA) amended Section 403(b) of the Code to add Section 403(b)(7), which states in part:

> For purposes of this title, amounts paid by an employer...to a custodial account...shall be treated as amounts contributed to an annuity contract for the employee if the amounts...are to be invested in regulated investment company stock (mutual fund) to be held in that custodial account.

Thus, the essential requirements to achieve the desired tax advantages similar to qualified retirement plans are as follows:

---

[1]Emphasis added. The exclusion allowance will be examined in greater detail subsequently in this chapter.

1. The employer must be a duly qualified educational or charitable organization or a public school system (or public college or university).
2. The participant must be a bona fide employee.
3. The participant's rights under the contract must be nonforfeitable.
4. The contributions paid in any year should not exceed the exclusion allowance for the year in question, the limits under IRC Section 415, or the maximum amount permitted under the nondiscrimination requirements.
5. The plan must meet the nondiscrimination requirements for plans that involve employer contributions. For plans that include only voluntary employee salary reductions, IRS regulations simply require that the opportunity for tax deferment be extended to essentially all employees.
6. The annuity contract must be purchased by such employer or the employer must make a deposit to a custodial account that will purchase mutual fund shares.

The next section analyzes these essential requirements of a 403(b) plan in greater detail.

25.2.2. Qualified Employers

If the employee is to qualify for tax-deferred treatment, his or her employer must be either:

1. A charitable organization qualified under Section 501(c)(3) of the Internal Revenue Code (for example, a tax-exempt hospital, church, school, or other such organization or foundation).
2. A public school system or public college or university (for example, one operated by the state, or by a county, city, town, school district, or other political subdivision or agency of a state). As used in this chapter, the term public school system includes such public colleges and universities.

Only those tax-exempt organizations that meet the requirements of Section 501(c)(3) are qualified employers for purposes of a 403(b) plan. In the case of questions concerning the qualification of an organization, a ruling should be sought from the IRS.[2]

25.2.3. Eligible Employees

To be eligible for participation in a 403(b) plan, an individual must be a bona fide employee of a qualified charitable organization or of a public school system. The individual may be the top-paid or the lowest paid employee. He or she may be a seasonal, part-time, or full-time employee but must be an *employee*--not an independent contractor. This point requires particular attention in connection with certain professional people (such as radiologists, pathologists, and anesthesiologists) who may or may not in certain circumstances, be employees.[3] Clerical, administrative, supervisory, and custodial employees of public school systems as well as teachers qualify.[4]

25.2.4. Employee's Rights Nonforfeitable

Attempted definitions of nonforfeitability are elusive. Without a trust, the employee's rights under an annuity contract, whether under the employer's basic retirement plan or a supplemental retirement annuity, would appear to be nonforfeitable if ownership of the contract is vested solely in him or her. The same would appear to be true if there is some form of joint ownership of the contract, together with an agreement between the employer and the employee whereby the employee could not be deprived of benefits provided by annuity premiums previously paid, even though the employer could exercise control over the time of enjoyment of those benefits.

---

[2] If the activity of the facility is such that if it were not publicly operated it could qualify under Section 501(c)(3), and if it has sufficient independence from the state, and so on, it may be able to obtain a ruling that it is a counterpart of a Section 501(c)(3) organization.

[3] Some professionals in the service of tax-exempt organizations may be barred by ethical or legal considerations from meeting the tests for the required employer-employee relationship. See Revenue Ruling 66-274, 1966-2 CB 446 for an outline of criteria for determining the relationship between a physician and a hospital. Also, see *Ravel* v. *Comm'r.*, 26 TCM 885 (1967) and *Azad* v. *U.S.*, 388 F. 2d 74 (1968).

[4] In addition, the regulations provide that one who is elected or appointed to certain public offices may qualify if there is a requirement that to hold the office such person must be trained or experienced in the field of education. For example, a commissioner or superintendent of education will generally be eligible, but a regent or trustee of a state university or a member of a board of education is not eligible. Reg. 1.403(b)-1(b)(5).

As a practical matter, it would appear that nonforfeitability would require that ownership ordinarily be vested solely in the employee, thus leaving him or her free of any restrictions or problems that might arise by virtue of insolvency or change of management of the employer. As sole owner of the contract, the employee is free to exercise any of his or her contractual rights, subject, of course, to restrictions on transferability. Thus, when an insurance company product is involved, the employee may be free, within the limitations of the contract, to elect a reduced paid-up annuity, to exchange the contract for a reduced annuity with an earlier maturity date, to surrender the contract in order to transfer the proceeds to another issuer, or to borrow from the insurer against its cash value.

25.2.5. Contributions

Two types of contributions can be made under 403(b) arrangements. These are often referred to as "nonelective" and "elective" contributions.

"Nonelective" contributions are those which the employer makes on behalf of the participant to the employer's basic retirement plan. "Elective" contributions to 403(b) plans are those voluntary contributions made by an eligible employee to a supplemental retirement annuity under a salary reduction agreement made with his or her employer. One such salary reduction agreement per year is permitted by IRC regulations. "Elective" contributions also include those an employee must make to receive employer contributions under the employer's basic retirement plan.

Both types of contributions must be made by the employer and are excluded from the employee's gross income for the current year as long as such contributions do not exceed the limitations outlined below and further discussed in the next several sections of this chapter.

Three possible limitations on the amount that can be contributed to a 403(b) arrangement are:

- A $9,500 limit under salary reduction arrangements
- An annual exclusion limitation
- An annual limit on employer contributions

25.2.6. Limitation on Employee Contributions

The maximum amount an individual may contribute on an annual basis to all 403(b) plans in which he or she participates is $9,500. The $9,500 limit does not apply to contributions made by an employer to a 403(b) plan. The employee's $9,500 limit, however, would be reduced by any additional "elective" deferrals the employee also may have made as a participant in a 401(k) plan[5] or a simplified employee pension (SEP) plan.

In special cases, an annual amount above $9,500 may be contributed by an employee to a 403(b) plan. For example, an employee of a qualifying organization who has entered into a salary reduction agreement with the employer and has at least 15 years of service with the organization, may make additional contributions above $9,500 in an amount not to exceed the smallest amount of the following:

- $3,000
- $15,000 decreased by the amount of additional salary reduction contributions made by the employee under the special rules.
- The excess of $5,000 times years of service minus prior employee tax-deferred employee contributions.

25.2.7. Exclusion Allowance

An employer's contributions to a 403(b) plan are excluded from an employee's gross income for federal income tax purposes in a particular year as long as such contributions do not exceed an employee's "exclusion allowance." To determine an employee's exclusion allowance, the following three-step process is generally used:

1. Multiply the employee's "reduced" compensation (gross compensation decreased by salary reduction contributions) for the most recent year of service by .20;
2. Multiply the result in 1 above by the employee's total years of service with the employer, and
3. Subtract the total amount contributed by the employer to the 403(b) plan or other retirement plan for that employee.

The following example illustrates how the three-step process works to determine an employee's exclusion allowance.

Assume Harry's gross compensation is $40,000. He has his salary reduced to $34,000 for the purpose of contributing $6,000 to the organization's 403(b) plan. Harry has worked for his employer for 4 years, during which time the employer contributed a total of $20,000 to the plan.

---

[5]401(k) plans were available prior to July 2, 1986.

In this situation, Harry's maximum exclusion allowance for the current year would be determined as follows:

1.	20 percent of reduced compensation for current year ($40,000 - $6,000) × .20 =	$6,800
2.	Multiplied by years of service	x 4
		$27,200
3.	Minus previous employer contributions	-20,000
	Harry's Exclusion Allowance for Current Year	$ 7,200

Since Harry's current contribution is $6,000, which is below the maximum exclusion allowance, the entire $6,000 would be excluded from Harry's current year's gross income for federal income tax purposes. Moreover, since Harry's current contribution of $6,000 is less than the $9,500 limitation previously discussed it also passes this requirement.

A common approach to determining an employee's annual maximum salary reduction contribution is to take 16 2/3 percent of an employee's gross pay. This approach assumes that an employer makes no other tax favored retirement plan contributions on behalf of the employee. For example, assume that Sue's gross compensation for the current year is $50,000. Her maximum exclusion allowance and, thus, her current contribution would be $8,333.33 (16 2/3% × 50,000). This figure is equal to 20 percent of the employee's reduced compensation ($50,000 - 8,333.33). Once again, since the amount is less than $9,500 the total amount could be contributed under a salary reduction 403(b) arrangement.

25.2.8. IRS Section 415 Limit

The third limitation is that annual contributions by an employer to a 403(b) plan including elective deferrals cannot exceed the IRS Section 415 limit, which is the lesser of $30,000 or 25 percent of the employee's taxable compensation for the year. The taxable compensation would be defined as gross compensation less any salary reduction contributions. This limit may apply to higher income employees whose exclusion allowance could exceed the IRS Section 415 limit.

For example, physician Jones has compensation for the current year of $180,000 and has worked for a University hospital for six years during which time a total of $66,000 has been contributed on Dr. Jones's behalf to the University's 403(b) plan. The University has not made any other contributions for Dr. Jones to any other qualified retirement plan. Using the approach outlined above, Dr. Jones's maximum exclusion allowance would be as follows:

1.	20 percent of $180,000 x 6 years =	$216,000
2.	Minus previous employer contributions	- 66,000
	Dr. Jones's exclusion allowance for the current year	$150,000

However, since the IRS Section 415's maximum dollar limit is $30,000 the maximum amount that the University can contribute on behalf of Dr. Jones is $30,000. It should be emphasized that the Section 415 limit applies to the total of elective deferrals and other employer retirement plan contributions; the $9,500 limit applies only to elective deferrals.

25.2.9. Special Catch-up Elections

Special consideration is given in ERISA to certain categories of employees (those who are employed in educational institutions, nonprofit hospitals, health and welfare service agencies, home health service agencies and churches) to allow those employees who have made less than the maximum allowable contributions in their early careers to make larger catch-up contributions. The three alternatives allowed are as follows:

1. *The $30,000 maximum rule.*   Under this approach, an eligible employee terminating employment can, on a one-time-only basis, make up the contributions that could have been made, but were not, during the 10-year period ending on the date of separation. (This amount is 20 percent of the employee's includible compensation multiplied by the number of years of service (not to exceed ten) for the employer minus the employer contributions already made during the relevant period.) Although no percentage limitation applies, this one-shot catch-up contribution is limited to a maximum of $30,000.

2. *The $15,000 maximum rule.*   Under this alternative, annual contributions can be made, at any time, equal to the lesser of 25 percent of compensation plus $4,000 or the exclusion allowance normally allowed under Internal Revenue Code Section 403(b).   The maximum annual deduction allowable under this approach is $15,000.

3. *The 25 percent/$30,000 rule.*   Under this approach, the maximum contribution is limited to the lesser of $30,000 or 25 percent of compensation. However, the 403(b) contribution must be aggregated with other qualified plan contributions to meet this test, and any employer contributions to a qualified defined benefit plan or other defined contribution plan must be subtracted from the 403(b) contribution. Since, in a defined benefit plan, the employee does not know the amount contributed by the employer, the IRS has established procedures to estimate the value of the employer's contribution.

Any election made under one of these special rules will be irrevocable. This means an employee electing to contribute under one of the special rules must continue to use the same rule in future years. However, the employee may always return to the general 403(b) limit.

25.2.10. Limits on Elective Deferrals

The maximum amount of elective deferrals an individual may make to a 403(b) plan in any taxable year is $9,500. The maximum amount will increase with the cost-of-living adjustments in future years but only after the limit for 401(k) cash or deferred arrangement (CODA) elective deferrals (see Chapter 12) reaches the $9,500 level. The limit applies to the sum of all the employee's elective deferrals for the taxable year, including CODAs and salary reduction SEPs.

If the employee makes an elective deferral in excess of the dollar limit for a taxable year, the excess must be allocated among the plans under which the deferrals were made by March 1 of the following year. The excess contributed must then be distributed by the plans to the employee by April 15. Such distributions (and investment income) will be included in the employee's taxable income for the year in which the excess deferral was made; however, if the excess is removed prior to the April 15 deadline, it will not be subject to the 10 percent penalty tax for premature distributions.

25.2.11. Nondiscrimination Requirements

For plan years after 1988, 403(b) annuity arrangements, except for church plans and students working fewer than 20 hours per week, are subject to extensive IRC nondiscrimination rules as outlined by the Tax Reform Act of 1986 (TRA '86). TRA '86 basically enacted three nondiscrimination rules that have an impact on 403(b) annuity plans. Two of the nondiscrimination rules apply primarily to prevent discrimination in favor of highly compensated employees (HCEs) as defined for qualified retirement plans. These rules apply to 403(b) annuities that are used as the employer's basic retirement plan. The third is a general rule that applies to 403(b) plans that permit elective deferrals.

The first nondiscrimination rule effective for plan years after 1990 applies the same series of rules and regulations concerning coverage and participation that apply to qualified retirement plans. These rules are discussed in detail in Chapter 5. Special transitional rules were allowed for plan years 1989 and 1990.

The second nondiscrimination rule requires that employer and employee contributions meet the average contribution percentage test (ACP) which compares contributions for "highly compensated employees" and "nonhighly compensated employees." This test is basically the same as applied to 401(k) plans and is discussed in detail in Chapter 12.

The final nondiscrimination rule requires that if the employer permits elective deferrals, this opportunity must be made available to all employees except for certain nonresident aliens and those covered by a Section 457 plan, a 401(k) plan, or another 403(b) plan sponsored by the same employer.

25.2.12. Annuity Contract Purchased by an Employer

In speaking of "an annuity...purchased...by an employer," the law gives no indication of what constitutes an annuity contract or a purchase by an employer. However, the IRS has stated that insurance companies or mutual funds must be used.[6] From the insurance company standpoint, it would appear to make no difference whether such a contract used for a 403(b) plan is a single-premium or annual-premium contract or whether it provides for fixed or variable annuity payments, provides for immediate or deferred payments, or includes a refund provision.

For many years the IRS took the position that a contract that provided a life insurance benefit did not qualify as a tax-deferred annuity. Section 403(b) now provides that "an individual contract issued after December 31, 1962, or a group contract which provides incidental life insurance protection may be purchased as an annuity contract." The expression "incidental life insurance protection" presumably has the same meaning as it has with respect to insurance purchased under qualified plans.[7] The IRS also has ruled that a modified endowment policy with an annuity rider providing a preretirement death benefit with an actuarial value of less than that of a typical retirement income policy meets the incidental death benefit test.[8]

Also, since December 31, 1962, the term annuity includes a so-called face-amount certificate but does not include a contract or certificate issued after that date that is transferable.[9] The regulations spell out in some detail

---

[6]Revenue Ruling 82-102.

[7]For a discussion of the meaning of incidental life insurance under qualified plans, see Chapter 6.

[8]Rev. Rul. 74--115, IRB. 1974-11,9.

[9]IRC 401(g), which reads in its entirety as follows:

> For purposes of this section and sections 402, 403, and 404, the term "annuity" includes a face-amount certificate, as defined in section 2(a)(15) of the Investment Company Act of 1940 (15 U.S.C. sec. 80a-2); but does not include any contract or

what is meant by the term *nontransferable*, and the language of the regulations has been used as a guide by insurers in appropriately wording their contracts.

Thus, any annuity contract, individual or group, ordinarily issued by an insurance company may be used to provide a tax-deferred annuity, provided it contains an appropriate restriction respecting transferability.

Contracts have been developed to accommodate the needs of the market. One can now find contracts with premiums payable for only 9 or 10 consecutive months of a year, which were designed to coincide with the payroll schedules of educational institutions. Contracts also are available that permit variations in the amount of premiums paid each year. Therefore, they are readily adaptable to varying incomes (hence, varying annual exclusion allowances).

It would appear that the payment of premiums will satisfy the "purchase" requirement of the statute. Thus, a qualified employer may assume the payment of premiums on an individual annuity contract already owned by one of its employees and will be considered as having purchased a tax-deferred annuity for the employee in each year that premiums are so paid, to the extent of the available exclusion allowance and provided that the contract contains the requisite restriction as to transferability.

ERISA, as mentioned previously, by adding section 403(b)(7) substantially expanded the range of permissible investments to include custodial accounts of regulated investment companies (mutual funds) as well as insurance company annuities or separate accounts.

25.3.   DISTRIBUTIONS AND TAXATION

25.3.1. Regular and Premature Distributions

For plan years after 1988, distributions from 403(b) arrangements are subject to basically the same rules as qualified plans, especially 401(k) plans

---

certificate issued after December 31, 1962, which is transferable, if any person other than the trustee of a trust described in section 401(a) which is exempt from tax under section 501(a) is the owner of such contract or certificate.

(See Chapter 12).[10] Distributions on behalf of an employee may be received from a 403(b) plan under the following circumstances:[11]

- Attainment of age 59½
- Death or disability
- Separation from service
- Financial hardship

Distributions from a 403(b) plan, unless rolled over (discussed later in this chapter) to an individual retirement account (IRA) or another 403(b) plan are taxed for federal income tax purposes, as ordinary income in the year received.

A premature distribution penalty tax of 10 percent of the amount distributed as well as the ordinary income tax due, applies to distributions before age 59½. Thus, for distributions prior to age 59½ for separation from service or financial hardship the penalty tax would apply except under the following conditions:

- If an individual age 55 or older receives a distribution upon separation from service of the employer.
- If the individual dies or is disabled.
- If upon separation from service from his or her employer, an individual receives a distribution in substantially equal periodic payments over the individual's life expectancy or over the joint life expectancies of the individual and his or her beneficiary.
- If an individual rolls over the distribution to an IRA or another 403(b) plan.
- If a distribution is used to pay medical expenses that are deductible for federal income tax purposes (currently over 7.5% of the individual's adjusted gross income) under IRS Code Section 213.
- If the payment is made to someone other than the participant under a Qualified Domestic Relations Order (see Chapter 6).

The 10 percent penalty tax also applies to other permitted nonmedical financial hardship distributions if prior to age 59½. (See Chapter 23). Additionally, any distribution for reason of financial hardship cannot exceed the amount of an individual's contributions, excluding investment earnings, under a salary reduction 403(b) plan.

---

[10]See John J. McFadden, *Retirement Plans for Employees*, Richard D. Irwin, Inc., Homewood, IL., pp. 269-270.

[11]If the account is *invested* in a custodial account (mutual fund) the withdrawal limitations apply to all 403(b) contributions. If the account is invested in an annuity contract, the withdrawal limitations apply only to salary reduction contributions.

25.3.2. Time When Distributions Must Commence

An individual must begin receiving a distribution from a 403(b) annuity plan not later than the April 1 following the year in which the individual attains age 70½.   If a distribution is taken in periodic payments, a minimum distribution must be made based on the individual's life expectancy or the joint life expectancies of the individual and his or her beneficiary. A penalty tax of 50 percent is imposed if the distribution is less than that required by law.

25.3.3. Taxation of Distributions

Any lump sum distribution from a 403(b) plan is taxable to the participant at ordinary income tax rates.   Neither capital gains income tax rates nor income averaging opportunities are available for a 403(b) plan distribution.[12] The only part of the distribution that may not be subject to taxation would be any cost basis the employee may have in the distribution because of taxes previously paid by the employee on his or her plan contributions or for any incidental life insurance costs (PS 58 costs) on life insurance included and already subjected to taxation.

Installment payments under a 403(b) plan are taxed in accordance with the annuity rules applicable for qualified plans. See Chapter 23 for a complete discussion of the annuity rules.

25.4.   LOANS

Because of the restrictions and limitations on distributions from 403(b) plans previously described, loan provisions are very popular under such plans. Loans under 403(b) plans are permitted on the same basis and with the same limits as qualified retirement plans. (See Chapter 9). Basically, such loans must meet the following IRC requirements:

- Loan may not exceed the lesser of 50 percent of the participant's account balance or $50,000
- Loan must bear a reasonable rate of interest
- Loan must be repaid within 5 years except for a loan used in the purchase of a principal residence

---

[12]McFadden, *Ibid.*, pp. 270-271.

- Loan repayment must be at least quarterly
- Loans must be on a level amortization basis

25.5.   TRANSFERS AND ROLLOVERS

25.5.1. Transfers

Transferability refers to the ability to move some or all of the participant's 403(b) accumulated plan assets among different funds or providers sponsored by the employer subject, of course, to the plan provisions. A participant also may be allowed to transfer his or her 403(b) plan assets to another 403(b) plan without federal income tax consequences, again subject to possible restrictions on the existing plan and the new plan.

25.5.2. Full Distribution Rollover

If instead of transferring 403(b) plan assets, the participant receives a total distribution of plan assets, it may be possible for the participant to complete a federal income tax free rollover to another 403(b) plan or to an IRA. A tax free rollover can be made for either total or partial distributions, subject to IRS requirements.

For a total distribution from a 403(b) plan to be eligible for a tax free rollover, it must be made within 60 days after the distribution is received by the plan participant. Moreover, the distribution must be complete, that is, all 403(b) plans set up on the employee's behalf by the employer are treated as one plan and must be made within one taxable year because of either the employee's separation from his or her employer's service or the attainment of age 59½.

25.5.3. Partial Distribution Rollover

If an employee receives a partial distribution under a 403(b) plan, it can be rolled over within 60 days to an IRA but not another 403(b) plan provided certain requirements are met. The requirements are that the partial distribution be equal to at least 50 percent of the participant's balance in his or her 403(b) plan and that the partial distribution be caused by the participant's disability or termination of employment.

QUESTIONS FOR REVIEW

1. Briefly summarize the provisions of the tax code that permit one to set up a tax-deferred annuity.
2. What are the essential requirements to achieve the desired tax shelter for a 403(b) plan? Explain.
3. What does it mean when the IRC requires that the employee's rights be nonforfeitable? Explain.
4. Describe the exclusion allowance for an employee for the taxable year under a 403(b) plan.
5. Explain how the use of the maximum exclusion in a year affects amounts of deductible contributions in future years.
6. How does the exclusion formula take into consideration what might be referred to as an allowance for past service? Explain.
7. Briefly describe the alternatives permitted for employees who have made little or no contributions under a 403(b) plan.

QUESTIONS FOR DISCUSSION

1. Discuss the conditions under which an employer may desire to establish a 403(b) plan?
2. Discuss how the elective deferral limitations are likely to affect plan design for 403(b) annuities.
3. Discuss how the nondiscrimination requirements are likely to affect plan design for 403(b) annuities.

26. Executive Retirement Arrangements*

Up to this point, the discussion in this text has been confined, for the most part, to tax-sheltered qualified retirement plans. Under the Internal Revenue Code (IRC or Code), such plans must be nondiscriminatory in order to maintain their tax-favored status; that is, they must not discriminate in favor of highly compensated employees. Several situations exist when an employer may *wish to* discriminate in favor of a specific executive or group of executives. For these situations, executive retirement arrangements can be used. Recent changes in tax policy and increasing restrictions on qualified plans has intensified interest in executive retirement arrangements from both employer and employee perspectives.

26.1. OBJECTIVES OF EXECUTIVE RETIREMENT ARRANGEMENTS

Because the design of an executive retirement arrangement must be responsive to the basic objectives of such a plan, it is necessary to establish these objectives before any questions of design, costing, and funding can be

---

*The authors wish to express their thanks to Garry N. Teesdale and Bernard E. Schaeffer of Hay Huggins, Inc. For an excellent discussion of executive retirement arrangements see Garry N. Teesdale and Bernard E. Schaeffer, "Executive Retirement Benefit Plans," in *The Handbook of Employee Benefits*, 3rd ed. Jerry S. Rosenbloom (Homewood, Ill.: Business One Irwin, 1992), Chapter 38 on which portions of this chapter are based.

considered. The objectives most frequently set forth for implementing an executive retirement arrangement are as follows:[1]

- Providing retirement income in excess of that permitted from qualified retirement plans under the Employee Retirement Income Security Act (ERISA) because of the IRC Section 415 limitations.[2]
- Recruiting an executive in mid- or late-career whose combined pension, from current and prior employers, falls short of reasonable retirement income objectives, since only his or her current period of service reflects the compensation levels he or she achieves before retiring.
- Establishing an additional element of executive compensation to attract and motivate qualified executives.
- Discouraging certain executives from terminating employment prior to qualifying for early retirement benefits.
- Encouraging the early retirement of some executives by providing unreduced benefits at an earlier age.

26.2. PLAN DESIGN CONSIDERATIONS

Once the plan's objectives are clearly established, it is necessary to understand the basic structure of executive retirement arrangements before the appropriate executive retirement plan design can be undertaken. Executive retirement plans are generally contractual arrangements between the employer and the employee (or independent contractor) under which the employer promises to make specific payments to the employee (or beneficiary) upon the occurrence of a specified future event such as retirement, disability, or death. Under some arrangements, the employee promises to render services to, or not compete with, the employer in the future.

---

[1]For a discussion of objectives, see Edward J. Emering, "Top Hat Pension Plans," *Journal of Pension Planning and Compliance*, May 1980, p. 168.

[2]The original ERISA legislation limited the maximum benefits payable under a qualified defined benefit plan to the lesser of 100 percent of an employee's three-year average pay or $75,000 (adjusted for cost-of-living changes) and an annual addition under a qualified defined contribution plan to the lesser of 25 percent or $25,000. In 1982 these adjusted figures were $136,425 and $45,475, respectively. The Tax Equity and Fiscal Responsibility Act of 1982 (TEFRA) rolled back these dollar limits to $90,000 (indexed) for defined benefit plans and $30,000 for defined contribution plans beginning in 1983. Under the Tax Reform Act of 1986, the $30,000 limit will not be increased until the defined benefit limit reaches $120,000. Moreover, a new $200,000 (indexed) pay limit was created. See Chapters 5 and 6 for a detailed discussion.

The typical executive retirement plan is unfunded, so as to avoid ERISA's benefit and contribution limits and compliance requirements and, hence, unfavorable income tax treatment. The employee is an unsecured creditor of the employer and has no rights to any specific asset even though the employer might use a funding vehicle discussed later in the chapter to set aside assets to meet its future obligation under the agreement.

An executive retirement arrangement may take the form of a supplemental executive retirement arrangement (SERP) or a deferred compensation agreement. Many practicing employee benefit specialists make a distinction between the two on the basis of whether the executive already earned the compensation in question. If the plan really provides additional benefits, it is referred to as a SERP. If compensation already earned by the employee is merely deferred primarily to save income taxes, the arrangement is referred to as a deferred compensation agreement. This chapter focuses mainly on the SERP and then briefly discusses the more individualized deferred compensation agreement. Many of the considerations discussed in the first instance, however, apply to both types of plan. In cases where this is not the case, the differences are pointed out.

26.3. SUPPLEMENTAL EXECUTIVE RETIREMENT ARRANGEMENTS

The basic concept of a SERP is that it provides a layer of benefit which, when added to other benefits, brings an executive's total retirement income to some predetermined level. A number of factors influence the ultimate design of a SERP. The primary consideration is, of course, the objectives of the plan. For example, if the problem of mid-career recruiting is of major importance, the SERP probably should have a relatively short service requirement to achieve full benefits.

Another important factor in the design of a SERP is the question of equity. Most SERPs provide the same level of benefits as a percentage of pay for all eligible executives. Frequently, only a relatively short period of service, such as 10 or 15 years, is required to achieve these benefits. It is possible that a long-service executive might perceive such a plan as being inequitable since his or her benefit will be no greater than the benefit provided for shorter-service executives. This problem is not prevalent under deferred compensation agreements since their emphasis is more on the idea of an individual arrangement than on a plan covering more than one executive.

The benefits of a SERP or other executive retirement arrangement, including those that might be provided on death or disability of the executive, should recognize all other company-provided benefits, including those provided only for executives. For example, the determination of whether a SERP should provide a spousal benefit could be influenced by the presence or absence of a supplemental life insurance plan for executives. Government-provided benefits, such as Social Security, usually are taken into account. The following discusses a variety of plan provisions that may be included in a SERP to fit the individual needs of the employer and the employees.

26.3.1. Eligibility for Participation

To be exempt from ERISA's various requirements an executive retirement plan must be maintained primarily for "a select group of management or highly compensated employees."[3] Thus, eligibility for participation normally is limited to members of top management who make significant contributions to the organization's success. This definition is subject to wide interpretation, however, and care should be taken to restrict eligibility to those executives for whom the plan is really intended. Eligibility requirements that are too broad or that are established so that they automatically expand the group covered (for example, a minimum salary requirement that could be eroded by inflationary pressure) can lead to substantial cost increases for an employer.

The most frequently used criteria to establish eligibility for participation is position. For the reason noted above, a minimum salary requirement is generally not desirable unless it is tied to some sort of price or wage index. Some organizations determine eligibility by whether the executive is eligible for the company's incentive compensation program.

Some plans avoid the use of specific eligibility requirements and require the executive to be designated for consideration by a group such as the compensation committee of the board of directors of the corporation. Even when specific eligibility requirements are used, it might be desirable to have the flexibility of permitting the designation of individual executives who might not otherwise be eligible but to whom, for unusual reasons, coverage should be extended.

No constraints are imposed by the IRC or ERISA on the selection of eligibility criteria; however, if the group covered is so large that it extends beyond "a select group of management or highly compensated employees,"

---

[3]ERISA compliance for plans covering "a select group of management or highly compensated employees" is minimal. Unfunded plans covering such employees are subject only to Part 1 (reporting and disclosure) and Part 5 (administration and enforcement) of subtitle B of Title I of ERISA. The reporting and disclosure rules can be met by complying with the regulation requiring the forwarding of a statement to the Department of Labor. The administration and enforcement requirements under ERISA are satisfied with a claims procedure statement.

the SERP could become a retirement plan under ERISA and subject to all its requirements.

26.3.2. Defined Benefit or Defined Contribution

As with qualified plans, SERPs may take the form of a defined benefit or defined contribution plan. In a defined benefit plan, the benefit could be: (1) a flat dollar amount; (2) an indexed dollar amount; or (3) a percentage of a portion of earnings either weighted for length of service or not and indexed or not. Offsets to the benefit might come from the employer's basic retirement plans, Social Security, benefits from a prior employer, and other employer incentive plans such as a profit-sharing plan, stock-option plan, or a deferred compensation agreement the executive has with the employer. For instance, a plan might provide a benefit based upon a certain percentage of final average earnings for each year of service, including credit for service with a previous employer, up to some combined maximum, minus any basic retirement plan benefits from both the current and any prior employer and primary Social Security benefits. Or, it might combine a higher percentage of final average earnings with a smaller number of maximum years less basic employer retirement plan benefits. Or, instead, some employers might use a given percentage of total compensation and subtract from this any benefits to which the executive is entitled either from the basic retirement plan or from a prior employer. In any case, the objectives of the plan will determine how the benefit is to be set.

In a defined contribution plan, the contribution rate is often a stated dollar or percentage-of-pay amount that may or may not be conditioned on the executive's or the employer's performance. As with a defined benefit plan, the objectives of the plan will determine the method by which the contribution is set, and although a dollar or percentage-of-pay amount commonly is used, there is no one rule for choosing the form of the contribution.

In order to maintain the unfunded status of the plan, the plan may not invest the contributions themselves, and several methods have arisen to determine the investment growth in a defined contribution plan. Earmarking and setting aside certain assets to determine investment growth and pay benefits is a frequently used approach, or the employer could make hypothetical investments and base benefits on the growth of these. A third method might base the growth on any of the following: (1) employer earnings; (2) a specified interest rate; (3) a specified index of either investment yield or asset fluctuation; or (4) a specified index of wage or cost-of-living fluctuation. It should be remembered that even though certain assets are informally set aside to provide for future benefits, the employer may not take a deduction for the contributions themselves and must pay tax on any investment earnings on these assets unless the investment is tax exempt or consists of the stock of other companies, in which case 80 percent of the dividend income is tax exempt.

In some instances, employers may purchase insurance contracts to cover the future costs of benefits. If the employee were the owner, he or she would be considered to be in constructive receipt of the benefits and incur a current tax liability. If, however, the employer is both the policyholder and the beneficiary, the income is not currently taxable to the employee. In addition, although premiums may not be deducted from the employer's taxable income, investment earnings are not currently taxable to the employer and policy dividends and death benefits are not taxable when received.[4]

As mentioned earlier, the use of a defined benefit or a defined contribution plan will be determined by the objectives of the employer and of the executive or executives to be covered. In some instances, when the plan covers only one executive or a group of executives with similar characteristics, the choice may be purely one of preference in approach. The defined benefit approach is perhaps a better way to achieve a given level of retirement income. The defined contribution method, on the other hand, may prove more useful in situations where the employer wishes to base the benefit on performance criteria. The many variables that must be considered in determining how a plan should be constructed, and that will influence the decision on whether to use a defined benefit or a defined contribution approach as well, follow.

26.3.3. Retirement Benefits

In determining the level of retirement benefits to be provided by a SERP, a number of elements must be considered. These include the basic income level (objectives), as a percentage of compensation, to be provided; the compensation base to be used to determine benefits; and the service necessary to receive full benefits. Also evaluated should be the sources of benefits considered in arriving at the amount of the supplemental benefit, the earliest age at which full, unreduced benefits will be payable, and the conditions, if any, under which benefits might be forfeited.

---

[4]If a corporation or partnership owns a deferred annuity contract, the annual increase in value of the contract is includable in the owner's gross income. Moreover, 50 percent of the inside buildup in value of company-held insurance and annuity policies and policy proceeds will be subject to the corporate alternative minimum tax; after 1989, 75 percent will be subject to the tax.

26.3.4. Income Objectives

The setting of income objectives for a SERP is approached in the same way as these objectives are set for basic qualified retirement plans. SERPs generally establish an income replacement target for executives of from 50 to 55 percent of gross pay. A higher replacement objective might draw criticism from shareholders and raise issues about the reasonableness of an executive's compensation from the viewpoint of the tax deductibility of corporate contributions.

26.3.5. Compensation Base

The benefits of a SERP should be based on the executive's basic salary. Since incentive compensation normally constitutes a significant part of an executive's total compensation, and since such incentive compensation influences the executive's standard of living, it is reasonable to include at least part of such incentive pay in the compensation base for benefits.

Once all the elements of includable compensation have been identified, it is necessary to establish the period over which this compensation base will be determined. The most common provision is to average pay over a period of time, such as three or five years (i.e., the highest three- or five-year average during the last 10 years of employment)--particularly when incentive pay is included as part of the base.

26.3.6. Service

To make sure the executive has made a significant contribution to the organization before retirement, some minimum service requirement is appropriate. If a major plan objective of a SERP is to assist in mid- or late-career recruiting, the plan probably should limit the service needed to achieve the full level of benefits. For this purpose, service periods of 10 or 15 years are common. The plan may exclude any executive who does not meet this minimum service requirement or it may provide such an individual with proportionate benefits.

When mid- or late-career recruiting is not a major plan objective, longer service periods may be required. However, many SERPs use a service period somewhat shorter than the service period required to accrue full benefits under the company's basic qualified retirement plan. Also, when longer service is required, it is more likely that shorter service executives receive proportionately reduced benefits rather than being excluded completely.

A commonly found variation in SERPs is to tie the service requirement to the income objective of the plan on a weighted basis so that a relatively large portion of the benefit is accrued in a short period of time. A formula that produces 5 percent of pay for each of the first 5 years of service and 2.5 percent for each of the next 10 years, thus producing 25 percent of pay in 5 years, 37.5 percent in 10 years, and 50 percent in 15 years would be an example.

26.3.7. Benefit Sources

The two major sources of basic benefits to be used for a SERP are the company's basic qualified retirement plan and Social Security. Any other company-provided retirement benefits also should be recognized, but voluntary plans such as savings plans and elective contributions to cash or deferred arrangements (CODAs) normally are not taken into account even though they represent a potential source of retirement income. Another possible source of benefit that should be considered is the amount of any vested benefits the executive might have by reason of prior employment. In a SERP designed with liberal benefits and short-service requirements, it would be reasonable to take such benefits into account. However, in actuality only a few plans make provision for this type of offset.

26.3.8. Age at Retirement

A major objective of many SERPs is to permit and/or encourage certain executives to retire prior to the company's normal retirement age. The SERP usually follows the pattern of the company's basic qualified retirement plan and sets age 65 as the normal retirement age. However, it is also common for the executive to be able to retire with full unreduced benefits as early as age 60 or 62 if any required service has been completed. Typically, although not necessarily, the age chosen for early retirement on this basis ties in with the age at which unreduced benefits are available under the company's basic qualified retirement plan.

The extent to which full unreduced benefits are made available and the establishment of age and/or service requirements that must be met reflect the degree to which the company wishes, from a personnel viewpoint, to encourage the early retirement of executives. If the primary interest is in encouraging early retirement on a selective basis, it might be appropriate to provide full, unreduced benefits only in company-initiated retirements.

When full, unreduced benefits are not available, for example for retirement after age 55 but before age 60, with less than the full amount of required service, or without necessary company consent, the company may provide a reduced benefit such as the benefit otherwise available reduced by 5 percent per year for each year that retirement precedes age 60. Generally, early retirement would not be made available, even on a reduced basis, before the employee also would be eligible to retire under the company's basic qualified retirement plan, for example, age 55 with 10 years of service.

26.3.9. Forfeitures

The forfeiture of retirement benefits when an employee goes to work for a competitor has never been very common in qualified retirement plans, and is prohibited by ERISA. However, such a prohibition does not apply to unfunded SERP benefits. In view of the executive levels and the amount of benefits involved, particularly in SERPs that include liberal early retirement provisions, such forfeiture provisions are frequently found in SERPs and provide some degree of protection for the company.

26.3.10.Forms of Payment

Generally, retirement benefits are paid in monthly installments for the lifetime of the executive. Because of the tie-in with the company's basic qualified retirement plan, the executive is usually given the right to elect optional forms of payment on the same terms, conditions, and actuarial bases available for basic retirement benefits.

The option of providing the SERP benefit in a lump sum is rarely made available to the executive. The primary reason is that no tax advantages exist with such a distribution and the entire amount would be treated as taxable income in one year. A second reason for not allowing this option is that the company would lose control over the executive's ability to enter into competitive employment after retirement. The issue of constructive receipt may also be a problem if this option is provided.

26.3.11.Death Benefits

It is possible to provide preretirement and/or postretirement death benefits under a SERP. Such benefits might take the form of providing or continuing a percentage of the retirement benefit the executive was entitled to receive or was receiving in the event of his or her death while eligible to retire or after having retired. Such a benefit is normally payable to the executive's spouse but could be paid to any one of a group of survivors, such as dependent children, brothers, and sisters. If paid to a spouse, such a benefit could be paid for life or for a fixed period such as 10 years. Benefits to children or other survivors could be paid for a fixed number of years or, in the case of children, until they reach a certain age, such as 21. Lump-sum death benefits are rarely paid as part of a SERP; as a rule, such benefits are more tax effective if provided under group life insurance programs.

Death benefits under a SERP can be provided at company cost or can be provided on a basis that requires some contribution by the executive. Typically, any cost to the executive is established by reducing the benefit otherwise payable by the use of option factors in the case of postretirement benefits or by a straight percentage reduction in the case of preretirement benefits.

26.3.12. Disability Benefits

Many organizations maintain long-term disability income programs that provide disability income payments until an employee reaches age 65. During the period of disability, the employee generally continues to accrue pension credits based on his or her last rate of pay and, at age 65, is considered as retired under the basic retirement plan. If a SERP is adopted, it is necessary to coordinate the SERP benefits with the long-term disability income program. One common approach is to provide the regular SERP benefits when the disabled executive reaches age 65.

Another approach is to provide all or part of the SERP benefits immediately upon disability, offsetting any disability income benefits payable to the executive until his or her basic retirement benefits begin.

If SERP benefits are provided under either approach, an important question to resolve is whether SERP benefits will be provided if the executive had not met the SERP service requirement prior to becoming disabled.

26.3.13. Vesting

If an executive terminates employment prior to the earliest retirement age possible, it is not customary to provide him or her with a vested interest in an unfunded SERP. An exception might be when a major objective of the SERP is to assist in mid- or late-career recruiting. In this situation, it may be necessary to offer some degree of protection to the executive. If vesting is desired, one approach is to provide an accrued benefit once the basic service requirement for SERP benefits has been attained.

26.3.14.Funding Considerations

Once a preliminary decision is made concerning the major provisions of a SERP, it is important that benefit illustrations and cost projections be made for the eligible participants. Such information enables the employer to test the tentative plan provisions and determine whether estimated costs are within acceptable parameters. Once the cost projections are deemed acceptable, funding alternatives can be considered.

A SERP of the type described in this chapter is generally funded on a current disbursement basis; that is, company contributions are made as benefit payments come due. Such a plan is considered an "unfunded" plan because of the absence of any prefunding of obligations.

26.4.   UNFUNDED PLAN

Funding a SERP could cause serious consequences. First, the plan would lose its exemption from ERISA compliance. More important, however, are the tax considerations applicable to a funded plan. Company contributions to a funded plan would not be deductible unless and until the executive achieves a nonforfeitable interest. And, as soon as the executive's rights become nonforfeitable, he or she could be considered in constructive receipt of the value of the then-accrued benefit even if the funds were not then available to the executive. Further, once his or her rights become nonforfeitable, all future company contributions could be taxable to the executive as they are made, even though not then paid to the executive. Since ERISA requires vested interests be created under funded plans, even if not tax qualified, the issue of nonforfeitable rights with the attendant tax consequences cannot be avoided. For these reasons, it is obvious that SERPs cannot be funded with the advantages of a qualified plan. However, even though not funded, certain accounting considerations must be observed.

26.5.   BENEFIT SECURITY ARRANGEMENTS

As mentioned above, since a SERP typically is unfunded, an executive's retirement income under the plan is dependent on the willingness and solvency of the company to pay promised benefits. An additional complicating factor is the length of time over which the benefits accrue and the ultimate pay-out date. The period could be 25 to 30 years in the future. Consequently, strong interest exists in methods that attempt to give an executive some assurance that SERP benefits will be paid.   Several techniques are now in use to accomplish this purpose.

Probably the most common method is the use of the so called "rabbi trust." Under this approach, the company creates an irrevocable trust for the benefit of an executive or a group of participating executives. The terms of the trust limit the use of the assets to providing benefits for the participating executives.   Thus, the trust assets cannot be used by current or future management, but remain subject to the claims of creditors in the event of the firm's insolvency.

Corporate-owned life insurance (COLI) is another commonly used technique for benefit security under a SERP. The basic concept under this approach is that the employer is the owner and beneficiary of a life insurance contract designed to accumulate sufficient cash values to pay the benefits promised the executive. The life insurance policy must be carried as a corporate asset and therefore provides only very limited benefit security for the executive since cash values and death benefits are within the employer's control.

Other techniques sometimes used to attempt to provide benefit security for a SERP include employee-owned trusts and employee-owned annuities. However these methods have tax disadvantages since they will cause the SERP to be considered a funded plan.[5]

26.6.   TAX CONSIDERATIONS

The income tax dimensions of a SERP must be evaluated. Corporate tax deductions are allowed under an unfunded SERP only as benefits are paid.[6] For the executive, the benefits are taxed as ordinary income when they are paid.   No special treatment is available for lump-sum distributions. Deferred compensation agreements involve other tax considerations and are discussed later in this chapter.

As with any other type of benefit program, the ultimate cost of a SERP equals the sum of the benefits paid plus any expenses associated with plan administration. The amount of benefits paid reflects elements of plan design such as eligibility requirements, benefit levels, early retirement age,

---

[5]Jerry S. Rosenbloom and G. Victor Hallman, *Employee Benefit Planning*, 3rd ed., Prentice Hall, Inc., Englewood Cliffs, N.J., p. 378.

[6]The requirements of *Statement of Financial Accounting Standards No. 87, Employers' Accounting for Pensions*, may apply to arrangements that are similar to pension plans regardless of their form and whether written or not; for example, deferred compensation arrangements or supplemental executive retirement plans, when they are the equivalent of pension plans (i.e., benefits are based on a general formula rather than being tailored to each individual in payout terms and timing of payments). See Chapter 22 for a complete discussion of accounting for retirement plans.

the inclusion of ancillary benefits, and the like. Since benefits are not prefunded, there is no offsetting element, as there would be in a tax-qualified retirement plan. While costs can and should be projected and considered from the viewpoint of cash flow, they also must be considered from the viewpoint of a charge against net income in accordance with accounting requirements. Accounting requirements may involve the recognition of cost accruals over the period of the executive's active employment. Federal tax law requires that the cost and benefits of a SERP or other executive retirement arrangement must be "reasonable" in amount when related to the total compensation of the executives.[7]

From the executive's standpoint, after the provisions of the plan have been determined, the employer must make sure that neither the tax doctrine of economic benefit nor the tax doctrine of constructive receipt applies. Under these two doctrines, an employee can be taxed currently on income he or she is deferring. This would, in essence, defeat the purpose of such a plan. The doctrine of economic benefit states that if a taxpayer is receiving a current benefit, he or she should be taxed currently on the value of that benefit; the doctrine of constructive receipt states that if a taxpayer could receive income at any time but elects to receive it later, he or she is still taxed currently because the employee has a nonforfeitable right to the income; this concept embodies the "payment in kind" or "cash equivalent" principle. Revenue Ruling 60-31 states that deferred compensation is not taxable before actual receipt whether it is forfeitable or nonforfeitable provided the deferral is agreed to before the compensation is earned, the deferral amount is not unconditionally placed in trust or in escrow for the benefit of the employee, and the promise to pay the deferred compensation is merely a contractual obligation not evidenced by notes or secured in any other manner. Thus, while certain assets may be earmarked and informally set aside to give some assurance that benefits will be paid, there must be no formal funding instrument and the executive must not have current access to the benefits.

26.7.   DEFERRED COMPENSATION AGREEMENTS

While the main purpose of SERPs is to provide the executive with an additional layer of retirement benefits over and above those provided by the employer's basic plan, deferred compensation agreements deal primarily with earnings deferral, usually to gain tax advantages, with retirement

---

[7]Federal Tax Regs. 1.162.7. See also Jerry S. Rosenbloom, "Distinguishing between Qualified and Nonqualified Deferred Compensation," in *Deferred Compensation*, ed. Herbert Chasman (Homewood, Ill.: Dow Jones-Irwin, 1978), pp. 3-4.

income as a secondary consideration. Postponing the receipt of current income not only reduces executives' current taxable income, but puts them in receipt of the funds after retirement when they may be in a lower tax bracket. However, any deferral of income to a future date must take into consideration the potential effects of increased interest and inflation rates as well as current tax considerations, all of which have cast some doubt upon the effectiveness of such deferral. These combined factors have led some to believe that the executive would be better off receiving the income as it is earned, paying the taxes due, and investing the remainder.

Other reasons for deferring current income from both the executive's and the employer's viewpoints are: (1) extending the executive's income beyond normal working years into retirement; (2) spreading bonuses over a wider span of years; (3) tying the executive to the employer by stipulating conditions on the receipt of deferred amounts; and (4) adding to the executive's retirement income.

The factors to be considered in drawing up the agreement are much the same as those that were discussed for supplemental executive retirement plans and include how much compensation will be deferred, whether investment growth will be added to such amounts, whether there will be conditions on receiving the funds, and what the various benefit options will be.

In order to avoid the possibility of the executives being judged to be in constructive receipt of the deferred funds, three rules contained in Revenue Ruling 60-31 must be followed in drawing up a deferred compensation agreement. They are that the deferral must be: (1) irrevocable; (2) agreed to before the compensation is earned; and (3) for a specified length of time. The agreement must also serve a business purpose.

26.8.   SUMMARY

Because of their nonqualified status, executive retirement arrangements permit a degree of flexibility unavailable in the more restricted qualified plans. When properly designed and administered, they can serve a number of needs that exist in the relationship between an employer and the executive that do not apply to the rest of the work force. From the employer's point of view, such arrangements can help attract and keep qualified executives, reward such executives for productivity and loyalty, and encourage the early retirement of certain executives. The executive, on the other hand, may look forward to retirement income higher than that provided by the employer's regular plan, or at least to full pension benefits in the case of a short-service executive; certain tax advantages; additional insurance coverage and dependent coverage; early retirement with full benefits; and the extension of income into retirement.

QUESTIONS FOR REVIEW

1. What are the typical objectives of an employer in establishing an executive retirement arrangement? Explain.
2. What is the ultimate cost of a SERP for an employer? Explain.
3. Describe the eligibility requirements typically used under a SERP.
4. Identify the considerations typically used to establish the level of retirement benefits and income objectives available under a SERP.
5. Describe how the compensation base applicable to benefits under a SERP usually is established.
6. Explain the reasons for including service requirements in SERPs and the types of service requirements used.
7. How can a SERP be used to encourage early retirement? Explain.
8. Are lump-sum options normally made available under SERPs? Explain.
9. Why are SERPs typically not prefunded? Explain.
10. Describe the advantages of deferred compensation arrangements.

QUESTIONS FOR DISCUSSION

1. Discuss the conditions under which an employer may desire to establish an executive retirement arrangement.
2. Compare the similarities and differences in plan design issues between qualified retirement plans and executive retirement arrangements.

INDEX

OZICK

Levitation

DATE DUE			

Levitation

FIVE FICTIONS

Cynthia Ozick

Alfred A. Knopf 🐎 New York 1982

THIS IS A BORZOI BOOK
PUBLISHED BY ALFRED A. KNOPF, INC.

Copyright © 1977, 1979, 1980, 1982 by Cynthia Ozick
All rights reserved under International and Pan-Ameri-
can Copyright Conventions. Published in the United
States by Alfred A. Knopf, Inc., New York, and
simultaneously in Canada by Random House of Canada
Limited, Toronto. Distributed by Random House, Inc.,
New York.

"Puttermesser: Her Work History, Her Ancestry, Her
Afterlife" has been previously published in
The New Yorker.

Other stories in this book have been previously published
in the *American Journal, Partisan Review, Quest,
Salmagundi,* and *Triquarterly.*

Library of Congress Cataloging in Publication Data

Ozick, Cynthia. Levitation, five fictions.
CONTENTS: Levitation.—Puttermesser.—Shots. [etc.]
I. Title.
PZ4.O994Le 1981 [PS3565.Z5] 813'.54 80–7997
ISBN 0–394–51413–0

Manufactured in the United States of America
First Edition

Mama, Shiphra, O my maminke

תַּרְהִבֵנִי בְּנַפְשִׁי עֹז

אֲשֹחֶה בְכָל־לַיְלָה מִטָּתִי,
בְּדִמְעָתִי עַרְשִׂי אַמְסֶה

Contents

Levitation

A pair of novelists, husband and wife, gave a party. The husband was also an editor; he made his living at it. But really he was a novelist. His manner was powerless; he did not seem like an editor at all. He had a nice plain pale face, likable. His name was Feingold.

For love, and also because he had always known he did not want a Jewish wife, he married a minister's daughter. Lucy too had hoped to marry out of her tradition. (These words were hers. "Out of my tradition," she said. The idea fevered him.) At the age of twelve she felt herself to belong to the people of the Bible. ("A Hebrew," she said. His heart lurched, joy rocked him.) One night from the pulpit her father read a Psalm; all at once she saw how the Psalmist meant *her*; then and there she became an Ancient Hebrew.

She had huge, intent, sliding eyes, disconcertingly luminous, and copper hair, and a grave and timid way of saying honest things.

They were shy people, and rarely gave parties.

Each had published one novel. Hers was about domestic life; he wrote about Jews.

All the roil about the State of the Novel had passed them by. In the evening after the children had been put to bed, while the portable dishwasher rattled out its smell of burning motor oil, they sat down, she at her desk, he at his, and began to write. They wrote not without puzzlements and travail; nevertheless as naturally as birds. They were devoted to accuracy, psychological realism, and earnest truthfulness; also to virtue, and even to wit. Neither one was troubled by what had happened to the novel: all those declarations about the end of Character and Story. They were serene. Sometimes, closing up their notebooks for the night, it seemed to them that they were literary friends and lovers, like George Eliot and George Henry Lewes.

In bed they would revel in quantity and murmur distrustingly of theory. "Seven pages so far this week." "Nine-and-a-half, but I had to throw out four. A wrong tack." "Because you're doing first person. First person strangles. You can't get out of their skin." And so on. The one principle they agreed on was the importance of never writing about writers. Your protagonist always has to be someone *real*, with real work-in-the-world—a bureaucrat, a banker, an architect (ah, they envied Conrad his shipmasters!)—otherwise you fall into solipsism, narcissism, tedium, lack of appeal-to-the-common-reader; who knew what other perils.

This difficulty—seizing on a concrete subject—was mainly Lucy's. Feingold's novel—the one he was writing now—was about Menachem ben Zerach, survivor of a massacre of Jews in the town of Estella in Spain in 1328. From morning to midnight he hid under a pile of corpses, until a "compassion-ate knight" (this was the language of the history Feingold relied on) plucked him out and took him home to tend his wounds. Menachem was then twenty; his father and mother and four younger brothers had been cut down in the terror. Six thousand Jews died in a single day in March. Feingold wrote well about how the mild winds carried the salty fra-grance of fresh blood, together with the ashes of Jewish houses, into the faces of the marauders. It was nevertheless a triumphant story: at the end Menachem ben Zerach becomes a renowned scholar.

"If you're going to tell about how after he gets to be a scholar he just sits there and *writes*," Lucy protested, "then you're doing the Forbidden Thing." But Feingold said he meant to concentrate on the massacre, and especially on the life of the "compassionate knight." What had brought him to this compassion? What sort of education? What did he read? Feingold would invent a journal for the compassionate knight, and quote from it. Into this journal the compassionate knight would direct all his gifts, passions, and private opinions.

"Solipsism," Lucy said. "Your compassionate knight is only another writer. Narcissism. Tedium."

They talked often about the Forbidden Thing. After a while they began to call it the Forbidden City, because not only were they (but Lucy especially) tempted to write—solipsisti-cally, narcissistically, tediously, and without common appeal —about writers, but, more narrowly yet, about writers in New York.

"The compassionate knight," Lucy said, "lived on the Upper West Side of Estella. He lived on the Riverside Drive, the West End Avenue, of Estella. He lived in Estella on Cen-tral Park West."

The Feingolds lived on Central Park West.

In her novel—the published one, not the one she was writing now—Lucy had described, in the first person, where they lived:

> By now I have seen quite a few of those West Side apartments. They have mysterious layouts. Rooms with doors that go nowhere—turn the knob, open: a wall. Someone is snoring behind it, in another apartment. They have made two and three or even four and five flats out of these palaces. The toilet bowls have antique cracks that shimmer with moisture like old green rivers. Fluted columns and fireplaces. Artur Rubinstein once paid rent here. On a gilt piano he raced a sonata by Beethoven. The sounds went spinning like mercury. Breathings all lettered now. Editors. Critics. Books, old, old books, heavy as centuries. Shelves built into the cold fireplace; Freud on the grate, Marx on the hearth, Melville, Hawthorne, Emerson. Oh God, the weight, the weight.

Lucy felt herself to be a stylist; Feingold did not. He believed in putting one sentence after another. In his publishing house he had no influence. He was nervous about his decisions. He rejected most manuscripts because he was afraid of mistakes; every mistake lost money. It was a small house panting after profits; Feingold told Lucy that the only books his firm respected belonged to the accountants. Now and then he tried to smuggle in a novel after his own taste, and then he would be brutal to the writer. He knocked the paragraphs about until they were as sparse as his own. "God knows what you would do to mine," Lucy said; "bald man, bald prose." The horizon of Feingold's head shone. She never showed him her work. But they understood they were lucky in each other. They pitied every writer who was not married to a writer. Lucy said: "At least we have the same premises."

Volumes of Jewish history ran up and down their walls;

they belonged to Feingold. Lucy read only one book—it was *Emma*—over and over again. Feingold did not have a "philosophical" mind. What he liked was event. Lucy liked to speculate and ruminate. She was slightly more intelligent than Feingold. To strangers he seemed very mild. Lucy, when silent, was a tall copper statue.

They were both devoted to omniscience, but they were not acute enough to see what they meant by it. They thought of themselves as children with a puppet theater: they could make anything at all happen, speak all the lines, with gloved hands bring all the characters to shudders or leaps. They fancied themselves in love with what they called "imagination." It was not true. What they were addicted to was counterfeit pity, and this was because they were absorbed by power, and were powerless.

They lived on pity, and therefore on gossip: who had been childless for ten years, who had lost three successive jobs, who was in danger of being fired, which agent's prestige had fallen, who could not get his second novel published, who was *persona non grata* at this or that magazine, who was drinking seriously, who was a likely suicide, who was dreaming of divorce, who was secretly or flamboyantly sleeping with whom, who was being snubbed, who counted or did not count; and toward everyone in the least way victimized they appeared to feel the most immoderate tenderness. They were, besides, extremely "psychological": kind listeners, helpful, lifting hot palms they would gladly put to anyone's anguished temples. They were attracted to bitter lives.

About their own lives they had a joke: they were "secondary-level" people. Feingold had a secondary-level job with a secondary-level house. Lucy's own publisher was secondary-level; even the address was Second Avenue. The reviews of their books had been written by secondary-level reviewers. All their friends were secondary-level: not the presidents or partners of the respected firms, but copy editors and production assistants; not the glittering eagles of the intellectual organs, but the wearisome hacks of small Jewish journals; not the fiercely cold-hearted literary critics, but those wan and chattering daily reviewers of film. If they knew a playwright, he was off-off-Broadway in ambition and had not yet been produced. If they knew a painter, he lived in a loft and had exhibited only once, against the wire fence in the outdoor show at Washington Square in the spring. And this struck them as mean and unfair; they liked their friends, but other people—why not they?—were drawn into the deeper caverns of New York, among the lions.

New York! They risked their necks if they ventured out to Broadway for a loaf of bread after dark; muggers hid behind the seesaws in the playgrounds, junkies with knives hung upside down in the jungle gym. Every apartment a lit fortress; you admired the lamps and the locks, the triple locks on the caged-in windows, the double locks and the police rods on the doors, the lamps with timers set to make burglars think you were always at home. Footsteps in the corridor, the elevator's midnight grind; caution's muffled gasps. Their parents lived in Cleveland and St. Paul, and hardly ever dared to visit. All of this: grit and unsuitability (they might have owned a snowy lawn somewhere else); and no one said their names, no one had any curiosity about them, no one ever asked whether they were working on anything new. After half a year their books were remaindered for eighty-nine cents each. Anonymous mediocrities. They could not call themselves forgotten because they had never been noticed.

Lucy had a diagnosis: they were, both of them, sunk in a ghetto. Feingold persisted in his morbid investigations into Inquisitional autos-da-fé in this and that Iberian marketplace. She herself had supposed the inner life of a housebound woman—she cited *Emma*—to contain as much comedy as the cosmos. Jews and women! They were both beside the point. It was necessary to put aside pity; to look to the center; to abandon selflessness; to study power.

They drew up a list of luminaries. They invited Irving Howe, Susan Sontag, Alfred Kazin, and Leslie Fiedler. They invited Norman Podhoretz and Elizabeth Hardwick. They invited Philip Roth and Joyce Carol Oates and Norman Mailer and William Styron and Donald Barthelme and Jerzy Kosinski and Truman Capote. None of these came; all of them had unlisted numbers, or else machines that answered the telephone, or else were in Prague or Paris or out of town. Nevertheless the apartment filled up. It was a Saturday night in a chill November. Taxis whirled on patches of sleet. On the inside of the apartment door a mound of rainboots grew taller and taller. Two closets were packed tight with raincoats and fur coats; a heap of coats smelling of skunk and lamb fell tangled off a bed.

The party washed and turned like a sluggish tub; it lapped at all the walls of all the rooms. Lucy wore a long skirt, violet-colored, Feingold a lemon shirt and no tie. He looked paler than ever. The apartment had a wide center hall, itself the breadth of a room; the dining room opened off it to the left, the living room to the right. The three party-rooms shone like a triptych: it was as if you could fold them up and enclose everyone into darkness. The guests were free-standing figures in the niches of a cathedral; or else dressed-up cardboard dolls, with their drinks, and their costumes all meticulously hung with sashes and draped collars and little capes, the women's hair variously bound, the men's sprouting and spilling: fashion stalked, Feingold moped. He took in how it all flashed, manhattans and martinis, earrings and shoe-tips—he marveled, but knew it was a falsehood, even a figment. The great world was somewhere else. The conversation could fool you: how these people talked! From the conversation itself—grains of it, carried off, swallowed by new eddyings, swirl devouring swirl, every moment a permutation in the tableau of those free-standing figures or dolls, all of them afloat in a tub—from this or that hint or syllable you could imagine the whole universe in the process of ultimate comprehension. Human nature, the stars, history—the voices drummed and strummed. Lucy swam by blank-eyed, pushing a platter of mottled cheeses. Feingold seized her: "It's a waste!" She gazed back. He said, "No one's here!" Mournfully she rocked a stump of cheese; then he lost her.

He went into the living room: it was mainly empty, a few lumps on the sofa. The lumps wore business suits. The dining room was better. Something in formation: something around the big table: coffee cups shimmering to the brim, cake cut onto plates (the mock-Victorian rosebud plates from Boots's drug store in London: the year before their first boy was born Lucy and Feingold saw the Brontës' moors; Coleridge's house in Highgate; Lamb House, Rye, where Edith Wharton had tea with Henry James; Bloomsbury; the Cambridge stairs Forster had lived at the top of)—it seemed about to become a regular visit, with points of view, opinions; a discussion. The voices began to stumble; Feingold liked that, it was nearly human. But then, serving round the forks and paper napkins, he noticed the awful vivacity of their falsetto phrases: actors, theater chatter, who was directing whom, what was opening where; he hated actors. Shrill puppets. Brainless. A double row of faces around the table; gurgles of fools.

The center hall—swept clean. No one there but Lucy, lingering.

"Theater in the dining room," he said. "Junk."

"Film. I heard film."

"Film too," he conceded. "Junk. It's mobbed in there."

"Because they've got the cake. They've got all the food. The living room's got nothing."

"My God," he said, like a man choking, "do you realize *no one came?*"

The living room had—had once had—potato chips. The chips were gone, the carrot sticks eaten, of the celery sticks nothing left but threads. One olive in a dish; Feingold chopped it in two with vicious teeth. The business suits had disappeared. "It's awfully early," Lucy said; "a lot of people had to leave." "It's a cocktail party, that's what happens," Feingold said. "It isn't *exactly* a cocktail party," Lucy said. They sat down on the carpet in front of the fireless grate. "Is that a real fireplace?" someone inquired. "We never light it," Lucy said. "Do you light those candlesticks ever?" "They belonged to Jimmy's grandmother," Lucy said, "we never light them."

She crossed no-man's-land to the dining room. They were serious in there now. The subject was Chaplin's gestures.

In the living room Feingold despaired; no one asked him, he began to tell about the compassionate knight. A problem of ego, he said: compassion being superconsciousness of one's own pride. Not that he believed this; he only thought it provocative to say something original, even if a little muddled. But no one responded. Feingold looked up. "Can't you light that fire?" said a man. "All right," Feingold said. He rolled a paper log made of last Sunday's *Times* and laid a match on it. A flame as clear as a streetlight whitened the faces of the sofa-sitters. He recognized a friend of his from the Seminary—he had what Lucy called "theological" friends—and then and there, really very suddenly, Feingold wanted to talk about God. Or, if not God, then certain historical atrocities, abominations: to wit, the crime of the French nobleman Draconet, a proud Crusader, who in the spring of the year 1247 arrested all the Jews of the province of Vienne, castrated the men, and tore off the breasts of the women; some he did not mutilate, and only cut in two. It interested Feingold that Magna Carta and the Jewish badge of shame were issued in the same year, and that less than a century afterward all the Jews were driven out of England, even families who had been settled there seven or eight generations. He had a soft spot for Pope Clement IV, who absolved the Jews from responsibility for the Black Death. "The plague takes the Jews themselves," the Pope said. Feingold knew innumerable stories about forced conversions, he felt at home with these thoughts, comfortable, the chairs seemed dense with family. He wondered whether it would be appropriate—at a cocktail party, after all!—to inquire after the status of the Seminary friend's agnosticism: was it merely that God had stepped out of history, left the room for a moment, so to speak, without a pass, or was there no Creator to begin with, nothing had been created, the world was a chimera, a solipsist's delusion?

Lucy was uneasy with the friend from the Seminary; he was the one who had administered her conversion, and every encounter was like a new stage in a perpetual examination. She was glad there was no Jewish catechism. Was she a backslider? Anyhow she felt tested. Sometimes she spoke of Jesus to the children. She looked around—her great eyes wheeled—and saw that everyone in the living room was a Jew.

There were Jews in the dining room too, but the unruffled, devil-may-care kind: the humorists, the painters, film reviewers who went off to studio showings of *Screw on Screen* on the eve of the Day of Atonement. Mostly there were Gentiles in the dining room. Nearly the whole cake was gone. She took the last piece, cubed it on a paper plate, and carried it back to the living room. She blamed Feingold, he was having one of his spasms of fanaticism. Everyone normal, everyone with sense—the humanists and humorists, for instance—would want to keep away. What was he now, after all, but one of those boring autodidacts who spew out everything they read? He was doing it for spite, because no one had come. There he was, telling about the blood-libel. Little Hugh of Lincoln.

How in London, in 1279, Jews were torn to pieces by horses, on a charge of having crucified a Christian child. How in 1285, in Munich, a mob burned down a synagogue on the same pretext. At Eastertime in Mainz two years earlier. Three centuries of beatified child martyrs, some of them figments, all called "Little Saints." The Holy Niño of LaGuardia. Feingold was crazed by these tales, he drank them like a vampire. Lucy stuck a square of chocolate cake in his mouth to shut him up. Feingold was waiting for a voice. The friend from the Seminary, pragmatic, licked off his bit of cake hungrily. It was a cake sent from home, packed by his wife in a plastic bag, to make sure there was something to eat. It was a guaranteed no-lard cake. They were all ravenous. The fire crumpled out in big paper cinders.

The friend from the Seminary had brought a friend. Lucy examined him: she knew how to give catechisms of her own, she was not a novelist for nothing. She catechized and catalogued: a refugee. Fingers like long wax candles, snuffed at the nails. Black sockets: was he blind? It was hard to tell where the eyes were under that ledge of skull. Skull for a head, but such a cushioned mouth, such lips, such orderly expressive teeth. Such a bone in such a dry wrist. A nose like a saint's. The face of Jesus. He whispered. Everyone leaned over to hear. He was Feingold's voice: the voice Feingold was waiting for.

"Come to modern times," the voice urged. "Come to yesterday." Lucy was right: she could tell a refugee in an instant, even before she heard any accent. They all reminded her of her father. She put away this insight (the resemblance of Presbyterian ministers to Hitler refugees) to talk over with Feingold later: it was nicely analytical, it had enough mystery to satisfy. "Yesterday," the refugee said, "the eyes of God were shut." And Lucy saw him shut his hidden eyes in their tunnels. "Shut," he said, "like iron doors"—a voice of such nobility that Lucy thought immediately of that eerie passage in Genesis where the voice of the Lord God walks in the Garden in the cool of the day and calls to Adam, "Where are you?"

They all listened with a terrible intensity. Again Lucy looked around. It pained her how intense Jews could be, though she too was intense. But she was intense because her brain was roiling with ardor, she wooed mind-pictures, she was a novelist. *They* were intense all the time; she supposed the grocers among them were as intense as any novelist; was it because they had been Chosen, was it because they pitied themselves every breathing moment?

Pity and shock stood in all their faces.

The refugee was telling a story. "I witnessed it," he said, "I am the witness." Horror; sadism; corpses. As if—Lucy took the image from the elusive wind that was his voice in its whisper—as if hundreds and hundreds of Crucifixions were all happening at once. She visualized a hillside with multitudes of crosses, and bodies dropping down from big bloody nails. Every Jew was Jesus. That was the only way Lucy could get hold of it: otherwise it was only a movie. She had seen all the movies, the truth was she could feel nothing. That same bulldozer shoveling those same sticks of skeletons, that same little boy in a cap with twisted mouth and his hands in the air—if there had been a camera at the Crucifixion Christianity would collapse, no one would ever feel anything about it. Cruelty came out of the imagination, and had to be witnessed by the imagination.

All the same, she listened. What he told was exactly like the movies. A gray scene, a scrubby hill, a ravine. Germans in helmets, with shining tar-black belts, wearing gloves. A ragged bundle of Jews at the lip of the ravine—an old grandmother, a child or two, a couple in their forties. All the faces stained with grayness, the stubble on the ground stained gray, the clothes on them limp as shrouds but immobile, as if they were already under the dirt, shut off from breezes, as if they were already stone. The refugee's whisper carved them like sculptures—there they stood, a shadowy stone asterisk of Jews, you could see their nostrils, open as skulls, the stony round ears of the children, the grandmother's awful twig of a neck, the father and mother grasping the children but strangers to each other, not a touch between them, the grandmother cast out, claiming no one and not claimed, all prayerless stone gums. There they stood. For a long while the refugee's voice pinched them and held them, so that you had to look. His voice made Lucy look and look. He pierced the figures through with his whisper. Then he let the shots come. The figures never teetered, never shook: the stoniness broke all at once and they fell cleanly, like sacks, into the ravine. Immediately they were in a heap, with random limbs all tangled together. The refugee's voice like a camera brought a German boot to the edge of the ravine. The boot kicked sand. It kicked and kicked, the sand poured over the family of sacks.

Then Lucy saw the fingers of the listeners—all their fingers were stretched out.

The room began to lift. It ascended. It rose like an ark on waters. Lucy said inside her mind, "This chamber of Jews." It seemed to her that the room was levitating on the little grains of the refugee's whisper. She felt herself alone at the bottom, below the floorboards, while the room floated upward, carrying Jews. Why did it not take her too? Only Jesus could take her. They were being kidnapped, these Jews, by a messenger from the land of the dead. The man had a power. Already he was in the shadow of another tale: she promised herself she would not listen, only Jesus could make her listen. The room was ascending. Above her head it grew smaller and smaller, more and more remote, it fled deeper and deeper into upwardness.

She craned after it. Wouldn't it bump into the apartment

upstairs? It was like watching the underside of an elevator, all dirty and hairy, with dust-roots wagging. The black floor moved higher and higher. It was getting free of her, into loftiness, lifting Jews.

The glory of their martyrdom.

Under the rising eave Lucy had an illumination: she saw herself with the children in a little city park. A Sunday afternoon early in May. Feingold has stayed home to nap, and Lucy and the children find seats on a bench and wait for the unusual music to begin. The room is still levitating, but inside Lucy's illumination the boys are chasing birds. They run away from Lucy, they return, they leave. They surround a pigeon. They do not touch the pigeon; Lucy has forbidden it. She has read that city pigeons carry meningitis. A little boy in Red Bank, New Jersey, contracted sleeping sickness from touching a pigeon; after six years, he is still asleep. In his sleep he has grown from a child to an adolescent; puberty has come on him in his sleep, his testicles have dropped down, a benign blond beard glints mildly on his cheeks. His parents weep and weep. He is still asleep. No instruments or players are visible. A woman steps out onto a platform. She is an anthropologist from the Smithsonian Institution in Washington, D.C. She explains that there will be no "entertainment" in the usual sense; there will be no "entertainers." The players will not be artists; they will be "real peasants." They have been brought over from Messina, from Calabria. They are shepherds, goatherds. They will sing and dance and play just as they do when they come down from the hills to while away the evenings in the taverns. They will play the instruments that scare away the wolves from the flock. They will sing the songs that celebrate the Madonna of Love. A dozen men file onto the platform. They have heavy faces that do not smile. They have heavy dark skins, cratered and leathery. They have ears and noses that look like dried twisted clay. They have gold teeth. They have no teeth. Some are young; most are in their middle years. One is very old; he wears bells on his fingers. One has an instrument like a butter churn: he shoves a stick in and out of a hole in a wooden tub held under his arm, and a rattling screech spurts out of it. One blows on two slender pipes simultaneously. One has a long strap, which he rubs. One has a frame of bicycle bells; a descendant of the bells the priests used to beat in the temple of Minerva.

The anthropologist is still explaining everything. She explains the "male" instrument: three wooden knockers; the innermost one lunges up and down between the other two. The songs, she explains, are mainly erotic. The dances are suggestive.

The unusual music commences. The park has filled with Italians—greenhorns from Sicily, settled New Yorkers from Naples. An ancient people. They clap. The old man with the bells on his fingers points his dusty shoe-toes and slowly follows a circle of his own. His eyes are in trance, he squats, he ascends. The anthropologist explains that up-and-down dancing can also be found in parts of Africa. The singers wail like Arabs; the anthropologist notes that the Arab conquest covered the southernmost portion of the Italian boot for two hundred years. The whole chorus of peasants sings in a dialect of archaic Greek; the language has survived in the old songs, the anthropologist explains. The crowd is laughing and stamping. They click their fingers and sway. Lucy's boys are bored. They watch the man with the finger-bells; they watch the wooden male pump up and down. Everyone is clapping, stamping, clicking, swaying, thumping. The wailing goes on and on, faster and faster. The singers are dancers, the dancers are singers, they turn and turn, they are smiling the drugged smiles of dervishes. At home they grow flowers. They follow the sheep into the deep grass. They drink wine in the taverns at night. Calabria and Sicily in New York, sans wives, in sweat-blotched shirts and wrinkled dusty pants, gasping before strangers who have never smelled the sweetness of their village grasses!

Now the anthropologist from the Smithsonian has vanished out of Lucy's illumination. A pair of dancers seize each other. Leg winds over leg, belly into belly, each man hopping on a single free leg. Intertwined, they squat and rise, squat and rise. Old Hellenic syllables fly from them. They send out high elastic cries. They celebrate the Madonna, giver of fertility and fecundity. Lucy is glorified. She is exalted. She comprehends. Not that the musicians are peasants, not that their faces and feet and necks and wrists are blown grass and red earth. An enlightenment comes on her: she sees what is eternal: before the Madonna there was Venus; before Venus, Aphrodite; before Aphrodite, Astarte. The womb of the goddess is garden, lamb, and babe. She is the river and the waterfall. She causes grave men of business—goatherds are men of business—to cavort and to flash their gold teeth. She induces them to blow, beat, rub, shake and scrape objects so that music will drop out of them.

Inside Lucy's illumination the dancers are seething. They are writhing. For the sake of the goddess, for the sake of the womb of the goddess, they are turning into serpents. When they grow still they are earth. They are from always to always. Nature is their pulse. Lucy sees: she understands: the gods are God. How terrible to have given up Jesus, a man like these, made of earth like these, with a pulse like these, God entering nature to become god! Jesus, no more miraculous than an ordinary goatherd; is a goatherd miracle? Is a leaf? A nut, a pit, a core, a seed, a stone? Everything is miracle! Lucy sees how she has abandoned nature, how she has lost true religion on account of the God of the Jews. The boys are on their bellies on the ground, digging it up with sticks. They dig and dig: little holes with mounds beside them. They fill them with peach pits, cherry pits, cantaloupe rinds. The Sicilians and Neapolitans pick up their baskets and purses and shopping bags and leave. The benches smell of eaten fruit, running juices, insect-mobbed. The stage is clean.

The living room has escaped altogether. It is very high and extremely small, no wider than the moon on Lucy's thumbnail. It is still sailing upward, and the voices of those on board are so faint that Lucy almost loses them. But she knows which word it is they mainly use. How long can they go on about it? How long? A morbid cud-chewing. Death and death and death. The word is less a human word than an animal's cry; a crow's. Caw caw. It belongs to storms, floods, avalanches. Acts of God. "Holocaust," someone caws dimly from above; she knows it must be Feingold. He always says this word over and over and over. History is bad for him: how little it makes him seem! Lucy decides it is possible to become jaded by atrocity. She is bored by the shootings and the gas and the camps, she is not ashamed to admit this. They are as tiresome as prayer. Repetition diminishes conviction; she is thinking of her father leading the same hymns week after week. If you said the same prayer over and over again, wouldn't your brain turn out to be no better than a prayer wheel?

In the dining room all the springs were running down. It was stale in there, a failed party. They were drinking beer or Coke or whiskey-and-water and playing with the cake crumbs on the tablecloth. There was still some cheese left on a plate, and half a bowl of salted peanuts. "The impact of Romantic Individualism," one of the humanists objected. "At the Frick?" "I never saw that." "They certainly are deliberate, you have to say that for them." Lucy, leaning abandoned against the door, tried to tune in. The relief of hearing atheists. A jacket designer who worked in Feingold's art department came in carrying a coat. Feingold had invited her because she was newly divorced; she was afraid to live alone. She was afraid of being ambushed in her basement while doing laundry. "Where's Jimmy?" the jacket designer asked. "In the other room." "Say goodbye for me, will you?" "Goodbye," Lucy said. The humanists—Lucy saw how they were all compassionate knights—stood up. A puddle from an overturned saucer was leaking onto the floor. "Oh, I'll get that," Lucy told the knights, "don't think another thought about it."

Overhead Feingold and the refugee are riding the living room. Their words are specks. All the Jews are in the air.

Puttermesser:
Her Work History,
Her Ancestry,
Her Afterlife

Puttermesser was thirty-four, a lawyer. She was also something of a feminist, not crazy, but she resented having "Miss" put in front of her name; she thought it pointedly discriminatory, she wanted to be a lawyer among lawyers. Though she was no virgin she lived alone, but idiosyncratically—in the Bronx, on the Grand Concourse, among other people's decaying old parents. Her own had moved to Miami Beach; in furry slippers left over from high school she roamed the same endlessly mazy apartment she had grown up in, her aging piano sheets still on top of the upright with the teacher's X marks on them showing where she should practice up to. Puttermesser always pushed a little ahead of the actual assignment; in school too. Her teachers told her mother she was "highly motivated," "achievement oriented." Also she had "scholastic drive." Her mother wrote all these things down in a notebook, kept it always, and took it with her to Florida in case she should die there. Puttermesser had a younger sister who was also highly motivated, but she had married an Indian, a Parsee chemist, and gone to live in Calcutta. Already the sister had four children and seven saris of various fabrics.

Puttermesser went on studying. In law school they called her a grind, a competitive-compulsive, an egomaniac out for aggrandizement. But ego was no part of it; she was looking to solve something, she did not know what. At the back of the linen closet she found a stack of her father's old shirt cardboards (her mother was provident, stingy: in kitchen drawers Puttermesser still discovered folded squares of used ancient waxed paper, million-creased into whiteness, cheese-smelling, nesting small unidentifiable wormlets); so behind the riser pipe in the bathroom Puttermesser kept weeks' worth of Sunday *Times* crossword puzzles stapled to these laundry boards and worked on them indiscriminately. She played chess against herself, and was always victor over the color she had decided to identify with. She organized tort cases on index cards. It was not that she intended to remember everything: situations—it was her tendency to call intellectual problems "situations"—slipped into her mind like butter into a bottle.

A letter came from her mother in Florida:

Dear Ruth,

I know you won't believe this but I swear it's true the other day Daddy was walking on the Avenue and who should he run into but Mrs. Zaretsky, the thin one from Burnside not the stout one from Davidson, you remember her Joel? Well he's divorced now no children thank God so he's free as a bird as they say his ex the poor thing couldn't conceive. *He* had tests he's O.K. He's only an accountant not good enough for you because God knows

I never forget the day you made Law Review but you should come down just to see what a tender type he grew into. Every tragedy has its good side Mrs. Zaretsky says he comes down now practically whenever she calls him long distance. Daddy said to Mrs. Zaretsky well, an accountant, you didn't overeducate your son anyhow, with daughters it's different. But don't take this to heart honey Daddy is as proud as I am of your achievements. Why don't you write we didn't hear from you too long busy is busy but parents are parents.

Puttermesser had a Jewish face and a modicum of American distrust of it. She resembled no poster she had ever seen: with a Negroid passion she hated the Breck shampoo girl, so blond and bland and pale-mouthed; she boycotted Breck because of the golden-haired posters, all crudely idealized, an American wet dream, in the subway. Puttermesser's hair came in bouncing scallops—layered waves from scalp to tip, like imbricated roofing tile. It was nearly black and had a way of sometimes sticking straight out. Her nose had thick, well-haired, uneven nostrils, the right one noticeably wider than the other. Her eyes were small, the lashes short, invisible. She had the median Mongol lid—one of those Jewish faces with a vaguely Oriental cast. With all this, it was a fact she was not bad-looking. She had a good skin with, so far, few lines or pits or signs of looseness-to-come. Her jaw was pleasing—a baby jowl appeared only when she put her head deep in a book.

In bed she studied Hebrew grammar. The permutations of the triple-lettered root elated her: how was it possible that a whole language, hence a whole literature, a civilization even, should rest on the pure presence of three letters of the alphabet? The Hebrew verb, a stunning mechanism: three letters, whichever fated three, could command all possibility simply by a change in their pronunciation, or the addition of a wing-letter fore and aft. Every conceivable utterance blossomed from this trinity. It seemed to her not so much a language for expression as a code for the world's design, indissoluble, predetermined, translucent. The idea of the grammar of Hebrew turned Puttermesser's brain into a palace, a sort of Vatican; inside its corridors she walked from one resplendent triptych to another.

She wrote her mother a letter refusing to come to Florida to look over the divorced accountant's tenderness. She explained her life again; she explained it by indirection. She wrote:

I have a cynical apperception of power, due no doubt to my current job. You probably haven't heard of the Office for Visas and Registration, OVIR for short. It's located on Ogaryova Street, in Moscow, U.S.S.R. I could enumerate for you a few of the innumerable bureaucratic atrocities of OVIR, not that anyone knows them all. But I could give you a list of the names of all those criminals, down to the women clerks, Yefimova, Korolova, Akulova, Arkhipova, Izrailova, all of them on Kolpachni Street in an office headed by Zolotukhin, the assistant to Colonel Smyrnov, who's under Ovchinikov, who is second in command to General Viryein, only Viryein and Ovchinikov aren't on Kolpachni Street, they're the ones in the head office—the M.D.V., Internal Affairs Ministry—on Ogaryova Street. Some day all the Soviet Jews will come out of the spider's clutches of these people and be free. Please explain to Daddy that this is one of the highest priorities of my life at this time in my personal history. Do you think a Joel Zaretsky can share such a vision?

Immediately after law school, Puttermesser entered the firm of Midland, Reid & Cockleberry. It was a blueblood Wall Street firm, and Puttermesser, hired for her brains and ingratiating (read: immigrant-like) industry, was put into a back office to hunt up all-fours cases for the men up front. Though a Jew and a woman, she felt little discrimination: the back office was chiefly the repository of unmitigated drudgery and therefore of usable youth. Often enough it kept its lights burning till three in the morning. It was right that the Top Rung of law school should earn you the Bottom of the Ladder in the actual world of all-fours. The wonderful thing was the fact of the Ladder itself. And though she was the only woman, Puttermesser was not the only Jew. Three Jews a year joined the back precincts of Midland, Reid (four the year Puttermesser came, which meant they thought "woman" more than "Jew" at the sight of her). Three Jews a year left—not the same three. Lunchtime was difficult. Most of the young men went to one or two athletic clubs nearby to "work out"; Puttermesser ate from a paper bag at her desk, along with the other Jews, and this was strange: the young male Jews appeared to be as committed to the squash courts as the others. Alas, the athletic clubs would not have them, and this too was preternatural— the young Jews were indistinguishable from the others. They bought the same suits from the same tailors, wore precisely the same shirts and shoes, were careful to avoid tie clips and to be barbered a good deal shorter than the wild men of the streets, though a bit longer than the prigs in the banks.

Puttermesser remembered what Anatole France said of Dreyfus: that he was the same type as the officers who condemned him. "In their shoes he would have condemned himself."

Only their accents fell short of being identical: the "a" a shade too far into the nose, the "i" with its telltale elongation, had long ago spread from Brooklyn to Great Neck, from Puttermesser's Bronx to Scarsdale. These two influential vowels had the uncanny faculty of disqualifying them for promotion. The squash players, meanwhile, moved out of the back offices into the front offices. One or two of them were groomed—curried, fed sugar, led out by the muzzle—for partnership: were called out to lunch with thin and easeful clients, spent an afternoon in the dining room of one of the big sleek banks, and, in short, developed the creamy cheeks and bland habits of the always-comfortable.

The Jews, by contrast, grew more anxious, hissed together meanly among the urinals (Puttermesser, in the ladies' room next door, could hear malcontent rumblings in the connecting plumbing), became perfectionist and uncasual, quibbled bitterly, with stabbing forefingers, over principles, and all in all began to look and act less like superannuated college athletes and more like Jews. Then they left. They left of their own choice; no one shut them out.

Puttermesser left too, weary of so much chivalry—the partners in particular were excessively gracious to her, and treated her like a fellow-aristocrat. Puttermesser supposed this was because *she* did not say "a" in her nose or elongate her "i," and above all she did not dentalize her "t," "d," or "l," keeping them all back against the upper palate. Long ago her speech had been "standardized" by the drilling of fanatical teachers, elocutionary missionaries hired out of the Midwest by Puttermesser's prize high school, until almost all the regionalism was drained out; except for the pace of her syllables, which had a New York deliberateness, Puttermesser could have come from anywhere. She was every bit as American as her grandfather in his captain's hat. From Castle Garden to blue New England mists, her father's father, hat-and-neckwear peddler to Yankees! In Puttermesser's veins Providence, Rhode Island, beat richly. It seemed to her the partners felt this.

Then she remembered that Dreyfus spoke perfect French, and was the perfect Frenchman.

For farewell she was taken out to a public restaurant—the clubs the partners belonged to (they explained) did not allow women—and apologized to.

"We're sorry to lose you," one said, and the other said, "No one for you in this outfit for under the canvas, hah?"

"The canvas?" Puttermesser said.

"Wedding canopy," said the partner, with a wink. "Or do they make them out of sheepskin—I forget."

"An interesting custom. I hear you people break the dishes at a wedding too," said the second partner.

An anthropological meal. They explored the rites of her tribe. She had not known she was strange to them. Their beautiful manners were the cautiousness you adopt when you visit the interior: Dr. Livingstone, I presume? They shook hands and wished her luck, and at that moment, so close to their faces with those moist smile-ruts flowing from the sides of their waferlike noses punctured by narrow, even nostrils, Puttermesser was astonished into noticing how strange *they* were—so many luncheon martinis inside their bellies, and such beautiful manners even while drunk, and, important though they were, insignificant though she was, the fine ceremonial fact of their having brought her to this carpeted place. Their eyes were blue. Their necks were clean. How closely they were shaven!—like men who grew no hair at all. Yet hairs curled inside their ears. They let her take away all her memo pads with her name printed on them. She was impressed by their courtesy, their benevolence, through which they always got their way. She had given them three years of meticulous anonymous research, deep deep nights going after precedents, dates, lost issues, faded faint politics; for their sakes she had yielded up those howling morning headaches and half a diopter's worth of sight in both eyes. Brilliant students make good aides. They were pleased though not regretful. She was replaceable: a clever black had been hired only that morning.

The palace they led her to at the end of it all was theirs by divine right: in which they believed, on which they acted. They were benevolent because benevolence was theirs to dispense.

She went to work for the Department of Receipts and Disbursements. Her title was Assistant Corporation Counsel—it had no meaning, it was part of the subspeech on which bureaucracy relies. Of the many who held this title most were Italians and Jews, and again Puttermesser was the only woman. In this great City office there were no ceremonies and no manners: gross shouts, ignorant clerks, slovenliness, litter on the floors, grit stuck all over antiquated books. The ladies' room reeked: the women urinated standing up, and hot urine splashed on the toilet seats and onto the muddy tiles.

The successive heads of this department were called Commissioners. They were all political appointees—scavengers after spoils. Puttermesser herself was not quite a civil servant and not quite *not* a civil servant—one of those amphibious creatures hanging between base contempt and bare decency; but she soon felt the ignominy of belonging to that mean swarm of City employees rooted bleakly in cells inside the honeycomb of the Municipal Building. It was a monstrous place, gray everywhere, abundantly tunneled, with multitudes of corridors and stairs and shafts, a kind of swollen doom through which the bickering of small-voiced officials whinnied. At the same time there were always curious farm sounds —in the summer the steady cricket of the air-conditioning, in the winter the gnash and croak of old radiators. Nevertheless the windows were broad and high and stupendously filled with light; they looked out on the whole lower island of Manhattan, revealed *as* an island, down to the Battery, all crusted over with the dried lava of shape and shape: rectangle over square, and square over spire. At noon the dark gongs of St. Andrew's boomed their wild and stately strokes.

To Puttermesser all this meant she had come down in the world. Here she was not even a curiosity. No one noticed a Jew. Unlike the partners at Midland, Reid, the Commissioners did not travel out among their subjects and were rarely seen. Instead they were like shut-up kings in a tower, and suffered from rumors.

But Puttermesser discovered that in City life all rumors are true. Putative turncoats are genuine turncoats. All whispered knifings have happened: officials reputed to be about to topple, topple. So far Puttermesser had lasted through two elections, seeing the powerful become powerless and the formerly powerless inflate themselves overnight, like gigantic winds, to suck out the victory of the short run. When one Administration was razed, for the moment custom seemed leveled with it, everything that smelled of "before," of "the old way"—but only at first. The early fits of innovation subsided, and gradually the old way of doing things crept back, covering everything over, like grass, as if the building and its workers were together some inexorable vegetable organism with its own laws of subsistence. The civil servants were grass. Nothing destroyed them, they were stronger than the pavement, they were stronger than time. The Administration might turn on its hinge, throwing out one lot of patronage eaters and gathering in the new lot: the work went on. They might put in fresh carpeting in the new Deputy's office, or a private toilet in the new Commissioner's, and change the clerks' light bulbs to a lower wattage, and design an extravagant new colophon for a useless old document—they might do anything they liked: the work went on as before. The organism breathed, it comprehended itself.

So there was nothing for the Commissioner to do, and he knew it, and the organism knew it. For a very great salary the Commissioner shut his door and cleaned his nails behind it with one of the shining tools of a fancy Swiss knife, and had a secretary who was rude to everyone, and made dozens of telephone calls every day.

The current one was a rich and foolish playboy who had given the Mayor money for his campaign. All the high officials of every department were either men who had given the Mayor money or else courtiers who had humiliated themselves for him in the political clubhouse—mainly by flattering the clubhouse boss, who before any election was already a secret mayor and dictated the patronage lists. But the current Commissioner owed nothing to the boss because he had given the Mayor money and was the Mayor's own appointee; and anyhow he would have little to do with the boss because he had little to do with any Italian. The boss was a gentlemanly Neapolitan named Fiore, the chairman of the board of a bank; but still, he was only an Italian, and the Commissioner cared chiefly for blue-eyed bankers. He used his telephone to make luncheon appointments with them, and sometimes tennis. He himself was a blue-eyed Guggenheim, a German Jew, but not one of the grand philanthropic Guggenheims. The name was a cunning coincidence (cut down from Guggenheimer), and he was rich enough to be taken for one of the real Guggenheims, who thought him an upstart and disowned him. Grandeur demands discreetness; he was so discreetly disowned that no one knew it, not even the Rockefeller he had met at Choate.

This Commissioner was a handsome, timid man, still young, and good at boating; on weekends he wore sneakers and cultivated the friendship of the dynasties—Sulzbergers and Warburgs, who let him eat with them but warned their daughters against him. He had dropped out of two colleges and finally graduated from the third by getting a term-paper factory to plagiarize his reports. He was harmless and simple-minded, still devoted to his brainy late father, and frightened to death of news conferences. He understood nothing: art appreciation had been his best subject (he was attracted to

Renaissance nudes), economics his worst. If someone asked, "How much does the City invest every day?" or "Is there any Constitutional bar against revenue from commuters?" or "What is your opinion about taxing exempt properties?" his pulse would catch in his throat, making his nose run, and he had to say he was pressed for time and would let them have the answers from his Deputy in charge of the Treasury. Sometimes he would even call on Puttermesser for an answer.

Now if this were an optimistic portrait, exactly here is where Puttermesser's emotional life would begin to grind itself into evidence. Her biography would proceed romantically, the rich young Commissioner of the Department of Receipts and Disbursements would fall in love with her. She would convert him to intelligence and to the cause of Soviet Jewry. He would abandon boating and the pursuit of bluebloods. Puttermesser would end her work history abruptly and move on to a bower in a fine suburb.

This is not to be. Puttermesser will always be an employee in the Municipal Building. She will always behold Brooklyn Bridge through its windows; also sunsets of high glory, bringing her religious pangs. She will not marry. Perhaps she will undertake a long-term affair with Vogel, the Deputy in charge of the Treasury; perhaps not.

The difficulty with Puttermesser is that she is loyal to certain environments.

Puttermesser, while working in the Municipal Building, had a luxuriant dream, a dream of *gan eydn*—a term and notion handed on from her great-uncle Zindel, a former shammes in a shul that had been torn down. In this reconstituted Garden of Eden, which is to say in the World to Come, Puttermesser, who was not afflicted with quotidian uncertainty in the Present World, had even more certainty of her aims. With her weakness for fudge (others of her age, class, and character had advanced to martinis, at least to ginger ale; Puttermesser still drank ice cream with cola, despised mints as too tingly, eschewed salty liver canapés, hunted down chocolate babies, Kraft caramels, Mary Janes, Milky Ways, peanut brittle, and immediately afterward furiously brushed her teeth, scrubbing off guilt)—with all this nasty self-indulgence, she was nevertheless very thin and unironic. Or: to postulate an afterlife was her single irony—a game in the head not unlike a melting fudge cube held against the upper palate.

There, at any rate, Puttermesser would sit, in Eden, under a middle-sized tree, in the solid blaze of an infinite heart-of-summer July, green, green, green everywhere, green above and green below, herself gleaming and made glorious by sweat, every itch annihilated, fecundity dismissed. And there Puttermesser would, as she imagined it, *take in*. Ready to her left hand, the box of fudge (rather like the fudge sold to the lower school by the eighth-grade cooking class in P.S. 74, The Bronx, circa 1942); ready to her right hand, a borrowed steeple of library books: for into Eden the Crotona Park Branch has ascended intact, sans librarians and fines, but with its delectable terrestrial binding-glue fragrances unevaporated.

Here Puttermesser sits. Day after celestial day, perfection of desire upon perfection of contemplation, into the exaltations of an uninterrupted forever, she eats fudge in human shape (once known—no use covering this up—as nigger babies), or fudge in square shapes (and in Eden there is no tooth decay); and she reads. Puttermesser reads and reads. Her eyes in Paradise are unfatigued. And if she still does not know what it is she wants to solve, she has only to read on. The Crotona Park Branch is as paradisal here as it was on earth. She reads anthropology, zoology, physical chemistry, philosophy (in the green air of heaven Kant and Nietzsche together fall into crystal splinters). The New Books section is peerless: she will learn about the linkages of genes, about quarks, about primate sign language, theories of the origins of the races, religions of ancient civilizations, what Stonehenge meant. Puttermesser will read Non-Fiction into eternity; and there is still time for Fiction! Eden is equipped above all with timelessness, so Puttermesser will read at last all of Balzac, all of Dickens, all of Turgenev and Dostoevski (her mortal self has already read all of Tolstoy and George Eliot); at last Puttermesser will read *Kristin Lavransdatter* and the stupendous trilogy of Dmitri Merezhkovski, she will read *The Magic Mountain* and the whole *Faerie Queene* and every line of *The Ring and the Book*, she will read a biography of Beatrix Potter and one of Walter Scott in many entrancing volumes and one of Lytton Strachey, at last, at last! In Eden insatiable Puttermesser will be nourished, if not glutted. She will study Roman law, the more arcane varieties of higher mathematics, the nuclear composition of the stars, what happened to the Monophysites, Chinese history, Russian, and Icelandic.

But meanwhile, still alive, not yet translated upward, her days given over to the shadow reign of a playboy Commissioner, Puttermesser was learning only Hebrew.

Twice a week, at night (it seemed), she went to Uncle Zindel for a lesson. Where the bus ran through peeling neighborhoods the trolley tracks sometimes shone up through a broken smother of asphalt, like weeds wanting renewal. From childhood Puttermesser remembered how trolley days were better days: in summer the cars banged along, self-contained little carnivals, with open wire-mesh sides sucking in hot winds, the passengers serenely jogging on the seats. Not so this bus, closed like a capsule against the slum.

The old man, Zindel the Stingy, hung on to life among the cooking smells of Spanish-speaking blacks. Puttermesser walked up three flights of steps and leaned against the crooked door, waiting for the former shammes with his little sack. Each evening Zindel brought up a single egg from the Cuban grocery. He boiled it while Puttermesser sat with her primer.

"You should go downtown," the shammes said, "where they got regular language factories. Berlitz. N.Y.U. They even got an *ulpan*, like in Israel."

"You're good enough," Puttermesser said. "You know everything they know."

"And something more also. Why you don't live downtown, on the East Side, fancy?"

"The rent is too much, I inherited your stinginess."

"And such a name. A nice young fellow meets such a name, he laughs. You should change it to something different, lovely, nice. Shapiro, Levine. Cohen, Goldweiss, Blumenthal. I don't say make it *different*, who needs Adams, who needs McKee, I say make it a name not a joke. Your father gave you a bad present with it. For a young girl, Butterknife!"

"I'll change it to Margarine-messer."

"Never mind the ha-ha. *My* father, what was your great-great-grandfather, didn't allow a knife to the table Friday night. When it came to *kiddush*—knifes off! All knifes! On Sabbath an instrument, a blade? On Sabbath a weapon? A point? An edge? What makes bleeding among mankind? What makes war? Knifes! No knifes! Off! A clean table! And something else you'll notice. By us we got only *messer*, you follow? By them they got sword, they got lance, they got halberd. Go to the dictionary, I went once. So help me, what don't one of them knights carry? Look up in the book, you'll see halberd, you'll see cutlass, pike, rapier, foil, ten dozen more. By us a pike is a fish. Not to mention what nowadays they got— bayonet stuck on the gun, who knows what else the poor soldier got to carry in the pocket. Maybe a dagger same as a pirate. But by us—what we got? A *messer! Puttermesser*, you slice off a piece butter, you cut to live, not to kill. A name of honor, you follow? Still, for a young girl—"

"Uncle Zindel, I'm past thirty."

Uncle Zindel blinked lids like insect's wings, translucent. He saw her voyaging, voyaging. The wings of his eyes shadowed the Galilee. They moved over the Tomb of the Patriarchs. A tear for the tears of Mother Rachel rode on his nose. "Your mother knows you're going? Alone on an airplane, such a young girl? You wrote her?"

"I wrote her, Uncle Zindel. I'm not flying anywhere."

"By sea is also danger. What Mama figures, in Miami who is there? The dead and dying. In Israel you'll meet someone. You'll marry, you'll settle there. What's the difference, these days, modern times, quick travel—"

Uncle Zindel's egg was ready, hard-boiled. The shammes tapped it and the shell came off raggedly. Puttermesser consulted the alphabet: *aleph, beys, gimel*; she was not going to Israel, she had business in the Municipal Building. Uncle Zindel, chewing, began finally to teach: "First see how a *gimel* and which way a *zayen*. Twins, but one kicks a leg left, one right. You got to practice the difference. If legs don't work, think pregnant bellies. Mrs. *Zayen* pregnant in one direction, Mrs. *Gimel* in the other. Together they give birth to *gez*, which means what you cut off. A night for knifes! Listen, going home from here you should be extra careful tonight. Martinez, the upstairs not the next door, her daughter they mugged and they took."

The shammes chewed, and under his jaws Puttermesser's head bent, practicing the bellies of the holy letters.

Stop. Stop, stop! Puttermesser's biographer, stop! Disengage, please. Though it is true that biographies are invented, not recorded, here you invent too much. A symbol is allowed, but not a whole scene: do not accommodate too obsequiously to Puttermesser's romance. Having not much imagination, she is literal with what she has. Uncle Zindel lies under the earth of Staten Island. Puttermesser has never had a conversation with him; he died four years before her birth. He is all legend: Zindel the Stingy, who even in *gan eydn* rather than eat will store apples until they rot. Zindel the Unripe. Why must Puttermesser fall into so poignant a fever over the cracked phrases of a shammes of a torn-down shul?

(The shul was not torn down, neither was it abandoned. It disintegrated. Crumb by crumb it vanished. Stones took some of the windows. There were no pews, only wooden folding chairs. Little by little these turned into sticks. The prayer books began to flake: the bindings flaked, the glue came unstuck in small brown flakes, the leaves grew brittle and flaked into confetti. The congregation too began to flake off—the women first, wife after wife after wife, each one a pearl and a consolation, until there they stand, the widowers, frail, gazing, palsy-struck. Alone and in terror. Golden Agers, Senior Citizens! And finally they too flake away, the shammes among them. The shul becomes a wisp, a straw, a feather, a hair.)

But Puttermesser must claim an ancestor. She demands connection—surely a Jew must own a past. Poor Puttermesser has found herself in the world without a past. Her mother was born into the din of Madison Street and was taken up to the hullabaloo of Harlem at an early age. Her father is nearly a Yankee: his father gave up peddling to captain a dry-goods store in Providence, Rhode Island. In summer he sold captain's hats, and wore one in all his photographs. Of the world that was, there is only this single grain of memory: that once an old man, Puttermesser's mother's uncle, kept his pants up with a rope belt, was called Zindel, lived without a wife, ate frugally, knew the holy letters, died with thorny English a wilderness between his gums. To him Puttermesser clings. America is a blank, and Uncle Zindel is all her ancestry. Unironic, unimaginative, her plain but stringent mind strains beyond the parents—what did they have? Only day-by-day in their lives, coffee in the morning, washing underwear, occasionally a trip to the beach. Blank. What did they know? Everything from the movies; something—scraps—from the newspaper. Blank.

Behind the parents, beyond and before them, things teem. In old photographs of the Jewish East Side, Puttermesser sees the teeming. She sees a long coat. She sees a woman pressing onions from a pushcart. She sees a tiny child with a finger in its mouth who will become a judge.

Past the judge, beyond and behind him, something more is teeming. But this Puttermesser cannot see. The towns, the little towns. Zindel born into a flat-roofed house a modest distance from a stream.

What can Puttermesser do? She began life as the child of an anti-Semite. Her father would not eat kosher meat—it was, he said, too tough. He had no superstitions. He wore the mother down, she went to the regular meat market at last.

The scene with Uncle Zindel did not occur. How Puttermesser loved the voice of Zindel in the scene that did not occur!

(He is under the ground. The cemetery is a teeming city of toy skyscrapers shouldering each other. Born into a wooden house, Zindel now has a flat stone roof. Who buried him? Strangers from the *landsmanshaft* society. Who said a word for him? No one. Who remembers him now?)

Puttermesser does not remember Uncle Zindel; Puttermesser's mother does not remember him. A name in the dead grandmother's mouth. Her parents have no ancestry. Therefore Puttermesser rejoices in the cadences of Uncle Zindel's voice above the Cuban grocery. Uncle Zindel, when alive, distrusted the building of Tel Aviv because he was practical, Messiah was not imminent. But now, in the scene that did not occur, how naturally he supposes Puttermesser will journey to a sliver of earth in the Middle East, surrounded by knives, missiles, bazookas!

The scene with Uncle Zindel did not occur. It could not occur because, though Puttermesser dares to posit her ancestry, we may not. Puttermesser is not to be examined as an artifact but as an essence. Who made her? No one cares. Puttermesser is henceforth to be presented as given. Put her back into Receipts and Disbursements, among office Jews and patronage collectors. While winter dusk blackens the Brooklyn Bridge, let us hear her opinion about the taxation of exempt properties. The bridge is not the harp Hart Crane said it was in his poem. Its staves are prison bars. The women clerks, Yefimova, Korolova, Akulova, Arkhipova, Izrailova, are on Kolpachni Street, but the vainglorious General Viryein is not. He is on Ogaryova Street. Joel Zaretsky's ex-wife is barren. The Commissioner puts on his tennis sneakers. He telephones. Mr. Fiore, the courtly secret mayor behind the Mayor, also telephones. Hey! Puttermesser's biographer! What will you do with her now?

Shots

I came to photography as I came to infatuation—with no special talent for it, and with no point of view. Taking pictures —when *I* take them, I mean—has nothing to do with art and less to do with reality. I'm blind to what intelligent people call "composition," I revile every emanation of "grain," and any drag through a gallery makes me want to die. As for the camera as *machine*—well, I know the hole I have to look through, and I know how to press down with my finger. The rest is thingamajig. What brought me to my ingenious profession was no idea of the Photograph as successor to the Painting, and no pleasure in darkrooms, or in any accumulation of clanking detritus.

Call it necrophilia. I have fallen in love with corpses. Dead faces draw me. I'm uninformed about the history of photography—1832, the daguerreotype, mercury vapor; what an annoyance that so blatant a thing as picture-taking is considered worth applying a history to!—except to understand how long a past the camera has, measured by a century-old length of a woman's skirt. People talk of inventing a time machine, as if it hadn't already been invented in the box and shutter. I have been ravished by the last century's faces, now motes in their graves—such lost eyes, and noses, and mouths, and earlobes, and dress-collars: my own eyes soak these up; I can never leave off looking at anything brown and brittle and old and decaying at the edges.

The autumn I was eleven I found the Brown Girl. She was under a mound of chestnut-littered leaves near five tall trash barrels in a corner of the yard behind the Home for the Elderly Female Ill. Though the old-lady inmates were kept confined to a high balcony above the browning grass of their bleak overgrown yard, occasionally I would see some witless half-bald refugee shuffling through a weed-sea with stockings rolled midway down a sinewy blue calf engraved by a knotted garter. They scared me to death, these sticks and twigs of brainless ancients, rattling their china teeth and howling at me in foreign tongues, rolling the bright gems of their mad old eyes inside their nearly visible crania. I used to imagine that if one of these fearful witches could just somehow get beyond the gate, she would spill off garters and fake teeth and rheumy eye-whites and bad smells and stupid matted old flesh, and begin to bloom all plump and glowing and ripe again: Shangri-La in reverse.

What gave me this imagining was the Brown Girl. Any one of these pitiful decaying sacks might once have been the Brown Girl. If only someone had shot a kind of halt-arrow through the young nipples of the Brown Girl at the crest of her years, if only she had been halted, arrested, stayed in her ripeness and savor!

The Brown Girl lived. She lay in a pile of albums dumped
into the leaves. It seemed there were hundreds of her: a girl in
a dress that dropped to the buttons of her shoes, with an
arched bosom and a hint of bustle, and a face mysteriously
shut: you never once saw her teeth, you never once saw the
lips in anything like the hope of a smile; laughter was out of
the question. A grave girl; a sepia girl; a girl as brown as the
ground. She must have had her sorrows.

Gradually (to my eyes suddenly) I saw her age. It wasn't
that the plain sad big-nosed face altered: no crinkles at the
lids, no grooves digging out a distinct little parallelogram from
nostril-sides to mouth-ends—or, if these were in sight, they
weren't what I noticed. The face faded out—became not
there. The woman turned to ghost. The ghost wore different
clothes now, too familiar to gape at. The fingers were ringless.
The eyes whitened off. Somehow for this melancholy spinster's
sake the first rule of the box camera was always being violated: not to put the sun behind your subject. A vast blurred
drowning orb of sun flooded massively, habitually down from
the upper right corner of her picture. Whoever photographed
her, over years and years and years, meant to obliterate her.
But I knew it was no sun-bleach that conspired to efface her.
What I was seeing—what I *had* seen—was time. And not time
on the move, either, the illusion of stories and movies. What I
had seen was time as stasis, time at the standstill, time at the
fix; the time (though I hadn't yet reached it in school) of
Keats's Grecian urn. The face faded out because death was
coming: death the changer, the collapser, the witherer; death
the bleacher, blancher, whitener.

The truth is, I'm looked on as a close-mouthed professional,
serious about my trade, who intends to shut up and keep se-
crets when necessary. I repel all "technical" questions—if
someone wants to discuss the make of my camera (it's Japa-

nese), or my favorite lens, or some trick I might have in developing, or what grade of paper I like, I'll stare her down. Moonings on Minor White's theories I regard as absolutely demeaning. I have a grasp on what I am about, and it isn't any of that.

What it is, is the Brown Girl. I kept her. I kept her, I mean, in a pocket of my mind (and one of her pictures in the pocket of my blouse); I kept her because she was dead. What I expect you to take from this is that I *could* keep her *even though* she was dead. I wasn't infatuated by her (not that she was the wrong sex: infatuation, like any passion of recognition, neglects gender); she was too oppressed and brown and quiet for that. But it was she who gave me the miraculous hint: a hint derived from no science of mechanics or physics, a rapturous hint on the other side of art, beyond metaphor, deep in the wonderfully literal. What she made me see was that if she wasn't a girl any more, if she wasn't a woman any more, if she was very likely not even a member of the elderly female ill any more (by the time her photos fell among the leaves, how long had she been lying under them?), still I *had* her, actually and physically and with the certainty of simple truth. I could keep her, just as she used to be, because someone had once looked through the bunghole of a box and clicked off a lever. Whoever had desultorily drowned her in too much sun had anyhow given her a monument two inches wide and three inches long. What happened then was here now. I had it in the pocket of my blouse.

Knowing this—that now will become then, that huge will turn little—doesn't cure. I walk around the wet streets with a historian now, a tenured professor of South American history: he doesn't like to go home to his wife. Somehow it always rains when we meet, and it's Sam's big blue umbrella, with a wooden horse's head for a handle, that preoccupies me this instant. Which is strange: he hasn't owned it for a whole year. It was left in a yellow garish coffee shop on the night side of a street you couldn't trust, and when Sam went back, only ten minutes later, to retrieve it, of course it wasn't there. At that time I didn't care about one thing in Sam's mind. I had to follow him, on assignment, all through a course of some public symposia he was chairing. We had—temporarily —the same employer. His college was setting up a glossy little booklet for the State Department to win South American friends with: I had to shoot Sam on the podium with Uruguayans, Sam on the podium with Brazilians, Sam on the podium with Peruvians, and so forth. It was a lackluster job—I had just come, not so long ago, from photographing an intergalactic physicist whose bravest hope was the invention of an alphabet to shoot into the kindergartens of the cosmos—so it was no trouble at all not to listen to the speeches while I shot the principals. Half the speeches were in Portuguese or Spanish, and if you wanted to you could put on earphones anywhere in the hall and hear a simultaneous translation. The translator sat at the squat end of the long symposium table up on the stage with Sam and the others, but kept his microphone oddly close to his lips, like a kiss, sweat sliding and gleaming along his neck—it seemed he was tormented by that bifurcated concentration. His suffering attracted me. He didn't count as one of the principals—the celebrity of the day (now it was night, the last of the dark raining afternoon) was the vice-consul of Chile—but I shot him anyhow, for my own reasons: I liked the look of that shining sweat on his bulging Adam's apple. I calculated my aim (I'm very fast at this), shot once, shot again, and was amazed to see blood spring out of a hole in his neck. The audience fell apart—it was like watching an anthill after you've kicked into it; there was a spaghetti of wires and police; the simultaneous translator was dead. It made you listen for the simultaneous silence of the principal speaker, but the Chilean vice-consul only swerved his syllables into shrieks, with his coat over his head; he was walked away in a tremor between two colleagues suddenly sprouting guns. A mob of detectives took away my film; it was all I could do to keep them from arresting my camera. I went straight to Sam —it was his show—to complain. "That's *film* in there, not bullets." "It's evidence now," Sam said. "Who wanted to do that?" I said. "God knows," Sam said; "they didn't do what they wanted anyhow," and offered six political possibilities, each of which made it seem worthwhile for someone to do away with the Chilean vice-consul. He found his umbrella under the table and steered me out. The rain had a merciless wind in it, and every glassy sweep of it sent fountains spitting upward from the pavement. We stood for a while under his umbrella (he gripping the horse's head hard enough to whiten his knuckles) and watched them carry the simultaneous translator out. He was alone on a stretcher; his duality was done, his job as surrogate consummated. I reflected how quickly vertical becomes horizontal. "You knew him," I said.

"Only in a public way. He's been part of all these meetings."

"So have I," I said.

"I've watched you watching me."

I resisted this. "That's professional watching. It's more like stalking. I always stalk a bit before I shoot."

"You talk like a terrorist," Sam said, and began a history of South American conspiracy, which group was aligned with whom, who gave asylum, who withheld it, who the Chilean vice-consul's intimates across several borders were, at this instant plotting vengeance. He had exactly the kind of mentality —cumulative, analytical—I least admired, but since he also had the only umbrella in sight, I stuck with him. He was more interested in political factionalism—he had to get everything

sorted out, and his fascination seemed to be with the victims—
than in his having just sat two feet from a murder. "My God,"
I said finally, "doesn't the power of inaccuracy impress you? It
could've been you on that stretcher."

"I don't suppose *you* ever miss your target," he said.

"No," I said, "but I don't shoot to kill."

"Then you're not one of those who want to change the
world," he said, and I could smell in this the odor of his melancholy. He was a melancholic and an egotist; this made me a
bit more attentive. His umbrella, it appeared, was going to
pilot him around for miles and miles; I went along as passen-
ger. We turned at last into a coffee shop—this wasn't the place
he lost the horse's head in—and then turned out again, heated
up, ready for more weather. "Don't you ever go home?" I
asked him.

"Don't you?"

"I live alone."

"I don't. I hate my life," he said.

"I don't blame you. You've stuffed it up with South American facts."

"Would you like North American facts better?"

"I can't take life in whole continents," I protested.

"The thing about taking it in continents is that you don't
have to take it face by face."

"The faces are the best part."

"Some are the worst," Sam said.

I looked into his; he seemed a victim of factionalism himself, as if you become what you study. He had rather ferocious
eyes, much too shiny, like something boiling in a pot—the
ferocity made you think them black, but really they were pale
—and black ripe rippled hair and unblemished orderly teeth,
not white but near-white. "Which faces are the worst?"

"Now I'll go home," he said.

The murder had cut short the series of symposia; the South

Americans scattered, which was too bad—they were Sam's source of vitality. But it never occurred to either of us that we might not meet again officially, and often enough we did—he on a platform, myself with camera. Whether this meant that all the magazine people I knew—the ones who were commissioning my pictures—were all at once developing a fevered concern for South American affairs (more likely it was for terrorism) is a boring question. I know *I* wasn't. I never wanted to listen to Sam on the subjects he was expert in, and I never did. I only caught what I thought of as their "moans"— impure and simmering and winnowing and sad. The sounds that came through his microphone were always intensely public: he was, his audience maintained—loyalists, they trotted after him from speech to speech—a marvelous generalist. He could go from predicting the demand for bauxite to tracing migrations of Indian populations, all in a single stanza. He could connect disparate packets of contemporary information with a linking historic insight that took your breath away. He was a very, very good public lecturer; all his claque said so. He could manage to make anyone (or everyone but me) care about South America. Still, I had a little trick in my head as he declaimed and as I popped my flashbulbs, not always at him— more often at the distinguished sponsors of the event. I could tell they were distinguished from the way they dragged me up to the dais to photograph them—it showed how important they were. Sometimes they wanted to be photographed just before Sam began, and sometimes, with their arms around him, when he was just finished, themselves grinning into Sam's applause. All the while I kept the little trick going.

The little trick was this: whatever he said that was vast and public and South American, I would simultaneously translate (I hoped I wouldn't be gunned down for it) into everything private and personal and secret. This required me to listen shrewdly to the moan behind the words—I had to blot out the words for the sake of the tune. Sometimes the tune would be civil or sweet or almost jolly—especially if he happened to get a look at me before he ascended to his lectern—but mainly it would be narrow and drab and resigned. I knew he had a wife, but I was already thirty-six, and who didn't have a wife by then? I wasn't likely to run into them if they didn't. Bachelors wouldn't be where I had to go, particularly not in public halls gaping at the per capita income of the interior villages of the Andes, or the future of Venezuelan oil, or the fortunes of the last Paraguayan bean crop, or the differences between the centrist parties in Bolivia and Colombia, or whatever it was that kept Sam ladling away at his tedious stew. I drilled through all these sober-shelled facts into their echoing gloomy melodies: and the sorrowful sounds I unlocked from their casings—it was like breaking open a stone and finding the music of the earth's wild core boiling inside—came down to the wife, the wife, the wife. That was the tune Sam was moaning all the while: wife wife wife. He didn't like her. He wasn't happy with her. His whole life was wrong. He was a dead man. If I thought I'd seen a dead man when they took that poor fellow out on that stretcher, I was stupidly mistaken; *he* was ten times deader than that. If the terrorist who couldn't shoot straight had shot *him* instead, he couldn't be more riddled with gunshot than he was this minute—he was smoking with his own death.

In the yellow garish coffee shop he went on about his wife —he shouldn't be telling me all this, my God, what the hell did he think he was doing; he was a fool; he was a cliché; he was out of a cartoon or an awful play; he was an embarrassment to himself and to me. It was either a trance or a seizure. And then he forgot his umbrella, and ran back after it, and it was gone. It wouldn't have had, necessarily, to be a desperate thief who stole his horse's head that night; it might easily have been a nice middle-class person like ourselves. A nice middle-class person especially would have hated to be out in such a drenching without a shred of defense overhead—Sam charged on into gales of cold rain, and made me charge onward too: for the first time he had me by the hand. I wouldn't let him keep it, though—I had to bundle my camera under my coat.

"How long are we going to walk in this?" I said.

"We'll walk and walk."

"I've got to go home or I'll soak my equipment," I complained.

"I'm not going home."

"Don't you ever go home?"

"My whole life is wrong," he said.

We spilled ourselves into another coffee place and sat there till closing. My shoes were seeping and seeping. He explained Verity: "I admire her," he said. "I esteem her, you wouldn't believe how I esteem that woman. She's a beautiful mother. She's strong and she's bright and she's independent and there's nothing she can't do."

"Now tell her good points," I said.

"She can fix a car. She always fixes the car. Puts her head into the hood and fixes it. She builds furniture. We live in a madhouse of excess property—she built every stick of it. She saws like a madwoman. She *sews* like a madwoman—I don't mean just *clothes*. She sews her own clothes and the girls' clothes too. What I mean is she *sews*—bedspreads and curtains and upholstery, even *car* upholstery. And she's got a whole budding career of her own. I've made her sound like a bull, but she's really very delicate at whatever she does—she does plates, you know."

"License plates?"

"She's done *some* metalwork—her minor was metallurgy—but what I'm talking about is ceramics. Porcelain. She does painted platters and pots and pitchers and sells them to Bloomingdale's."

"She's terrific," I said.

"She's terrific," he agreed. "There's nothing she can't do."

"Cook?"

"My God, *cook*," he said. "French, Italian, Indian, whatever you want. And bakes. Pastries, the difficult stuff, crusts made of cloud. She's a domestic genius. We have this big harp —hell, it was busted, a skeleton in a junk shop, so she bought it cheap and repaired it—she plays it like an angel. You think you're in heaven inside that hell. She plays the piano, too— classics, ragtime, rock. She's got a pretty nice singing voice. She's good at basketball—she practically never misses a shot. Don't ask me again if I admire her."

I asked him again if he admired her.

"I'm on my knees," he groaned. "She's a goddamn goddess. She's powerful and autonomous and a goddamn genius. Christ," he said, "I hate my life."

"If I had someone like that at home," I said, "I'd never be out in the rain."

"She could abolish the weather if she wanted to, only she doesn't want to. She has a terrific will."

I thought this over and was surprised by my sincerity: "You ought to go home," I told him.

"Let's walk."

After that we met more or less on purpose. The South American fad wore off—there was a let-up in guerrilla activity down there—and it got harder to find him in public halls, so I went up to his college now and then and sat in on his classes, and afterward, rain or shine, but mostly rain, we walked. He told me about his daughters—one of them was nearly as terrific as Verity herself—and we walked with our arms hooked. "Is something happening here?" I inquired. "Nothing will ever happen here," he said. We had a friend in common, the editor who'd assigned me to photographing that intergalactic physicist I've mentioned; it turned out we were asked, Sam with

Verity, myself as usual, to the editor's party, in honor of the editor's ascension. There were some things the editor hadn't done which added immensely to his glory; and because of all the things he hadn't done they were making him vice-chancellor of Sam's college. I did justice to those illustrious gaps and omissions: I took the host, now majestic, and his wife, their children, their gerbil, their maid. I shot them embedded in their guests. I dropped all those pictures behind me like autumn leaves. I hadn't brought my usual Japanese spy, you see; I'd carried along a tacky Polaroid instead—instant development, a detective story without a detective, ah, I disliked that idea, but the evening needed its jester. I aimed and shot, aimed and shot, handing out portraits deciduously. Verity had her eye on all this promiscuity; she was blond and capacious and maybe capricious; she seemed without harm and without mercy.

"You're the one who shot the simultaneous translator," she said.

"Judicial evidence," I replied.

"Now let me," she said, "ask you something about your trade. In photography, do you consistently get what you expect?"

I said: "It's the same as life."

Verity expressed herself: "The viewfinder, the viewfinder!"

"I always look through that first," I admitted.

"And then do you get what you see? I mean can you predict exactly, or are you always surprised by what comes out?"

"I can never predict," I told her, "but I'm never surprised."

"That's fatalism," Verity said. Her voice was an iron arrow; she put her forefinger into my cheek as humbly as a bride. "Talk about shots, here's a parting one. You take a shot at Sam, no expectations. He's not like life. He's safe. He's *good*."

He was safe and he was good: Sam the man of virtue. She knew everything exactly, even when everything was nothing she knew it exactly, she was without any fear at all; jealousy wasn't in her picture; she was more virtuous than he was, she was big, she had her great engine, she was her own cargo. And you see what it is with infatuation: it comes on you as quick as a knife. It's a bullet in the neck. It gets you from the outside. One moment you're in your prime of health, the next you're in anguish. Until then—until I had the chance to see for myself how clear and proud his wife was—Sam was an entertainment, not so entertaining after all. Verity was the Cupid of the thing, Verity's confidence the iron arrow that dragged me down. She had her big foot on her sour catch. I saw in her glow, in her sureness, in her pride, in her tall ship's prow of certitude, the plausibility of everything she knew: he'd have to go home in the end.

But the end's always at the end; in the meantime there's the meantime.

How to give over these middle parts? I couldn't see what I looked like, from then on, to Sam: all the same I had my automatic intelligence—light acting on a treated film. I was treated enough; Verity had daubed me. Since I was soaked in her solution, infatuation took, with me, a mechanical form—if you didn't know how mechanical it was, you would have imagined it was sly. I could listen now to everything Sam said. Without warning, I could *follow* him; I discovered myself in the act of wanting more. I woke up one morning in a fit of curiosity about the quantity of anthracite exports on the Brazilian littoral. I rooted in hard-to-find volumes of Bolívar's addresses. I penetrated the duskier hells of the public library and boned up on every banana republic within reach. It was astounding: all at once, and for no reason—I mean for *the* reason—Sam interested me. It was like walking on the lining of his brain.

On the South American issue he was dense as a statue. He had never noticed that I hadn't paid attention to his subject before; he didn't notice that I was attentive now. His premise was that everyone alive without exception was all the time infatuated with the former Spanish Empire. On *my* subject, though, Sam was trying; it was because of Verity; she had made him ambitious to improve himself with me.

"Verity saw at that party," he said, "that you had the kind of camera that gets you the picture right away."

"Not exactly right away. You have to wait a minute," I corrected.

"Why don't you use a camera like that all the time? It's magic. It's like a miracle."

"Practical reasons of the trade. The farther you are from having what you think you want, the more likely you are to get it. It's just that you have to wait. You really have to *wait*. What's important is the waiting."

Sam didn't get it. "But it's *chemistry*. The image is already on the film. It's the same image one minute later or two months later."

"You're too miracle-minded even for a historian," I admonished him. "It's not like that at all. If you have a change of heart between shooting your picture and taking it out of the developer, the picture changes too." I wanted to explain to him how, between the exposure and the solution, history comes into being, but telling that would make me bleed, like a bullet in the neck, so I said instead, "Photography is *literal*. It gets what's *there*."

Meanwhile the rain is raining on Sam and me. We meet in daylight now, and invent our own occasions. We hold hands, we hook arms, we walk through the park. There is a mole on his knuckle which has attached itself to my breathing; my lungs grasp all the air they can. I want to lay my tears on the hairs of his fingers. Because of the rain, the daylight is more like twilight; in this perpetual half of dusk, the sidewalks a kind of blackened purple, like fallen plums, we talk about the past and the future of the South American continent. Verity is in her house. I leave my camera behind too. Our faces are rivers, we walk without an umbrella, the leaves splash. When I can't find Sam on my own, I telephone Verity; she stops the motor of her sewing machine and promises to give him the message when he returns. He comes flying out to meet me, straight from his Committee on Inter-American Conditions; I'm practically a colleague now, and a pleasure to talk to about Ecuadorian peonage. He tells me he's never had a mistress and never will; his wife is too remarkable. I ask him whether he's ever walked in a summer rain this way with anyone else. He admits he has; he admits it hasn't lasted. "The rain hasn't lasted? Or the feeling?" He forgets to answer. I remember that *he* is only interested; it's I who feel. We talk some more about the native religions still hiding out in the pampas; we talk about the Jewish gauchos in nineteenth-century Argentina. He takes it all for granted. He doesn't realize how hard I've had to study. A big leaf like a pitcher overturns itself all over our heads, and we make a joke about Ponce de León and the Fountain of Youth. I ask him then if he'll let me take his picture in the park, under a dripping linden tree, in a dangerous path, so that I can keep him forever, in case it doesn't last.

I see that he doesn't understand. He doesn't understand: unlike me, he's not under any special spell, he's not in thrall to any cult. That's the rub always—infatuation's unilateral or it doesn't count as real. I think he loves me—he may even be "in love"—but he's not caught like me. He'd never trace my life over as I've traced over his brain waves. He asks me why I want to shoot him under the linden tree. I tell him the truth I took from his wife: virtue ravishes me. I want to keep its portrait. I am silent about the orphaned moment we're living in now, how it will leave us. I feel, I feel our pathos. We are virtue's orphans. The tree's green shoots are fleeting; all green corrupts to brown. Sam denies that he's a man of virtue. It's only his guilt about Verity: she's too terrific to betray.

He consents to having his picture taken in the sopping park if I agree to go home with him afterward.

I say in my amazement, "I can't go home with you. She's *there*."

"She's always there."

"Then how can I go home with you?"

"You have to *see*. It's all been too obscure. I want you to know what I know."

"I know it, you've told me. You've told and told."

"You have to get the smell of it. Where I am and how I live. Otherwise you won't believe in it. You won't know it," he insists. "Such cozy endurances."

"You endure them," I said.

"Yesterday," he said, "she brought home a box of old clothes from the Salvation Army. From a thrift shop. From an old people's home, who knows where she got it from. Pile of rags. She's going to sew them into God's bright ribbons. A patchwork quilt. She'll spin straw into gold, you'll see."

"She's terrific."

"She's a terrific wife," he says.

We walk to my place, pick up my camera—I stop to grab my light meter for the rain's sake—and walk crosstown to the park again. I shoot Sam, the man of virtue, under the dripping linden tree. Although I am using my regular equipment, it seems to me the picture's finished on the spot. It's as if I roll it out and fix it then and there. Sam has got his back against the bark, and all the little wet leaves lick down over his bumpy hair. He resembles a Greek runner resting. His face is dappled by all those heart-shaped leaves, and I know that all the rest of my life I'll regret not having shot him in the open, in a field. But my wish for now is to speckle him and see him darkle

under the rainy shade of a tree. It comes to me that my desire
—oh, my desire! it stings me in the neck—is just now not even
for Sam's face: it's for the transitoriness of these thin vulnerable leaves, with their piteous veins turned upward toward a
faintness of liverish light.

We walk the thirty-one blocks, in the quickening rain, to his
place. It's only a four-room apartment, but Verity's made a
palace of it. Everything plain is converted into a sweetness, a
furriness, a thickness of excess. She weaves, she knits. She's an
immense spider building out of her craw. The floors are piled
with rugs she's woven, the chairs with throws she's knit. She's
cemented up a handy little fireplace without a flue; it really
works, and on a principle she invented herself. She's carpen-
tered all the bookcases—I catch the titles of the four books
Sam's written; he's a dignitary and a scholar, after all—and
overhead there wafts and dazzles the royal chandelier she
found in the gutter and refurbished. Each prism slid through
her polishing and perfecting fingers. Verity resurrects, Verity's
terrific—you can't avoid thinking it. She's got her big shoul-
ders mounted over her sewing machine in the corner of the
living room, hemming brown squares. "It's weird, you
wouldn't believe it," she says, "*all* the stuff in this box they
gave me is brown. It's good rich fabric, though—a whole load
of clothes from dead nuns. You know what happened? A con-
vent dissolved, the young nuns broke their vows and ran to get
married."

"That's *your* story," Sam says.

Verity calls her daughter—only one of the girls is at home,
the other is away at college. Clearly this one isn't the daughter
that's so much like Verity. She has a solemn hard flank of
cheek, and no conversation. She carries out a plate of sliced
honey cake and three cups of tea; then she hides herself in her
bedroom. A radio is in there; gilded waves of Bach tremble
out of it. I look around for Verity's harp.

"Hey, let's dress you up," Verity says out of her teacup;

she's already downed a quantity of cake. "There's stuff in that box that would just fit you. You've got a waist like our girls. I wish *I* had a waist like that." I protest; I tell her it's too silly. Sam smolders with his sour satisfaction, and she churns her palms inside the box like a pair of oars. She pulls out a long skirt, and a blouse called a bodice, and another blouse to wear under that, with long sleeves. Sam pokes my spine and nudges me into the girl's bedroom, where there's a tall mirror screwed into the back of the door. I look at myself.

"Period piece!" says Verity.

I'm all in brown, as brown as leaves. The huge high harp, not gold as I imagined it but ivory, is along the wall behind me. I believe everything Sam has told about the conquistadores. I believe everything he's told about Verity. He's a camera who never lies. His wet hair is black as olives. He belongs to his wife, who's terrific. She's put a nun's bonnet on herself. She has an old-fashioned sense of fun—the words come to me out of, I think, Louisa May Alcott: she likes costume and dress-up. Soon she will have us guessing riddles and playing charades. They are a virtuous and wholesome family. The daughter, though her look is bone, is fond of Bach; no junk music in such a household. They are sweeter than the whole world outside. When Sam is absent the mother and her daughter climb like kittens into a knitted muff.

I shoot Verity wearing the nun's bonnet.

"Look at *you!*" she cries.

I return to the mirror to see. I am grave; I have no smile. My face is mysteriously shut. I'm suffering. Lovesick and dreamsick, I'm dreaming of my desire. I am already thirty-six years old, tomorrow I will be forty-eight years old, and a crafty parallelogram begins to frame the space between my nose and mouth. My features are very distinct—I will live for years and years before they slide out of the mirror. I'm the Brown Girl in the pocket of my blouse. I reek of history. If, this minute, I could glide into a chemical solution, as if in a gondola, splashed all over and streaming with wet silver, would the mirror seize and fix me, like a photographic plate? I watch Sam's eyes, poached and pale and mottled with furious old civilizations, steaming hatred for his wife. I trip over the long drapery of my nun's hem. All the same I catch up my camera without dropping it—my ambassador of desire, my secret house with its single shutter, my chaste aperture, my dead infant, husband of my bosom. Their two heads, hers light, his black, negatives of each other, are caught side by side in their daughter's mirror. I shoot into their heads, the white harp behind. Now they are exposed. Now they will stick forever.

From a Refugee's Notebook

Redactor's Comment: These fragments, together with the above unprepossessing title, were found (in a purple-covered spiral tablet of the kind used by university students of an earlier generation and in another country) behind a mirror in a vacant room-for-rent on West 106th Street, New York City. The author, of European or perhaps South American origin, remains unidentified.

I. FREUD'S ROOM

Not long ago they turned Freud's house in Vienna into a museum, but few visitors come. It is even hard to know it is there: the big hotels don't list it on their bulletin boards, no one thinks of it as part of the tourist circuit. If you want to find it, the only place to ask is at the police station.

I have not been there myself (I do not go to any land which once suckled the Nazi boot), but I have dreamed over photographs of those small rooms where Sigmund Freud wrote his treatises and met with his patients and kept, in a glass case, his collection of ancient stone animals and carved figurines. There is a picture of Freud sitting at his desk, looking downward through dark-rimmed perfectly round lenses at a manuscript; behind him is the shining case with a good-sized camel, wood or stone, on top of it, and a great Grecian urn to the side. There are a wall of books, a vase of pussy willows, and on every shelf and surface cups, goblets, beasts, and hundreds of those strange little gods.

The museum, I suppose, is clear now of all that Egyptian debris, unless somehow it has all been brought back to fill the emptiness of the refugee's rooms.

In another of these famous photographs there is a curious juxtaposition. The picture is divided exactly in two by a lamp pole. On the left there is the crowd of stone godlets, on the right the couch on which Freud's patients lay during analysis. The wall behind the couch is covered by a Persian carpet hung in lieu of a tapestry; the couch itself is draped, in a heavy, ugly way, by another carpet hiding a hump of bolster beneath it and wearing a soft flat velveteen pillow as a kind of depressed beret. The very center of the picture is occupied by the low plush armchair in which Freud himself sat. The arms of the chair look worn, the whole small space seems cramped by so many objects, so many picture frames dangling in clumsy dis-order up and down and across the wall behind the armchair and the couch. In one of the frames, under glass, the flanks of a greyhound dog glimmer. All this, of course, is what we have come to think of as Victorian clutter, and one pities the house-maid who came timidly in with her perilous duster. Yet if you take a second look, there is no clutter. Everything in the room is necessary: the couch and the gods. Even the slim dog who runs and yelps on the wall.

Especially the gods. The gods, the gods!

It is not the juxtaposition you suppose. What you are think-ing is this: these primitive stone things, ranged like small determined marchers on shelves and tables (is it not amazing how many of them have one foot thrust forward, like the men who marched afterward in Vienna, or is it simply that the sculptor requires this posture for balance, else his god would shatter?)—these stone things, then, represent the deep primitive grain of the mind Freud sought. The woman or man on the couch was an archaeological enterprise—layer after layer to be spaded and sifted through, ever so delicately as archaeologists do, with feather brush, like the maid who slips in every morning to touch the top of each stone head with a sculptor's tender fear of despoiling the very matter the god-spirit has entrusted to him.

(The German word for matter is excellent, and illumines our English usage: *der Stoff*. Stuff. As in: the stuff of the universe. The wonder of the term is its thinginess. The awesome little gods in Freud's consulting room are matter, stuff, crumbs of rock; rubble.)

No, the juxtaposition I am thinking of is not merely the tangency of primitive with primitive. It is something else. The proliferation of gods, in mobs and bevies, the carpets with their diamond and flower figures, their languid tassels drooping down, the heavy figured table shawl with even longer fringes, over which a handful of gods blindly parade, the varnished brown wood frames, the vases curved and straight-sided, the libation cups standing dry, the burdensome tomes with their oppressive squatness mimicking pyramids—it is the room of a king.

The breath of this room drones with dreams of a king who lusts to become a god absolute as stone. The dreams that rise up from couch and armchair mix and braid in the air: the patient recounts her dream of a cat, signifying the grimness of a bad mother, and behind this dream, lurking in the doctor, is the doctor's dream. The gods walking over the long-fringed table shawl have chosen their king.

Respected reader: if I seem to be saying that Sigmund Freud wished to be a god, do not mistake me. I am no poet, and despise metaphors. I am a literal-minded person. I have no patience with figures of speech. Music is closed to me, and of art I have seen little. I have suffered the harsh life of a refugee and have made my living in bolts of cloth. I am familiar with texture: I can, with eyes shut, tell you which is rayon and which silk, which the genuine wool and which the synthetic, which pure nylon and which graduated toward cotton, which the coarse lace and which the fine. My whole bent is toward the tangible and the palpable. I know the difference between what is there and what is not there; between the empty and the full. I have nothing to do with make-believe.

I tell you that Sigmund Freud wished to become a god.

Some few men in history have wished it and would, but for mortality, have achieved it—some by tyranny: the Pharaohs indisputably, and also that Louis who was Sun King of France. Some by great victories: Napoleon and Hannibal. Some by chess: those world masters who murder in effigy the potent queens of their imaginings. Some by novel-writing: that conquistador Tolstoy who used only himself, costumed and dyed, under other names, and his aunties and his brothers and his poor wife Sonya (pragmatic and sensible like myself). Some by medicine and dentistry, wizardries of prosthesis and transplantation.

But others scheming to become gods utilize another resource altogether. Kings, generals, chess masters, surgeons, even those who wreak immense works of imagination—their resources are ultimately their sanity; their sobriety; their bourgeois probity. (Bourgeois? The sacred monarchs too? Yes; to live a decent life in dynastic Egypt, with food not likely to fester, clean drains, and comfortable beds, it was necessary to own ten thousand slaves.) The notion of the mad genius is a foolish and false commonplace. Ambition sniffs out the grain of logic and possibility. Genius summons up not grotesqueries but verisimilitudes: the lifelike, the anti-magical. Whoever seeks to become an earthly god must follow the earth itself.

Some few do not. At least two have not. The inventor of the

Sabbath—call him Moses if you wish—declared the cycle of the earth null. What do the birds, the worms their prey, the corn in the field, men and animals who sleep and wake up hungry, know of a Sabbath, this arbitrary call to make a stop in the diurnal rhythm, to move consciously apart from the natural progression of days? It is only God, standing apart from nature, who tells nature to cease, who causes miracles, who confounds logic.

After Moses, Freud. They are not alike. What the Sabbath and its emanations sought to suppress, Freud meant to reveal: everything barbarous and dreadful and veiled and terror-bearing: the very tooth and claw. What the roiling half-savage village Christianity of the Dark Ages called Hell, Freud called Id, which he similarly described as a "cauldron." And just as the village priest with a gift for the drama of fright peopled Hell with this and that demon, Beelzebub, Eblis, Apollyon, Mephisto, those curiously-named assistants or doubles of Satan, so Freud peopled the Unconscious with the devils of Id and Ego and Superego, potent dancing ghosts who cavort unrecorded in our anatomies while we pretend they are not there. And this too is to go against the diurnal rhythm of things. Nature does not stop to suspect itself of daily subterfuge. Inventing such a stop, Freud imposed on all our surface coherencies a Sabbath of the soul.

Which is to moon over the obvious: Freud was lured by what was clearly not "sane." The draw of the irrational has its own deep question: how much is research, how much search? Is the scientist, the intelligent physician, the skeptical philosopher who is attracted to the irrational, himself a rational being? How explain the attraction? I think of that majestic scholar of Jerusalem sitting in his university study composing, with bookish distance and objectivity, volume after volume on the history of Jewish mysticism . . . is there an objective "scientific interest" or is all interest a snare? And Freud: is the student of the dream-life—that subterranean grotto all drowned and darkling, torn with the fury of anguish and lust —is the student of the dream-life not himself a lovesick captive of it? Is the hidden cauldron not an enticement and a seduction to its inventor? Is the doctor of the Unconscious not likely to be devoured by his own creation, like that rabbi of Prague who constructed a golem?

Or, to say it even more terribly: it may be that the quarry is all the time in the pursuer.

[Here the first fragment ends.]

II. THE SEWING HAREMS

It was for a time the fashion on the planet Acirema for the more sophisticated females to form themselves into Sewing Harems. Each Sewing Harem would present itself for limited rental, in a body, to a rich businessman capable of housing it in a suitably gracious mansion or tasteful duplex apartment or roomy ranch or luxurious penthouse. Prices ran high. The typical Sewing Harem could be had for a little over seventy-five thousand dollars, but hiring one of these groups was splendidly prestigious, and was worth sacrificing foreign travel for, a new car, or even college for one's children.

What the Sewing Harems sewed was obvious. Do not visualize quilting bees, samplers, national flags.

What I have failed to mention so far is that the atmosphere of this planet contained a profusion of imperva molecules, which had the property of interacting with hormonal chemistry in such a way as to allow the women of that place to sew their own bodies with no anguish whatsoever. Imperva molecules had been present only since the last ice age, and their inherent volatility offered no guarantee that they could withstand the temperature assaults of the next ice age; but since no one was predicting a new ice age, and since the last one had been over for at least a hundred million years, no immediate atmospheric peril was anticipated.

Once rented, the Sewing Harem would incarcerate itself in

comfortable chambers, feast abundantly but privately, and rest prodigiously. After a day or so of hungerless inactivity, the sewing would begin.

There was considerable virtuosity in the style of stitches, but the most reliable, though not the most aesthetic, was the backstitch, which consists of two, sometimes three, running stitches, the final one repeated over upon itself. One woman would sew another, with the most cooperative cheerfulness imaginable, though occasionally an agile woman—an athlete or acrobat or dancer—managed, with fastidious poise, in exquisite position, to sew herself.

There was, as I have explained, no anguish in the flesh. Still, there was the conventional bleeding while the needle penetrated again and again, and the thread, whatever color was used, had to be tugged along swollen by wet blood, so that the whole length of it was finally dyed dark red. Healing took the usual week or so, and then the man who had leased the Sewing Harem was admitted to try whatever licentious pleasure his fancy and theirs could invent—except, of course, bodily entry. Inaccessibility increased wit, discrimination, maneuverability, and intellectuality on both sides.

The terms of the rental did not allow for snipping open stitches.

At the close of the rental period (between three and six months), a not insignificant number of the women would have become pregnant. How this could have happened I leave to the reader's nimble imagination, but surely in several instances stitches had been opened in defiance of contractual obligations, and perhaps even with the complicity and connivance of the women in question.

The terms of rental further stipulated that should any children be born to any of the women as a consequence of the activity of the leasing period, said children would be held in common by all the women: each one, equal with every other, would be designated as mother.

Now it should be immediately evident that all of this was far, far less than ordinary custom. The lighthearted hiring of Sewing Harems was practiced in a number of the great cities of that planet, but could be found hardly at all in the under-developed countries. The formation of Sewing Harems—or so it was charged by the Left and the Right—was the fad of the self-indulgent and the irrepressibly reckless. Not altogether so: since after the period of the lease expired, the members of each Sewing Harem, in their capacity as equal mothers, often attempted to remain together, and to continue as a serious social body, in order to raise its children intelligently.

Given the usual temperamental difficulties, the peregrinations of restless individuals, the nomadic habits of the group as a whole, and the general playfulness (their own word being the more ironic "frivolousness") of the membership, a Sewing Harem was frequently known to disband not many years after the nearly simultaneous birth of its children.

But the chief reason for the dissolution of a Sewing Harem was jealousy over the children. The children were few, the mothers many. Each child was everyone's child in the mind of the community, but by no means in the mind of the child. At first the babies were kept together in a compound, and all the mothers had equal access to them for dandling, rocking, and fondling. But of course only the mothers who could breast-feed were at all popular with the babies, since the theorists of these societies, who had a strong and authoritative caucus, frowned on bottles. Consequently, the mothers who had not experienced parturition, and who had no breast-milk, were avoided by the babies, and soon the community of mothers began to be divided into those the babies preferred and those the babies shunned; or, into milkers and non-milkers; or, into elite mothers and second-class mothers.

Somehow, even after the children were weaned, the original classifications persisted, causing depression among the second-class mothers.

As the children grew older, moreover, it was discovered that they *interrupted*. By now, several of the second-class mothers, feeling disappointed, had gone off to join other Sewing Harems just then in the process of putting themselves out for rental. And only these defeated mothers, by virtue of being no longer on the scene, were not interrupted. All the rest were. It was found that the children interrupted careers, journeys, appointments, games, telephone calls, self-development, education, meditation, sexual activity, and other enlightened, useful, and joyous pursuits. But since the children were all being brought up with the highest self-expectations, they believed themselves to be ("as indeed you are," the mothers told them) in every way central to the community.

They believed this, in spite of their understanding that, morally and philosophically, they had no right to exist. Morally: each one had been conceived by breach of contract. Philosophically: each one had been born to a mother theoretically committed to the closure of the passage leading to the womb. In brief, the children knew that they were the consequence of unpredictable deviations from a metaphysical position; or, to state it still more succinctly, the fruit of snipped stitches.

That the children interrupted the personal development of the mothers was difficulty enough. In a less dialectical community, there might have been a drive toward comfortable if imperfect solutions. But these were (as it ought by now to be radiantly clear) no ordinary women. Ordinary women might have taken turns in caring for the children, or hired men and other women for this purpose, or experimented with humane custodial alternatives. A Sewing Harem, however, was a community of philosophers. And just as bottle-feeding had been condemned as an inferior compromise, so now were the various permutations of day-care proposals scorned. Each child was regarded as the offspring not simply of a single philosopher, but of a community of philosophers; hence not to be subjected to rearing by hirelings, or by any arrangement inferior to the loftiest visions of communal good.

As for taking turns, though it might be fair, it was inconceivable: just as each child was entitled to the highest self-expectation without compromise, so was each philosopher entitled to the highest self-development without compromise or interruption.

The children as they grew not only interrupted the mothers; they interfered with the mothers' most profound ideals. The blatant fact of the birth of a large group of children hindered ecological reform, promoted pollution, and frustrated every dramatic hope of rational population reduction. In short, the presence of the children was anti-progressive. And since not only joy and self-development, but also friendship and truth, were the dearest doctrines of a Sewing Harem, the children were made to understand that, in spite of their deserving the highest self-expectations, they represented nevertheless the most regressive forces on the planet.

It is hardly necessary to note, given the short life of any novelty, that by the time the children became adults, the fad of the Sewing Harems had virtually died out (excepting, now and then, an occasional nostalgic revival). Not surprisingly, the term "Harem" itself was by now universally repudiated as regressive and repugnant, despite the spirited voluntarism and economic self-sufficiency of the original societies. But the historic influence of those early societies was felt throughout the planet.

Everywhere, including the most backward areas, women were organizing themselves for sewing, with the result, of course, that there were fewer and fewer natural mothers and more and more adoptive mothers. The elitist distinctions observed by the founding groups no longer pertained, and were, in fact, reversed by the overwhelming vote of the underdeveloped countries. Devotion to egalitarian principles put the sewn majority in the saddle; and since the majority were adoptive mothers, or women whose lives were peripheral to children, or women who had nothing to do with children at all, natural motherhood (though it continued to be practiced, with restraint, in all circles except the very literary) was little noticed and less remarked on, neither as neurosis nor as necessity. It was neither patronized nor demeaned, and it was certainly not persecuted. It was not much on anyone's mind.

It goes without saying that society at large instantly improved. The planet took on a tidier appearance: more room for gardens and trees, a diminution of garbage and poverty, fewer smoky factories, highways decently uncrowded for a holiday drive. In the international sphere, matters were somewhat less satisfactory, at least in the view of the men and women who ran the planet. Though the wicked remained dominant, as always, it was not much worthwhile making wars any more, since in any conflict it is preferable that vast and vaster quantities of lives be butchered, and the numbers of young soldiers available for losing the bottom halves of their torsos went on diminishing.

To put it as briefly and delightfully as possible: the good (those self-respecting individuals who did not intend to waste their years) had greater opportunities to add to their goodness via self-improvement and self-development, the wicked were thwarted, and the planet began to look and smell nicer than anyone had ever expected.

And all this was the legacy of a handful of Sewing Harems which had once been dismissed as a self-indulgent ideological fad.

Meanwhile, something rather sad had happened, though it applied only to a nearly imperceptible minority and seldom drew anyone's constructive attention.

The children of the Sewing Harems had become pariahs.

How this occurred is of not much interest: whether they were regarded as a laughingstock anachronism, the spawn of geishas, scions of an antiquated and surely comical social contrivance, the very reminder of which was an embarrassment to the modern temper; whether they were taken as the last shameful relic of an aggressively greedy entrepreneurial movement; whether they were scorned as personalities mercilessly repressed by the barbaric extremes of the communal impulse; whether they were damned as the offspring of the pornographic imagination; whether they were jeered at as the deformed cubs of puritanical bluestockings; whether all of these or none, no one can rightly say.

Sociologists with enough curiosity to look into the origins of the sect pointed, predictably, to their upbringing: they were taught that they were at the root of the planet's woes, and yet they were taught that they had earned not one, but many, mothers. As a consequence of the first teaching, they fulfilled themselves as irrational demons and turned themselves into outcasts. As a consequence of the second teaching, they idolized motherhood.

You will have noticed that I have referred to these unfortunates as a "sect." This is exactly true. They were content to marry only one another; or, perhaps, no one else was content to marry any of *them*. Since numbers of them had the same father, or the same natural mother, or both, they were already afflicted with the multitudinous ills of inbreeding, and their fierce adherence to endogamy compounded these misfortunes. They had harelips, limps, twisted jaws and teeth, short arms, diseases of the blood, hereditary psychoses; some were wretchedly strabismic, others blind or deaf. They were an ugly, anxious, stern-minded crew, continually reproducing themselves.

Any woman of the sect who sewed herself they would kill; but this was generally unheard of among them, since sewing was their most ferocious taboo. Male babies born in any way sexually deformed were admitted to early surgery, but female babies born with unusually small or sealed vaginas were fed cyanide. The only remaining resemblance to the gaily lucid and civilizing Sewing Harems from which these savages derived was their prohibition of bottle-feeding.

They were organized into strong family units, and emphasized family orderliness and conventionality. All this was within the tribe. Otherwise they were likely to be criminals— members of the sect were frequently convicted of having murdered sewn women. If they had any gift at all, it was for their indulgence in unusual art forms. They had a notorious talent for obscene stonecutting.

Worst of all was their religious passion. They had invented a Superior Goddess: a single unimaginative and brutish syllable of three letters, two of them identical, formed her name —ingenious nonetheless, since it was a palindrome, pronounced identically whether chanted forward or backward. The goddess was conceived as utterly carnal, with no role other than to nurture the urge to spawn; under her base auspices the tribe spewed forth dozens of newborn savages in a single day.

In addition to murdering sewn women, the descendants of the Sewing Harems were guilty of erecting religious statuary on highways in the dead of night. These appeared in the likenesses of immense round gate-pillars, which, looming without warning in the blaze of day where there had been nothing the evening before, were the cause of multiple bloody traffic accidents. The best were carved out of enormous rocks quarried no one knew where, hauled on trucks, and set in place by cranes. The cheapest were made of concrete, mixed on the spot, and left to dry behind sawhorses hung with bright rags. In police reports these structures were usually described as mammary replicas; in actuality they had the shapes of huge vulvae. Sometimes the corpse of a sewn woman, stinking of some foul incense, a shiny magazine picture of an infant nailed into her thigh, would be found between the high walls of the two horrendous labia.

I have already remarked that these primitives did not number significantly in the general population (though they were disproportionately present in the prison population). They were pests, rather than a pestilence, and their impact on the planet would without doubt have continued negligible had the imperva molecules not suddenly begun first to deteriorate in the skies, and then to disintegrate entirely. All this was inexplicable; until now every firm scientific expectation was that no such dissolution could occur except under the climatic threat of a new ice age. Such a comment was always taken for a joke. In point of fact it remained a joke. There were no extraordinary atmospheric upheavals; the normal temperature of the planet was undisturbed.

But it became of course impossible for women to sew themselves as casually, uncomplicatedly, and joyfully as they had been capable of doing for immemorial generations—ever since, in fact, that planet's version of Eden: a humane Eden, incidentally, which had passed on no unkindnesses or encumbrances, whether to women or to men.

And because of irresistible advances in technology, the vulval thread had been so improved (composed of woven particles of infertels encased in plastic, it could now withstand blood-dye) that the stitches could not be undone, except by the most difficult and dangerous surgery, which the majority eschewed, because of the side effects of reversed infertels when they are burst. The treacherous stitch-snipping of the Sewing Harems, so long a subject of mockery and infamy among those who admired both progress and honest commitment, was all at once seen to be a lost treasure of the race.

Nearly all of the sewn women remained sewn until their deaths.

And the pariahs, the only source of mothers, bred like monkeys in their triumph, until the great stone vulvae covered the planet from end to end, and the frivolous memory of the Sewing Harems was rubbed away, down to the faintest smear of legend.

[Here ends the second fragment.]

Puttermesser and Xanthippe

for Mark Podwal

I. PUTTERMESSER'S BRIEF LOVE LIFE, HER TROUBLES, HER TITLES

Puttermesser, an unmarried lawyer and civil servant of forty-six, felt attacked on all sides. The night before, her lover, Morris Rappoport, a married fund-raiser from Toronto, had walked out on her. His mysterious job included settling Soviet Jewish refugees away from the big metropolitan centers; he claimed to have fresh news of the oppressed everywhere, as well as intimate acquaintance with malcontents in numerous cities in both the Eastern and Western hemispheres. Puttermesser suspected him of instability and overdependency: a future madman. His gripe was that she read in bed too much; last night she had read aloud from Plato's *Theaetetus*:

THEODORUS: What do you mean, Socrates?
SOCRATES: The same thing as the story about the Thracian

maidservant who exercised her wit at the expense of Thales, when he was looking up to study the stars and tumbled down a well. She scoffed at him for being so eager to know what was happening in the sky that he could not see what lay at his feet. Anyone who gives his life to philosophy is open to such mockery. It is true that he is unaware what his next-door neighbor is doing, hardly knows, indeed, whether the creature is a man at all; he spends all his pains on the question, what man is, and what powers and properties distinguish such a nature from any other. You see what I mean, Theodorus?

Rappoport did not see. He withdrew his hand from Puttermesser's belly. "What's the big idea, Ruth?" he said.

"That's right," Puttermesser said.

"What?"

"That's just what Socrates is after: the big idea."

"You're too old for this kind of thing," Rappoport said. He had a medium-sized, rather square, reddish mustache over perfect teeth. His teeth were more demanding to Puttermesser's gaze than his eyes, which were so diffidently pigmented that they seemed whited out, like the naked eyes on a Roman bust. His nose, however, was dominant, eloquent, with large deep nostrils that appeared to meditate. "Cut it out, Ruth. You're behaving like an adolescent," Rappoport said.

"*You'll* never fall down a well," Puttermesser said. "You never look up." She felt diminished; those philosophical nostrils had misled her.

"Ruth, Ruth," Rappoport pleaded, "what did I do?"

"It's what you didn't do. You didn't figure out what powers and properties distinguish human nature from any other," Puttermesser said bitterly; as a feminist, she was careful never to speak of "man's" nature. She always said "humankind" instead of "mankind." She always wrote "he or she" instead of just "he."

Rappoport was putting on his pants. "You're too old for sex," he said meanly.

Puttermesser's reply was instantly Socratic: "Then I'm *not* behaving like an adolescent."

"If you know I have a plane to catch, how come you want to read in bed?"

"It's more comfortable than the kitchen table."

"Ruth, I came to make love to you!"

"All I wanted was to finish the *Theaetetus* first."

Now he had his coat on, and was crossing his scarf carefully at his throat, so as not to let in the cold. It was a winter night, but Puttermesser saw in this gesture that Rappoport, at the age of fifty-two, still obeyed his mother's doctrines, no matter that they were five decades old. "You wanted to finish!" he yelled. He grabbed the book from her lap. "It goes from page 847 to page 879, that's thirty-three pages—"

"I read fast," Puttermesser said.

In the morning she understood that Rappoport would never come back. His feelings were hurt. In the end he would have deserted her anyway—she had observed that, sooner or later, he told all his feelings to his wife. And not only to his wife. He was the sort of man who babbles.

The loss of Rappoport was not Puttermesser's only trouble. She had developed periodontal disease; her dentist reported—with a touch of pleasure in disaster—a sixty percent bone loss. Loss of bone, loss of Rappoport, loss of home! "Uncontrollable pockets," the dentist said. He gave her the name of a periodontist to consult. It was an emergency, he warned. Her gums were puffy, her teeth in peril of uprooting. It was as if, in the dread underworld below the visible gums, a volcano lay, watching for its moment of release. She spat blood into the sink.

The sink was a garish fake marble. Little blue fish-tiles swam around the walls. The toilet seat cover had a large blue mermaid painted on it. Puttermesser hated this bathroom. She hated her new "luxury" apartment, with its windowless slot of a kitchen and two tiny cramped rooms, the bathroom without a bathtub, the shower stall the size of a thimble, the toilet's flush handle made of light blue plastic. Her majestic apartment on the Grand Concourse in the Bronx, with its Alhambra spaciousness, had been ravaged by arsonists. Even before that, the old tenants had been dying off or moving away, one by one; junkies stole in, filling empty corridors with blood-stained newspapers, smashed bottles, dead matches in random rows like beetle tracks. On a summer evening Puttermesser arrived home from her office without possessions: her shoes were ash, her piano was ash, her piano teacher's penciled "Excellent," written in fine large letters at the top of "Humoresque" and right across the opening phrase of "Für Elise," had vanished among the cinders. Puttermesser's childhood, burned away. How prescient her mother had been to take all of Puttermesser's school compositions with her to Florida! Otherwise every evidence of Puttermesser's early mental growth might have gone under in that criminal conflagration.

The new apartment was crowded with plants: Puttermesser, who was once afflicted with what she called a "black thumb," and who had hitherto killed every green thing she put her hand to, determined now to be responsible for life. She dragged in great clay urns and sacks of vitamin-rich soil bought at Woolworth's and emptied dark earth into red pots. She seeded and conscientiously watered. Rappoport himself had lugged in, on a plastic-wheeled dolly, a tall stalk like a ladder of green bear's ears: he claimed it was an avocado tree he had grown from a pit in Toronto. It reminded Puttermesser of her mother's towering rubber plants on the Grand Concourse, in their ceiling-sweeping prime. Every window sill of Puttermesser's new apartment was fringed with fronds, foliage, soaring or drooping leaf-tips. The tough petals of blood-veined coleus strained the bedroom sunset. Puttermesser, astonished, discovered that if she remained attentive enough, she had the power to stimulate green bursts. All along the bosky walls vegetation burgeoned.

Yet Puttermesser's days were arid. Her office life was not peaceable; nothing bloomed for her. She had fallen. Out of the blue, the Mayor ousted the old Commissioner—Puttermesser's boss, the chief of the Department of Receipts and Disbursements—and replaced him with a new man, seven years younger than Puttermesser. He looked like a large-eared boy; he wore his tie pulled loose, and his neck stretched forward out of his collar; it gave him the posture of a vertical turtle. His eyes, too, were unblinkingly turtlish. It was possible, Puttermesser conceded to herself, that despite his slowly reaching neck and flattish head, the new man did not really resemble a turtle at all; it was only that his name—Alvin Turtelman—suggested the bare lidless deliberation of that immobile creature of the road. Turtelman did not preen. Puttermesser saw at once, in all that meditated motionlessness, that he was more ambitious than the last Commissioner, who had been satisfied with mere prestige, and had used his office like a silken tent decorated with viziers and hookahs. But Turtelman was patient; his steady ogle took in the whole wide trail ahead. He spoke of "restructuring," of "functioning," of "goals" and "gradations," of "levels of purpose" and "versus equations." He was infinitely abstract. "None of this is personal," he liked to say, but his voice was a surprise; it was more pliable than you would expect from the stillness of his stare. He stretched out his vowels like any New Yorker. He had brought with him a score of underlings for what he called "mapping out." They began the day late and ended early, moving from cubicle to cubicle and collecting résumés. They were all bad spellers, and their memos, alive with solecisms, made Puttermesser grieve, because they were lawyers, and Puttermesser loved the law and its language. She caressed its meticulousness. She thought of law as Apollo's chariot; she had read all the letters of Justice Oliver Wendell Holmes, Jr., to Harold Laski (three volumes) and to Sir Frederick Pollock (two). In her dream once she stood before a ship captain and became the fifth wife of Justice William O. Douglas; they honey-mooned on the pampas of Argentina. It was difficult to tell whether Turtelman's bad spellers represented the Mayor himself, or only the new Commissioner; but clearly they were scouts and spies. They reported on lateness and laxness, on backlogs and postponements, on insufficiencies and excesses, on waste and error. They issued warnings and sounded alarms; they brought pressure to bear and threatened and cautioned and gave tips. They were watchful and envious. It soon became plain that they did not understand the work.

They did not understand the work because they were, it turned out, political appointees shipped over from the Department of Hygienic Maintenance; a handful were from the Fire Department. They had already had careers as oligarchs of street-sweeping, sewers and drains, gutters, the perils of sleet, ice, rainslant, gas, vermin, fumigation, disinfection, snow removal, water supply, potholes, steam cleaning, deodorization, ventilation, abstersion, elutriation; those from the Fire Department had formerly wielded the scepter over matters of arson, hydrants, pumps, hose (measured by weight, in kilograms), incendiary bombs, rubber boots, wax polish, red paint, false alarms, sappers, marshals. They had ruled over all these corporealities, but without comprehension; they asked for frequent memos; they were "administrators." This meant they were good at arrest; not only at making arrests (the fire marshals, for instance), but at bringing everything to a standstill, like the spindle-prick in Sleeping Beauty. In their presence the work instantly held its breath and came to a halt, as if it were a horse reined in for examination. They walked round and round the work, ruminating, speculating. They could not judge it; they did not understand it.

But they knew what it was for. It was for the spoils quota. The work, impenetrable though it was to its suzerains, proliferated with jobs; jobs blossomed with salaries; salaries were money; money was spoils. The current Mayor, Malachy ("Matt") Mavett, like all the mayors before him, was a dispenser of spoils, though publicly, of course, he declared himself morally opposed to political payoffs. He had long ago distributed the plums, the high patronage slots. All the commissioners were political friends of the Mayor. Sometimes a mayor would have more friends than there were jobs, and then this or that commissioner would suddenly be called upon to devise a whole new management level: a many-pegged perch just between the heights of direct mayoral appointment and the loftier rungs of the Civil Service. When that happened, Puttermesser would all at once discover a fresh crew of intermediate bosses appointed to loiter between herself and the Commissioner. Week after week, she would have to explain the work to them: the appointed intermediate bosses of the Department of Receipts and Disbursements did not usually know what the Department of Receipts and Disbursements *did*. By the time they found out, they vanished; they were always on the move, like minor bedouin sheikhs, to the next oasis. And when a new commissioner arrived right after an election (or, now and then, after what was officially described as "internal reorganization"—demoralization, upheaval, bloodbath), Puttermesser would once again be standing in the sanctuary of the Commissioner's deep inner office, the one with the mottled carpeting and the private toilet, earnestly explaining his rich domain to its new overlord.

Puttermesser was now an old hand, both at the work and at

the landscape of the bureaucracy. She was intimate with every folly and every fall. (Ah, but she did not expect her own fall.) She was a witness to every succession. (Ah, but she did not expect to be succeeded herself.) The bureaucracy was a faded feudal world of territory and authority and hierarchy, mainly dusty, except at those high moments of dagger and toppling. Through it all, Puttermesser was seen to be useful: this accounted for her climb. She had stuck her little finger into every cranny of every permutation of the pertinent law. Precedents sped through her brain. Her titles, movable and fictitious, traveled upward: from Assistant Corporation Counsel she became Administrative Tax Law Associate, and after that Vice Chief of Financial Affairs, and after that First Bursary Officer. All the while she felt like Alice, swallowing the potion and growing compact, nibbling the mushroom and swelling: each title was a swallow or a nibble, and not one of them signified anything but the degree of her convenience to whoever was in command. Her titles were the poetry of the bureaucracy.

The truth was that Puttermesser was now a fathomer; she had come to understand the recondite, dim, and secret journey of the City's money, the tunnels it rolled through, the transmutations, investments, multiplications, squeezings, fattenings and battenings it underwent. She knew where the money landed and where it was headed for. She knew the habits, names, and even the hot-tempered wives of three dozen bank executives on various levels. She had acquired half a dozen underlings of her own—with these she was diffident, polite; though she deemed herself a feminist, no ideology could succeed for her in aggrandizing force. Puttermesser was not aggressive. She disdained assertiveness. Her voice was like Cordelia's. At home, in bed, she went on dreaming and reading. She retained a romantic view of the British Civil Service in its heyday: the Cambridge Apostles carrying the probities of G. E. Moore to the far corners of the world, Leonard Woolf doing justice in Ceylon, the shy young Forster in India. Integrity. Uprightness. And all for the sake of imperialism, colonialism! In New York, Puttermesser had an immigrant's grandchild's dream of merit: justice, justice shalt thou pursue. Her heart beat for law, even for tax law: she saw the orderly nurturing of the democratic populace, public murals, subway windows bright as new dishes, parks with flowering borders, the bell-hung painted steeds of dizzying carousels.

Every day, inside the wide bleak corridors of the Municipal Building, Puttermesser dreamed an ideal Civil Service: devotion to polity, the citizen's sweet love of the citizenry, the light rule of reason and common sense, the City as a miniature country crowded with patriots—not fools and jingoists, but patriots true and serene; humorous affection for the idiosyncrasies of one's distinctive little homeland, each borough itself another little homeland, joy in the Bronx, elation in Queens, O happy Richmond! Children on roller skates, and over the Brooklyn Bridge the long patchwork-colored line of joggers, breathing hard above the homeland-hugging green waters.

II. PUTTERMESSER'S FALL, AND THE
HISTORY OF THE GENUS GOLEM

Turtelman sent his secretary to fetch Puttermesser. It was a new secretary, a middle-aged bony acolyte, graying and testy, whom he had brought with him from the Department of Hygienic Maintenance: she had coarse eyebrows crawling upward. "This isn't exactly a good time for me to do this," Puttermesser complained. It was as if Turtelman did not trust the telephone for such a purpose. Puttermesser knew his purpose: he wanted teaching. He was puzzled, desperate. Inside his ambitiousness he was a naked boy, fearful. His office was cradled next to the threatening computer chamber; all along the walls the computer's hard flanks glittered with specks and lights. Puttermesser could hear, behind a partition, the spin of a thousand wheels, a thin threadlike murmur, as if the software men, long-haired chaps in sneakers, had set lyres out upon the great stone window sills of the Municipal Building. Walking behind the bony acolyte, Puttermesser pitied Turtelman: the Mayor had called for information—figures, indexes, collections, projections—and poor Turtelman, fresh from his half-education in the land of abstersion and elutriation, his frontal lobes still inclined toward repair of street-sweeping machinery, hung back bewildered. He had no answers for the Mayor, and no idea where the answers might be hidden; alas, the questions themselves fell on Turtelman's ears as though in a foreign tongue.

The secretary pushed open Turtelman's door, stood aside for Puttermesser, and went furiously away.

Poor Turtelman, Puttermesser thought.

Turtelman spoke: "You're out."

"Out?" Puttermesser said. It was a bitter Tuesday morning in mid-January; at that very moment, considerably south of the Municipal Building, in Washington, D.C., they were getting ready to inaugurate the next President of the United States. High politics emblazoned the day. Bureaucracies all over the world were turning on their hinges, gates were lifting and shutting, desks emptying and filling. The tide rode upon Turtelman's spittle; it glimmered on his teeth.

"As of this afternoon," Turtelman said, "you are relieved of your duties. It's nothing personal, believe me. I don't know you. We're restructuring. It's too bad you're not a bit older. You can't retire at only forty-six." He had read her résumé, then; at least that.

"I'm old enough," Puttermesser said.

"Not for collecting your pension. You people have a valuable retirement system here. I envy you. It drains the rest of us dry." The clack of his teeth showed that he was about to deliver a sting: "We ordinary folk who aren't lucky enough to be in the Civil Service can't afford you."

Puttermesser announced proudly, "I earn my way. I scored highest in the entire city on the First-Level Management Examination. I was editor-in-chief of Law Review at Yale Law School. I graduated from Barnard with honors in history, *summa cum laude,* Phi Beta Kappa—"

Turtelman broke in: "Give me two or three weeks, I'll find a little spot for you somewhere. You'll hear from me."

Thus the manner of Puttermesser's fall. Ignoble. She did not dream there was worse to come. She spilled the papers out of her drawers and carried them to a windowless cubicle down the hall from her old office. For a day or so her ex-staff averted their eyes; then they ceased to notice her; her replacement had arrived. He was Adam Marmel, late of the Bureau of Emergencies, an old classmate of Turtelman's at New York University, where both had majored in Film Arts. This interested Puttermesser: the Department of Receipts and Disbursements was now in the hands of young men who had been trained to pursue illusion, to fly with a gossamer net after fleeting shadows. They were attracted to the dark, where fraudulent emotions raged. They were, moreover, close friends, often together. The Mayor had appointed Turtelman; Turtelman had appointed Marmel; Marmel had succeeded Puttermesser, who now sat with the *Times,* deprived of light, isolated, stripped, forgotten. An outcast. On the next Friday her salary check came as usual. But no one called her out of her cubicle.

Right in the middle of business hours—she no longer had

any business, she was perfectly idle—Puttermesser wrote a
letter to the Mayor:

The Honorable Malachy Mavett
Mayor, City of New York
City Hall

Dear Mayor Mavett:
Your new appointee in the Department of Receipts
and Disbursements, Commissioner Alvin Turtelman, has
forced a fine civil servant of honorable temperament, with
experience both wide and impassioned, out of her job.
I am that civil servant. Without a hearing, without due
process, without a hope of appeal or redress (except, Mr.
Mayor, by you!), Commissioner Turtelman has destroyed
a career in full flower. Employing an affectless vocabulary
by means of which, in a single instant, he abruptly ousted
a civil servant of high standing, Commissioner Turtelman
has politicized a job long held immune to outside pre-
ferment. In a single instant, honor, dignity, and continuity
have been snatched away! I have been professionally
injured and personally humiliated. I have been rendered
useless. As of this writing I am costing the City's taxpayers the price of my entire salary, while I sit here working
a crossword puzzle; while I hold this very pen. No one
looks at me. They are embarrassed and ashamed. At first
a few ex-colleagues came into this little abandoned office
(where I do nothing) to offer condolences, but that was
only at first. It is like being at my own funeral, Mr. Mayor,
only imagine it!
Mr. Mayor, I wish to submit several urgent questions
to you; I will be grateful for your prompt views on these
matters of political friendships, connections, and power.
1. Are you aware of this inequitable treatment of

professional staff in the Bureau of Summary Sessions of the Department of Receipts and Disbursements?

2. If so, is this the nature of the Administration you are content to be represented by?

3. Is it truly your desire to erode and undermine the professional Civil Service—one of democratic government's most just, most equitable, devices?

4. Does Commissioner Alvin Turtelman's peremptory action really reflect your own sensibility, with all its fairness and exuberant humaneness?

In City, State, and World life, Mr. Mayor (I have observed this over many years), power and connections are never called power and connections. They are called principle. They are called democracy. They are called judgment. They are called doing good. They are called restructuring. They are called exigency. They are called improvement. They are called functioning. They are called the common need. They are called government. They are called running the Bureau, the Department, the City, the State, the World, looking out for the interests of the people.

Mr. Mayor, getting the spoils is called anything but getting the spoils!

Puttermesser did not know whether Malachy ("Matt") Mavett's sensibility was really fair and exuberantly humane; she had only put that in to flatter him. She had glimpsed the Mayor in the flesh only once or twice, at a meeting, from a distance. She had also seen him on Sunday morning television, at a press conference, but then he was exceptionally cautious and sober; before the cameras he was neuter, he had no sensibility at all; he was nearly translucent. His white mustache looked tangled; his white hair twirled in strings over his temples.

Puttermesser's letter struck her as gripping, impressive; copying it over on the typewriter at home that night, she felt how the Mayor would be stabbed through by such fevered eloquence. How remorseful he would be, how moved!

Still another salary check arrived. It was not for the usual amount; Puttermesser's pay had been cut. The bony acolyte appeared with a memo from Turtelman: Puttermesser was to leave her barren cubicle and go to an office with a view of the Woolworth Building, and there she was to take up the sad life of her demotion.

Turtelman had shoved her into the lowliest ranks of Taxation. It was an unlikely post for a mind superfetate with Idea; Puttermesser felt the malignancy behind this shift. Her successor had wished her out of sight. "I do not consort with failure," she heard Adam Marmel tell one of the auditors. She lived now surrounded by auditors—literal-minded men. They read best-sellers; their fingers were smudged from the morning papers, which they clutched in their car pools or on the subway from Queens. One of them, Leon Cracow, a bachelor from Forest Hills who wore bow ties and saddle shoes, was engaged in a tedious litigation: he had once read a novel and fancied himself its hero. The protagonist wore bow ties and saddle shoes. Cracow was suing for defamation. "My whole love life's maligned in there," he complained to Puttermesser. He kept the novel on his desk—it was an obscure book no one had ever heard of, published by a shadowy California press. Cracow had bought it remaindered for eighty-nine cents and ruminated over it every day. Turning the pages, he wet two of his fingers repeatedly. The novel was called *Pyke's Pique*; a tax auditor named John McCracken Pyke was its chief character. "McCracken," Cracow said, "that's practically Cracow. It sounds practically identical. Listen, in the book this guy goes to prostitutes. I don't go to prostitutes! The skunk's got me all wrong. He's destroying my good name." Sometimes Cracow asked Puttermesser for her opinion of his lawyer's last move. Puttermesser urged him on. She believed in the uses of fantasy. "A person should see himself or herself everywhere," she said. "All things manifest us."

The secret source of this motto was, in fact, her old building on the Grand Concourse. Incised in a stone arch over the broad front door, and also in Puttermesser's loyal brain, were these Roman-style tracings: LONGWOOD ARMS, No. 26. GREENDALE HALL, No. 28. ALL THINGS MANIFEST US. The builder had thought deep thoughts, and Cracow was satisfied. "Ruth," he said, "you take the cake." As usual, he attempted to date her. "Any concert, any show, you name it," he said; "I'm a film buff." "You fit right in with Turtelman and Marmel," Puttermesser said. "Not me," Cracow retorted, "with me it's nostalgia only. My favorite movie is Deanna Durbin, Leopold Stokowski, and Adolphe Menjou in *One Hundred Men and a Girl*. Wholesome, sweet, not like they make today. Light classical. Come on, Ruth, it's at the Museum of Modern Art, in the cellar." Puttermesser turned him down. She knew she would never marry, but she was not yet reconciled to childlessness. Sometimes the thought that she would never give birth tore her heart.

She imagined daughters. It was self-love: all these daughters were Puttermesser as a child. She imagined a daughter in fourth grade, then in seventh grade, then in second-year high school. Puttermesser herself had gone to Hunter College High School and studied Latin. At Barnard she had not renounced Catullus and Vergil. *O infelix Dido*, chanted the imaginary daughter, doing her Latin homework at Puttermesser's new Danish desk in the dark corner of the little bedroom. It was a teak rectangle; Puttermesser still had not bought a lamp for it. She hated it that all her furniture was new.

No reply came from the Mayor: not even a postcard of acknowledgment from an underling. Malachy ("Matt") Mavett was ignoring Puttermesser.

Rappoport had abandoned the Sunday *Times*, purchased

Saturday night at the airport; he had left it, unopened, on the Danish desk. Puttermesser swung barefoot out of bed, stepped over Plato, and reached for Rappoport's *Times*. She brooded over his furry chest hair, yellowing from red. Now the daughter, still in high school, was memorizing Goethe's *Erlkönig*:

> *Dem Vater grauset's, er reitet geschwind,*
> *Er hält in Armen des ächzende Kind,*
> *Erreicht den Hof mit Mühe und Not:*
> *In seinem Armen das Kind war tot.*

The words made Puttermesser want to sob. The child was dead. In its father's arms the child was dead. She came back to bed, carrying Rappoport's *Times*. It was as heavy as if she carried a dead child. The Magazine Section alone was of a preternatural weight. Advertising. Consumerism. Capitalism. Page after page of cars, delicately imprinted chocolates, necklaces, golden whiskey. Affluence while the poor lurked and mugged, hid in elevators, shot drugs into their veins, stuck guns into old grandmothers' tremulous and brittle spines, in covert pools of blackness released the springs of their bright-flanked switchblades, in shafts, in alleys, behind walls, in ditches.

A naked girl lay in Puttermesser's bed. She looked dead— she was all white, bloodless. It was as if she had just undergone an epileptic fit: her tongue hung out of her mouth. Her eyelids were rigidly ajar; they had no lashes, and the skin was so taut and thin that the eyeballs bulged through. Her palms had fallen open; they were a clear white. Her arms were cold rods. A small white square was visible on the tongue. The girl did not resemble Puttermesser at all; she was certainly not one of the imaginary daughters. Puttermesser moved to one side of the bed, then circled back around the foot to the other side. She put on her slippers; summoning reason, she continued to move around and around the bed. There was no doubt that a real body was in it. Puttermesser reached out and touched the right shoulder—a reddish powder coated her fingers. The body seemed filmed with sand, or earth, or grit; some kind of light clay. Filth. A filthy junkie or prostitute; both. Sickness and filth. Rappoport, stalking away in the middle of the night, had been careless about closing the apartment door. God only knew where the creature had concealed herself, what had been stolen or damaged. When Puttermesser's back was turned, the filthy thing had slid into her bed. Such a civilized bed, the home of Plato and other high-minded readings. The body had a look of perpetuity about it, as if it had always been reclining there, in Puttermesser's own bed; yet it was a child's body, the limbs stretched into laxity and languor. She was a little thing, no more than fifteen: Puttermesser saw how the pubic hair was curiously sparse; but the breasts were nearly not there at all. Puttermesser went on calculating and circling: should she call the super, or else telephone for an ambulance? New York! What was the good of living in a tiny squat box, with low ceilings, on East Seventy-first Street, a grudging landlord, a doorman in an admiral's uniform, if there were infiltrators, addicts, invaders, just the same as on the fallen Grand Concourse?

Puttermesser peered down at the creature's face. Ugly. The nose and mouth were clumsily formed, as if by some coarse hand that had given them a negligent tweak. The vomerine divider was off-center, the nostrils unpleasantly far apart. The mouth was in even worse condition—also off-center, but somehow more carelessly made, with lips that failed to match, the lower one no better than a line, the upper one amazingly fat, swollen, and the narrow tongue protruding with its white patch. Puttermesser reached out a correcting hand, and then withdrew it. Once again the dust left deep red ovals on her fingertips. But it was clear that the nostrils needed pinching to bring them closer together, so Puttermesser tentatively pinched. The improvement was impressive. She blew into the left nostril to get rid of a tuft of dust; it solidified and rolled out like a clay bead. With squeamish deliberation she pushed the nose in line with the middle space where the eyebrows ought to have been. There were no eyebrows, no eyelashes, no fingernails, no toenails. The thing was defective, unfinished. The mouth above all required finishing. Forming and re-forming the savage upper lip, getting into the mood of it now, Puttermesser wished she were an artist or sculptor: she centered the mouth, thickened the lower lip with a quick turn, smoothed out the hunch of the upper one—the tongue was in the way. She peeled off the white square and, pressing hard, shoved the tongue back down into the mouth.

The bit of white lay glimmering in Puttermesser's palm. It seemed to be nothing more than an ordinary slip of paper, but she thought she ought to put it aside to look it over more carefully after a while, so she left the bed and set it down on the corner of the teak desk. Then she came back and glanced up and down the body, to see whether there was anything else that called for correction. A forefinger needed lengthening, so Puttermesser tugged at it. It slid as if boneless, like taffy, cold but not sticky, and thrillingly pliable. Still, without its nail a finger can shock; Puttermesser recoiled. Though the face was now normal enough, there was more to be done. Something had flashed upward from that tongue-paper—the white patch was blank; yet it was not only blank. Puttermesser carried it in her palm to the window, for the sake of the light. But on the sill and under the sill every pot was cracked, every green plant sprawled. The roots, skeletal and hairy, had been torn from their embracing soil—or, rather, the earth had been scooped away. The plain earth, stolen. Puttermesser, holding the white scrap, wandered from window to window. There was no pot that had not been vandalized in the same way— Rappoport's big clay urn was in shards, the avocado tree broken. A few sparse grains of soil powdered the floor. Not a plant anywhere had been left unmolested—all the earth in Puttermesser's apartment was gone; taken away; robbed.

In the bedroom the girl's form continued its lethal sleep. Puttermesser lifted the tiny paper to the bright panes. Out of the whiteness of the white patch another whiteness flickered, as though a second version of absence were struggling to swim up out of the aboriginal absence. For Puttermesser, it was as if the white of her own eye could suddenly see what the purposeful retina had shunned. It was in fact not so much a seeing as the sharpness of a reading, and what Puttermesser read—she whose intellectual passions were pledged to every alphabet—was a single primeval Hebrew word, shimmering with its lightning holiness, the Name of Names, that which one dare not take in vain. Aloud she uttered it:

חשם,

whereupon the inert creature, as if drilled through by electricity, as if struck by some principle of instantaneous vitality, leaped straight from the bed; Puttermesser watched the fingernails grow rapidly into place, and the toenails, and the eyebrows and lashes: complete. A configuration of freckles appeared on the forehead. The hair of the head and of the mons Veneris thickened, curled, glistened dark red, the color of clay; the creature had risen to walk. She did it badly, knocking down the desk-chair and bumping into the dresser. Sick, drugged, drunk; vandal; thief of earth!

"Get your clothes on and get out," Puttermesser said. Where were the thing's clothes? She had none; she seemed less pale moment by moment; she was lurching about in her skin. She was becoming rosy. A lively color was in her cheeks and hands. The mouth, Puttermesser's own handiwork, was vivid. Puttermesser ran to her closet and pulled out a shirt, a skirt, a belt, a cardigan. From her drawers she swept up bra, pantyhose, slip. There was only the question of shoes. "Here," she said, "summer sandals, that's all I can spare. Open toes, open heels, they'll fit. Get dressed. I can give you an old coat—go ahead. Sit down on the bed. Put this stuff on. You're lucky I'm not calling the police."

The creature staggered away from the bed, toward the teak desk.

"Do what I say!"

The creature had seized a notepad and a ballpoint pen, and was scribbling with shocking speed. Her fingers, even the newly lengthened one, were rhythmically coordinated. She clenched the pen, Puttermesser saw, like an experienced writer: as if the pen itself were a lick of the tongue, or an extension of the thinking digits. It surprised Puttermesser to learn that this thief of earth was literate. In what language? And would she then again try to swallow what she wrote, leaving one untouchable word behind?

The thing ripped away the alphabet-speckled page, tottered back with the pad, and laid the free sheet on the pillow.

"What's the matter? Can't you walk?" Puttermesser asked; she thought of afflicted children she had known, struck by melancholy witherings and dodderings.

But the answer was already on the paper. Puttermesser read: "I have not yet been long up upon my fresh-made limbs. Soon my gait will come to me. Consider the newborn colt. I am like unto that. All tongues are mine, especially that of my mother. Only speech is forbidden me."

A lunatic! Cracked! Alone in the house with a maniac; a deaf-mute to boot. "Get dressed," Puttermesser again commanded.

The thing wrote: "I hear and obey the one who made me."

"What the hell *is* this," Puttermesser said flatly.

The thing wrote: "My mother," and rapidly began to jerk herself into Puttermesser's clothes, but with uneven sequences of the body—the more vitality the creature gained, the more thinglike she seemed.

Puttermesser was impatient; she longed to drive the creature out. "Put on those shoes," she ordered.

The thing wrote: "No."

"Shoes!" Puttermesser shouted. She made a signpost fist and flung it in the direction of the door. "Go out the way you came in!"

The thing wrote: "No shoes. This is a holy place. I did not enter. I was formed. Here you spoke the Name of the Giver of Life. You blew in my nostril and encouraged my soul. You circled my clay seven times. You enveloped me with your spirit. You pronounced the Name and brought me to myself. Therefore I call you mother."

Puttermesser's lungs began to roil. It was true she had circled the creature on the bed. Was it seven times around? It was true she had blown some foreign matter out of the nose. Had she blown some uncanny energy into an entrance of the dormant body? It was true she had said aloud one of the Names of the Creator.

The thing wrote again: "Mother. Mother."

"Go away!"

The thing wrote: "You made me."

"I didn't give birth to you." She would never give birth. Yet she had formed this mouth—the creature's mute mouth. She looked at the mouth: she saw what she had made.

The thing wrote: "Earth is my flesh. For the sake of my flesh you carried earth to this high place. What will you call me?"

A new turbulence fell over Puttermesser. She had always imagined a daughter named Leah. "Leah," she said.

"No," the creature wrote. "Leah is my name, but I want to be Xanthippe."

Puttermesser said, "Xanthippe was a shrew. Xanthippe was Socrates' wife."

"I want to be Xanthippe," the thing wrote. "I know everything you know. I am made of earth but also I am made out of your mind. Now watch me walk."

The thing walked, firmly, with a solid thump of a step and no stumbling. She wrote on the pad: "I am becoming stronger. You made me. I will be of use to you. Don't send me away. Call me what I prefer, Xanthippe."

"Xanthippe," Puttermesser said.

She succumbed; her throat panted. It came to her that the creature was certainly not lying: Puttermesser's fingernails were crowded with grains of earth. In some unknown hour after Rappoport's departure in the night, Puttermesser had shaped an apparition. She had awakened it to life in the conventional way. Xanthippe was a golem, and what had polymathic Puttermesser *not* read about the genus golem?

Puttermesser ordered: "All right, go look on the bookshelves. Bring me whatever you see on your own kind."

The creature churned into the living room and hurried back with two volumes, one in either hand; she held the pen ready in her mouth. She dumped the books on the bed and wrote: "I am the first female golem."

"No you're not," Puttermesser said. It was clear that the creature required correction. Puttermesser flew through the pages of one of the books. "Ibn Gabirol created a woman. This was in Spain, long ago, the eleventh century. The king gave him a dressing-down for necromancy, so he dismantled her. She was made of wood and had hinges—it was easy to take her apart."

The creature wrote: "That was not a true golem."

"Go sit down in a corner," Puttermesser said. "I want to read."

The creature obeyed. Puttermesser dived into the two volumes. She had read them many times before; she knew certain passages nearly verbatim. One, a strange old text in a curiously awkward English translation (it was printed in Austria in 1925), had the grass-green public binding of a library book; to Puttermesser's citizenly shame, she had never returned it. It had been borrowed from the Crotona Park Branch decades ago, in Puttermesser's adolescence. There were photographs in it, incandescently clear: of graves, of a statue, of the lamp-hung interior of a synagogue in Prague— the Altneuschul—, of its tall peaked contour, of the two great clocks, one below the cupola, the other above it, on the venerable Prague Jewish Community House. Across the street from the Community House there was a shop, with a sign that said V. PRESSLER in large letters; underneath, his hand in his pocket, a dapper mustached dandy in a black fedora lounged eternally. Familiar, static, piercingly distinct though these illustrations were, Puttermesser all the same felt their weary old ache: phantoms—V. PRESSLER a speck of earth; the houses air; the dandy evaporated. Among these aged streets and deranged structures Puttermesser's marveling heart had often prowled. "You have no feelings," Rappoport once told her: he meant that she had the habit of flushing with ideas as if they were passions.

And this was true. Puttermesser's intelligence, brambly with the confusion of too much history, was a private warted tract, rubbled over with primordial statuary. She was painfully anthropological. Civilizations rolled into her rib cage, stone after graven stone: cuneiform, rune, cipher. She had pruned out allegory, metaphor; Puttermesser was no mystic, enthusiast, pneumaticist, ecstatic, kabbalist. Her mind was clean; she was a rationalist. Despite the imaginary daughters —she included these among her losses—she was not at all attached to any notion of shade or specter, however corporeal it might appear, and least of all to the idea of a golem—

hardly that, especially now that she had the actual thing on her hands. What transfixed her was the kind of intellect (immensely sober, pragmatic, unfanciful, rationalist like her own) to which a golem ordinarily occurred—occurred, that is, in the shock of its true flesh and absolute being. The classical case of the golem of Prague, for instance: the Great Rabbi Judah Loew, circa 1520–1609, maker of that renowned local creature, was scarcely one of those misty souls given over to untrammeled figments or romances. He was, instead, a reasonable man of biting understanding, a solid scholar, a pragmatic leader—a learned quasi-mayor. What he understood was that the scurrilous politics of his city, always tinged with religious interests, had gone too far. In short, they were killing the Jews of Prague. It had become unsafe for a peddler to open his pack, or a merchant his shop; no mother and her little daughter dared turn into an alley. Real blood ran in the streets, and all on account of a rumor of blood: citizens of every class—not just the guttersnipes—were muttering that the Jews had kneaded the bodies of Christian infants into their sacral Passover wafers. Scapegoat Jews, exposed, vulnerable, friendless, unarmed! The very Jews forbidden by their dietary code to eat an ordinary farmyard egg tainted with the minutest jot of fetal blood! So the Great Rabbi Judah Loew, to defend the Jews of Prague against their depredators, undertook to fashion a golem.

Puttermesser was well acquainted with the Great Rabbi Judah Loew's method of golem-making. It was classical; it was, as such things go, ordinary. To begin with, he entered a dream of Heaven, wherein he asked the angels to advise him. The answer came in alphabetical order: *afar, esh, mayim, ruach*: earth, fire, water, wraith. With his son-in-law, Isaac ben Shimshon, and his pupil, Jacob ben Chayim Sasson, the Great Rabbi Judah Loew sought inner purity and sanctification by means of prayer and ritual immersion; then the three its recurrence. The golem recurred, of course. It moved from the Exile of Babylon to the Exile of Europe; it followed the Jews. In the third century Rabbi Rava created a golem, and sent it to Rabbi Zera, who seemed not to know it was a golem until he discovered that it could not speak. Then realization of the thing's true nature came to him, and he rebuked it: "You must have been made by my comrades of the Talmudic Academy; return to your dust." Rabbi Hanina and Rabbi Oshaya were less successful than Rabbi Rava; they were only able to produce a very small calf, on which they dined. An old kabbalistic volume, the Book of Creation, explains that Father Abraham himself could manufacture human organisms. The Book of Raziel contains a famous workable prescription for golem-making: the maker utilizes certain chants and recitations, imprinted medals, esoteric names, efficacious shapes and totems. Ben Sira and his father, the prophet Jeremiah, created a golem, in the logical belief that Adam himself was a golem; their golem, like Adam, had the power of speech. King Nebuchadnezzar's own idol turned into a living golem when he set on its head the diadem of the High Priest, looted out of the Temple in Jerusalem; the jeweled letters of the Tetragrammaton were fastened into the diadem's silver sockets. The prophet Daniel, pretending to kiss the king's golem, swiftly plucked out the gems that spelled the Name of God, and the idol was again lifeless. Even before that, thieves among the wicked generation that built the Tower of Babel swiped some of the contractor's materials to fashion idols, which were made to walk by having the Name shoved into their mouths; then they were taken for gods. Rabbi Aharon of Baghdad and Rabbi Hananel did not mold images; instead, they sewed parchments inscribed with the Name into the right arms of corpses, who at once revived and became members of the genus golem. The prophet Micah made a golden calf that could dance, and Bezalel, the designer of the Tabernacle, knew how to combine letters of the alphabet so as to duplicate Creation, both heaven and earth. Rabbi Elazar of Worms had a somewhat similar system for golem-making: three adepts must gather up "virginal mountain earth," pour running water over it, knead it into a man, bury it, and recite two hundred and twenty-one alphabetical combinations, observing meticulously the prescribed order of the vowels and consonants. But Abraham Abulafia could make a man out of a mere spoonful of earth by blowing it over an ordinary dish of water; undoubtedly this had some influence on Paracelsus, the sixteenth-century German alchemist, who used a retort to make a homunculus: Paracelsus's manikin, however, was not telluric, being composed of blood, sperm, and urine, from which the Jewish golem-makers recoiled. For the Jews, earth, water, and the divine afflatus were the only permissible elements—the afflatus being summoned through the holy syllables. Rabbi Ishmael, on the other hand, knew another way of withdrawing that life-conferring holiness and rendering an active golem back into dust: he would recite the powerful combinations of sacred letters backward, meanwhile circling the creature in the direction opposite to the one that had quickened it.

There was no end to the conditions of golem-making, just as there was no end to the appearance of one golem after another in the pullulating procession of golem-history; but Puttermesser's brain, crowded with all these acquisitions and rather a tidy store of others (for instance, she had the noble Dr. Gershom Scholem's bountiful essay "The Idea of the Golem" virtually by heart), was unattracted either to number or to method. What interested Puttermesser was something else: it was the plain fact that the golem-makers were neither visionaries nor magicians nor sorcerers. They were neither fantasists nor fabulists nor poets. They were, by and large, scientific realists—and, in nearly every case at hand, serious scholars and intellectuals: the plausible forerunners, in fact, of their great-grandchildren, who are physicists, biologists, or logical positivists. It was not only the Great Rabbi Judah Loew, the esteemed golem-maker of Prague, who had, in addition, a reputation as a distinguished Talmudist, reasoner, philosopher; even Rabbi Elijah, the most celebrated Jewish intellect of Eastern Europe (if Spinoza is the most celebrated on the Western side), whose brilliance outstripped the fame of every other scholar, who founded the most rigorous rabbinical academy in the history of the cold lands, who at length became known as the Vilna *Gaon* (the Genius of the city of Vilna, called, on his account, the Jerusalem of the North)— even the Vilna *Gaon* once attempted, before the age of thirteen, to make a golem! And the Vilna *Gaon*, with his stern refinements of exegesis and analysis, with his darting dazzlements of logical penetration, was—as everyone knows—the scourge of mystics, protester (*mitnagid*) against the dancing hasidim, scorner of those less limber minds to the Polish south, in superstitiously pious Galicia. If the Vilna *Gaon* could contemplate the making of a golem, thought Puttermesser, there was nothing irrational in it, and she would not be ashamed of what she herself had concocted.

She asked Xanthippe: "Do you eat?"

The golem wrote, "*Vivo, ergo edo.* I live, therefore I eat."

"Don't pull that on me—my Latin is as good as yours. Can you cook?"

"I can do what I must, if my mother decrees it," the golem wrote.

"All right," Puttermesser said. "In that case you can stay. You can stay until I decide to get rid of you. Now make lunch. Cook something I like, only better than I could do it."

III. THE GOLEM COOKS, CLEANS, AND SHOPS

The golem hurried off to the kitchen. Puttermesser heard the smack of the refrigerator, the clatter of silver, the faucet turned on and off; sounds of chopping in a wooden bowl; plates set out, along with an eloquent tinkle of glassware; a distant whipping, a distant sizzling; mushroom fragrances; coffee. The golem appeared at the bedroom door with a smug sniff, holding out her writing pad:

"I can have uses far beyond the mere domestic."

"If you think you're too good for kitchen work," Puttermesser retorted, "don't call yourself Xanthippe. You're so hot on aspiration, you might as well go the whole hog and pick Socrates."

The golem wrote: "I mean to be a critic, even of the highest philosophers. Xanthippe alone had the courage to gainsay Socrates. Nay, I remain Xanthippe. Please do not allow my Swedish mushroom soufflé to sink. It is best eaten in a steaming condition."

Puttermesser muttered, "I don't like your prose style. You write like a translation from the Middle Finnish. Improve it," but she followed the golem into the little kitchen. The golem's step was now light and quick, and the kitchen too seemed transformed—a floating corner of buoyancy and quicksilver: it was as if the table were in the middle of a Parisian concourse, streaming, gleaming: it had the look of a painting, both transient and eternal, a place where you sat for a minute to gossip, and also a place where the middle-aged Henry James came every day so that nothing in the large world would be lost on him. "You've set things up nicely enough,"

Puttermesser said; "I forgot all about these linen placemats." They were, in fact, part of her "trousseau"; her mother had given her things. It was expected, long ago, that Puttermesser would marry.

The golem's soufflé was excellent; she had also prepared a dessert that was part mousse, part lemon gelatin. Puttermesser, despite her periodontic troubles, took a greedy second helping. The golem's dessert was more seductive even than fudge; and fudge for Puttermesser was notoriously paradisal.

"First-rate," Puttermesser said; the golem had been standing all the while. "Aren't you having any?"

Immediately the golem sat down and ate.

"Now I'm going for a walk," Puttermesser announced. "Clean all this up. Make the bed. Be sure to mop under it. Look in the hamper, you'll find a heap of dirty clothes. There's a public washing machine in the basement. I'll give you quarters."

The golem turned glum.

"Well, look," Puttermesser argued, "I can use you for anything I please, right?"

The golem wrote, "The Great Rabbi Judah Loew's wife sent the golem of Prague to fetch water, and he fetched, and he fetched, until he flooded the house, the yard, the city, and finally the world."

"Don't bother me with fairy tales," Puttermesser said.

The golem wrote, "I insist I am superior to mere household use."

"No one's superior to dirty laundry," Puttermesser threw back, and went out into the great city. She intended to walk and brood; though she understood at last how it was that she had brought the golem to life, it disturbed her that she did not recall *making* her—emptying all the plant pots, for instance. Nor was Puttermesser wise to her own secret dictates in creating the golem. And now that the golem was actually in the house, what was to be done with her? Puttermesser worried about the landlord, a suspicious fellow. The landlord allowed no dogs or—so the lease read—"irregular relationships." She thought of passing Xanthippe off as an adopted daughter —occasionally she would happen on an article about single parents of teen-age foster children. It was not so unusual. But even that would bring its difficulty, because—to satisfy the doorman and the neighbors—such a child would have to be sent to school; and it was hardly reasonable, Puttermesser saw, to send the golem to an ordinary high school. They would ship her off to an institution for deaf-mutes, to learn sign language—and it would become evident soon enough, wouldn't it, that the golem was not the least bit deaf? There was really no place for her in any classroom; she probably knew too much already. The erratic tone of her writing, with its awful pastiche, suggested that she had read ten times more than any other tenth-grader of the same age. Besides, did the golem *have* an age? She had the shape of a certain age, yes; but the truth was she was only a few hours old. Her public behavior was bound to be unpredictable.

Puttermesser was walking northward. Her long introspective stride had taken her as far as Eighty-sixth Street. She left Madison and veered up Lexington. She had forgotten her gloves; her fingers were frozen. February's flying newspapers scuttled over broken bottles and yogurt cups squashed in the gutter. A bag lady slept in a blue-black doorway, wrapped in a pile of ragged coats. Dusk was coming down; all the store windows, without exception, were barred or shuttered against the late-afternoon Sunday emptiness. Burglars, addicts, marauders, the diverse criminal pestilences of uptown and downtown, would have to find other ways of entry: breaking through a roof; a blowtorch on a steel bar; a back toilet window with a loose grill. Ingenuity. Puttermesser peered around behind her for the mugger who, in all logic, should have been stalking her; no one was there. But she was ready: she had left her wallet at home on purpose; a police whistle dangled on a cord around her neck; she fondled the little knife in her pocket. New York! All the prisons in the metropolitan area were reputed to be hopelessly overcrowded.

At Ninety-second Street she swung through the revolving doors of the Y to warm up. The lobby was mostly uninhabited; a short line straggled toward the ticket office. Puttermesser read the poster: a piano concert at eight o'clock. She headed downtown. It was fully dark now. She reflected that it would be easy enough to undo, to reverse, the golem; there was really no point in keeping her on. For one thing, how would the golem be occupied all day while Puttermesser was at work? And Puttermesser was nervous: she had her demotion to think about. Stripped. Demoralized. That pest Cracow. Turtelman and Marmel. The Civil Service, founded to eradicate patronage, nepotism, favoritism, spoils, payoffs, injustice, corruption! Lost, all lost. The Mayor had no intention of answering Puttermesser's urgent letter.

Taking off her coat, Puttermesser called to the golem, "What's going on in there?" An unexpected brilliance spilled out of the bedroom: a lamp in the form of the Statue of Liberty stood on the teak desk. "What's this?"

"I bought it," the golem wrote. "I did everything my mother instructed. I cleaned up the kitchen, made the bed"—a new blue bedspread, with pictures of baseball mitts, covered it—"mopped the whole house, did the laundry, ironed everything, hung my mother's blouses and put my mother's pantyhose into the drawer—"

Puttermesser grabbed the sheet of paper right off the golem's pad and tore it up without reading the rest of it. "What do you mean you bought it? What kind of junk is this? I don't want the Statue of Liberty! I don't want baseball mitts!"

"It was all I could find," the golem wrote on a fresh page. "All the stores around here are closed on Sunday. I had to go down to Delancey Street on the Lower East Side. I took a taxi."

"Taxi! You'll shop when I tell you to shop!" Puttermesser yelled. "Otherwise you stay home!"

"I need a wider world," the golem wrote. "Take me with you to your place of employment tomorrow."

"My foot I will," Puttermesser said. "I've had enough of you. I've been thinking"—she looked for a euphemism—"about sending you back."

"Back?" the golem wrote; her mouth had opened all the way.

"You've got a crooked tooth. Come here," Puttermesser said, "I'll fix it."

The golem wrote, "You can no longer alter my being or any part of my being. The speaking of the Name fulfills; it precludes alteration. But I am pleasant to look on, am I not? I will not again gape so that my crooked tooth can offend my mother's eye. Only use me."

"You've got rotten taste."

The golem wrote, "It was my task to choose between baseball mitts and small raccoons intermingled with blue-eyed panda bears. The baseball mitts struck me as the lesser evil."

"I never *wanted* a bedspread," Puttermesser objected. "When I said to make the bed I just meant to straighten the blankets, that's all. And my God, the Statue of Liberty!"

The golem wrote, "A three-way bulb, 150 watts. I thought it so very clever that the bulb goes right into the torch."

"Kitsch. And where'd you get the money?"

"Out of your wallet. But see how pleasantly bright," the golem wrote. "I fear the dark. The dark is where pre-existence abides. It is not possible to think of pre-existence, but one dreads its facsimile: post-existence. Do not erase, obliterate, or annihilate me. Mother, my mother. I will serve you. Use me in the wide world."

"You stole my money right out of my wallet, spent a fortune on a taxi, and brought home the cheapest sort of junk. If you pull this kind of thing in the house, don't talk to me about the wide world!"

IV. XANTHIPPE AT WORK

But the next morning the golem was in Puttermesser's office.

"Who's the kid?" Cracow asked.

"Marmel's letting me have a typist," Puttermesser said.

"Marmel? That don't make sense. After demoting you?"

"I was reassigned," Puttermesser said; but her cheeks stung.

"Them's the breaks," Cracow said. "So how come the royal treatment? You could use the typing pool like the rest of us."

"Turtelman's put me on a special project."

"Turtelman? Turtelman kicked you in the head. What special project?"

"I'm supposed to check out any employee who broods about lawsuits on City time," Puttermesser said.

"Oh come on, Ruth, can the corn. You know damn well I've been maligned. My lawyer says I have a case. I damn well have a case. What's the kid's name?"

"Leah."

"Leah." Cracow pushed his face right into the golem's. "Do they hire 'em that young? What are you, Leah, a high-school dropout?"

"She's smart enough as is," Puttermesser said.

"Whyn't you let the kid answer for herself?"

Puttermesser took Cracow by the elbow and whispered, "They cut out her throat. Malignancy of the voicebox."

"Whew," Cracow said.

"Get going," Puttermesser ordered the golem, and led her to the ladies' room. "I told you not to come! I'm in enough hot water around here, I don't need you to make trouble."

The golem plucked a paper towel from the wall, fetched Puttermesser's ballpoint pen from the pocket of Puttermesser's cardigan (the golem was still wearing it), and wrote: "I will ameliorate your woe."

"I didn't say woe, I said hot water. *Trouble.* First kitsch, now rococo. Observe reality, can't you? Look, you're going to sit in front of that typewriter and that's it. If you can type half as well as you cook, fine. I don't care *what* you type. Stay out of my way. Write letters, it doesn't matter, but stay out of my way."

The golem wrote, "I hear and obey."

All day the golem, a model of diligence, sat at the typewriter and typed. Puttermesser, passing en route from one fruitless meeting to another, saw the sheets accumulating on the floor. Was Xanthippe writing a novel? a memoir? To whom, after all, did she owe a letter? The golem looked abstracted, rapt. Puttermesser was hoping to patch together, bit by bit, her bad fortune. The gossips ran from cubicle to cubicle, collecting the news: Turtelman's niece, an actress—she had most recently played a medieval leper, with a little bell, in a television costume drama—was engaged to the Mayor's cousin. Marmel's aunt had once stayed in the same hotel in Florida with Mrs. Minnie Mavett, the Mayor's elderly widowed adoptive mother. (The Mayor had been an adopted child, and campaigned with his wife and four natural children as a "lucky orphan.") Marmel and Turtelman were said to have married twin sisters; surely this was a symbolic way of marrying each other? Or else Marmel was married to a Boston blueblood, Turtelman to a climber from Great Neck. On the other hand, only Marmel was married; Turtelman was an austere bachelor. One of the secretaries in the Administrative Assistant's office had observed that Marmel, Turtelman, and the Mayor all wore identical rings; she denied they were school rings. Turtelman's "restructuring," moreover, had begun (according to Polly in Personnel) to assume telltale forms. He was becoming bolder and bolder. He was like some crazed plantation owner at harvest time, who, instead of cutting down the standing grain, cuts down the conscientious reapers. Or he was like a raving chessmaster who throws all the winning pieces in the fire. Or he was like a general who leads a massacre against his own best troops. All these images failed. Turtelman was destroying the Department of Receipts and Disbursements. What he looked for was not performance but loyalty. He was a mayoral appointee of rapacious nature conniving at the usual outrages of patronage; he was doing the Mayor's will. He did not love the democratic polity as much as he feared the Mayor. Ah, Walt Whitman was not in his kidneys. Plunder was.

Cracow, meanwhile, reported that several times Adam Marmel had telephoned for Puttermesser. It was urgent. "That new girl's no good, Ruth. I'm all in favor of hiring the handicapped, but when it comes to answering the telephone what's definitely needed is a larynx. I had to pick up every damn time. You think Marmel wants to put you back up there in the stratosphere?"

Puttermesser said nothing. Cracow thought women ought to keep their place; he took open satisfaction in Puttermesser's flight downward. He nagged her to tell him what Turtelman's special project was. "You'd rather do special projects for the higher-ups than date a nice guy like me," he complained. "At least let's have lunch." But Puttermesser sent the golem out to a delicatessen for sandwiches; it was a kosher delicatessen—Puttermesser thought the golem would care about a thing like that. By the middle of the afternoon the golem's typed sheets were a tall stack.

At a quarter to five Turtelman's bony acolyte came puffing in. "Mr. Turtelman lent me to Mr. Marmel just to give you this. I hope you appreciate I'm not normally anyone's delivery boy. You're never at your desk. You can't be reached by phone. You're not important enough to be incommunicado, believe me. Mr. Marmel wants you to prepare a portfolio for him on these topics toot sweet."

Marmel's memo:

Dear Ms. Puttermesser:

Please be good enough to supply me with the following at your earliest convenience. A list of the City's bank depositories. Average balance in each account for the last three years. List of contact people at banks—names, titles, telephone numbers. List of contacts for Department of Receipts and Disbursements (referred to below as "we," "our," and "us") in Office of Mayor, Department of Budget, relevant City Council committees, Office of Comptroller. Copies of all evaluation reports published during past year. Current organization chart showing incumbent, title, and salary for each of our Office Heads. Why do we not have any window poles? Where have all the window poles gone? How to get toilet paper and soap regularly replaced in executive washroom? What kind of Management Information System files do we have on the assessed value of City real estate? How effective was our last Investors' Tour? Old notes disclose visit to sewage disposal plant, helicopter ride, fireboat demonstration, lunch and fashion show for the ladies— how to win goodwill this year from these heavy pockets? What hot litigation should I know about in re our Quasi-Judicial Division?

It was the old story: the floundering new official perplexed and beleaguered. Puttermesser felt a touch of malicious pleasure in Marmel's memo; she had known it would come to this—Turtelman, having thrown her out, now discovered he could not clear a space for himself without the stirring of Puttermesser's little finger. Marmel, spurred by Turtelman (too high-and-mighty to ask on his own), had set out to pick Puttermesser's brain. He was appealing to Puttermesser to diaper him. Each item in Marmel's memo would take hours and hours to answer! Except for the window poles. Puttermesser could explain about the window poles in half a second.

"Stand by," she said to the bony acolyte. And to Xanthippe: "Take a letter!"

Mr. Adam Marmel
First Bursary Officer
Bureau of Summary Sessions
Department of Receipts and Disbursements
Municipal Building

Dear Mr. Marmel:

Window poles are swiped by the hottest and sweatiest secretaries. The ones located directly above the furnace room, for instance. Though lately the ones who jog at lunchtime are just as likely to pinch poles. When they get them they hide them. Check out the second-floor ladies' room.

The fresh air of candor is always needed whenever the oxygen of honest admission has been withdrawn. Precisely WHY ["Make that all capitals," Puttermesser said, dictating] have I been relieved of my position? Precisely WHY have you stepped into my job? Let us have some fresh air!

Yours sincerely,
R. Puttermesser, Esq.

The bony acolyte snatched the sheet directly from the golem's typewriter. "There's a lot more he wants answers to. You've left out practically everything."

"Window poles are everything," Puttermesser said. "The fresh air of candor is all." She observed—it was a small shock —that the golem's style had infected her.

The bony acolyte warned, "Fresh is right. You better answer the rest of what he wants answered."

"Go home," Puttermesser told the golem. "Home!"

During dinner in the little kitchen Puttermesser was nearly as silent as the golem. Injustice rankled. She paid no attention to the golem's scribblings. The nerve! The nerve! To throw her out and then come and pick her brain! "No more Swedish soufflé," she growled. "Cook something else for a change. And I'm getting tired of seeing you in my old sweater. I'll give you money, tomorrow go buy yourself some decent clothes."

"Tomorrow," the golem wrote, "I will again serve you at your place of employment."

But in the morning Puttermesser was lackadaisical; ambition had trickled away. What, after so much indignity, was there to be ambitious *for*? For the first time in a decade she came to the office late. "What's the special project, Ruth?" Cracow wanted to know right away. "The kid was burning up the typewriter yesterday. What is she anyhow, an illegal alien? She don't look like your ordinary person. Yemenite Israeli type? What is this, already she don't show up, it's only the second day on the job? The phone calls you missed! Memos piled up! That gal from Personnel back and forth two, three times! They're after you today, Ruth! The higher-ups! What's the special project, hah? And the kid leaves you high and dry!"

"She'll turn up." Puttermesser had given the golem a hundred and twenty dollars and sent her to Alexander's. "No taxis or else," Puttermesser said; but she knew the golem would head downtown to Delancey Street. The thronged Caribbean faces and tongues of the Lower East Side drew her; Xanthippe, a kind of foreigner herself, as even Cracow could see, was attracted to immigrant populations. Their tastes and adorations were hers. She returned with red and purple blouses, narrow skirts and flared pants of parrot-green and cantaloupe-orange, multicolored high-heeled plastic shoes, a sunflower-yellow plastic shoulder bag with six double sets of zippers, a pocket mirror, and a transparent plastic comb in its own peach tattersall plastic case.

"Hispanic absolutely," Cracow confirmed—Cracow the bigot—watching Xanthippe lay open boxes and bags.

But Puttermesser was occupied with a trio of memos. They appeared to originate with Marmel but were expressed through Polly, the Atropos of Personnel, she who had put aside her shears for the flurry of a thousand Forms, she who brooded like Shiva the Destroyer on a world of the lopped.

Memo One:

You are reported as having refused to respond to requests for information relating to Bureau business. You now are subject to conduct inquiry. Please obtain and fill out Form 10V, Q17, with particular reference to Paragraph L, and leave it *immediately* with Polly in Personnel.

Memo Two:

In consideration of your seniority, Commissioner Alvin Turtelman, having relieved you of Level Eleven status in the Bureau of Summary Sessions, Department of Receipts and Disbursements, due to insufficient control of bursary materials, weak administrative supervision as well as output insufficiency, has retained you at Level Four. However, your work shows continued decline. Lateness reported as of A.M. today. Fill out Below-Level-Eight Lateness Form 14TG. (Submit Form to Polly in Personnel.)

Memo Three:

As a result of a determination taken by Commissioner Alvin Turtelman in conjunction and in consultation with First Bursary Officer Adam Marmel, your Level Four appointment in the Department of Receipts and Disbursements is herewith terminated. Please submit Below-Level-Six Severance Form A97, Section 6, with particular reference to Paragraph 14b, to Polly in Personnel.

Severed! Sacked! Dismissed! Let go! Fired! And all in the space of three hours! "Output insufficiency," a lie! "Decline," a fiction! "Conduct inquiry"—like some insignificant clerk or window-pole thief! Late once in ten years and Cracow, litigious would-be lover, snitches to Polly, the Atropos, the Shiva, of Personnel! Who else but Cracow? Lies. Fabrications. Accusations. Marmel the hollow accuser. Absence of due process!

The Honorable Malachy Mavett
Mayor, City of New York
City Hall

Dear Mayor Mavett:

Where is your pride, to appoint such men? Men who accuse without foundation? An accuser who seizes the job of the accused? Suspect! Turtelman wanted me out in order to get Marmel in! I stand for Intellect and Knowledge, they stand for Politics and Loyal Cunning. Hart Crane, poet of New York, his harp the Brooklyn Bridge, does that harp mean nothing to you? Is Walt

Whitman dead in your kidneys? Walt Whitman who cried out "numberless crowded streets, high growths of iron, slender, strong, light, splendidly uprising toward clear skies," who embraced "a million people—manners free and superb—open voices—hospitality . . . " Oh, Mayor Mavett, it is Injustice you embrace! You have given power to men for whom Walt Whitman is dead in their kidneys! This city of masts and spires opens its breast for Walt Whitman, and you feed it with a Turtelman and a Marmel! Ruth Puttermesser is despised, demoted, thrown away at last! Destroyed. Without work. Doer of nought, maker of nothing.

This letter remained locked inside Puttermesser's head. Cracow was trying hard not to look her way. He had already read Marmel's memos manifested through Polly the Destroyer; he had surely read them. He stood behind the golem's chair, attentive to her fingers galloping over the typewriter keys—including the newly lengthened one; how glad Puttermesser was that she had fixed it! "Hey Ruth, take a gander at this stuff. What's this kid *doing?* That's some so-called special project for Turtelman."

"The special project for Turtelman," Puttermesser said coldly, "is my vanquishment. My vanishing. My send-off and diminishment. So long, Leon. May you win your case against the mediocre universality of the human imagination."

"You been canned?"

"You know that."

"Well, when Polly walks in you figure what's up. You figure who's out."

"Beware of *Schadenfreude*, Leon. You could be next."

"Not me. I don't look for trouble. You look for trouble. I knew right away this whole setup with the kid was phony. She's typing up a craziness—whatever it is, Bureau business it isn't. You let in the crazies, you get what you expect."

At that moment—as Cracow's moist smile with its brown teeth turned and turned inside Cracow's dark mouth—a clarification came upon Puttermesser: no: a clarity. She was shut of a mystery. She understood; she saw. "Home!" Puttermesser ordered the golem. Xanthippe gathered up her clothes and shoved the typewritten sheets into one of the blouse bags.

V . WHY THE GOLEM WAS CREATED; PUTTERMESSER'S PURPOSE

That night the golem cooked spaghetti. She worked barefoot. The fragrance of hot buttered tomato sauce and peppers rushed over a mound of shining porcelain strands. "What are you doing?" Puttermesser demanded; she saw the golem heaping up a second great batch. "Why are you so hungry?"

The golem looked a little larger today than she had yesterday.

Then Puttermesser remembered that it was in the nature of a golem to grow and grow. The golem's appetite was nevertheless worrisome—how long would it take for Xanthippe to grow out of over one hundred dollars' worth of clothes? Could only a Rothschild afford a golem? And what would the rate of growth be? Would the golem eventually have to be kept outdoors, so as not to crash through the ceiling? Was the golem of Prague finally reversed into lifelessness on account of its excessive size, or because the civic reforms it was created for had been accomplished?

Ah, how this idea glowed for Puttermesser! The civic reforms of Prague—the broad crannied city of Prague, Prague distinguished by numberless crowded streets, high growths of iron, masts and spires! The clock-tower of the Jewish Community House, the lofty peaked and chimneyed roof of the

Altneuschul! Not to mention Kafka's Castle. All that mani-
fold urban shimmer choked off by evil, corruption, the blood
libel, the strong dampened hearts of wicked politicos. The
Great Rabbi Judah Loew had undertaken to create his golem
in an unenlightened year, the dream of America just unfolding, far away, in all its spacious ardor; but already the seed of
New York was preparing in Europe's earth: inspiration of
city-joy, love for the comely, the cleanly, the free and the
new, mobs transmuted into troops of the blessed, citizens
bursting into angelness, sidewalks of alabaster, buses filled
with thrones. Old delicate Prague, swept and swept of sin,
giving birth to the purified daylight, the lucent genius, of New
York!

By now Puttermesser knew what she knew.

"Bring me my books," she ordered the golem. And read:

A vision of Paradise must accompany the signs. The
sacred formulae are insufficient without the trance of
ecstasy in which are seen the brilliance of cities and their
salvation through exile of heartlessness, disorder, and the
desolation of sadness.

A city washed pure. New York, city (perhaps) of seraphim.
Wings had passed over her eyes. Her arms around Rappoport's heavy *Times*, Puttermesser held to her breast heartlessness, disorder, the desolation of sadness, ten thousand knives,
hatred painted in the subways, explosions of handguns, bombs
in the cathedrals of transportation and industry, Pennsylvania
Station, Grand Central, Rockefeller Center, terror in the
broadcasting booths with their bustling equipment and seductive provincial voices, all the metropolitan airports assaulted,
the decline of the Civil Service, maggots in high management.
Rappoport's *Times*, repository of a dread freight! All the

Xanthippe in her bed as if the golem were some transient mirage, an aggressive imagining, or else a mere forward apparition—this had, with a wearisome persistence, been teasing at the edge of Puttermesser's medulla oblongata all along, ever since the first mulling of it on her desolate walk to the Y. It was like a pitcher that will neither fill nor pour out. But it was now as plain as solid earth itself that the golem was no apparition. Apparitions do not, in hideous public jargon, type up exhaustive practical documents concerning civic reform! Puttermesser knew what she knew—it unraveled before her in the distance, the *PLAN*, approaching, approaching, until it crowded her forebrain with its importuning force: how she had set Rappoport's *Times*, record of multiple chaos and urban misfortune, down on the floor beside the bed, where the *Theaetetus* already lay. How, with a speed born of fever and agitation, she had whirled from window sill to window sill, cracking open clay plant pots as though they were eggs, and scooping up the germinative yolks of spilling earth. How she had fetched it all up in her two palms and dumped it into the bathtub. How only a half-turn of the tap stirred earth to the consistency of mud—and how there then began the blissful shudder of Puttermesser's wild hands, the molding and the shaping, the caressing and the smoothing, the kneading and the fingering, the straightening and the rounding, but quickly, quickly, with detail itself (God is in the details) unachieved, blurred, completion deferred, the authentic pleasure of the precise final form of nostril and eyelid and especially mouth left for afterward. Into the hole of the unfinished face of clay Puttermesser pressed a tag of paper, torn from the blank upper margin of Rappoport's *Times*, on which she had written in her own spittle two oracular syllables. The syllables adhered and were as legible as if inscribed in light. Then Puttermesser raised up out of the tub the imponderous damp relentless clay of a young girl—a lifeless forked creature in the semblance of a girl—and smelled the smell of mud, and put her down in her own bed to dry. The small jar to that small weight loosened crumbs of earth wherever a limb was joined to the trunk, and where the neck was joined, and where the ears had their fragile connecting stems. The crumbs sprinkled down. They crept under Puttermesser's fingernails. And all this Puttermesser performed (aha, now it beat in hindbrain and in forebrain, she saw it, she knew it again!) because of agitation and fever: because of the wilderness inside Rappoport's *Times*. Why should the despoiled misgoverned miscreant City not shine at dawn like washed stones? Tablets of civilization, engraved with ontological notations in an ancient tongue. Puttermesser craved. Her craving was to cleanse the wilderness; her craving was to excise every black instance of injustice; her craving was to erase outrage. In the middle of her craving—out of the blue—she formulated the *PLAN*.

She was thumbing it now, it was in her hands:

PLAN

FOR THE

RESUSCITATION,

REFORMATION,

REINVIGORATION

& REDEMPTION

OF THE

CITY OF NEW YORK

"Where did you get this?" Puttermesser demanded.

"I am your amanuensis," the golem wrote. "I express you. I copy and record you. Now it is time for you to accomplish your thought."

"Everyone has funny thoughts," Puttermesser croaked; an uneasiness heated her. She was afraid of the last page.

"No reality greater than thought," the golem wrote.

"Lay off the Middle Finnish. I want to hear the truth about all this. Where'd this stuff come from? You *couldn't* copy it, I never put any of it down."

The golem wrote: "Two urges seeded you. I am one, this is the other. A thought must claim an instrument. When you conceived your urge, simultaneously you conceived me."

"Not simultaneously," Puttermesser objected; perhaps the golem could not be trusted with chronology. She breathed outside history. Puttermesser re-imagined the electric moment exactly: the *PLAN* swimming like an inner cosmos into being, the mere solid golem an afterthought.

"No matter; I will serve your brain. I am your offspring, you are my mother. I am the execution of the grandeur of your principles. Grand design is my business. Leave visionary restoration to me." After which the golem put the ballpoint pen in her mouth and patiently sucked.

A fatigue seeped into Puttermesser; a tedium. It struck her that the golem was looking sly. She noticed that the seams along the armholes in the golem's orange blouse had begun to open. Growth. Enlargement. Swelling. Despite distraction Puttermesser read on. The *PLAN*, though it had originated in her own mind, nevertheless smacked of Marmel's lingo, Turtelman's patois. It appeared to derive, in truth, from the Form-language of Polly the Destroyer. A starkness penetrated Puttermesser; the dead words themselves depressed her. Her wrists shook. Was it not possible to dream a dream of City without falling into the mouth of the Destroyer? Behold the conservation of residential property through the exclusion of depreciating factors. Compute twelve hundred and fifty zoning codes. Note physical aspects. Social aspects. Retail and wholesale business. Manufacturing. Shipping. Single and multiple residences. Cultural institutions. Parks, public buildings, amusements, schools, universities, community objectives, rapidity and feasibility of transportation via streets and transit lines. Health, traffic, safety, public assembly conveniences. Sanitation. Prevention of slums. Transformation of slums. Eradication of poverty. Morality and obedience to law. Ordinances. Trust and pension funds. Treasury, public works, water. Public library. Police. Inspection. Councils and commissions. Welfare. Trustees. Revenue forecasting. Remote teleprocessing systems, computerized key-entry, restructuring of assessment districts, liens, senior-citizen rent-increase exemptions, delinquency centralization, corporate billings!

"My God," Puttermesser said.

"My mother has mastered and swallowed all of it," the golem wrote. "All of it is inside my mother's intelligence."

"I only meant—" Weak, Puttermesser wondered what it was she had meant. "Gardens and sunlight. Washed stones. Tablets. No; tables. Picnic tables."

Xanthippe stood nodding. The slyness powered her eyes. "My mother will become Mayor," she wrote.

The golem took the stack of typed sheets from Puttermesser's unquiet hands and held out the last page:

BY ORDER OF

RUTH PUTTERMESSER,

MAYOR

OF THE

CITY OF NEW YORK

"Drivel. Now you've gone too far. I never thought of that."

"Sleep on it," the golem wrote.

"That's *your* idea. You're the one who put that one in."

"Creator and created," the golem wrote, "merge," scribbling this with a shrug; the shrug made the ripped seams in her orange blouse open a little more.

The Honorable Malachy Mavett
Mayor
City Hall

Dear Mayor Mavett:

It is not respectful of a citizen's conception of the Mayor's office as "responsive" that you ignore my letter about possible spoils and other abuses. Still less is it respectful of me as a living human being and as a (former, now dismissed) Civil Servant. Shame! Shame!

Very sincerely yours,

THE HONORABLE RUTH PUTTERMESSER

This letter too remained locked inside Puttermesser's head. The signature was experimental—just to see what it looked like.

"No use, no use," the golem wrote on her notepad. "Mayor Puttermesser, by contrast, will answer all letters."

VI. MAYOR PUTTERMESSER

And so Puttermesser becomes Mayor of New York. The "and so" encloses much—but not so much as one might think. It is only a way of hastening Puttermesser's blatant destiny, of avoiding—never mind that God is in the details!—a more furrowed account of how the golem, each day imperceptibly enlarging, goes about gathering signatures for a citizens' petition. The golem is above all a realist; Puttermesser will run as an independent. There is not the minutest hope that the county leaders of either the Democratic or the Republican party will designate, as preferred candidate for Mayor of the City of New York, Ruth Puttermesser, Esq., a currently unemployed attorney put out in the street, so to speak, by Commissioner Alvin Turtelman of the Department of Receipts and Disbursements, in conjunction and in consultation with First Bursary Officer Adam Marmel. The golem is Puttermesser's campaign manager. She has burst out of all her new clothes, and has finally taken to extra-large men's denim overalls bought in the Army-Navy store on the corner of Suffolk and Delancey. The golem's complexion has coarsened a little. It is somehow redder, and the freckles on her forehead, when gazed at by an immobile eye, appear to have the configuration of a handful of letters from a generally unrecognizable alphabet:

$$\dagger \; \xi \; \mathsf{K}$$

Puttermesser has not failed to take note of how these letters, *aleph, mem,* and *tav,* in their primal North Semitic form, read from right to left, have extruded themselves with greater and greater clarity just below the golem's hairline. Puttermesser attributes this to pressure of the skin as the golem gains in height and thickness. She orders the golem to cut bangs. Though she is periodically alarmed at what a large girl Xanthippe is growing into, otherwise Puttermesser is pleased by her creation. Xanthippe is cheerful and efficient, an industrious worker. She continues to be a zealous cook. She remains unsure about time (occasionally she forgets that Wednesday intrudes between Tuesday and Thursday, and she has not quite puzzled out the order of all the months, though she has it splendidly fixed that November will embrace what has now become the sun of Puttermesser's firmament—Election Day); she is sometimes cocky; often intrepid; now and then surly; mainly she smiles and smiles. She can charm a signature out of anyone. At her own suggestion she wears around her neck a card that reads DEAF-MUTE, and with this card dangling on her bosom, in overalls, she scrambles up and down tenement steps as far away as Bensonhurst and Canarsie, in and out of elevators of East Side and West Side apartment buildings. She churns through offices, high schools and universities (she has visited Fordham, L.I.U., Pace, N.Y.U., Baruch College, Columbia; she has solicited the teaching staffs of Dalton, Lincoln, Brearley, John Dewey, Julia Richman, Yeshiva of Flatbush, Fieldston, Ramaz, as well as Puttermesser's own alma mater, Hunter High), supermarkets, cut-rate drugstores, subway stations, the Port Authority bus terminal. Wherever there are signers to be found, the golem appears with her ballpoint pen.

The petition is completed. The golem has collected fourteen thousand five hundred and sixty-two more signatures than the law calls for.

All this must be recorded as lightly and swiftly as possible; a dry patch to be gotten through, perhaps via a doze or a skip. For Puttermesser herself it is much more wretched than a mere dry patch. She suffers. Her physiological responses are: a coldness in the temples, blurring of the eyes, increased periodontic difficulties. She is afflicted with frequent diarrhea. Her spine throbs. At night she weeps. But she keeps on. Xanthippe gives her no peace, urges her to rephrase her speeches with an ear for the lively, insists that she sport distinctive hats, glossy lipstick, even contact lenses (Puttermesser, edging into middle age, already owns reading glasses).

The golem names Puttermesser's party as follows: Independents for Socratic and Prophetic Idealism—ISPI for short. A graphic artist is hired to devise a poster. It shows an apple tree with a serpent in it. The S in ISPI is the serpent. Puttermesser has promised to transform the City of New York into Paradise. She has promised to cast out the serpent. On Election Day, Malachy ("Matt") Mavett, the incumbent, is routed. Of the three remaining candidates, two make poor showings. Puttermesser is triumphant.

Puttermesser is now the Mayor of the City of New York! Old ardors and itches wake in her. She recites to herself: Justice, justice shalt thou pursue. Malachy ("Matt") Mavett takes his wife and family to Florida, to be near Mrs. Minnie Mavett, his adoptive mother. He is no longer a lucky orphan. He gets a job as a racetrack official. It is a political job, but he is sad all the same. His wife bears his humiliation gracelessly. His children rapidly acquire accents that do not mark them as New Yorkers. Turtelman and Marmel vanish into rumor. They are said to be with the F.B.I. in Alaska, with the C.I.A. in Indonesia. They are said to have relocated at Albany. They are said to be minor factotums in the Federal Crop Insurance Corporation, with offices in Sourgrass, Iowa. They are said to have mediocre positions in the Internal Revenue Service, where they will not be entitled to Social Security. They are said to have botched a suicide pact. No one knows what has become of Turtelman and Marmel. But Puttermesser is relieved; she herself, by means of a memo from City Hall, has dismissed them. Turtelman and Marmel are sacked! Let go! Fired!

Malachy ("Matt") Mavett, following protocol, telephones to congratulate Puttermesser on her victory. But he confesses to bafflement. Where has Puttermesser come from? An ordinary drone from the Bureau of Summary Sessions of the Department of Receipts and Disbursements! How can she, "an unknown," he asks, "a political nonentity," have won the public over so handily? Puttermesser reminds him that some months ago she wrote him a letter asking for justice, condemning patronage and spoils. "You did not reply," she accuses him in a voice hoarse from speech-making. The ex-Mayor does not remember any letter.

Though Puttermesser is disconcerted by the move to Gracie Mansion (in her dreams her mother is once again rolling up winter rugs and putting down summer rugs in the wide sun-periled apartment on the Grand Concourse), the golem immediately chooses the most lavish bedroom in the Mayor's residence for herself. It contains an antique dresser with gryphon feet and a fourposter arched by a lofty tester curtained in white velvet. Old brass bowls glint on the dressertop. The golem fills one whole closet with fresh overalls. She wanders about studying the paintings and caressing the shining banister. She exhorts Puttermesser to rejoice that she no longer has her old suspicious landlord on East Seventy-first Street to worry about. Millions of citizens are her landlord now!

Puttermesser cannot pay attention to the golem's sprightliness. She is in a frenzy over the job of appointing commissioners and agency heads. She implores Xanthippe to keep away from City Hall—the campaign is over, she will only distract from business. The new Mayor intends to recruit noble psyches and visionary hearts. She is searching for the antithesis of Turtelman and Marmel. For instance: she yearns after Wallace Stevens—insurance executive of probity during office hours, enraptured poet at dusk. How she would like to put Walt Whitman himself in charge of the Bureau of Summary Sessions, and have Shelley take over Water Resource Development—Shelley whose principle it is that poets are the legislators of mankind! William Blake in the Fire Department. George Eliot doing Social Services. Emily Brontë over at Police, Jane Austen in Bridges and Tunnels, Virginia Woolf and Edgar Allan Poe sharing Health. Herman Melville overseeing the Office of Single Room Occupancy Housing. "*Integer vitae scelerisque purus*," the golem writes on her notepad, showing off. "That's the ticket," Puttermesser agrees, "but what am I supposed to do, chase around town like Diogenes with a lantern looking for an honest man?" Xanthippe writes philosophically, "The politics of Paradise is no longer politics." "The politics of Paradise is no longer Paradise," Puttermesser retorts; "don't annoy me anyhow, I have to get somebody fast for Receipts and Disbursements." "You could promote Cracow," the golem writes. "I already have. I moved him over to Bronx Landfill and Pest Control. That's two levels up. He's got a good idea for winter, actually— wants to convert that garbage mountain out near the bay to a ski jump. And he's stopped asking me out. Thank God he's scared of dating the Mayor." "If you would seek commissioners of integrity and rosy cleverness," the golem writes, "fashion more of my kind." Fleetingly, Puttermesser considers this; she feels tempted. The highest echelons of City management staffed by multiple members of the genus golem! Herself the creator, down to the last molecule of ear-wax, of every commissioner, deputy, bureau chief, executive director! Every mayoral assistant, subordinate, underling, a golem! She looks over at Xanthippe. Twice already Xanthippe has quarreled with the Mansion's official cook. The cook has refused to follow the golem's recipes. "One is enough," Puttermesser says, and hurries down the subway and off to City Hall.

Despite its odious language reminiscent of Turtelman and Marmel, Puttermesser repeatedly consults the

PLAN

FOR THE

RESUSCITATION,

REFORMATION,

REINVIGORATION

& REDEMPTION

OF THE

CITY OF NEW YORK.

She blames Xanthippe for such a preposterous text: only two days spent in the Bureau of Summary Sessions, and the golem has been infected by periphrasis, pleonasm, and ambagious tautology. But behind all that there glimmers a loveliness. To Puttermesser's speeding eye, it is like the spotted sudden flank of a deer disturbing a wood. There *will* be resuscitation! There *will* be redemption!

And it begins. Mayor Puttermesser sends the golem out into the City. At first she tends to hang out among the open-air stalls of Delancey Street, but Puttermesser upbraids her for parochialism; she instructs the golem to take subways and buses—no taxis—out to all the neighborhoods in all the boroughs. It goes without saying that a robust reformist administration requires a spy. The golem returns with aching tales of what she has seen among the sordid and the hopeless; sometimes she even submits a recommendation on a page of her notepad. Puttermesser does not mind. Nothing the golem reports is new to Mayor Puttermesser. What is new is the discovery of the power of office. Wrongdoing and bitterness can be overturned: it is only a matter of using the power Puttermesser owns.

Crowds of self-seeking importuners float up the steps of City Hall; Mayor Puttermesser shoos them away. She admits visionary hearts only. She tacks signs up all around her desk: NO MORE SPOILS QUOTA. MERIT IS SWEETER THAN GOLD. WHAT YOU ARE, NOT WHOM YOU KNOW.

Lost wallets are daily being returned to their owners. Now it is really beginning—the money and credit cards are always intact. The golem ascends from the subway at Sixty-eighth and Lexington (this is the very corner where Puttermesser's alma mater, Hunter High, used to stand), looking slightly larger than the day before, but also irradiated. The subways have been struck by beauty. Lustrous tunnels unfold, mile after mile. Gangs of youths have invaded the subway yards at night and have washed the cars clean. The wheels and windows have been scrubbed by combinations of chemicals; the long seats have been fitted with velour cushions of tan and blue. Each car shines like a bullet. The tiles that line the stations are lakes of white; the passengers can cherish their own reflections in the walls. Every Thursday afternoon the youths who used to terrorize the subways put on fresh shirts and walk out into Central Park, reconnoitering after a green space; then they dance. They have formed themselves into dancing clubs, and crown one another's heads with clover pulled up from the sweet ground. Foliage is browning, Thursday afternoons grow cold and dusky. But the youths who used to terrorize the subways are whirling in rings over darkening lawns.

The streets are altered into garden rows: along the curbs, between sidewalk and road, privet hedges shake their little leaves. The open sanitation carts are bright, like a string of scarlet chariots. They are drawn by silent horses who sniff among the new hedges. Flutes and clarinets announce the coming of the cart procession every day at noon, and children scramble to pick up every nub of cigarette or scrap of peel or paper wrapper, pressing with fistfuls toward the singing flutes and gravely marching horses, whose pairs of high nostrils flare outward like trumpets.

The great cargo trucks still spill into the intersections, carrying bolts of cloth, oranges, fowl, refrigerators, lamps, pianos, cards of buttons, lettuces, boxes of cereal, word processors, baby carriages, pillowcases with peacocks imprinted on them; some deliver uptown, others downtown; they pant and rumble freely, unimpeded; buses and taxis overtake them effortlessly. Except for fire engines and ambulances, there are no other motored vehicles. Little girls dare, between buses, to jump rope in the middle of the street. Some roads, though, have been lushly planted, so that lovers seek them out to hide in one another's breast. The tall grasses and young maples of the planted roads are haunted by pretzel sellers, hot-chestnut peddlers, hawkers of books in wheelbarrows. The children are often indoors after school, carpentering bookshelves. The libraries are lit all night, and the schools are thronged in the evenings by administrative assistants from the great companies, learning Spanish, Portuguese, Russian, Hebrew, Korean, and Japanese. There are many gardeners now, and a hundred urban gardening academies. There is unemployment among correction officers; numbers of them take gardening jobs. No one bothers to drag the steel shutters down over storefronts after closing. The Civil Service hums. Intellect and courtliness are in the ascendancy. Mayor Puttermesser has staffed the Department of Receipts and Disbursements with intelligent lawyers, both women and men, who honor due process. Turtelman and Marmel are replaced by visionary hearts. Never again will an accuser take the job of the accused, as Marmel did with Puttermesser! There is no more rapaciousness in the Bureau of Summary Sessions.

A little-known poet who specializes in terza rima is put in charge of Potter's Field. For each sad burial there, she composes a laudatory ode; even the obscure dead are not expendable or forlorn. The parks, their arbors and fields, are speckled with wide-mouthed terra-cotta urns; no one injures them. Far away in the Bronx, the grape-wreathed heads of wine gods are restored to the white stelae of the Soldiers' Monument, and the bronze angel on top of the Monument's great stone needle glistens. Nothing is broken, nothing is despoiled. No harm comes to anything or anyone. The burnt-out ruins of Brownsville and the South Bronx burst forth with spinneys of pines and thorny locusts. In their high secret pride, the slums undo themselves: stoops sparkle, new factories and stores buzz, children gaze down in gladness at shoes newly bought, still unscratched; the shoe stores give away balloons, and the balloons escape to the sky. Everywhere former louts and loiterers, muggers and thieves, addicts and cardsharps are doing the work of the world, absorbed, transformed. The biggest City agency is what used to be called Welfare; now it is the Department of Day Play, and delivers colored pencils and finger paints and tambourines to nurseries clamorous as bee-loud glades, where pianos shake the floors, and story-tellers dangle toddlers in suspense from morning to late afternoon, when their parents fetch them home to supper. Everyone is at work. Lovers apply to the City Clerk for marriage licenses. The Bureau of Venereal Disease Control has closed down. The ex-pimps are learning computer skills.

Xanthippe's heels have begun to hang over the foot of her fourposter bed in Gracie Mansion. The golem is worn out. She lumbers from one end of the City to the other every day, getting ideas. Mayor Puttermesser is not disappointed that the golem's ideas are mainly unexciting. The City is at peace. It is in the nature of tranquility—it is in the nature of Paradise— to be pacific; tame; halcyon. Oh, there is more to relate of how Mayor Puttermesser, inspired by the golem, has resuscitated, reformed, reinvigorated and redeemed the City of New York! But this too must be left to dozing and skipping. It is essential to record only two reflections that especially engage Mayor Puttermesser. The first is that she notices how the City, tranquil, turns toward the conventional and the orderly. It is as if tradition, continuity, propriety blossom of themselves: old courtesies, door-holding, hat-tipping, a thousand pleases and pardons and thank-yous. Something in the grain of Paradise is on the side of the expected. Sweet custom rules. The City in its redeemed state wishes to conserve itself. It is a rational daylight place; it has shut the portals of night.

Puttermesser's second reflection is about the golem. The coming of the golem animated the salvation of the City, yes— but who, Puttermesser sometimes wonders, is the true golem? Is it Xanthippe or is it Puttermesser? Puttermesser made Xanthippe; Xanthippe did not exist before Puttermesser made her: that is clear enough. But Xanthippe made Puttermesser Mayor, and Mayor Puttermesser too did not exist before. And that is just as clear. Puttermesser sees that she is the golem's golem.

In the newborn peaceable City, Xanthippe is restless. She is growing larger. Her growth is frightening. She can no longer fit into her overalls. She begins to sew together pairs of sheets for a toga.

VII. RAPPOPORT'S RETURN

On a late spring afternoon about halfway through her mayoral term, and immediately after a particularly depressing visit to the periodontist (she who had abolished crime in the subways was unable to stem gum disease in the hollow of her own jaw), Puttermesser came home to Gracie Mansion to find Rappoport waiting in her private sitting room.

"Hey, you've got some pretty tough security around here. I had a hell of a time getting let in," Rappoport complained.

"Last time I saw you," Puttermesser said, "you had no trouble letting yourself out."

"How about we just consider that water under the bridge, Ruth, what do you say?"

"You walked out on me. In the middle of the night."

"You were liking Socrates better than me," Rappoport said.

"Then why are you back?"

"My God, Ruth, look who you've become! I can't pass through New York without seeing the Mayor, can I? Ruth," he said, spreading his impressive nostrils, "I've thought about you a lot since the election. We read all about you up in Toronto."

"You and Mrs. Rappoport?"

"Oh come on, let's give it another try. Not that I don't understand you have to be like Caesar's wife. Above susp—"

"I have to be Caesar," Puttermesser broke in.

"Well, even Caesar gives things another try."

"You're no Cleopatra," Puttermesser said.

There was a distant howl; it was the cook. She was fighting with the golem again. In a moment Xanthippe stood in the doorway, huge and red, weeping.

"Leave that woman alone. She'll cook what she'll cook, you can't tell her anything different," Puttermesser scolded. "She runs a strictly kosher kitchen and that's enough. Go and wash your face."

"Plump," Rappoport said, staring after Xanthippe in her toga. "Right out of Caesar's Forum."

"A growing girl. She wears what she pleases."

"Who is she?"

"I adopted her."

"I like a big girl like that." Rappoport stood up. "The town looks terrific. I came to congratulate you, Ruth."

"Is that why you came?"

"It turns out. Only I figured if you could bring a whole city back to life—"

"There are some things, Morris, that even the Mayor can't revive."

Rappoport, his briefcase under his arm, wheeled and hesitated. "It didn't make it through the move? My avocado tree that I grew from a pit in Toronto? It was doing fine in your old apartment."

"I don't have it any more."

"Aha, you wanted to dispose of me lock, stock, and barrel. You got rid of every symptom and sign. The least bit of green leaf—"

"All my plants are gone."

"No kidding. What happened?"

"I took their earth and made a golem."

Rappoport, flaunting his perfect teeth under his mustache, laughed out loud. In the middle of his laughter his head suddenly fell into the kind of leaning charm Puttermesser recalled from long ago, when they had first become lovers; it almost made her relent.

"Goodbye, Ruth. I really do congratulate you on civic improvement." Rappoport held out his hand. "It's one terrific town, I mean it. Utopia. Garden of Eden. In Toronto they run articles on you every day."

"You can stay for dinner if you like," Puttermesser offered. "Though I've got a meeting right after—municipal bonds. Myself, it's eat and get on down to City Hall."

Someone had seized Rappoport's outstretched hand and was shaking it; it was not Puttermesser. Xanthippe, practiced politician, her wide cheeks refreshed and soap-fragrant, had sped forward out of nowhere. Rappoport looked stunned; he looked interested. He slipped his fingers out of the golem's grasp and moved them upward against her chest, to catch hold of the card that twirled there: DEAF-MUTE.

"That's awfully generous of you, Ruth, adopting someone like that. You're a wonderful person. We really ought to get together again. I *will* stay for a bite, if you don't mind."

The golem did not bring her ballpoint to the table. She dealt with her soup spoon as if it were her enemy, the cook. Disgruntled, she heaped a fourth helping of mashed potatoes onto her plate. But her eye was on Rappoport, and her mouth was round with responsiveness: was it his teeth? was it his reddish mustache, turning gray? was it his wide welcoming nostrils? was it his briefcase bulging with worldly troubles?

Rappoport was talkative. His posture was straight-backed and heroic: he told of his last clandestine trip to Moscow, and of the turmoil of the oppressed.

When Puttermesser returned at midnight from the meeting on municipal bonds, the golem was asleep in her fourposter bed, her heels thrust outward in their pink socks over the footboard, and Rappoport was snoring beside her.

Eros had entered Gracie Mansion.

VIII. XANTHIPPE LOVESICK

Consider now Puttermesser's situation. What happens to an intensely private mind when great celebrity unexpectedly invades it? Absorbed in the golem's *PLAN* and its consequences—consequences beyond the marveling at, so gradual, plausible, concrete, and sensible are they, grounded in a policy of civic sympathy and urban reasonableness—Puttermesser does not readily understand that she induces curiosity and applause. She has, in fact, no expectations; only desires as strong and as strange as powers. Her desires are pristine, therefore acute; clarity is immanent. Before this inward illumination of her desires (rather, of the *PLAN*'s desires), everything else—the clash of interests that parties, races, classes, are said to give rise to—falls away into purposelessness. Another way of explaining all this is to say that Mayor Puttermesser finds virtue to be intelligible. Still another way of explaining is to say that every morning she profoundly rejoices. There is fruitfulness everywhere. Into the chaos of the void (defeat, deception, demoralization, loss) she has cast a divinely clarifying light. Out of a dunghill she has charmed a verdant citadel. The applause that reaches her is like a seasound at the farthest edge of her brain; she both hears it and does not hear it. Her angelic fame—the fame of a purifying angel—is virtue's second face. Fame makes Puttermesser happy, and at the same time it brings a forceful sense of the penultimate, the tentative, the imperiled.

It is as if she is waiting for something else: for some conclusion, or resolution, or unfolding.

The golem is lovesick. She refuses to leave the Mansion. No more for her the daily voyage into the broad green City as the Mayor's ambassador and spy. She removes the DEAF-MUTE card and substitutes another: CONTEMPLATIVE. Puttermesser does not smile at this: she is not sure whether it is meant to be a joke. There is too much gloom. There are hints of conspiracy. Anyhow the golem soon takes off the new sign. In the intervals between Rappoport's appearances Xanthippe languishes. Rappoport comes often—sometimes as often as three or four times a week. Xanthippe, moping, thumps out to greet him, trailing a loose white tail of her toga; she escorts him straight into her bedroom. She turns on the record player that Rappoport has brought her as a birthday gift. She is two years old and insatiable. God knows what age she tells her lover.

Rappoport steals out of the golem's bedroom with the dazzled inward gaze of a space traveler.

The Mayor upbraids Xanthippe: "It's enough. I don't want to see him around here. Get rid of him."

Xanthippe writes: "Jealousy!"

"I'm tired of hearing complaints from the cook. This is Gracie Mansion, it's not another kind of house."

"Jealousy! He used to be yours."

"You're stirring up a scandal."

"He brings me presents."

"If you keep this up, you'll spoil everything."

"My mother has purified the City."

"Then don't foul it."

"I am in contemplation of my future."

"Start contemplating the present! Look out the window! Fruitfulness! Civic peace! You saw it happening. You caused it."

"I can tear it all down."

"You were made to serve and you know it."

"I want a life of my own. My blood is hot."

The Mansion thickens with erotic airs. Heavy perfumes float. Has Rappoport journeyed to mysterious islands to offer

the golem these lethargic scents, these attars of weighty drooping petals? The golem has discarded her sewn-together sheets
and looms with gemlike eyes in darkling passageways,
wrapped in silks, vast saris that skim the carpets as she goes;
each leg is a pillar wound in a bolt of woven flowers.

The summer deepens. A dry dust settles on the leaves in the
Bronx Botanical Gardens, and far away the painted carousels
of Brooklyn cry their jollities.

The Mayor: "I notice Rappoport hasn't been around
lately."

Xanthippe writes: "He left."

"Where?"

"He clouded over his destination. Vienna. Rome. Jerusalem. Winnipeg. What do I care? A man of low position.
Factotum of refugee philanthropy, twelve bosses over him."

"What happened?"

"I wore him out."

"I need you right away," Puttermesser urges. "We're putting in new tiles on the subway line out toward Jamaica
Avenue. With two-color portraits baked right into the glaze—
Thoreau, Harriet Beecher Stowe, Emerson so far. You can
decide who else."

"No."

"You haven't been anywhere in months."

"My mother speaks the truth. I thirst for the higher world.
Office and rank. Illustrious men."

Puttermesser is blighted with melancholy. She fears. She
foresees. In spite of fruitfulness and civic peace (rather, on
their account), it is beginning to be revealed to her what her
proper mayoral duty directs.

She does nothing.

In pity, she waits. Sometimes she forgets. How long did the
Great Rabbi Judah Loew of Prague wait, how often did he
forget? There are so many distinguished visitors. The Em-

peror of Japan takes the elevator to the top of the Empire State Building. Puttermesser gives an astronaut a medal on the steps of City Hall; he has looked into the bosom of Venus. The mayors of Dublin, San Juan, and Tel Aviv arrive. In the Blue Room, Puttermesser holds a news conference about interest rates. She explains into the television cameras that the City of New York, in its abundance, will extend interest-free loans to the Federal government in Washington.

Now and then Xanthippe disappears. She does not return to the Mansion at night. Frequently her fourposter stands empty.

Early one morning, the golem, her eyes too polished, her cheeks too red, her silk windings torn, the tiny letters on her forehead jutting like raw scars, thumps home.

"Four days gone without a word!" Puttermesser scolds.

Xanthippe writes impatiently: "Been down to Florida."

"Florida!"

"Been to visit ex-Mayor Malachy ('Matt') Mavett."

"What for?"

"Remember Marmel?"

"What's this about?"

"Been out West to visit him. Him and Turtelman."

"What *is* this?"

But Puttermesser knows.

There are curious absences, reports of exhaustion, unexplained hospitalizations. The new Commissioner of Receipts and Disbursements whispers to Puttermesser, in confidence, that he will divorce his wife. His eyeballs seem sunken, his lips drop back into a hollow face. He has lost weight overnight. He will not say what the trouble is. He resigns. The Executive Director of the Board of Education resigns. It is divulged that he suffers from catarrh and is too faint to stand. The Commissioner of the Department of Cultural Affairs has been struck stone-deaf by a horrible sound, a kind of exultant hiss; he will not say what it was. The City's managers and executives all appear to sicken together: commissioner after commissioner, department after department. Puttermesser's finest appointments—felled; depleted. There is news of an abortion in Queens. A pimp sets himself up in business on Times Square again, in spite of the cherry trees the Department of Sanitation has planted there; the Commissioner of Sanitation himself stalks under the hanging cherries, distracted, with a twisted spine and the start of a hunch. Two or three of the proud young men of the dancing clubs defect and return to mugging in the subways. The City's peace is unraveling. The commissioners blow their noses into bloody tissues, drive their little fingers into their ears, develop odd stammers, instigate backbiting among underlings.

The golem thirsts.

"Stay home," the Mayor pleads. "Stay out of the City."

The golem will no longer obey. She cannot be contained. "My blood is hot," Xanthippe writes; she writes for the last time. She tosses her ballpoint pen into the East River, back behind the Mansion.

IX. THE GOLEM DESTROYS HER MAKER

Mayor Puttermesser's reputation is ebbing. The cost of municipal borrowing ascends. A jungle of graffiti springs up on the white flanks of marble sculptures inside museums; Attic urns are smashed. Barbarians cruise the streets. O New York! O lost New York!

Deputy commissioners and their secretaries blanch at the sound of a heavy footstep. Morning and afternoon the golem lumbers from office to office, searching for high-level managers. In her ragged sari brilliant with woven flowers, her great head garlanded, drenched in a density of musky oils, Xanthippe ravishes prestigious trustees, committee chairmen, council members, borough presidents, the Second Deputy Comptroller's three assistants, the Director of the Transit Authority, the Coordinator of Criminal Justice, the Chief of the Office of Computer Plans and Controls, the Head of Intergovernmental Relations, the Chancellor of the City University, the Rector of the Art Commission, even the President of the Stock Exchange! The City is diseased with the golem's urge. The City sweats and coughs in her terrifying embrace. The City is in the pincer of the golem's love, because Xanthippe thirsts, she thirsts, she ravishes and ravages, she ambushes management level after management level. There is no Supervising Accountant or Secretary to the Minority Leader who can escape her electric gaze.

Sex! Sex! The golem wants sex! Men in high politics! Lofty officials! Elevated bureaucrats!

Mayor Puttermesser is finished. She can never be re-elected. She is a disgrace; her Administration is wrecked. Distrust. Desolation. It is all over for Mayor Puttermesser and the life of high politics. The prisons are open again. The press howls. Mayor Puttermesser is crushed. The golem has destroyed her utterly.

X. THE GOLEM SNARED

Puttermesser blamed herself. She had not forestalled this devastation. She had not prepared for it; she had not acted. She had seen what had to be done, and put it off and put it off. Dilatory. She could not say to herself that she was ignorant; hadn't she read in her books, a thousand times, that a golem will at length undo its creator? The turning against the creator is an "attribute" of a golem, comparable to its speechlessness, its incapacity for procreation, its soullessness. A golem has no soul, therefore cannot die—rather, it is returned to the elements of its making.

Xanthippe without a soul! Tears came to Puttermesser, her heart in secret shook. She was ready to disbelieve. A golem cannot procreate? Ah, but its blood is as hot as human blood. Hotter! A golem lusts tremendously, as if it would wrest the flame of further being from its own being. A golem, an earthen thing of packed mud, having laid hold of life against all logic and natural expectation, yearns hugely after the generative, the fructuous. Earth is the germ of all fertility: how then would a golem not dream itself a double? It is like a panting furnace that cries out for more and more fuel, that spews its own firebrands to ignite a successor-fire. A golem cannot procreate! But it has the will to; the despairing will; the violent will. Offspring! Progeny! The rampaging energies of Xanthippe's eruptions, the furious bolts and convulsions of her visitations—Xanthippe, like Puttermesser herself, longs for daughters! Daughters that can never be!

Shall the one be condemned by the other, who is no different?

Yet Puttermesser weeps. The golem is running over the City. She never comes home at all now. A ferry on its way from the Battery to Staten Island is terrorized; some large creature, bat or succubus, assaults the captain and causes him to succumb. Is it Xanthippe? Stories about "a madwoman on the loose, venomous against authority" ("unverifiable," writes the City Hall Bureau of the *Times*) wash daily over Mayor Puttermesser's desk. The secret chamber where sleeps the President of the Chase Manhattan Bank has had its windows brutally smashed; a bit of flowered silk clings to the jagged glass.

Xanthippe! Xanthippe! Puttermesser calls in her heart.

Every night pickets parade in front of Gracie Mansion, with torches and placards:

MAYOR PUTTERMESSER WHAT HAS HAPPENED TO THE SUBWAYS?
HIGH HOPES THE HIGH ROAD TO HELL.
SHE WHO SPARKED SNUFFED.
PUTTERMESSER'S BITTER MESSES.
RUTHIE WITH SUCH A DOWN WE NEEDED YOUR UP?
FROM SMASH HIT TO SMASH.
KAPUT-TERMESSER!

Every day there are speakers on the steps of City Hall, haranguing; when the police chase them, they vanish for ten minutes and reappear. Mobs bubble, hobble, guffaw.

Puttermesser composes a letter to ex-Mayor Malachy ("Matt") Mavett:

Gracie Mansion
City of New York

Dear Matt [she permits herself this liberty]:

My campaign manager's recent Florida visit may have caused you some distress. I did not authorize it. Your defeat via the ballot box, which eliminated the wrong-doers Turtelman and Marmel from City officialdom, was satisfaction enough. Please excuse any personal indignities my campaign manager (who is now on my personal staff) may have inflicted. She expresses her nature but cannot assume responsibility for it.

Dilatory! Procrastinator! Imaginary letters! Puttermesser's tears go on falling.

Gracie Mansion
City of New York

Dear Morris:
   Please come.

           In friendship
           Ruth

She hands this to one of the window-pole thieves to mail. In a few days it brings Rappoport, out of breath, his once-pouting briefcase hollow, caved in; Rappoport himself is hollow, his stout throat caved in, as if he had ejected his Adam's apple. His nose and chin, and the furless place between his eyebrows, have a papery cast. His beautiful teeth are nicked. His mustache looks squirrelly, gray.

"Xanthippe's left home," Puttermesser announces.

"You're the Mayor. Call the Missing Persons Bureau."

"Morris. Please."

"What do you want?"

"Bring her back."

"Me?"

"You can do it."

"How?"

"Move in."

"What? Here? In Gracie Mansion?"

"In Xanthippe's bed. Morris. Please. She likes you. You're the one who started her off."

"She got too big for her britches. In more than a manner of speaking, if you don't mind my saying so. What d'you mean, started her off?"

"You excited her."

"That's not my fault."

"You created desire. Morris, bring her back. You can do it."

"What for? I've had enough. No more. Drained. Drained, believe me, Ruth."

"Lie in her bed. Just once."

"What's in it for me? I didn't come back to this rotten town for the sake of a night's sleep in Gracie Mansion. The novelty's worn off. The bloom is no longer on the rose, you follow? Besides, you've gone downhill, Ruth, did you see those pickets out there?" He shows her his sleeve—two buttons ripped off. "They treated me like a scab, walking in here—"

"Just lie down in her bed, Morris. That's all I'm asking."

"No."

"I'll make it worth your while."

"What're you getting at? You're getting at something."

"You're a fund-raiser by profession," Puttermesser says meditatively; a strangeness rises in her. A noxious taste.

"Something like that. There's a lot of different things I do."

"That's right. Plenty of experience. You're qualified for all sorts of fine spots."

"I'm qualified for what?"

"The truth is," Puttermesser says slowly, "I'm in possession of a heap of resignations. Several of my commissioners," Puttermesser says slowly, "have fallen ill."

"I hear there's typhoid in some of those buildings along Bruckner Boulevard. What've you got, an epidemic? I heard cholera in Forest Hills."

"Rumors," Puttermesser spits out. "People love to badmouth. That's what makes the City go down. The banks are leaving, nobody worries about *that*. I'm talking resignations. *Openings*, Morris. You can take your pick, in fact. How about the Department of Investigation? Run the Inspectors General. Or I can appoint you judge. How about Judge of the Criminal Court? Good spot, good pay. Prestige, God knows. Look, if you like you can take over Receipts and Disbursements."

Rappoport stared. "Commissioner of Receipts and Disbursements?"

"I can go higher if you want. Fancier. Board of Water Supply's a dandy. Nice remuneration, practically no show."

"Ruth, Ruth, what is this?"

Justice, justice shalt thou pursue!

It is Mayor Puttermesser's first political deal.

"Stay a night in Xanthippe's bed and any job you want is yours. The orchard's dropping into your lap, Morris, I'm serious. Plums."

"A spot in your Administration actually?"

"Why not? Choose."

"Receipts and Disbursements," Rappoport instantly replies.

Puttermesser says sourly, "You're at least as qualified as Turtelman."

"What about my wife?"

"Keep her in Toronto."

Standing in solitude in the night fragrance behind Gracie Mansion, Puttermesser catches river-gleams: the Circle Line yacht with its chandelier decks; a neon sign pulsing; the distant caps of little waves glinting in moonwake, in neonwake. White bread baking on the night shift casts its faintly animal aroma on the waters: rich fumes more savory than any blossom. It is so dark in the back garden that Puttermesser imagines she can almost descry Orion's belt buckle. One big moving star twins as it sails: the headlights of an airliner nosing out toward Europe. Plane after plane rises, as if out of the black river. Puttermesser counts them, each with its sharp beams like rays scattered from the brow of Moses, arching upward into the fathomless universe. She counts planes; she counts neon blinks; she counts the silhouettes of creeping scows; she counts all the mayors who have preceded her in the City of New York. Thomas Willett, Thomas Delavall . . .

William Dervall, Nicholas De Meyer, Stephanus Van Cortlandt . . . Francis Rombouts . . . Isaac de Reimer, Thomas Noell, Philip French, William Peartree, Ebenezer Wilson . . . DeWitt Clinton . . . Gideon Lee . . . Smith Ely . . . Jimmy Walker . . . John P. O'Brien, Fiorello H. LaGuardia . . . Robert F. Wagner, John V. Lindsay, Abraham D. Beame, Edward I. Koch! She counts and waits. She is waiting for the golem to be lured homeward, to be ensnared, to lumber groaning with desire into her fourposter bed.

In the golem's fourposter, Commissioner Morris Rappoport, newly appointed chief of the Department of Receipts and Disbursements, lies in sheets saturated with a certain known pungency. He has been here before. He recoils from the familiar scented pillows.

Indoors and out, odors of what has been and what is about to be: the cook's worn eggplant au gratin, river smells, the garden beating its tiny wings of so many fresh hedge-leaves, airplane exhaust spiraling downward, the fine keen breath of the bread ovens, the golem's perfumed pillows—all these drifting smokes and combinations stir and turn and braid themselves into a rope of awesome incense, drawing Xanthippe to her bed. Incense? Fetor and charged decay! The acrid signal of dissolution! Intimations of the tellurian elements! Xanthippe, from wherever she has hurtled to in the savage City (savage once again), is pulled nearer and nearer the Mansion, where the portraits of dead mayors hang. Scepter and status, all the enchantments of influence and command, lead her to her undoing: in her bed lies the extremely important official whose job it is to call the tune that makes the City's money dance. She will burst on him her giant love. On the newly appointed Commissioner of Receipts and Disbursements the golem will spend her terrible ardor. Then she will fall back to rest, among the awful perfumes of her cleft bed.

Whereupon Mayor Puttermesser, her term of office

blighted, her comely *PLAN* betrayed, will dismantle the golem, according to the rite.

XI. THE GOLEM UNDONE, AND THE BABBLING OF RAPPOPORT

The City was ungovernable; the City was out of control; it was no different now for Mayor Puttermesser than it had ever been for any mayor. In confusion and hypocrisy, Puttermesser finished out what was left of her sovereign days.

One thing was different: a certain tumulus of earth introduced by the Parks Commissioner in the mournful latter half of Mayor Puttermesser's Administration.

Across the street from City Hall lies a little park, crisscrossed by paths and patches of lawn fenced off by black iron staves. There are benches set down here and there with a scattered generosity. There is even an upward-flying fountain. Perhaps because the little park is in the shadow of City Hall and, so to speak, under its surveillance, the benches have not been seriously vandalized, and the lawns not much trampled on. Best of all, and most alluring, are the flower beds, vivid rectangles of red geraniums disposed, it must be admitted, in the design of a miniature graveyard. Civil servants peering down from high windows of the elephant-gray Municipal Building can see the crimson slash that with wild brilliance cuts across the concrete bitterness below. Some distance behind the flower beds rise those great Stonehenge slabs of the Twin Towers; eastward, the standing zither that is Brooklyn Bridge.

From the Mayor's office inside City Hall the park is not visible, and for Puttermesser this is just as well. It would not have done for her to be in sight of Xanthippe's bright barrow while engaged in City business. Under the roots of the flower beds lay fresh earth, newly put down and lightly tamped. Mayor Puttermesser herself, in the middle of the night, had telephoned the Parks Commissioner (luckily just back from Paris) and ordered the ground to be opened and a crudely formed and crumbling mound of special soil to be arranged in the cavity, as in an envelope of earth. The Parks Commissioner, urgently summoned, thought it odd, when he arrived at Gracie Mansion with his sleepy diggers, that the Mayor should be pacing in the back garden behind the Mansion under a veined half-moon; and odder yet that she should be accompanied by a babbling man with a sliding tongue, who identified himself as the newly appointed Commissioner of Receipts and Disbursements, Morris Rappoport.

"Did you bring spades? And a pickup truck?" the Mayor whispered.

"All of that, yes."

"Well, the spades won't do. At least not yet. You don't shovel up a floor. You can use the spades afterward, in the park. There's some dried mud spread out on a bedroom floor in the Mansion. I want it moved. With very great delicacy. Can you make your men understand that?"

"Dried mud?"

"I grant you it's in pieces. It's already falling apart. But it's got a certain design. Be delicate."

What the Parks Commissioner saw was a very large and shapeless, or mainly shapeless, mound of soil, insanely wrapped (so the Parks Commissioner privately judged) in a kind of velvet shroud. The Parks Commissioner had been on an official exchange program in France, and had landed at Kennedy Airport less than two hours before the Mayor telephoned. The exchange program meant that he would study the enchanting parks of Paris, while his Parisian counterpart was to consider the gloomier parks of New York. The Parks Commissioner, of course, was Puttermesser's own appointee, a botanist and city planner, an expert on the hardiness of

certain shade trees, a specialist in filigreed gazebos, a lover of
the urban nighttime. All the same, he was perplexed by the
Mayor's caprice. The mound of dirt on the bedroom floor did
not suggest to him his own good fortune and near escape. In
fact, though neither would ever learn this, the Parks Commissioner and his Parisian counterpart were both under a
felicitous star—the Parisian because his wife's appendectomy
had kept him unexpectedly and rather too lengthily in Paris so
that he never arrived in New York at all (he was an anxious
man), and the Parks Commissioner because he had not been
at home in his lower Fifth Avenue bed when the golem came
to call. Instead, he had been out inspecting the Bois de
Boulogne—consequently, the Parks Commissioner was in fine
mental health, and was shocked to observe that the newly
appointed Commissioner of Receipts and Disbursements was
not.

Rappoport babbled. He followed after Puttermesser like a
dog. He had performed exactly as she had instructed, it
seemed, but then her instructions became contradictory. First
he was to circle. Then he was not to circle. Rather, he was to
scrape with his penknife. There he was, all at once a satrap
with a title; the title was as palpable as a mantle, and as
sumptuous; overhead drooped the fourposter's white velvet
canopy with its voluptuous folds and snowy crevices—how
thickly warm his title, how powerful his office! Alone, en-
closed in the authority of his rank, Rappoport awaited the
visitation of the golem. Without a stitch, not a shred of sari
remaining, her burnished gaze on fire with thirst for his grandeur, she burst in, redolent of beaches, noisy with a fiery hiss;
Rappoport tore the white velvet from the tester and threw it
over burning Xanthippe.

Rappoport babbled. He told all the rest: how they had con-
tended; how he had endured her size and force and the horror
of her immodesty and the awful sea of her sweat and the
sirocco of her summer breath; and how he—or was it she?

—had chanted out the hundred proud duties of his new jurisdiction: the protocol and potency of the City's money, where it is engendered, where it is headed, where it lands: it could be said that she was teaching him his job. And then the Mayor, speaking through the door, explaining the depth of tranquility after potency that is deeper than any sleep or drug or anesthesia, directing him to remove Xanthippe in all her deadweight mass from the fourposter down to the bare floor, and to wind her in the canopy.

Rappoport babbled: how he had lifted Xanthippe in her trance, the torpor that succeeds ravishment, down to the bare floor; how he had wound her in white velvet; how pale Puttermesser, her reading lenses glimmering into an old green book, directed him with sharpened voice to crowd his mind with impurity—with everything earthly, soiled, spoiled, wormy; finally how Puttermesser directed him to trail her as she weaved round Xanthippe on the floor, as if circling her own shadow.

Round and round Puttermesser went. In the instant of giving the golem life, the just, the comely, the cleanly, the Edenic, had, all unwittingly, consummated Puttermesser's aspiring reflections—even the radiant *PLAN* itself! Now all must be consciously reversed. She must think of violent-eyed loiterers who lurk in elevators with springblades at the ready, of spray cans gashing red marks of civilization-hate, of civic monuments with their heads knocked off, of City filth, of mugging, robbery, arson, assault, even murder. Murder! If, for life, she had dreamed Paradise, now she must feel the burning lance of hell. If, for life, she had walked seven times clockwise round a hillock of clay, now she must walk seven times counterclockwise round captive Xanthippe. If, for life, she had pronounced the Name, now she must on no account speak or imagine it or lend it any draught or flame of breath; she must erase the Name utterly.

And what of Rappoport, Rappoport the golem's lure and snare, Rappoport who had played himself out in the capture of Xanthippe? He too must walk counterclockwise, behind Puttermesser, just as the Great Rabbi Judah Loew had walked counterclockwise with his disciples when the time came for the golem of Prague to be undone. The golem of Prague, city-savior, had also run amok!—terrorizing the very citizens it had been created to succor. And all the rites the Great Rabbi Judah Loew had pondered in the making of the golem, he ultimately dissolved in the unmaking of it. All the permutations and combinations of the alphabet he had recited with profound and holy concentration in the golem's creation, he afterward declaimed backward, for the sake of the golem's discomposition. Instead of meditating on the building up, he meditated on the breaking down. Whatever he had early spiraled, he late unraveled: he smashed the magnetic links that formed the chain of being between the atoms.

Puttermesser, circling round the torpid Xanthippe in her shroud of white velvet, could not help glancing down into the golem's face. It was a child's face still. Ah, Leah, Leah! Xanthippe's lids flickered. Xanthippe's lips stirred. She looked with her terrible eyes—how they pulsed—up at Puttermesser.

"My mother."

A voice!

"O my mother," Xanthippe said, still looking upward at Puttermesser, "why are you walking around me like that?"

She spoke! Her voice ascended!—a child's voice, pitched like the pure cry of a bird.

Puttermesser did not halt. "Keep moving," she told Rappoport.

"O my mother," Xanthippe said in her bird-quick voice, "why are you walking around me like that?"

Beginning the fifth circle, Rappoport gasping behind her, Puttermesser said, "You created and you destroyed."

"No," the golem cried—the power of speech released!—"it was you who created me, it is you who will destroy me! Life! Love! Mercy! Love! Life!"

The fifth circle was completed; still the golem went on bleating in her little bird's cry. "Life! Life! More!"

"More," Puttermesser said bitterly, beginning the sixth circle. "More. You wanted more and more. It's more that brought us here. More!"

"You wanted Paradise!"

"Too much Paradise is greed. Eden disintegrates from too much Eden. Eden sinks from a surfeit of itself."

"O my mother! I made you Mayor!"

Completing the sixth circle, Puttermesser said, "You pulled the City down."

"O my mother! Do not cool my heat!"

Beginning the seventh circle, Puttermesser said, "This is the last. Now go home."

"O my mother! Do not send me to the elements!"

The seventh circle was completed; the golem's small voice piped on. Xanthippe lay stretched at Puttermesser's feet like Puttermesser's own shadow.

"Trouble," Puttermesser muttered. "Somehow this isn't working, Morris. Maybe because you're not a priest or a Levite."

Rappoport swallowed a tremulous breath. "If she gets to stand, if she decides to haul herself up—"

"Morris," Puttermesser said, "do you have a pocket knife?"

Rappoport took one out.

"O my mother, mother of my life!" the golem bleated. "Only think how for your sake I undid Turtelman, Marmel, Mavett!"

Huge sly Xanthippe, gargantuan wily Xanthippe, grown up out of the little seed of a dream of Leah!

Rappoport, obeying Puttermesser, blew aside the golem's

bangs and with his small blade erased from Xanthippe's forehead what appeared to be no more than an old scar—the first on the right of three such scars—queerly in the shape of a sort of letter K.

Instantly the golem shut her lips and eyes.

The *aleph* was gone.

"Dead," Rappoport said.

"Returned," Puttermesser said. "Carry her up to the attic."

"The attic? *Here?* In Gracie Mansion? Ruth, think!"

"The Great Rabbi Judah Loew undid the golem of Prague in the attic of the Altneuschul. A venerable public structure, Morris, no less estimable than Gracie Mansion."

Rappoport laughed out loud. Then he let his tongue slide out, back and forth, from right to left, along the corners of his mouth.

"Bend down, Morris."

Rappoport bent down.

"Pick up her left hand. By the wrist, that's the way."

Between Rappoport's forefinger and thumb the golem's left hand broke into four clods.

"No, it won't do. This wasn't well planned, Morris, I admit it. If we try to get her up the attic stairs—well, you can see what's happening. Never mind, I'll call the Parks Commissioner. Maybe City Hall Park—"

Then began the babbling of Rappoport.

XII. UNDER THE FLOWER BEDS

Garbage trucks are back on the streets. Their ferocious grinders gnash the City's spew. Traffic fumes, half a hundred cars immobile in a single intersection, demoralization in the ladies' lavatories of the Municipal Building, computers down,

Albany at war with City Hall, a drop in fifth-grade reading scores—the City is choking. It cannot be governed. It cannot be controlled. There is a rumor up from Florida that ex-Mayor Malachy ("Matt") Mavett is scheming to recapture City Hall. As for current patronage, there is the egregious case of the newly appointed Commissioner of Receipts and Disbursements, said to be the Mayor's old lover; he resigns for health reasons even before taking office. His wife fetches him home to Toronto. Mayor Puttermesser undergoes periodontal surgery. When it is over, the roots of her teeth are exposed. Inside the secret hollow of her head, just below the eye sockets, on the lingual side, she is unendingly conscious of her own skeleton.

The *Soho News* is the only journal to note the Mayor's order, in the middle of a summer night, for an extra load of dirt to be shoveled under the red geraniums of City Hall Park. Parks Department diggers have planted a small wooden marker among the flower beds: DO NOT TOUCH OR PICK. With wanton contempt for civic decorum, passersby often flout the modest sign. Yet whoever touches or picks those stems of blood-colored blossoms soon sickens with flu virus, or sore throat, or stuffed nose accompanied by nausea—or, sometimes, a particularly vicious attack of bursitis.

And all the while Puttermesser calls in her heart: O lost New York! And she calls: O lost Xanthippe!

A Note on the Type

The text of this book was set in Electra, a Linotype
face designed by W. A. Dwiggins. This face cannot be
classified as either modern or old-style. It is not based
on any historical model, nor does it echo any particular
period or style. It avoids the extreme contrasts between
thick and thin elements that mark most modern faces
and attempts to give a feeling of fluidity,
power, and speed.

Composed by Maryland Linotype Composition
Company, Inc., Baltimore, Maryland
Printed and bound by The Haddon Craftsmen, Inc.,
Scranton, Pennsylvania

Designed by Judith Henry